Student's name: ____________________ Assignment date: ___

Primary Grades Math Test Review Assessment

低年级数学 測試複習考核

Frank Ho Amanda Ho

何数棋谜 培训

Ho Math Chess Learning Centre

Student's name: ____________________ Assignment date: _______________

Table of contents

Student's name: ____________________ Assignment date: ________________

Student's name: ____________________ Assignment date: ________________

Student's name: ____________________ Assignment date: ________________

Student's name: ____________________ Assignment date: ________________

Student's name: ____________________ Assignment date: ________________

Student's name: ____________________ Assignment date: ________________

Student's name: ____________________ Assignment date: ________________

Student's name: ___________________ Assignment date: _______________

Student's name: ____________________ Assignment date: ________________

Preface

We have seen that many students did their homework but still could not get A mark consistently. One of the problems is that even though they did their homework or assignments, but the problems given in quizzes or tests by their day school teachers are different from what they did in their homework. Some students also need more practice or tests, and there are not enough test problems in their textbooks. Often it because some students could use a quick review to boost their marks.

This workbook was not written just for reviewing, testing, or assessing purposes. Students can also use it to learn new concepts and get ahead.

It is challenging to produce a workbook to be used worldwide by instructors all over the world. This workbook can be used worldwide to meet the needs of students with advanced abilities in many countries. How did we produce such a workbook? We have combed through many math books produced by many countries and areas, including China, the USA, Canada, Hong Kong, Taiwan, Singapore etc., to compare their contents and studied their exam papers. We also studied many math problems in the IB program, SSAT math part, and regional and international math assessments. Doing these researches allows us to produce some problems that have a very high standard and some average problems for beginner's level.

All drawings in this workbook may not represent the exact scales.

This workbook can be used for lower and middle grades.

Frank Ho
Amanda Ho

December 22, 2015

Please email your comments or suggestions about this workbook to fho1928@gmail.com.

Ho Math Chess Primary Grades Math

Test Review assesssment 何数棋謎低年级数学测试複習考核

Student's name: ____________________ Assignment date: ________________

***** Part 1 Whole numbers operations *****

Results of additions or subtractions less than or equal to 20

3 + 7 = 10	9 + 7 = 18	11– 3 = 8	13 – 4 = 9
13 + 7 = 20	3 + 6 = 9	8 + 6 = 14	11 – 5 = 6
18 – 9 = 9	8 + 6 = 14	9 + 5 = 14	7 + 6 = 13
3 + 7 = 10	14 – 5 = 9	11 – 5 = 6	8 + 3 = 11
11 + 7 = 18	17 – 3 = 14	12 – 7 = 5	12 + 6 = 18
5 + 7 = 12	17 – 5 = 12	14 + 6 = 20	5 + 9 = 14
15 – 2 = 13	4 + 6 = 10	6 + 7 = 13	14 – 5 = 9
11 + 6 = 17	13 – 4 = 9	9 + 6 = 15	7 + 4 = 11
6+ 8 = 14	15 – 6 = 9	5 + 16 = 21	5 + 6 = 11
17 – 3 = 14	12 + 6 = 18	17 – 6 = 11	12 + 6 = 18
13 – 4 = 9	4 + 12 = 16	13 + 5 = 18	5 + 14 = 19
7 + 6 = 13	11 – 6 = 5	5 + 13 =18	15 – 8 = 7
5 + 6 = 11	19 – 7 = 12	14 + 6 = 20	14 + 6 =20
18 – 5 =13	12 – 5 = 7	5 + 14 =19	5 + 15 = 20
16 – 7 = 9	14 + 6 = 20	12 – 7 = 5	9 + 7 =16
14 + 6 = 20	6+ 13 = 19	13– 4 = 9	5 + 6 = 11
15 + 4 = 19	16 – 2 =14	11 + 6 = 17	13 – 5 = 8
10 – 4 = 6	6 + 6 = 12	5 + 6 = 11	12 – 5 = 7
17 – 2 = 15	5 + 6 = 11	12 + 6 = 18	17 – 4 = 13
13 + 6 = 19	18– 9 =9	5 + 12 = 17	11 + 8= 19
5 + 8 = 13	12– 5 = 7	20 – 4 = 16	5 + 6 = 11
12– 5 + 2 = 9	6 + 9 – 3 = 12	11 + 7 – 6 = 12	12– 5 + 5 = 12
3 + 13 – 2 = 14	14 – 9 + 2 = 7	12 + 4 – 2 = 14	5 + 9 – 7 =7
17 – 8 + 1 = 10	10 + 9 – 6 = 13	13– 4 + 5 =14	1 +19 – 2 =18
1 + 9 – 2 = 8	18 – 5 + 3 = 16	1 + 9 – 2 =8	11– 5 + 5 = 11

Ho Math Chess Primary Grades Math

Test Review assesssment 何数棋謎低年级数学测试複習考核

Student's name: ____________________ Assignment date: ________________

3-digit addition or subtraction with borrowing from or carrying over

587 − 497 90	210 − 199 11	301 − 198 103	507 − 368 139	255 − 146 109	371 − 183 188
202 − 106 96	821 − 738 83	542 − 453 89	345 − 254 91	222 − 133 89	344 − 255 89
204 − 115 89	221 − 216 5	369 − 298 71	333 − 287 46	567 − 476 91	345 − 298 47
911 − 799	412 − 234	587 + 497	210 + 199	301 + 198	345 + 254
911 + 799	507 + 368	255 + 146	371 + 183	202 + 106	821 + 738
542 + 453	222 + 133	344 + 255	204 + 115	221 + 216	369 + 298
333 + 287	567 + 476	345 + 298	487 + 234	534 + 287	321 + 478
487 − 234	534 − 287	521 − 478	471 − 289	505 − 386	431 − 278

112, 178, 1084, 409, 499, 599
1710, 875, 401, 554, 308, 1559
995, 355, 599, 319, 437, 667
620, 1043, 643, 721, 821, 799
243, 244, 43, 182, 119, 153

Student's name: ____________________ Assignment date: ________________

Repeated addition, multiplication

Problems	Skip counting from n	m groups of n circles each	Repeated additions	Arrays (row × column)
3 × 5	Skip counting from 5 5, 10, 15	3 groups of 5 circles each ○○○○○ ○○○○○ ○○○○○	3 repeated additions of 5 5 + 5 + 5 = 15	3 rows by 5 columns ○○○○○ ○○○○○ ○○○○○
5 × 3	3, 6, 9, 12, 15	5 groups of 3	5 repeated additions of 3	5 rows by 3 columns
3 x 6	6, 12, 18	3 groups of 6 each	3 repeated additions of 6	○○○○○○ ○○○○○○ ○○○○○○
6 x 3	3, 6, 9, 12, 15, 18	6 groups of 3 each	6 repeated additions of 3	○○○ ○○○ ○○○ ○○○ ○○○ ○○○
4 x 5	5, 10, 15, 20	4 group of 5 each	4 repeated additions of 5	○○○○○ ○○○○○ ○○○○○ ○○○○○

Student's name: ____________________ Assignment date: ________________

Repeated subtraction and division

Problems	Skip counting from n	m groups of n equal number of items (circles) in each group	Repeated subtractions
Divide 24 pies into a group of 4 each. How many groups?	Skip counting from 4 4, 8, 12, 16, 20, 24 6 groups	24 items with 4 in each group	Repeated subtractions of 4 24 – 4 – 4 – 4 – 4 – 4 – 4 = 0
Share 12 oranges by 3 persons. How many oranges does each person get?	4 oranges 4, 4, 4		12 – 4 -- 4 – 4
21 cookies with 3 in each group. How many groups are there?	7 groups		21 – 3 -- 3 – 3 – 3 – 3 – 3 - 3 = 0
Divide 20 balls into 5 groups with an equal number of balls in each group.	4 balls		20 – 4 – 4 – 4 – 4 -- 4= 0

Student's name: ____________________ Assignment date: ________________

Multiplication

4 × 7	10 × 9	21 × 8	87 × 4	45 × 8
69 × 8	21 × 6	55 × 6	45 × 9	7 × 68
497 × 9	301 × 5	12 × 11	71 × 83	21 × 38
42 × 53	45 × 54	33 × 87	67 × 76	799 × 54
202 × 106	222 × 133	344 × 255	204 × 115	471 × 289
505 × 386	431 × 278	709 × 806	507 × 497	890 × 608

28, 90, 168, 348, 360
552, 126, 330, 405, 476
4473, 1505, 132, 5893, 798
2226, 2430, 2871, 5092, 43146
21412, 29526, 87720, 23460, 20519
194930, 119818, 571454, 251979, 541120

Student's name: ____________________ Assignment date: ________________

Divisions with 0 in the quotient

21 2 ⟌ 42	2 21 ⟌ 42	2002 21 ⟌ 42042
140 3 ⟌ 420	35 12 ⟌ 420	350350 12 ⟌ 4204200
12012 3 ⟌ 36036	3003 12 ⟌ 36036	3000300 12 ⟌ 36003600
1200102 4 ⟌ 4800408	1600136 3 ⟌ 4800408	200017 24 ⟌ 4800408
1011003 5 ⟌ 5055015	1685005 3 ⟌ 5055015	37001 15 ⟌ 555015
453 37 ⟌ 16761	387 29 ⟌ 11223	587 19 ⟌ 11153

Student's name: ____________________ Assignment date: ________________

Mixed operations

4 × 3 =12	18 ÷ 3 = 6	26 − 9 = 17	43 + 8 = 51
3 + 9 = 12	17 − 9 = 8	24 × 5 =120	16 ÷ 2 = 8
15 − 4 = 11	12 × 9 =108	23 + 8 = 31	12 ÷ 4 = 3
25 ÷ 5 = 5	26 − 9 = 17	24 × 3 =72	21 + 3 = 24
4 × 4 =16	45 ÷ 9 = 5	18 + 7 = 25	19 − 8 =11
14 × 5 =70	18 + 7 =25	15 − 7 = 8	25 + 9 = 34
16 + 5 = 21	14 − 9 = 5	17 × 4 =68	21 ÷ 3 = 7
23 + 8 = 31	23 − 9 = 14	14 × 6 =84	48 ÷ 6 = 8
14 × 7 =98	16 ÷ 8 = 2	23 − 7 = 16	17 + 8 = 25
14 ÷ 7 = 2	23 − 9 = 14	18 × 3 =54	23 + 5 = 28
26 × 3 =78	24 + 8 = 32	23 − 9 = 14	28 ÷ 4 =7
12 ÷ 6 = 2	15− 9 = 6	17 × 3 =51	77 + 8 = 85
4 × 9 =36	25 ÷ 5 =5	14 − 8 = 6	55 + 8 = 63
13 − 4 = 9	24 × 8 =192	23 + 8 = 31	27 ÷ 3 = 9
4 × 3 =12	36 ÷ 6 = 6	27 − 9 = 18	29 + 8 = 37
18 − 9 = 9	14 × 7 =98	33 + 7 = 40	21 ÷ 3 = 7
24 × 3 =72	15 ÷ 5 = 3	24 − 9 = 15	23 + 8 = 31
23 + 8 = 31	13− 9 =4	23 − 6 =17	49 ÷ 7 =7
40 ÷ 8 =5	24 × 5 =120	31 − 9 = 22	34 + 5 = 39
24 × 5 =120	13 + 8 = 21	27 − 8 = 19	54 ÷ 9 = 6
15 − 9 =6	36 ÷ 9 =4	24 × 5 =120	29 + 8 = 37

Ho Math Chess Primary Grades Math

Test Review assesssment 何数棋謎低年级数学测试複習考核

Student's name: ____________________ Assignment date: ________________

Test of mixed operations

14 × 3 =42	12 ÷ 3 = 4	96 – 9 = 87	13 + 8 = 21
32 + 9 = 41	12 – 9 = 3	44 × 5 =220	36 ÷ 2 = 18
55 – 4 = 51	14 × 9 =126	13 + 8 = 21	12 ÷ 4 = 3
55 ÷ 5 = 11	21 – 9 = 12	14 × 3 =42	69 + 3 = 72
24 × 4 =96	27 ÷ 9 = 3	18 + 8 = 26	19 – 8 =11
34 × 5 =170	17 + 7 =24	23 – 7 = 16	15 + 9 = 24
56 + 5 = 61	91 – 9 = 82	15 × 4 =60	69 ÷ 3 = 23
43 + 8 = 51	41 – 9 = 32	34 × 6 =204	72 ÷ 6 = 12
14 × 7 =98	24 ÷ 8 = 3	21 – 7 = 14	37 + 8 = 45
84 ÷ 7 = 12	33 – 9 = 24	14 × 3 =42	53 + 5 = 58
16 × 3 =48	74 + 8 = 82	26 – 9 = 17	72 ÷ 4 =18
72 ÷ 6 = 12	21– 9 = 12	14 × 3 =42	78 + 8 = 86
14 × 9 =126	75 ÷ 5 =15	16 – 8 = 8	85 + 8 = 93
47 – 4 = 43	24 × 8 =192	33 + 8 = 41	24 ÷ 3 = 8
24 × 3 =72	96 ÷ 6 = 16	77 – 9 = 68	23 + 8 = 31
28 – 9 = 19	14 × 5 =70	73 + 7 = 80	81 ÷ 3 = 27
84 × 3 =252	25 ÷ 5 = 5	24 – 9 = 15	93 + 8 = 101
93 + 8 = 101	23– 9 =14	33 – 6 =27	42 ÷ 7 =6
40 ÷ 8 =5	34 × 5 =170	81 – 9 = 72	64 + 5 = 69
34 × 5 =170	93 + 8 = 101	77 – 8 = 69	54 ÷ 9 = 6
35 – 9 =26	36 ÷ 9 =4	34 × 5 =170	39 + 8 = 47

Student's name: ____________________ Assignment date: ________________

Mixed operations

24 × 3 =72	39 ÷ 3 = 13	42 − 9 = 33	53 + 8 = 61
33 + 9 = 42	12− 7 = 5	34 × 5 =170	36 ÷ 4 = 9
53 − 6 = 47	24 × 9 =216	23 + 8 = 31	54 ÷ 6 = 9
45 ÷ 5 = 9	12 − 9 = 3	24 × 3 =72	59 + 4 = 63
14 × 4 =56	36÷ 9 = 4	28 + 8 = 36	91 − 8 =83
33 × 5 =165	27 + 7 =34	13 − 7 = 6	35 + 9 = 44
57 + 5 = 62	92 − 9 = 83	16 × 4 =64	96 ÷ 3 = 32
25 + 8 = 33	43 − 9 = 34	32 × 6 =192	36 ÷ 6 = 6
13 × 7 =91	40 ÷ 8 = 5	23 − 7 = 16	39 + 8 = 47
63 ÷ 7 = 9	23 − 9 = 14	41 × 3 =123	57 + 5 = 62
18 × 3 =54	75 + 8 = 83	27 − 9 = 18	32 ÷ 4 =8
84 ÷ 6 = 14	28 − 9 = 19	17 × 3 =51	77 + 8 = 85
17 × 9 =153	85 ÷ 5 =17	17 − 8 = 9	85 + 8 = 93
20 − 4 = 16	16 × 8 =128	34 + 8 = 42	21 ÷ 3 = 7
23 × 3 =69	84 ÷ 6 = 14	75 − 9 = 66	24 + 8 = 32
28 − 9 = 19	14 × 5 =70	73 + 7 = 80	84 ÷ 3 = 28
83 × 3 =243	75 ÷ 5 = 15	31 − 9 = 22	95 + 8 = 103
92 + 8 = 100	28− 9 =19	21 − 9 =12	49 ÷ 7 =7
48 ÷ 8 =6	35 × 5 =175	83 − 9 = 74	63 + 5 = 68
32 × 5 =160	99 + 8 = 107	71 − 8 = 63	45 ÷ 9 = 5
23 − 9 =14	45 ÷ 9 =5	30 × 5 =150	33 + 8 = 41

Student's name: ____________________ Assignment date: _______________

Number representations

Number in one, ten, hundred, and thousand representing by number blocks

A number can be expressed by using graphics representation, and it is called number blocks.

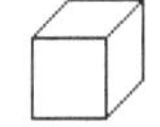

1 or 1 unit

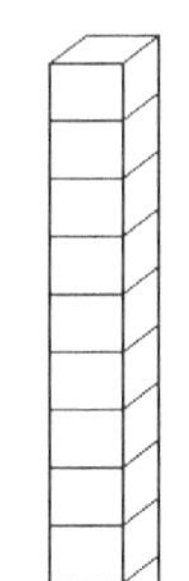

1 ten

or 10 units

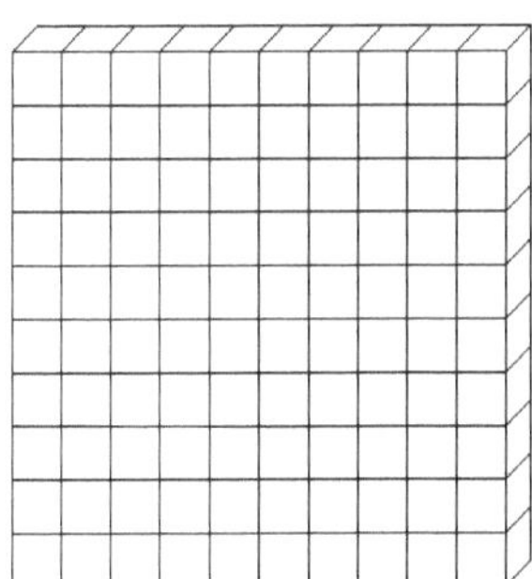

1 hundred

100
or _______ units

10
or _______ tens

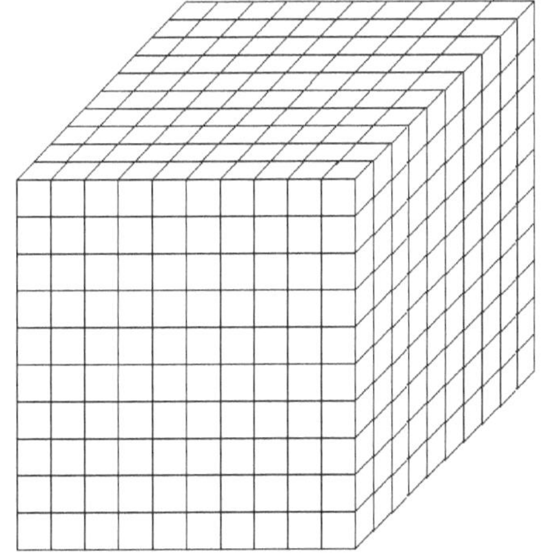

000
1 _______ thousand

or 1000 units

100
or _______ tens

10
or _______ hundreds

Student's name: ____________________ Assignment date: ________________

Convert number blocks to the standard number representing by digits.

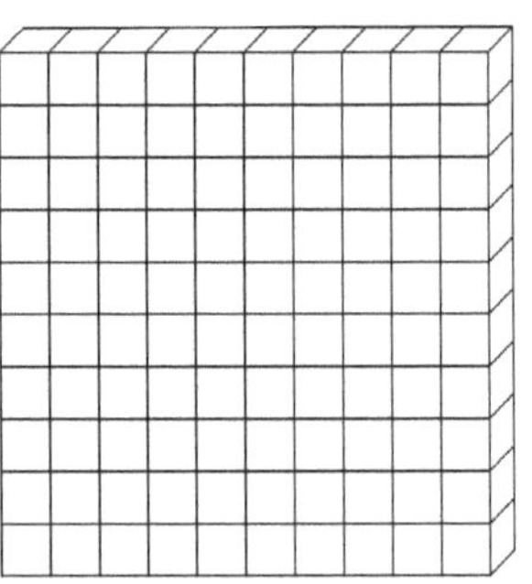
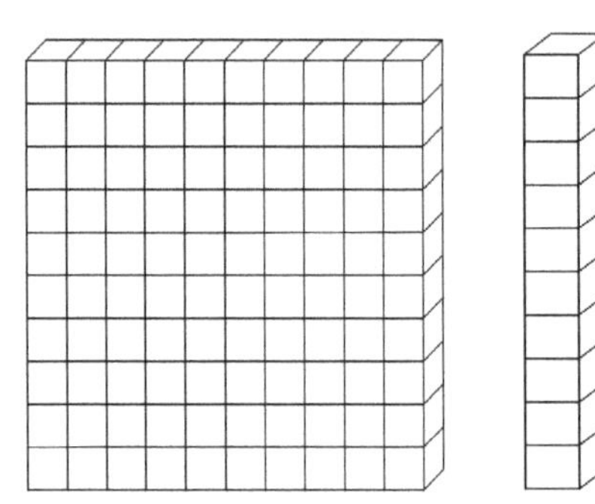

211
______

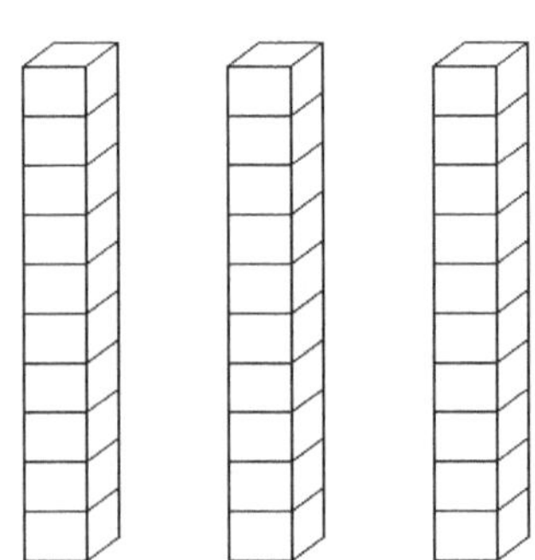
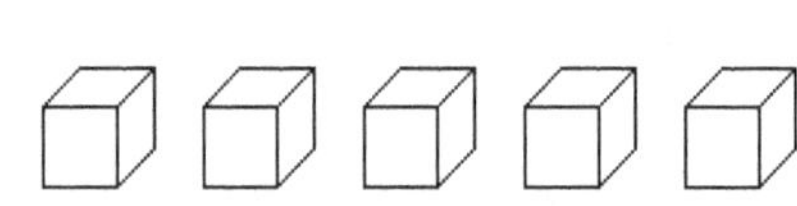

35
______

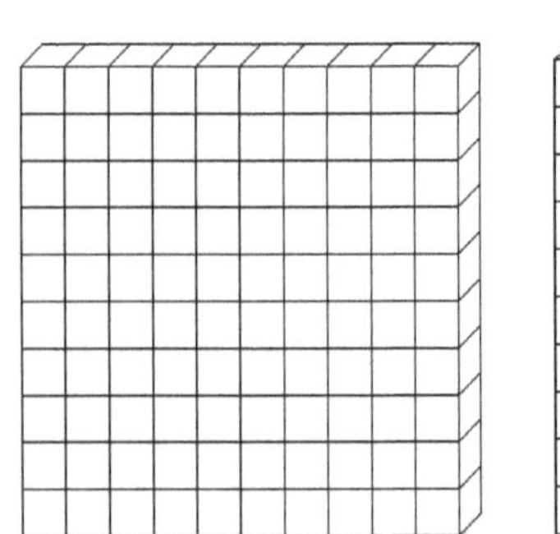
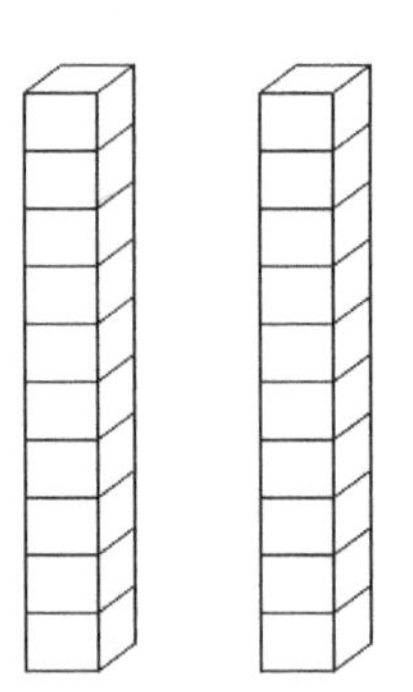
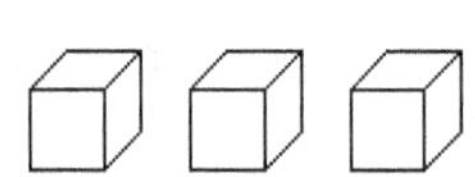

123
______

Student's name: ____________________ Assignment date: ________________

Convert number blocks to the standard number representing by digits.

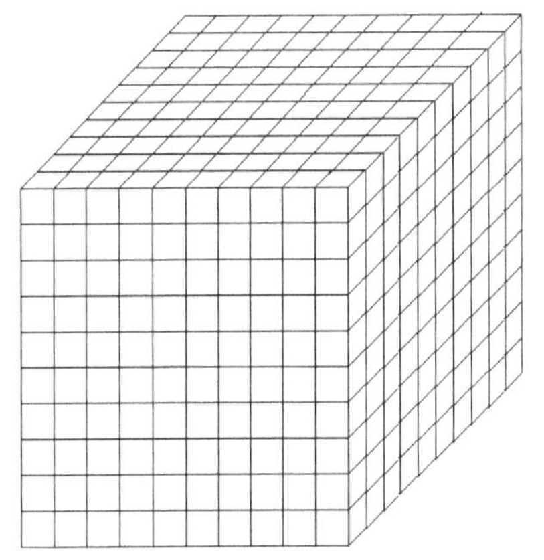
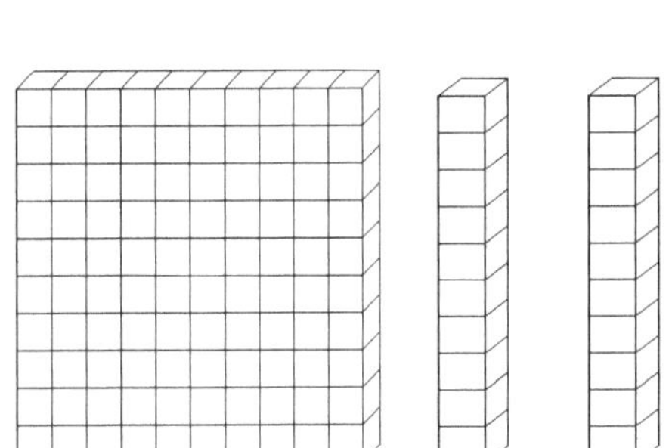

1123
____

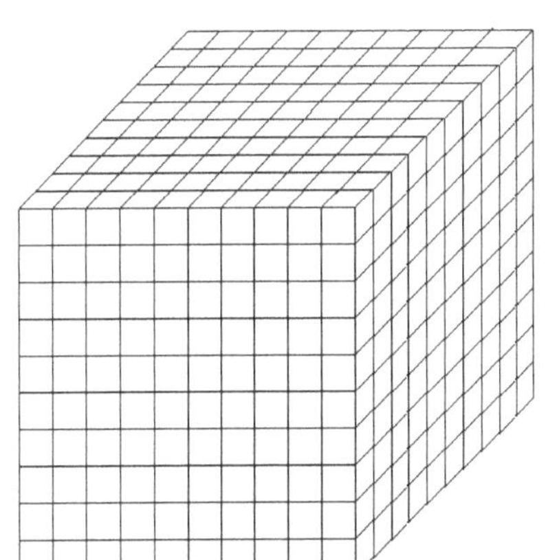
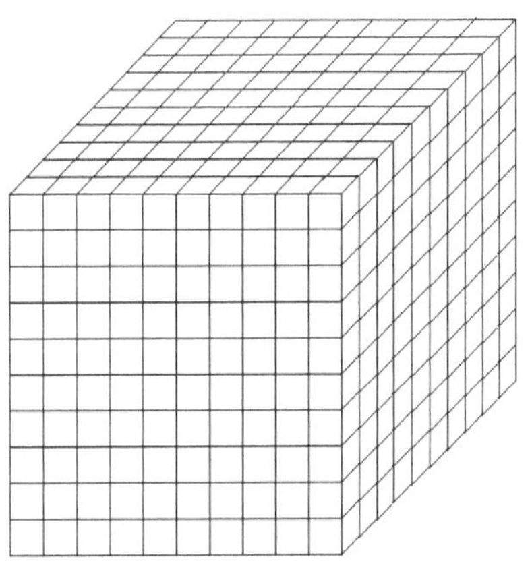
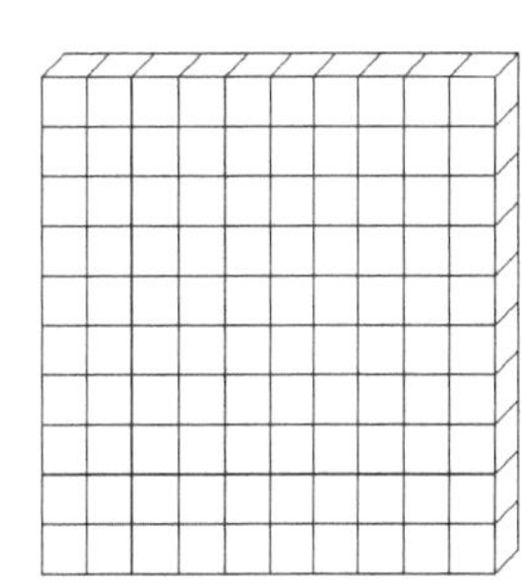

2100
____

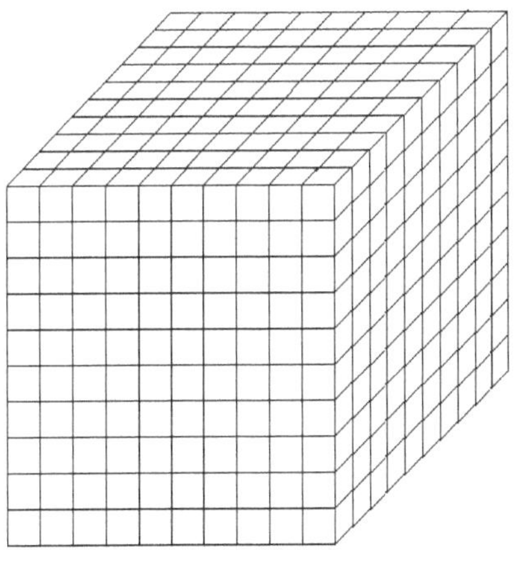
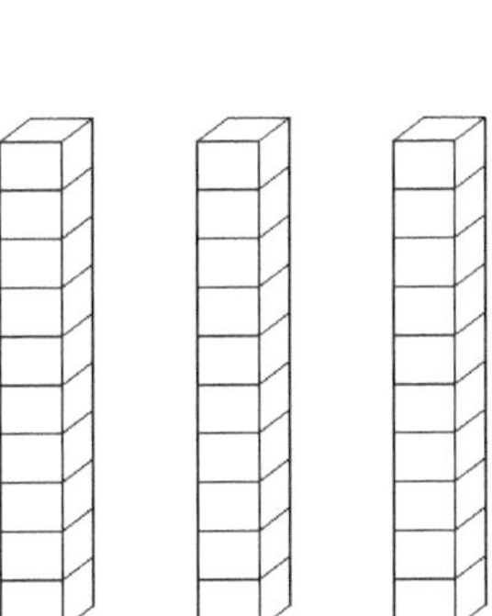

1032
____

Student's name: ____________________ Assignment date: ________________

Convert words to standard numbers.

1. four thousand two hundred seventy-three __________.4273
2. six thousand eight hundred thirty-one __________.6831
3. one thousand ninety-five __________.1095
4. two thousand two hundred three __________.2203
5. five thousand six hundred ten __________.5610
6. four thousand five hundred nine __________.4509
7. eleven thousand two hundred thirty-four __________.11234
8. three hundred seventeen __________.317
9. thirteen hundred fifty-three __________.1353
10. eight thousand two __________.8002
11. four thousand twelve __________.4012
12. six thousand three hundred three __________.6303
13. nine thousand eighty-five __________.9085
14. three thousand one hundred six __________.3106
15. six thousand nine __________.6009

Student's name: ____________________ Assignment date: ________________

Convert the standard number to English words.

1. 3000 Three thousand.
2. 2574 Two thousand five hundred seventy-four.
3. 743 Seven hundred forty-three.
4. 2500 Two thousand five hundred.
5. 2308 Two thousand three hundred eight.
6. 3089 Three thousand eighty-nine.
7. 6800 Six thousand eight hundred.
8. 5614 Five thousand six hundred fourteen.
9. 8009 Eight thousand nine.
10. 60 Sixty.
11. 7800 Seven thousand eight hundred.
12. 0 Zero.
13. 3604 Three thousand six hundred four.
14. 5740 Five thousand seven hundred forty.
15. 6396 Six thousand three hundred ninety-six.
16. 7009 Seven thousand nine.

Student's name: ___________________ Assignment date: _______________

Whole number place value

A number may have one or more digits written from left to right, and each digit has a value depending on where it is placed. Understanding the concept of place value allows us to be able to read a number.
The names for place values are called differently when the same digit is placed at different locations.

Example

1234.4321

The above number is read as four thousand two hundred thirty-four and four thousand three hundred twenty-one thousandths

The names of place values for the whole numbers part and decimals part can be read as follows:

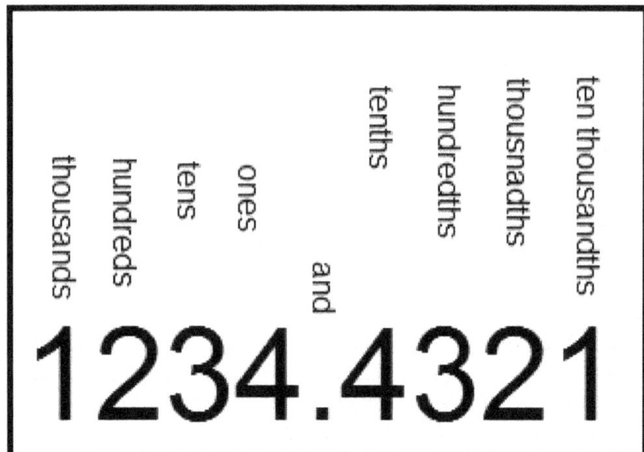

The ones place is also called the units' place.

If there are no place values, then how do you say the following number?

11111.1111

It would be awkward to say one one one one one point one one one one.

Student's name: ____________________ Assignment date: ________________

Choose the correct *place value* of 6 in each of the following numbers.

1.	1356	a. ones ●	b. tens	c. hundreds	d. thousands
2.	2657	a. ones	b. tens	c. hundreds ●	d. thousands
3.	6732	a. ones	b. tens	c. hundreds	d. thousands ●
4.	3651	a. ones	b. tens	c. hundreds ●	d. thousands
5.	7896	a. ones ●	b. tens	c. hundreds	d. thousands
6.	6312	a. ones	b. tens	c. hundreds	d. thousands ●
7.	2561	a. ones	b. tens ●	c. hundreds	d. thousands
8.	7463	a. ones	b. tens ●	c. hundreds	d. thousands

Ho Math Chess Primary Grades Math

Test Review assesssment 何数棋谜低年级数学测试複習考核

Student's name: ____________________ Assignment date: ________________

Choose the correct face *value* of 6 (The value at each place value representing by each digit.) in each of the following numbers.

1356	a. 6 ones ●	b. 6 tens	c. 6 hundreds	d. 6 thousands
2657	a. 6 ones	b. 6 tens	c. 6 hundreds ●	d. 6 thousands
6732	a. 6 ones	b. 6 tens	c. 6 hundreds	d. 6 thousands ●
3651	a. 6 ones	b. 6 tens	c. 6 hundreds ●	d. 6 thousands
7896	a. 6 ones ●	b. 6 tens	c. 6 hundreds	d. 6 thousands
6312	a. 6 ones	b. 6 tens	c. 6 hundreds	d. 6 thousands ●
2561	a. 6 ones	b. 6 tens ●	c. 6 hundreds	d. 6 thousands
7463	a. 6 ones	b. 6 tens ●	c. 6 hundreds	d. 6 thousands

Student's name: ____________________ Assignment date: ________________

Expanded forms of standard whole numbers

A standard number can be rewritten by the sum of its digits. This representation is called expanded from.

Example

Standard form: 3618 (English Words: three thousand six hundred twenty-eight) Expanded form in *face value* of each digit: 3000 + 600 + 20 + 8 Expanded form in *place value* of each digit using English words: 3 thousands + 6 hundreds + 2 tens + 8 ones

Write the following number in expanded from using face value.

1. 6358 = 6000 + 300 + 50 + 8
   7000 + 400 + 20
2. 7420 = ____________________
   5000 + 800 + 30 + 7
3. 5837 = ____________________
   7000 + 200 + 50 + 6
4. 7256 = ____________________
   1000 + 900 + 40 + 3
5. 1943 = ____________________
   9000 + 100 + 60 + 2
6. 9162 = ____________________
   7000 + 900 + 3
7. 7903 = ____________________
   6000 + 800 + 20
8. 6820 = ____________________
   5000 + 800 + 20 + 9

Circle the number which is the greatest in the following.

- $3 \times 1000 + 4 \times 100 + 2 \times 10 + 5 \times 1$
- $3 \times 1000 + 5 \times 100 + 1 \times 10 + 5 \times 1$
- 3 thousands + 5 hundreds + 5 tens + 4 ones
- 3505
- 3560

Circle the last one.

Student's name: ____________________ Assignment date: ________________

Write each number in expanded form using English words.

1. 7042 = 7 thousands + 4 tens + 2 ones

3 thousands + 8 hundreds + 5 ones

2. 3805 = ____

1 thousand + 2 hundreds + 3 tens + 7 ones

3. 1237 = ____

3 thousands + 6 tens + 5 ones

4. 3065 = ____

4 thousands + 2 hundreds

5. 4200 = ____

3 thousands + 8 tens

6. 3080 = ____

5 thousands + 3 ones

7. 5003 = ____

4 thousands + 2 hundreds + 5 tens + 1 one

8. 4251 = ____

Student's name: ____________________ Assignment date: ________________

Convert expanded form to standard form.

1. 6000 + 200 + 50 + 3 = 6253
2. 2000 + 500 + 30 + 8 = __________ 2538
3. 4000 + 600 + 10 + 2 = __________ 4612
4. 7000 + 200 + 9 = __________ 7209
5. 3000 + 400 + 8 = __________ 3408
6. 9000 + 200 + 50 = __________ 9250
7. 1000 + 7 = __________ 1007
8. 2000 + 80 + 6 = __________ 2086
9. 8000 + 100 + 5 = __________ 8105
10. 6 thousands + 5 hundreds + 2 tens + 9 ones = __________ 6529
11. 8 thousands + 3 hundreds + 1 ten + 7 ones = __________ 8317
12. 6 thousands + 2 hundreds + 4 tens + 5 ones = __________ 6245
13. 3 thousands + 8 hundreds + 5 ones = __________ 3805
14. 2 thousands + 4 hundreds + 3 tens + 9 ones = __________ 2439
15. 7 thousands + 7 tens + 6 ones = __________ 7076
16. 5 thousands + 3 hundreds + 8 tens = __________ 5308
17. 1 thousand + 8 tens + 1 one = __________ 1081

Student's name: ____________________ Assignment date: ______________

Write each number in all English words.

1. 21 tens two hundred ten
2. 32 tens Three hundred twenty
3. 470 tens Four thousand seven hundred
4. 36 hundreds Three thousand six hundred
5. 67 hundreds Six thousand seven hundred
6. 18 hundreds One thousand eight hundred
7. 371 hundreds Thirty seven thousand one hundred
8. 4562 ones Four thousand five hundred sixty-two
9. 35 hundreds Three thousand five hundred
10. 720 tens Seven thousand two hundred
11. 29 hundreds Two thousand nine hundred
12. 75 tens Seven hundred fifty
13. 10 hundreds One thousand
14. 20 tens Two hundred
15. 305 tens Three thousand fifty
16. 50 hundreds Five thousand
17. 1009 ones One thousand nine
18. 107 tens One thousand seventy

Student's name: ____________________ Assignment date: ________________

Find as many ways as you can to show the following numbers.

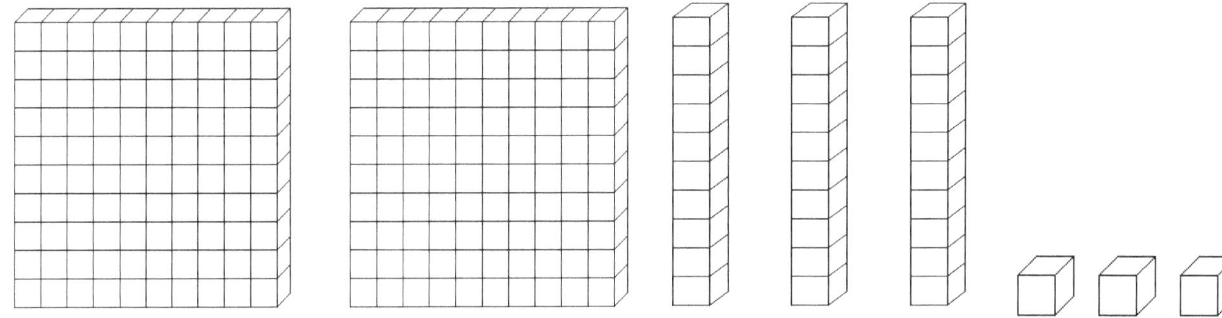

1.	Hundreds	Tens	Ones
2.	2	3	3
3.	2	2	13
4.	2	0	33
5.	1	13	3
6.	1	0	33
7.	0	0	233
8.	0	20	33
9.	0	10	133
10.	0	1	223
11.	0	15	83
12.	0	6	173
13.	0	23	3
14.	0	5	183
15.	0	11	23

Student's name: ____________________ Assignment date: ________________

Find as many ways as you can to show the following numbers.

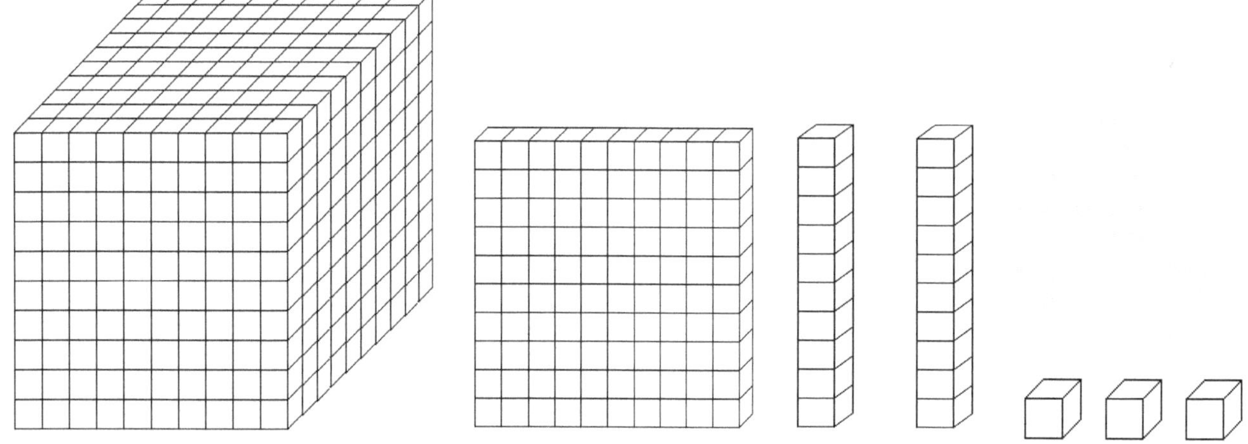

	Thousands	Hundreds	Tens	Ones
1.	1	1	2	3
2.	1	1	1	13
3.	0	0	0	1123
4.	1	0	0	123
5.	1	1	0	23
6.	0	11	0	23
7.	0	0	112	3
8.	0	0	110	23
9.	0	10	12	3
10.	0	1	100	23
11.	0	3	81	13
12.	0	4	70	23
13.	0	5	62	3
14.	0	10	10	23

Ho Math Chess Primary Grades Math

Test Review assesssment 何数棋謎低年级数学测试複習考核

Frank Ho, Amanda Ho

Student's name: ____________________ Assignment date: ________________

Circle the number that is closest to the leftmost number.

1.	560	a. 660	b. 521	c. 570	d. 568 ●
2.	374	a. 384	b. 375 ●	c. 743	d. 4374
3.	2560	a. 5236	b. 600	c. 3560	d. 2568 ●
4.	3646	a. 364	b. 4578	c. 3656 ●	d. 6613
5.	6894	a. 7012 ●	b. 894	c. 8964	d. 9864
6.	2573	a. 2563	b. 2571 ●	c. 2671	d. 2753
7.	8649	a. 9864	b. 8650 ●	c. 8641	d. 4689
8.	2000	a. 999	b. 2111	c. 2005	d. 1999 ●
9.	50	a. 25	b. 35	c. 45 ●	d. 65
10.	4673	a. 4670 ●	b. 4637	c. 4736	d. 7463
11.	6830	a. 6803	b. 6930	c. 6840	d. 6831 ●
12.	6009	a. 9006	b. 6090 ●	c. 9060	d. 6900
13.	2584	a. 2588 ●	b. 2594	c. 2684	d. 3584
14.	2895	a. 1895	b. 2995	c. 2589	d. 2890 ●
15.	6825	a. 7000 ●	b. 6000	c. 6500	d. 5682
16.	4792	a. 7294	b. 4800 ●	c. 4700	d. 4900

Student's name: ____________________ Assignment date: ________________

Count up or count down.

Example: Start at 10 and count up by 2's. 10 , 12 , 14 , 16 , 18 .

Start at 100 and count c by 5's. 100 , 95 , 90 , 85 , 80 .

45 55 65 75 85

1. Start at 45 and count up by 10's. ______ , ______ , ______ , ______ , ______.

29 34 39 44 49

2. Start at 29 and count up by 5's. ______ , ______ , ______ , ______ , ______.

300 400 500 600 700

3. Start at 300 and count up by 100's. ______ , ______ , ______ , ______ , ______.

10 110 210 310 410

4. Start at 10 and count up by 100's. ______ , ______ , ______ , ______ , ______.

4 9 14 19 24

5. Start at 4 and count up by 5's. ______ , ______ , ______ , ______ , ______.

19 16 13 10 7

6. Start at 19 and count down by 3's. ______ , ______ , ______ , ______ , ______.

102 97 92 87 82

7. Start at 102 and count v by 5's. ______ , ______ , ______ , ______ , ______.

115 105 95 85 75

8. Start at 115 and count down by 10's. ______ , ______ , ______ , ______ , ______.

925 825 725 625 525

9. Start at 925 and count back by 100's.______ , ______ , ______ , ______ , ______.

95 92 89 86 83

10. Start at 95 and count back by 3's. ______ , ______ , ______ , ______ , ______.

197 222 247 272 297

Student's name: ____________________ Assignment date: ________________

11. Start at 197 and count up by 25's. ______ , ______ , ______ , ______ , ______.

256 306 356 406 456

12. Start at 256 and count up by 50's. ______ , ______ , ______ , ______ , ______.

720 920 1120 1320 1520

13. Start at 720 and count up by 200's. ______ , ______ , ______ , ______ , ______.

528 548 568 588 608

14. Start at 528 and count down by 20's. ______ , ______ , ______ , ______ , ______.

239 229 219 209 199

15. Start at 239 and count down by 10's. ______ , ______ , ______ , ______ , ______.

137 187 237 287 337

16. Start at 137 and count up by 50's. ______ , ______ , ______ , ______ , ______.

Student's name: ____________________ Assignment date: ________________

Greater than, more than, less than, between

Fill in each blank.

1. 10 greater than 4000 ____________________. 4010

2. 300 less than 1000 ____________________. 700

3. 3 more than 200 ____________________. 203

4. 200 more than 5000 ____________________. 5200

5. between 199 and 201 ____________________. 200

6. 1 less than 400 ____________________. 399

7. 40 more than 1060 ____________________. 1100

8. between 6832 and 6834 ____________________. 6833

9. 2 more than 998 ____________________. 1000

10. 5 less than 2001 ____________________. 1996

Student's name: ____________________ Assignment date: ________________

What number am I given place values (word problems of place values)?

I am a 3-digit number and have twice as many hundreds as tens, three times as many tens as ones. What am I? 631
I have half as many tens as hundreds, half as many hundreds as ones. I am over four-hundred. What am I? 428
I have 8 thousands, twice as many ones as thousands, half as many hundreds as ones and 3 more tens than ones. What am I? 8874
I have a consecutive 4-digit number with the thousands place value as the largest digit. My ones of this number is calculated as follows: $4 - 2 \div 2$. What am I? 6543
I have 15 hundreds, 9 tens, and 17 ones. What am I? 1607
I am a 4-digit consecutive number and my ones digit is 1. What am I? 4321

Student's name: ____________________ Assignment date: ________________

Place value word problems

1. There is a 2-digit number. The last digit is five. The number is between thirty and forty. What can that number be?

35

2. There are two zeros in a number and the number is less than two hundred. What can that number be?

100

3. There is a 3-digit number. The sum of its digits is three and there are no zeros in it. What can that number be?

are
111

4. The tens digit is twice as much as the ones digit. What could be the sum of the tens digit and the ones digit?

Circle the correct answer.

4, 5, 7, 8, 9

The answer is 9. 21 (3), 42(6), 63 (9), 84(12)

5. The left most digit 1 of the number 1234.4221 is how many times of the right-most 1?

$$\frac{1000}{0.0001} = \frac{10000000}{1} = 10{,}000{,}000$$

6. I am a 4-digit number and my ones is 3 more than 2. My tens is 3 more than 1. My hundreds
is 2 less than 10. My thousands is the result of splitting my hundreds equally. What am I?

4745

Student's name: ____________________ Assignment date: ________________

The greatest and the least number

	digits	the greatest number	the least number with no leading 0's. No leading zeros.
1.	2, 4, 6, 8	8642	2468
2.	2, 3, 5, 8	8532	2358
3.	4, 0, 7, 3	7430	3047
4.	5, 1, 4, 7	7541	1457
5.	3, 0, 2, 5	5320	2035
6.	7, 4, 8, 3	8743	3478
7.	5, 7, 2, 1	7521	1257
8.	3, 9, 0, 2	9320	2039
9.	2, 5, 5, 7	7552	2557
10.	6, 1, 1, 8	8611	1168
11.	2, 0, 0, 5	5200	2005
12.	3, 6, 4, 5	6543	3456
13.	6, 7, 5, 5	7655	5567
14.	6, 0, 0, 6	6600	6006

Ho Math Chess Primary Grades Math

Test Review assesssment 何数棋謎低年级数学测试複習考核

Student's name: ____________________ Assignment date: _______________

Compare the following numbers using > (greater than) or < (less than).

1.	6324	__ >	4879	2.	7303	__ >	4898
3.	5463	__ >	5364	4.	12685	__ <	12856
5.	120	__ <	1200	6.	999	__ <	1000
7.	2231	__ <	2241	8.	4478	__ <	4487
9.	5655	__ <	6555	10.	7538	__ <	7601
11.	3250	__ <	4103	12.	96	__ <	120

Circle the number that is greater than the number on the left most

1.	3518	a. 5138 •	b. 1468	c. 8351 •	d. 3185
2.	6484	a. 3684	b. 6548 •	c. 8446 •	d. 6348
3.	7951	a. 3758	b. 7953 •	c. 7591	d. 8001 •
4.	6083	a. 3806	b. 3386	c. 6088 •	d. 6830 •
5.	2753	a. 5237 •	b. 3572 •	c. 2537	d. 2235
6.	9732	a. 9741 •	b. 7933	c. 9823 •	d. 9703
7.	2063	a.3000 •	b.2300 •	c.2100 •	d.2000
8.	1650	a.1500	b.1600	c.1560	d.1056

Student's name: ____________________ Assignment date: ________________

Order each set of numbers from least to greatest.

1. 1643, 789, 6732, 5673
 789, 1643, 5673, 6732
____.

2. 4573, 4628, 6274, 2890
 2890, 4573, 4628, 6274
____.

3. 55365, 56365, 55465, 55366
 55365, 55355, 55465, 56365
____.

4. 4731, 4745, 4754, 5474
 4731, 4745, 4754, 5474
____.

5. 5720, 3792, 7558, 5721
____.

Order each set of numbers from greatest to least.

1. 6743, 7643, 4673, 4763
 7643, 6743, 4763, 4673
____.

2. 5304, 4998, 8994, 4899
 8994, 5304, 4998, 4899
____.

3. 1000, 9999, 1002, 2001
 9999, 2001, 1002, 1000
____.

4. 85735, 85635, 85935, 76895,
 85935, 85735, 85635, 76895
____.

5. 5782, 4628, 5728, 6482
 6482, 5782, 5728, 4628
____.

Ho Math Chess Primary Grades Math

Test Review assesssment 何数棋謎低年级数学测试複習考核

Student's name: ____________________ Assignment date: ________________

Test of number representation and place value

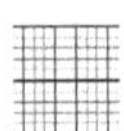

Solve the following number riddle. I have 13 tens, 7 ones, 3 hundreds. What am I? 437
I am 237 and I have 1 hundred and 9 ones. How many tens do I need to make up to 237? 2 tens

Number written in standard form	Whole number written in English words	Number written in expanded form	Written in number and words using place values	Represented by Base Ten blocks	Value of the underlined digit
463	Four hundred sixty-three	400+60+3	4 hundreds + 6 tens + 3 ones		3
259	Two hundred fifty-nine	200+50+9	2 hundreds + 5 tens + 9 ones		50
310	Three hundred ten	300 + 10	3 hundreds + 1 tens	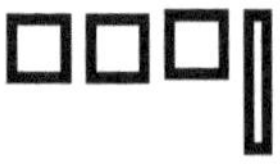	300
4302	Four thousand three hundred two	4000+300 +2	4 thousands + 3 hundreds + 2 ones	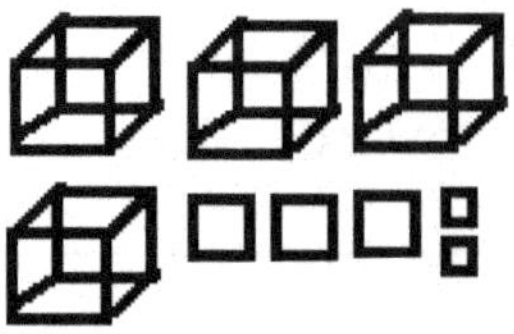	4000

Student's name: ____________________ Assignment date: ________________

+ 12.2 of 1 hundred + 15 of tens + 10 of tenths

= ___ hundreds ____ tens ___ ones ___ hundredths

1371.12
13 hundreds + 7 tens + 1 ones + 12 hundredths

120 + 15 + [image] = ?

135.4

Find A and B.

$$\begin{array}{r} BA \\ -\ 74 \\ \hline 16 \end{array} \qquad \begin{array}{r} 6A \\ -\ B5 \\ \hline 18 \end{array}$$

B=9, A=0, 90-74=16,
A=3, B=4, 63-45=18

Standard numbers	English words of place values of the underlined digit.	Face values	Rounding
375,231,872.2134 (3 underlined)	Hundreds millions	Three hundred millions	Round at 1,000,000. 375,000,000
375,231,872.2135 (3 underlined)	thousandths	Three thousandths	Round at 100th. 375,341,873.21

Student's name: ____________________ Assignment date: ________________

Number written in standard form	Number written in English words	Number written in expanded form	Written in number and words using place values	Represented by Base Ten blocks	Value of the underlined digit
352	Three hundred fifty two	300 + 50 + 2	3 hundreds + 5 tens + 2 ones		Not available
96	Ninety six	90 + 6	9 tens + 6 ones		Not available

Represented the following base ten blocks by fewer blocks

Standard number is? 1114

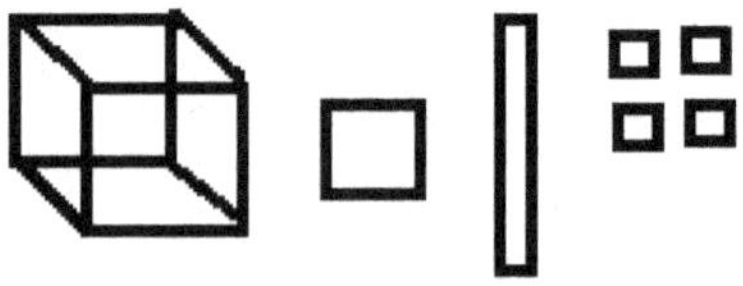

answer

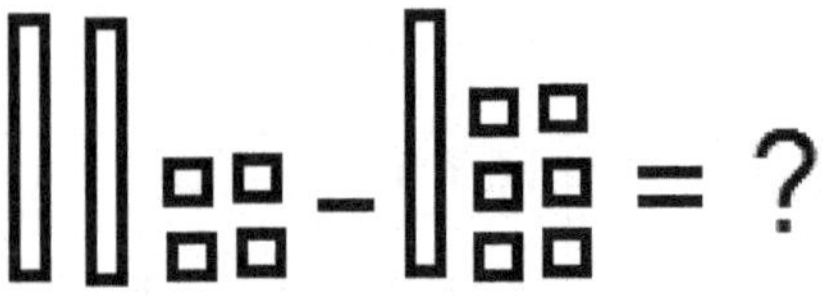

= ?

Answer 8

Student's name: ____________________ Assignment date: ________________

Use only digits 0 1 4 5 9 to create numbers and each digit cannot be repeated in each number.

Problems	Answers
What is the largest 4-digit number?	9541
What is the largest 3-digit number?	954
What is the largest 4-digit even number?	9540
What is the largest 4-digit odd number?	9541
What is the largest 4-digit number with 4 in the hundreds place?	9451
What is the largest 4-digit number with 8 in the thousands place?	8954
What is the largest 4-digit number that is divisible by 4?	9540
What is the largest 3-digit odd number that is divisible by 3?	951
What is the largest 3-digit even number that is divisible by 4?	940

4213 – 2918 = 10 × ____ + 100 × ____ + 1000 × __+ 1 × ____

1, 2, 9, 5

Student's name: ____________________ Assignment date: ________________

***** Part 2 Number Theory *****

Factor and primes

A natural number can always be expressed as a product of two other natural numbers. These two natural numbers are called factors. If a natural number can only be a product of the other two numbers, then this number is a prime number. If the factor is a prime, then it is called a prime factor.

The "Repeated Division`` method is used to find factors or prime factors.

What is the greatest odd factor of 48? 3
How many primes are there from 10 to 30? 6 11, 13, 17, 19, 23, 29
The number x is a prime factor of 9, then what is the prime factor x + 3 =? 6
The greatest odd factor of 60 is ___________. 15

Student's name: ____________________ Assignment date: ________________

Multiplier

A number can be multiplied by 1, 2, 3, …etc.. These products are also called multiples. A number has infinite multiples. The results in the times table from 1×1 to 1×9 are multiples of 1.

I am a multiple of 5 between 0 and 39 and am also an odd number. What numbers could I be? 5, 15, 25, 35
I am a multiple of 5 between 0 and 39 and am also an even number. What numbers could I be? 10, 20, 30
I am a multiple of 5 greater than 39 and less than 58 and am an even number. What numbers could I be? 40, 50
I am a multiple of 5 greater than 39 and less than 58 and am an odd number. What numbers could I be? 45, 55
I am a multiple of both 3 and 5 between 0 and 39 and am also an odd number. What numbers could I be? 15
I am a multiple of both 4 and 5 between 29 and 59. What numbers could I be? 40, 60
I am a multiple of both 4 and 7 and am less than 100. What numbers could I be? 28, 56, 84

Student's name: ___________________ Assignment date: _______________

Odd and even numbers

Many students will answer that even numbers are 2, 4, 6, 8,… etc., but what happens to 1212? Is it even or odd? To understand that if the last digit (the rightmost one) of a number is 0, 2, 4, 6, 8, then it is an even number is important. In contrast, if the last digit (the rightmost one) of a number is 1, 3, 5, 7, 9, then it is an odd number.

.

Circle the following numbers, which are even. 2, 14, 13, 29, 24, 102, 0, 100, 231 437, 500, 502, 609, 111, 102, 134 2 13 29 231 437 609 111
There is a 2-digit number. If the one place digit must be even and the tens place digit must be odd, what could be the largest 2-digit number? 98 .
How many even numbers are there from 100 to 200? $\left[\frac{200}{2}\right] - \left[\frac{98}{2}\right] = 100 - 49 = 51$
Is the sum of an even number + an even number odd or even? even
Is the difference of an even number – an even number odd or even? even
Is the sum of an even number + an odd number odd or even? odd
Is the sum of an even number – an odd number odd or even? odd
Is the sum of an odd number + an odd number odd or even? even
Is the sum of an odd number – an odd number odd or even? even
Is the produce of an even number × an odd number odd or even? even

Student's name: ____________________ Assignment date: ________________

Divisibility Rules

Divisor	Numbers Divisible	Example	Reason
2	The last digit is even	8336	the last digit is even
3	The sum of digits is divisible by 3	411	4 + 1 + 1 = 6, 6 is divisible by 3
4	The last two digits are '00' or exactly divisible by 4	2132	32 ÷ 4 = 8
5	The last digit is '5' or '0'	3265	The unit digit is '5'
6	Any even number divisible by 3	1248	Is even and 1+2+4+8 = 15 is divisible by 3.
8	The last three digits are '00' or exactly divisible by 8	4624	624 ÷ 8 = 78
9	Sum of digits is divisible by 9	3141	3+1+4+1= 9 is divisible by 9.
10	The last digit is '0'	3620	unit digit is '0'

Student's name: ____________________ Assignment date: ______________

Divisibility rules word problems

Circle the following numbers which are divisible by 2 or 5. 10, 25, 50, 15, 30, 14, 16, 20, 55, 56, 100, 90
The ratio of the number of even numbers divisible by 4 between 17 to 29 to the number of odd numbers divisible by 3 between 24 and 36 is ________. The even numbers divisible by 4 between 17 to 29 are 20, 24, 28 The odd numbers divisible by 3 between 17 to 29 are 18, 21, 24, 27 The ratio is 3 to 4.
When a number is divided by 13 the quotient is 3 and the remainder is 2. What is the remainder of the same number is divided by 5? The number is $13 \times 3 + 2 = 41$ $8 \times 5 + 1 = 41$ The remainder is 1.
What numbers between 111 and 279 are divisible by both 3 and 5? The number divisible by 5 must end in 0 or 5. 120, 135, 150, 165, 185, 210, 225, 245, 269, 275. Find the first smallest number above 111 and is divisible by both 3 and 5 which is 120, then just add the LCM of 3 and 5 which is 15 .
There are three consecutive numbers and each of them is less than 100.The smallest is divisible by 3, the middle number is divisible by 2, and the largest is divisible by 5. What are these three numbers? The middle one is divisible by 2 which is an even number. The largest must end in 0 or 5. The set of the three smallest values are 3, 4, 5. 33, 34, 35; 63, 64, 65; 93, 94, 95
How many numbers less than 200 are divisible by either 2 or 5 but not both? $\left[\frac{198}{2}\right] + \left[\frac{195}{5}\right] - \left[\frac{190}{10}\right] = 99 + 39 - 19 = 119$

Student's name: ____________________ Assignment date: ________________

2, 3, and 5 are used to make a three-digit number $\overline{abc}$. The three digit number $\overline{abc}$ is divisible by 2. $\overline{ab}$ is divisible by 5. What is $\overline{abc}$? 352
Find the sum of all counting numbers less than 20, which are not divisible by 2 or 3. 5+7+11+13+17+19 =73
The number 2325 is divisible by 3 and also 5. What is the next larger number which is divisible 3 and 5? 2340
What is the smallest number that is divisible by 3, 5, and 7, but not divisible by 4, 6, or 8? 105

Student's name: ____________________ Assignment date: _______________

Mark "√" if the number is divisible by the following.

	36	29	72	45	51	70
By 2	√		√			√
By 3	√		√	√	√	
By 5				√		√
By 10						√

Mark "√" if the number is divisible by the following.

	310	512	341	524	136	372
By 2	√	√		√	√	√
By 4		√		√	√	√
By 8		√			√	

Mark "√" if the number is divisible by the following.

	258	441	639	139	204	342
By 3	√	√	√		√	√
By 6	√				√	√
By 9		√	√			√

1. Write the largest 3- digit number that is divisible by 2. 998
2. Write the largest 3- digit number that is divisible by 3. 999
3. Write the largest 3- digit number that is divisible by 6. 996

Student's name: ____________________ Assignment date: ________________

***** Part 3 Order of operations *****

When finding the value for an expression (called evaluating), the way to do it is from left to right and use the rule of BEDMAS (bracket, exponent, division, multiplication, addition, subtraction). It means:

Do the bracket first.
Do the exponents second
Then do division or multiplication, depending on whichever comes first.
Finally, do addition or subtraction depending on whichever comes first.

For example, $3 + 2 - 4 + (2 + 3) \div 5 \times 2 - 1 + 2^2$
$= 5 - 4 + 5 \div 5 \times 2 - 1 + 4$
$= 1 + 1 \times 2 - 1 + 4$
($5 \div 5$ must be done before multiplication and been added to others)
$= 1 + 2 - 1 + 4$
$= 3 - 1 + 4$
$= 2 + 4$
$= 6$

If there are addition, subtraction, multiplication, and division in the expression, do multiplication and division first, then do addition and subtraction. The order is usually from left to right.

Evaluate the following expressions.

Expressions	Value	Comments
$7 - 2 \times 3$	1	
$7 - (2 \times 3)$	1	Are the brackets necessary? _______
$(7 - 2) \times 3$	15	
$2 \times 7 - 3$	11	
$(2 \times 7) - 3$	11	Are the brackets necessary? ______
$2 \times (7 - 3)$	8	
$4 \times 5 + 6 \times 7$	12	

Student's name: ____________________ Assignment date: ________________

Test of evaluating the following expressions

Expressions	Value	Comments
4 × (5 + 6) × 7	308	
4 × (5 + 6 × 7)	188	
(4 × 5 + 6) × 7	182	
45 ÷ 5 + 9 ÷ 3	12	
(45 ÷ 5) + (9 ÷ 3)	12	Are brackets necessary? ________
42 ÷ (5 + 9) ÷ 3	1	
48 ÷ (5 + 9 ÷ 3)	6	
(45 ÷ 5 + 9) ÷ 3	6	
1 + 2 + 3 ÷ 3 – 2 – 1	1	
(1 + 2 + 3) ÷ (3 – 2) – 1	5	
1 + 2 + 3 ÷ (3 – 2)– 1	5	
1 + 2 + 3 ÷ 3 x 2 – 1	4	
1 + 2 + 3 ÷ 3 x(2 – 1)	4	
$\frac{2+4\div 2}{8+6\times 2}$ =?	1/5	

Student's name: ____________________ Assignment date: ________________

Evaluate mixed operations by using the order of operations.

$7 \times 4 + 3 \times 8$
$= 28 + 24$
$= 52$

$7 \times 9 - 16 \div 2$
$= 63 - 8$
$= 55$

1. $6 \times 5 + 9 \times 4 \quad = 66$

2. $8 \div 2 - 9 \div 3 \quad = 1$

3. $5 \times 7 - 6 \div 2 \quad = 32$

4. $5 \times 9 + 3 \times 6 \quad = 63$

5. $8 \div 4 - 7 \div 7 \quad = 1$

6. $5 \times 7 + 8 \div 4 \quad = 37$

7. $6 \div 3 + 9 \times 6 \quad = 56$

8. $8 \div 2 + 4 \times 7 \quad = 32$

9. $9 \times 2 + 3 \times 7 \quad = 39$

10. $8 \times 3 + 6 \div 2 \quad = 27$

Student's name: ____________________ Assignment date: ________________

Evaluate mixed operations by using the order of operations.

8 + 2 × 7 + 6	5 + 9 ÷ 3 – 2
= 8 + 14 + 6	= 5 + 3 – 2
= 28	= 6

1. 5 + 7 × 8 + 3 = 64
2. 5 + 8 ÷ 2 + 6 = 15
3. 4 + 16 ÷ 2 – 5 = 7
4. 7 + 3 × 7 – 9 = 19
5. 8 + 6 ÷ 2 + 7 = 18
6. 8 + 4 × 6 + 5 = 37
7. 7 + 12 ÷ 3 – 5 = 6
8. 9 – 15 ÷ 3 + 8 = 12
9. 7 + 24 ÷ 6 + 8 = 19
10. 9 + 21 ÷ 3 – 7 = 9

Student's name: ____________________ Assignment date: ________________

***** Part 4 Shortcuts for number computation *****

Some shortcuts can be used to do computation mentally. These shortcuts allow students to do computation more efficiently and improve their computation skills.

Student's name: ____________________ Assignment date: ________________

Multiplied by 5.

Try to find a matching 2 so that 2 × 5 = 10.

Example

5 × 16 = 5 × 2 × 8 = 10 × 8 = 80

124 × 5 = 62 × 2 × 5 = 62 × 10 = 620

1. 5 × 46 = 230
2. 5 × 58 = 290
3. 64 × 5 = 320
4. 78 × 5 = 390
5. 102 × 5 = 510
6. 372 × 5 = 1860
7. 5 × 612 = 3060
8. 5 × 406 = 2030
9. 306 × 5 = 1530
10. 1004 × 5 = 5020
11 92 × 5 = 460
12. 5 × 3040= 15200

Student's name: ____________________ Assignment date: ________________

Multiplied by 25

Try to find a matching 4 so that 4 × 25 = 100

Example:

25 × 8 = 25 × 4 × 2 = 100 × 2 = 200
132 × 25 = 33 × 4 × 25 = 33 × 100 = 3300

1. 28 × 25 = 700
2. 44 × 25 = 1100
3. 25 × 36 = 900
4. 25 × 72 = 1800
5. 25 × 124 = 3100
6. 84 × 25 = 2100
7. 172 × 25 = 4300
8. 452 × 25 = 11300
9. 208 × 25 = 5200
10. 356 × 25 = 8900
11 25 × 332 = 8300
12. 704 × 25 = 17600

Student's name: ____________________ Assignment date: ________________

Multiplied by 125

Try to find a matching 8 so that 8 × 125 = 1000

Example

125 × 48 = 125 × 8 × 6 = 1000 × 6 = 6000
168 × 125 = 21 × 8 × 125 = 21 × 1000 = 21000

1. 125 × 16 = 2000
2. 125 × 48 = 6000
3. 88 × 125 = 11000
4. 72 × 125 = 9000
5. 96 × 125 = 12000
6. 125 × 56 = 7000
7. 125 × 24 = 3000
8. 64 × 125 = 8000
9. 80 × 125 = 10000
10. 125 × 160 = 20000
11 32 × 125 = 4000
12. 125 × 720 = 90000

Student's name: ____________________ Assignment date: ________________

Multiplied an even number by a number ending with 5.

Example

26 × 35 = 13 × 2 × 35 = 13 × 70 = 910
45 × 38 = 45 × 2 × 19 = 90 × 19 = 1710

1. 15 × 28 = 420
2. 35 × 74 = 2590
3. 15 × 34 = 510
4. 25 × 52 = 1300
5. 36 × 45 = 1620
6. 66 × 35 = 2310
7. 128 × 35 = 4480
8. 14 × 85 = 1190
9. 75 × 12 = 900
10. 135 × 16 = 2160
11 325 × 6 = 1950
12. 715 × 4 = 2860

Student's name: ____________________ Assignment date: ________________

Numbers ending in 5 multiply by the number itself

Example

15 × 15 = 1 × (1+1) 25 = 225
35 × 35 = 3 × (3+1) 25 = 1225

1. 25 × 25 = 625
2. 45 × 45 = 2025
3. 35 × 35 = 1225
4. 95 × 95 = 9025
5. 55 × 55 = 3025
6. 65 × 65 = 4225
7. 85 × 85 = 7225
8. 75 × 75 = 5625
9. 15 × 15 = 225
10. 195 × 195 = 38025

11 105 × 105 = 11025

12. 205 × 205 = 42025

Student's name: ____________________ Assignment date: ________________

Multiplied by 11

Example

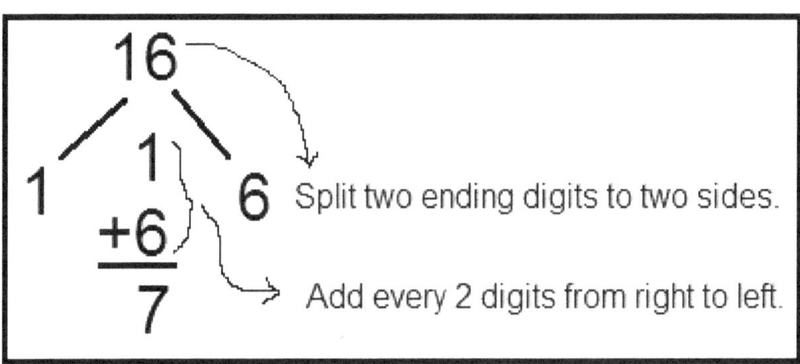

16 × 11 = 1(1 + 6) 6 = 176

11 × 37 = 3 (3 + 7) 7 = 3 (10) 7 = 407

1. 24 × 11 = 264
2. 11 × 18 = 198
3. 32 × 11 = 352
4. 11 × 27 = 297
5. 61 × 11 = 671
6. 11 × 81 = 891
7. 56 × 11 = 616
8. 78 × 11 = 858
9. 11 × 77 = 847
10. 11 × 84 = 924
11. 11 × 123 = 1353
12. 458 × 11 = 5038

Student's name: ____________________ Assignment date: ________________

Shortcut for adding numbers ending with 0's

This shortcut can also be used for subtraction.

Thousands adding thousands

1. 4000 + 9000 = 1300	2. 5000 + 9000 = 14000	3. 5000 + 3000 = 8000
4. 7000 + 4000 = 11000	5. 3000 + 2000 = 5000	6. 6000 + 800 = 6800
7. 8000 + 5000 = 13000	8. 7000 + 3000 = 10000	9. 7000 + 7000 = 14000
10. 6000 + 3000 = 9000	11. 5000 + 4000 = 9000	12. 3000 + 7000 = 10000
13. 8000 + 4000 = 12000	14. 9000 + 7000 = 16000	15. 9000 + 8000 = 17000

Fill in each blank to add up to thousands or ten thousand.

1. 5000 + 5000 = 10000	2. 3000 + 7000 = 10000
3. 6700 + 3300 = 10000	4. 5200 + 4800 = 10000
5. 7420 + 2580 = 10000	6. 3810 + 6190 = 10000
7. 8409 + 1591 = 10000	8. 3617 + 6383 = 10000
9. 2509 + 2491 = 5000	10. 2175 + 825 = 3000
11. 3096 + 3904 = 7000	12. 3289 + 2711 = 6000
13. 2078 + 1922 = 4000	14. 2843 + 2157 = 5000
15. 1745 + 6255 = 8000	16. 2004 + 4996 = 7000

Student's name: ____________________ Assignment date: ________________

The following does subtraction to get nice numbers ending with 0 first.

25 + 36 – 16
= 25 + 20
= 45

31 – 17 + 47
= 31 + 47 – 17
= 31 + 30
= 61

1. 42 + 37 – 17 = 62

2. 23 – 16 + 36 = 43

3. 41 – 28 + 38 = 51

4. 63 – 35 + 45 = 73

5. 72 – 38 + 58 = 92

6. 57 + 21 – 47 = 31

7. 53 – 24 + 44 = 73

8. 56 + 33 – 46 = 43

9. 39 + 41 – 29 = 51

10. 37 – 29 + 49 = 57

Student's name: ____________________ Assignment date: ________________

multiplied or divided by 10, 100, or 1000

Multiplied by the power of multiples of 10 Add the sum of ending zeros two factors to the end of the non-zero product. 2 × 5 = 10 4 × 25 = 100, 5 × 20 = 100 8× 125 = 1000	Divided by the power of multiples of 10 Cross out the same number of ending zeros of both dividend and divisor. 3120000 ÷ 300 = 10400
10 × 10 = 24100	10 ÷ 10 = 1
100 × 10 =1000	100 ÷ 10 = 10
200 × 2 × 5 = 1000	200 ÷ 2 ÷ 50 = 2
7200 × 900 = 6480000	7200 ÷ 900 = 8
300 × 570000 = 171000000	570000 ÷ 300 = 1900
40000 ×1560000 = 62400000000	1560000 ÷ 40000 = 39
8005 ×76000 = 608,380,000	576000 ÷ 800 = 720
6500 × 4 × 25 = 650,000	6500 ÷ 8÷ 125 = 6.5
105000× 700 = 73,500,000	105000÷ 700 = 150
472000 × 400 = 188,800,000	472000 ÷ 400 = 1180
50000 × 2000 = 100,000,000	50000 ÷ 2000 = 25
640000 × 40010 = 254,06,400,000	640000 ÷ 40010 =16
10 × 8 × 125 = 10,000	100 ÷ 10 = 10
100 × 4 × 25 = 10,000	1000 ÷ 4÷ 25 = 10
200 × 5 × 20 = 2,000,000	2000 ÷ 10 = 200
7200 × 9000 = 64,800,000	72000 ÷ 900 = 80
570000 × 3000 = 1,710,000,000	5700000 ÷ 300 = 19000
1560000 ×400000 = 624,000,000,000	15600000 ÷ 40000 = 390
576000 × 8000 = 4,608,000,000	5760000 ÷ 800 = 7200
6500 × 500 = 3,250,000	65000 ÷ 50 = 1300
105000× 7000 = 735,000,000	1050000÷ 700 = 1500
472000 × 4000 = 18,888,000,000	4720000 ÷ 400 = 11800
50000 × 20000 = 1,000,000,000	500000 ÷ 2000 = 250

,

Student's name: ____________________ Assignment date: ________________

Shortcuts for mixed operation

The following expressions can be thought of as vertical formats so that the top and the bottom number can be reduced by a common factor first.

$28 \times \underline{36 \div 9}$

$= 28 \times 4$

$= 112$

$57 \div 3 \times 6$

$= 57 \times \underline{6 \div 3}$

$= 57 \times 2$

$= 114$

1. $56 \times 12 \div 4 \quad = 168$
2. $64 \div 4 \times 8 \quad = 128$
3. $81 \div 3 \times 9 \quad = 243$
4. $51 \times 26 \div 13 \quad = 102$
5. $84 \div 7 \times 21 \quad = 252$
6. $75 \times 15 \div 5 \quad = 225$
7. $53 \times 36 \div 12 \quad = 159$
8. $84 \div 6 \times 48 \quad = 672$
9. $68 \div 4 \times 24 \quad = 408$
10. $35 \times 66 \div 11 \quad = 210$

Student's name: ____________________ Assignment date: ________________

***** Part 5 Different methods of computing and number models *****

Other than the traditional method of computing from right to left, there are other computing methods.
For the exploratory study, these methods are often mentioned in math textbooks.

Student's name: ____________________ Assignment date: ________________

Front end Addition

Front end computation is a good way to do mental math, and this technique can also be used for estimating.

Example 1

Vertical format

$$\begin{array}{r} 24 \\ +\ 35 \\ \hline 54 \\ +\ \ 5 \\ \hline 59 \end{array}$$

54 ⇦ Add the leftmost digit digits (tens place) first,

\+ 5 ⇦ then add the digits (ones place) next to the right.

Horizontal format

24 + 35 = 24 + 30 + 5 = 54 + 5 = 59

Example 2

Vertical format

$$\begin{array}{r} 37 \\ +\ 87 \\ \hline 117 \\ +\ \ 7 \\ \hline 124 \end{array}$$

117 ⇦ Add the leftmost digits (tens place) first,

\+ 7 ⇦ then add the digits (ones place) next to the right.

Horizontal format

37 + 87 = 37 + 80 + 7 = 117 + 7 = 124

Student's name: ____________________ Assignment date: ________________

Example 3

Vertical format

```
   498
 + 789
 -----
  1198  ⇦ Add the leftmost digit (hundreds place) first.
    80  ⇦ Add the tens place.
 +   9  ⇦ Add the ones place.
 -----
  1278
 +   9
 -----
  1287
```

Horizontal format

498 + 789 = 498 + 700 + 80 + 9 = 1198 + 80 + 9 = 1278 + 9 = 1287

Student's name: ____________________ Assignment date: ________________

Test of front end addition

Calculate the following in horizontal format.

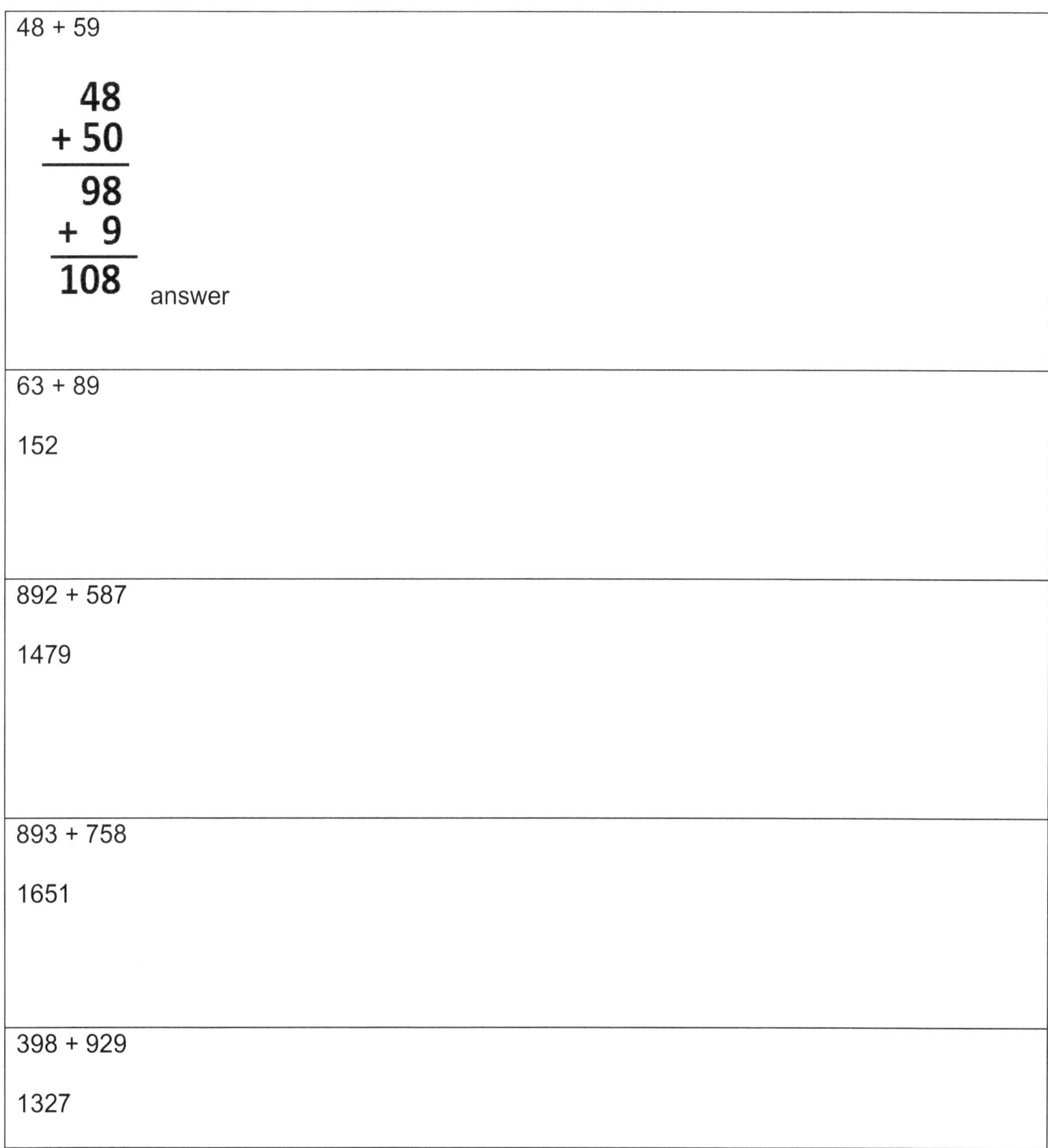

48 + 59

$$\begin{array}{r} 48 \\ +\ 50 \\ \hline 98 \\ +\ 9 \\ \hline 108 \end{array}$$ answer

63 + 89

152

892 + 587

1479

893 + 758

1651

398 + 929

1327

Student's name: ____________________ Assignment date: ________________

Front end subtraction

Example 1

Vertical format

```
   98
 - 86
 ----
   18  ⇦ Subtract the leftmost digit (tens place) first. (98 - 80 = 18).
 -  6  ⇦ Subtract the next right digit (ones place).
 ----
   12  ⇦ Add the 2 differences.
```

Horizontal format

98- 86 = 98 – 80 – 6 = 18 – 6 = 12

Example 2

Vertical format

```
   87
 - 39
 ----
   57  ⇦ Subtract the leftmost digit (tens place) first.
 -  9  ⇦ Subtract the next right digit (ones place).
 ----
   48  ⇦ Subtract
```

Horizontal format

87 – 39 = 87 – 30 -9 = 57 – 9 = 48

Student's name: ____________________ Assignment date: ________________

Example 3

Vertical format

```
  762
- 685
-----
  162   ⇦ Subtract the leftmost digit (hundreds place) first. (762 - 600 = 162)
-  85   ⇦ Subtract the next right digit (tens place).
-----
   82
-   5   ⇦ Subtract the next right digit (ones place).
-----
   77
```

Horizontal format

762 – 685 = 762 -600 – 80 – 5 = 162 – 80 – 5 = 82 – 5 = 78

Student's name: ____________________ Assignment date: ________________

Test of front end subtraction

Calculate the following in horizontal format.

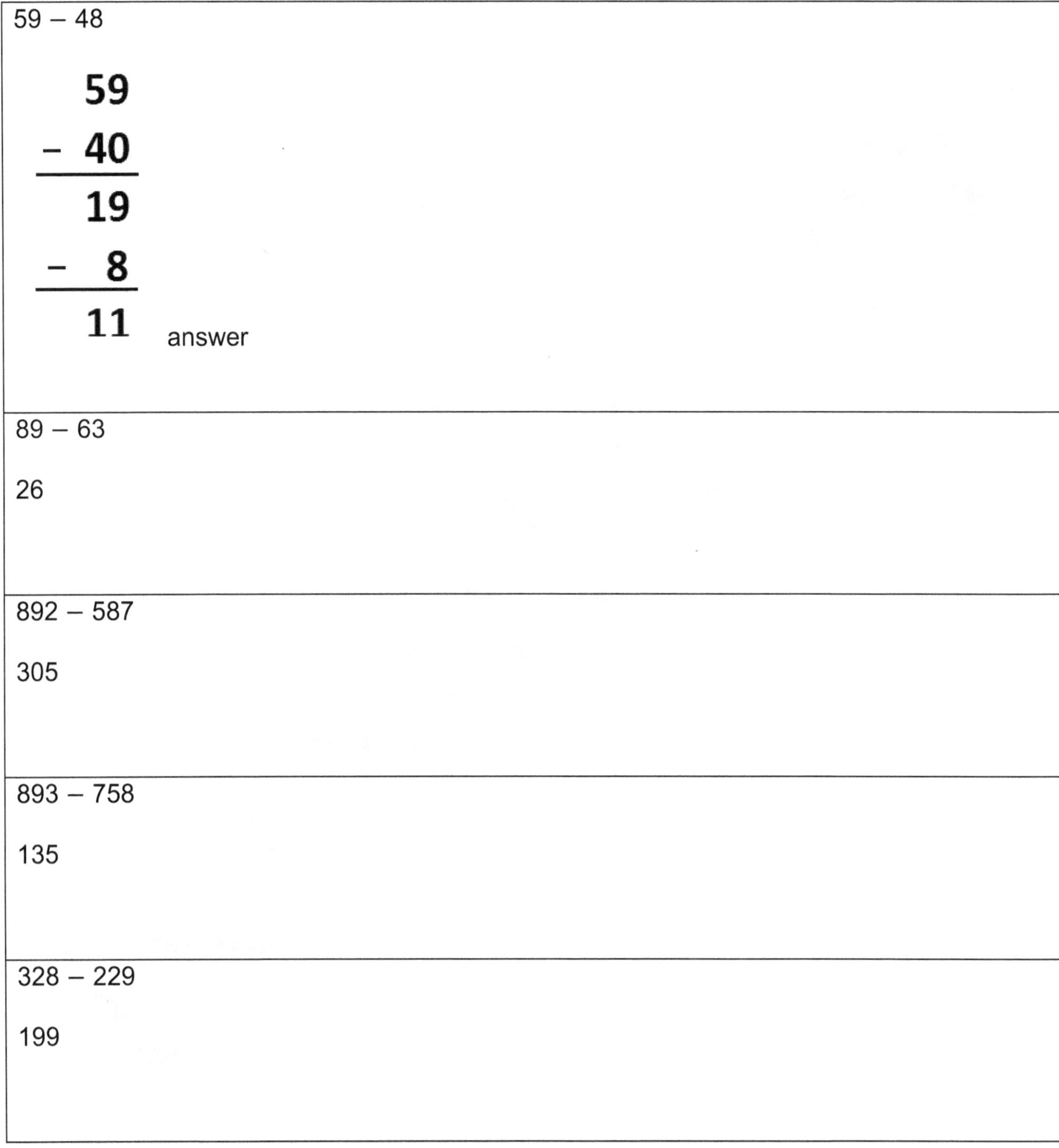

59 – 48

$$\begin{array}{r} 59 \\ -\ 40 \\ \hline 19 \\ -\ 8 \\ \hline 11 \end{array}$$ answer

89 – 63

26

892 – 587

305

893 – 758

135

328 – 229

199

Student's name: ____________________ Assignment date: ________________

Different subtraction methods

The following methods could be used to master subtraction skills.

Strategies	Procedure	Comments
Intuitive	Some students have done enough computations to the extent they just Know the answers.	Requires the student's willingness to learn and memorize.
Borrowing 10	1 1 – 7 1 ten is borrowed to minus 7 (to get 3) and then add 1 to get the answer 4.	A universal method can be used to subtract all facts.
Making ten (adding the bottom to 10)	1 1 – 7 3 added to 7 is 10, so 3 plus 1 is 4. This method is similar to the above borrowing 10	A universal method can be used to subtract all facts.
Counting back	1 1→1 0→ 9 – 2 Subtract 1 from 11 to make 10, and then subtract 1 again to make 9.	A universal method but still doing the counting and using less reasoning and logic.
Adding the bottom to 10	1 1 →□□1 3 – 8→ – 1 0	Making the bottom number to be 10 by addition. A universal approach for all subtraction facts but requires multiple operators.
Subtracting top to 10	1 2 →□□1 0 – 3→ – 1	A reverse method similar to the above idea but by subtracting the top number down to 10.
Turn subtraction into addition	13 + 4 6 +3 = 9	A universal method and also fast in getting answers.

Student's name: ____________________ Assignment date: ________________

A different method of subtraction by subtracting a nice number ending with 0 first

Example: 65 – 28 = $65 \overset{+2}{-} 28 \overset{+2}{=} 67 - 30 = 37$

Evaluate using shortcut where applicable.

71 – 19

52

85 – 57

28

63 – 29

34

75 – 38

37

61 – 27

34

83 – 48

35

73 – 59

14

82 – 37

45

85 – 49

36

72 – 28

44

Student's name: ____________________ Assignment date: ________________

Addition or subtraction word problems

1. At Kitchener Elementary school, there are 230 boys and 250 girls. How many children are there in the school altogether?

   480

2. Ms. Munson's kindergarten class painted 18 pictures on Wednesday and 20 pictures on Thursday. How many more pictures did they paint on Thursday?

   2

3. For Show & Tell, twins Lenny and Lonny each brought 24 rocks to school. How many rocks did they bring in all?

   48

4. Mr. Singh started with 150 pieces of chalk. By the end of the week, he had broken 86 of them. How many pieces of chalk does Mr. Singh have left?

   64

480, 2, 48, 64

Student's name: ____________________ Assignment date: _______________

5. Gina Gardener spots 24 spotted butterflies and 14 plain butterflies in her flower garden. What is the sum number of butterflies in her garden?

38

6. Erin Entomologist finds 89 red ants, 38 brown ants and 84 black ants marching back to their anthill in her yard. How many more black ants than brown ants are there? How many more red ants than black ants are there? What is the total number of ants of any colour in her yard?

46 more blacks than browns, 5 more reds than blacks

211 altogether

7. In the morning, Professor Chris counted 23 neutrinos in the mine. In the afternoon, his grad student counted 17 neutrinos. How many neutrinos did they count that day?

40 altogether

38, 46 more blacks than browns, 5 more reds than blacks, 211 altogether, 40

Student's name: ____________________ Assignment date: ________________

Mixed Word Problems

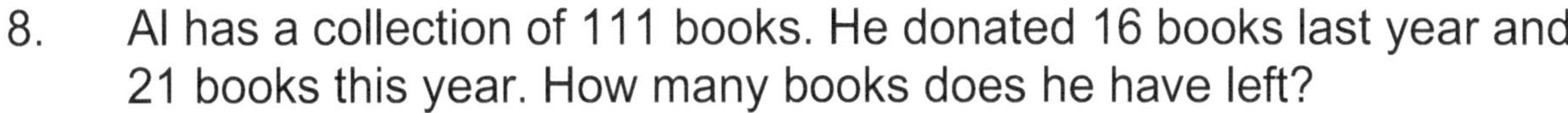

8. Al has a collection of 111 books. He donated 16 books last year and 21 books this year. How many books does he have left?

74

9. Michelle loves collecting small plastic animals. She has 35 cats and 30 ducks. How many animals does she have in her collection?

65

10. A school has three dining halls. Each dining hall has 22 tables. If there are four children at each table, how many children can stay for lunch?

88

11. Chris made thirty-two statements in class. Mark said that eleven of them were wrong. How many correct statements did Chris make?

21

84, 65, 88, 21

Student's name: ____________________ Assignment date: ________________

12. There are 23 doves and 419 crows in Harlandale Woods. How many birds are there in total in Harlandale Woods?

    442

13. It takes 4 minutes to make a glass of pineapple juice. How many glasses of juice can be made in 3 hours and 4 minutes?

    46

14. Last month, John worked for 186 hours, Gord worked for 134 hours, and Alexei worked 32 hours more than John. How many hours did they work altogether?

    538

15. There are 80 hens and 25 sheep on a farm. How many animals are there on the farm?

    105

442, 16, 538, 105

Student's name: ____________________ Assignment date: ________________

16. Invitations were sent to 106 relatives for a family get-together. Only 93 relatives came. How many relatives did not come?

13

17. A zoo has 59 brown monkeys and 34 black monkeys. How many monkeys are there in the zoo?

93

18. Mr. Bloomburg will be 72 next year. His son is 34 years younger than he is. How old is his son right now?

37

19. There are 30 ice cream cakes in Dairy King. If each cake is cut into 8 pieces and then each part is further cut into 2 pieces, how many pieces of cake are there in all?

480

13, 93, 37, 480

Student's name: ____________________ Assignment date: ________________

20. There are 66 vans and 54 buses in the parking lot. How many vehicles are there in the parking lot?

120

21. A jungle has 784 deer, of which 523 are spotted. How many deer do not have spots?

261

22. There are 69 men and 30 women in a Boeing 737 jet airplane. How many passengers are there altogether?

99

23. Mr. Lee drove his new car 31 kilometres on Tuesday and 85 kilometres on Wednesday. How many kilometres did he drive over these two days?

216

120, 261, 99, 216

Student's name: ____________________ Assignment date: ________________

24. Clara-Anne has 18 teddy bears. She gives away 5 of them to her best friend. How many teddy bears does she have now?

    13

25. Regina is a mechanic. She repaired 39 cabs and 28 cars last month. How many vehicles did she repair all together?

    67

26. There are five members of Ronaldo's family. The family's total weight is 284 kg, and Ronaldo weighs 40 kg. How many kilograms do the other four members weigh?

    244

27. Mr. Mandela used 93 litres of fuel last month. He used 56 litres this month. How many litres of fuel were consumed in the two months?

    149

13, 67, 24, 149

Student's name: ____________________ Assignment date: ________________

28. The sum of two numbers is 31, and their product is 240. What are these two numbers?

15, 16

29. When divided by 5 leaves a remainder of 3. It is a two-digit number less than 50. The two digits are equal.

33

30. The product of three children's ages is 36. The sum of their ages is 11. How old are they?

2, 3, 6

31. When divided by 5 leaves a remainder of 4. It is a two-digit number less than 50. The two digits are equal.

44

15, 33, 2, 3, 6; 15, 16; 44

Student's name: ____________________ Assignment date: ________________

32. Arthur bought a computer paper package for $15 and 3 pens at $2 each. He got a $5 change back after he paid. How much did he pay?

$26

33. Eileen divided her paper clips equally into 17 boxes, with five clips in each box with 4 clips left over. How many paper clips did she have at the beginning?

89

34. It is now 7:20 p.m. In 2 hours 45 minutes, Marylou will go to a concert. At what time will she go to a concert?

10:05

35. Julie can finish her 20 practice questions in half an hour. At this speed, how many practice questions can he finish in 3 and a half hours?

140

$26; 89, 10:05, 140

Student's name: ____________________ Assignment date: ________________

4 basic operations word problems with the wording as or x times as many (As …as)

Kumar has $309. Pauline has twice as much as Kumar. How much does Pauline have? $618
Kumar has $44. Pauline has half as much as Kumar. How much does Pauline have? $22
Kumar has 212 marbles. Pauline has 3 less than half as many as Kumar. How many does Pauline have? $103
Kumar has $214. Pauline has $15 more than half as much as Kumar. How much does Pauline have? $122
Kumar has $129. Pauline has 3 times as much as Kumar. How much does Pauline have? $387
After Pauline gave $3 to Kumar, then Kumar had $214. Kumar had $4 less than twice as much as Pauline had. How much did Pauline have at the beginning? $\frac{214+4}{2} = 109$
Joanne told her mother. "If I had done twice as correct as I answered in the test, I would have 6 more points than I have now".. How many points did Joanne actually get on the test? 6

Student's name: ____________________ Assignment date: ________________

Brent rode 15 km to a park, and on the way home, he rode three times as far to his uncle's home. How far did he ride to his uncle's house from the park? 15x3=45
Brent sold 219 raffle tickets. Pauline sold 9 times as many. How many tickets did Pauline sell? 219x9=1971
Pauline and her 4 friends like to share 705 candies equally. How many candies would each person get? 705/5=141
Pauline memorizes 23 vocabularies per day. How many vocabularies will she memorize in 25 days? 23x25=575
Brent buys lunch meat at $0.99 per 100 g. How much will it cost him if he buys 1.2 kg? 0.99x1200/100=$11.88
Brent makes half as much as Pauline per hour. Pauline makes $75 per 5 hours. How much will Brent make in 5 hours? $37.5
Pauline finishes reading a book in 10 days. At half of the reading speed, how long will it take Pauline to finish reading the same book? 20 days
Brent runs 15 km per day. At the same rate, how many days would Brent have run if his total distance is 225 km? 15 days

Student's name: ____________________ Assignment date: ________________

Test of advanced word problems

Bob has 149 more stamps than Adam. Cathy has 229 more stamps than Bob. Altogether they have 767 stamps. How many stamps does each one of them have? Hint: Use the Line Segment Diagram to solve. Bob = (767 – 229 + 149) /3 = 229 Adam = 229 – 149 = 80 Cathy = 229 + 229 = 458
9119 people were in the sports stadium last night. 3557 of them were women, and there were 879 fewer women than men. The rest were children. How many children were in the sports stadium last night? 1126, W: 3557, M: 4436, C: 1126
Vera wants to give two cans of fruit juice to each of her 13 friends invited to her birthday party. How many 6-pack of juice cans must she buy? 5 of 6-pack

Student's name: ____________________ Assignment date: ________________

***** Part 6 Decimal *****

Division models

The division is a reverse operation or works backwards of multiplication, such as the following multiplication equation.

The number of groups (sets, factor 1) × objects shared in each group (object 2) = total number of objects (product).

To find the number of groups (sets) when a number of objects and the number of objects shared (divided) by each group are given, we have to find *the number of groups* model.

To find the number of objects shared (divided, averaged) by each group when several objects and the number of groups (sets) are given, then we have the *finding the number of objects shared (divided, averaged) by each group* (set) model.

.

Model 1 Finding the number of groups (sets)

English Word Problems	How to solve it? Method 1 - Draw a model. This method is slow, so it is only used for teaching division concept purposes. Draw loops around the counters to show the numbers in each group (set). Each object is represented by a circle (counter).	Method 2 – Use work backwards of the multiplication method This method is used for all computations. Complete the division mathematical equation sentence.	Objects are what has been shared or divided. Set is the number of groups. The average is the number of things or objects being divided in each set (group).
Frank bought 12 cat cans. He wants to place 3 cans in a bag. How many bags does he need?	Step 1. Draw 12 circles to represent 12 real cans. Step 2. Loop every 3 cans. Step 3. Count the number of loops, and the total number of loops is the number of bags (groups, sets) needed. ○○○○○○ ○○○○○○	_____ ÷ _____ = _____	What has been divided into sets? _____ How many sets are there? ____ How many are in each set? ____

Student's name: ____________________ Assignment date: ______________

Frank bought 20 cat cans. He wants to place 5 cans in a bag. How many bags does he need?		___ ÷ __ = __	What has been divided into sets? _____ How many sets are there? ____ How many are in each set? ____
Frank bought 15 cat cans. He wants to place 3 cans in a bag. How many bags does he need?	Draw the counters (circles) yourself.	___ ÷ __ = __	What has been divided into sets? _____ How many sets are there? ____ How many are in each set? ____
Pauline earned 6 stamps for each hour of work. She earned 27 stamps in total. How many hours did she work?		__ ÷ __ = __	What has been divided into sets? _____ How many sets are there? ____ How many are in each set? ____

Student's name: ____________________ Assignment date: ________________

Model 2 Finding the number of objects shared (divided) in each group (set)

Problems	Draw loops around the counters to show the numbers shared by each group. Each object is represented by a circle (counter).	Complete the division sentence.	What has been divided into sets? _____ How many sets are there? ____ How many are in each set? ____
Frank bought 12 pencils to have them shared by 4 classes equally. How many pencils does each class get?	○○○○○○ ○○○○○○	__ ÷ __ = __	What has been divided into sets? _____ How many sets are there? ____ How many are in each set? ____
Frank bought 20 pencils to have them shared by 5 classes equally. How many pencils does each class get?	○○○○○ ○○○○○ ○○○○○ ○○○○○	__ ÷ __ = __	What has been divided into sets? _____ How many sets are there? ____ How many are in each set? ____
Frank bought 16 pencils to have them shared by 4 classes equally. How many pencils does each class get?	Draw the counters yourself.	__ ÷ __ = __	What has been divided into sets? _____ How many sets are there? ____ How many are in each set? ____
Pauline earned 30 stamps for her work. She worked for 5 hours. How many stamps did she earn each hour? Assume she earned the same number of stamps for each hour.		__ ÷ __ = __	What has been divided into sets? _____ How many sets are there? ____ How many are in each set? ____

Student's name: ____________________ Assignment date: ________________

Multiplication and division models

model	Write multiplication equations or division equations
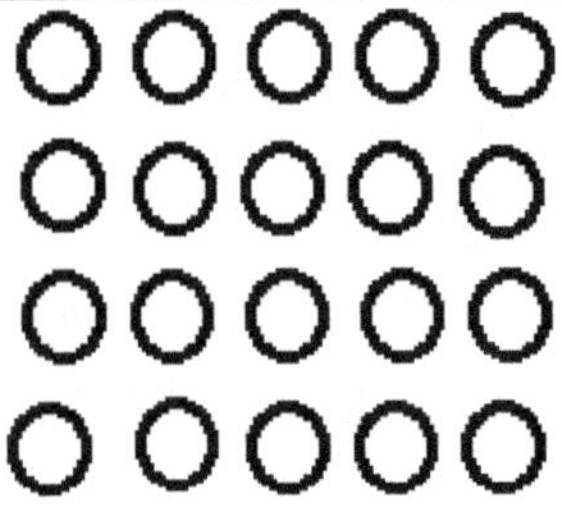	$4 \times 5 = 20$ 4 repeated 5 times. $5 \times 4 = 20$ 5 repeated 4 times.
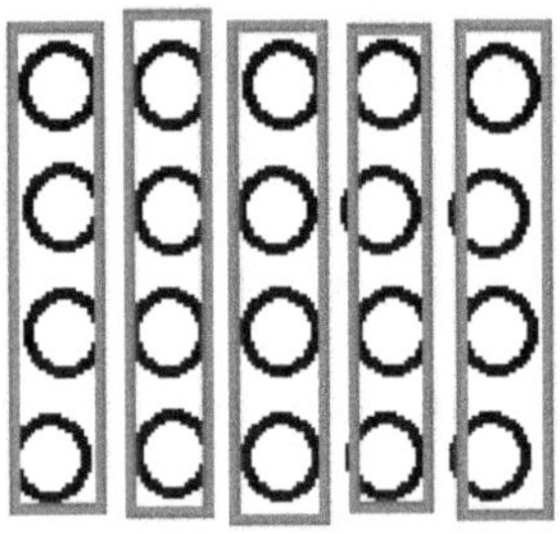	$20 \div 5 = 4$ 20 divided into groups of 5. There are 4 in each group. $20 \div 4 = 5$ 20 divided into 4 each group. There are 5 groups.

Model	Mathematical sentence (equation)
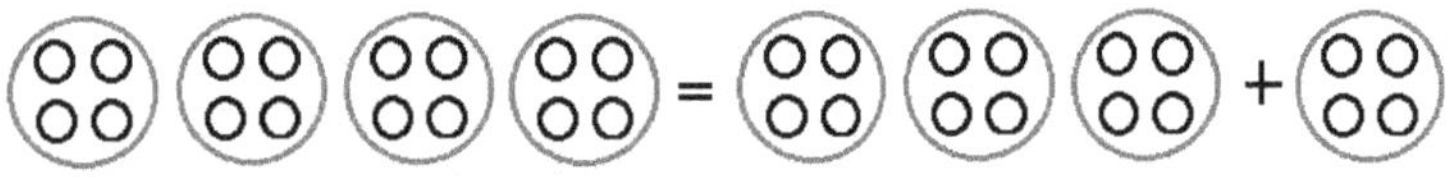 = +	
	In the multiplication model
	In the division model
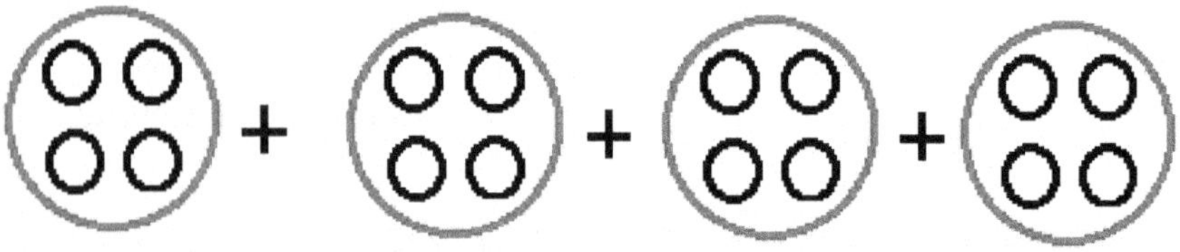 + + +	In multiplication equation
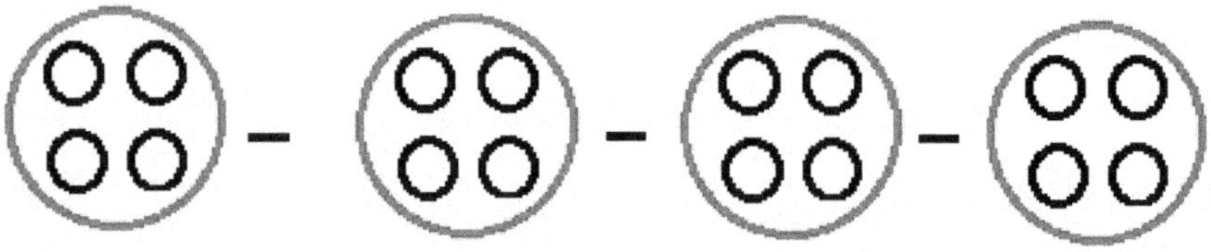 – – –	In division equation

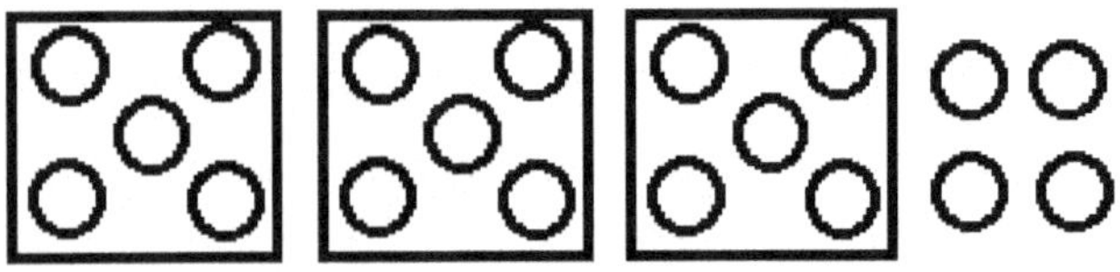

Student's name: ____________________ Assignment date: ________________

	The left model shows $4 \times 4 = 16$. Draw to show how it can also show $2 \times 8 = 16$ Draw to show how it can also show $20 \div 3$ has the quotient of 6 with the remainder 1

Student's name: ____________________ Assignment date: ________________

Decimals

A number can be a whole number such as 0, 1, 2, 3, etc. What happens if we want to show just part of a whole? For example, one chocolate bar is cut into 10 smaller pieces, then how to say each smaller part in math?

We can say it in fraction as $\frac{1}{10}$.

The notation of $\frac{1}{10}$ can be explained in the following ways:

1. Read it from the bottom-up. There are 10 parts and only one part I is taken.
2. Reading it from top to down, we say one-tenth.
3. Divide without leaving any remainder if it is divisible. To stop division when used up all digits of dividend and leave the quotient with the remainder is a fraction.

decimal	fraction
$10 \div 3 = ?$ Hint: To think 1 as 1.0000 so you can drop down as many zeros as you want when there are no more digits in dividend. Place a decimal point once you start to drop down 0. $$\begin{array}{r} 3.33 \\ 3\overline{)10} \\ 9 \\ \hline 10 \\ 9 \\ \hline 10 \\ 9 \\ \hline 1 \end{array}$$	When dividing, leave the answer in remainder format. For example, $10 \div 3 = 3\frac{1}{3}$ $$\begin{array}{r} 3 \\ 3\overline{)10} \\ 9 \\ \hline 1 \end{array}$$

In the above case 3, since 1 = 1.00000, we produce a division quotient 0.1 and this format of the number is called decimal number or just called it decimal.

Student's name: ____________________ Assignment date: ________________

Why we need decimals when we already have fractions?

It is because we found in some cases, the use of fractions are awkward in our verbal communications, for example, a 3-digit fraction $\frac{129}{419}$ is a mouthful to say, but it is easier to say using its equivalent value when converting to decimal as *******. In our monetary system, it is also easier to use $25.13 instead of $\$25\frac{13}{100}$.

Student's name: ____________________ Assignment date: ________________

A decimal number = whole number + fraction (including a decimal point in tenths, hundredths, thousandths, etc.)

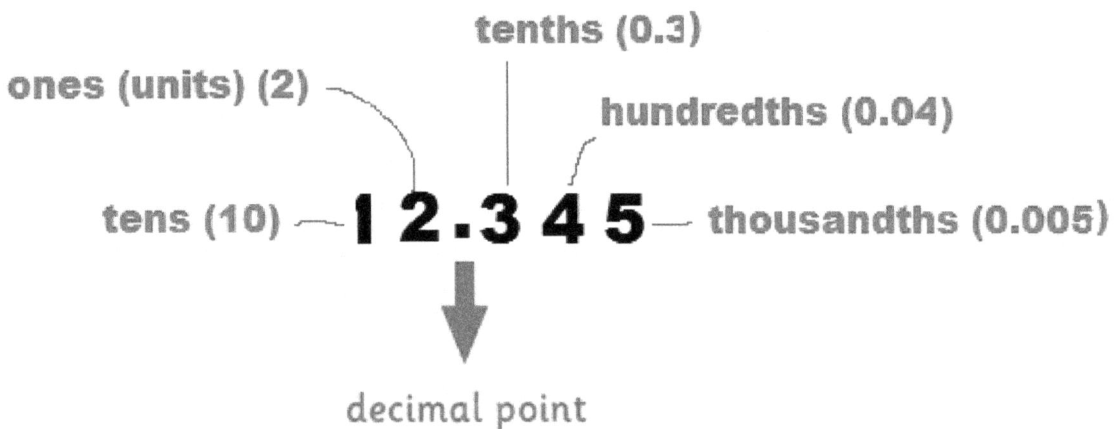

十位,个位桌,十分位, 百分位,千分位

As we can see from the above place value diagram, the decimal point is only to separate the whole number from the fraction. Each number from left to right is scaled down 10 times, Ten times smaller than ones place will be tenth ($\frac{1}{10}$), that is why there is no "oneth" in the fraction part of a decimal number.

Decimal representations

Since decimals can be converted into fractions and also the other way around, so the graphic representation of both numbers is identical. We can use block tens or number lines to illustrate decimals, just as in fractions.

In primary schools, we normally learn tenths (one decimal place), hundredths (2-decimal place), or even thousandths (3-decimal place).

Student's name: ____________________ Assignment date: ________________

Division to decimal to fraction

problem	Decimal division	fraction
$1 \div 10 = 0.1$	10) 1 □ ; quotient □□ ; □□ ; 0.1	$\frac{1}{10}$
$1 \div 100 = 0.01$	100) 1 □□ ; quotient □□□ ; □□□ ; 0.01	$\frac{1}{100}$
$2 \div 100 = 0.02$	100) 2 □□ ; quotient □□□ ; □□□ ; 0.02	$\frac{2}{100}$
$22 \div 220 = 0.1$	220) 2 2 □ ; quotient □□□ ; □□□ ; 0.1	$\frac{22}{220} = \frac{1}{10}$

Student's name: ____________________ Assignment date: ______________

Tenths

Students could be introduced to the money system of dollars and cents to get to know the decimals. Students also should have the concept of the place value so they could understand the decimals much better. For example, the 1's in the following number mean very differently due to its place value.

1111.11

Students should study the place value to understand the tenth, hundredth, or thousandths and higher place values.

Each digit in a number has its own place value. The following is an example.

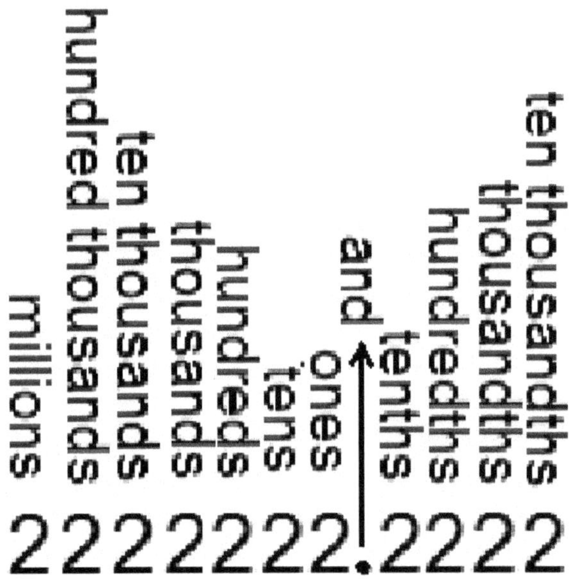

millions
hundred thousands
ten thousands
thousands
hundreds
tens
ones
and
tenths
hundredths
thousandths
ten thousandths

2222222.2222

Student's name: ____________________ Assignment date: ________________

Tenths

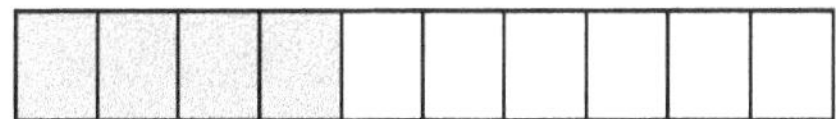

$0.4 = \frac{4}{10}$ It is read as four-tenths.

Ones	Decimal point	Tenths
0	•	4

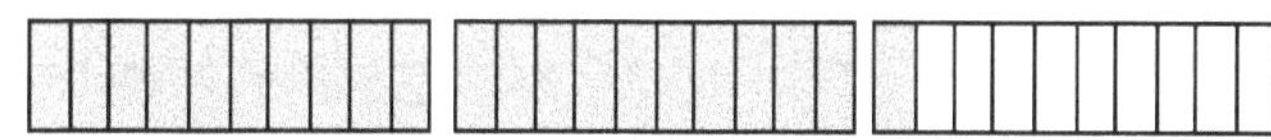

$2.1 = 2\frac{1}{10}$ It is read as two and one-tenth.

Ones	Decimal point	Tenths
2	•	1

1. Express the shaded part in fractions and decimals.

1. $\frac{1}{10}$ 0.1

2. $\frac{7}{10}$ 0.7

3. $\frac{4}{10}$ 0.4

4. $\frac{9}{10}$ 0.9

5. $\frac{15}{10}$ 1.5

6. 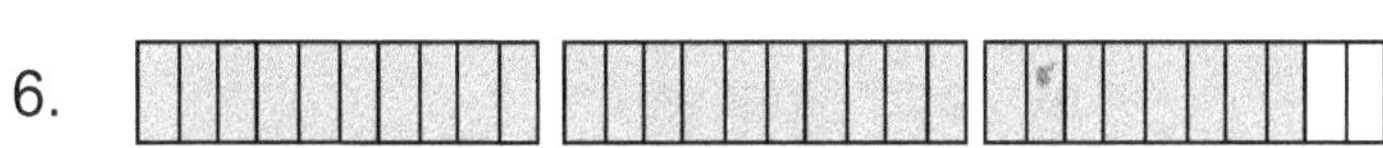 $\frac{28}{10}$ 2.8

7. $\frac{17}{10}$ 1.7

8. $\frac{32}{10}$ 3.2

Student's name: ____________________ Assignment date: ________________

2. Write the value of each point as a decimal.

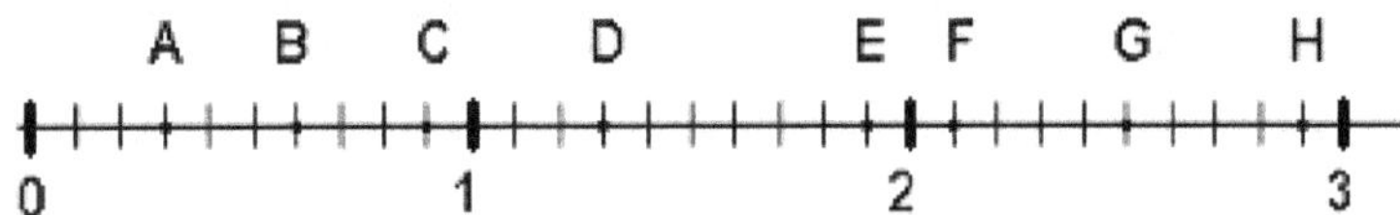

A: 0.3 B: 0.6 C: 0.9 D: 1.3 E: 1.9 F: 2.1 G: 2.5 H: 2.9

3. Draw the length of AB.

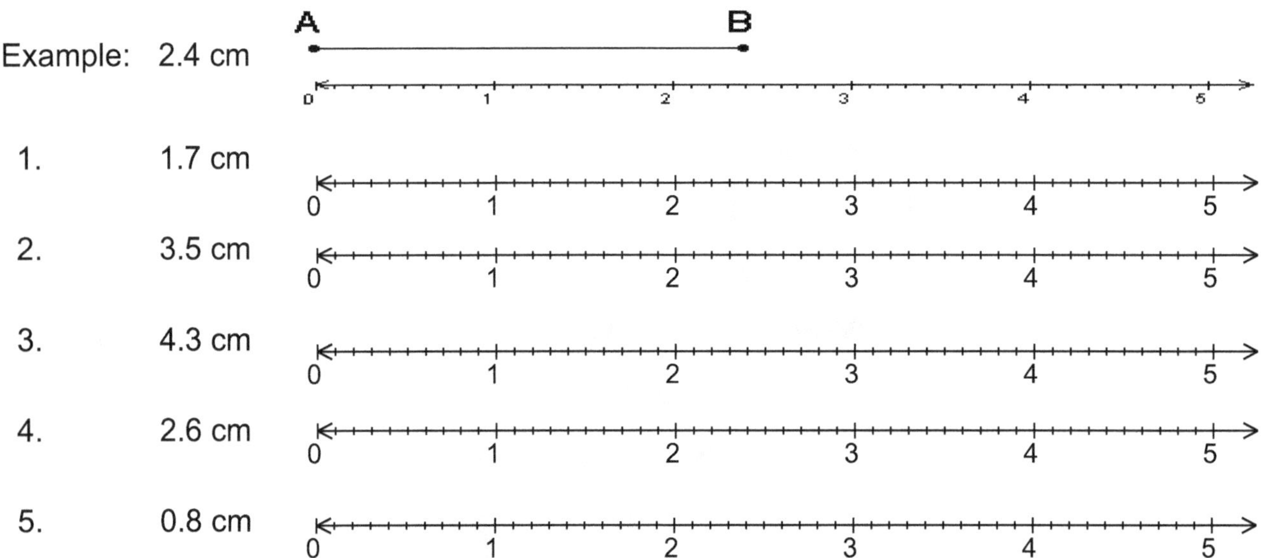

4. Complete the following chart.

	Fraction	Decimal	Words
1.	$2\frac{8}{10}$	2.8	two and eight tenths
2.	$1\frac{5}{10}$	1.5	one and five-tenths
3.	$2\frac{5}{10}$	2.5	two and five-tenths
4.	$6\frac{4}{10}$	6.4	six and four-tenths
5.	$4\frac{3}{10}$	4.3	four and three tenths

Student's name: ____________________ Assignment date: ________________

Hundredths (% = per hundredth)

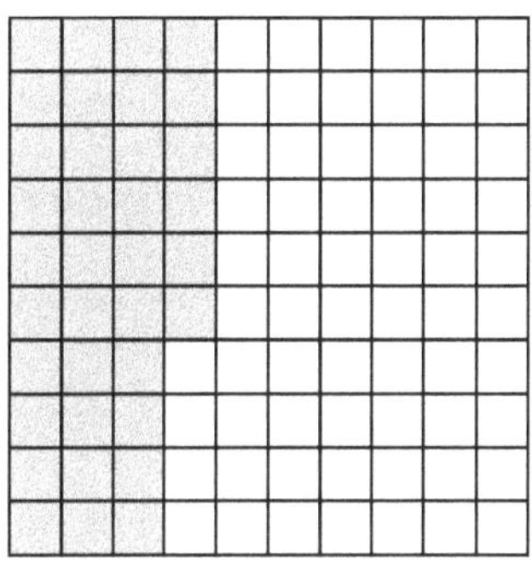

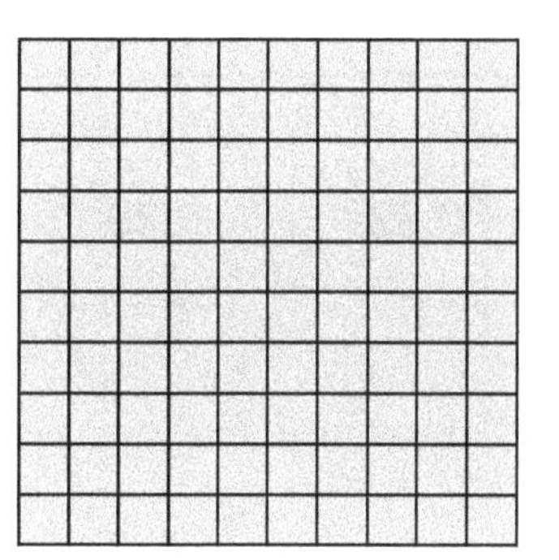

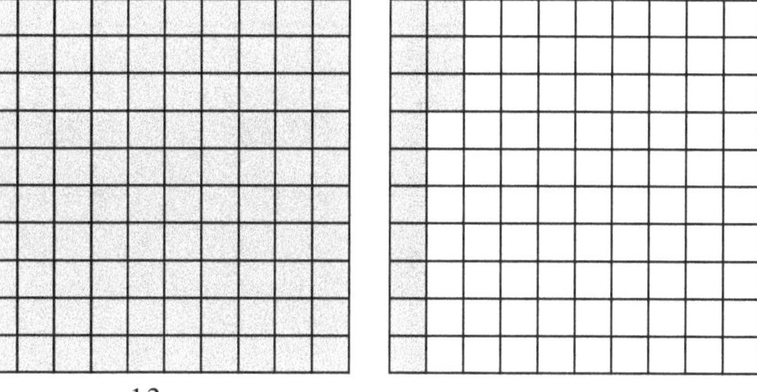

$0.36 = \frac{36}{100}$ It is read as thirty-six hundredths.

$1.13 = 1\frac{13}{100}$ It is read as one and thirteen hundredths.

Ones	Decimal point	Tenths	Hundredths
0	•	3	6

Ones	Decimal point	Tenths	Hundredths
1	•	1	3

1. Express the shaded part in fractions and decimals.

1.

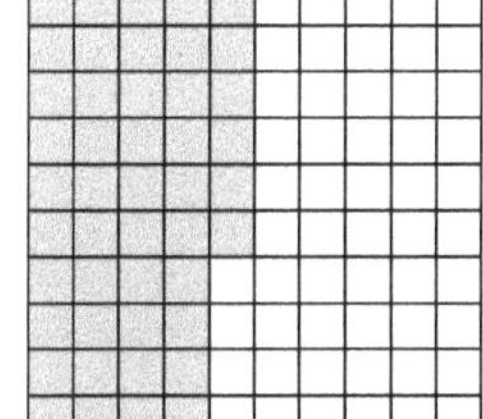

$\frac{46}{100}$ or 0.46

2.

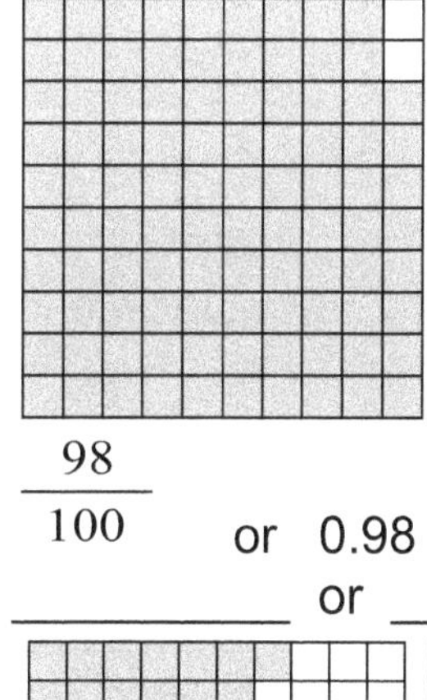

$\frac{98}{100}$ or 0.98

___________ or __________

3.

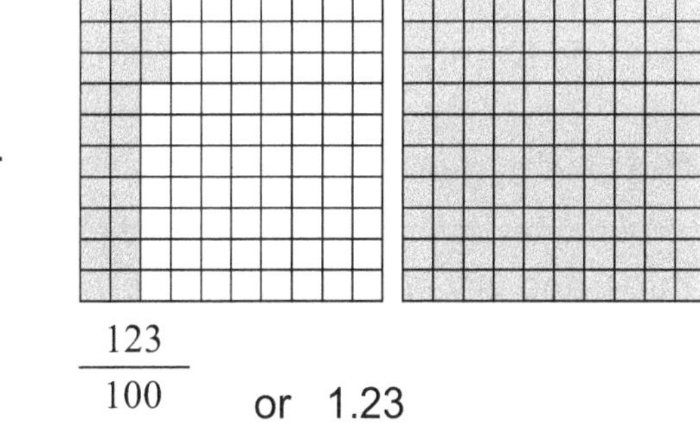

$\frac{123}{100}$ or 1.23

___________ or __________

4.

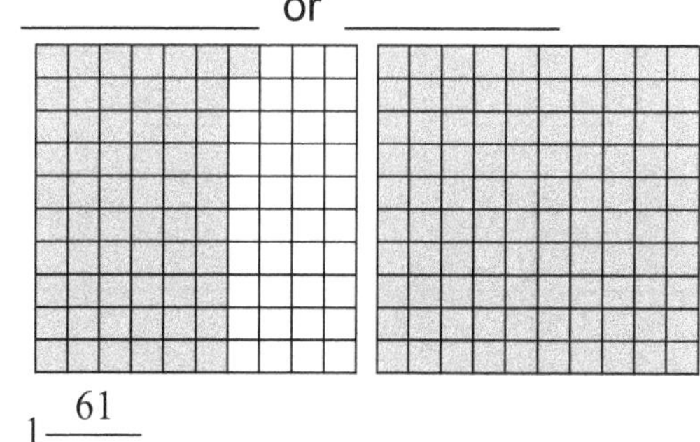

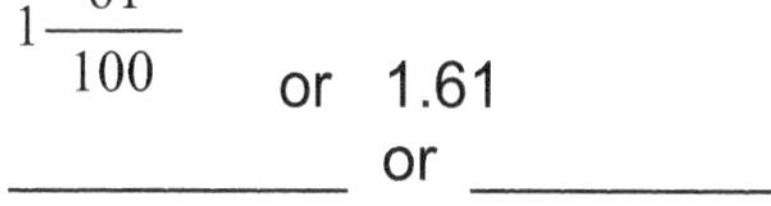

$1\frac{61}{100}$ or 1.61

___________ or __________

Student's name: ____________________ Assignment date: ________________

2. Write the value of each point as a decimal.

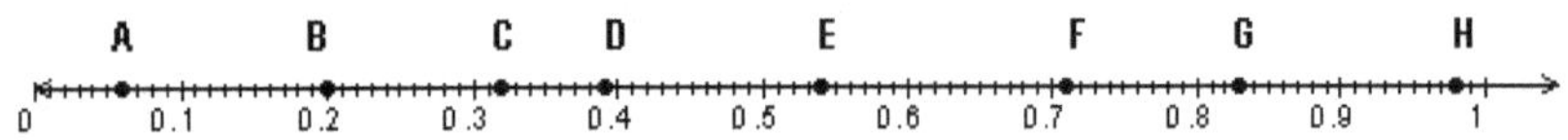

A: 0.05 B: 0.20 C: 0.32 D: 0.39 E: 0.54 F: 0.71 G: 0.83 H: 0.98

3. Draw the length of AB.

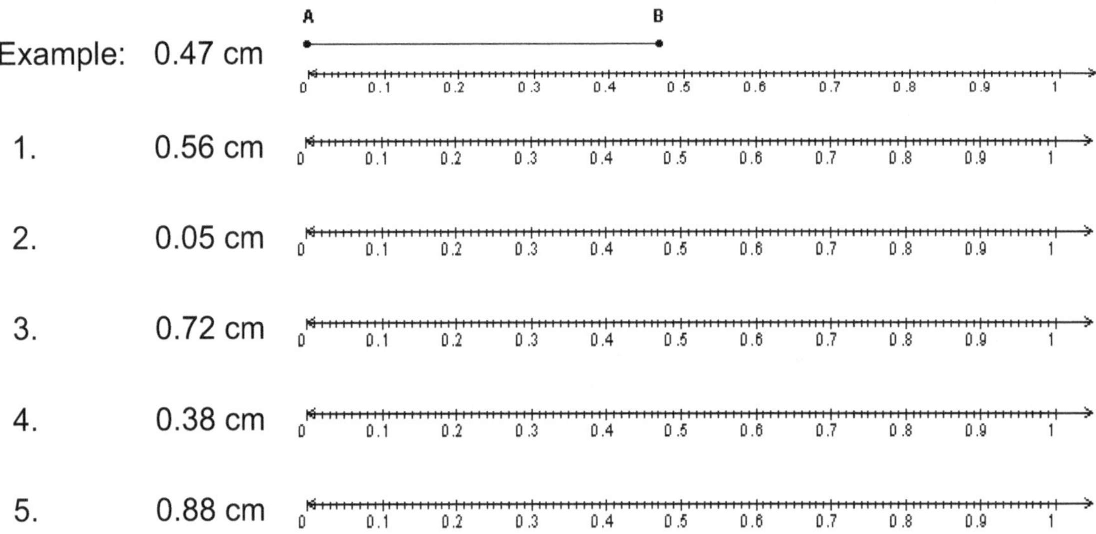

Example: 0.47 cm

1. 0.56 cm

2. 0.05 cm

3. 0.72 cm

4. 0.38 cm

5. 0.88 cm

4. Complete the following chart.

	Fraction	Decimal	Words
1.	$5\frac{23}{100}$	5.23	five and twenty-three hundredths
2.	$8\frac{9}{100}$	8.09	eight and nine hundredths
3.	$2\frac{27}{100}$	2.27	two and twenty-seven hundredths
4.	$4\frac{31}{100}$	4.31	four and thirty-one hundredths
5.	$3\frac{59}{100}$	3.59	three and fifty-nine hundredths

Ho Math Chess Primary Grades Math

Test Review assesssment 何数棋谜低年级数学测试複習考核

Student's name: ____________________ Assignment date: ________________

Compare decimals.

1. 0.53 [>] 0.27

2. <
0.24 □ 0.79

3. <
0.36 □ 0.81

4. >
0.18 □ 0.05

5. >
0.71 □ 0.52

6. >
0.53 □ 0.06

7. <
0.84 □ 4.57

8. >
5.09 □ 0.37

9. >
2.05 □ 0.72

10. <
0.74 □ 1.85

11. >
5.07 □ 0.59

12. >
3.90 □ 0.78

13. <
0.35 □ 2.13

14. <
0.47 □ 3.18

15. >
7.90 □ 7.09

16. >
3.75 □ 3.71

17. <
3.36 □ 3.47

18. >
6.09 □ 6.03

19. >
1.95 □ 1.92

20. >
2.67 □ 2.63

21. >
7.04 □ 0.74

22. >
8.52 □ 8.51

23. <
1.52 □ 7.43

24. <
2.49 □ 3.74

25. <
5.03 □ 5.30

26. <
2.87 □ 3.52

Student's name: ____________________ Assignment date: ______________

Order the following decimals from least to greatest.

1. 0.26, 0.62, 2.06

0.26, 0.62, 2.06
____

2. 9.52, 5.43, 7.86

5.43, 7.86, 9.52
____

3. 2.78, 2.74, 2.79

2.74, 2.78, 2.79
____

4. 4.74, 4.61, 4.83

4.61, 4.74, 4.83
____

5. 5.09, 5.73, 3.17

3.17, 5.09, 5.73
____

6. 9.07, 1.75, 4.68

1.75, 4.68, 9.07
____

Order the following decimals from greatest to least.

1. 6.30, 0.68, 2.96

6.30, 2.96, 0.68
____

2. 5.04, 0.45, 4.05

5.04, 4.05, 0.45
____

3. 0.36, 0.06, 0.63

0.63, 0.36, 0.06
____

4. 3.16, 3.18, 3.11

3.18, 3.16, 3.11
____

5. 8.45, 4.58, 4.85

8.45, 4.85, 4.58
____

6. 5.14, 0.14, 8.14

0.14, 5.14, 8.14
____

Student's name: ____________________ Assignment date: ________________

Decimal computations for advanced students

The whole number divided by the whole number	Decimal divided by whole	Whole divided by decimal	Decimal divided by decimal	Operated by the power of 10
$1 \div 3$	$12.12 \div 3$	$300 \div 0.3 = \frac{300}{0.3} =$	$3.9 \div 0.3$	$3.9 \div 10$
$1 \div 5$	$10.05 \div 5$	$1515 \div 0.03$	$15.15 \div 0.03$	$15.15 \div 10000$
$1 \div 7$	$21.021 \div 7$	$1414 \div 0.7$	$14.14 \div 0.3$	$14.14 \div 0.1$
$21 \div 5$	$0.002525 \div 5$	$25251414 \div 0.5$	$252514.14 \div 0.5$	$252514.14 \div 0.001$
$31 \div 4$	$2829.028 \div 4$	$2829028 \div 0.04$	$28.29028 \div 0.04$	28.29028×0.01
$205 \div 25$	$0.502625 \div 5$	$502625 \div 0.05$	$5026.25 \div 0.05$	5026.25×10000
$125 \div 8$	$125.125 \div 25$	$125125 \div 2.5$	$1251.25 \div 2.5$	$1251.25 \div 10$
$18 \div 15$	$30.015 \div 15$	$30015 \div 1.5$	$300.15 \div 1.5$	$30015 \div 100$

Student's name: ____________________ Assignment date: ________________

Adding and subtracting decimal by lining up decimal point using models

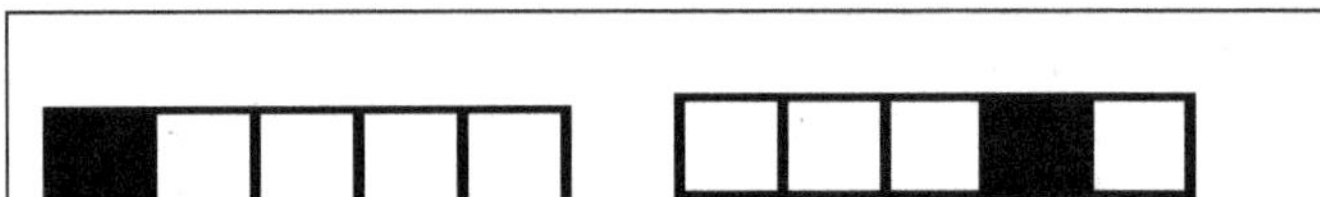

+ = ______ + ______ = _____

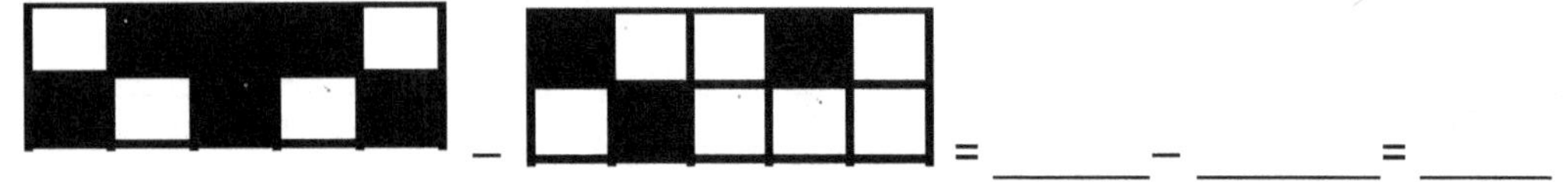

– = ______ – ______ = _____

4 + 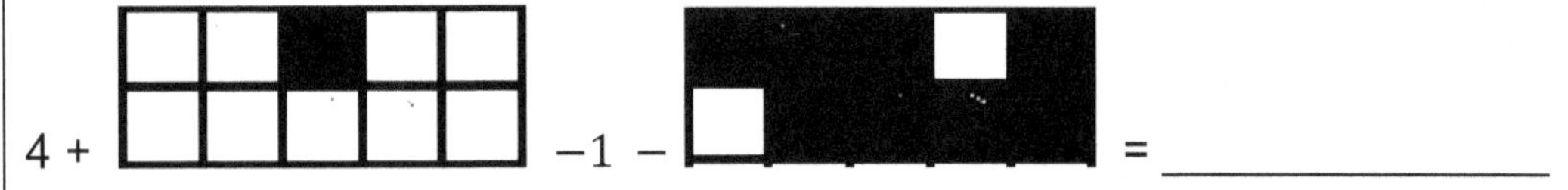 –1 – = ____________

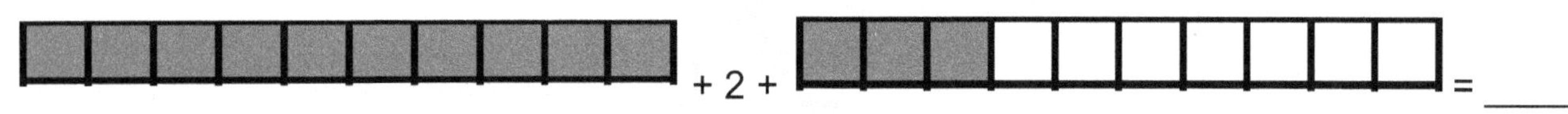

+ 2 + = ____

1+2+0.3=3.3

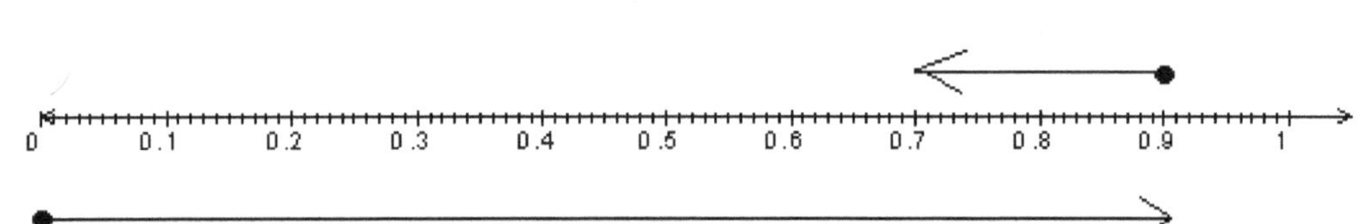

Circle the correct answer for the above number line operation.

0.9 + 0.2 = 1.1
0.9 – 0.2 = 0.7
0.9 – 0.7 = 0.2
0.9 + 0.7 = 1.6

The second one from the top is correct.

Ho Math Chess Primary Grades Math

Test Review assesssment 何数棋謎低年级数学测试複習考核

Student's name: ____________________ Assignment date: ________________

Adding and subtracting decimal hundredths using grid or plot

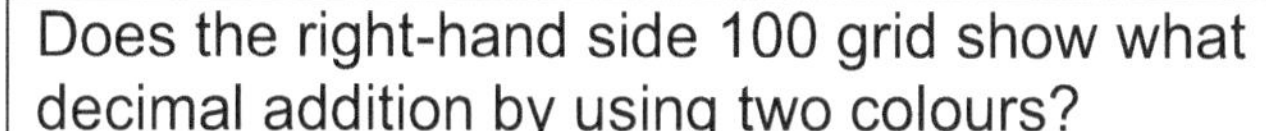 Does the right-hand side 100 grid show what decimal addition by using two colours? ____________ + __________ = _______ 0.46 + 0.20 = 0.66	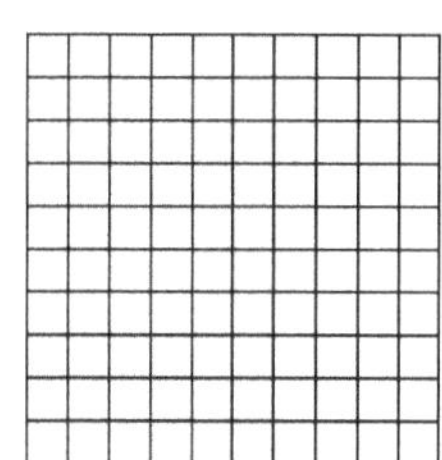
The right-hand side 100 grid shows decimal subtraction by using crossed-out squares for subtracting numbers. ____________ – __________ = _______ 0.41 – 0.18 = 0.23	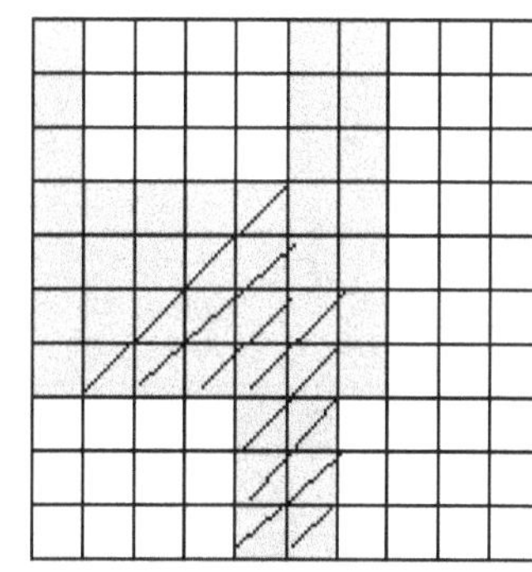
What decimal is the shaded area on the right figure? 25 ÷ 50 = 0.5	
What decimal is the shaded area on the right figure?	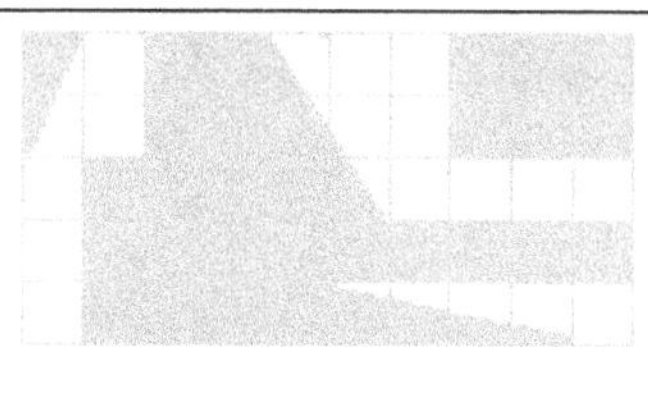
What decimal is the shaded area on the right figure?	

Student's name: ____________________ Assignment date: ________________

Circle the following equivalent decimals on the right side to the farthest left side decimal.

0.01	0.010, $\frac{1}{10}$, $\frac{1}{100}$, $\frac{2}{200}$, 0.001
0.91	0.9100, 0.091, 0.910, $\frac{91}{10}$, $\frac{91}{100}$, 91%
0.333…	$\frac{1}{3}$, $\frac{3}{9}$, $\frac{3}{10}$, 0.3, 0.33, $0.\bar{3}$
1.90	1.9, 1.900, 1.09, $1\frac{90}{100}$, $1\frac{9}{10}$
2.1 – 1.91	0.19, 0.91, 0.190, $\frac{19}{10}$, $\frac{19}{100}$
2.31 – 2.3	0.1, 0.010, 0.01, $\frac{1}{100}$
2.109	2.0109, 2.1090, $2\frac{109}{1000}$, $2 + 109$, $2 + 0.109$
2 – 1.091	1.099, 1.009, 1.909, 1.9090
11.11 + 1.11	12.22, 12.022, 12.220, $12\frac{22}{100}$
1.98 × 2	1.98+1.9, 1.98× 2 ÷ 2
1.98 ÷ 2	0.99, $\frac{99}{100}$, 0.990, 0.099, 0.999
1.212 × 1000	1212, 121, 12120, 1.212000
10 × 1.11 × 10	111, 121, 1.1100, 1.110× 10
2.213 × 10	212.3, 2.213, 2.1230, 21.23

Student's name: ____________________ Assignment date: ________________

Answers

Circle the following equivalent decimals on the right side to the farthest left side decimal.

0.01	0.010 $\frac{1}{10}$ $\frac{1}{100}$ $\frac{2}{200}$ 0.001
0.91	0.9100, 0.091, 0.910, $\frac{91}{10}$, $\frac{91}{100}$, 91%
0.333…	$\frac{1}{3}$, $\frac{3}{9}$, $\frac{3}{10}$, 0.3, 0.33, $0.\overline{3}$
1.90	1.9, 1.900, 1.09, $1\frac{90}{100}$, $1\frac{9}{10}$
2.1 – 1.91	0.19, 0.91, 0.190, $\frac{19}{10}$, $\frac{19}{100}$
2.31 – 2.3	0.1, 0.010, 0.01, $\frac{1}{100}$
2.109	2.0109, 2.1090, $2\frac{109}{1000}$, 2 + 109, 2 + 0.109
2 – 1.091	1.099, 1.009, 1.909, 1.9090
11.11 + 1.11	12.22, 12.022, 12.220, $12\frac{22}{100}$
1.98 × 2	1.98+1.9, 3.96, 1.98× 2 ÷ 2
1.98 ÷ 2	0.99, $\frac{99}{100}$, 0.990, 0.099, 0.999
1.212 × 1000	1212, 121, 12120, 1.212000
10 × 1.11 × 10	111, 121, 1.1100, 1.110× 10
2.213 × 10	212.3, 2.213, 2.1230, 21.23

Answers

Student's name: ____________________ Assignment date: ________________

Decimals Addition

When do decimal addition, we should line the decimal points up.

$$\begin{array}{r} 2.3 \\ +\ 5.8 \\ \hline 8.1 \end{array}$$

1. $\begin{array}{r} 1.5 \\ +\ 6.3 \\ \hline 7.8 \end{array}$

2. $\begin{array}{r} 3.4 \\ +\ 4.6 \\ \hline 8.0 \end{array}$

3. $\begin{array}{r} 3.7 \\ +\ 6.3 \\ \hline 10.0 \end{array}$

4. $\begin{array}{r} 5.8 \\ +\ 2.6 \\ \hline 8.4 \end{array}$

5. $\begin{array}{r} 4.6 \\ +\ 0.3 \\ \hline 4.9 \end{array}$

6. $\begin{array}{r} 6.3 \\ +\ 3.6 \\ \hline 9.9 \end{array}$

7. $\begin{array}{r} 4.1 \\ +\ 2.5 \\ \hline 6.6 \end{array}$

8. $\begin{array}{r} 2.5 \\ +\ 0.7 \\ \hline 3.2 \end{array}$

9. $\begin{array}{r} 4.8 \\ +\ 3.2 \\ \hline 8.0 \end{array}$

10. $\begin{array}{r} 2.4 \\ +\ 6.7 \\ \hline 9.1 \end{array}$

11. $\begin{array}{r} 5.5 \\ +\ 2.5 \\ \hline 8.0 \end{array}$

12. $\begin{array}{r} 0.2 \\ +\ 9.4 \\ \hline 9.6 \end{array}$

13. $\begin{array}{r} 5.4 \\ +\ 9.3 \\ \hline 14.7 \end{array}$

14. $\begin{array}{r} 2.3 \\ +\ 8.7 \\ \hline 11.0 \end{array}$

15. $\begin{array}{r} 4.4 \\ +\ 8.9 \\ \hline 13.3 \end{array}$

16. $\begin{array}{r} 3.1 \\ +\ 0.9 \\ \hline 4.0 \end{array}$

17. $\begin{array}{r} 0.8 \\ +\ 0.3 \\ \hline 1.1 \end{array}$

18. $\begin{array}{r} 4.5 \\ +\ 7.8 \\ \hline 12.3 \end{array}$

Ho Math Chess Primary Grades Math

Test Review assesssment 何数棋謎低年级数学测试複習考核

Frank Ho, Amanda Ho www.homathchess.com

Student's name: ____________________ Assignment date: ________________

Decimals Addition

Example:

  1.62
+ 5.24
  6.86

1.
  2.52
+ 7.13
  9.65

2.
  2.52
+ 5.18
  7.70

3.
  2.72
+ 5.49
  8.21

4.
  8.95
+ 1 05
 10.00

5.
  7.35
+ 4.79
 12.14

6.
  7.48
+ 4.37
 11.85

7.
  3.25
+ 2.43
  5.68

8.
  3.63
+ 5.45
  9.08

9.
  3.62
+ 7.48
 11.10

10.
  4.36
+ 7.57
 11.93

11.
  5.89
+ 7.25
 13.14

12.
  5.35
+ 9.28
 14.63

13.
  2.37
+ 6.41
  8.78

14.
  1.37
+ 5.25
  6.62

15.
  2.19
+ 6.67
  8.86

16.
  3.43
+ 8.89
 12.32

17.
  3.57
+ 8.89
 12.46

18.
  4.38
+ 7.76
 12.14

Student's name: ____________________ Assignment date: ________________

Across Addition

1) 4.6 + 3.3 = ____ 7.9	2) 6.2 + 2.5 = ____ 8.7	3) 2.8 + 3.1 = ____ 5.9
4) 0.7 + 3.8 = ___ 4.5	5) 0.9 + 0.2 = ___ 1.1	6) 9.6 + 2.2 = _____ 11.8
7) 6.3 + 7.5 = ____ 13.8	8) 8.1 + 3.6 = ___ 11.7	9) 7.7 + 4.6 = _____ 12.3
10)5.2 + 3.8 = _____ 9.0	11)6.4 + 0.6 = ____ 7.0	12)9.4 + 1.7 = ____ 11.1
13)9.3 + 0.8 = ____ 10.1	14)8.2 + 2.8 = ____ 11.0	15)5.0 + 6.3 = _____ 11.3

Student's name: ____________________ Assignment date: ________________

horizontal Addition

1) 4.72 + 3.25 = ____ 7.97	2) 4.15 + 3.43 = ____ 7.58	3) 4.72 + 3.11 = ____ 7.83
4) 4.72 + 0.46 = ___ 5.18	5) 4.25 + 7.09 = ___ 11.34	6) 5.13 + 7.34 = _____ 12.47
7) 4.62 + 0.28 = ____ 4.90	8) 4.52 + 0.37 = ___ 4.89	9) 0.56 + 7.35 = _____ 7.91
10) 6.48 + 3.09 = ____ 9.57	11) 5.73 + 1.64 = ____ 7.37	12) 4.72 + 5.76 = ____ 10.48
13) 0.09 + 2.65 = ____ 2.74	14) 6.42 + 5.78 = ____ 12.2	15) 4.27 + 8.09 = ____ 12.36

Student's name: ____________________ Assignment date: ________________

Decimal Subtraction

The same as addition, always line the decimals up.

$$\begin{array}{r} 5.6 \\ -\ 2.1 \\ \hline 3.5 \end{array}$$

1. $$\begin{array}{r} 6.8 \\ -\ 2.5 \\ \hline 4.3 \end{array}$$

2. $$\begin{array}{r} 6.4 \\ -\ 3.6 \\ \hline 2.8 \end{array}$$

3. $$\begin{array}{r} 7.5 \\ -\ 6.9 \\ \hline 0.6 \end{array}$$

4. $$\begin{array}{r} 6.0 \\ -\ 4.7 \\ \hline 1.3 \end{array}$$

5. $$\begin{array}{r} 7.6 \\ -\ 5.7 \\ \hline 1.9 \end{array}$$

6. $$\begin{array}{r} 16.1 \\ -\ 9.3 \\ \hline 6.8 \end{array}$$

7. $$\begin{array}{r} 5.9 \\ -\ 1.8 \\ \hline 4.1 \end{array}$$

8. $$\begin{array}{r} 5.3 \\ -\ 1.8 \\ \hline 3.5 \end{array}$$

9. $$\begin{array}{r} 8.5 \\ -\ 7.6 \\ \hline 0.9 \end{array}$$

10. $$\begin{array}{r} 3.5 \\ -\ 0.7 \\ \hline 2.8 \end{array}$$

11. $$\begin{array}{r} 8.2 \\ -\ 1.9 \\ \hline 6.3 \end{array}$$

12. $$\begin{array}{r} 25.7 \\ -\ 13.2 \\ \hline 12.5 \end{array}$$

13. $$\begin{array}{r} 7.8 \\ -\ 4.4 \\ \hline 3.4 \end{array}$$

14. $$\begin{array}{r} 5.5 \\ -\ 4.7 \\ \hline 0.8 \end{array}$$

15. $$\begin{array}{r} 3.7 \\ -\ 3.3 \\ \hline 0.4 \end{array}$$

16. $$\begin{array}{r} 0.9 \\ -\ 0.3 \\ \hline 0.6 \end{array}$$

17. $$\begin{array}{r} 19.1 \\ -\ 6.9 \\ \hline 12.2 \end{array}$$

18. $$\begin{array}{r} 14.7 \\ -\ 8.1 \\ \hline 6.6 \end{array}$$

Student's name: ____________________ Assignment date: ________________

Decimal Subtraction

```
    7.59
 -  2.43
 -------
    5.16
```

```
1.    5.67      7.    6.78      13.    7.89
    - 1.43          - 3.41           - 3.75
    ------          ------           ------
      4.24            3.37             4.14

2.    6.79      8.    4.17      14.    6.16
    - 0.33          - 3.64           - 2.64
    ------          ------           ------
      6.46            0.53             3.52

3.    5.58      9.    2.73      15.    2.15
    - 0.07          - 0.18           - 1.07
    ------          ------           ------
      5.51            2.55             1.08

4.   10.73      10.  12.07      16.   17.01
    - 3.66          - 8.28           -14.85
    ------          ------           ------
      7.07            3.79             2.16

5.   26.00      11.  35.63      17.   17.20
    -21.05          -11.68           -16.48
    ------          ------           ------
      4.95           23.95             0.72

6.   35.19      12.  63.43      18.   27.72
    - 7.04          -33.68           - 2.69
    ------          ------           ------
     28.15           29.75            25.03
```

Student's name: ____________________ Assignment date: ________________

Horizontal Subtraction

1) 6.7 – 3.28 = ____ 3.42	2) 4.8 – 1.05 = ____ 3.75	3) 3.8 – 2.29 = _____ 1.51
4) 6.3 – 3.812 = ______ 2.488	5) 8.31 – 4.79 = ______ 3.52	6) 6.41 – 5.919 = ____ 0.491
7) 9.1 – 0.63 = ______ 8.47	8) 4.8 – 0.92 = ______ 3.88	9) 7.3 – 0.24 = ____ 7.06
10)5.03 – 3.1 = _____ 1.93	11)8.04 – 6.2 = ______ 1.84	12)4.09 – 1.9 = ____ 2.19
13)11.6 – 7.5 = _____ 4.1	14)12.7 – 8.8 = ______ 3.9	15)13.2 – 4.5 = _____ 8.7

Student's name: ____________________ Assignment date: ________________

1)5.703 – 3.124 = ____ 2.579	2)6.407 – 2.353 =____ 4.054	3)5.407 – 1.254 = _____ 4.153
4)6.306 – 6.2723 = ______ 0.0337	5)7.605 – 3.5887 = ______ 4.0163	6)3.517 – 0.6334 = ____ 2.8836
7)5.4 – 1.57 = ______ 3.83	8)8.0 – 0.07 = ______ 7.93	9)5.7 – 1.86 = ____ 3.84
10) 12.64 – 6.07 = _____ 6.57	11) 37.58 – 3.19 = _____ 34.39	12) 16.48 – 6.03 = ____ 10.45
13) 52.71 – 23.49 = ____ 29.22	14) 25.43 – 18.20 = ____ 7.23	15) 10.01 – 4.13 = _____ 5.88

Student's name: ____________________ Assignment date: ________________

Place value computation including decimals and fractions including decimals and fractions

Do not ask students to work on this page until they understand the decimal place values.

2 hundreds and 2 thousands + 4 hundreds and 15 hundredths = ___________   2600.15
213 thousandths + 49 hundredths = -______________   0.703
Fifty and 50 hundredths – twenty-nine and 39 thousandths = ____________   21.11
one hundred twenty-three times 9 + $\frac{97}{100}$ = ____________________   1107.97
two hundred thirty-three – $9\frac{7}{100}$ = ____________________   223.93
If [grid] + $\frac{7}{100}$ + $\frac{?}{100}$ = 1, what is the value of "?"?   89

Decimal and fraction conversion

Decimal	fraction
0.21	? $\frac{21}{100}$
0.212	? $\frac{53}{250}$
? 0.1	$\frac{1}{10}$
? 0.25	$\frac{5}{20}$
? 1.2	$1\frac{1}{5}$
$\frac{52}{25} + 1.02$	? $3\frac{1}{10}$
$\frac{2}{0.25}$	? $\frac{8}{1}$

Student's name: ____________________ Assignment date: ________________

Estimating Sums by rounding to ones

5 . 6 →	6		5.6 is close to 6
+ 2 . 3 →	+ 2		2.3 is close to 2
.	8		6 + 2 = 8. So 5.6 + 2.3 is about 8.

1.	4 . 2 → + 7 . 5 →	4 + 8 = 12	2.	5 . 2 → + 1 . 6 →	5 + 2 = 7
3.	2 . 4 → + 5 . 1 →	2 + 5 = 7	4.	7 . 3 → + 0 . 6 →	7 + 1 = 8
5.	5 . 9 → + 3 . 7 →	6 + 4 = 10	6.	4 . 5 → + 7 . 7 →	5 + 8 = 13
7.	4 . 2 → + 3 . 6 →	4 + 4 = 8	8.	4 . 7 → + 7 . 1 →	5 + 7 = 12
9.	5 . 6 → + 8 . 2 →	6 + 8 = 14	10.	5 . 4 → + 3 . 2 →	5 + 3 = 8
11	6 . 9 → + 2 . 4 →	7 + 2 = 9	12.	4 . 5 → + 7 . 3 →	5 + 7 = 12

Ho Math Chess Primary Grades Math

Test Review assesssment 何数棋謎低年级数学测试複習考核

Student's name: ____________________ Assignment date: ________________

Estimating differences

$$\begin{array}{rcr} 8.7 & \rightarrow & 9 \\ -\ 3.2 & \rightarrow & -\ 3 \\ \hline . & & 6 \end{array}$$

8.7 is close to 9
3.2 is close to 3
9 – 3 = 6 . So 8.7 – 3.2 is close to 6.

1. $$\begin{array}{rcr} 5.3 & \rightarrow & 5 \\ -\ 1.6 & \rightarrow & -\ 2 \\ \hline & & 3 \end{array}$$

2. $$\begin{array}{rcr} 7.5 & \rightarrow & 8 \\ -\ 3.8 & \rightarrow & -\ 4 \\ \hline & & 4 \end{array}$$

3. $$\begin{array}{rcr} 7.2 & \rightarrow & 7 \\ -\ 5.3 & \rightarrow & -\ 5 \\ \hline & & 2 \end{array}$$

4. $$\begin{array}{rcr} 6.6 & \rightarrow & 7 \\ -\ 1.8 & \rightarrow & -\ 2 \\ \hline & & 5 \end{array}$$

5. $$\begin{array}{rcr} 7.2 & \rightarrow & 7 \\ -\ 0.3 & \rightarrow & -\ 0 \\ \hline & & 7 \end{array}$$

6. $$\begin{array}{rcr} 5.2 & \rightarrow & 5 \\ -\ 4.5 & \rightarrow & -\ 5 \\ \hline & & 0 \end{array}$$

7. $$\begin{array}{rcr} 5.1 & \rightarrow & 5 \\ -\ 3.6 & \rightarrow & -\ 4 \\ \hline & & 1 \end{array}$$

8. $$\begin{array}{rcr} 8.1 & \rightarrow & 8 \\ -\ 3.6 & \rightarrow & -\ 4 \\ \hline & & 4 \end{array}$$

9. $$\begin{array}{rcr} 7.7 & \rightarrow & 8 \\ -\ 1.3 & \rightarrow & -\ 1 \\ \hline & & 7 \end{array}$$

10. $$\begin{array}{rcr} 3.4 & \rightarrow & 3 \\ -\ 0.7 & \rightarrow & -\ 1 \\ \hline & & 2 \end{array}$$

11 $$\begin{array}{rcr} 8.2 & \rightarrow & 8 \\ -\ 5.6 & \rightarrow & -\ 6 \\ \hline & & 2 \end{array}$$

12. $$\begin{array}{rcr} 3.4 & \rightarrow & 3 \\ -\ 2.8 & \rightarrow & -\ 3 \\ \hline & & 0 \end{array}$$

Student's name: ____________________ Assignment date: ________________

Relating decimals to measuring length

Metric measurement ladder diagram

The Metric system uses the same prefix words to memorize all three weight, length, and capacity measurements.

As you move the list of prefixes, the next unit is 10 times the current one. As you move down the list, the next unit is the 10th of the current one.

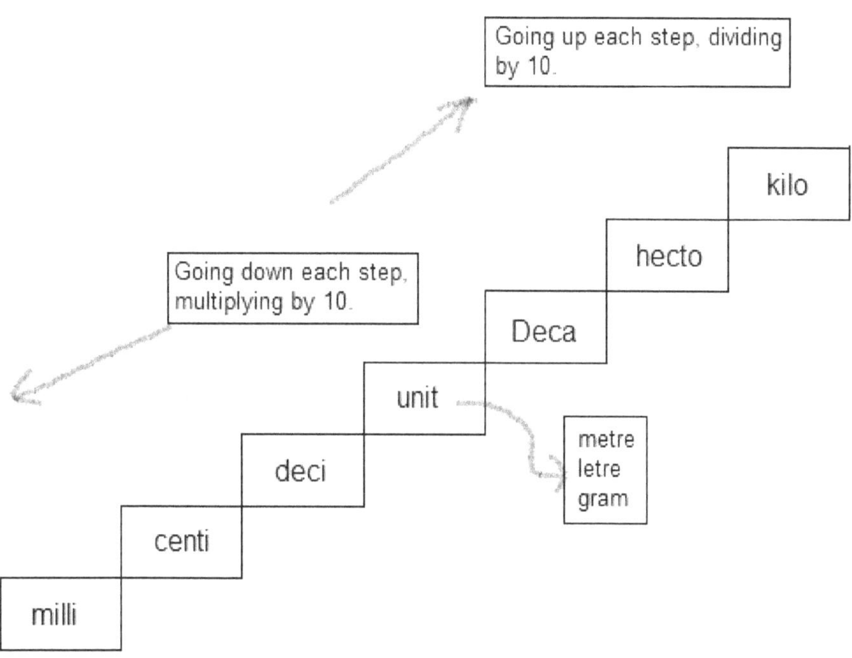

1 m = 10 dm = 100 cm, 1 dm =0.1 m
1 dm = 10 cm, 1 cm = 0.1 dm
1 cm = 10 mm, 1 mm = 0.1 cm

Student's name: ____________________ Assignment date: ________________

4 m 8 dm = 4 m + _____ m = _____m 0.8, 4.8
2 cm 6 mm = 2 cm + ______ cm = _____ cm 0.6, 2.6.
4 km 4 m = 4 km + _____ km = _____ km 0.004, 4.004
4.5 m 3 cm = ____ 4.5 m + ______m = _______ m 0.03, 4.53
31 mm = ______ cm _____ mm 3, 1
2500 cm = ______ km ______m = _______ km 2, 5, 2.05
45 cm = _____ dm _____cm = _______ dm = ______m 4, 5, 4.5, 0.45
1100 mm = ______ cm = _______ dm = ______ m = ________ km 110, 11, 1.1, 0.0011
1100 mm – 99 cm = ____ cm 1001
12.1m = ______ cm = ______ mm 121, 1210
34.55 mm +1.3 cm = _________ cm 4.755
1345 mm + 12.3 cm + 1 km = ______ km 1.1468
1000 mm + 100 dm + 100 m = ______ km 0.111

Student's name: ____________________ Assignment date: ________________

Relating decimals to money

\$1 = 100 cents (¢), 1 cent = 1 ¢ =\$0.01
1 dime = 10 cents= 10 ¢, 1 nickel = 5 cents = 5 ¢
1 penny = 1 cent = 1 ¢

\$1.55 + 5 cents = \$ _________ 1.60
\$1.60 + ______ cents = \$2.00 40
\$1.400 + _____ cents = \$5.00 360
400 ¢ + 900 ¢ = \$ _______ 1.30
692 ¢ + _____ cents = \$9.01 209
\$12.35 + _______ ¢ = \$12.40 5
\$ 12.40 + ______ cents = \$13.50 110
\$13.00 + \$ _____ = \$ 14.10 1.10
\$5.15 – ______ cents = 232 cents 283
\$1.10 – 99 cents = \$ _______ 1.10
\$4.12 – \$ ______ = 213 cents 1.99

Student's name: ____________________ Assignment date: ________________

Decimal word problems

1. A rope is 4.6 cm long. Another rope is 5.2 cm long. If the two ropes are connected, what is the maximum length of the rope?
   9.8 cm

2. An apple is 0.32 lb. An orange is 0.24 lb. What is the total weight of the two fruits?
   0.56 lb

3. A table is 0.8 m high. A box is 1.3 m high. If the box is put on the table, what is the height from the top of the box to the ground?
   2.1 m

4. An ant walks 6.2 cm in one minute. A snail crawls 2.4 cm. How much further does an ant walk?
   3.8 cm

5. A shirt is $15.32. A hat is $7.45. What is the total price of the two items?
   $22.77

6. A watermelon is 3.6 kg. A pineapple is 1.2 kg. How much heavier is the watermelon?
   2.4 kg

7. Pauline bought 7 packs of jumbo gums for 79 cents each. How much change did she get from $7.00?

$1.47

Student's name: ____________________ Assignment date: ________________

Rounding decimal number (5 up, 4 down)

The rounding decimal number is the same as rounding the whole number as long as we realize that the zeros after the decimal point do not make sense.

Question: Round the following numbers to the nearest tenths (one decimal place)	Step 1: Point to the place value (underlined) to be rounded.	Step 2: Look at the digit (single number) to the right of the pointed number.	Step 3: 5 up, 4 down If it is 5 or more, add 1 to the pointed number (round up); if it is less than 5, do not add 1 to the pointed number (round down).	Step 4: All digits to the right of the pointed number should be changed to 0.	Final answer
4128.59	4128.<u>5</u>9	9	4128.6	4128.60	4128.6

Question:
Round the following numbers to the nearest tens (underlined)

4128.59	41<u>2</u>8.59	8	4138.59	4130.00	4130

Question:
Round the following numbers to the nearest hundredths (2 decimal places)

4128.5987	4128.5<u>9</u>87	8	4128.6087	4128.6000	4128.60

Round to the underlined place value

10.<u>3</u>4	______	______	_______	______	10.30
0.3<u>5</u>5	______	______	_______	______	0.40

Student's name: ____________________ Assignment date: ________________

Test of rounding to the thousands

Circle the numbers from the list below that meet requirements. When rounded to tens, they equal 60. 51, 59, 56, 54, 55, 59, 54, 61, 67, 65, 60 51, 59, 56, 54, 55, 59, 54, 61, 67, 65, 60 answer
Circle the numbers from the list below that meet requirements. When rounded to tens, they equal 100. 91, 99, 96, 94, 95, 90, 94, 101, 145, 151, 120, 110 91, 99, 96, 94, 95, 90, 94, 101, 145, 151, 120, 110 answer
Circle the numbers from the list below that meet requirements. When rounded to hundreds, they equal 100. 91, 99, 96, 94, 95, 90, 94, 101, 145, 151, 120, 110, 89, 199 91, 99, 96, 94, 95, 90, 94, 101, 145, 151, 120, 110, 89, 199 answer
Circle the numbers from the list below that meet requirements. When rounded to thousands, they equal 2000. 1991,1499,1896,1094, 2995, 2090, 1594, 2101, 1145, 1651, 1220, 2110, 2189, 2199 1991,1499,1896,1094, 2995, 2090, 1594, 2101, 1145, 1651, 1220, 2110, 2189, 2199 answer

Find all possible numbers which meet the requirement: the numbers, when rounded to the nearest tens, are equal to 80. The numbers are from 75 to 84
Find all possible numbers between 350 to 499 which meet the requirement: the numbers, when rounded to the nearest hundreds, are equal to 400. The numbers are from 350 to 449.
If a number 13?9 is rounded to 1300, what could be the tens? 0, 1, 2, 3, 4

Student's name: ____________________ Assignment date: ________________

***** Part 7 Pattern *****

Pattern attributes (for higher grades)

Figure pattern has some attributes such as colours, sizes, shapes, directions, and fonts. For example, the following pattern has the attributes of sizes, shapes, and colours.

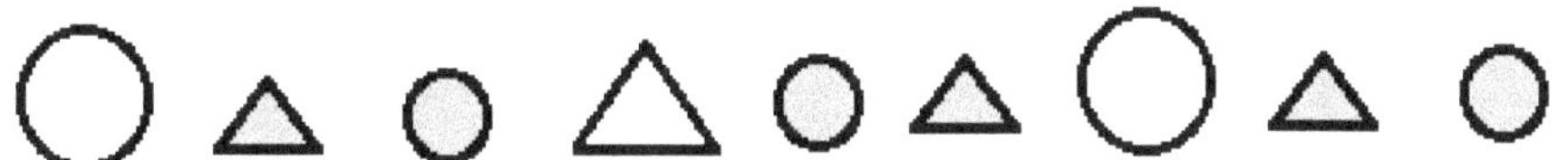

A. The above pattern has 3 attributes size, colour, shape.

B. How does the size change?
It changes in the order of Large, small, small, Large, small, small, ….

How does the shape change?
It changes in the order of large circle, small triangle, small circle, large circle, small triangle, small circle, ….

C. What are the next three shapes in the pattern?

answer 

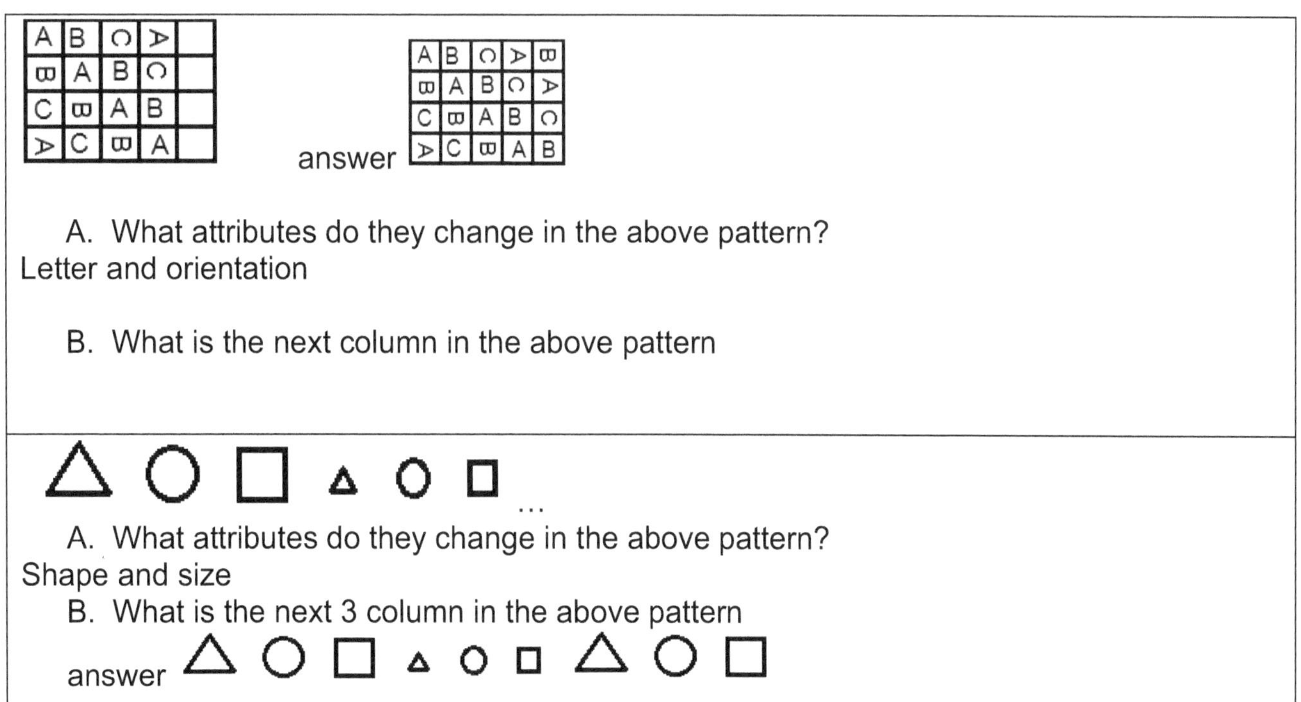

answer

A. What attributes do they change in the above pattern?
Letter and orientation

B. What is the next column in the above pattern

A. What attributes do they change in the above pattern?
Shape and size

B. What is the next 3 column in the above pattern

answer

Student's name: ____________________ Assignment date: ______________

Pattern core and pattern rule (for higher grades)

There are many different kinds of patterns such as all numbers pattern, pattern with figures, pattern with repeated core pattern or 2-dimensional pattern etc.

Pattern core

Example

What is the pattern core of the pattern ABCABCABCABCABC….?

The pattern core of the above pattern is ABC.

What is the 110th letter of the pattern ABCABCABCABCABC….? Use the division method by dividing 110 by 3, and the remainder is 2, so the letter is B because the pattern core is ABC. $110 = 36 \times 3 + 2$
Predict the colour of the 112th block of the following pattern. red | yellow | yellow | red | red | yellow | yellow | red | red | yellow | yellow | red $\frac{112}{4}$ has remainder 0, so the colour is red because the pattern core is ryyr. .
predict the 57th term of A1B2A1B2A1B2… Each letter or number is considered as one term. 57 divided by 4 with the remainder of 1, so the 57th term is A.
How many letters are in the 20th term in the following pattern? RY, RRYY, RRRYYY, RRRRYYYY, … 40 by making a table.RY, RRYY, RRRYYY, RRRRYYYY 2 letters for term 1, 4 letters for term 2, 6 letters for term 3 ….so there will be 40 letters for term 20.

Student's name: ____________________ Assignment date: ________________

How to find the number pattern?

How to find the next number?

Step 1

To find the next number of a number pattern, it is often to use the difference or quotient (or called gap) between two adjacent numbers.

Step 2

To predict the next number, one should figure out the pattern rule.

1-dimensional pattern

3, 5, 7, 9, 11, _____

The gap is always 2 by using the larger – small number.
The pattern rule is as follows.
Start at 3, add 2 to get the next number.
The answer is 13.

2, 4, 8, 16, _________ 32
The pattern rule is ________________
Start at 2, multiplied by 2 to get the next number.

Row 1	1	2	3	4	5
Row 2	3	4	5	6	?

The pattern rule is ____________________________________.
row 2 = row 1 + 2

Continue the pattern in the following table.

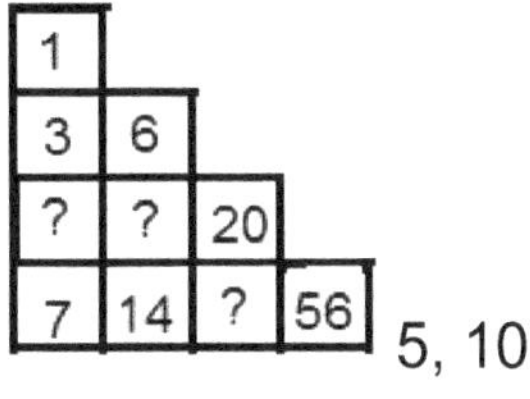

5, 10

28 The number times 2 of the last column.

Student's name: ____________________ Assignment date: ________________

In and out boxes

In	1	3	5	7
Out	3	5	7	?

Pattern rule: Out = In + 2
9

In	1	3	5	7
Out	3	5	7	?

Pattern rule: Out = In + 2
9, 11

In	1	3	5	7
Out	3	5	7	?

Pattern rule: Out = In + 2
9

In	1	3	5	7
Out				

Pattern rule: Out = In + 2
3, 5, 7, 9

In	1	3	5	7
Out				

Pattern rule: Out = In × 2
2, 6, 10, 14

In	4	6	7	8
Out				

Pattern rule: Out = In - 1
3, 5, 6, 7

In	Out
2	
4	
5	
7	

Pattern rule: Out = In × 3
6, 12, 15, 21

In	Out
12	
9	
6	
5	

Pattern rule: Out = In add 2
14, 11, 8, 7

In	Out
19	
18	
17	
13	

Pattern rule: Out = In subtract 6
13, 12, 11, 7

Student's name: ____________________ Assignment date: ________________

Number patterns or letter pattern(for lower grades)

1.	1	2	3	_____	_____	_____	4,5,6
2.	2	4	6	_____	_____	_____	8,10,12
3.	5	10	15	_____	_____	_____	20,25,30
4.	10	100	1000	_____	_____	_____	10000,100000,1000000
5.	325	335	345	_____	_____	_____	355,365,375
6.	4236	5236	6236	_____	_____	_____	7236,8236,9236
7.	270	280	290	_____	_____	_____	300,310,320,
8.	1150	1200	1250	_____	_____	_____	1300,1350,1400
9.	7385	7375	7365	_____	_____	_____	7355,7345,7335
10.	4350	4250	4150	_____	_____	_____	4050,3950,3850
11.	1007	1008	1009	_____	_____	_____	1010,1011,1012
12.	4256	4506	4756	_____	_____	_____	5006,5526
13.	21	32	43	_____	_____	_____	54,65,76
14.	613	524	435	_____	_____	_____	346,257,168
15.	987	876	765	_____	_____	_____	654,543,432

Student's name: ____________________ Assignment date: ________________

Letters pattern

1. Continue the following patterns.

B, D, F. H, ____ J
ABAABA __ __ __ __ __ __ __ __ AABAAAAB
GH1GH2GH3 __ __ __ GH4
BAABBAAABBB___ ___ ___ ___ ___ ___ ___ ___ AAAABBBB

Student's name: ____________________ Assignment date: ________________

Looking for patterns

1.	3	_____	15	31	63	127	255	7
2.	10	20	40	80	160	_____		320
3.	2	4	16	_____	65536			256
4.	16	8	_____	_____	1			4, 2
5.	_____	12	36	108	324	972		4
6.	_____	_____	20	24	96	100	400	1, 5
7.	600	600	300	100	25	_____		5
8.	784529	78452	7452	452	_____	_____		42, 2
9.	11	18	25	32	39	_____	53	46
10.	810	270	_____	30	10			90
11.	1	4	16	64	256	_____		1024
12.	$400	$200	$100	$50	_____			$25
13.	100	99	97	94	90	_____	_____	85, 79
14.	15	12	14	11	13	_____	_____	10, 12
15.	1	3	7	15	31	_____	_____	63, 127
16.	67	35	19	11	7	_____	_____	5, 4

Student's name: ____________________ Assignment date: ________________

Looking for patterns.

Triangle	Answers
1	
2 2	
3 4 3	
4 7 __ 4	7
5 11 __ 11 5	14
6 __ 25 __ 16 6	16, 25
7 22 41 __ 41 __ 7	50

The above is called the Pascal triangle if two 1's are added on both ends of each row.

Triangle	Answers
1	
2 4	
3 9 27	
4 16 __ 256	64
5 __ __ 625 3125	25, 125

Triangle	Answers
1	
2 4	
3 6 9	
4 8 __ 16	12
5 __ 15 __ __	10, 20, 25
6 __ __ __ __ __	12, 18, 24, 30, 36

Student's name: ____________________ Assignment date: ________________

Figure pattern

1.						
2.						
3.						
4.						
5.						
6.						
7.						
8.						
9.						

Student's name: ____________________ Assignment date: ________________

Put R in the following board in such a way that each row, each column has one and only one R. Can you find more than one way?

1.

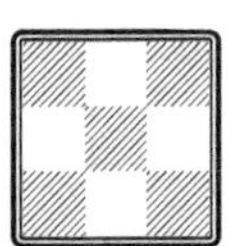
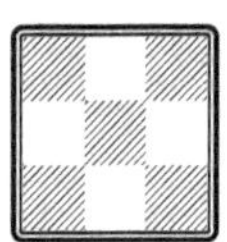

2.

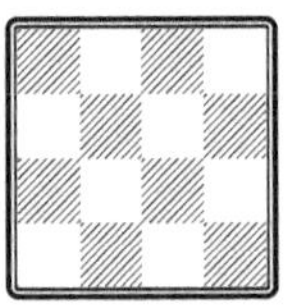
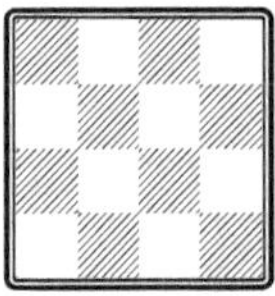
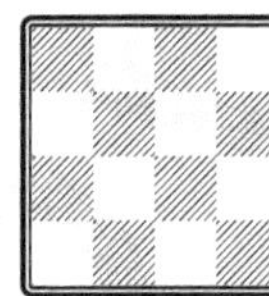

3.

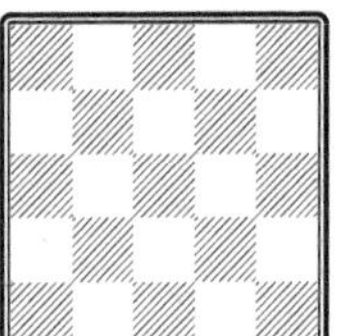
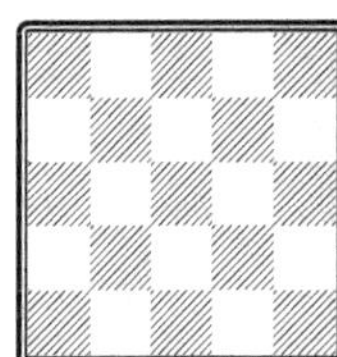
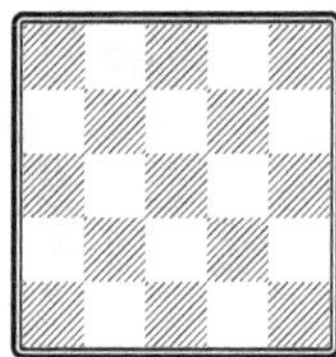

Put A,B,C in the following board in such a way that each row, each column has one and only one of each kind. Can you find more than one way?

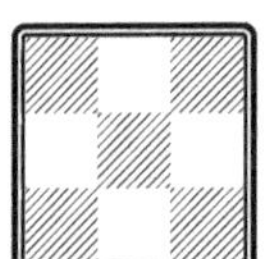
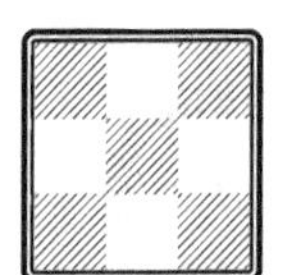
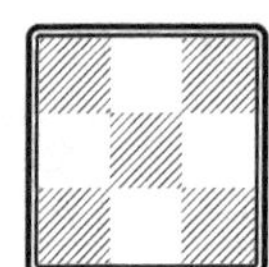

Put A, B, C and D in the following board in such a way that each row, each column, and each main diagonal has one and only one of each kind. Can you find more than one way?

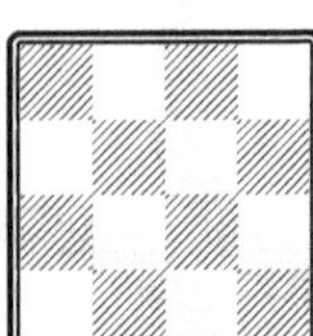
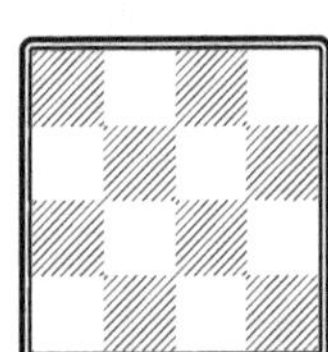
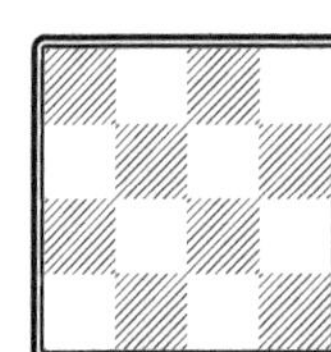
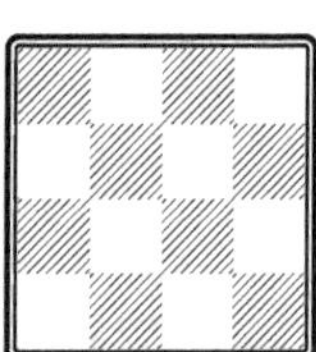

Answers may vary.

Student's name: ____________________ Assignment date: ________________

2-dimensional pattern

Look for Pattern and Complete T-table.

2.

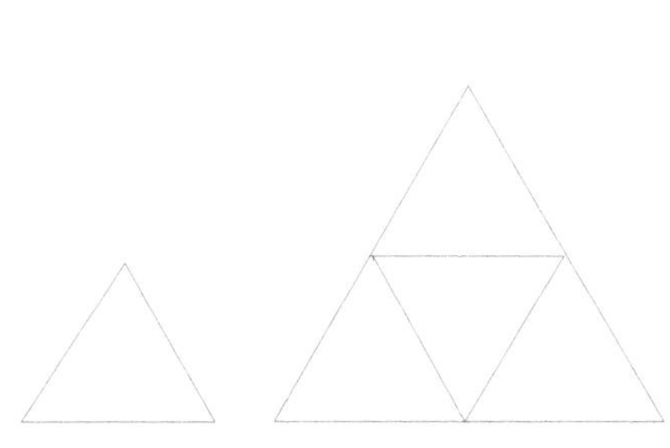

Number of columns	Number of squares
1	3
2	6
3	9
4	12
5	15
6	18

3.

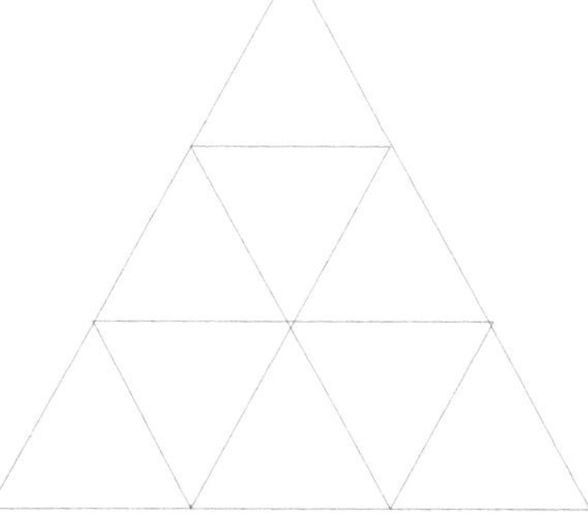

Number of rows	Number of triangles
1	1
2	4
3	9
4	16
5	25
6	36

4.

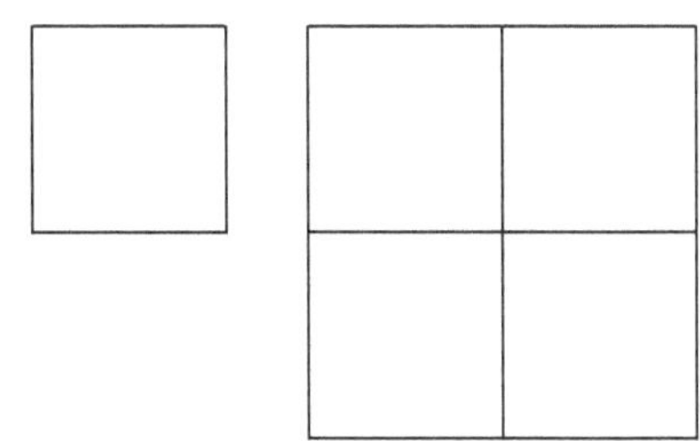

Number of rows	Number of squares
1	1
2	4
3	9
4	16
5	25
6	36

Student's name: ____________________ Assignment date: ________________

Look for Pattern and Complete T-table.

5.

Number of rows	Number of apples
3	5
4	7
5	9
6	11
7	13
8	15

6.

Number of rows	Number of stars
2	4
3	8
4	12
5	16
6	20
7	24

7.

Number of rows	Number of dots
3	5
4	8
5	11
6	14
7	17
8	20

Student's name: ____________________ Assignment date: ________________

Look for Pattern and Complete T-table.

8.

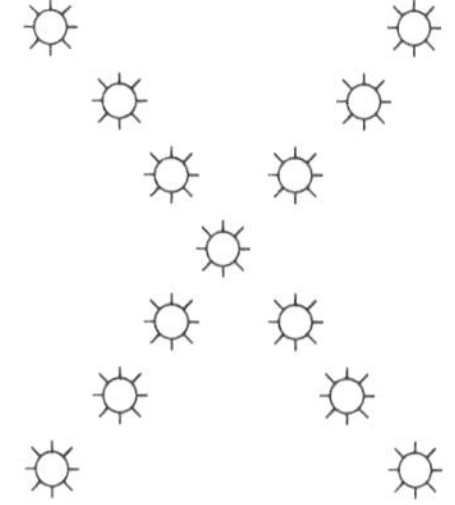

Number of rows	Number of apples
3	5
5	9
7	13
9	17
11	21
13	25

9.

Number of rows	Number of stars
3	6
5	12
7	18
9	24
11	30
13	36

10

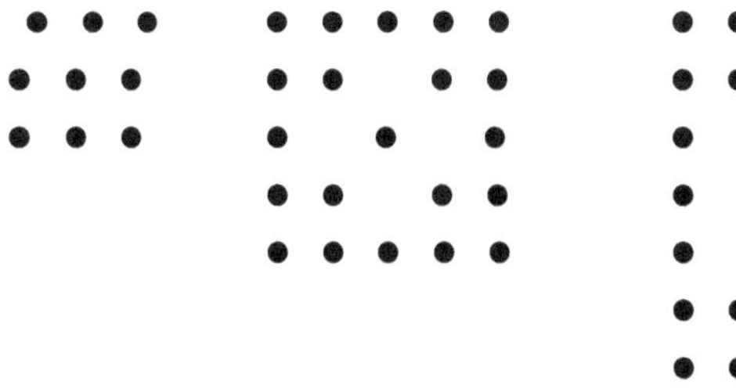

Number of rows	Number of dots
3	9
5	21
7	33
9	45
11	57
13	69

Student's name: ____________________ Assignment date: ________________

Pattern word problems

Alvin saves $11 in February, and he saves $5 after that every month. How much will he have saved by the end of August? 11 + 5 x 6 = $41
Adam saves $17 in January and $5 each month after that. Bob saves $15 in January and $7 each month after that. Who has saved more money by the end of November? Adam = 17 + 5 x 11=72 Bob = 15 + 7 x 11 = 92 ..... Bob saved more.
Heather has biked 10 km from her home. After that, she cycles 7 km per hour. If she biked 38 km, how many more hours had she biked after the initial 10 km? 38 = 10 + 7 x 4 Heather would have biked 4 more hours. 38
Kiko and Snow cats share cat food one can for every 5 days. How many cans should Frank buy in December if there are no more cans left? $\begin{array}{r} 6 \\ 5 \overline{)31} \\ -30 \\ \hline 1 \end{array}$ Frank needs to buy 7 cans.
Kiko, the cat, likes to go out in the very early morning. She will usually come back every 45 minutes, rest for 5 minutes, and then go out again until noon. Then she likes to take a nap. Suppose Kiko goes out at 6:30 a.m. If this pattern continues, how many times would she have gone out, and how many times would she have come back if Kiko stayed at home the last time before noon? From 12 noon to 6:30 a.m., she would have come back 6 times, and come back 6 times. 630 715, 720 805, 810 855, 900 945, 950 1035, 1040 1125.

Student's name: ____________________ Assignment date: ________________

The two cats Kiko and Snow, like to collect leaves. Yesterday Kiko collected 3 leaves, and Snow collected 1 leaf. If starting from today, Kiko collects 1 leaf every day and Snow collects 2 leaves every day, then on what day will they collect the same number of leaves? Snow: 1, 2, 2 Kiko: 3, 1, 1 The second day.
In Ethan`s class, three out of every five students are male. There are 125 students in his class. How many of them are female
Today, Adam has read 8 pages of his book and will read one page after that. Bob has read 4 pages and will read 2 pages after that. How many days later will Adam and Bob read the same number of pages?
Kiko, the cat, goes out every 6 minutes, and the cat Snow goes out every 8 minutes. If both of them go out at 6:30 a.m. when would be the next time they go out altogether? Use LCM or pattern to solve it. 7:18 a.m.
Banno has 8 books and buys 1 new book every week. Benni has 4 books and buys a new book every week. After how many weeks will Banno and Benni have the same number of books?

Student's name: ____________________ Assignment date: ________________

The pattern in **ax + by model**

Renee is working to raise money for her gymnastics competition trip. She has two options:
Option A – She works 7 days, and each day, she makes $8.
Option B – She makes different money each day.

Day 1	Day 2	Day 3	Day 4	Day 5	Day 6	Day 7
$1	$3	$5	$7	$9	?	?

To raise the most money, which option should Renee choose? Show all your work.

Option A: $8 x 7 = $56
Option B: 1+ 3 + 5 + 7 + 9 + 11 + 13 = $49

Option A is better.

Renee wants to grow 50 seedlings in two kinds of trays. One tray can hold 4 seedlings, and the other tray can hold 6 seedlings. How many different ways can she fill in the two trays if each tray must be in full?

Each drop of two of the six-seedling tray would require the fill of 3 of four-seedling trays.

Number of 6 seedlings	Number of 4 seedlings
7	2
5	5
3	8
1	11

There are 4 ways to plant.

Student's name: ____________________ Assignment date: ________________

Pattern test

Figure out the pattern rule first, then write the next three numbers.

27, 24, 21, 18, ____, _____, _____ 15, 12, 9

Start at 27 and subtract 3 each time to get the next one.

Figure out the pattern rule first, then write the next three numbers.

4, 5, 7, 10, 14, ____, _____, _____ 19, 25, 32

Start at 4 and add 1, 2, 3 ,4 … each time.

Figure out the pattern rule first, then write the next three numbers.

31, 35, 39, ____, _____, _____ 43, 47, 51

Start at 31 and add 4 each time.

Look for patterns of the following pattern figure, then complete the number chain.

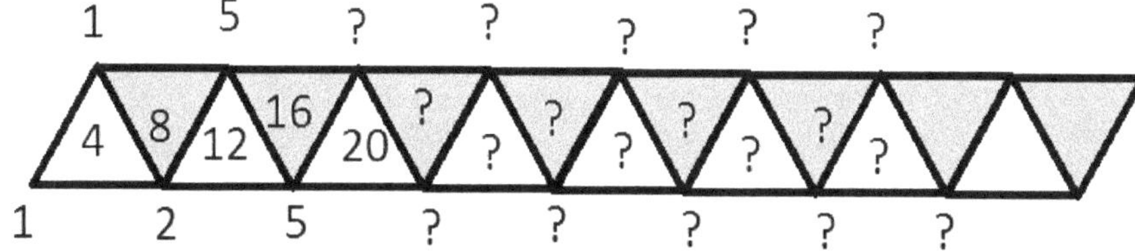

The pattern rule inside the chain. ______________________. Start at 4 and add 4 each time.
The pattern rule above the chain ______________________. Start at 1, increase by 4, 1, 3 each time.
The pattern below the chain ______________________. Start at 1, increase by 1, 3, 4 each time.
The pattern of zigzagging numbers ______________________. Start at 1, increase by 0, 1, 3 ach time._

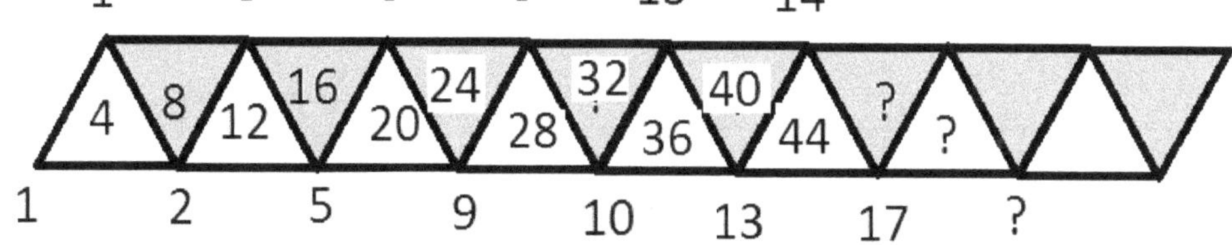

Student's name: ____________________ Assignment date: ________________

Describe how the attributes change in the following diagram pattern?

□ ● □ ◇ □ ● □ ◇ □ ● □ ....

____

Repeat the pattern core □ ● □ ◇ answer

Draw the next three shapes. ____

◇ □ ● answer

Describe the pattern rule of the following T-chart. You should think about how to get the number of paws from the number of cats.

cats	paws
1	4
2	?
3	?
4?	?

The pattern rule is ______________________________ Paws = $4 \times cat$

8, 12, 16

Describe the pattern rule of the following T-chart.

weeks	days
1	?
2	14
3	?
4?	?

____ days = $7 \times weeks$

7, 21, 28

Create a problem that can be solved by using the above pattern rule.

______________________________ How many days are there if there are 8 weeks?

32

Student's name: ____________________ Assignment date: ________________

Renee can make 3 paper kites in 1 hour. Create a chart to show how many kites can make of increased hours each hour up to 5 hours.

hours	kites
1	3
?	?
?	?
?	?

____ kites = 3 × $hours$

2 6, 3 9, 4 12

Create a problem that can be solved by using the above pattern rule.

______________________________ How many kites can Renee make at week 7?

Student's name: ____________________ Assignment date: ________________

***** Part 8 Venn Diagram *****

Place the multiples of 3 in the following table and the multiples of 2 in the following table in the Venn diagram.

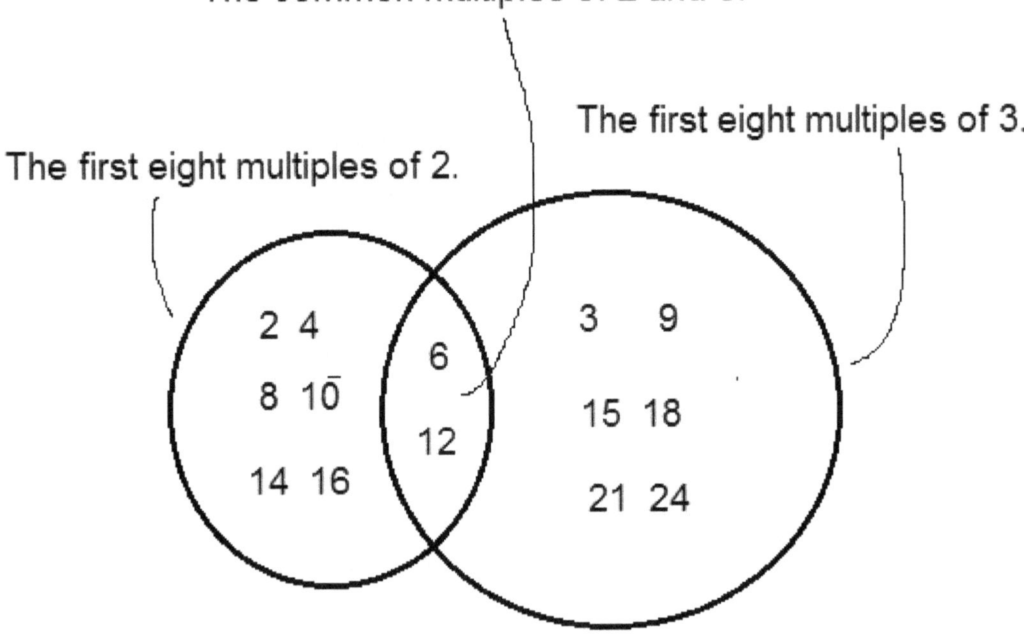

Place the first eight multiples of 6 in the following table and the first eight multiples of 9 in the following table in the Venn diagram.

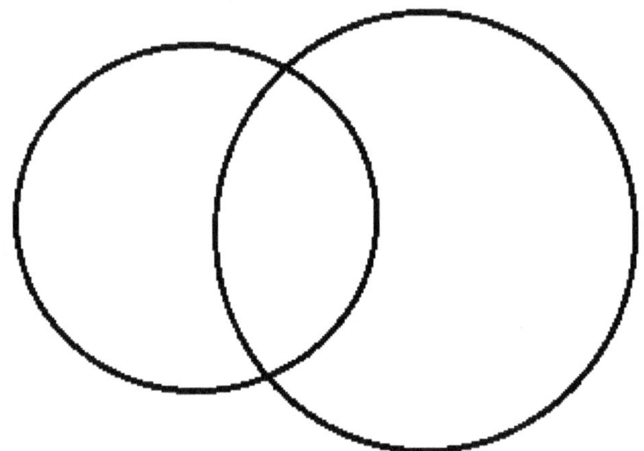

Student's name: ____________________ Assignment date: ________________

Venn diagram

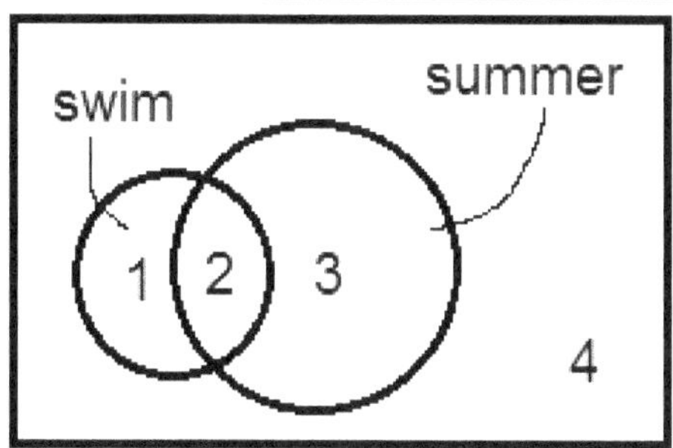

Use the above Venn diagram to answer the following questions.

A. In which part of the Venn diagram would you put on a summer swimming suit.
B. In which part of the Venn diagram would you put on your beachwear?
C. In which part of the Venn diagram would you swim outdoor?

Student's name: ____________________ Assignment date: ________________

Test of Venn diagram

There are some three-digit numbers sorted into the following Venn diagram. Write numbers into each circle to replace the question marks.

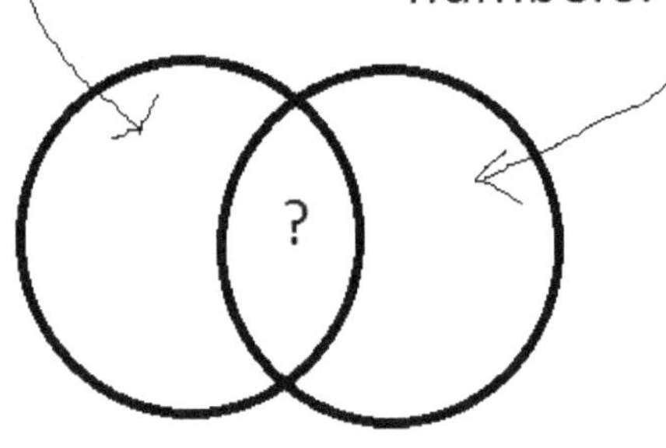

222
444
666
888 answer

Use the following numbers to create a Venn diagram using the sorting rule (attributes) you created. Label each part of the circle and the intersection in the middle.
21, 27, 302, 80, 35, 235, 16, 107, 212
Answers may vary.

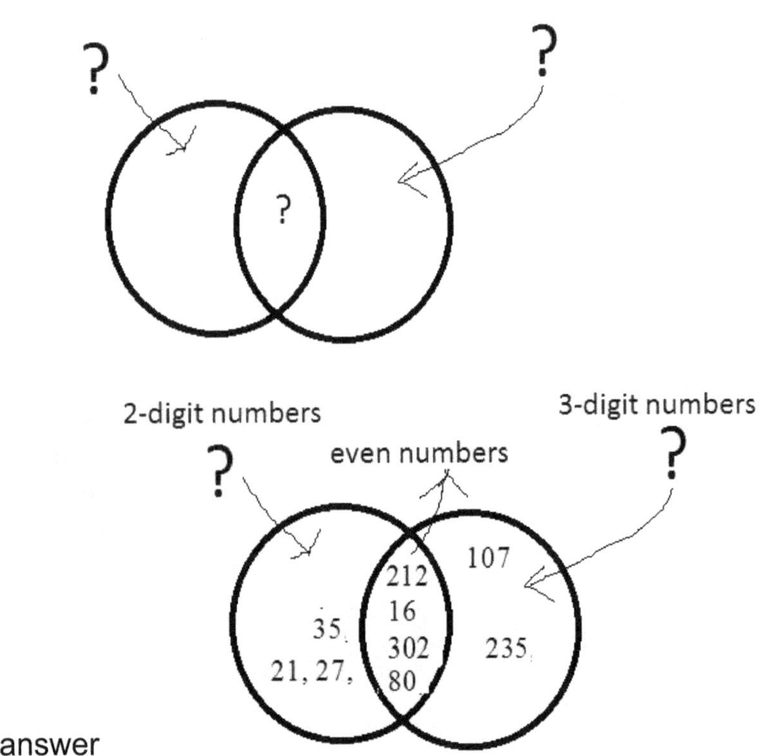

answer

Ho Math Chess Primary Grades Math

Test Review assesssment 何数棋謎低年级数学测试複習考核

Student's name: ____________________ Assignment date: ________________

***** Part 9 Simple equation using figures *****

If ◯ = 9 then ◯ + 1 = ______. 10
If ◯ = 11 then ◯ – 2 = ______. 9
If ● = 1 then ◯ = ●●● then ◯ + ●●● = ______. 6
If ◯ = ●●● then ◯ + ●●●●● = ______ 8
If ◯ = ●●● and ● = 1 then ◯ + ●●● – ● = ______ 5
Write a number in the box to make the equation true. ◯ +7 = 11 ◯ + 6 = 13 ◯ + 9 = 16 2 + ◯ = 13 6 + ◯ = 14 11 = ◯ + 2 17 = 8 + ◯
◯ – 8 = 3 ◯ – 2 = 9 13 – ◯ – 8 = 3 6 – ◯ – 1 = 3

Student's name: ____________________ Assignment date: _______________

Solving equation

Equations

It makes sense for students to learn some equations before ratio and proportion, so many students got confused on proportions simply because they do not know how to solve the equations of proportion, especially the method of using cross multiplication. This section aims to give students the knowledge of using equations to solve proportion and percent problems.

An equation is a mathematical sentence using = sign to connect two quantities. The left side of the = sign or the right side of the = sign is called an algebraic expression. The expression consists of numbers, operators, or variables (unknown quantity representing by a letter, normally by x). The operators can have brackets (parentheses), exponents, plus, minus, multiplication, or division,, which are used in elementary school mathematics. To solve an equation is to find all values of the variables so that both sides are equal.

To solve the equation, quite often, we use the following equation of properties:

The equation does not change when both sides add the same quantity.

The equation does not change when both sides subtract the same quantity.

The equation does not change when both sides multiply the same quantity.

The equation does not change when both sides are divided by the same quantity.

Student's name: ____________________ Assignment date: ________________

Arithmetic operations properties

A few properties govern the arithmetic operations with real numbers, and they are presented below.

Closure for addition, subtraction, and multiplication.
For real numbers a and b:

$a + b$ is a unique real number.
$a - b$ is a unique real number.
$a \times b$ Is a unique real number.

If two real numbers are added, subtracted, or multiplied, then the result is always a real number. The result is "enclosed" in the universe of the real numbers.
For division, it may not be true, such as $\frac{8}{0}$.

The commutative property for addition and multiplication of 2 numbers
(The associative property is used for 3 or more numbers)

For real numbers a and b.
$a + b = b + a$
$ab = ba$
The results are not changed when the order of 2 numbers is changed.

Which one of the following operations is commutative and which one is not?

Problems	Commutative or not
To put on soap and wash hands	☐
To put on gloves and put on a coat.	☐
To wash hands and eat.	☐

Student's name: ____________________ Assignment date: ________________

To wash clothes and dry them.	☐
To eat rice and eat chicken.	☐
To hang up the phone and say good-bye.	☐
To multiply 2 and 3.	☐
To mix blue and green paint.	☐
The number of different outfits of pairing pants and shirts.	☐
The number of ways of choosing food from a menu.	☐
To check and checkmate the king.	☐
To flip ● ● ● ● / ● ● ● ● around	☐
To get an area of a rectangle.	☐

No, yes, no, yes, yes, no, yes, no, yes ,no

Student's name: ____________________ Assignment date: ________________

Associative property (grouping property) for addition and multiplication of 3 numbers

For real numbers a, b, c
$(a + b) + c = a + (b + c)$
$(ab)c = a(bc)$

Use the associative property to make 10 first and then add the third number.

4 6 + 3	4 3 + 6	9 7 + 1	4 8 + 2	7 8 + 3

Use the associative property to make a nice number (number with trailing zeros) first, then multiply the third number.

$12 \times 6 \times 5$ =	$11 \times 4 \times 25$ =	$7 \times 25 \times 4$ =
$13 \times 2 \times 5$ =	$14 \times 2 \times 25$ =	$7 \times 15 \times 4$ =
$2 \times 7 \times 5$ =	$8 \times 4 \times 25$ =	$8 \times 8 \times 25$ =

More problems can be found in this workbook under the heading multiplied by 5.
13, 13, 17, 14, 18
360, 1100, 700
130, 700, 480
70, 800, 800

Student's name: ____________________ Assignment date: ________________

Addition by regrouping using the associative property

The order of operation is normally from left to right, but because the sign always goes with the number so the numbers can be regrouped for addition by using the associative property (1+7 + 9 = (1+9) +7= 10+7=17.

Example: 23 + 42 + 77 + 38 = (23 + 77) + (42 + 38) = 100 + 80 = 180

1. 42 + 73 + 27 + 58
=(42 + 58) + (73 + 27)
= 100 + 100
= 200

2. 26 + 39 + 44 + 61

3. 85 + 36 + 115 + 34

4. 51 + 23 + 49 + 57

5. 73 + 42 + 28 + 27

6. 49 + 36 + 51 + 74

7. 153 + 57 + 63 + 47

8. 535 + 58 + 52 + 65

9. 73 + 69 + 51 + 127

10. 56 + 368 + 32 + 84

170, 270, 180, 170, 210, 320, 710, 320, 540

Student's name: ____________________ Assignment date: ________________

Identity of addition

For real number a

$a+0=0+a=a$

Zero is the addition identity. Any number add a 0. Its answer is still the number itself.

Identity of multiplication

For real number a

$a(1)=(1)a=a$

One is the multiplication identity. Any number multiplies 1, and its answer is still the number itself.

Additive inverse

For any real number a, there exists a unique real number $-a$ such that

$a+(-a)=a-a=0$

The number - a is known as the additive inverse.
a and -a are additive inverse to each other and also the opposite of each other.

Multiplicative inverse

For any nonzero real number a, there exists a unique real number $\frac{1}{a}$ such that

$a\left(\frac{1}{a}\right)=\left(\frac{1}{a}\right)a=1$, the number $\frac{1}{a}$ is known as the multiplicative inverse or reciprocal of a.

a and $\frac{1}{a}$ are multiplicative inverse or reciprocal to each other. Since 1 is the product of $a\times\frac{1}{a}$ so to get $\frac{1}{\frac{a}{b}}$, we just have to inverse $\frac{a}{b}$ to get the answer $\frac{b}{a}$.

Student's name: ____________________ Assignment date: _______________

Distributive property

For real numbers a, b, c

$a(b+c)=ab+ac$	$a(b-c)=ab-ac$	$(a+b)c = ac+bc$	(a – b) c = ac - bc

The vertical multiplication is an example of using associative property.

$a(b+c)=ab+ac$	24 × 37 = 24 × (7 + 30) = 168 + 720 = 888 Note on the right-hand side, when 3 × 24, it means 30 × 24.	24 × 37 168 72 888	One can clearly see the reason why the product lined up with tens place value when 3 × 24.
$a(b+c)=ab+ac$	24 × 37 = 24 × (30+7) = 720 + 168 = 888	24 × 37 72 168 888	
	Note how 3 and 24 is multiplied first.		

Student's name: ____________________ Assignment date: ________________

Using distributive property to factor out common number on addition

Examples

36 × 8 + 36 × 12

= 36 × (8 + 12)

= 36 × 20

= 720

56 × 48 + 56 × 52

= 56 × (48 + 52)

= 56 × 100

= 5600

73 × 7 + 73 × 3

730

81 × 4 + 81 × 6

810

693 × 2 + 693 × 8

6930

239 × 8 + 239 × 2

2390

421 × 9 + 421 × 1

4210

326 × 5 + 326 × 5

3260

Student's name: ____________________ Assignment date: ________________

7. 43 × 26 + 43 × 74

4300

61 × 45 + 61 × 55

6100

9. 48 × 36 + 48 × 64

4800

68 × 28 + 28 × 32

2800

11. 57 × 35 + 43 × 35

3500

69 × 41 + 41 × 31

4100

13. 58 × 31 + 58 × 69

5800

29 × 47 + 71 × 47

4700

Student's name: ____________________ Assignment date: ________________

Using distributive property to factor out the common number on subtraction

Examples

$45 \times 13 - 45 \times 3$

$= 45 \times (13 - 3)$

$= 45 \times 10$

$= 450$

$129 \times 147 - 129 \times 47$

$= 129 \times (147 - 47)$

$= 129 \times 100$

$= 12900$

1. $61 \times 17 - 61 \times 7$

   610

2. $87 \times 16 - 87 \times 6$

   870

3. $52 \times 15 - 52 \times 5$

   520

4. $43 \times 27 - 43 \times 7$

   860

5. $67 \times 25 - 67 \times 5$

   1340

6. $66 \times 74 - 66 \times 4$

   4620

Student's name: ____________________ Assignment date: ________________

7. 48 × 132 – 48 × 32

4800

8. 63 × 143 – 63 × 43

6300

9. 77 × 124 – 77 × 24

7700

10. 57 × 119 – 57 × 19

5700

11. 48 × 265 – 48 × 65

9600

12. 71 × 335 – 71 × 35

21300

13. 63 × 47 – 47 × 13

2350

14. 78 × 32 – 32 × 38

1280

15. 53 × 26 – 33 × 26

520

16. 27 × 59 – 59 × 17

590

Student's name: ____________________ Assignment date: ________________

Variable and expression

In algebra, an unknown quantity or number is represented by a letter such as x, y. An algebraic expression is a mathematical sentence consisting of numbers, operators, or variables with no equal sign.

Fill in ____________ with an answer.

Word phrases	Expressio n	Comments
The product of 10 and a number	$10x$	Do not write the product as $10 \times x$. The number (called coefficient) is placed in front of the variable, and there is an implied $\times$ sign between the number and variable. $3x$ means 3 times x.
A number is doubled.	$2x$	Write variable (unknown) X as x or X since X looks like a multiplication sign. We normally use x, y z as variables, but not always.
One hundred divided by a number	$\frac{100}{x}$	Do not write division as $a \div b$. Use $\frac{a}{b}$ as a division in algebra since we need to work with LCD in the future.

Student's name: ____________________ Assignment date: ________________

Variable and expression

Word phrases	Algebraic expression
A number is tripled.	$3x$
4 times x	$4x$
x times 2 (a number is doubled.)	$2x$
x times x (a number is multiplied by itself.)	x^2
one-sixth of a number (a number divided by 6)	____________ x/6
Maria's age 7 years from her age now	____________ x + 7
1 times x	____________ x
x times 1	____________ x
2x times 4	____________ 4 x 2x
2 times a	____________ 2a
a times 2	____________ 2a
thirty-one kilometres less than the distance	____________ $x - \frac{1}{3}$
4 times 2 x	____________ 4 x 2x
3 minus x	____________ 3 - x
1 more than a number	____________ x + 1
a number decreased by four	____________ x - 4

Student's name: ____________________ Assignment date: ________________

Writing algebraic expressions

Word phrase	Algebraic expression
99 subtracted from a number	X - 99
a number divided by 23	x/23
The sum of a number y and 15	y + 15
one multiplies a number.	x
the difference between a number and forty	X - 40
99 multiplied by a number	99x
a number multiplied by 1	x
the product of 2 and 5 and a number	10x
If x is an odd number, what is the next larger odd number?	X+2
a number divided by 5523	x/5523
5523 divided by a number	5523x
I rode roller coaster x times, and the total time is 300 minutes. What is the average time?	300/x
It took me 30 minutes to finish my grocery shopping, and it included the time of x waiting in line. What is the time I actually spent on shopping?	30 - x

Student's name: ____________________ Assignment date: ________________

Writing algebraic expressions

Word phrase	Algebraic expression
Let t be the time taken between school and home round trip. How long did it take for 7 round trips?	7x _______________
It took Stanley and Edward 5 hours altogether to finish typing a science project report. How much time did Stanley spend on typing, assume Edward typed x hours?	5 - x _______________

Word phrase	Algebraic expression
____	$x + 9$
____	$5 - x$
____	$9x + 4$
____	$\frac{1}{2x}$
____	$5a$
a number x multiplied by itself	x^2
____	$x^2 + 30$

Student's name: ____________________ Assignment date: ________________

Writing word phrases

______________________________	$u + \frac{u}{4}$
111 less than a number	
______________________________	$200m$
______________________________	$\frac{1}{2x}$
______________________________	$3x - 1$
______________________________	x^2
______________________________	$u - 4u$

Student's name: ____________________ Assignment date: ________________

Evaluate the following expressions.

Expressions	Value	Comments
7 – 2 × 3	1	
7 – (2 × 3)	1	Are the brackets necessary? _____
(7 – 2) × 3	15	
2 × 7 – 3	11	
(2 × 7) – 3	11	Are the brackets necessary? _____
2 × (7 – 3)	8	
4 × 5 + 6 × 7	62	

Student's name: ____________________ Assignment date: ________________

Evaluate the following expressions

Expressions	Value	Comments
4 × (5 + 6) × 7	308	
4 × (5 + 6 × 7)	1288	
(4 × 5 + 6) × 7	182	
45 ÷ 5 + 9 ÷ 3	12	
(45 ÷ 5) + (9 ÷ 3)	12	Are brackets necessary? ________
42 ÷ (5 + 9) ÷ 3	1	
48 ÷ (5 + 9 ÷ 3)	6	
(45 ÷ 5 + 9) ÷ 3	6	
1 + 2 + 3 ÷ 3 – 2 – 1	1	
(1 + 2 + 3) ÷ (3 – 2) – 1	5	
1 + 2 + 3 ÷ (3 – 2) – 1	5	
1 + 2 + 3 ÷ 3 × 2 – 1	4	
1 + 2 + 3 ÷ 3 × (2 – 1)	4	

Student's name: ____________________ Assignment date: ________________

Evaluate the following expressions

Evaluate. Use $x = 1$, $y = 2$, $z = 3$	Value	Comments
$1x$	1	$1x$ means x.
$y - x$	1	
$z - x$	2	
$z - x - y$	0	
$4x + 3x + 2x$	9	
$4x + 3x - 2x$	5	
$4x - 3x - 2x$	-1	
$4x - 3x + 2x$	3	
$\frac{z}{3} + 9$	10	
$\frac{z}{3} + 9 + 2x$	12	
$2x + \frac{z}{3} - 1$	2	
$z + 2\frac{2}{3}$	5 2/3	
$-z + 2\frac{2}{3} + x$	2/3	
$\frac{x+y+z}{2} + 3$	9	

Student's name: ____________________ Assignment date: ______________

***** Part 10 Cross multiplication for proportion *****

When an equation is in the form of $\frac{a}{b}=\frac{c}{d}$, the cross multiplication method can be used to get the result. The basic idea is to get the cross product $ad=bc$.

Notice a and d, b and c can be exchanged in $\frac{a}{b}=\frac{c}{d}$ to get the same result. If $\frac{a}{b}=\frac{c}{d}$, a and d exchanged to get $\frac{d}{b}=\frac{c}{a}$ or if $\frac{a}{b}=\frac{c}{d}$, b and c exchanged to get $\frac{a}{c}=\frac{b}{d}$.

Proportion can be reduced in 2 ways, top with bottom (a,c) and (b,d) such as, for example, $\frac{x}{2}=\frac{\not{6}\,2}{\not{3}\,1}$ or left with right numbers such as $(a,b),(c,d)$, for example, $\frac{3}{\not{4}\,2}=\frac{x}{\not{2}\,1}$.

The technique of cross multiplication is very important, and it plays a very important role in elementary school math. Still, unfortunately, some students have ignored its importance when the elementary schools, later many problems students encountered in high school is because they did not master the technique of cross multiplication. Cross multiplication concept can be used to solve a large number of different types of problems. Some of them are as follows:

Proportions in ratio, rate, similarity, scale etc.

Solving equations in the form of $\frac{x}{a}=b$ or $\frac{x}{a}=\frac{b}{c}$ etc.

This method is extremely important in solving equations taught in elementary school. For example, the equations model in elementary school are all in the forms of $\frac{x}{a}=b$ or $\frac{x}{a}=\frac{b}{c}$, so a simple of the method of using cross multiplication could be used to solve all equation problems. If the model is changed to $\frac{x}{a}=\frac{b}{c}+dx$, then the cross multiplication concept will not work for the model $\frac{x}{a}=\frac{b}{c}+dx$

Rational equations in high school such as $\frac{x^2-3x+2}{x-2}=\frac{x}{2}$

Student's name: ____________________ Assignment date: ________________

Trinomial factoring in high school

Factor x^2+3x-2

$$\begin{matrix} 1 & -2 \\ & \times & \\ 1 & -1 \end{matrix}$$

Finding equations when the slope and one point are given in high school

$$\frac{y-1}{x-2}=\frac{3}{4}$$

Trigonometric ratios

For example, Sin 30^0 = $\frac{1}{2}$, the product concept could be used to get the answer when 2 of them are unknown and one of them is known, but the concept of cross multiplication still helps in solving trigonometric ratios.

Student's name: ____________________ Assignment date: ________________

Example

Tina bought 2 pencils for $2.50. At the same price rate, how much would a dozen of pencils cost?

Method 1: Use unit-rate

$\frac{2.50}{2} \times 12 = 2.5 \times 6 = 15$ dollars

Method 2: Use equivalent ratio

$$\frac{2.50}{2} = \frac{x}{12}$$

(× 6)

$x = 2.50 \times 6 = 15$

Since 12 is a multiple of 2, so it is easier to use multiple factors to figure out x.

Method 3: Use cross multiplication

When the equivalent ratio does not have an integral multiple factor then cross multiplication can be used.

$\frac{2.50}{2} = \frac{x}{12}$

$2x = 12 \times 2.5$

$x = 15$

Student's name: ____________________ Assignment date: ________________

Method 1 Multiply both sides by LCD	Method 2 Cross Multiplication
$\frac{x}{2}=\frac{3}{4}$ Multiply both sides by LCD, which is 4. (The reason the cross multiplication is introduced is because the above concept of multiplying 4 on both sides is difficult for the elementary students to understand: it involves equation property, fraction cancellation, and then numerator ×. It takes 3 extra steps to achieve the result of cross multiplication.) $4\times\frac{x}{2}=\frac{3}{4}\times 4$ $2x=3$ $x=\frac{3}{2}$	$\frac{x}{2}=\frac{3}{4}$ $4x$ 6 $\frac{x}{2}=\frac{3}{4}$ Cross multiply as shown above $4x=6$ $2x=3$ $x=\frac{3}{2}$
Multiply both sides by LCD is the more accurate and the general method to solve equation problems since it does not require further reducing later and it can also handle more complicated equation model such as $\frac{x}{a}=\frac{b}{c}+dx$ etc.	The cross multiplication method always assumes the LCD is the product of the 2 bottom numbers and in some cases it is not true. As we can see that the above cross multiplication assume the LCD is 8. so the reducing is required later. However, for elementary student the cross multiplication offers an advantage of being easily to operate for equation model like $\frac{x}{a}=\frac{b}{c}$.

Student's name: ____________________ Assignment date: ________________

Cross multiplication

After we understand how cross multiplication works using LCD in the last section, here 2 ways of cross multiplication is introduced. Do both method 1 and method 2 for the same question.

Method 1: Just blindly do cross multiplication without any analyzing.	Method 2: Only do cross multiplication on number × number and leave the side with variable alone and later exchange number and variable to get the answer.
$\frac{n}{2}=\frac{4}{3}$ $3n = 8$ $n=\frac{8}{3}$	$\frac{n}{2}=\frac{4}{3}$ We still do cross multiplication but only do the number and leave the variable side alone. 8 $\frac{n}{\not{2}}=\frac{\not{4}}{3}$ We did not do $3\times n$. So $n = \frac{8}{3}$
$\frac{x}{2}=\frac{4}{5}$	Only multiply 2 and 4 and leave 5 and x alone. Exchange 5 and x to get the answer. 8/5

Student's name: ____________________ Assignment date: ________________

Cross multiplication

Method 1: Just blindly do cross multiplication without any analysis.	Method 2: Only do cross multiplication on number and leave the side with variable alone and later exchange number and variable to get the answer.
$\frac{y}{3}=\frac{5}{7}$	
$\frac{3}{2}=\frac{x}{5}$	
$\frac{7}{2}=\frac{a}{13}$	
$\frac{9}{2}=\frac{y}{9}$	

15/7, 15/2, 91/2, 81/2

Student's name: ____________________ Assignment date: ________________

Solve equations

Equations	Solve	Comments
$x + 1 = 2$	1. Isolate x by leaving x to the left side, but not always. Usually, we move x to the side, where it has a positive sign. We normally write the solution as x = a number, so it is a good idea to move x to the left. 2. Move the numbers to the right. There are 2 ways the number can be moved. Method 1 (adding/subtracting) $x + 1 = 2$ The first way is to add – 1 to both sides, so the number 1 on the left side disappears. $x + 1 - 1 = 2 - 1$ $x = 1$ Method 2 (moving numbers) Notice that the above, on the left side, the number added – 1 is cancelled with the original number 1. So we can really think of it as having moved the number 1 to the right side and changes its sign from – to +. So the 1 – 1 part on the left side can be omitted. $x + 1 = 2$ $x = 2 - 1$ $x = 1$	Method 1 (adding/subtracting) Subtract 1 on both sides so that 1 will be cancelled and x on the left side is isolated. $x + 1 = 2$ $x + 1 - 1 = 2 - 1$ $x + \cancel{1} - \cancel{1} = 2 - 1$ $x = 1$ Method 2 (moving numbers) Note the above the right-hand side 1 is cancelled with –1 anyway. An operation is just like to move 1 to the other side and also change its sign whenever the number is moved to the other side. $x + 1 = 2$ $x = 2 - 1$ $x = 1$

Student's name: ____________________ Assignment date: ________________

Fill in answer in □ and _______.

Equation	Unknown or variable	Comments
? + 1 = 3	? = 3 - □ = □	Subtract 1 from both sides. ? + 1 – 1 = 3 – 1 ? = 3 – 1 It can be thought as if it were moved to the right-hand side, and its sign is changed from + to –. ? + 1 = 3 (–1)
$\chi + 1 = 3$	χ = 3 - □ = □	χ + 1 = 3 (–1)
$\chi + 2 = 3$	χ = 3 - □ = □	
$\chi + 3 = 5$	χ = 5 - □ = □	
$\chi + 4 = 7$	χ = 7 - □ = □	

2 2 1 2 3

Student's name: ____________________ Assignment date: ________________

$5 + \chi = 9$	$\chi = 9 - \square$ $= \square$	Move 5 to the right side.
$\chi + 6 = 9$	$\chi = 9 - \square$ $= \square$	
$7 + \chi = 9$	$\chi = 9 - \square$ $= \square$	
$\chi + 8 = 9$	$\chi = 9 - \square$ $= \square$	
$\chi + 9 = 9$	$\chi = 9 - \square$ $= \square$	
$10 + \chi = 19$	$\chi = 19 - \square$ $= \square$	
$\chi + 12 = 19$	$\chi = 19 - \square$ $= \square$	

4 3 1 1 0 9 7

Student's name: ____________________ Assignment date: ________________

Equation	Unknown or variable	Comments
? – 1 = 3	? = 3 + □ = □	Add 1 from both sides. ? – 1 + 1 = 3 + 1 ? = 3 + 1 It can be thought as if 1 was moved to the right-hand side, and its sign is changed from – to +. ? – 1 = 3 (+1)
χ – 1 = 3	χ = 3 + □ = □	χ – 1 = 3 (+1)
χ – 2 = 3	χ = 3 + □ = □	
χ – 3 = 5	χ = 5 + □ = □	
– 4 + χ = 7	χ = 7 + □ = □	

4, 4, 5, 8, 11

Student's name: ____________________ Assignment date: ________________

$\chi - 5 = 9$	$\chi = 9 + \square$ $= \square$	Move 5 to the right side.
$-6 + \chi = 9$	$\chi = 9 + \square$ $= \square$	
$\chi - 7 = 9$	$\chi = 9 + \square$ $= \square$	
$\chi - 8 = 9$	$\chi = 9 + \square$ $= \square$	
$-9 + \chi = 9$	$\chi = 9 + \square$ $= \square$	
$\chi - 10 = 19$	$\chi = 19 + \square$ $= \square$	
$\chi - 12 = 19$	$\chi = 19 + \square$ $= \square$	

14, 16, 17, 18, 29, 31

Student's name: ____________________ Assignment date: ________________

$2 \times ? = 6$	$? = \frac{6}{\square} = \square$	Divide both sides by 2. $\frac{2 \times ?}{2} = \frac{6}{2}$ $? = 3$ It can be thought as if 2 were moved to the right-hand side at the bottom position. Use the concept of cross multiplication. When moving a factor of a product, the factor always goes to the other side's denominator. It can be shown step by step as follows: $\frac{2 \times ?}{1} = \frac{6}{1}$ $\frac{?}{1} = \frac{6}{2 \times 1}$ $? = \frac{6}{2}$ $2 \times ? = \frac{6}{②}$
$2\chi = 8$	$\chi = \frac{6}{\square} = \square$	The idea of moving comes from the cross multiplication. $\frac{\not{2}x}{1} = \frac{8}{1}$ $\square$ 2
$\frac{3x}{1} = \frac{9}{1}$	$\frac{\not{3}x}{1} = \frac{9}{3} = \square$	

4, 3

Student's name: ____________________ Assignment date: ________________

Without working on enough cross multiplication exercise, the concept of moving factor seems to be difficult for students to grasp. Alternatively, students could be taught by dividing the same number to both sides of the equation. The result x will be isolated any way after the division, so we do not really need to write an extra step for the division $\frac{3x}{3}=\frac{9}{3}$. For example, $3x=9$, both sides divide 3, then 3 x will become x. so on the left side, we could just write x and on the right side we write $\frac{9}{3}$. The equation becomes $x=\frac{9}{3}=3$.

$3\chi = 9$	$\chi = \frac{9}{\square} = \square$	
$\frac{3x}{1}=\frac{12}{1}$	$\frac{\not{3}x}{1}=\frac{12}{3} = \square$	
$3\chi = 12$	$\chi = \frac{12}{\square} = \square$	
$3\chi = 15$	$\chi = \frac{15}{\square} = \square$	
$3 \times \chi = 18$	$\chi = \frac{18}{\square} = \square$	
$4\chi = 16$	$\chi = \frac{16}{\square} = \square$	
$5 \times \chi = 20$	$\chi = \frac{20}{\square} = \square$	

3, 4, 4, 5, 6, 4, 4

Student's name: ____________________ Assignment date: ________________

$7\chi = 28$	$\chi = \dfrac{28}{\square} = \square$	
$9\chi = 36$	$\chi = \dfrac{36}{\square} = \square$	

4, 4

Student's name: ____________________ Assignment date: ________________

Equation division

The idea of working on fractional equations (rational equations) is to convert the fractions to whole numbers by multiplying LCD to both sides of the equation. However, with the equation in $\frac{a}{b}=\frac{c}{d}$ form, the exchange of ad and bc could be used to solve the unknown.

$\frac{?}{2}=6$	? = 6 X □ = □	Multiply both sides by 2. ? = 2 X 6 = 12 It can be thought as if 2 were moved to the right-hand side and then multiply 6. $\frac{?}{2}=6$ The idea comes from cross multiplication and is demonstrated as follows. ? = 12 $\frac{?}{2}=\frac{6}{1}$
$\frac{\chi}{2}=6$	χ = 6 X □ = □	$\frac{\chi}{2}=6$
$\frac{x}{2}=8$	χ = 8 X □ = □	
$\frac{x}{3}=7$	χ = 7 X □ = □	

12, 16, 21

Student's name: ____________________ Assignment date: ________________

Equation division

$\frac{x}{4}=8$	$x = 8 \times \square$ $= \square$	
$\frac{x}{5}=10$	$x = 10 \times \square$ $= \square$	
$\frac{x}{6}=12$	$x = 12 \times \square$ $= \square$	
$\frac{x}{7}=13$	$x = 13 \times \square$ $= \square$	
$\frac{x}{8}=14$	$x = 14 \times \square$ $= \square$	
$\frac{x}{9}=11$	$x = 11 \times \square$ $= \square$	
$\frac{x}{10}=12$	$x = 12 \times \square$ $= \square$	

32, 50, 72, 91, 112, 99, 120

Student's name: ____________________ Assignment date: ________________

Solve Equations – addition and subtraction.
$x + 4 = 0$
$x - 4 = 0$
$x + 4 = 2$
$x - 4 = 2$
$4 + x = 0$
$4 - x = 0$
$4 + x = 2$
$4 - x = 2$

-4, 4, -2, 6, -4, 4, -2, 2

Student's name: ____________________ Assignment date: ________________

Solve Equations – addition and subtraction.
$x + 4 = 0$
$x - 4 = 0$
$x + 4 = 6$
$x - 4 = 2$
$4 + x = 0$
$4 - x = 0$
$4 + x = 2$
$4 - x = 2$

-4, 4, 2, 6, -4, 4, -2, 2

Student's name: ____________________ Assignment date: ________________

Solve Equations – multiplication and division
$4x = 12$
$x \times 4 = 16$
$4x + 4 = 2$
$6x - 4 = 8$
$4 + 2x = 0$
$4 - 8x = 0$
$4 + 4x = 2$
$4 - 4x = 2$

3, 4, -1/2, 2, -2, ½, ½, 1/2

Student's name: ____________________ Assignment date: _______________

Addition problems

A number is 27 more than 35. What is the number?

The difference between a number and 49 is 137. What is the number?

A number minus 45 equals 132. What is the number?

Subtraction problems

The sum of a number and 37 is 961. What is the number?

The difference between 462 and a number is 344. What is the number?

A number plus 186 equals 251. What is the number?

A number is 18 less than 91. What is the number?

62, 186, 177, 924, 118, 65, 73

Student's name: ____________________ Assignment date: ________________

Multiplication problems

A number divided by 4 equals 502. What is the number?

How much is 456 multiplied by 12?

How much is 63 times 34?

What is the sum of nine 148's?

Number A is 128 and is twice as much as number B. How much is number B?

2008, 5472, 2142, 1332, 64

Student's name: ____________________ Assignment date: ________________

Division problems

9744 divided by 14, what is its quotient?

756 divided by a number. Its quotient is 3. What is the number?

How many times is 508 of 8?

A number multiplied by 9. Its product is 1458. What is the number?

8 multiplied by a number equals 356. What is the number?

The product of a number and 12 is 276. What is the number?

Number A is 128, and number B is twice as number A. How much is number B?

Number A is 48, and number B is 12. How many times is number A of number B?

696, 252, 4064, 162, 33 1/2, 23, 256, 4

Student's name: ____________________ Assignment date: ________________

Techniques in solving linear equations

To solve linear equations $(ax + b = 0)$, we rely on the equation properties as follows:

- Add a number to both sides of an equation
- Subtract a number from both sides of an equation.
- Multiply both sides of an equation by a number.
- Divide both sides of an equation by a non-zero number.

Move variable to the side where the sign will be positive

Move x to the left side	Move x to the right side
$3x = 2x + 2$	$2x + 2 = 3x$
$4x = 3x - 2$	$4x - 2 = 2x$
$5x = 2x - 2$	$3x = 5x + 2$
$5x = 2x - 2$	$4x = 5x + 2$
$6x + 2 = 5x$	$7x = 9x - 2$
$9x + 2 = 7x$	$6x = 8x - 2$

Student's name: ____________________ Assignment date: ________________

Advanced equation

(□×5)÷ 3 = 4 + □ □=6
2□+7=6□-9 □=4
Solve □. 2□- 1 thousand + 3 hundreds + 8 tens + 7 hundredths = 5 hundredths □=460.04
(4 thousand-cubes, 4 ten-rods, 4 unit squares) − (3 thousand-cubes, 5 ten-rods, 10 unit squares) =2□ □ = 492
If $\frac{1}{3} \times x = 6$, then $x\frac{x+2}{2}$=?

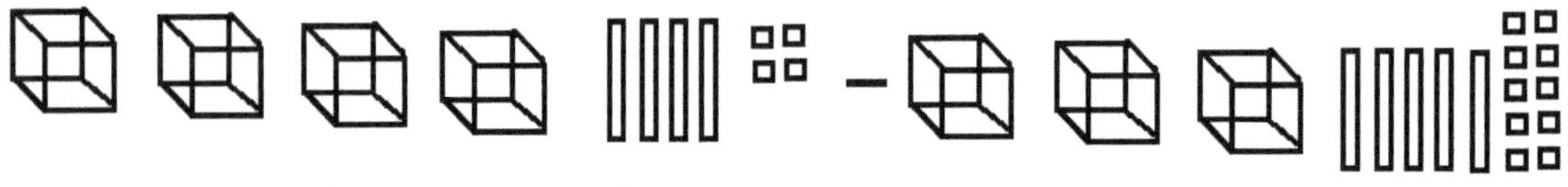

Student's name: ____________________ Assignment date: ________________

Test of equation

If $5 \times x = 120$ and $\frac{x}{y}$ = 3, then what is y? 8
Find N if $3 \times (25 + N - 13) = 96$. $N = 20$
What is x if there are three equations as follows: $x - y = 5$ $y + z = 4$ $z + 1 = 3$ 7
What is n if $0 = 1 \times n \times 1$? 0
What is n if $1 = 1 \times n \times 1$? 1
What is □ if 21 – □ $= 54 \div 3$? 3
When a number is added to twice of itself, the result is the difference of the number less than 12, what is the number? 3

Student's name: ____________________ Assignment date: ________________

If □6 + 78 = 114, then what value is the missing part □? In this problem □6 is a 2-digit number. 3
If $\frac{28}{48} = \frac{\Delta}{12}$, what is the value of Δ? 7
If $1 + 2 \times p = 25$, then $p - 11 = ?$ 1

Ho Math Chess Primary Grades Math

Test Review assesssment 何数棋謎低年级数学测试複習考核

Frank Ho, Amanda Ho www.homathchess.com

Student's name: ____________________ Assignment date: ________________

Roman numerals

Complete the following table.

I	II	III	IV	V	VI	VII	VIII	IX	X
XI	XII	XIII	XIV	XV	XVI	XVII	XVIII	XIX	XX
XXI	XXII	XXIII	XXIV	XXV	XXVI	XXVII	XXVIII	XXIX	XXX
XXXI	XXXII	XXXIII	XXXIV	XXXV	XXXVI	XXXVII	XXXIII	XXXIX	XL
XLI	XLII	XLIII	XLIV	XLV	XLVI	XLVII	XLVIII	XLIX	L
LI	LII	LIII	LIV	LV	LVI	LVII	LVIII	LIX	LX
LXI	LXII	LXIII	LXIV	LXV	LXVI	LXVII	LXVIII	LXIX	LXX
LXXI	LXXII	LXXIII	LXXIV	LXXV	LXXVI	LXXVII	LXXVIII	LXXIX	LXXX
LXXXI	LXXXII	LXXXIII	LXXXIV	LXXXV	LXXXVI	LXXXVII	LXXXVIII	LXXXIX	XC
XCI	XCII	XCIII	XCIV	XCV	XCVI	XCVII	XCVIII	XCIX	C

Complete the following clock with Roman numerals.

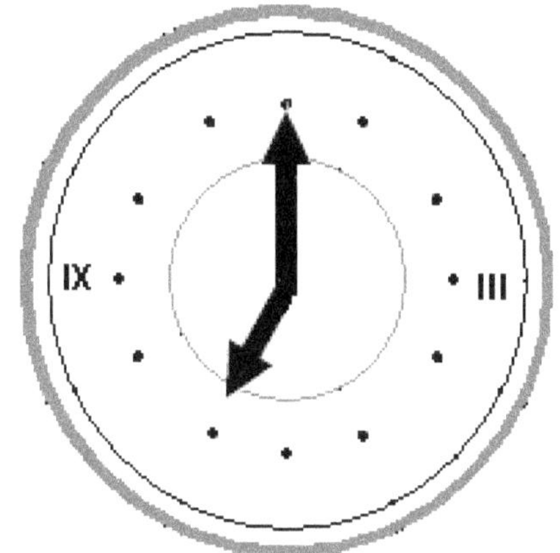

I, II, III, IV, V, VI, VII, VIII, IX, X, XI, XII

Student's name: ____________________ Assignment date: ________________

Connect the following drawings in order.

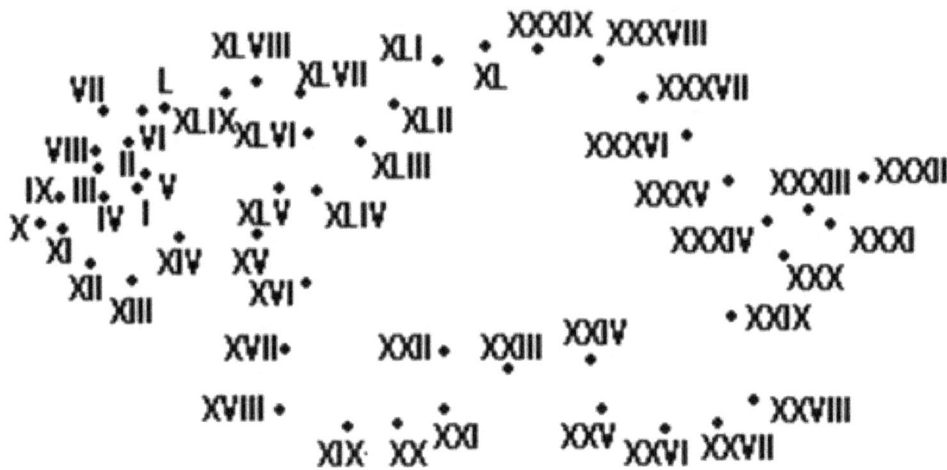

Translate the following Roman numerals to numbers.

1.	I	= 1	10.	X	= 10	19.	LX	= 60
2.	II	= 2	11.	XX	= 20	20.	LXX	= 70
3.	III	= 3	12.	XXX	= 30	21.	LXXX	= 80
4.	IV	= 4	13.	XL	= 40	22.	XC	= 90
5.	V	= 5	14.	L	= 50	23.	C	= 100
6.	IV	= 4	15.	VI	= 6	24.	VII	= 7
7.	IX	= 9	16.	XI	= 11	25.	XII	= 12
8.	XL	= 40	17.	LX	= 60	26.	LXX	= 70
9.	XC	= 90	18.	CX	= 110	27.	CXX	= 102

Ho Math Chess Primary Grades Math

Test Review assesssment 何数棋謎低年级数学测试複習考核

Student's name: ____________________ Assignment date: ________________

Translate the following numbers into Roman numerals.

1.	1	= I	10.	10	= X	19.	60	= LX
2.	2	= II	11.	20	= XX	20.	70	= LXX
3.	3	= III	12.	30	= XXX	21.	80	= LXXX
4.	4	= IV	13.	40	= XL	22.	90	= XC
5.	5	= V	14.	50	= L	23.	100	= C
6.	11	= XI	15.	12	= XII	24.	14	= XIV
7.	21	= XXI	16.	22	= XXII	25.	24	= XXIV
8.	31	= XXXI	17.	32	= XXXII	26.	34	= XXXIV
9.	41	= XLI	18.	42	= XLII	27.	44	= XLIV

Translate the following numbers below.

1.	XII	= 12	10.	7	= VII	19.	9	= IX
2.	XXXIII	= 33	11.	3	= III	20.	XXV	= 25
3.	XV	= 15	12.	19	= XIX	21.	18	= XVIII
4.	XVI	= 16	13.	28	= XXVIII	22.	75	= LXXV
5.	LI	= 51	14.	54	= LIV	23.	LXVII	= 67
6.	VIII	= 8	15.	69	= LXIX	24.	LXXXV	= 85
7.	IX	= 9	16.	77	= LXXVII	25.	42	= LXII
8.	CC	= 200	17.	36	= XXXVI	26.	63	= LXIII
9.	XCV	= 95	18.	81	= LXXXI	27.	LV	= 55

Student's name: ____________________ Assignment date: ________________

***** Part 11 Measurement *****

Metric measurement ladder diagram

The Metric system uses the same prefix words to memorize all three weight, length, and capacity measurements. As you move the list of prefixes, the next unit is 10 times the current one. As you move down the list, the next unit is 10th of the current one. Every time, the measurement reduces 10 times by going up one step; the measurement increases 10 times by going down one step.

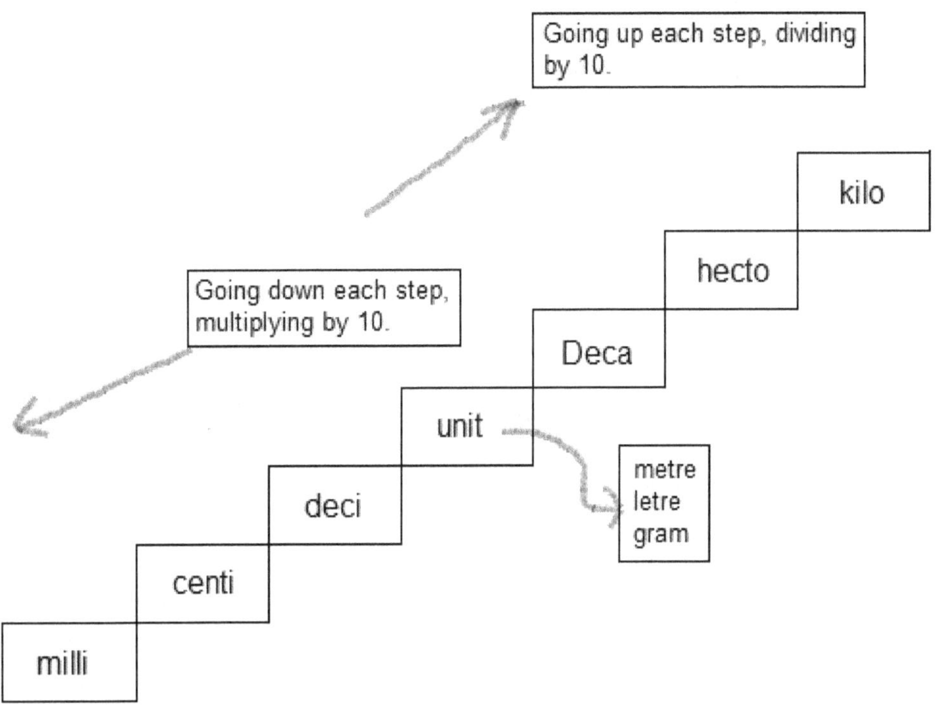

Length	kilometre (km) 1 km = 1000 m	hectometre (hm)	decametre (dam)	metre (m) 1 m = 100 cm	decimetre (dm)	centimetre (cm) 1 cm = 10 mm	millimetre (mm)
Weight (mass)	kilogram (kg) 1 kg = 1000 g 1 t = 1000 kg	hectogram	decagram	gram (g) 1 g = 1000 mg	decigram	centigram	milligram
Volume (Capacity)	kilolitre 1 kL = 1000 L	hectolitre	decalitre	Litre (L) 1 L = 10000 mL	decilitre	centilitre	millilitre

Student's name: ____________________ Assignment date: ________________

Capacity, volume, and mass

You will remember the following conversion formula, then convert it to get other units.
10 cm × 10 cm × 10 cm = 1000 cm^3 (volume) =1 L (capacity) = 1 kg (weight, mass)

Because 1 m = 100 cm, so 10 cm = 0.1 m, 0.001 m^3= 1 L

Because 1 L = 1000 mL so 10 cm × 10 cm × 10 cm = 1000 cm^3 = 1000 mL
so 1 mL = 1 cm^3

9800 cm^3= _________ L = ________kg 9.8, 9.8
980 cm^3= _________ L = ________kg 0.98, 0.98
8.6m^3= _________ L = ________kg 8 600, 8600
380 cm^3= _________ L = ________kg 0.38, 0.38
38 cm^3= _________ L = ________kg 0.038, 0.038
6.9 m^3= _________ L = ________kg 6900, 6900
490 cm^3= _________ mL = ________ g 490, 490
0.49 m^3= _________ L = ________kg 490 L, 490 kg
948 L = _______________ m^3 0.948 m^3
8.6 mL = _______________ m^3 8.6 mL =86 cm^3=$\frac{86}{1000000}$ m^3= 0.000086 m^3
380 L = _______________ m^3 = 0.38 m^3
8000 L = _______________ m^3 8

Student's name: ____________________ Assignment date: ________________

km	m	cm	mm	t	kg	g	mg	kL	L	mL
1	1000	100,000	1,000,000	0.0012				5		
3	3000	30,000	3,000,000		3600				37000	
2.3	2300	23000	230,000		2.11 kg+250 g			5.1		
0.409	4090	40900	409000			5.2			3.8	
0.00042	0.42	4 cm+20 mm	42				3191			5000
2.21	2 km+210 m	221000	2210000		2500					3200
0.30002	300.02	30002	300020	3.1				1.1		
		198.21			3.5				2.2	
0.311204	3.11204	311.204	3112.04			1000				3.3
512.12	512120	51212000	51212000 0				7000		400.21	

Student's name: ____________________ Assignment date: ______________

Test of measurement word problem

Melody wanted to buy some lunch meat that was priced per 100 g. if she wanted to buy $\frac{3}{4}$ kg of lunch meat, how many times the price per 100 g would she pay?

1.5

Shelby wanted to buy some roasted pumpkin seeds that were priced per 100 g. If she wanted to buy 1.2 kg of pumpkin seeds, how many times the price per 100 g would she pay?

$$\frac{1.2 \times 1000}{100} = 12$$

Wayne bought some pieces of candies. Each piece weighed 150 g, and she bought 2.4 kg in total weight. How many pieces of candies did she buy in all?

$$\frac{2.4 \times 1000}{150} = 16\,pieces$$

If the total amount of juice in 7 containers was 24.5 L, how many millilitres of juice did one container hold on average?
24.5/7=3.5
3.5 x 1000 = 3500 mL

---

l15 cm + 0.08 m + 1100 mm = ________ metres = ________ cm = ________ mm
2.33, 233, 2330

0.8 L – 550 mL = ________ L = _____ mL1.35, 1350

Ten-tenth of 100 cm + one-tenth of 2 metres = _______ cm 120

Han compared the costs of the following sizes of juice.

Size	Cost	calculation
250 mL	3 for $1.10	0.15 cents / mL
150 mL	4 for $2.50	1.56 cents / mL
1 L	$4.50	2.22 cents / mL, 1L = 1000 mL
2 L	$8.00	4 cents / mL

Which size would be the best to buy?

Student's name: ____________________ Assignment date: ________________

Each bag requires a piece of fabric 30 cm by 50 cm. What is the greatest number of bags that could be shown from a piece of fabric measuring 4 m by 5.5 m? 88
How can many cubed fudges with 3 inches side length be packed into an icebox 9 inches deep by 12 inches wide and 8 inches high such that the lid can still be closed? 24
One drawstring bag requires 150 cm of the cord. Cord for the drawstrings is sold in spools of 80 m. What is the greatest number of bags that can be completed with one spool of the cord? 53
If a ceramic tile costs \$8.50 per square yard, what will a kitchen floor that is 12 feet by 15 feet long cost? 1 yard = 3 feet 1 $yard^2$ = 9 ft^2 $\frac{12\times15\times8.5}{9}$ = 17
There are 8 ounces in a $\frac{1}{2}$ pound. How many ounces are in 5 $\frac{3}{4}$ lbs? 92 ounces
Grace and her friend walked from the parking lot to the beginning of a 4 km hiking trail. They realized that they left their water bottles in the car, so they went back to get their bottles, then they hiked the trail and returned to their car. How far did they walk in total? 50 m + 50 m+50 m+ 5km + 5km + 50 m = 10 km 200 m = 10.2 km

Student's name: ____________________ Assignment date: ______________

Length

 THE LENGTH OF A SMALL CAR IS ABOUT 5 METRES.	 THE LENGTH OD A TENNIS RACQUET IS ABOUT 150 CENTIMETER.
 The length of a bed is about 2 metres.	 The height of a door is about 2 meters.
 A calculator is about 10 centimetres long.	 The diameter of a baseball is about 10 centimetres.

Student's name: ____________________ Assignment date: ________________

Length

1 km = 1000 m = 10,000 dm = 100,000 cm =1,000,000 mm
1 m = 10 dm = 100 cm = 1000 mm
1 dm = 10 cm = 100 mm
1 cm = 10 mm

1. Metre to decimetre.

1. 1 m = 10 dm
2. 5 m = 50 dm
3. 30 m = 300 dm
4. 60 m = 600 dm
5. 45 m = 450 dm
6. 67 m = 670 dm
7. 70 m = 700 dm
8. 88 m = 880 dm
9. 300 m = 3000 dm
10. 400 m = 4000 dm
11. 55 m = 550 dm
12. 19 m = 190 dm

2. Decimetre to the metre.

1. 10 dm = 1 m
2. 30 dm = 3 m
3. 100 dm = 10 m
4. 60 dm = 6 m
5. 300 dm = 30 m
6. 610 dm = 61 m
7. 150 dm = 15 m
8. 680 dm = 68 m
9. 1000 dm = 100 m
10. 740 dm = 74 m
11. 230 dm = 23 m
12. 600 dm = 60 m

Student's name: ____________________ Assignment date: ________________

3. Metre to Centimetre.

1. 1 m = 100 cm
2. 3 m = 300 cm
3. 10 m = 1000 cm
4. 20 m = 2000 cm
5. 15 m = 1500 cm
6. 26 m = 2600 cm
7. 50 m = 5000 cm
8. 63 m = 6300 cm
9. 100 m = 10000 cm
10. 91 m = 9100 cm
11. 40 m = 4000 cm
12. 16 m = 1600 cm

4. Centimetre to the metre.

1. 100 cm = 1 m
2. 700 cm = 7 m
3. 400 cm = 4 m
4. 2600 cm = 26 m
5. 5400 cm = 54 m
6. 7300 cm = 73 m
7. 2400 cm = 24 m
8. 14000 cm = 140 m
9. 1000 cm = 10 m
10. 53000 cm = 530 m
11. 5000 cm = 50 m
12. 3700 m = 37 m

5. Metre to the millimetre.

1. 1 m = 1000 mm
2. 6 m = 6000 mm
3. 60 m = 60000 mm
4. 40 m = 40000 mm
5. 33 m = 33000 mm
6. 55 m = 55000 mm
7. 48 m = 48000 mm
8. 89 m = 89000 mm
9. 200 m = 200000 mm
10. 900 m = 900000 mm
11. 40 m = 40000 mm
12. 18 m = 18000 mm

Student's name: ____________________ Assignment date: ________________

6. Millimetre to the metre.

1. 1000 mm = ____1____ m
2. 8000 mm = ____8____ m
3. 33000 mm = ____33____ m
4. 72000 mm = ____72____ m
5. 29000 mm = ____29____ m
6. 16000 mm = ____16____ m
7. 57000 mm = ____57____ m
8. 60000 mm = ____60____ m
9. 45000 mm = ____45____ m
10. 90000 mm = ____90____ m
11. 20000 mm = ____20____ m
12. 66000 mm = ____66____ m

7. Kilometre to the metre.

1. 1 km = ____1000____ m
2. 3 km = ____3000____ m
3. 10 km = ____10000____ m
4. 20 km = ____20000____ m
5. 15 km = ____15000____ m
6. 26 km = ____26000____ m
7. 50 km = ____50000____ m
8. 63 km = ____63000____ m
9. 100 km = ____100000____ m
10. 91 km = ____91000____ m
11. 72 km = ____72000____ m
12. 30 km = ____30000____ m

8. Metre to a kilometre.

1. 1000 m = ____1____ km
2. 4000 m = ____4____ km
3. 5000 m = ____5____ km
4. 63000 m = ____63____ km
5. 34000 m = ____34____ km
6. 47000 m = ____47____ km
7. 52000 m = ____52____ km
8. 30000 m = ____30____ km
9. 180000 m = ____180____ km
10. 120000 m = ____120____ km
11. 30000 m = ____30____ km
12. 160000 m = ____160____ km

Student's name: ____________________ Assignment date: ________________

9. Centimetre to the millimetre.

1. 1 cm = 10 mm
2. 7 cm = 70 mm
3. 30 cm = 300 mm
4. 80 cm = 8000 mm
5. 51 cm = 510 mm
6. 78 cm = 780 mm
7. 73 cm = 730 mm
8. 570 cm = 5700 mm
9. 860 cm = 8600 mm
10. 950 cm = 9500 mm
11. 600 cm = 6000 mm
12. 210 m = 2100 mm

10. Millimetre to Centimetre.

1. 10 mm = 1 cm
2. 70 mm = 7 cm
3. 60 mm = 6 cm
4. 20 mm = 2 cm
5. 160 mm = 16 cm
6. 400 mm = 40 cm
7. 3700 mm = 370 cm
8. 5100 mm = 510 cm
9. 8400 mm = 840 cm
10. 5600 mm = 560 cm
11. 2500 mm = 250 cm
12. 4400 m = 440 cm

11. Metre to decimetre, centimetre, and millimetre.

1. 1m = 10 dm = 100 cm = 1000 mm
2. 5m = 50 dm = 500 cm = 5000 mm
3. 30m = 300 dm = 3000 cm = 30000 mm
4. 56m = 560 dm = 5600 cm = 56000 mm
5. 450m = 4500 dm = 45000 cm = 450000 mm

Student's name: ____________________ Assignment date: ________________

Length

1. 9 m = __90__ dm	2. 40 dm = __400__ cm
3. 7 cm = __70__ mm	4. 700 mm = __70__ cm
5. 150 cm = __15__ dm	6. 50 dm = __50__ m
7. 5 m = __500__ cm	8. 20 m = __2000__ cm
9. 56 dm = __5600__ mm	10. 8000 cm = __80__ m
11. 9000 mm = __90__ dm	12. 10 dm = __100__ cm
13. 600 m = __6000__ dm	14. 800 dm = __80__ m
15. 400 dm = __4000__ cm	16. 5000 cm = __500__ dm
17. 6000 cm = __60000__ mm	18. 9000 mm = __900__ cm
19. 30 km = __30000__ m	20. 50 m = __500__ dm
21. 2000 m = __2__ km	22. 8000 m = __80__ km
23. 50 000 m = __50__ km	24. 3000 km = __3000000__ m
25. 6 dm = __60__ cm	26. 7 cm = __70__ mm
27. 7 m = __700__ cm	28. 600 mm = __60__ cm
29. 400 dm = __40__ m	30. 40 cm = __4__ dm
31. 8 km = __8000__ m	32. 60 000 m = __60__ km
33. 30 dm = __3000__ mm	34. 60 m = __6000__ cm
35. 3000 mm = __30__ dm	36. 8000 cm = __80__ m
37. 5 dm = __50__ cm	38. 8 dm = __80__ cm

Ho Math Chess Primary Grades Math

Test Review assesssment 何数棋谜低年级数学测试複習考核

Student's name: ____________________ Assignment date: ________________

Length

1. 9 cm = 90 mm
2. 3 m = 300 cm
3. 35 dm = 3500 mm
4. 3 km = 3000 m
5. 400 cm = 40 dm
6. 5000 cm = 500 dm
7. 90 mm = 9 cm
8. 4000 cm = 40 m
9. 5000 mm = 5 m
10. 560 000 dm = 56 km
11. 70 cm = 700 mm
12. 12 m = 1200 cm
13. 102 dm = 10200 mm
14. 40 km = 40000 m
15. 6200 cm = 620 dm
16. 780 cm = 78 dm
17. 690 mm = 69 cm
18. 42000 cm = 420 m
19. 56000 mm = 56 m
20. 470 000 dm = 47 km
21. 45000 m = 45 km
22. 60 000 m = 60 km
23. 780 000 m = 780 km
24. 150 000 km = 150000000 m
25. 120 dm = 1200 cm
26. 510 cm = 5100 mm
27. 690 m = 69000 cm
28. 4 600 mm = 460 cm
29. 47 000 dm = 4700 m
30. 29 000 cm = 2900 dm
31. 830 cm = 8300 mm
32. 8 700 mm = 870 cm
33. 11 000 cm = 1100 dm
34. 450 dm = 45 m
35. 60 m = 6000 cm
36. 22 000 m = 2200000 cm
37. 730 dm = 73000 mm
38. 8800 cm = 88 m

Student's name: ____________________ Assignment date: ______________

Fill in ( ) with >, < or =.

1. 2000 mm __=__ 2 m
2. 30 dm __<__ 4 m
3. 15 dm __>__ 110 cm
4. 40 cm __=__ 4 dm
5. 60 m __<__ 6 km
6. 80 mm __=__ 8 cm
7. 8 m __<__ 80 km
8. 90 mm __<__ 9 dm
9. 50 000 dm __<__ 6 km
10. 3 km __>__ 400 m

Fill in the following blank.

1.	km	m	dm	cm	mm
2.	5	5000	50000	500000	5 000 000
3.	40	40000	400 000	4000000	40000000
4.	3	3000	30000	300 000	3000000
5.	80	80000	500000	8000000	80000000
6.	9	9 000	90000	900000	9000000
7.	45	45000	450000	4500000	45 000 000
8.	560	560000	5600 000	56000000	560000000
9.	34	34000	340 000	3400000	34000000
10.	72	72000	720000	7 200 000	72000000
11.	43	43 000	430000	4300000	43000000
12.	90	90000	900000	9000000	90 000 000
13.	220	220000	2200000	22000000	220000000
14.	66	66000	660 000	6600000	66000000
15.	52	52000	520000	5200000	52000000

Ho Math Chess Primary Grades Math

Test Review assesssment 何数棋謎低年级数学测试複習考核

Student's name: ____________________ Assignment date: _______________

Choose the appropriate answer.

1.	The length of a book is	a. 20 cm	b. 2 m	c. 20 m	a ___
2.	The length of a desk is	a. 20 cm	b. 2 m	c. 20 m	b ___
3.	The length of a bed is	a. 20 cm	b. 2 m	c. 20 m	b ___
4.	The height of a door is	a. 20 cm	b. 2 m	c. 20 m	b ___
5.	The length of a swimming pool is	a. 20 cm	b. 2 m	c. 20 m	c ___
6.	The length of a soccer field is	a. 20 cm	b. 2 m	c. 20 m	c ___
7.	The length of a bus is	a. 10 cm	b. 1 m	c. 10 m	c ___
8.	The length of a car is	a. 50 cm	b. 5 m	c. 50 m	b ___
9.	The length of your feet is about	a. 20 cm	b. 2 m	c. 20 m	b ___
10.	The thickness of a piece of 2 x 4 board is	a. 1 mm	b. 1 cm	c. 1 dm	a ___
11.	The thickness of a laptop computer	a. 5 mm	b. 5 cm	c. 5 dm	b ___
12.	The thickness of a piece of CD is	a. 1 mm	b. 1 cm	c. 1 m	a ___
13.	The height of Seymour mountain is	a. 15 cm	b. 15 m	c. 1500 m	c ___
14.	The height of a house door is about	a. 2 m	b. 2 m	c. 1500 m	b ___
15.	Car distance of travelling for one hour is	a 2 km	b. 2 m	c. 60 km	c ___
16.	The length of a cell phone is about	a 10 cm	b. 2 m	c. 10 km	a ___
17.	The diameter of the earth is about	a. 13 m	b. 13 km	c. 13000 km	c ___

1.

Student's name: ____________________ Assignment date: ________________

Test of measuring length

km	m	cm	mm	comment
0.00004	0.04	4	40	
0.00002	0.02	2	20	
2	2000	200000	2000000	
0.2	200	2000	20000	
0.04	4	400	4000	
80	80000	8000000	80000000	
0.0007 × 1000	70	7000	70000	
5 × 0.01	500	5000	50000	

Student's name: ____________________ Assignment date: ________________

Capacity

ONE CARTON CAN HOLD ABOUT 1 LITRE OF MILK.	A CAN OF POP MIGHT CONTAIN 350 MILLILITERS.
A small car oil container can hold 20 litres of gasoline.	A small bottle of medicine is about 30 millilitres.
A bottle of water is about 20 litres.	A kettle can hold about 3 litres of water.

Student's name: ____________________ Assignment date: ________________

Capacity

1 L = 1000 mL	1000 mL = 1L

1. Litre to millilitre.

1. 1 l = 1000 ml
2. 4 l = 4000 ml
3. 7 l = 7000 ml
4. 10 l = 10000 ml
5. 81 l = 81000 ml
6. 210 l = 210000 ml
7. 700 l = 700000 ml
8. 305 l = 305000 ml
9. 380 l = 380000 ml
10. 402 l = 402000 ml
11. 54 l = 54000 ml
12. 800 l = 800000 ml
13. 70 l = 70 000 ml
14. 26 l = 26000 ml

2. Millilitre to litre.

1. 1 000 ml = 1 l
2. 3 000 ml = 3 l
3. 5 000 ml = 5 l
4. 10 000 ml = 10 l
5. 35 000 ml = 35 l
6. 41 000 ml = 41 l
7. 67 000 ml = 67 l
8. 605 000 ml = 605 l
9. 740 000 ml = 740 l
10. 706 000 ml = 706 l
11. 880 000 ml = 880 l
12. 510 000 ml = 510 l
13. 60 000 ml = 60 l
14. 94 000 ml = 94 l

Student's name: ____________________ Assignment date: ________________

Capacity

1. 5 000 ml = 5 l
2. 8 000 ml = 8 l
3. 70 l = 70000 ml
4. 4 l = 4000 ml
5. 60 000 ml = 60 l
6. 10 000 ml = 10 l
7. 18 l = 18000 ml
8. 64 l = 64000 ml
9. 309 000 ml = 309 l
10. 203 000 ml = 203 l
11. 6000 l = 6000000 ml
12. 4000 l = 4 000 000 ml
13. 12 000 ml = 12 l
14. 58 l = 58000 ml
15. 76 l = 76000 ml
16. 91 000 ml = 91 l
17. 430 000 ml = 430 l
18. 200 l = 200000 ml
19. 504 l = 504000 ml
20. 35 000 ml = 35 l
21. 700 l = 700000 ml
22. 2000 l = 2000000 ml
23. 4000 l = 4000000 ml
24. 4070 l = 4070000 ml
25. 45 000 ml = 45 l
26. 50 000 ml = 50 l
27. 67 l = 67000 ml
28. 48 000 ml = 48 l
29. 20 l = 20000 ml
30. 123 l = 123000 ml
31. 508 l = 508000 ml
32. 612 l = 612000 ml
33. 97 000 ml = 97 l
34. 1 l = 1000 ml
35. 60 000 ml = 60 l
36. 33 000 ml = 33 l
37. 28 l = 28000 ml
38. 43 000 ml = 43 l

Student's name: ____________________ Assignment date: ________________

Mass (weight)

 AN APPLE HAS A MASS OF ABOUT 200 GRAMS.	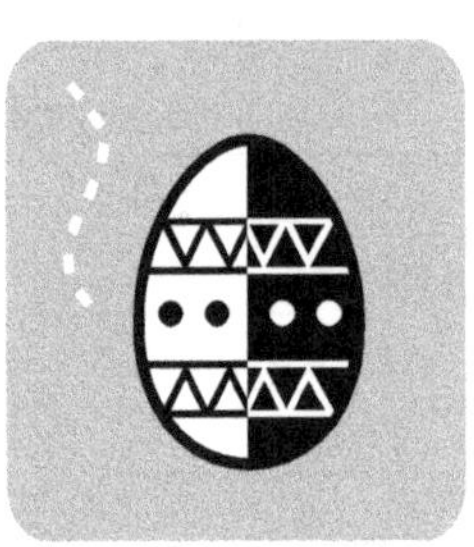 AN EGG HAS A MASS OF ABOUT 50 GRAMS.
 A book is about 1 kilogram.	 A piece of paper has a mass of about 5 grams.
 A bag of rice has a mass of about 10 kilograms.	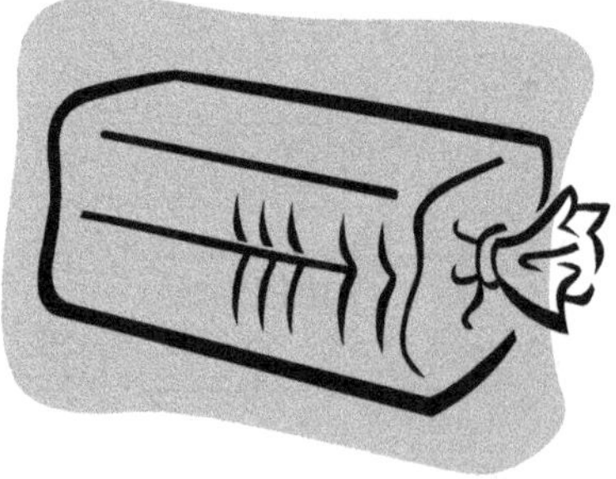 A loaf of bread is about 500 grams.

Student's name: ____________________ Assignment date: ________________

Mass

1kg=1000 g	1000 g= 1 kg

1. Kilogram to the gram.

1. 1 kg = 1000 g
2. 5 kg = 5000 g
3. 12 kg = 12000 g
4. 20 kg = 20000 g
5. 200 kg = 200000 g
6. 3300 kg = 3300000 g
7. 305 kg = 305000 g
8. 409 kg = 409000 g
9. 600 kg = 600000 g
10. 70 kg = 70000 g
11. 43 kg = 43000 g
12. 607 kg = 607000 g

2. Gram to the kilogram.

1. 1 000 g = 1 kg
2. 3 000 g = 3 kg
3. 15 000 g = 15 kg
4. 45 000 g = 45 kg
5. 201 000 g = 201 kg
6. 307 000 g= 307 kg
7. 280 000 g = 280 kg
8. 606 000 g = 606 kg
9. 6 000 000 g = 6000 kg
10. 9 006 000 g = 9006 kg
11. 48 000 g = 48000 kg
12. 5 060 000 g = 5060 kg

Ho Math Chess Primary Grades Math

Test Review assesssment 何数棋謎低年级数学测试複習考核

Frank Ho, Amanda Ho www.homathchess.com

Student's name: ____________________ Assignment date: ________________

Mass

1. 5 000 g = 5 kg
2. 6 000 g = 6 kg
3. 43 000 g = 43 kg
4. 65 kg = 65000 g
5. 77 kg = 77000 g
6. 80 kg = 80000 g
7. 80 000 g = 80 kg
8. 75 kg = 75000 g
9. 3 000 000 g = 3000 kg
10. 2 006 000 g = 2006 kg
11. 48 000 kg = 48000000 g
12. 5 060 000 g = 5060 kg
13. 505 kg = 505000 g
14. 6 000 kg = 6000000 g
15. 70 kg = 70000 g
16. 90 kg = 90000 g
17. 201 000 g = 201 kg
18. 307 000 g= 307 kg
19. 28 000 kg = 28000000 g
20. 606 000 g = 606 kg
21. 71 000 g = 71 kg
22. 480 kg = 480000 g
23. 810 kg = 810 000 g
24. 70 000 g = 70 kg

Fill in the blank with >, < or =

1. 5 kg > 500 g
2. 200 kg > 200 g
3. 30 kg > 3000 g
4. 53 kg = 53000 g
5. 2 kg > 99 g
6. 8000 g < 80 kg
7. 5 kg < 6000 g
8. 5 kg > 4 000 g
9. 7 kg < 30 000 g
10. 9 kg = 9 000 g
11. 7 kg > 900 g
12. 6000 g < 40 kg

Ho Math Chess Primary Grades Math

Test Review assesssment 何数棋谜低年级数学测试複習考核

Student's name: ____________________ Assignment date: ________________

Choose the appropriate answer. All numbers are approximate.

1.	A box of table salt (10 cm by 5 cm by 17 cm) weighs	a. 1 g	b. 1 kg	b
2.	The mass of an egg is	a. 50 g	b. 50 kg	a
3.	A loaf of bread weighs	a. 500 g	b. 500 kg	a
4.	A jellybean weighs	a. 1 g	b. 1 kg	a
5.	The average mass of an adult is about	a. 70 g	b. 70 kg	b
6.	The mass of a muffin is about	a. 100 g	b. 100 kg	a
7.	The mass of a notebook computer is	a. 3 g	b. 3 kg	b
8.	The mass of a poker chip	a. 10 g	b. 10 kg	a
9.	The mass of a can of juice is about	a. 300 g	b. 300 kg	a
10.	The mass of a jar of peanut butter is	a. 1 g	b. 1 kg	b
11.	The mass of a 30 cm ruler is	a. 50 g	b. 10 kg	a
12.	A litre of juice has a mass of about	a. 1 g	b. 1 kg	b
13.	A hen has a mass of about	a. 3 g	b. 3 kg	b
14.	A miniature Yorkshire terrier is about	a. 1 g	b. 1 kg	b
15.	The mass of an apple is about	a. 200 g	b. 200 kg	a
16.	A newborn baby has a mass of about	a. 3 g	b. 3 kg	b
17.	The mass of a large bag of cat food is about	a. 8 g	b. 8 kg	b
18.	The mass of an orange is about	a. 50 g	b. 50 kg	a

Student's name: ____________________ Assignment date: ________________

Conversion of units

1. 6 km + 2 km = ___8___ km
2. 4 km + 300 m = ___4300___ m
3. 5 dm + 1 cm = ___51___ cm
4. 9 m + 5 dm + 3 cm = ___953___ cm
5. 8 m + 6 dm + 5 cm + 4 mm = ___8654___ mm
6. 7 km – 1300 m = ___5700___ m
7. 12 km – 4500 m = ___7500___ m
8. 72 m + 8 dm + 15 cm = ___7295___ cm
9. 10 m + 78 cm + 17 mm= ___10797___ mm
10. 35 m – 4 dm – 18 mm= ___34582___ mm
11. 3 kg + 400 g = ___3400___ g
12. 4 kg – 120 g = ___3880___ g
13. 33 kg – 2500 g = ___30500___ g
14. 27 kg + 560 g – 3 kg = ___24560___ g
15. 6 L + 18 L = ___24000___ mL
16. 52 L + 1600 mL = ___53600___ mL
17. 35000 mL + 69000 mL= ___104___ L
18. 7 l – 780 mL = ___6220___ mL
19. 3 L – 20 mL = ___2980___ mL

Student's name: ____________________ Assignment date: ________________

Imperial system

Length
1 foot = 12 inches
1 yard = 3 feet
1 mile = 5289 feet

Volume

1 gallon = 4 quarts

Mass and Weight

1 pound (lb) = 16 ounces (oz)

Student's name: ____________________ Assignment date: ________________

***** Part 12 Perimeter and Area *****

Perimeter is the distance around the figure.

1. Trace the perimeter of the following figure with a colour pen.

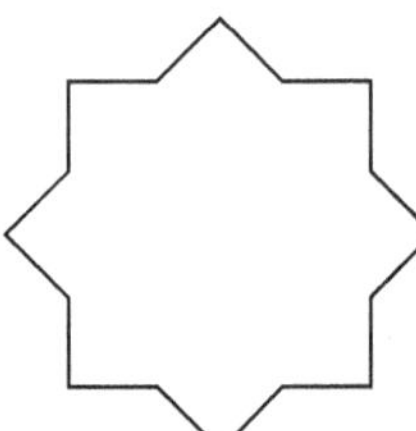
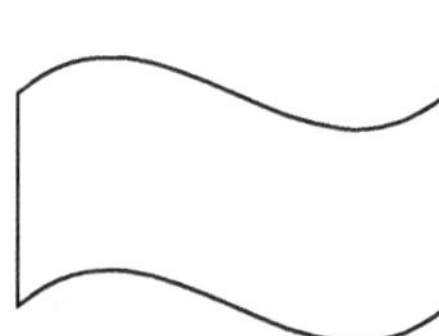

2. The side of each small square is 1 cm. Find the perimeters of the following shapes.

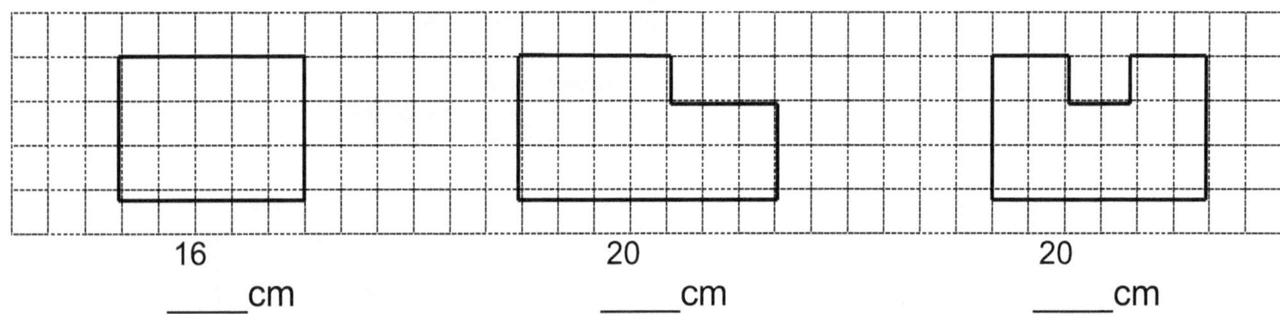

16 ____cm 20 ____cm 20 ____cm

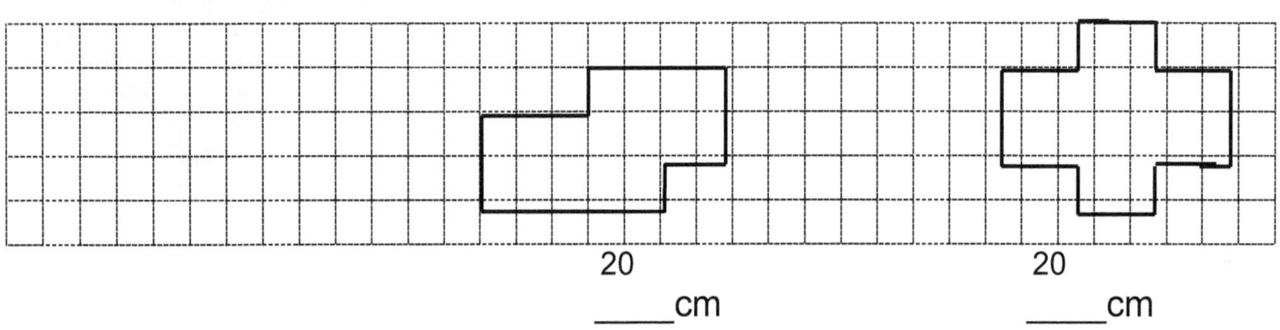

20 ____cm 20 ____cm

Student's name: ____________________ Assignment date: ________________

Perimeter

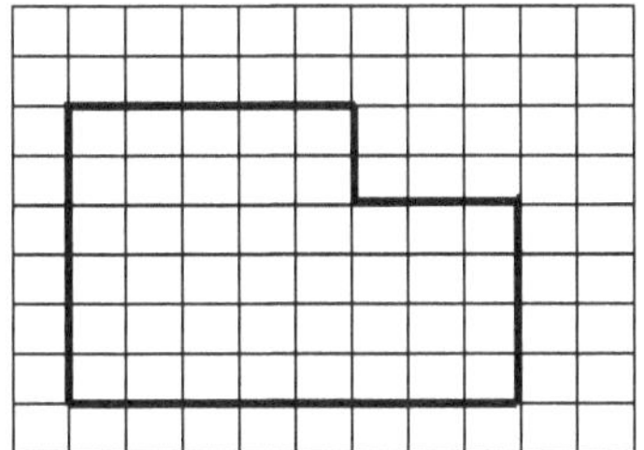

Perimeter = 28

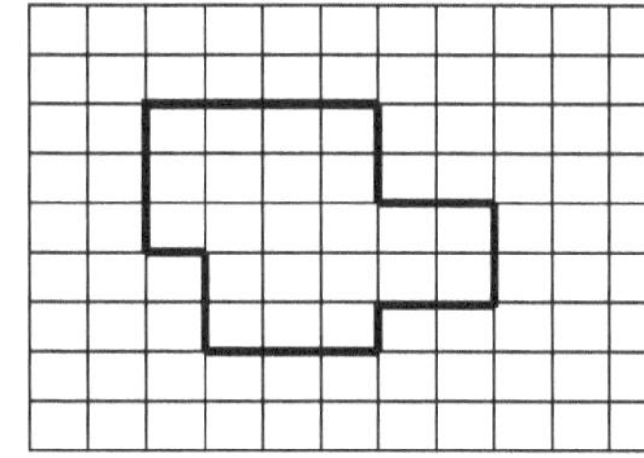

Perimeter = 22

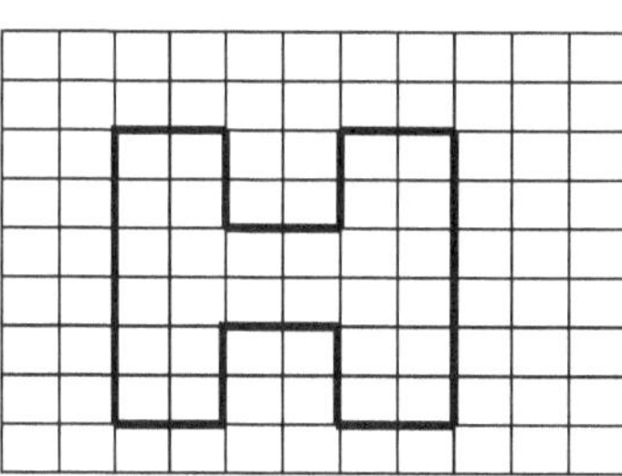

Perimeter = 32

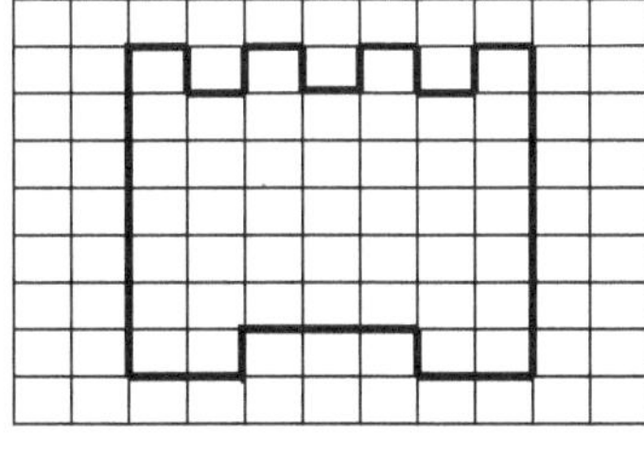

Perimeter = 36

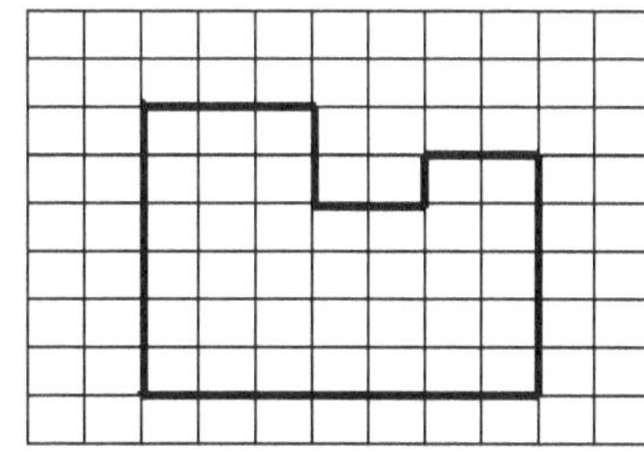

Perimeter = 28

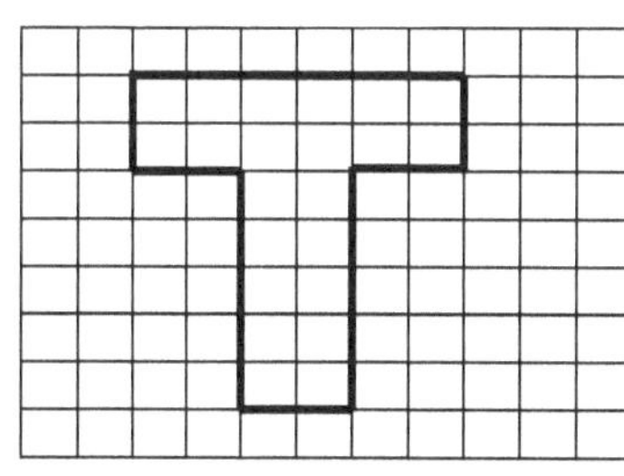

Perimeter = 26

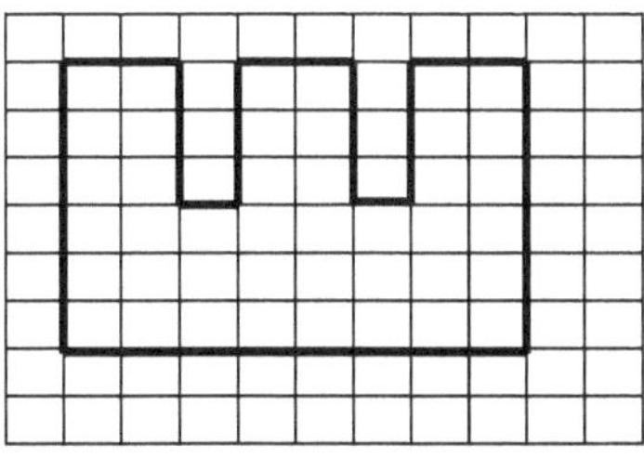

Perimeter = 40

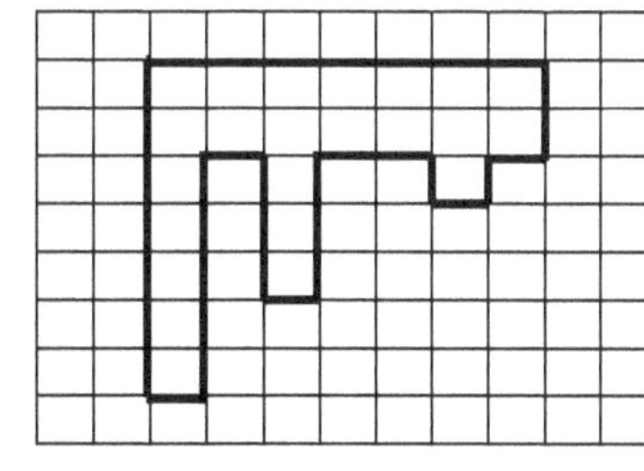

Perimeter = 36

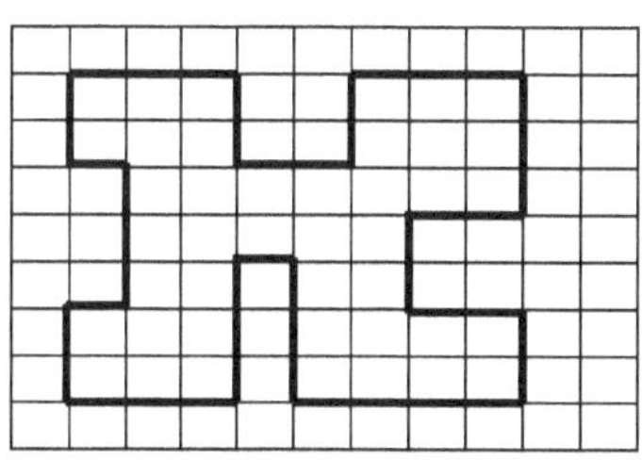

Perimeter = 46

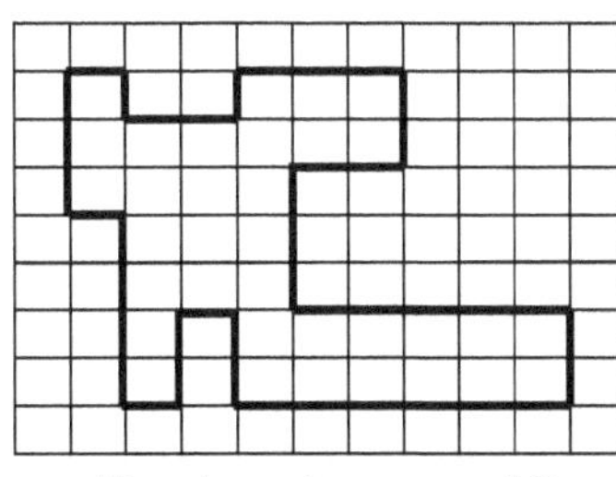

Perimeter = 42

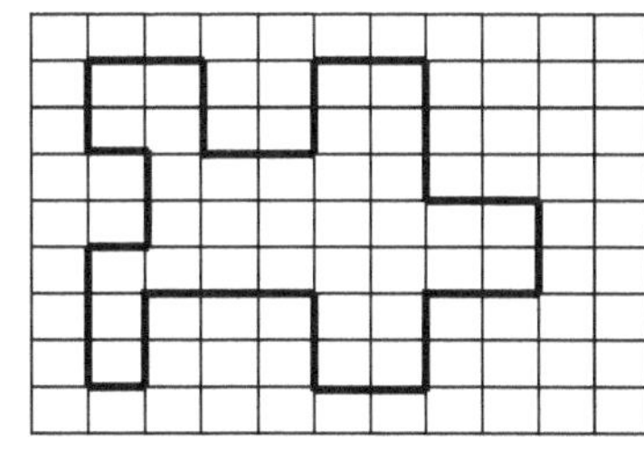

Perimeter = 40

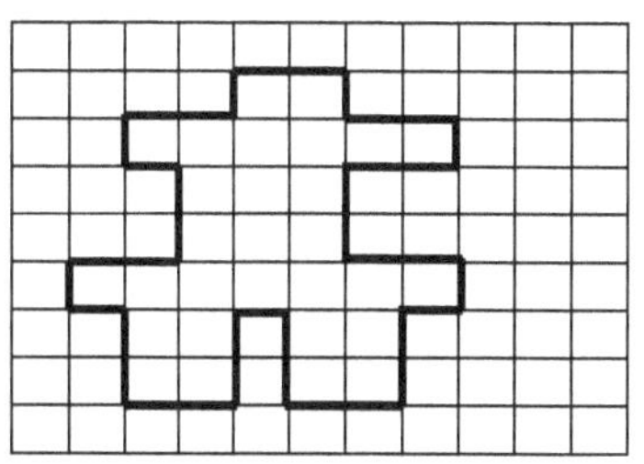

Perimeter = 38

Ho Math Chess Primary Grades Math

Test Review assesssment 何数棋謎低年级数学测试複習考核

Student's name: ____________________ Assignment date: ________________

Measure the lengths of the sides. Then find the perimeters of the figures.

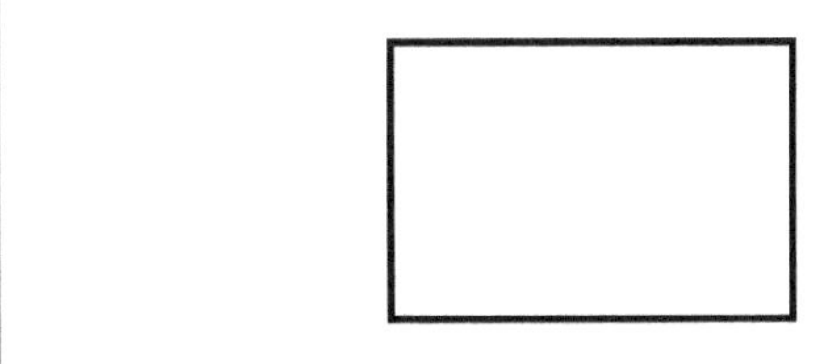

Perimeter
=____cm+____cm+____cm+____cm
= 10

Perimeter
=____cm+____cm+____cm
= 12

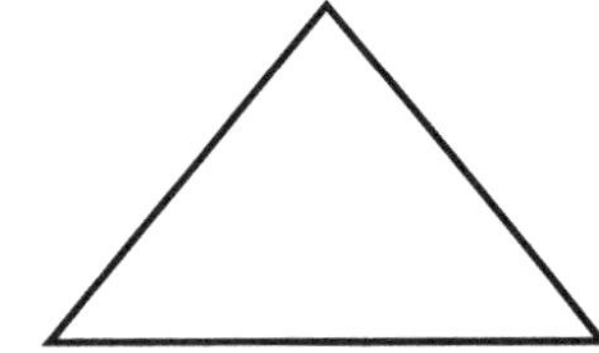

Perimeter
=____cm+____cm+____cm
=10

Perimeter =
____cm+____cm+____cm+ ____cm
+____cm+____cm
=13

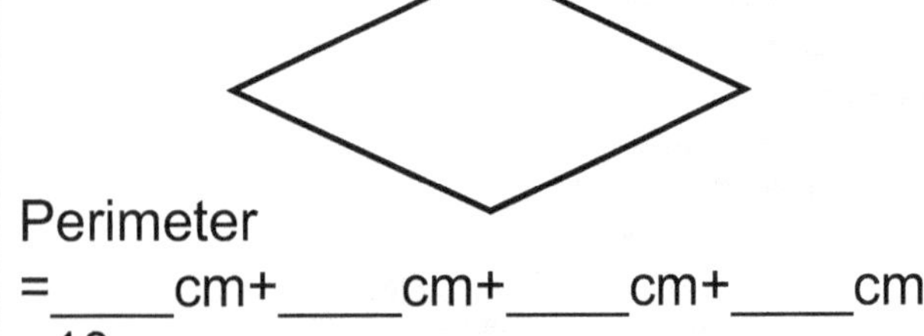

Perimeter
=____cm+____cm+____cm+____cm
=10

Perimeter =____cm+____cm+____cm
+____cm+ ____cm
=11

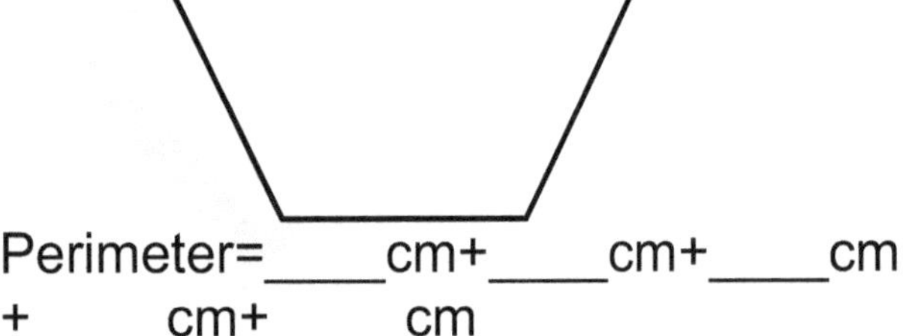

Perimeter=____cm+____cm+____cm
+ ____cm+ ____cm
=12

Perimeter =____cm+____cm+____cm
+____cm + ____cm + ____cm
=13

Student's name: ____________________ Assignment date: ________________

The perimeter of a Rectangle

Perimeter of a rectangle = 2 × (Length + Width)

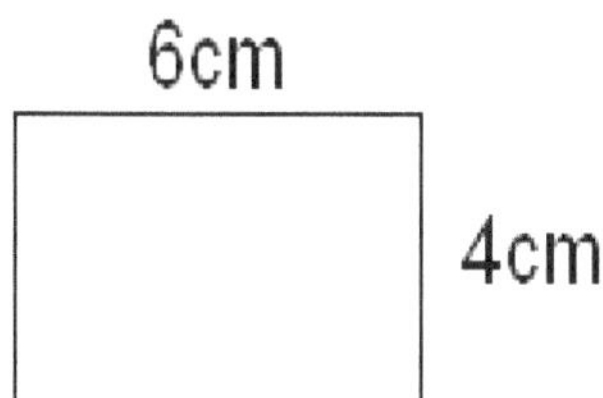

Perimeter = 2 × (6 + 4)
= 20 cm

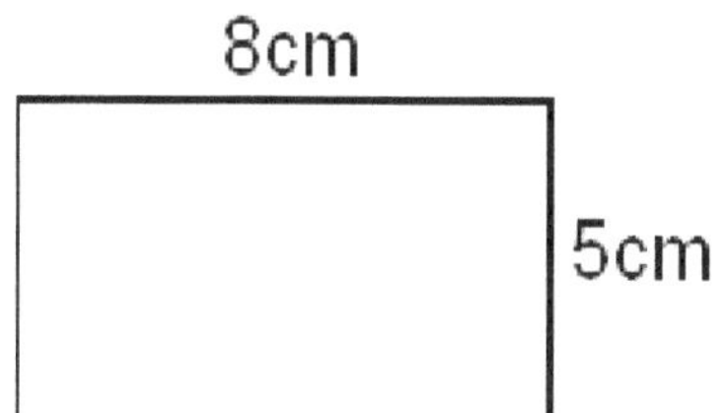

Perimeter = 2 × (8 + 5)
= 26 cm

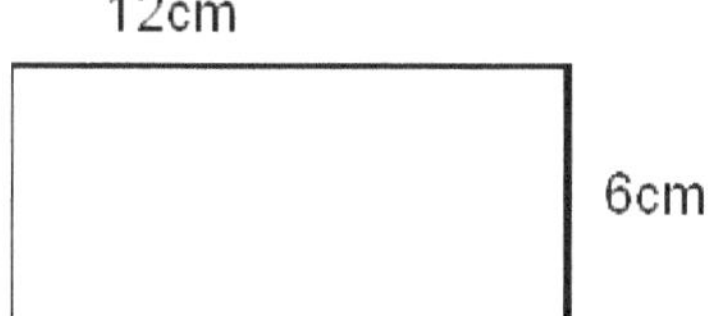

Perimeter = 36

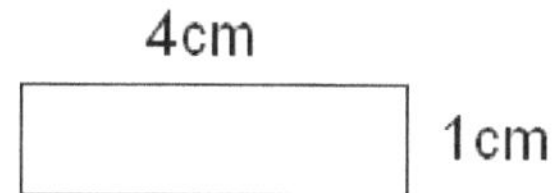

Perimeter = 10

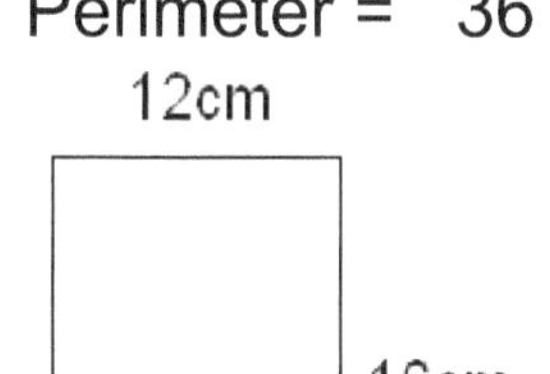

Perimeter = 56

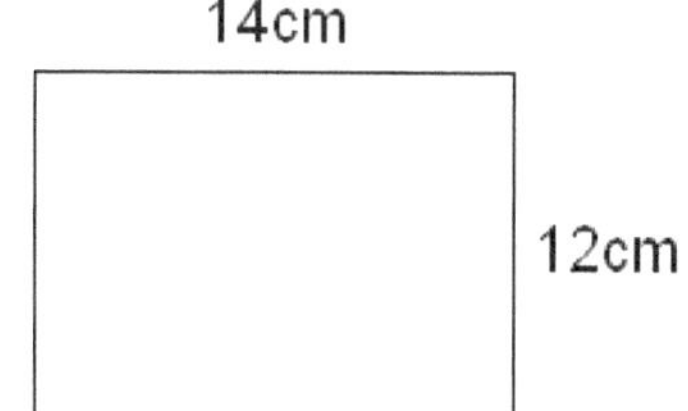

Perimeter = 52

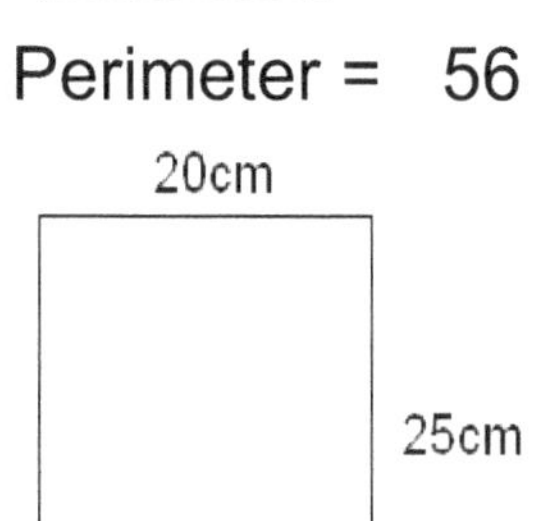

Perimeter = 90

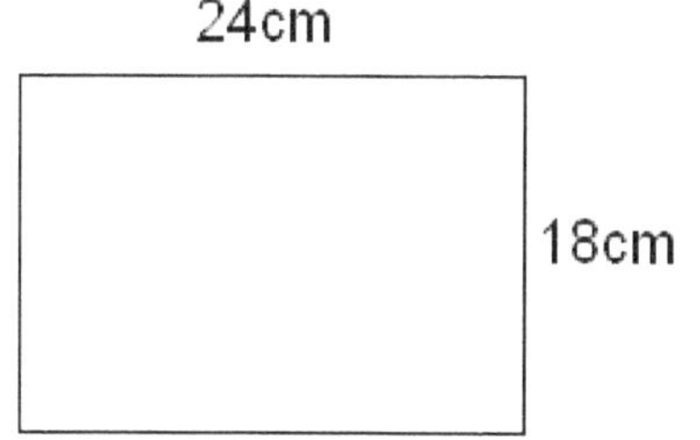

Perimeter = 84

Student's name: ____________________ Assignment date: ________________

The perimeter of a Square

The perimeter of a square = 4 × side Length

4cm

Perimeter = 4 × _4_ = _16_ cm

7cm

Perimeter = 4× _7_ = _28_ cm

20cm

Perimeter = 80

14cm

Perimeter = 56

26cm

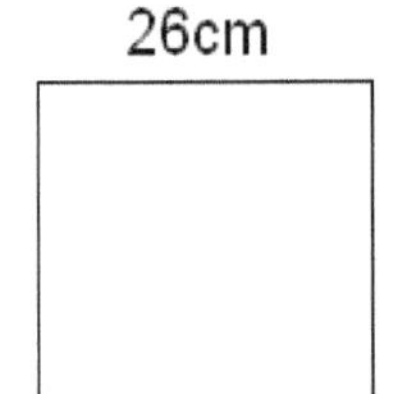

Perimeter = 104

32cm

Perimeter = 128

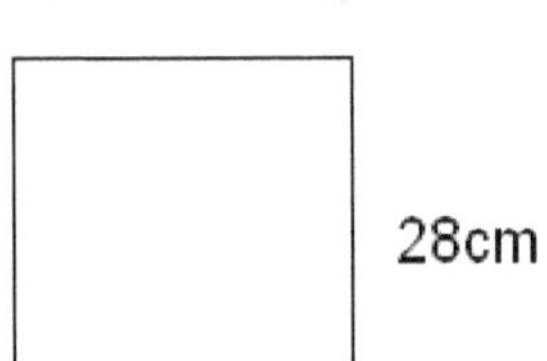

28cm

Perimeter = 112

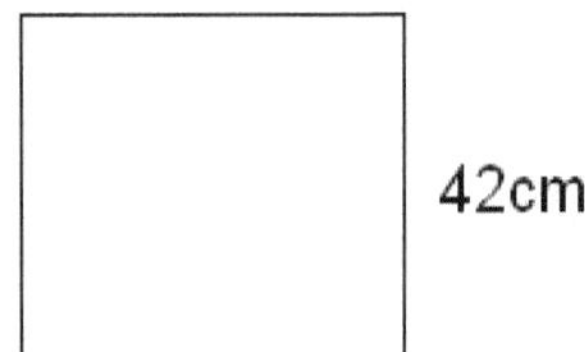

42cm

Perimeter = 168

Student's name: ____________________ Assignment date: ________________

Areas of rectangles or squares

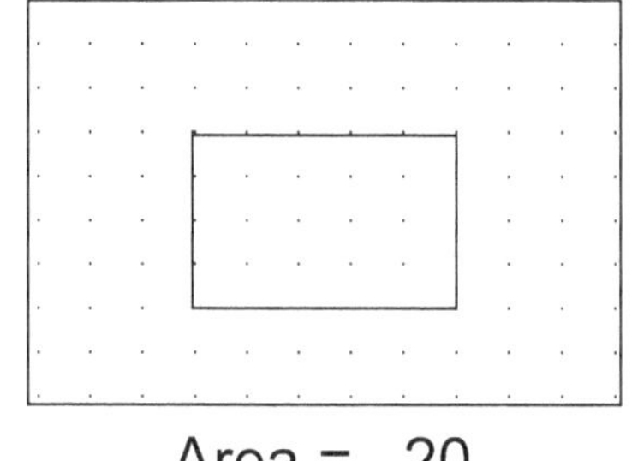
Area = 20

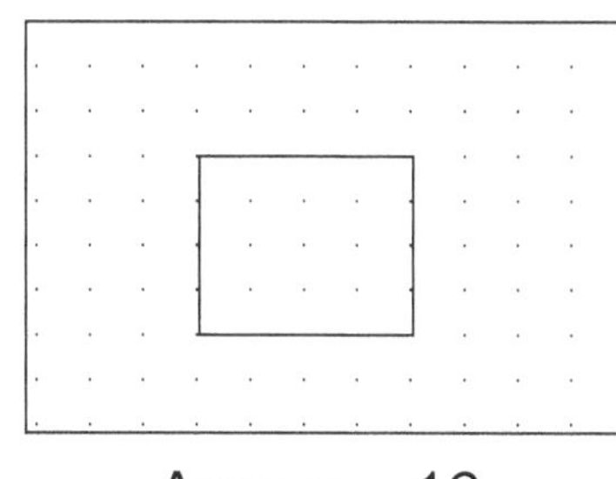
Area = 16

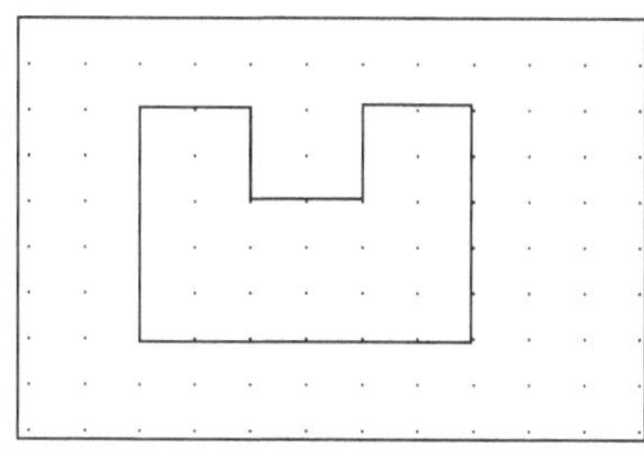
Area = 26

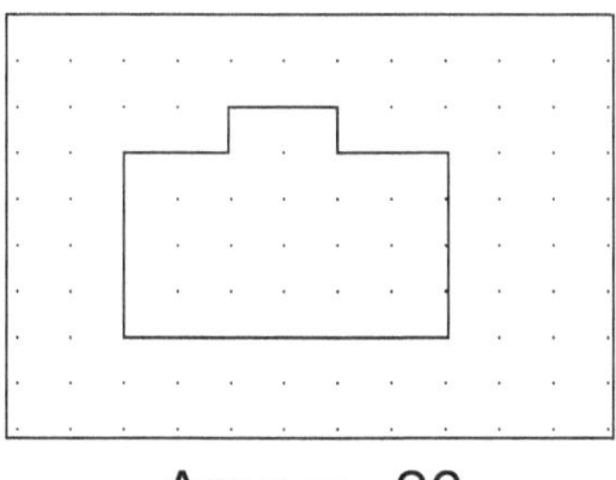
Area = 26

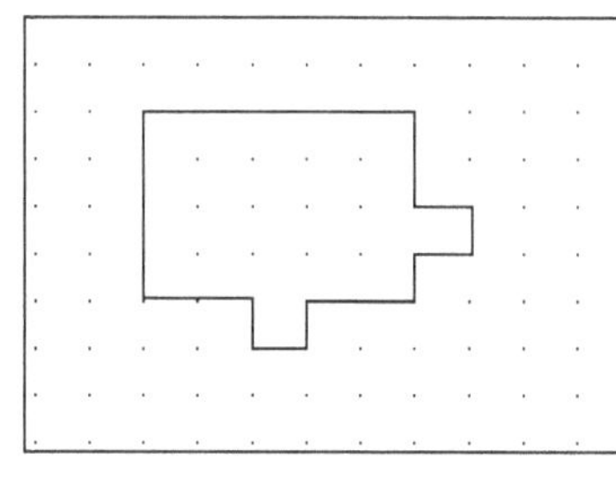
Area = 22

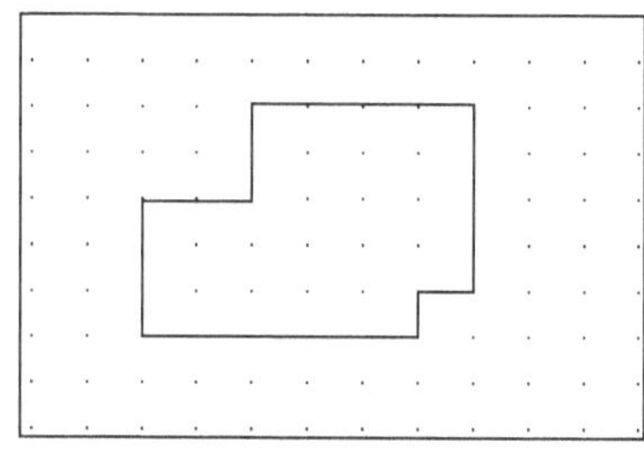
Area = 25

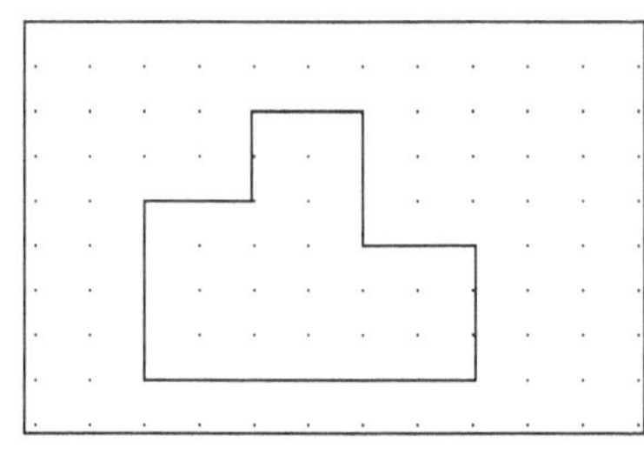
Area = 26

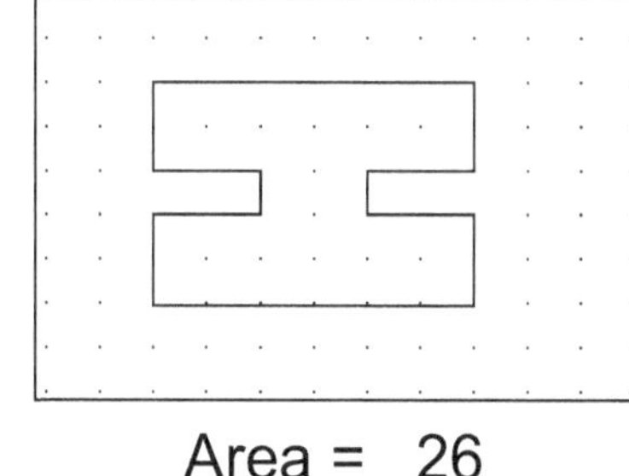
Area = 26

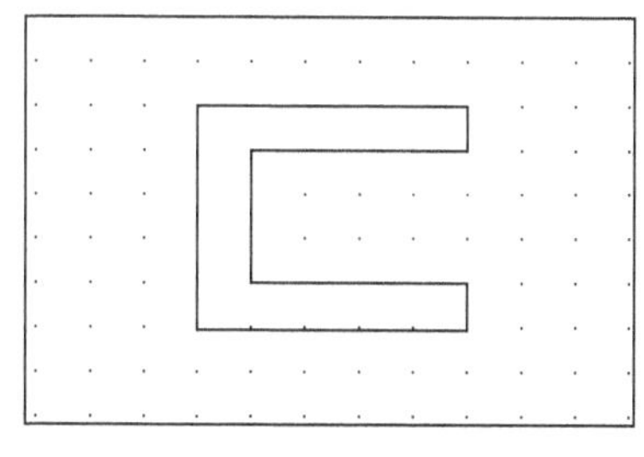
Area = 13

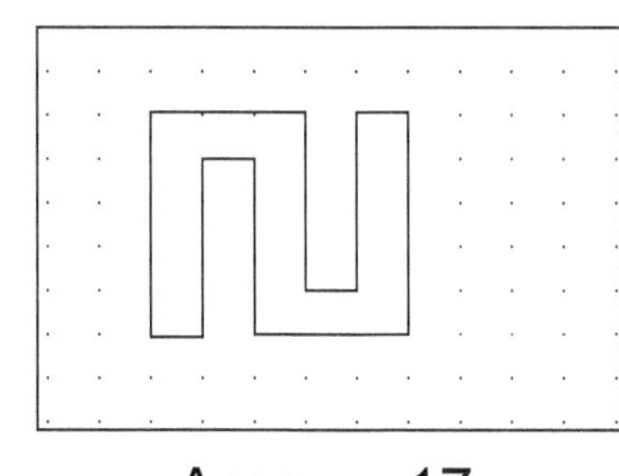
Area = 17

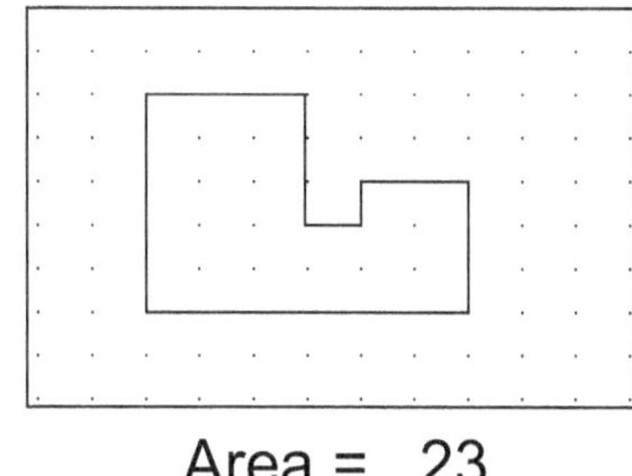
Area = 23

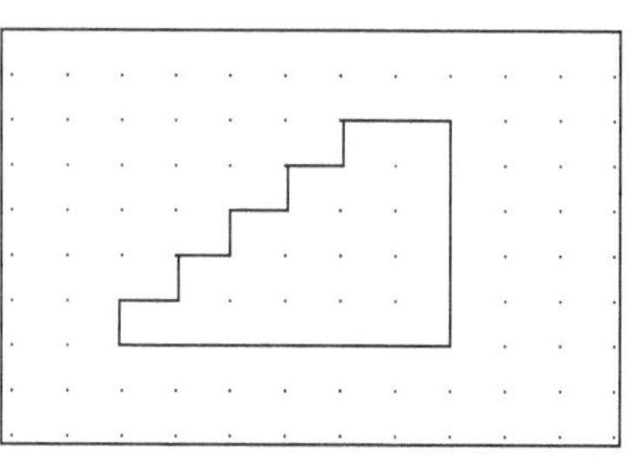
Area = 20

Student's name: ____________________ Assignment date: ________________

Area of a triangle

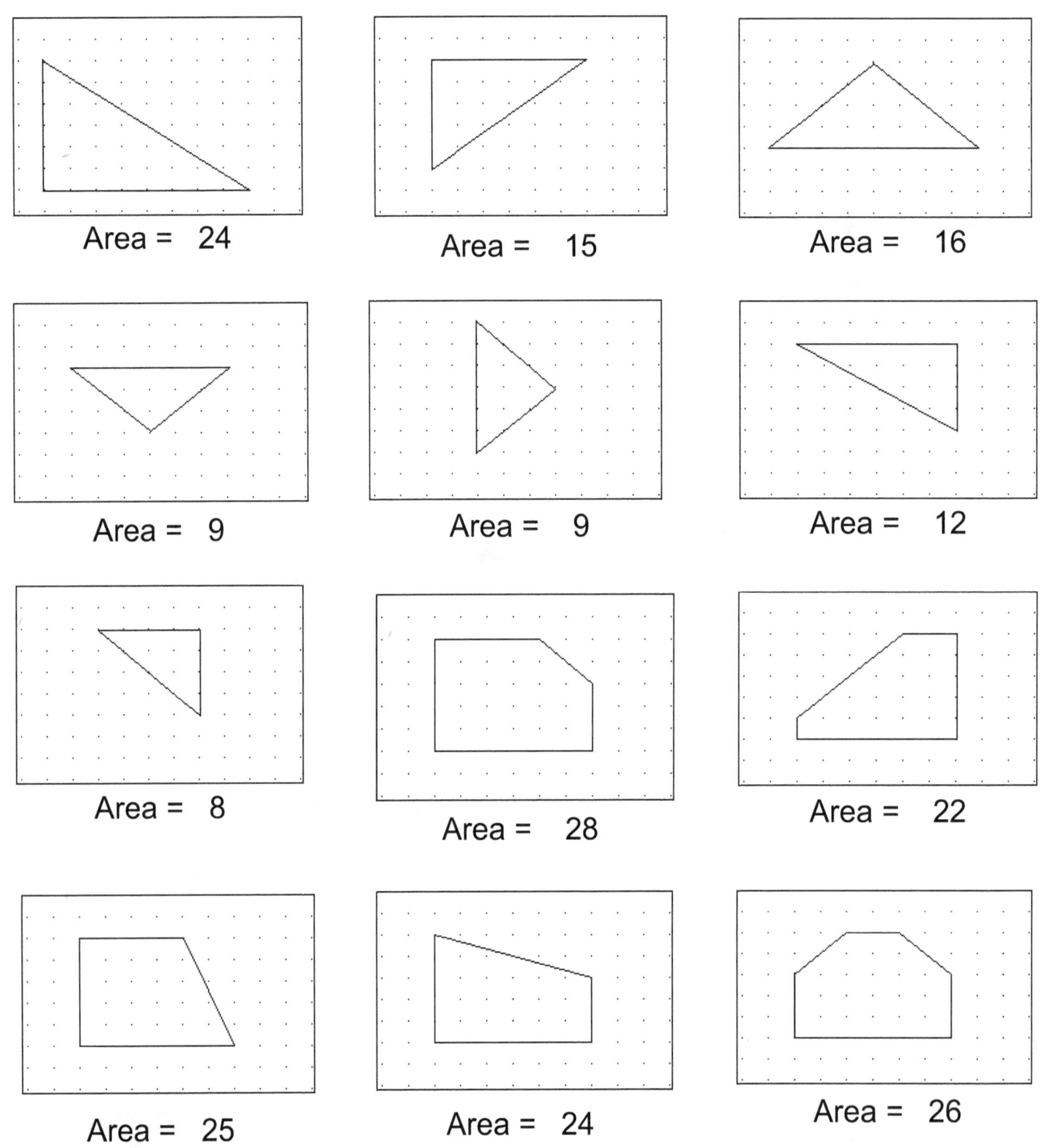

Student's name: ____________________ Assignment date: ________________

Area

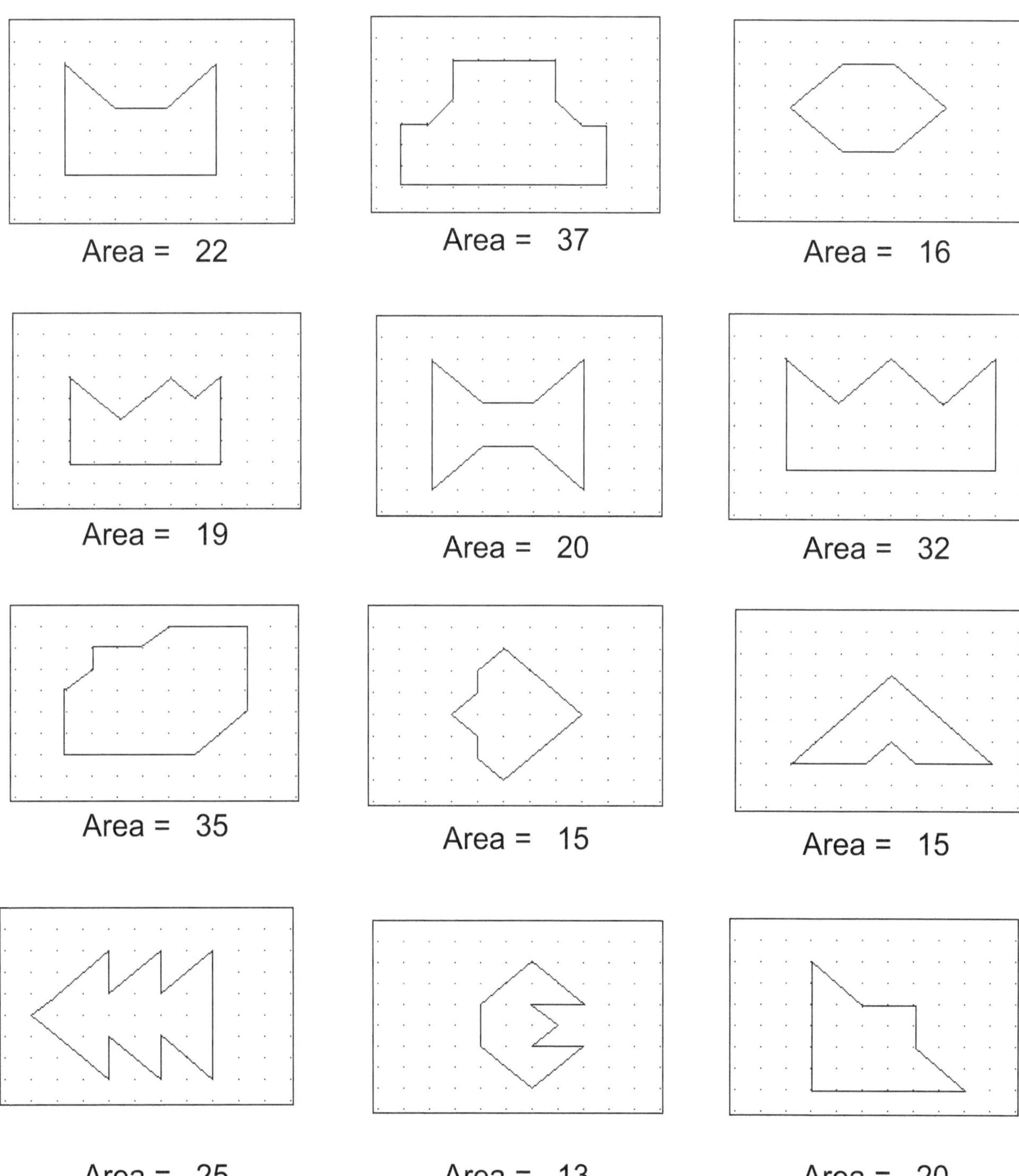

Student's name: ____________________ Assignment date: ________________

Area of a Rectangle

Area of a rectangle = Length × Width

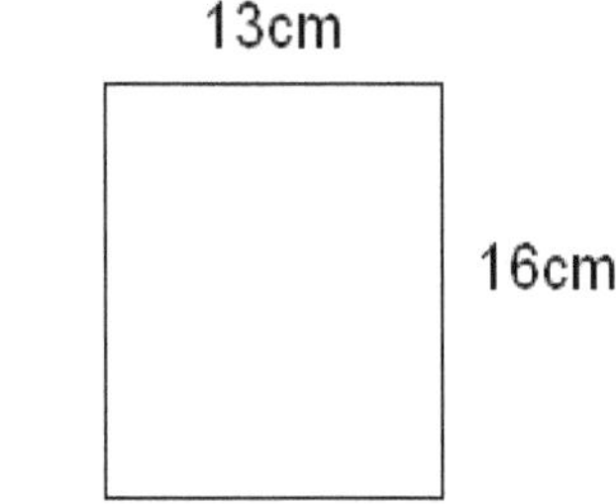

7cm
4cm

Area = 7 × 4 = 28 cm^2

Area = 13 × 16 = 208 cm^2

Area = 420 cm^2

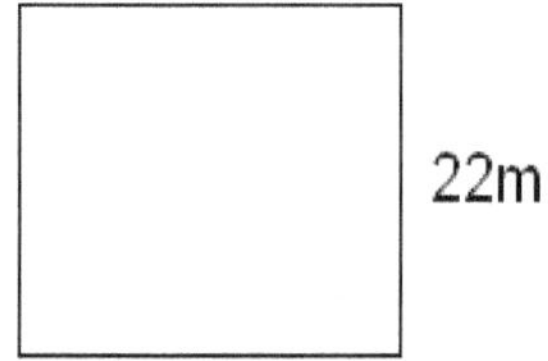

Area = 528 m^2

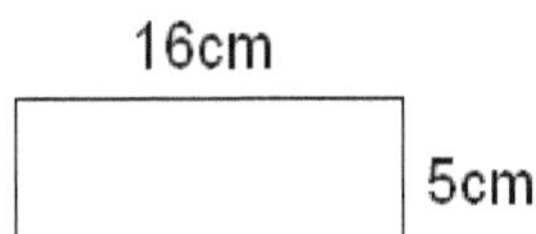

Area = 80 cm^2

Area = 200 m^2

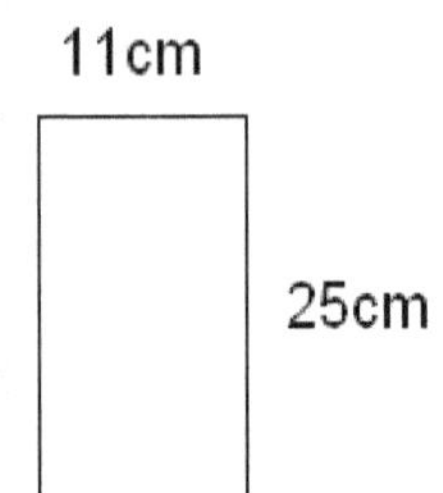

Area = 275 cm^2

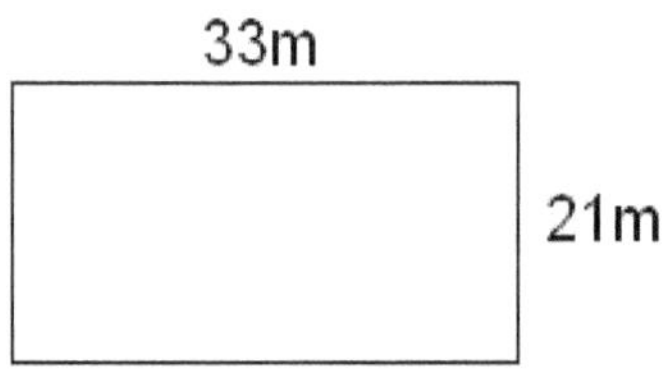

Area = 693 m^2

Student's name: ____________________ Assignment date: ________________

Find the perimeter and area of each rectangle.

1. 12 cm in wide, 15 cm in long 54 Perimeter = ________cm 180 Area = ________ cm^2	2. 14 cm in wide, 20 cm in long 68 Perimeter = ________cm 280 Area = ________ cm^2
3. 24 cm in wide, 36 cm in long 120 Perimeter = ________ 864 Area = ________	4. 31 cm in wide, 40 cm in long 142 Perimeter = ________ 1240 Area = ________
5. 32 m in wide, 45 m in long 154 Perimeter = ________ 1440 Area = ________	6. 100 m in wide, 120 m in long 440 Perimeter = ________ 12000 Area = ________
7. 15 km in wide, 30 km in long 90 Perimeter = ________ 450 Area = ________	8. 40 km in wide, 140 km in long 360 Perimeter = ________ 5600 Area = ________
9. 400 cm in wide, 500 cm in long 1800 Perimeter = ________ 200000 Area = ________	10. 72 km in wide, 150 km in long 444 Perimeter = ________ 10800 Area = ________
11. Find the following rectangular area with the dimension of width 50 cm and the length 5 m. 25000 cm^2	12. Find the following rectangular area with the dimension of width 2 m and the length 900 cm. 18000 cm^2

Ho Math Chess Primary Grades Math

Test Review assesssment 何数棋謎低年级数学测试複習考核

Student's name: ____________________ Assignment date: ________________

Area of a rectangle and square

Area of a rectangle = Length × width
Area of a square = side Length × side length

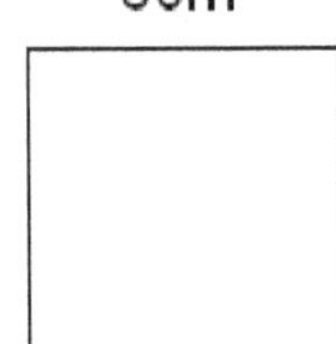

Area = 6 × 6 = 36 cm^2

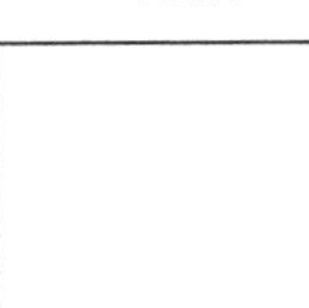

Area = 225 m^2

Area = 324 m^2

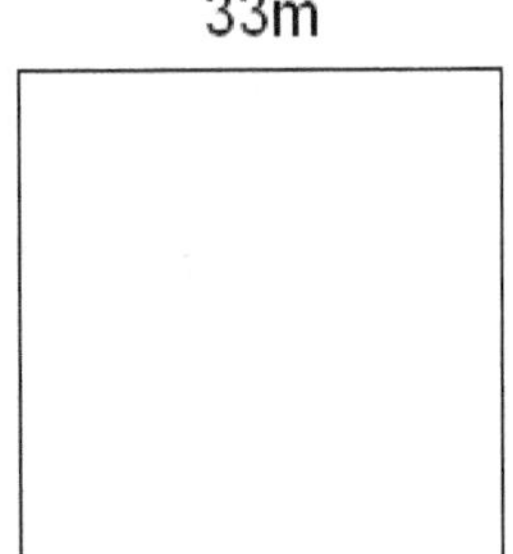

Area = 1089 m^2

Area = 12 × 12 = 144 cm^2

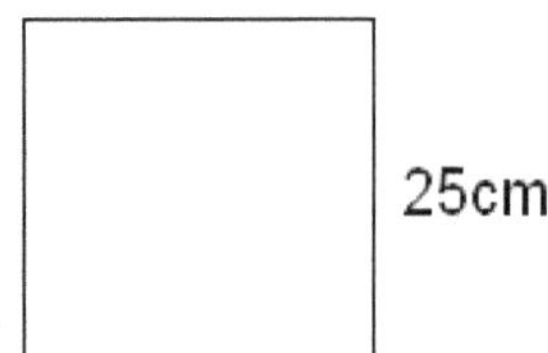

Area = 625 cm^2

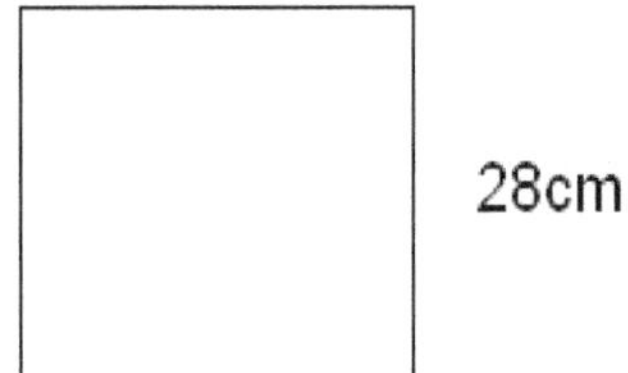

Area = 784 cm^2

Area = 1764 cm^2

Student's name: ____________________ Assignment date: ________________

Find the perimeter and area of each square.

1. Side length is 20 cm Perimeter = 80 cm Area = 400 cm^2	2. Side length is 50 cm Perimeter = 200 cm Area = 2500 cm^2
3. Side length is 13 cm Perimeter = 52 Area = 169	4. Side length is 48 m Perimeter = 192 Area = 2304
5. Side length is 63 km Perimeter = 252 Area = 3969	6. Side length is 36 km Perimeter = 144 Area = 1296
7. Side length is 28 cm Perimeter = 112 Area = 784	8. Side length is 32 m Perimeter = 128 Area = 1024
9. Side length is 37 km Perimeter = 148 Area = 1369	10. Side length is 93 km Perimeter = 372 Area = 8649

Student's name: ____________________ Assignment date: ______________

Area and Perimeter

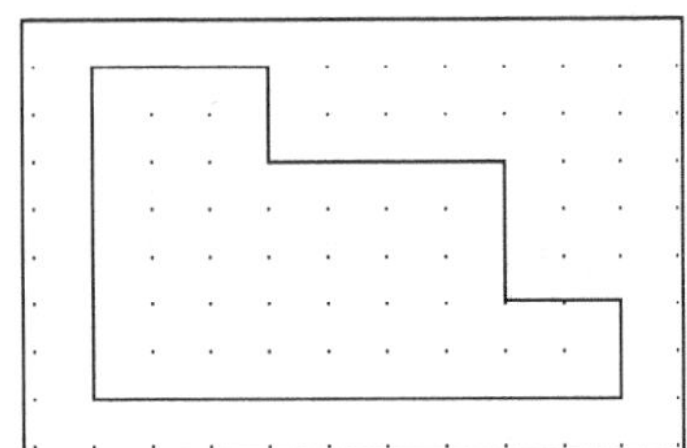

Perimeter ______ units 32
Area ______units² 45

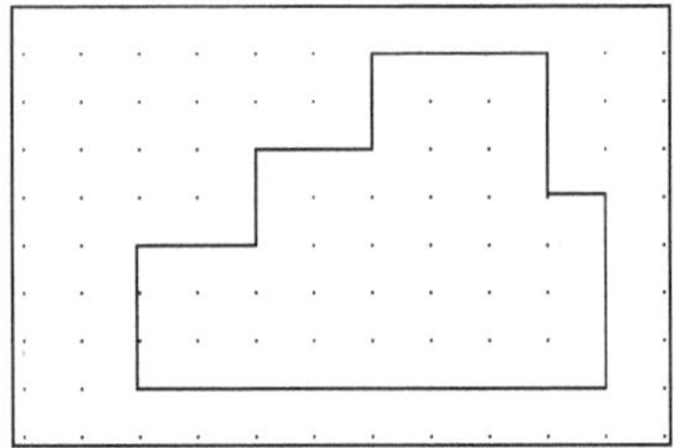

Perimeter ______ units 30
Area ______units² 41

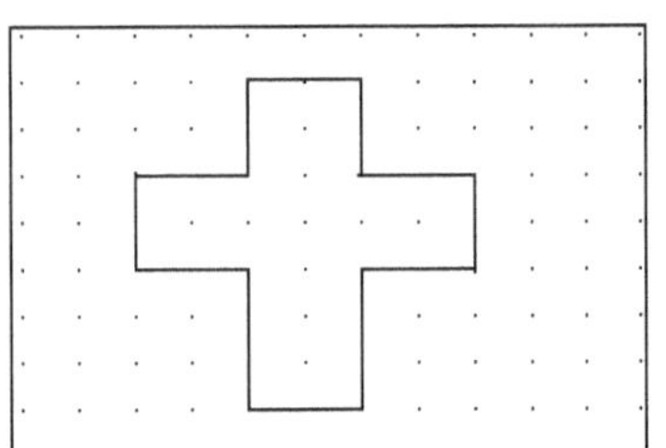

Perimeter ______ units 26
Area ______units² 22

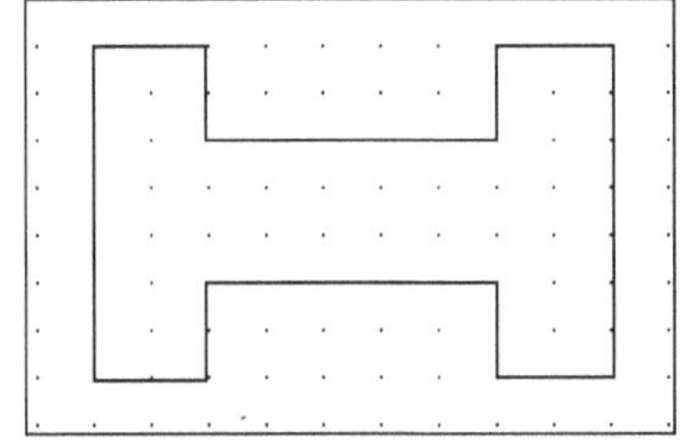

Perimeter ______ units 32
Area ______units² 43

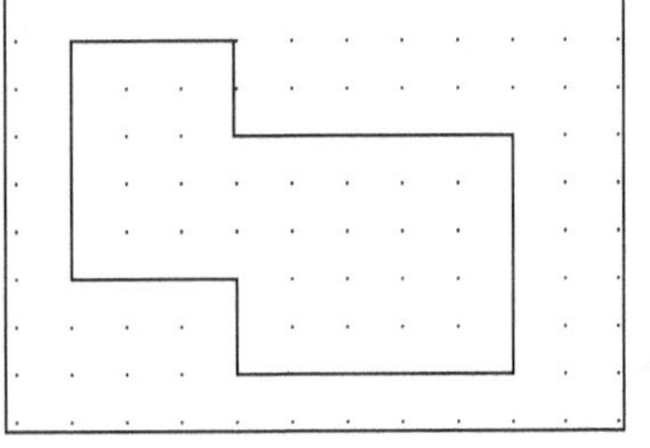

Perimeter ______ units 30
Area ______units² 40

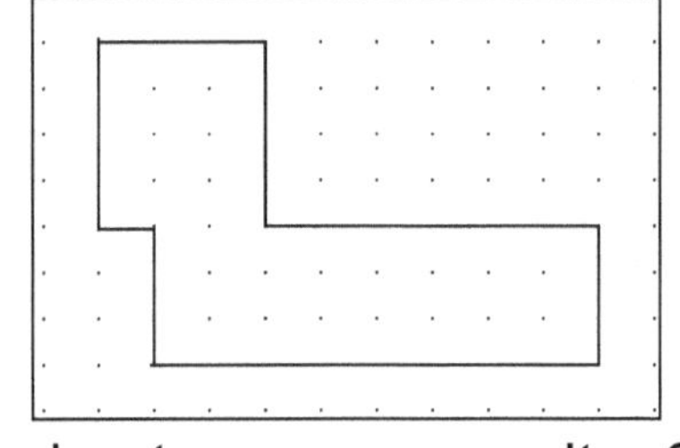

Perimeter ______ units 32
Area ______units² 36

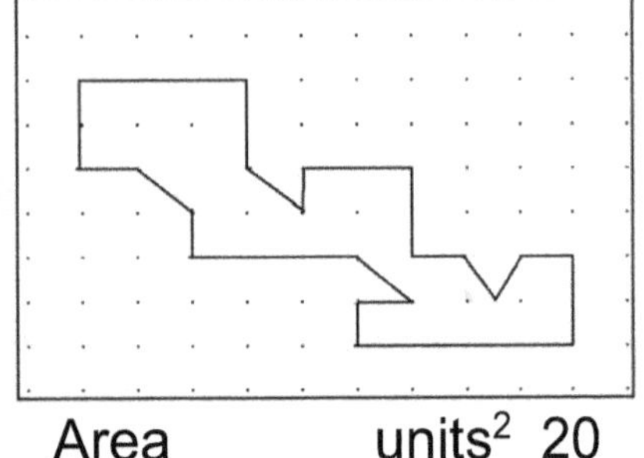

Area ______units² 20

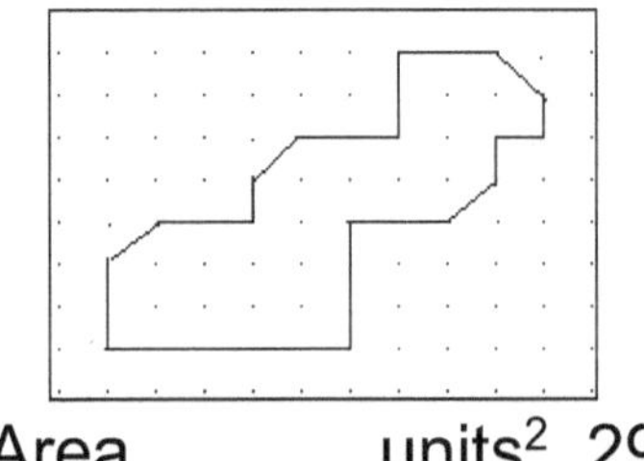

Area ______units² 29

Student's name: ____________________ Assignment date: ________________

Fill in the missing values for a rectangle.

	Length	Width	Perimeter	Area
1.	8	4	24	32
2.	12	7	38	84
3.	8	4	24	32
4.	9	6	30	54
5.	8	7	30	56
6.	13	5	36	65
7.	6	4	20	24
8.	20	4	48	80

Fill in the missing values for a square.

	Side length	Perimeter	Area
1.	4	16	16
2.	7	28	49
3.	9	36	81
4.	12	48	144
5.	7	28	49
6.	9	36	81

Student's name: ____________________ Assignment date: ________________

Area and perimeter word problems

1. Averill Garden is in the shape of a rectangle with 30 m in length and 40m in width. The owner wants to fence the Garden. How many meters of the fence does he need to buy?

140 cm

____

2. Mystery City is in the shape of a square. The length of one side is 180 km. There is a road around the city. How long is the road?

720 km

____

3. A tower is in the shape of a triangle. The total distance around the tower is 480 m. What is the length of the missing side?

120m
170m
?

190 cm

____

4. Janet walks her dog around a block 4 times a day. The block is 240 m long and 320m wide. What is the total distance does she walk with her dog every day?

4480 m

____

5. A table is 120 cm long and 60 cm wide. Lucy wants to cover the table with a table cloth. At least how much cloth does she need?

7200 cm^2

____

6. Nick wants to floor his bedroom. His bedroom is 15 m long and 11 m wide. How many square meters of the wood panel does he need?

165 m^2

____

Student's name: ____________________ Assignment date: ______________

7. A basketball court measures 40 m by 20 m.

What is the perimeter? 120 m

What is the area? 800 m^2

8. A volleyball court measures 18 m by 9 m.

What is the perimeter? 54 m

What is the area? 162 m^2

9. The distance around a tennis court is 100 m. It is 30 meters long. What is its width?

20 m

10. A bear pen is 9 m long if its area is 108 m^2.

What is its width? 20 cm

What is its perimeter? 12 m

11. Linda wants to build a fence for her backyard against the wall of her house. The wall is 12 m long. Suppose she needs a 30 m fence. What is the width of her backyard?

9 m

What is the area of her backyard? 108 m^2

12. Lois wants to fence his rectangular garden against the river. No fence is needed along the river. The area of the garden is 240 m^2. The length along the river is 40 m. . What is the width of his garden?

6 m

What is the total length of his fence? 52 m

Student's name: ____________________ Assignment date: ________________

Advanced word problems of areas for rectangles or squares
Answers are in whole numbers only.

<table>
<tr><td>shapes</td><td>perimeter</td><td>area</td><td>What could be the dimension of the shape?</td></tr>
<tr><td>rectangle</td><td>48 m

$48 \div 2 = 24$
<table><tr><td>length</td><td>width</td></tr><tr><td>23</td><td>1</td></tr><tr><td>22</td><td>2</td></tr><tr><td>21</td><td>3</td></tr><tr><td>20</td><td>4</td></tr><tr><td>19</td><td>5</td></tr><tr><td>18</td><td>6</td></tr><tr><td>17</td><td>7</td></tr><tr><td>16</td><td>8</td></tr><tr><td>15</td><td>9</td></tr><tr><td>14</td><td>10</td></tr><tr><td>13</td><td>11</td></tr><tr><td>12</td><td>12</td></tr></table></td><td>What could be the areas?

23x1=23
22x2=44
21x3=63
20x4=80
.
.
.
12x12=144
There is 12 dimension.</td><td>Not applicable</td></tr>
<tr><td>rectangle</td><td>What could be the largest perimeter?

1+1+36+36 = 74

What could be the least perimeter?

2(4+9) = 26</td><td>36 m^2</td><td>Not applicable</td></tr>
</table>

Student's name: ____________________ Assignment date: ________________

<table>
<tr><td>shapes</td><td>perimeter</td><td>area</td><td>What could be the dimension of the shape?</td></tr>
<tr><td>rectangle</td><td>6 m</td><td>2 m²</td><td>What could be the dimensions of the shape?

1m by 2 m</td></tr>
<tr><td>Rectangle</td><td>12 m</td><td>12÷ 2 = 6
<table><tr><td>length</td><td>width</td></tr><tr><td>5</td><td>1</td></tr><tr><td>4</td><td>2</td></tr></table></td><td>What could be the dimension of the square?

5 m by 1 m
4 m by 2 m</td></tr>
<tr><td>square</td><td></td><td>49 m²</td><td>What could be the dimension of the square?

7 m by 7 m</td></tr>
</table>

Student's name: ____________________ Assignment date: ________________

Volume of a rectangle and a square

The volume of a rectangle or cube = LWH (Length × Width × Height)

A rectangular tank has dimensions 5 feet by 10 feet by 15 feet. The tank will be filled with water at a rate of 5 cubic feet per minute. How long will it take to fill up the tank?

Student's name: ____________________ Assignment date: ________________

Temperature

Write the temperatures.

1. 50 ____ ^{0}C

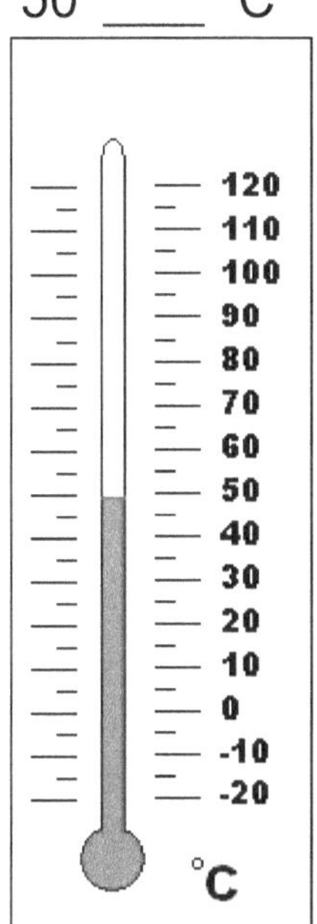

2. 80 ____ ^{0}C

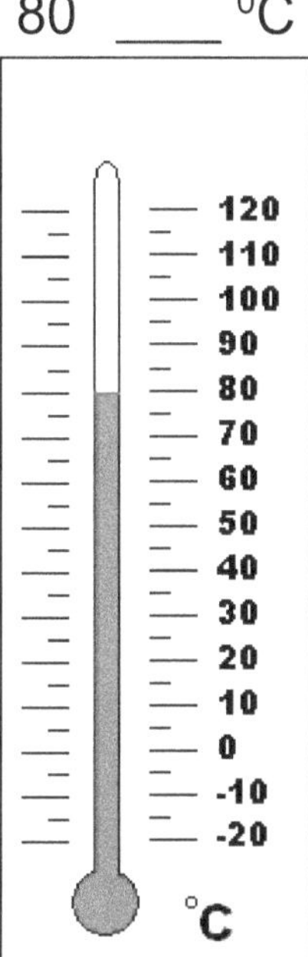

3. 40 ____ ^{0}C

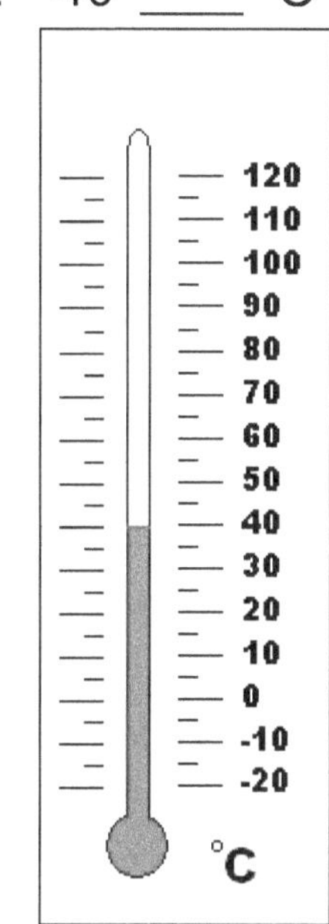

4. 95 ____ ^{0}C

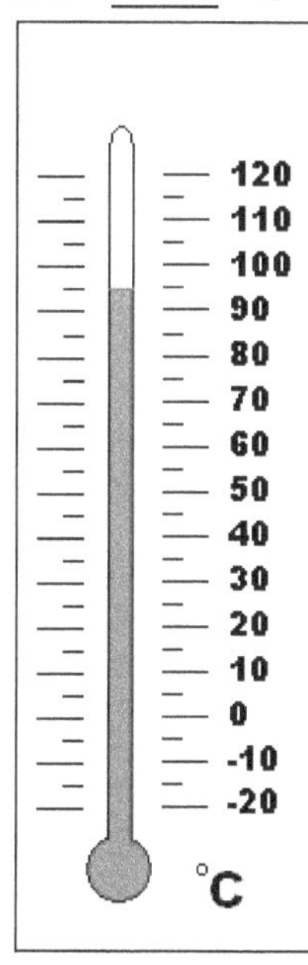

5. 75 ____ ^{0}C

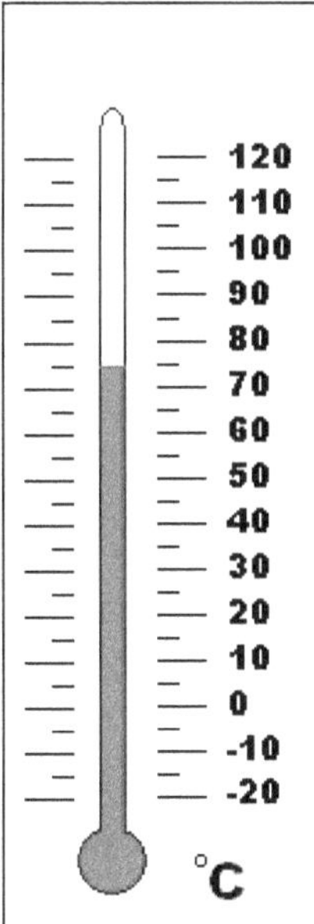

6. 5 ____ ^{0}C

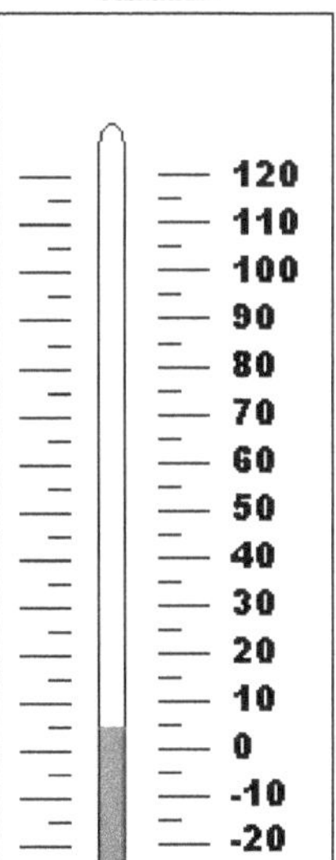

7. 70 ____ ^{0}C

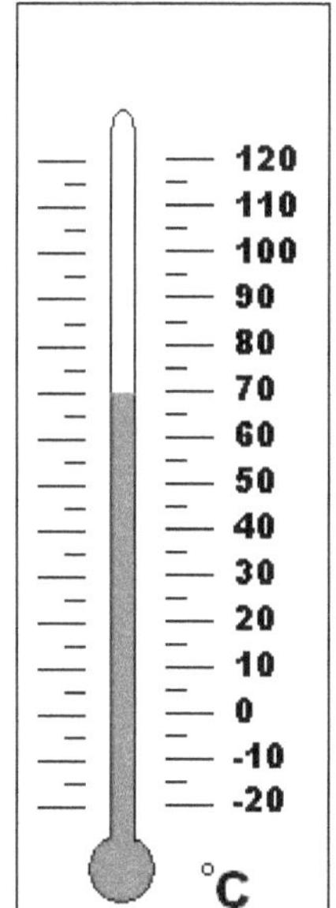

8. 115 ____ ^{0}C

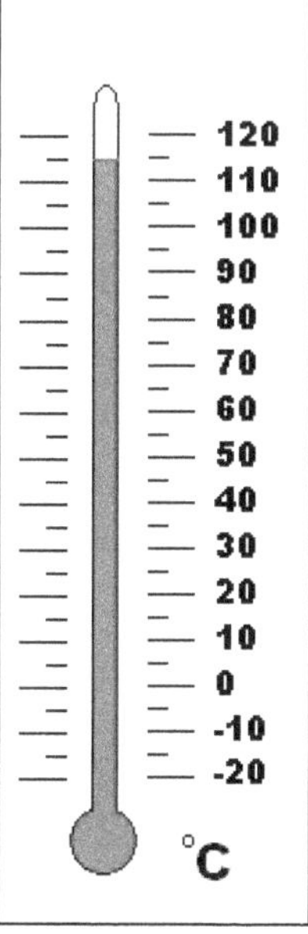

Student's name: ____________________ Assignment date: ________________

Colour the thermometer to show the temperature.

1. 40 °C

2. 80 °C

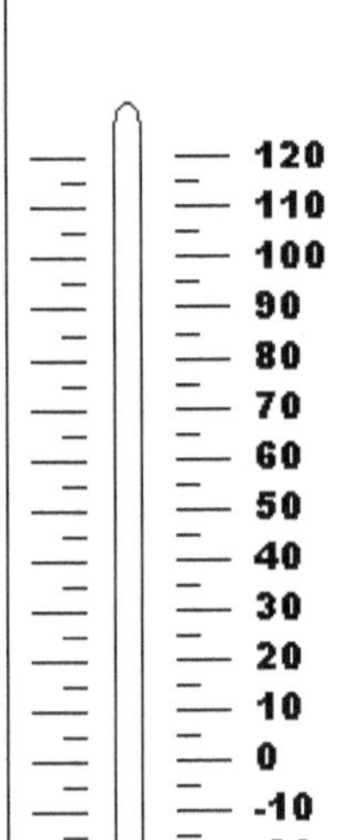

3. 55 °C

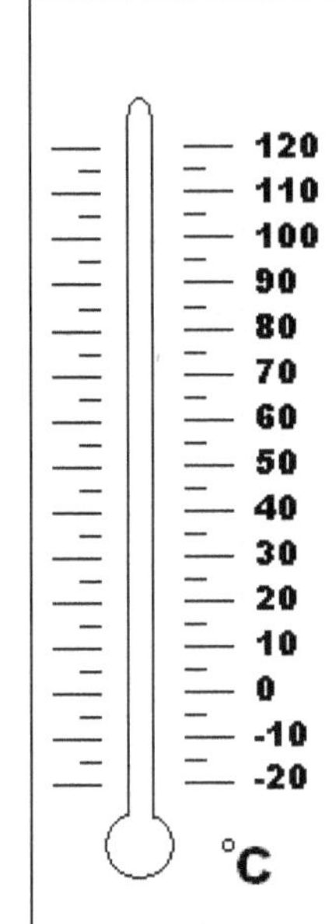

4. 75 °C

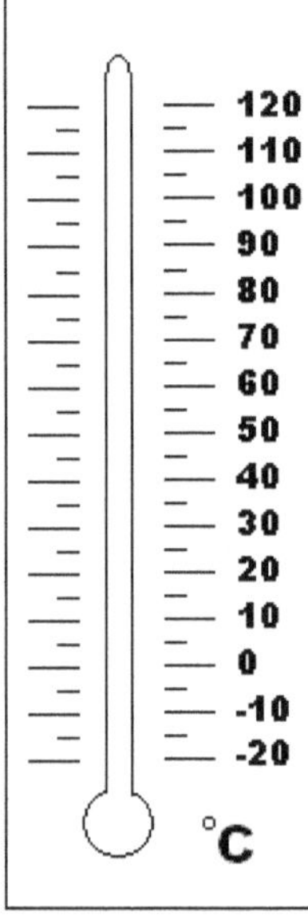

5. 5 °C

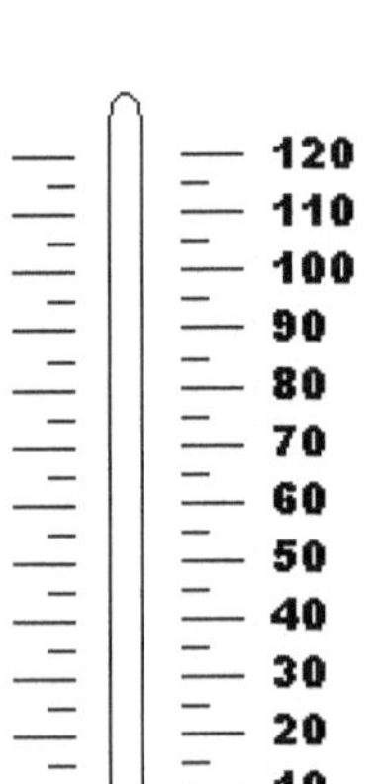

6. 60 °C

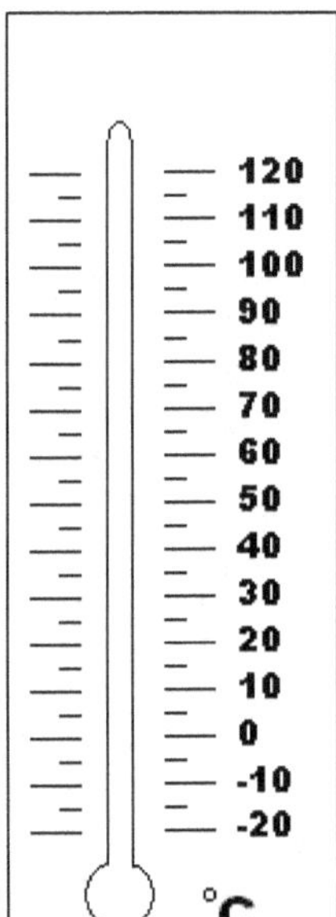

7. 95 °C

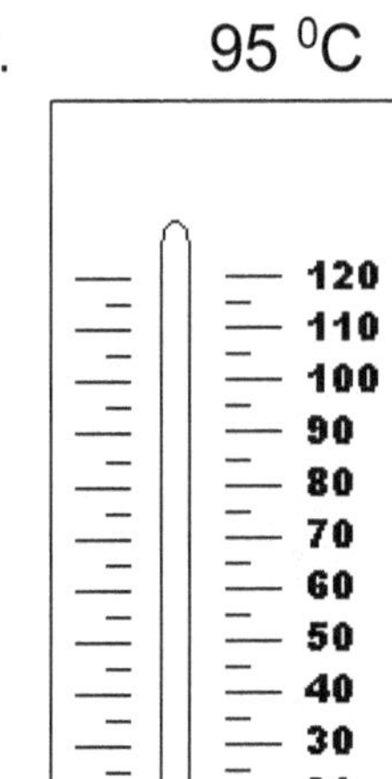

8. 100 °C

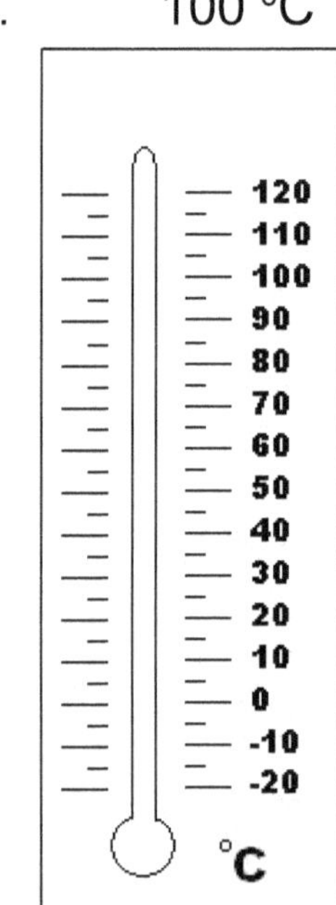

Student's name: ____________________ Assignment date: ________________

The following thermometers show the temperatures of midnight in four different cities: Vancouver, Winnipeg, Chicago, and San Carlos.

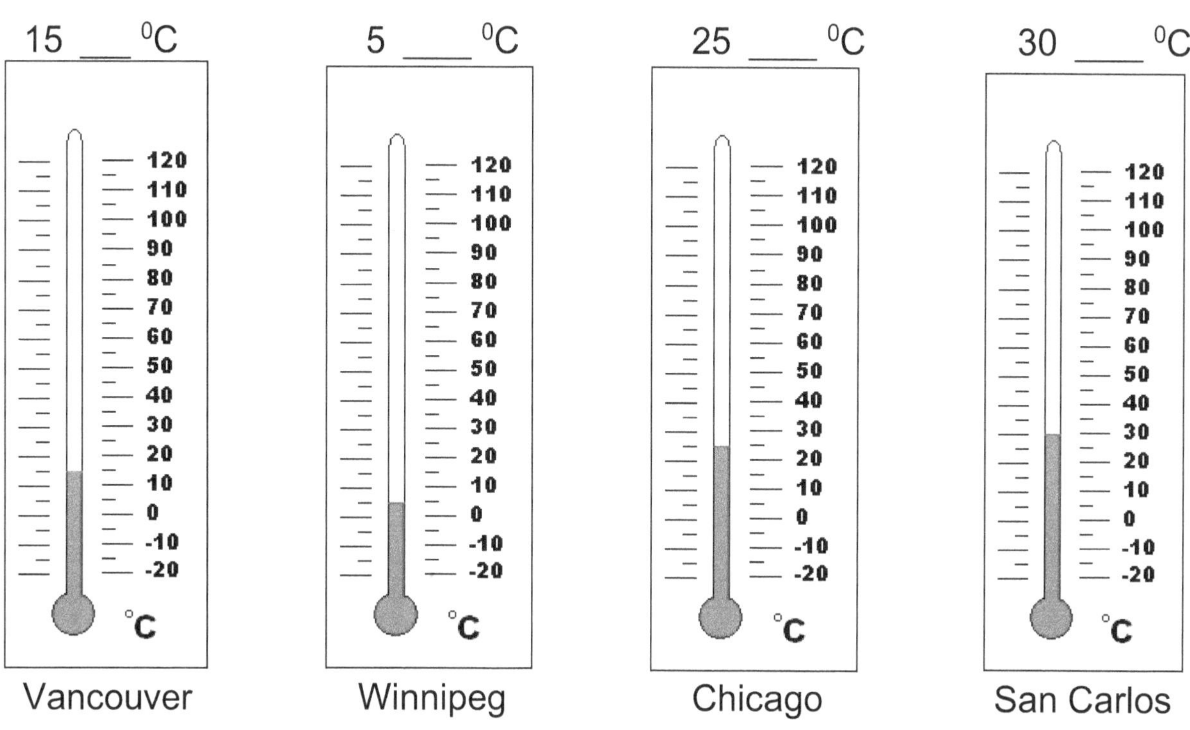

1. What is the temperature of Vancouver? 15 ^{0}C
2. What is the temperature of Chicago? 25 ^{0}C
3. What is the highest temperature? Which city? 30 ^{0}C San Carlos
4. What is the lowest temperature? Which city? 5 ^{0}C Winnipeg
5. How many ^{0}C higher is the temperature of San Carlos than Winnipeg?
   25 ^{0}C
6. How many ^{0}C lower is the temperature of Vancouver than Chicago?
   10 ^{0}C

Student's name: ____________________ Assignment date: ________________

Cold or hot? Then estimate the temperature.

a. hot√ b. cold

Temperature: ____________ 100 ^{0}C

a. hot b. cold√

Temperature: ____________ 0 ^{0}C

a. hot b. cold√

Temperature: ____________ below 0 ^{0}C

a. hot√ b. cold

Temperature: ____________ 30 ^{0}C

a. hot√ b. cold

Temperature: ____________ 39 ^{0}C

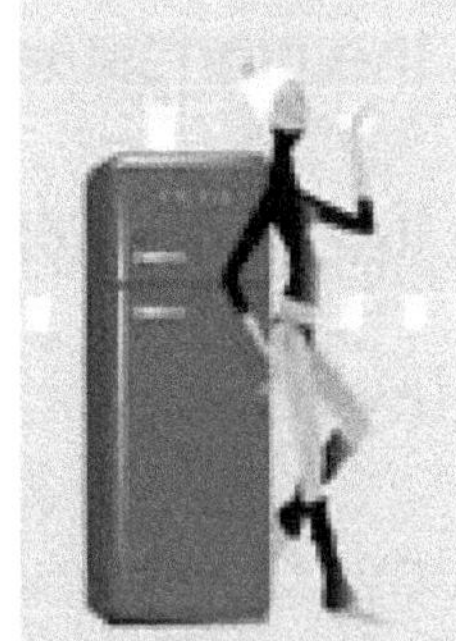

a. hot b. cold√

Temperature: ____________ 0 ^{0}C

Student's name: ____________________ Assignment date: ________________

***** Part 13 Money *****

Even though Canadian money is represented here, its math knowledge can be transferred into any country's money system. Only dollar sign ($) or cent sign (¢) are used in presenting money amount.

	Money cent notation	Money dollar notation
One hundred cents	100¢	$1.00 10 cents (dimes) $1.00 dollar cents (pennies) A dime is a tenth of a dollar. A penny is a hundredth of a dollar or a tenth of a dime, A dollar is 10 dimes or a 100 dents. A dime is 10 cent.

Student's name: ____________________ Assignment date: ________________

Write each amount in two ways (dollars and cents).

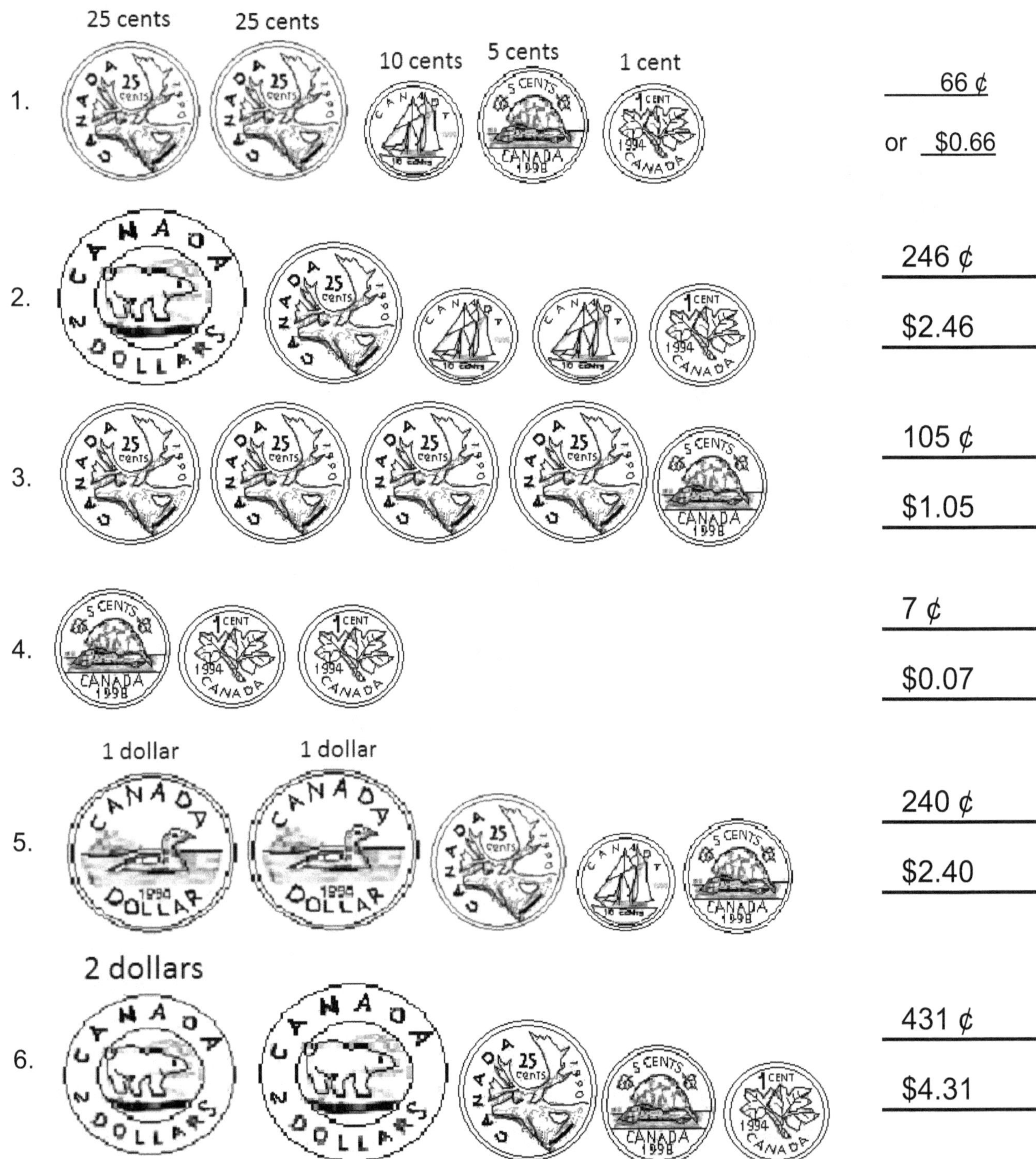

1. 66 ¢ or $0.66

2. 246 ¢ $2.46

3. 105 ¢ $1.05

4. 7 ¢ $0.07

5. 240 ¢ $2.40

6. 431 ¢ $4.31

Ho Math Chess Primary Grades Math

Test Review assesssment 何数棋謎低年级数学测试複習考核

Student's name: ____________________ Assignment date: ________________

Write each amount in two ways.

7.  111 ¢ / $1.11

8.  500 ¢ / $5.00

9. 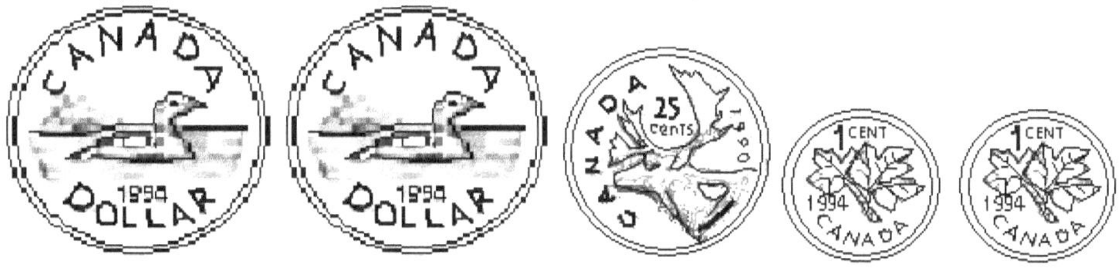 227 ¢ / $2.27

10.  336 ¢ / $3.36

11. 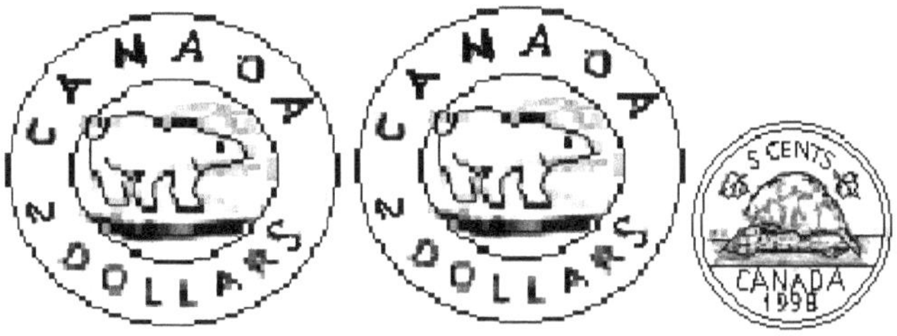 405 ¢ / $4.05

12.  15 ¢ / $0.15

Student's name: ____________________ Assignment date: ________________

Fill in the missing number.

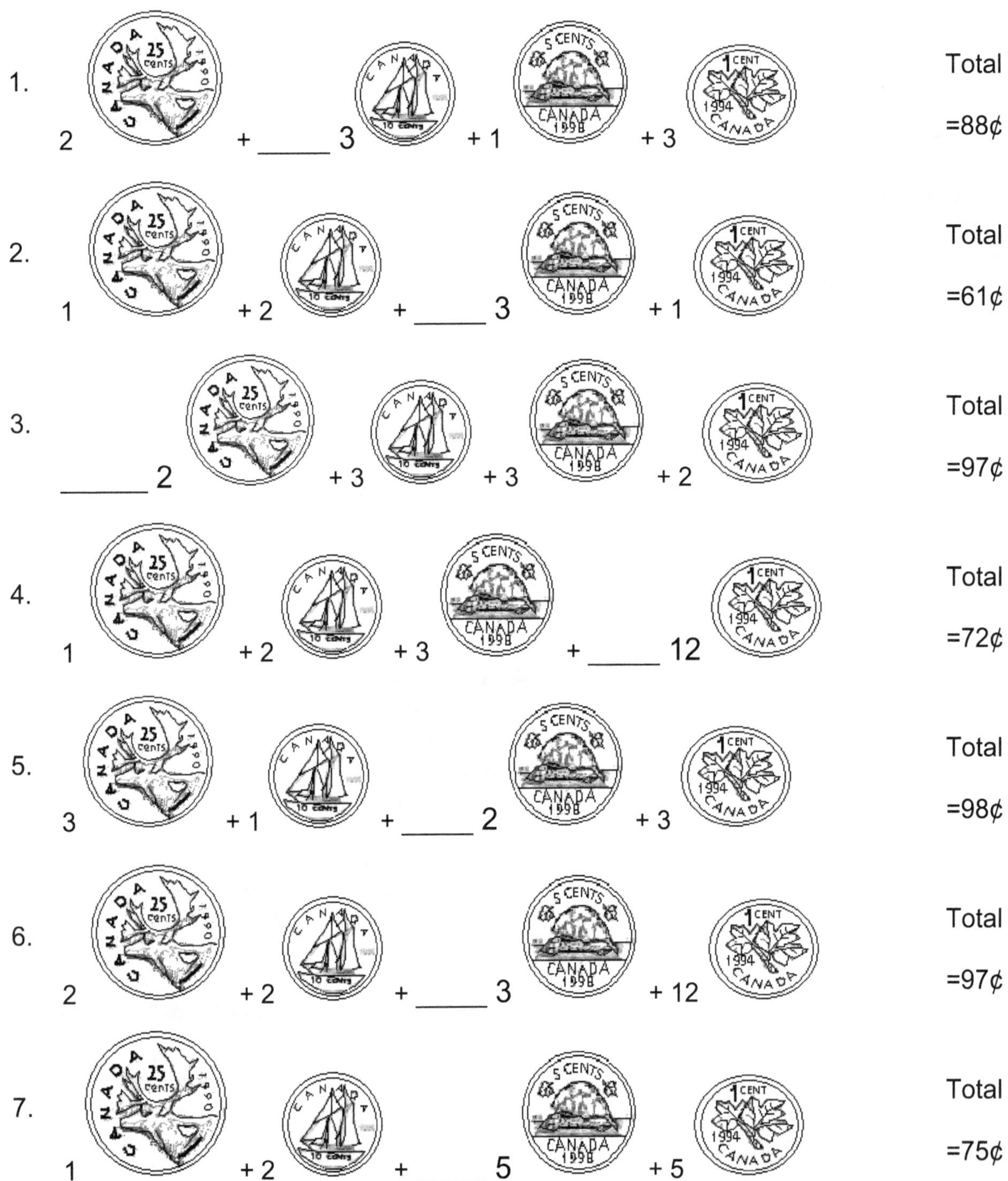

Ho Math Chess Primary Grades Math

Test Review assesssment 何数棋谜低年级数学测试複習考核

Student's name: ____________________ Assignment date: ________________

Fill in the missing number.

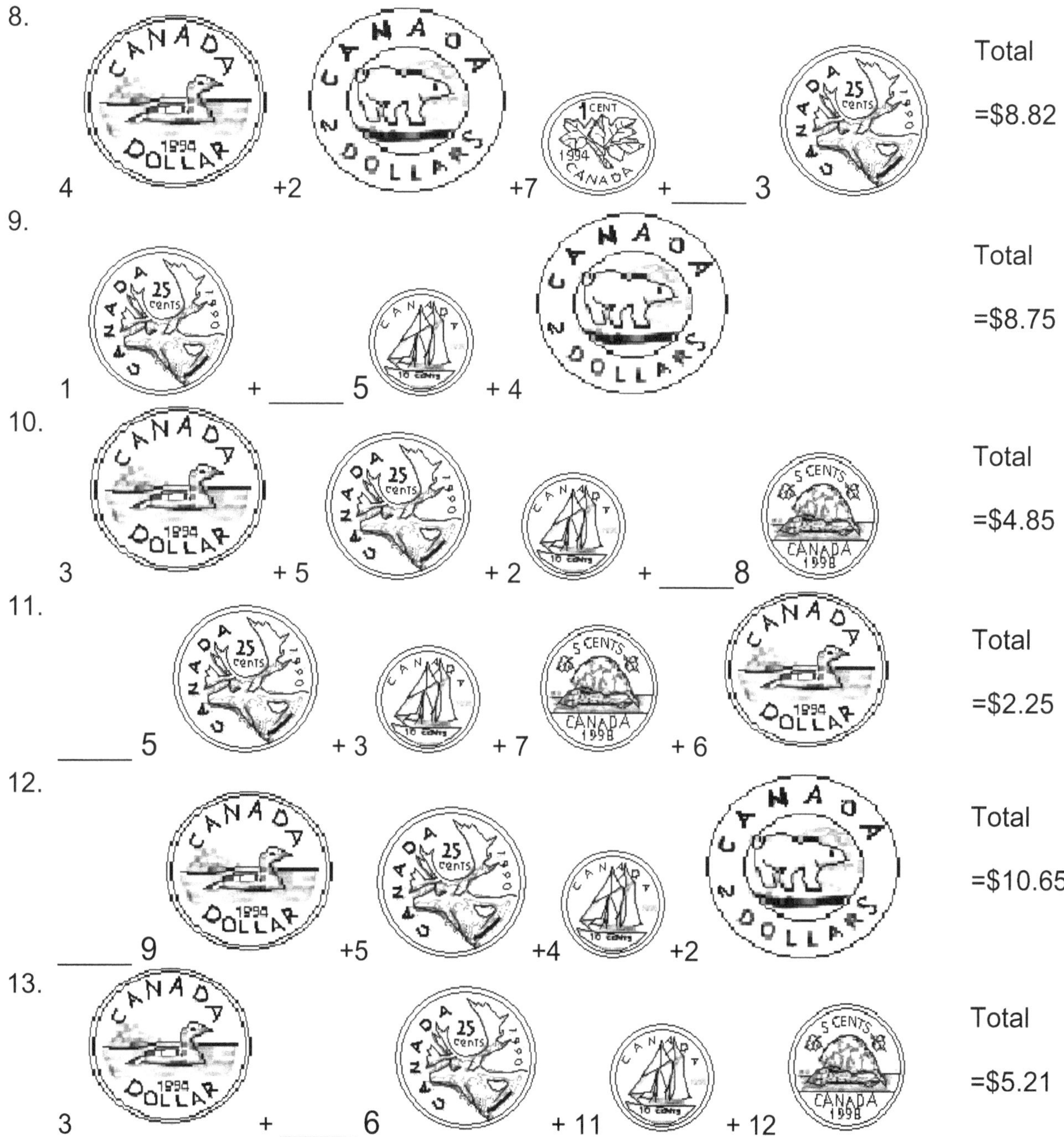

Student's name: ____________________ Assignment date: ________________

Fill in the missing number.

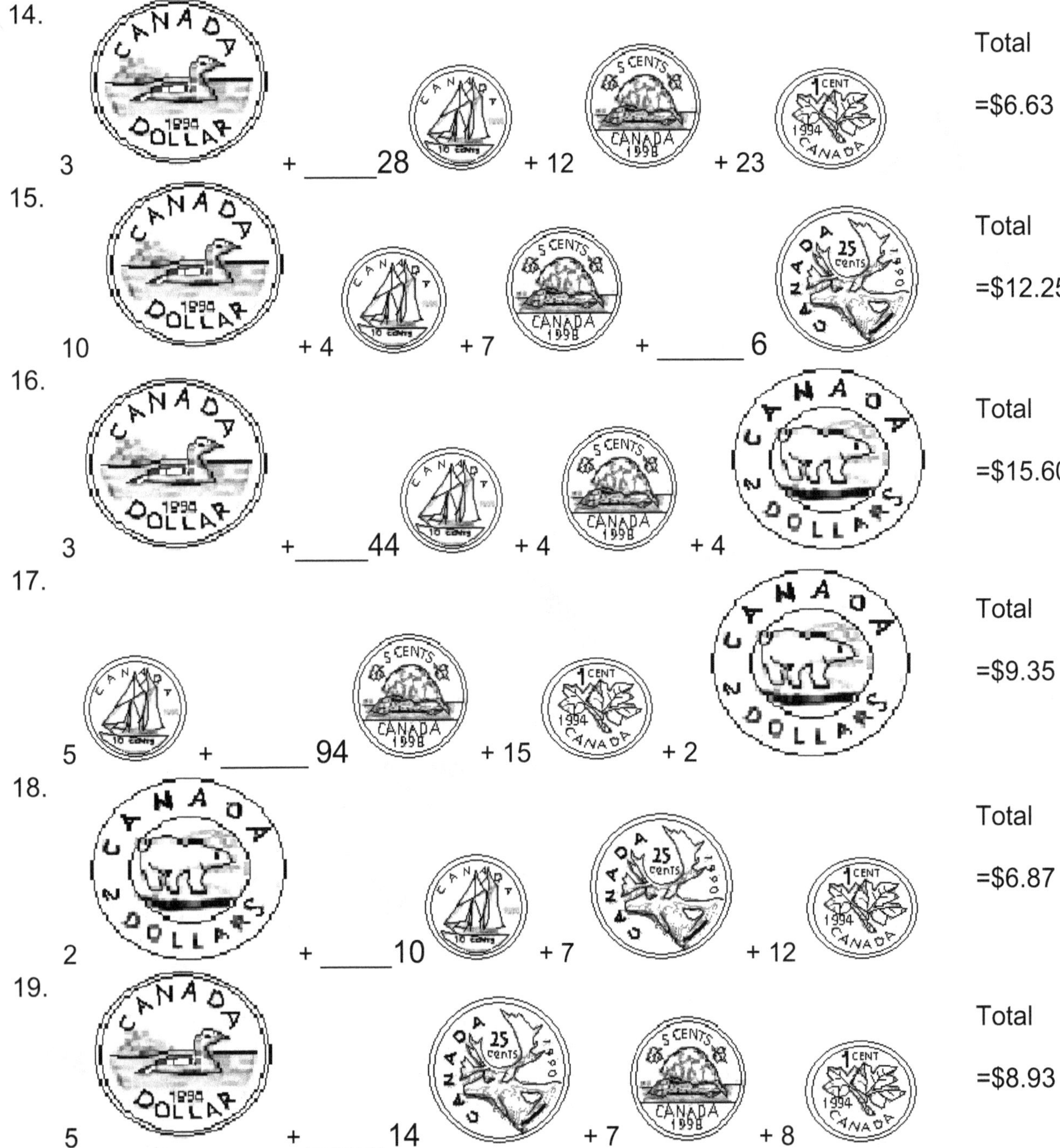

Student's name: ____________________ Assignment date: ________________

Write each amount in decimal form.

1. 2 quarters, 3 dimes, 4 nickels, 5 pennies $1.05	2. 4 quarters, 1 nickel, 2 dimes, 3 pennies $1.28
3. 1 quarter, 6 dimes, 2 nickels, 7 pennies $1.02	4. 3 quarters, 8 dimes, 12 pennies $1.67
5. 2 quarters, 7 nickels, 9 pennies $0.94	6. 6 quarters, 2 nickels, 1 dime, 22 pennies $1.92
7. 2 loonies, 1 quarter, 4 nickels, 4 pennies $2.49	8. 1 toonie, 3 loonies, 5 nickels, 6 dimes $5.85
9. 3 toonies, 5 quarters, 6 nickels, 8 pennies $7.63	10. 5 loonies, 2 quarters, 6 dimes, 1 nickel $6.15
11. 1 10-dollar bill, 3 toonies, 2 loonies, 1 quarter, 4 nickels, 3 dimes, 12 pennies $18.87	12. 3 5-dollar bills, 2 toonies, 3 loonies, 5 quarters, 2 nickels, 8 pennies $23.43
13. 2 10-dollar bills, 3 5-dollar bills, 4 toonies, 6 loonies, 2 quarters, 5 dimes, 8 pennies $50.08	14. 2 20-dollar bills, 5 5-dollar bills, 3 toonies, 7 quarters, 9 dimes, 31 pennies $73.96
15. 2 20-dollar bills, 3 10-dollar bills, 4 loonies, 8 nickels, 3 dimes, 24 pennies $74.94	16. 3 10-dollar bills, 6 toonies, 3 loonies, 7 quarters, 5 nickels, 5 pennies $47.05

Student's name: ____________________ Assignment date: ________________

Use the fewest number of coins to make each amount.

1. 62 ¢
2 pennies, 1 dimes, 0 nickels, 2 quarters

2. 36 ¢
1 pennies, 1 dimes, 0 nickels, 1 quarters

3. 48 ¢
3 pennies, 2 dimes, 0 nickels, 1 quarters

4. 74 ¢
4 pennies, 2 dimes, 0 nickels, 2 quarters

5. 91 ¢
1 pennies, 1 dimes, 1 nickels, 3 quarters

6. 56 ¢
1 pennies, 0 dimes, 1 nickels, 2 quarters

7. 87 ¢
2 pennies, 1 dimes, 0 nickels, 3 quarters

8. 19 ¢
4 pennies, 1 dimes, 1 nickels, 0 quarters

9. $ 1.45
0 pennies, 2 dimes, 0 nickels, 1 quarters, 1 loonies, 0 toonies

10. $ 5.39
4 pennies, 1 dimes, 0 nickels, 1 quarters, 1 loonies, 2 toonies

11. $ 6.72
2 pennies, 2 dimes, 0 nickels, 2 quarters, 0 loonies, 3 toonies

12. $ 3.56
1 pennies, 0 dimes, 1 nickels, 2 quarters, 1 loonies, 1 toonies

Ho Math Chess Primary Grades Math

Test Review assesssment 何数棋謎低年级数学测试複習考核

Student's name: ____________________ Assignment date: ________________

Use exactly the number of coins to make each amount.(Answer may Vary.)

1. 47 ¢ with 5 coins

2 pennies	2 dimes
0 nickels	1 quarters

2. 53 ¢ with 5 coins

3 pennies	0 dimes
0 nickels	2 quarters

3. 36 ¢ with 4 coins

1 pennies	0 dimes
2 nickels	1 quarters

4. 51 ¢ with 7 coins

1 pennies	4 dimes
2 nickels	0 quarters

5. 53 ¢ with 8 coins

3 pennies	5 dimes
0 nickels	0 quarters

6. 58 ¢ with 9 coins

3 pennies	5 dimes
1 nickels	0 quarters

7. 86 ¢ with 14 coins

6 pennies	8 dimes
0 nickels	0 quarters

8. 71 ¢ with 11 coins

1 pennies	4 dimes
6 nickels	0 quarters

9. $ 1.25 with 10 coins

1 pennies	7 dimes
0 nickels	2 quarters
0 loonies	0 toonies

10. $ 2.08 with 6 coins

3 pennies	0 dimes
1 nickels	0 quarters
2 loonies	0 toonies

11. $ 3.21 with 10 coins

1 pennies	0 dimes
4 nickels	4 quarters
0 loonies	1 toonies

12. $ 5.81 with 10 coins

1 pennies	0 dimes
1 nickels	3 quarters
5 loonies	0 toonies

Student's name: ____________________ Assignment date: ________________

Use two ways to present each amount. (Use 'P' present penny, 'N' present nickel, 'D' present dime, 'Q' present quarter and 'T' present total.)

1. 30 ¢ with 6 coins

6 N

or 1 Q + 5 P

2. 40 ¢ with 4 coins

4 D

or 1 Q + 3 N

3. 45 ¢ with 9 coins

9 N

or 4 D + 5 P

4. 55 ¢ with 7 coins

2 Q + 5 P

or 3 N + 4 D

or 1Q+6N

5. 80 ¢ with 8 coins

8 D

or 3 N + 1 Q + 4 D

or 5P+3Q

or 2Q+6N

6. 85 ¢ with 13 coins

9 N + 4 D

or 12 N + 1 Q

or 5P+8D

or 3Q+10P

Student's name: ____________________ Assignment date: ________________

How many ways can you make each amount? ('P' present penny, 'N' present nickel, 'D' present dime, 'Q' present quarter and 'T' present total)

1. 57 ¢ with 9 coins

	P	N	D	Q	T
1.	7	0	0	2	
2.	2	3	4	0	
3.	2	6	0	1	
4.					
5.					
6.					
7.					

3
____________ ways

2. 85 ¢ with 12 coins

	P	N	D	Q	T
1.	0	10	1	1	
2.	5	2	6	0	
3.	5	5	2	1	
4.					
5.					
6.					
7.					

3
____________ ways

3. 73 ¢ with 15 coins

	P	N	D	Q	T
1.	3	10	2	0	
2.	8	1	6	0	
3.	8	4	2	1	
4.					
5.					
6.					
7.					
8.					
9.					

3
____________ ways

4. $ 1.00 with 18 coins

	P	N	D	Q	T
1.	0	16	2	0	
2.	5	10	2	1	
3.	10	4	2	2	
4.	5	7	6	0	
5.	10	1	6	1	
6.					
7.					
8.					
9.					

5
____________ ways

Student's name: ____________________ Assignment date: ________________

Money calculation by making changes

A good way of learning decimal calculations.

	Purchase	paid	Change
1.	$3.12	5	$1.88
2.	$0.89	CANADA 2 DOLLARS	$1.11
3.	$4.58	10	$5.42
4.	$6.12	10	$3.88
5.	$15.68	20	$4.32
6.	$12.45	20	$7.55
7.	$0.69	CANADA 2 DOLLARS	$0.31
8.	$12.68	20	$7.32

Student's name: ____________________ Assignment date: ________________

Money calculation by making changes

	Purchase	paid	Change
9.	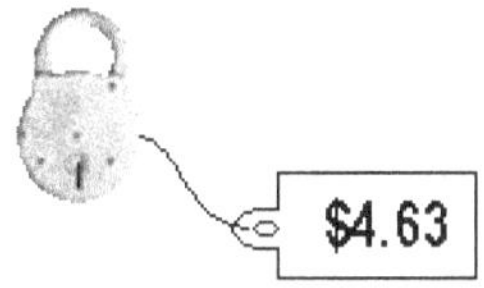 $4.63	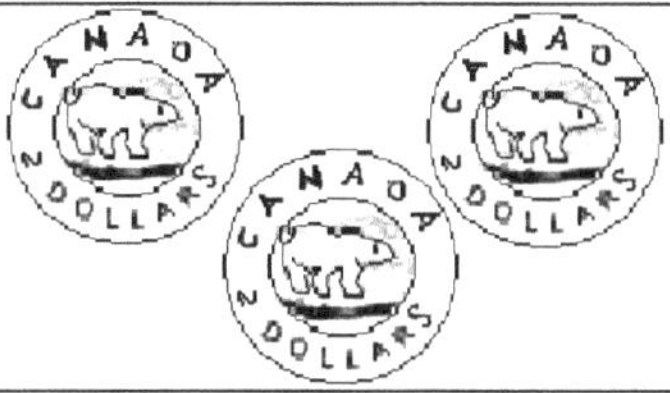	$1.37
10.	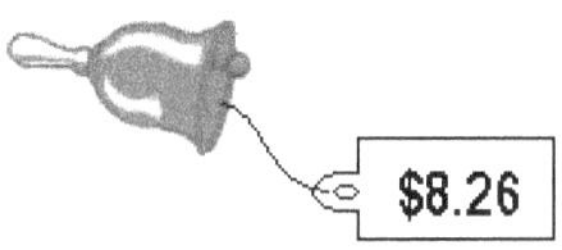 $8.26		$1.74
11.	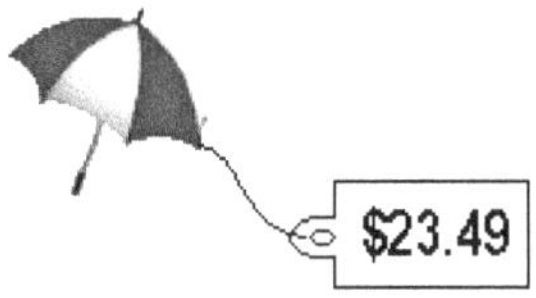 $23.49		$6.51
12.	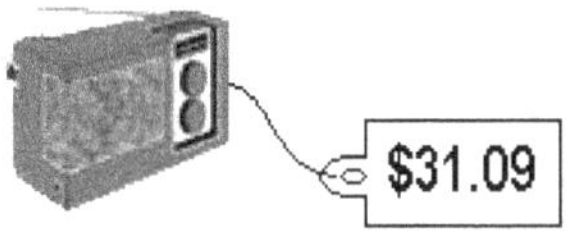 $31.09		$0.91
13.	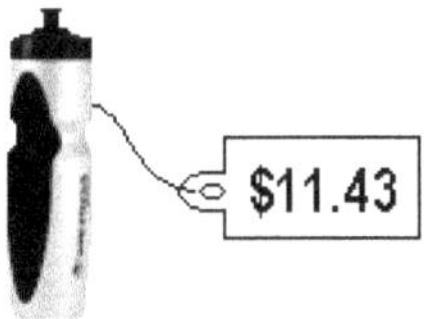 $11.43		$13.57
14.	 $46.18		$13.82
15.	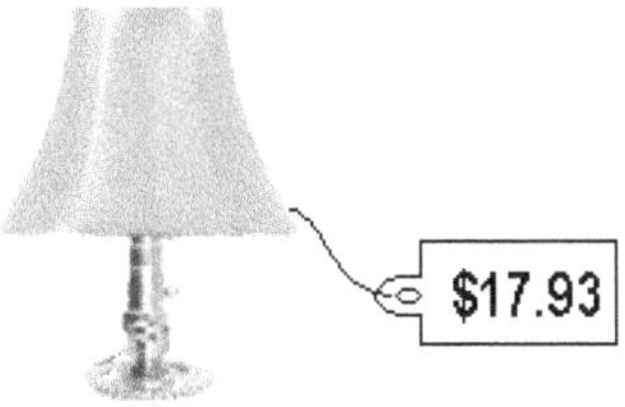 $17.93		$1.07

Student's name: ____________________ Assignment date: ________________

Money word problems

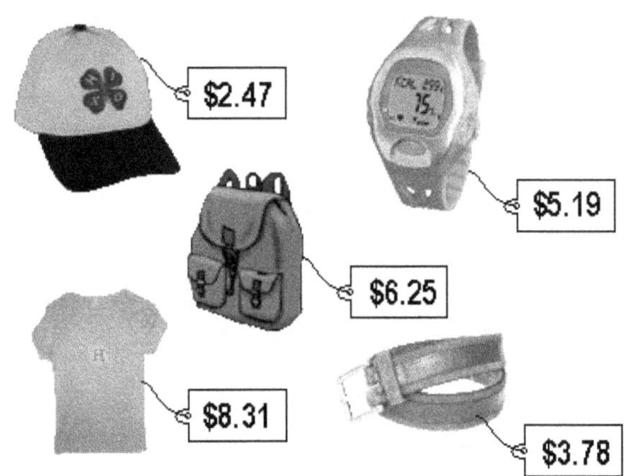

1. Linda bought a T-shirt and paid $10. How much change would she get?

   $1.69

2. Grace gave the clerk $6.25 for two items. Which two items did she buy?

   Cap and belt

3. Tom bought a bag and a watch. How much did the two items cost him?

   $11.44
   If he gave the clerk $15. How much change should he get?
   $3.56

4. Steve bought 2 T-shirt and a bag. He had $20 with him. Is it enough? How much should he borrow to make the deal?

   No. $2.87

5. Isabel bought 3 items with $12. Which 3 items did she buy? How much change did she get?

   Cap Belt and watch $0.56

Student's name: ____________________ Assignment date: ________________

Money word problems

1. James bought a notebook for $1.75 and a pen for $2.46. How much did he spend?

   $4.21

2. Lollipop is $2.58 per pound. Chocolate bar is $7.84 per pound. Frank bought 5 pounds of lollipop and 2 pounds of chocolate bar. How much did it cost him?

   $28.58

3. Kevin has some coins in his purse: 3 toonies, 4 loonies, 7 quarters, 3 dimes, 5 nickels, and 15 pennies. How much does he have?

   $12.45

4. Three friends went for shopping for picnic. They bought 3 loaves of bread for $1.27 each, 5 bottles of juice for $2.35 each, 2 pounds of sausage for &7.46 per pound. How much should each person pay?

   $10.16

5. Aaron bought four goldfish for $0.28 each and a bag of fish food for $1.63. He gave the clerk $5. How much change did he get?

   $2.25

Student's name: ____________________ Assignment date: ________________

Rounding to the nearest dollar

Example: Is $3.42 is closer to $3 or $4?

$3 $3.42 $4

$0.42 $0.58

The difference between $3 and $3.42 is: $3.42 - $3 = $0.42
The difference between $4 and $3.42 is: $4 - $3.42 = $0.58
And we know that 0.58 > 0.42. So when $3.42 is rounded to nearest dollar, the answer is $3.

1. $ 4.78 $5
2. $ 0.63 $1
3. $ 23.52 $24
4. $ 8.41 $8
5. $ 7.89 $8
6. $ 5.09 $5
7. $ 27.91 $28
8. $ 81.32 $81
9. $ 48.19 $48
10. $ 31.87 $32
11. $ 157.37 $157
12. $ 642.61 $623

Round to the nearest ten dollar or tens place.

1. $ 36.72 $40
2. $ 81.32 $80
3. $ 68.07 $70
4. $ 55.67 $60
5. $ 43.98 $40
6. $ 37.21 $40
7. $ 582.71 $580
8. $ 695.86 $700
9. $ 472.96 $470
10. $ 892.65 $890
11. $ 531.53 $530
12. $ 637.09 $640

Student's name: ____________________ Assignment date: ________________

Rounding to the nearest dime

Example: Is $3.42 is closer to $3.4 or $3.5?

$3 — $3.42 — $4

$0.42 | $0.58

The difference between $3.4 and $3.42 is: $0.42 $3.42 - $3.4 = $0.02
The difference between $3.5 and $3.42 is: $3.5 - $3.42 = $0.08
We know that 0.08 > 0.02, so when $3.42 is rounded to nearest dime, the answer is $3.4

13. $ 4.78 $5.0 ____________ 14. $ 0.63 $0.6 ____________

15. $ 23.52 $23.5 ____________ 16. $ 8.41 $8.4 ____________

17. $ 7.89 $8.0 ____________ 18. $ 5.09 $5.1 ____________

19. $ 27.91 $27.9 ____________ 20. $ 81.32 $81.3 ____________

21. $ 48.19 $48.2 ____________ 22. $ 31.87 $31.9 ____________

23. $ 157.37 $157.4 ____________ 24. $ 642.61 $642.6 ____________

Circle the amount where the cent is more than 50 cents.

13. $ 36.72 = 14. $ 81.32

15. $ 68.07 16. $ 55.67 =

17. $ 43.98 = 18. $ 37.21

19. $ 582.71 = 20. $ 695.86 =

21. $ 472.96 = 22. $ 892.65 =

23. $ 531.53 = 24. $ 637.09 =

Student's name: ____________________ Assignment date: ________________

***** Part 14 Estimating *****

Estimating the sums or differences.

Example:

$$\begin{array}{r} \$2.37 \\ +\ \$3.82 \\ \hline \end{array} \rightarrow \begin{array}{r} \$2.00 \\ \$4.00 \\ \hline \text{about } \$6.00 \end{array}$$

$$\begin{array}{r} \$6.67 \\ -\ \$2.71 \\ \hline \end{array} \rightarrow \begin{array}{r} \$7.00 \\ -\ \$3.00 \\ \hline \text{about } \$4.00 \end{array}$$

$ 2.74 + $ 5.08 + $ 12.57

= $ 3 + $ 5 + $ 13

= $21

$ 15.63 - $ 6.98

= $ 16 - $ 7

= $ 9

1.

$$\begin{array}{r} \$7.46 \\ +\ \$4.73 \\ \hline \end{array} \rightarrow \begin{array}{r} 7 \\ +\ 5 \\ \hline 12 \end{array}$$

2.

$$\begin{array}{r} \$9.86 \\ -\ \$5.47 \\ \hline \end{array} \rightarrow \begin{array}{r} 10 \\ -\ 5 \\ \hline 5 \end{array}$$

3.

$$\begin{array}{r} \$32.65 \\ +\ \$67.28 \\ \hline \end{array} \rightarrow \begin{array}{r} 30 \\ +\ 70 \\ \hline 100 \end{array}$$

4.

$$\begin{array}{r} \$72.58 \\ -\ \$18.36 \\ \hline \end{array} \rightarrow \begin{array}{r} 70 \\ -\ 20 \\ \hline 50 \end{array}$$

5. $ 4.75 + $ 3.17 + $ 8.69

=

=17

6. $ 6.85 + $ 0.26 + $ 7.94

=

=15

7. $ 17.95 - $ 3.62

=

=21

8. $ 25.73 - $ 12.39

=

=14

Student's name: ____________________ Assignment date: ________________

Estimating the products.
Example:

$$\begin{array}{r} \$2.83 \\ \times\quad 6 \\ \hline . \end{array} \quad \text{about} \quad \begin{array}{r} \$3.00 \\ \times\quad 6 \\ \hline \$18.00 \end{array}$$

$ 18.93 × 52
= $20 × 50
= $ 1000

1. $\begin{array}{r} \$5.08 \\ \times\quad 9 \\ \hline \end{array} \rightarrow \begin{array}{r} 5 \\ \times\ 9 \\ \hline 45 \end{array}$

2. $\begin{array}{r} \$8.73 \\ \times\quad 4 \\ \hline \end{array} \rightarrow \begin{array}{r} 9 \\ \times\ 4 \\ \hline 36 \end{array}$

3. $\begin{array}{r} \$12.66 \\ \times\quad 7 \\ \hline \end{array} \rightarrow \begin{array}{r} 10 \\ \times\ 7 \\ \hline 70 \end{array}$

4. $\begin{array}{r} \$47.23 \\ \times\quad 8 \\ \hline \end{array} \rightarrow \begin{array}{r} 50 \\ \times\ 8 \\ \hline 400 \end{array}$

5. $ 5.14 × 12
=
= 60

6. $ 6.71 × 8
=
= 56

7. $ 15.31 × 5
=
= 75

8. $ 19.57 × 13
=
= 260

9. $ 21.47 × 32
=
= 600

10. $ 68.04 × 79
=
= 5600

Student's name: ____________________ Assignment date: ________________

Estimating the quotients.
Example:

$6\overline{)\$23.27}$ *use compatible number* $6\overline{)\$24.00}$ with quotient \$4.00; 24, 0

\$ 46.73 ÷ 7

= \$ 49.00 ÷ 7 (round dividend with compatible number)

= \$ 7

1. $5\overline{)\$62.73}$ → 12

2. $4\overline{)\$33.59}$ →8

3. $8\overline{)\$67.23}$ →8

4. $7\overline{)\$81.36}$ →12

5. \$ 53.87 ÷ 6

=

= 9

6. \$ 70.62 ÷ 9

=

= 8

7. \$ 43.09 ÷ 5

=

= 9

8. \$ 68.47 ÷ 6

=

= 11

9. \$ 39.72 ÷ 4

=

= 10

10. \$ 61.78 ÷ 7

=

= 9

Student's name: ____________________ Assignment date: ________________

***** Part 15 Rounding whole numbers *****

Example:

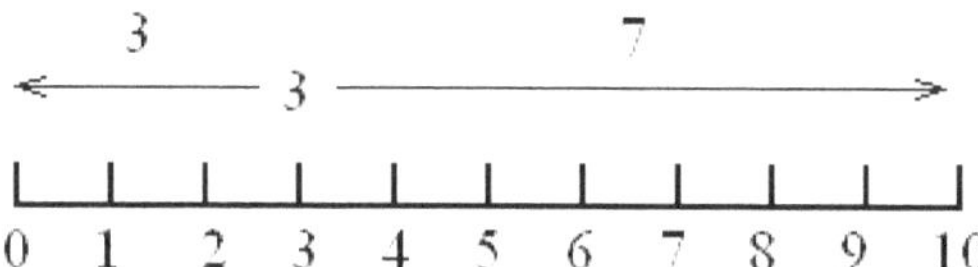

From 3 to 0 is 3, from 3 to 10 is 7, so 3 is closer to 0.

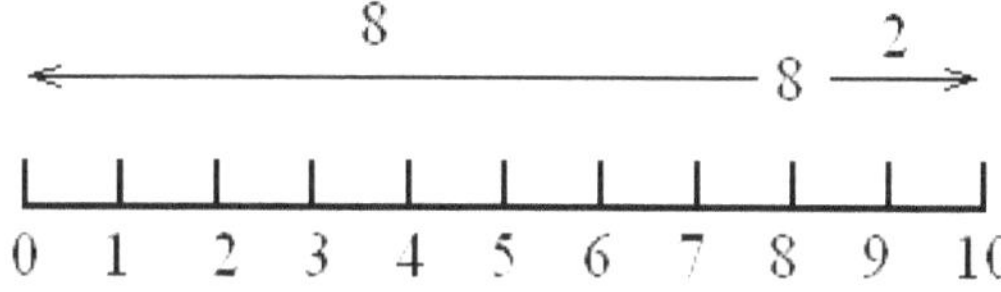

From 8 to 0 is 8, from 8 to 10 is 2, so 8 is closer to 10.

The number 1, 2, 3, 4 are rounded down to 0.
The umber 5, 6, 7, 8, 9 are rounded up to 10.

Rounding the following numbers to either 0 or 10

1.	2 $\xrightarrow{rounded}$ 0	2.	8 $\xrightarrow{rounded}$ 10
3.	4 $\xrightarrow{rounded}$ 0	4.	3 $\xrightarrow{rounded}$ 0
5.	9 $\xrightarrow{rounded}$ 10	6.	7 $\xrightarrow{rounded}$ 10
7.	6 $\xrightarrow{rounded}$ 10	8.	5 $\xrightarrow{rounded}$ 10

Rounding the following numbers to the nearest ten

We look at the tens place digit, if it is less than five, then round it up; otherwise, rounded it down.

5<u>4</u> is rounded down to 50; 6<u>7</u> is rounded up to 70.

1.	32 $\xrightarrow{rounded}$ 30	2.	47 $\xrightarrow{rounded}$ 50
3.	38 $\xrightarrow{rounded}$ 40	4.	24 $\xrightarrow{rounded}$ 20
5.	19 $\xrightarrow{rounded}$ 20	6.	76 $\xrightarrow{rounded}$ 80
7.	52 $\xrightarrow{rounded}$ 50	8.	65 $\xrightarrow{rounded}$ 70

Student's name: ____________________ Assignment date: ______________

Rounding the following numbers to the nearest hundred

We look at the hundreds place digit, if it is less than five, then round it up; otherwise, rounded it down.

6<u>8</u>3 is rounded down to 700; 2<u>3</u>9 is rounded up to 200.

1. 256 $\xrightarrow{\text{rounded}}$ 300
2. 218 $\xrightarrow{\text{rounded}}$ 200
3. 363 $\xrightarrow{\text{rounded}}$ 400
4. 649 $\xrightarrow{\text{rounded}}$ 600
5. 409 $\xrightarrow{\text{rounded}}$ 400
6. 832 $\xrightarrow{\text{rounded}}$ 800
7. 271 $\xrightarrow{\text{rounded}}$ 300
8. 551 $\xrightarrow{\text{rounded}}$ 600
9. 759 $\xrightarrow{\text{rounded}}$ 800
10. 725 $\xrightarrow{\text{rounded}}$ 700
11. 647 $\xrightarrow{\text{rounded}}$ 600
12. 527 $\xrightarrow{\text{rounded}}$ 500

Rounding the following numbers to the nearest thousand

We look at the thousands place digit, if it is less than five, then round it up; otherwise, rounded it down.

2<u>4</u>64 is rounded down to 2000; 6<u>8</u>37 is rounded up to 7000.

1. 4680 $\xrightarrow{\text{rounded}}$ 5000
2. 1843 $\xrightarrow{\text{rounded}}$ 2000
3. 3279 $\xrightarrow{\text{rounded}}$ 3000
4. 8419 $\xrightarrow{\text{rounded}}$ 8000
5. 1862 $\xrightarrow{\text{rounded}}$ 2000
6. 6708 $\xrightarrow{\text{rounded}}$ 7000
7. 7498 $\xrightarrow{\text{rounded}}$ 7000
8. 5275 $\xrightarrow{\text{rounded}}$ 5000
9. 2673 $\xrightarrow{\text{rounded}}$ 3000
10. 2751 $\xrightarrow{\text{rounded}}$ 3000
11. 4501 $\xrightarrow{\text{rounded}}$ 5000
12. 9999 $\xrightarrow{\text{rounded}}$ 10000

Student's name: ____________________ Assignment date: ________________

Filling the following blank

2 9 6
1. 296 is composed of _____ hundreds, _____ tens and _____ ones.

6 9 8
2. 698 is composed of _____ hundreds, _____ tens and _____ ones.

5 1 3
3. 513 is composed of _____ hundreds, _____ tens and _____ ones.

2 0 3
4. 203 is composed of _____ hundreds, _____ tens and _____ ones.

7 1 6
5. 716 is composed of _____ hundreds, _____ tens and _____ ones.

1 2 3 8
6. 1238 is composed of ___ thousands, ___ hundreds, ___ tens and ___ ones.

4 3 6 8
7. 4368 is composed of ___ thousands, ___ hundreds, ___ tens and ___ ones.

9 8 6 1
8. 9861 is composed of ___ thousands, ___ hundreds, ___ tens and ___ ones.

1 4
9. 14 321 is composed of _____ ten thousands, _____ thousands,
3 2 1
_____ hundreds, _____ tens and _____ ones.

9 9
10. 99 999 is composed of _____ ten thousands, _____ thousands,
9 9 9
_____ hundreds, _____ tens and _____ ones.

4
11. 396 is nearly _____ hundred.

9
12. 91 is nearly _____ ten.

3
13. 3003 is nearly _____ thousand.

2
14. 1997 is nearly _____ thousand. 3

Student's name: ____________________ Assignment date: ________________

15. 301 is nearly _____ hundred.

2

16. 19 is nearly _____ ten.

4

17. 396 is nearly _____ hundred.

5

18. 531 is nearly _____ hundred.

7

19. 698 is nearly _____ hundred.

2

20. 203 is nearly _____ hundred.

7

21. 716 is nearly _____ hundred.

1 2 4

22. 1238 is nearly _____ thousand, _____ hundred, _____ ten.

4 3 7

23. 4368 is nearly _____ thousand, _____ hundred, _____ ten.

9 8 6

24. 9861 is nearly _____ thousand, _____ hundred, _____ ten.

1 4 3 2

25. 14 321 is nearly ___ ten thousands, ___ thousand, ___ hundred, ___ ten.

9 9 9 9

26. 99 989 is nearly ___ ten thousands, ___ thousand, ___ hundred, ___ ten.

2

27. 2002 is nearly _____ thousands.

3

28. 2998 is nearly _____ thousands.

9

29. 898 is nearly _____ hundreds.

5

30. 489 is nearly _____ hundreds.

6

31. 58 is nearly _____ tens.

8

32. 82 is nearly _____ tens.

Student's name: ____________________ Assignment date: ________________

Estimating Sums

351 →	400	351 is close to 400
+ 168 →	+ 200	168 is close to 200
	600	400 + 200 = 600.
		So 351 + 168 is about 600.

13
$$\begin{array}{r} 252 \\ +\ 476 \\ \hline \end{array} \rightarrow \begin{array}{r} 300 \\ +\ 500 \\ \hline 800 \end{array}$$

14.
$$\begin{array}{r} 337 \\ +\ 575 \\ \hline \end{array} \rightarrow \begin{array}{r} 300 \\ +\ 600 \\ \hline 900 \end{array}$$

15
$$\begin{array}{r} 537 \\ +\ 159 \\ \hline \end{array} \rightarrow \begin{array}{r} 500 \\ +\ 200 \\ \hline 700 \end{array}$$

16.
$$\begin{array}{r} 379 \\ +\ 582 \\ \hline \end{array} \rightarrow \begin{array}{r} 400 \\ +\ 600 \\ \hline 1000 \end{array}$$

17
$$\begin{array}{r} 373 \\ +\ 727 \\ \hline \end{array} \rightarrow \begin{array}{r} 400 \\ +\ 700 \\ \hline 1100 \end{array}$$

18.
$$\begin{array}{r} 368 \\ +\ 208 \\ \hline \end{array} \rightarrow \begin{array}{r} 400 \\ +\ 200 \\ \hline 600 \end{array}$$

19
$$\begin{array}{r} 347 \\ +\ 563 \\ \hline \end{array} \rightarrow \begin{array}{r} 300 \\ +\ 600 \\ \hline 900 \end{array}$$

20.
$$\begin{array}{r} 358 \\ +\ 537 \\ \hline \end{array} \rightarrow \begin{array}{r} 400 \\ +\ 500 \\ \hline 900 \end{array}$$

21
$$\begin{array}{r} 306 \\ +\ 247 \\ \hline \end{array} \rightarrow \begin{array}{r} 300 \\ +\ 200 \\ \hline 500 \end{array}$$

22.
$$\begin{array}{r} 369 \\ +\ 274 \\ \hline \end{array} \rightarrow \begin{array}{r} 400 \\ +\ 300 \\ \hline 700 \end{array}$$

23
$$\begin{array}{r} 281 \\ +\ 435 \\ \hline \end{array} \rightarrow \begin{array}{r} 300 \\ +\ 400 \\ \hline 700 \end{array}$$

24.
$$\begin{array}{r} 628 \\ +\ 241 \\ \hline \end{array} \rightarrow \begin{array}{r} 600 \\ +\ 200 \\ \hline 800 \end{array}$$

Ho Math Chess Primary Grades Math

Test Review assesssment 何数棋謎低年级数学测试複習考核

Student's name: ____________________ Assignment date: ________________

Estimate Sums

```
  3 5 2 →     3 5 0
+   7 9 →  +    8 0
           -------
              4 3 0
```

352 is close to 350
79 is close to 80
350 + 80 = 430.
So 352 + 79 is about 430.

```
25   4 6 9 →     4 7 0        26.  4 7 9 →     4 8 0
   +   2 6 →  +    3 0           +   4 7 →  +    5 0
              5 0 0                            5 3 0

27   3 6 1 →     3 6 0        28.  3 6 2 →     3 6 0
   +   5 7 →  +    6 0           +   3 4 →  +    3 0
              4 2 0                            3 9 0

29   6 3 7 →     6 4 0        30.  3 0 9 →     3 1 0
   +   6 8 →  +    7 0           +   3 1 →  +    3 0
              7 1 0                            3 4 0

31     8 1 →       8 0        32.    1 8 →       2 0
   + 3 5 2 →  +  3 5 0           + 3 7 6 →  +  3 8 0
              4 3 0                            4 0 0

33   3 7 2 →     3 7 0        34.  4 0 8 →     4 1 0
   +     9 →  +    1 0           +     3 →  +      0
              3 8 0                            4 1 0

35   4 8 1 →     4 8 0        36.  3 7 2 →     3 7 0
   +   1 6 →  +    2 0           +   4 4 →  +    4 0
              5 0 0                            4 1 0
```

Ho Math Chess Primary Grades Math

Test Review assesssment 何数棋谜低年级数学测试複習考核

Student's name: ____________________ Assignment date: ________________

Estimating Differences

$$\begin{array}{r} 579 \\ -\ 312 \\ \hline \end{array} \rightarrow \begin{array}{r} 600 \\ -\ 300 \\ \hline 300 \end{array} \qquad \begin{array}{r} 542 \\ -\ 75 \\ \hline \end{array} \rightarrow \begin{array}{r} 540 \\ -\ 80 \\ \hline 460 \end{array}$$

1. $$\begin{array}{r} 481 \\ -\ 226 \\ \hline \end{array} \rightarrow \begin{array}{r} 500 \\ -\ 200 \\ \hline 300 \end{array}$$

2. $$\begin{array}{r} 731 \\ -\ 472 \\ \hline \end{array} \rightarrow \begin{array}{r} 700 \\ -\ 500 \\ \hline 200 \end{array}$$

3. $$\begin{array}{r} 482 \\ -\ 369 \\ \hline \end{array} \rightarrow \begin{array}{r} 500 \\ -\ 400 \\ \hline 100 \end{array}$$

4. $$\begin{array}{r} 465 \\ -\ 273 \\ \hline \end{array} \rightarrow \begin{array}{r} 500 \\ -\ 300 \\ \hline 200 \end{array}$$

5. $$\begin{array}{r} 538 \\ -\ 407 \\ \hline \end{array} \rightarrow \begin{array}{r} 500 \\ -\ 400 \\ \hline 100 \end{array}$$

6. $$\begin{array}{r} 629 \\ -\ 124 \\ \hline \end{array} \rightarrow \begin{array}{r} 600 \\ -\ 100 \\ \hline 500 \end{array}$$

7. $$\begin{array}{r} 624 \\ -\ 64 \\ \hline \end{array} \rightarrow \begin{array}{r} 620 \\ -\ 60 \\ \hline 560 \end{array}$$

8. $$\begin{array}{r} 383 \\ -\ 58 \\ \hline \end{array} \rightarrow \begin{array}{r} 380 \\ -\ 60 \\ \hline 320 \end{array}$$

9. $$\begin{array}{r} 539 \\ -\ 27 \\ \hline \end{array} \rightarrow \begin{array}{r} 540 \\ -\ 30 \\ \hline 510 \end{array}$$

10. $$\begin{array}{r} 741 \\ -\ 73 \\ \hline \end{array} \rightarrow \begin{array}{r} 740 \\ -\ 70 \\ \hline 670 \end{array}$$

11 $$\begin{array}{r} 582 \\ -\ 105 \\ \hline \end{array} \rightarrow \begin{array}{r} 600 \\ -\ 100 \\ \hline 500 \end{array}$$

12. $$\begin{array}{r} 537 \\ -\ 362 \\ \hline \end{array} \rightarrow \begin{array}{r} 500 \\ -\ 400 \\ \hline 100 \end{array}$$

Student's name: ____________________ Assignment date: ________________

Estimating Products

$$\begin{array}{r} 325 \\ \times\ 24 \\ \hline \end{array} \rightarrow \begin{array}{r} 300 \\ \times\ 20 \\ \hline 6000 \end{array}$$

325 is close to 300
24 is close to 20
325 × 20 = 6000.
So 325 × 20 is about 6000.

1.
$$\begin{array}{r} 460 \\ \times\ 29 \\ \hline \end{array} \rightarrow \begin{array}{r} 400 \\ \times\ 30 \\ \hline 12000 \end{array}$$

2.
$$\begin{array}{r} 391 \\ \times\ 32 \\ \hline \end{array} \rightarrow \begin{array}{r} 400 \\ \times\ 30 \\ \hline 12000 \end{array}$$

3.
$$\begin{array}{r} 417 \\ \times\ 53 \\ \hline \end{array} \rightarrow \begin{array}{r} 400 \\ \times\ 50 \\ \hline 20000 \end{array}$$

4.
$$\begin{array}{r} 716 \\ \times\ 61 \\ \hline \end{array} \rightarrow \begin{array}{r} 700 \\ \times\ 60 \\ \hline 42000 \end{array}$$

5.
$$\begin{array}{r} 826 \\ \times\ 209 \\ \hline \end{array} \rightarrow \begin{array}{r} 800 \\ \times\ 200 \\ \hline 160000 \end{array}$$

6.
$$\begin{array}{r} 431 \\ \times\ 572 \\ \hline \end{array} \rightarrow \begin{array}{r} 400 \\ \times\ 600 \\ \hline 240000 \end{array}$$

7.
$$\begin{array}{r} 280 \\ \times\ 72 \\ \hline \end{array} \rightarrow \begin{array}{r} 300 \\ \times\ 70 \\ \hline 21000 \end{array}$$

8.
$$\begin{array}{r} 328 \\ \times\ 183 \\ \hline \end{array} \rightarrow \begin{array}{r} 300 \\ \times\ 200 \\ \hline 60000 \end{array}$$

9.
$$\begin{array}{r} 631 \\ \times\ 826 \\ \hline \end{array} \rightarrow \begin{array}{r} 600 \\ \times\ 800 \\ \hline 480000 \end{array}$$

10.
$$\begin{array}{r} 495 \\ \times\ 52 \\ \hline \end{array} \rightarrow \begin{array}{r} 500 \\ \times\ 50 \\ \hline 250000 \end{array}$$

11
$$\begin{array}{r} 274 \\ \times\ 33 \end{array} \rightarrow \begin{array}{r} 300 \\ \times\ 30 \\ 9000 \end{array}$$

12.
$$\begin{array}{r} 472 \\ \times\ 83 \\ \hline \end{array} \rightarrow \begin{array}{r} 500 \\ \times\ 80 \\ \hline 40000 \end{array}$$

Student's name: ____________________ Assignment date: ________________

Estimating Products

If the multiplier or multiplicand is close to 15, 25, 35 (or 150, 250, 350), etc., use the first digit times the other number, plus half of the other number times ten.

Example:

630 × 24

630 is close to 600
24 is close to 25

600 × 20 = 12000
600 ÷ 2 × 10 = 3000
12000 + 3000 = 15000

So, 630 × 24 is about 15000.

1. 483 × 15
→ 500 × 10 + 500 ÷ 2 × 10
= 5000 + 2500
= 7500

2. 692 × 16
→10500

3. 417 × 25
→8200

4. 306 × 35
→ 10500

5. 782 × 34
→28000

6. 487 × 153
→ 75000

7. 242 × 793
→160000

8. 156 × 389
→ 60000

9. 245 × 421
→ 100000

10. 784 × 257
→ 200000

11. 320 × 348
→ 105000

12. 247 × 721
→ 175000

Student's name: ____________________ Assignment date: ________________

Estimating Quotients with 1-digit divisors

Example:

3747 ÷ 6 — Round the front-end of dividend to the nearest multiple of divisor. — Round front-end 37 hundred to nearest multiple of 6. 3747 → 3600, and 3600 ÷ 6 = 600

1. 372 ÷ 5

   → 350 ÷ 5

   = 70

2. 572 ÷ 7

   → 80

3. 4726 ÷ 6

   → 800

4. 3729 ÷ 9

   → 400

5. 4371 ÷ 5

   → 900

6. 5231 ÷ 9

   → 600

7. 6217 ÷ 8

   → 800

8. 2416 ÷ 5

   → 500

9. 4642 ÷ 3

   → 1500

10. 5725 ÷ 2

    → 2800

11. 6438 ÷ 7

    → 900

12. 5373 ÷ 9

    → 600

Student's name: ____________________ Assignment date: ________________

Estimating Quotients with 2-digit divisors

Example:

6429 ÷ 28 Round the divisor first. Then round the front-end of dividend to the nearest multiple of divisor.

28 is rounded to 30. Round front-end 64 hundred to nearest multiple of 30. 6429 → 6300, and 6300 ÷ 30 = 210

1.	2351 ÷ 32 → 70	2.	4725 ÷ 73 → 70
3.	3825 ÷ 93 → 40	4.	7925 ÷ 87 → 90
5.	5330 ÷ 62 → 90	6.	6528 ÷ 78 → 80
7.	3709 ÷ 59 → 60	8.	3642 ÷ 51 → 70
9.	3178 ÷ 38 → 80	10.	5189 ÷ 42 → 130
11.	6235 ÷ 73 → 90	12.	4627 ÷ 19 → 230

Student's name: ____________________ Assignment date: ________________

Test of rounding word problems

1. I'm a 3-digit number. The sum of my digits is 10. When rounded to the nearest hundred, I am 900. When rounded to the nearest ten, I am 900 too. What number am I?

901

2. When a number is rounded to the nearest thousand, it round to 4000. All of its digits are the same. What number is it?

4444

3. Rounding a number to the nearest ten, hundred, or thousand will give the same answer 3000. The number is not 3000. What is the number?

2995

4. When a number is rounded to the nearest hundred, the number is doubled. What is the number?

50

5. To the nearest hundred, a number round to 2800. Three digits of the number are the same. What is the number?

2822

6. When a number is rounded to the nearest tens, hundreds, or thousands place, it gives the same answer 1000. When you read it forward, it sounds the same as you read it backwards. What is the number?

999

7. Austin has $1 with at least one kind of quarters, dimes, and nickels. What could be the greatest number of coins he could have?

15 coins
1 of quarter, 1 of dime, 13 of nickels

8. The sum of 89297 + 98729 = _______
The difference of 270270 – 3 = ________
The product of 270270 × 3 = __________
The quotient of 270270 ÷ 3 = ___________

Student's name: ____________________ Assignment date: ________________

9. Johnny would like to place 15 chocolates into 4 boxes. Each box can hold 4 or 3 chocolates. How many boxes will hold exactly 3 chocolates.

bbb

1 box (4, 4, 4, 3)

Student's name: ____________________ Assignment date: ________________

***** Part 16 Fractions *****

Fraction can be represented by the following two models.

Model 1 – Choosing one or more equal parts of 1 whole.

A fraction is shown by $\frac{a}{b}$. The top part is *numerator* which tells how many parts are chosen. The bottom part is called *denominator* which tells how many parts are in a whole. The *denominator* is also the fraction unit of that fraction. For example, the following fraction three-quarter example shows that there are three of one quarter (basic fraction unit) .

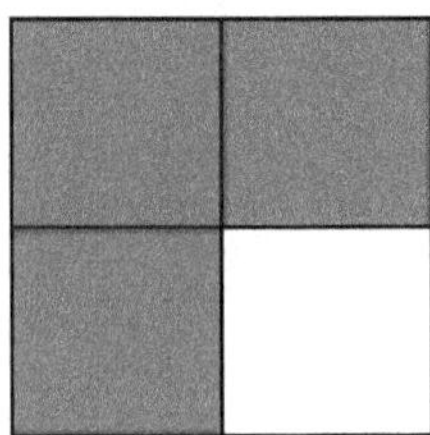

What is meaning of 2 in the following fraction?
$\frac{1}{2}$

The above digit is 2 but the real meaning is actually "half", so $\frac{3}{2}$ means there are three of half. The fraction unit concept can be used to understand fraction addition or subtraction better. For example, $\frac{2}{2} + \frac{1}{2}$ = two of half plus 1 of half = 3 of half = $\frac{3}{2}$.

Model 2 – Choosing one or more equal parts of a set.

What part is the circle figure in the following set?

The answer is $\frac{2}{7}$.

Ho Math Chess Primary Grades Math

Test Review assesssment 何数棋謎低年级数学测试複習考核

Frank Ho, Amanda Ho www.homathchess.com

Student's name: ____________________ Assignment date: ________________

Model 1 – Choosing one or more equal parts of 1 whole.
Example: Divide 1 whole into equal parts.

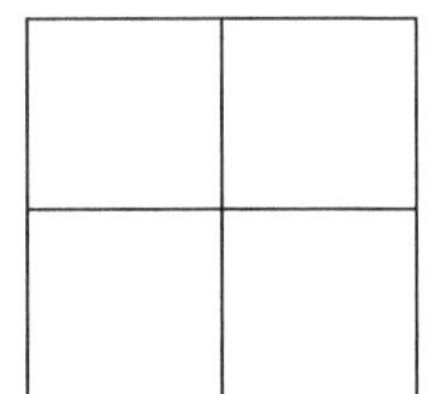

4 equal parts
4 fourth or 4 quarters

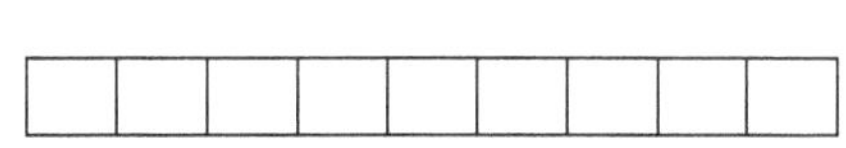

9 equal parts
Nine ninth

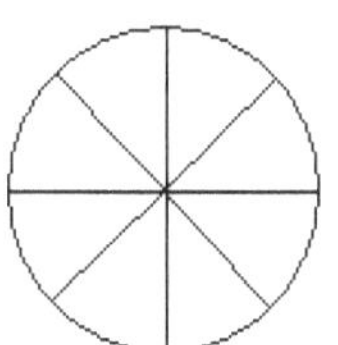

8 equal parts
10 eighth

1. Circle the following figures with equal parts.

1.
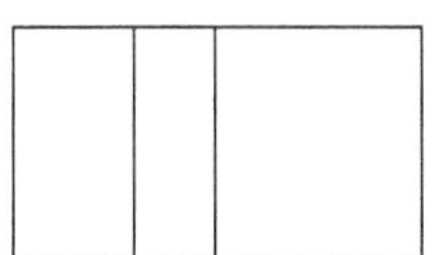

2.
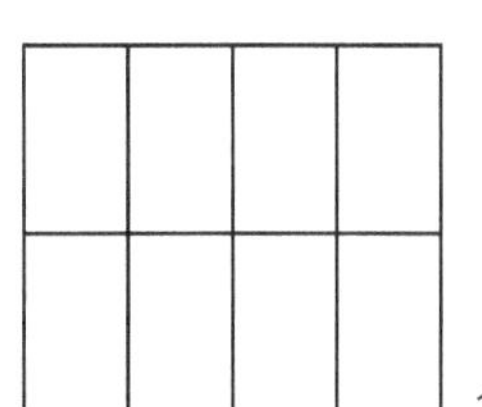
√

3.
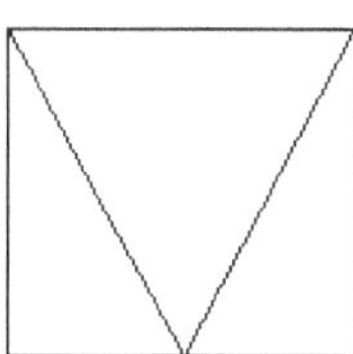

4.
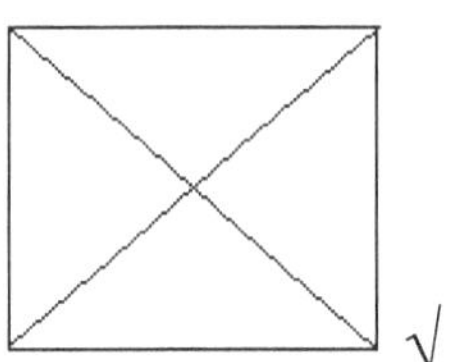
√

5.
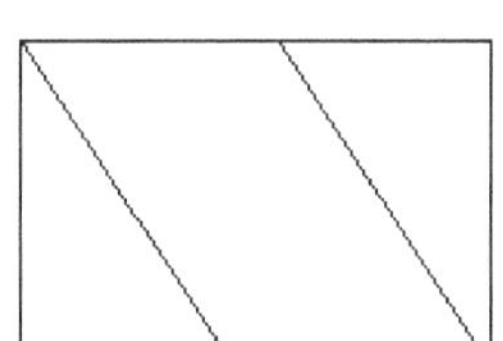

6.
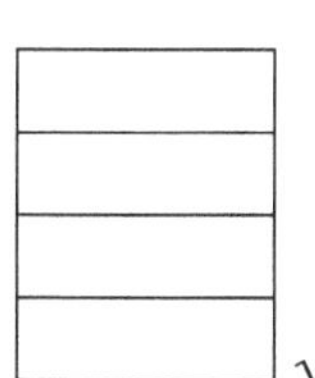
√

7.
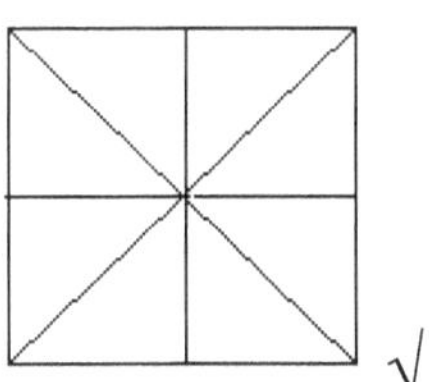
√

8.
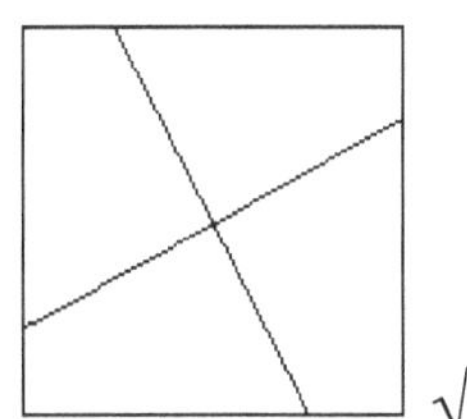
√

9.
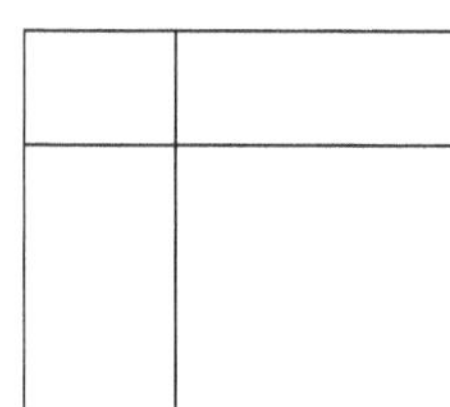

10.
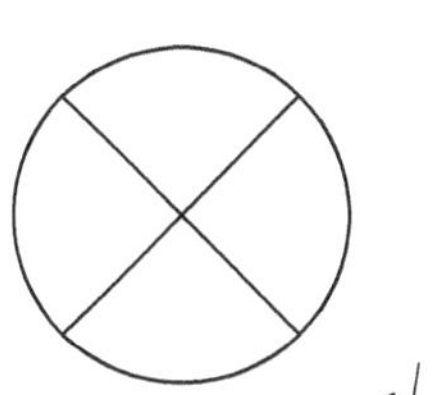
√

11
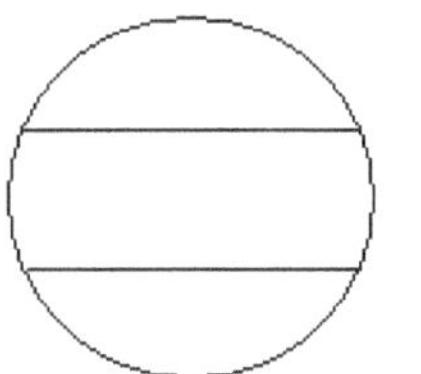

12.
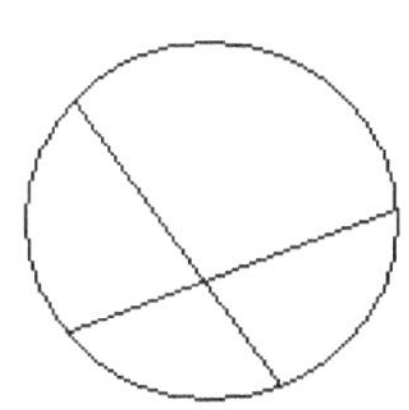

13.
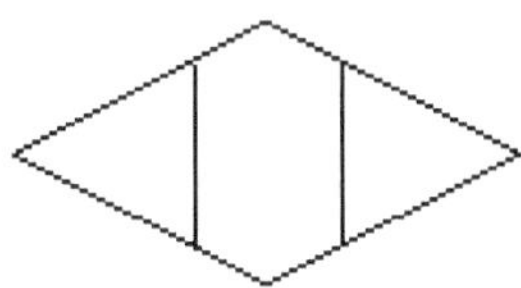

14
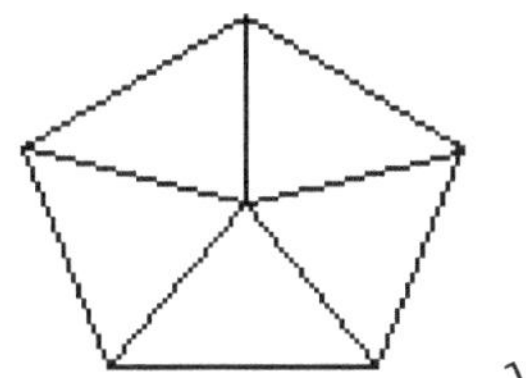
√

15.
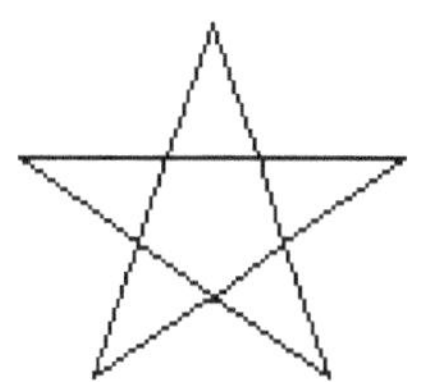

Student's name: ____________________ Assignment date: ________________

2. Name the equal parts of each whole.

1.

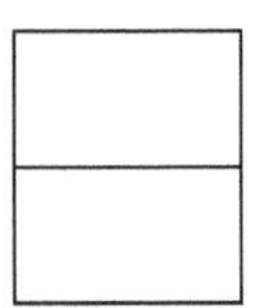

2 halves

2.

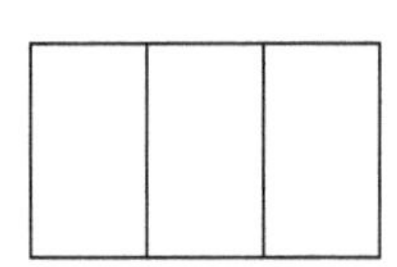

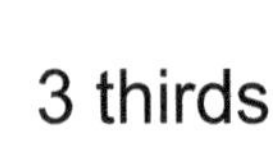

3 thirds
____

3.

4 fourths
____

4.

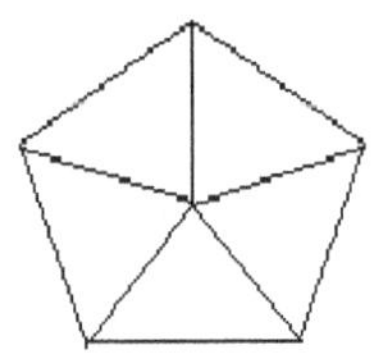

5 fifths
____

5.

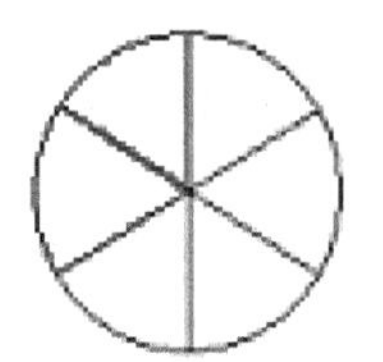

6 sixths
____

6.

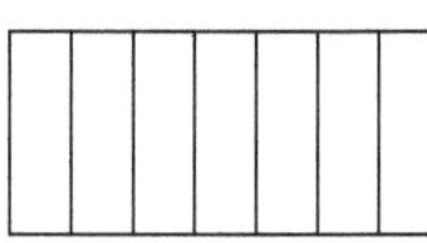

7 sevenths
____

7.

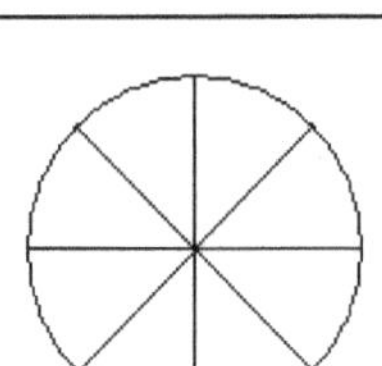

8 eighths
____

8.

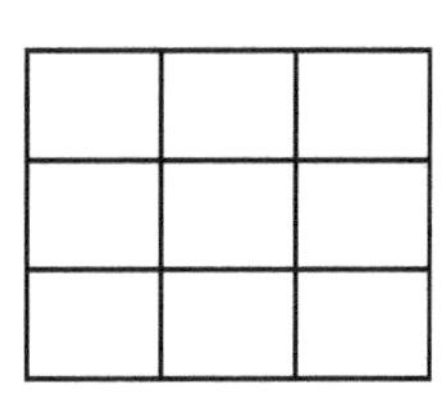

9 ninths
____

9.

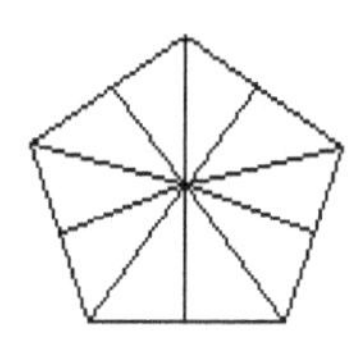

10 tenths
____

10.

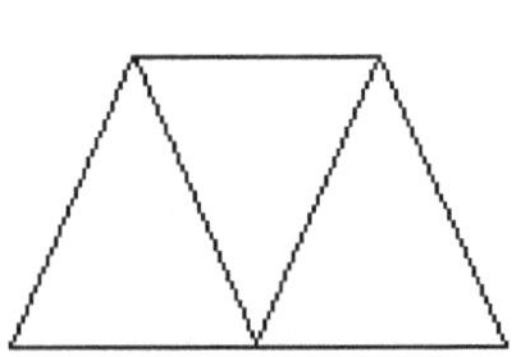

3 thirds
____

11.

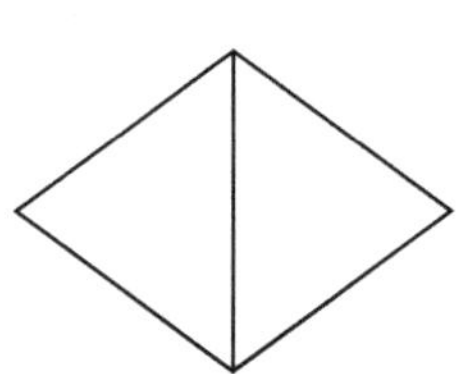

2 halves
____

12.

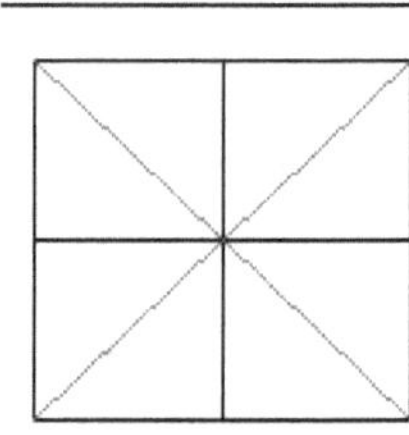

8 eighths
____

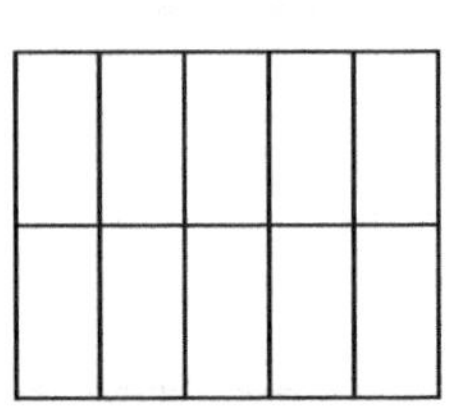

10 tenths
____

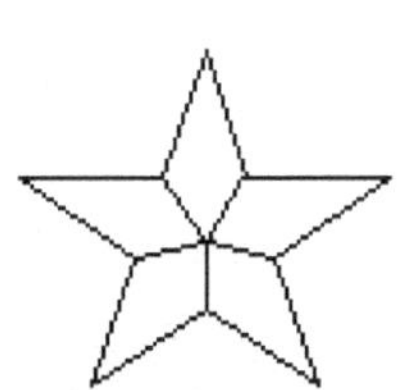

5 fifths
____

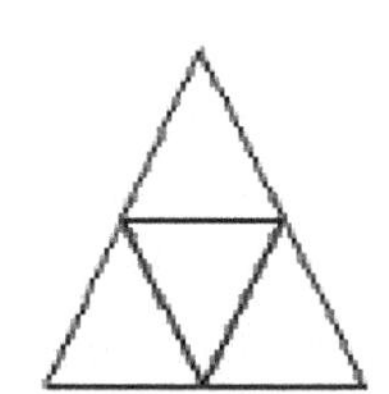

4 fourths
____

Student's name: ____________________ Assignment date: ________________

Equal Parts

1. Name the equal parts of each whole.

Example: 3 equal parts 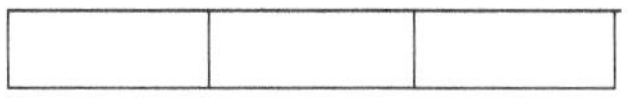 three thirds

1.  5 fifths
2. 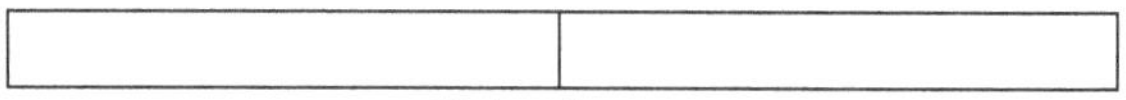 2 halves
3. 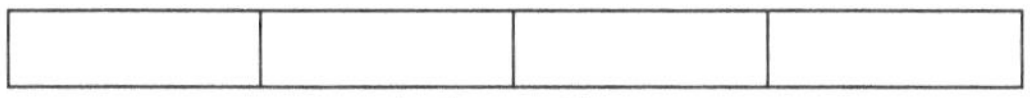 4 fourths
4. 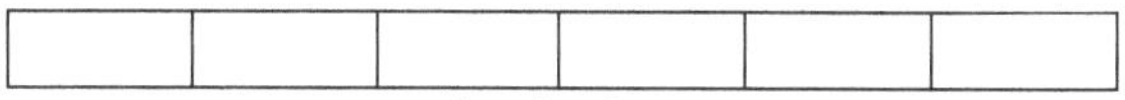 6 sixths
5.  7 sevenths
6. 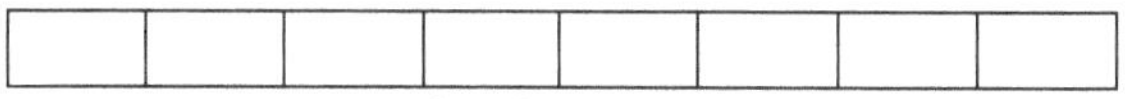 8 eighths

2. Divide each square into 2 halves (at least the same size) in five ways.

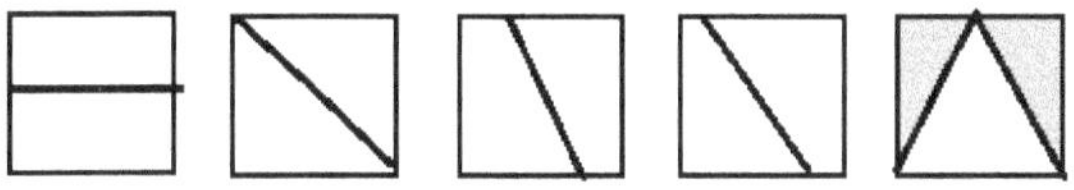

answer

3. Divide each square into four fourths (the same size and shape) in five ways.

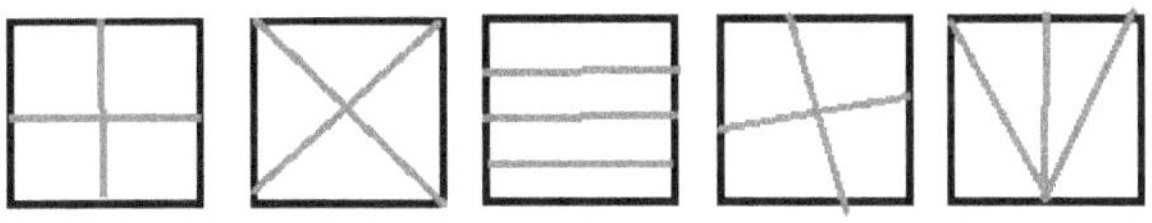

answer

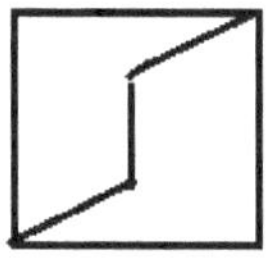

4. Divide each square into six sixths (at least the same size) in four ways.

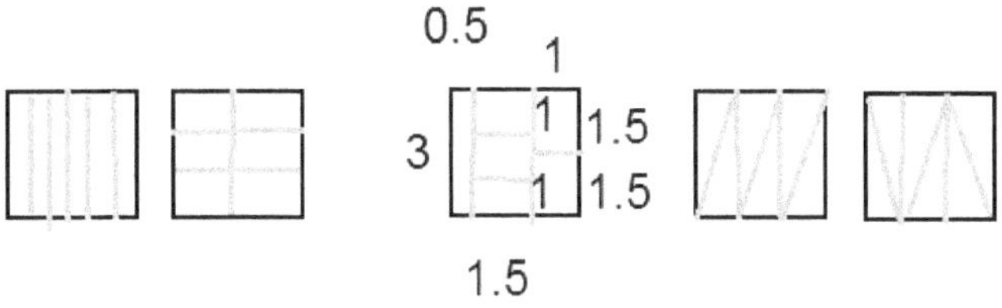

0.5 1 1 1.5 3 1 1.5 1.5

answer

Student's name: ____________________ Assignment date: ______________

Representing Fractions

$$\frac{\text{numerator}}{\text{denominator}} = \frac{\text{the number of favorite parts}}{\text{the number of equal parts in a whole}}$$

1. What fraction of each figure is shaded?

1.
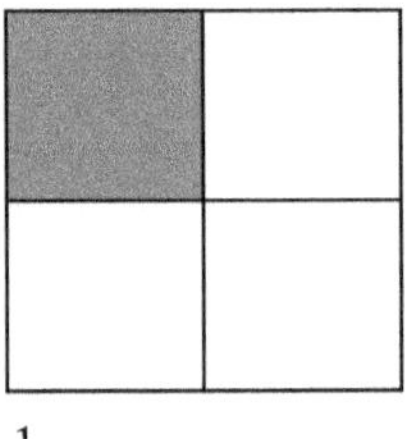
$\frac{1}{4}$ ________

2.
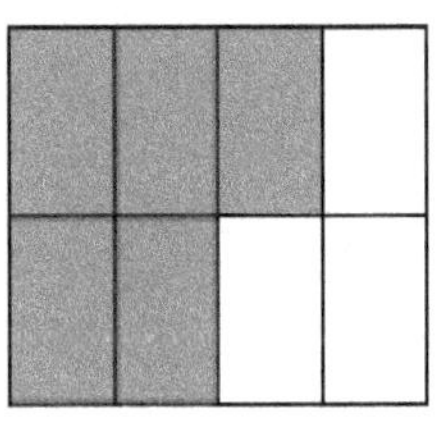
$\frac{5}{8}$ ________

3.
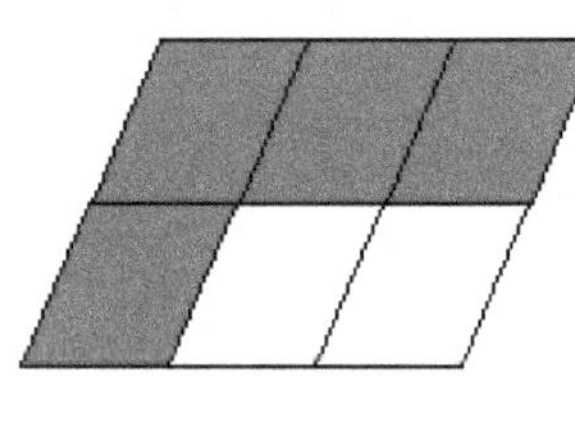
$\frac{4}{6}$ ________

4.
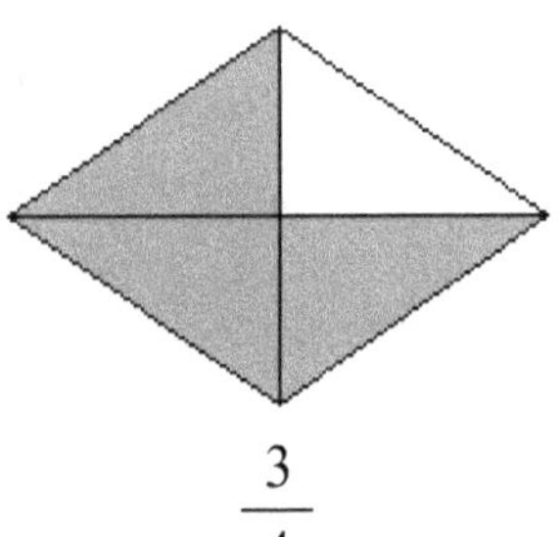
$\frac{3}{4}$

5.
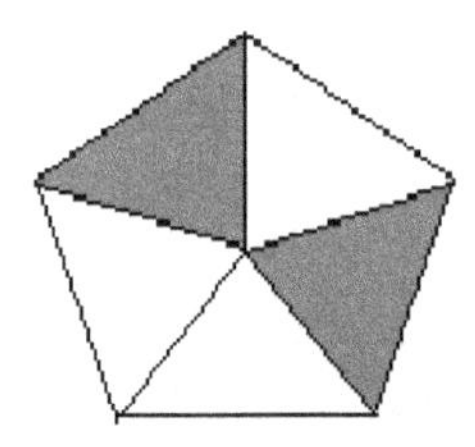
$\frac{2}{5}$

6.
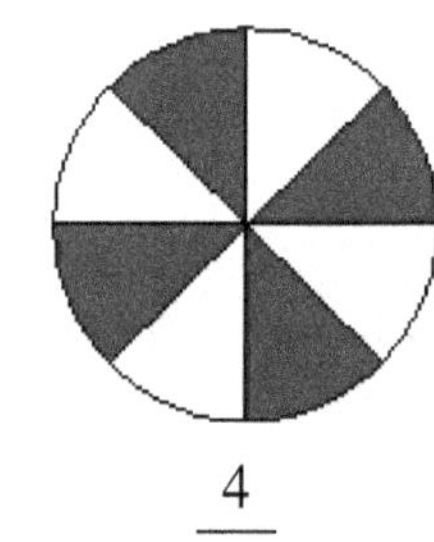
$\frac{4}{8}$

____

7.
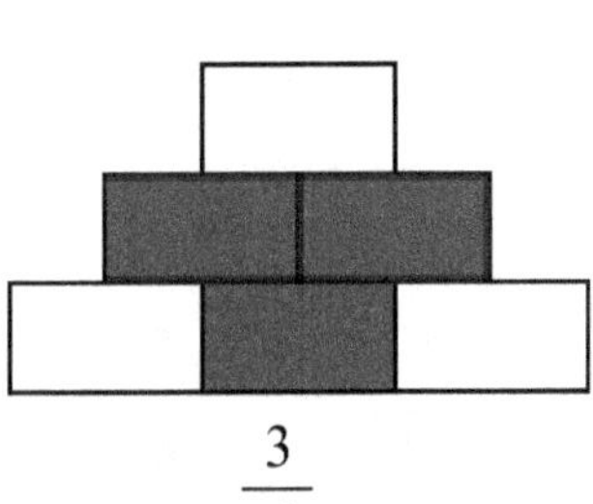
$\frac{3}{6}$

____

8.
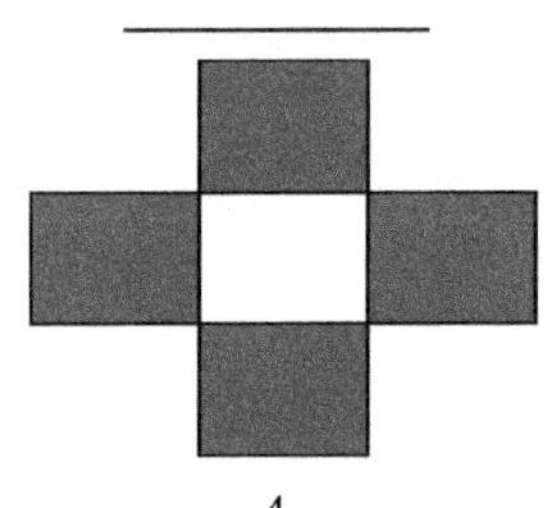
$\frac{4}{5}$

____

9.
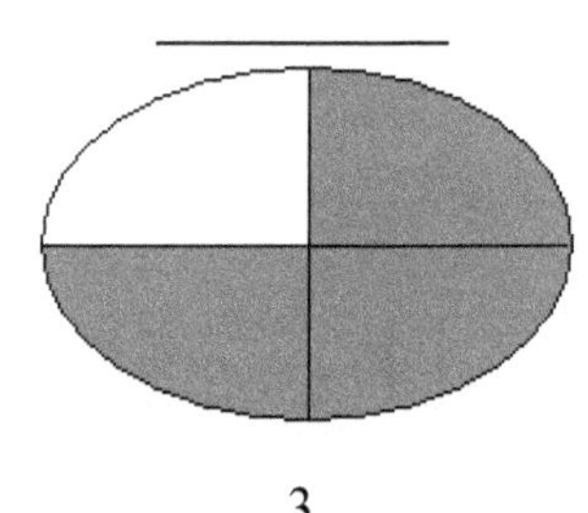
$\frac{3}{4}$

____

10.
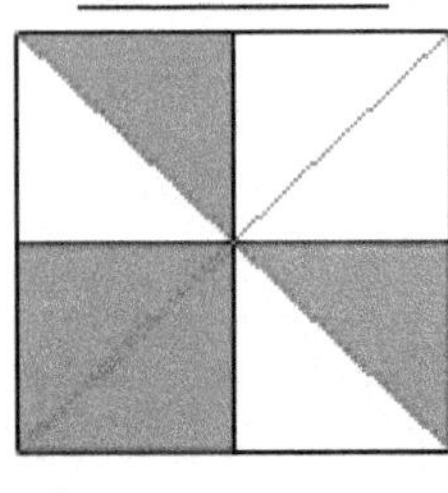
$\frac{4}{8}$ ________

____

11.
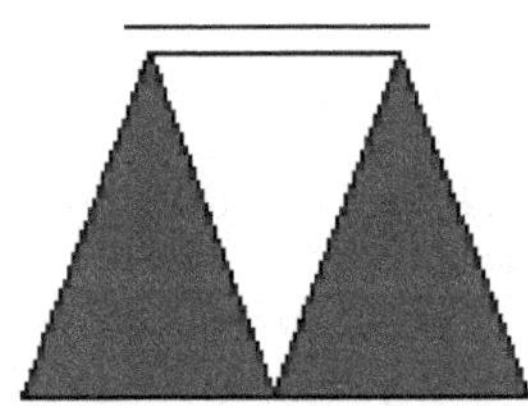
$\frac{2}{3}$ ________

____

12.
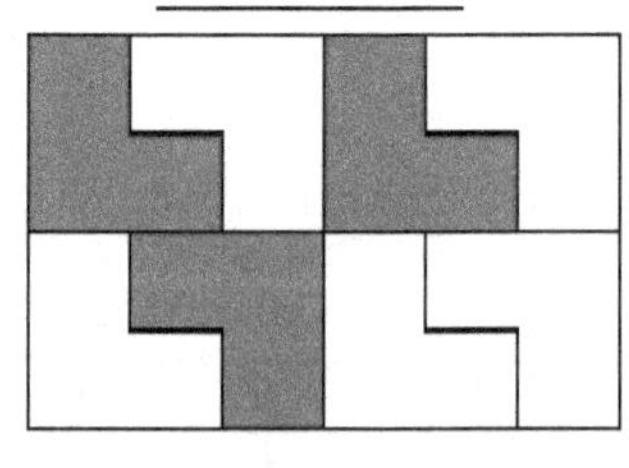
$\frac{3}{8}$ ________

Student's name: ____________________ Assignment date: _______________

2. What fraction of each figure is shaded? Express in words and in fraction form.

1. 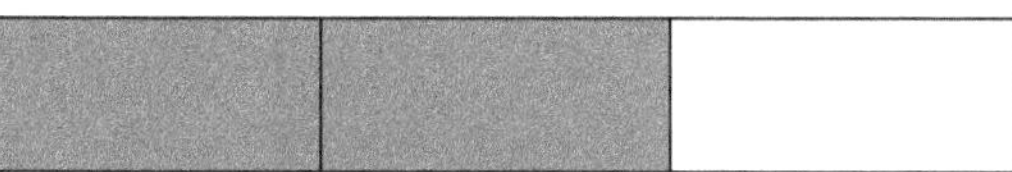 two thirds $\frac{2}{3}$

2. 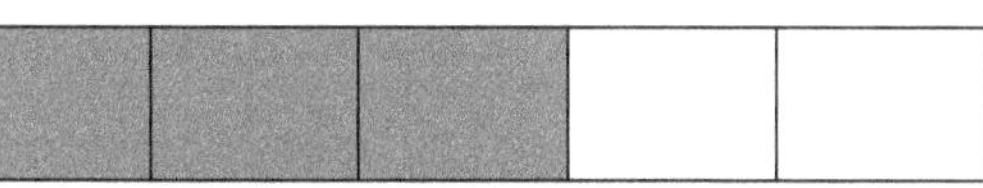 three fifths $\frac{3}{5}$

3. 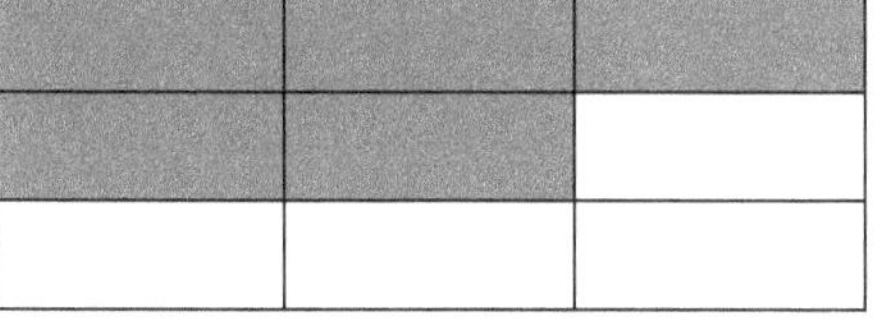 five ninths $\frac{5}{9}$

4. 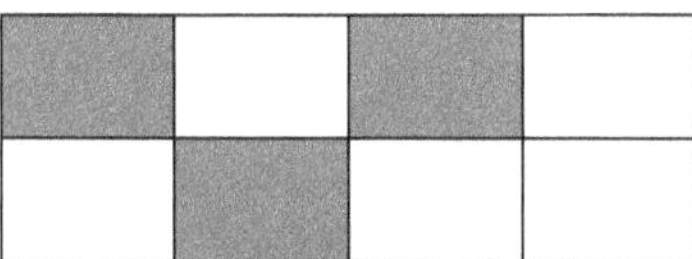 three eighths $\frac{3}{8}$

5. 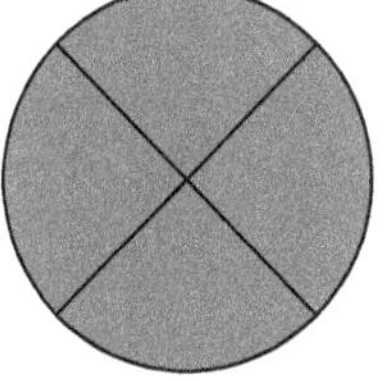 four fourths $\frac{4}{4}$

6. 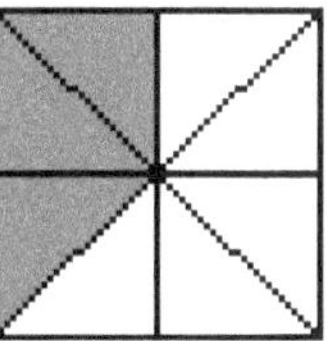 three eighths $\frac{3}{8}$

7. 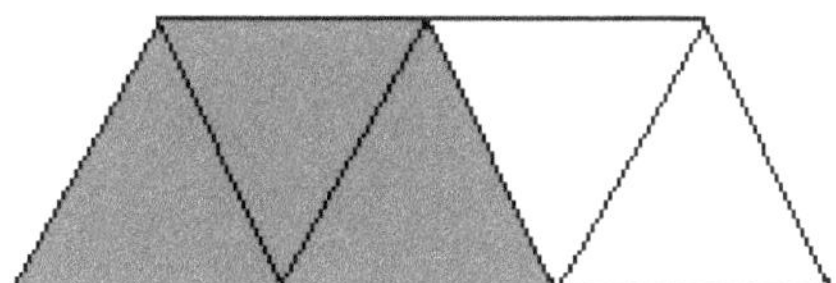 three fifths $\frac{3}{5}$

8. 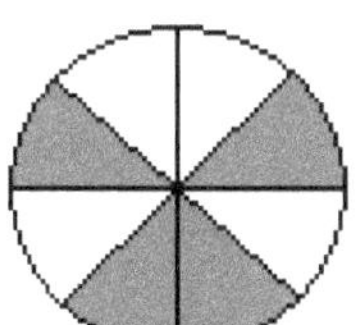 four eighths $\frac{4}{8}$

Student's name: ____________________ Assignment date: ________________

1. Divide each figure and shade the portion the fraction presented.

1.

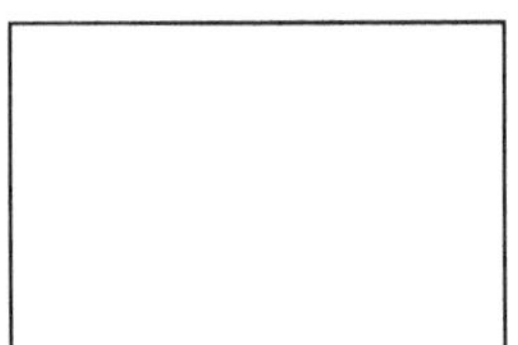

$\frac{1}{2}$

2.

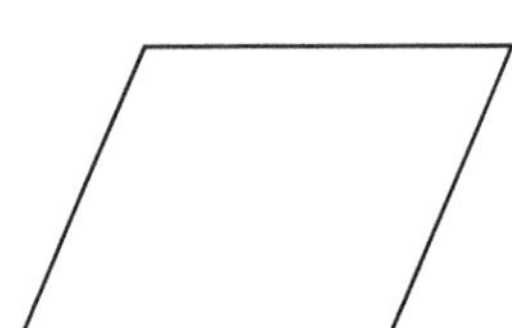

$\frac{2}{4}$

3.

$\frac{4}{6}$

4.

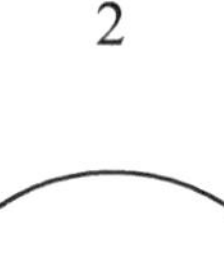

$\frac{3}{4}$

5.

$\frac{1}{4}$

6.

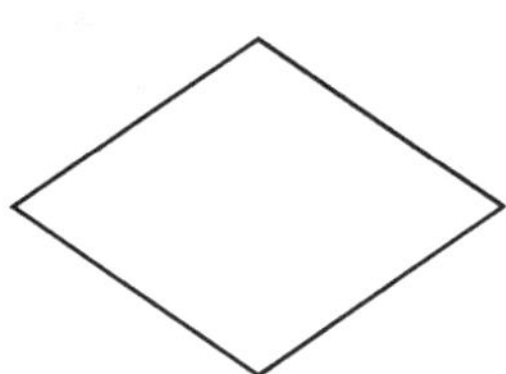

$\frac{3}{4}$

7.

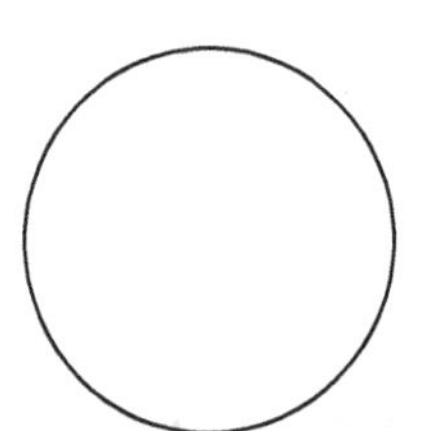

$\frac{5}{6}$

8.

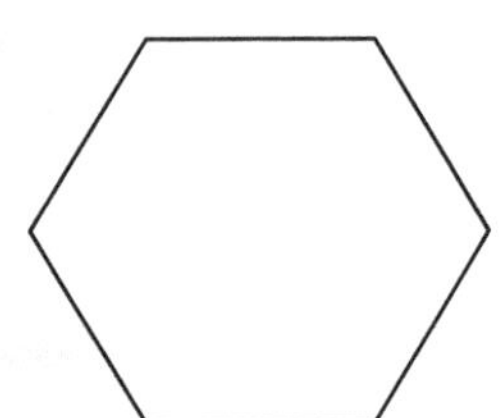

$\frac{2}{6}$

9.

$\frac{2}{5}$

10.

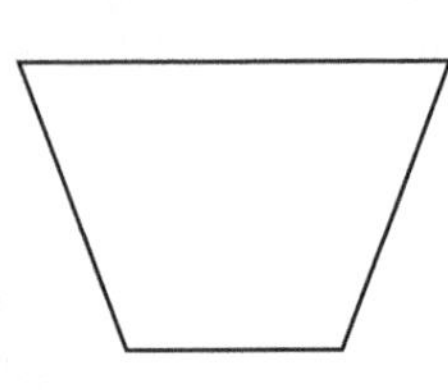

$\frac{1}{3}$

11.

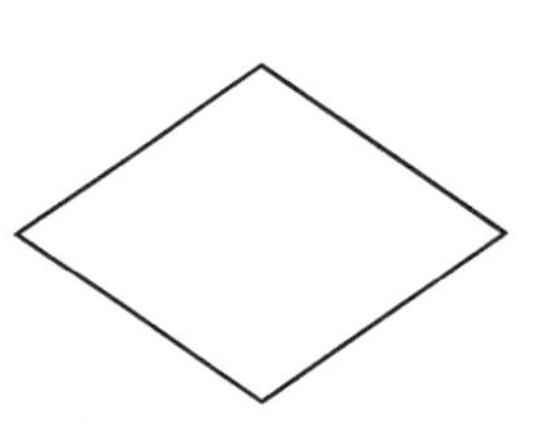

$\frac{7}{8}$

12.

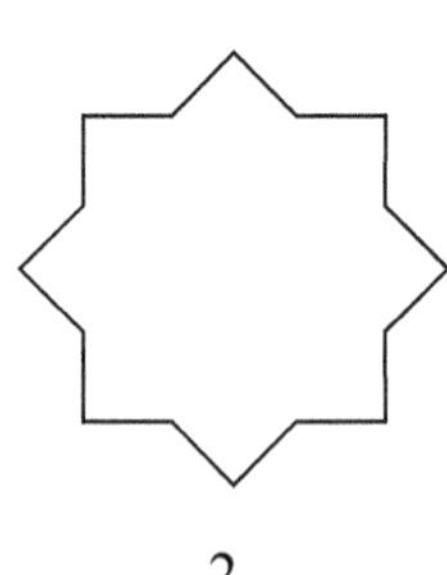

$\frac{2}{4}$

Student's name: ____________________ Assignment date: ________________

2. Divide each figure and shade it as indicated.

1. one half

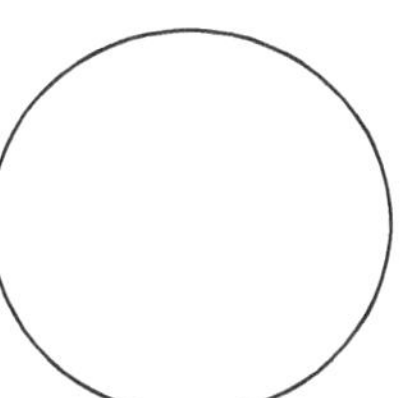

2. two fifths

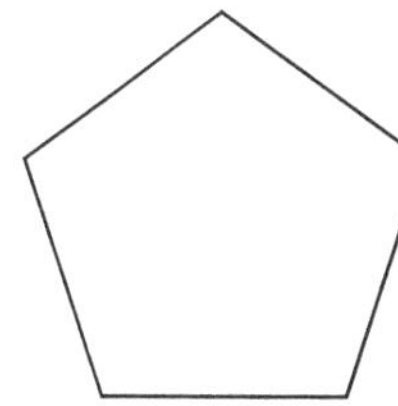

3. three eighths

4. one fourth

5. three fourths

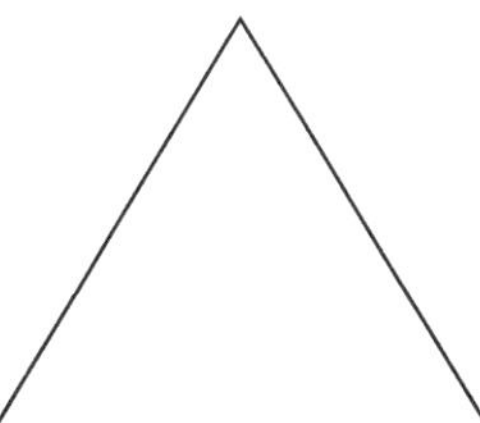

6. two thirds

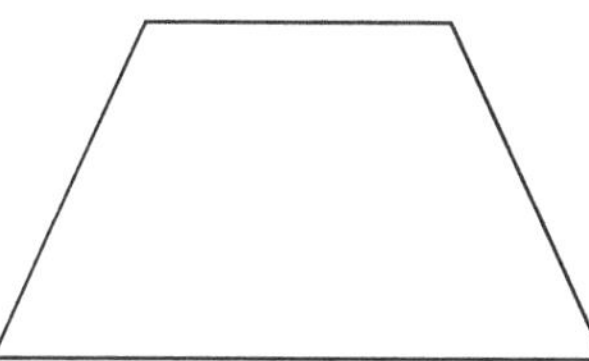

7. four fifteenths

8. seven eighths

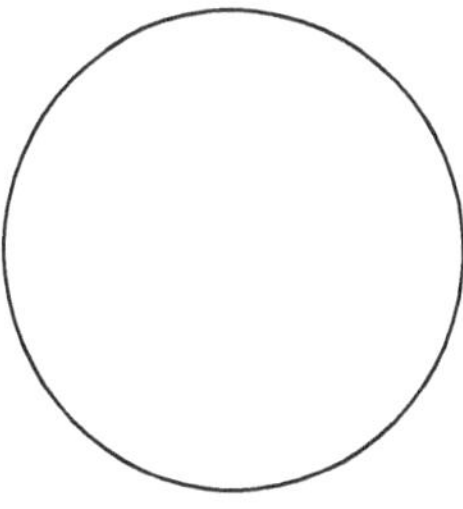

9. three fifths

10. two halves

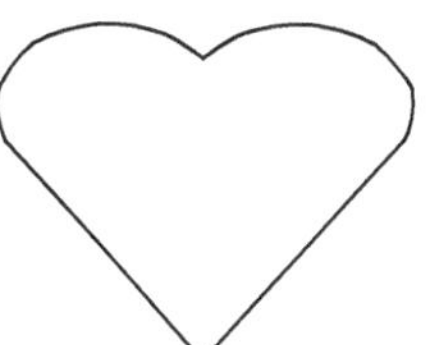

Student's name: ____________________ Assignment date: ______________

Proper fraction, improper fraction and mixed numbers using models

Here are two type of fractions as follows.

Proper Fraction	$\frac{\text{small numerator}}{\text{big denominator}}$		$\frac{3}{4}$
Improper fraction	$\frac{\text{big numerator}}{\text{small denominator}}$		$\frac{9}{4}$

Mixed number	whole number + $\frac{\text{numerator}}{\text{denominator}}$ of whole = whole number $\frac{\text{numerator}}{\text{denominator}}$		$2\frac{1}{4}$

1. Write each as an improper fraction and a mixed number.

	figure	Improper fraction	Mixed number
1.		$\frac{7}{4}$	$1\frac{3}{4}$
2.		$\frac{4}{3}$	$1\frac{1}{3}$
3.		$\frac{14}{6}$	$2\frac{2}{6}$
4.		$\frac{13}{5}$	$2\frac{3}{5}$
5.		$\frac{31}{9}$	$3\frac{4}{9}$
6.		$\frac{13}{4}$	$3\frac{1}{4}$

Student's name: ____________________ Assignment date: ________________

2. Draw pictures to show each improper fraction and write a mixed number.

	Improper fraction	Figure	Mixed number
1.	$\frac{5}{2}$	____________	$2\frac{1}{2}$
2.	$\frac{5}{3}$	____________	$1\frac{2}{3}$
3.	$\frac{7}{4}$	____________	$1\frac{3}{4}$
4.	$\frac{8}{5}$	____________	$1\frac{3}{5}$
5.	$\frac{10}{3}$	____________	$3\frac{1}{3}$

2. Draw pictures to show each mixed number and write an improper fraction.

	Mixed number	Figure	Improper fraction
1.	$1\frac{1}{3}$	____________	$\frac{4}{3}$
2.	$1\frac{4}{5}$	____________	$\frac{9}{5}$
3.	$2\frac{3}{4}$	____________	$\frac{11}{4}$
4.	$3\frac{1}{2}$	____________	$\frac{7}{2}$
5.	$2\frac{5}{6}$	____________	$\frac{17}{6}$

Student's name: ____________________ Assignment date: ________________

Proper fraction, improper fraction and mixed numbers using division

Mixed number	Improper fraction	Division	Ratio	Ratio converted to Part to whole fractions
$2\frac{1}{3}$	$\frac{7}{2}$	$2\overline{)7}$ quotient 3; 6; remainder 1	7 to 2	$\frac{7}{9}$ *to* $\frac{2}{9}$
	$\frac{13}{3}$			
	$\frac{17}{4}$			
$4\frac{2}{7}$				
		$3\overline{)20}$ quotient 6; 18; remainder 2		
			21 : 2	

Student's name: ____________________ Assignment date: ________________

Equivalent Fractions

Example:

$\frac{1}{2}$ 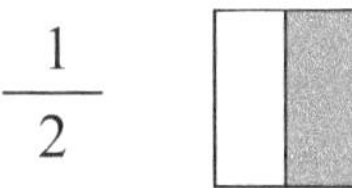 is equivalent to (the same as) $\frac{2}{4}$ We say, $\frac{1}{2} = \frac{2}{4}$

1. Write an equivalent fraction for each fraction.

$\frac{1}{3}$		$\frac{1}{3}$		$\frac{1}{3}$	
$\frac{1}{6}$	$\frac{1}{6}$	$\frac{1}{6}$	$\frac{1}{6}$	$\frac{1}{6}$	$\frac{1}{6}$

$\frac{1}{3} = \frac{2}{6}$ ________ $\frac{2}{3} = \frac{4}{6}$ ________ $\frac{3}{3} = \frac{6}{6}$ ________

$\frac{1}{4}$		$\frac{1}{4}$		$\frac{1}{4}$		$\frac{1}{4}$	
$\frac{1}{8}$	$\frac{1}{8}$	$\frac{1}{8}$	$\frac{1}{8}$	$\frac{1}{8}$	$\frac{1}{8}$	$\frac{1}{8}$	$\frac{1}{8}$

$\frac{1}{4} = \frac{2}{8}$ ________ $\frac{2}{4} = \frac{4}{8}$ ________ $\frac{3}{4} = \frac{6}{8}$ ________ $\frac{4}{4} = \frac{8}{8}$ ________

2. Shade the second figure which is equivalent to the first figure and fill in blank.

1.

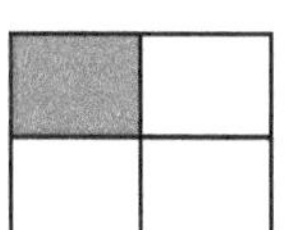 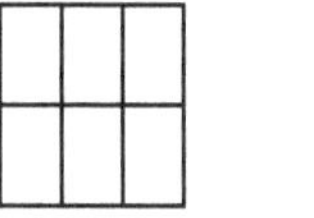

$\frac{1}{4} = \frac{2}{8}$ ________

2.

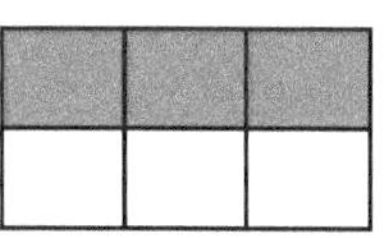 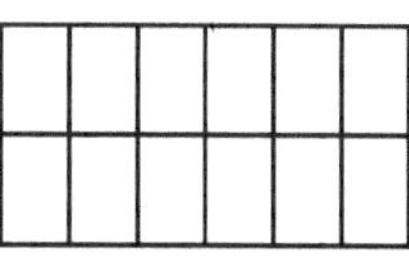

$\frac{3}{6} = \frac{6}{12}$ ________

3.

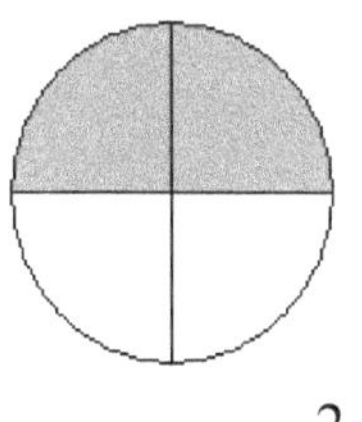 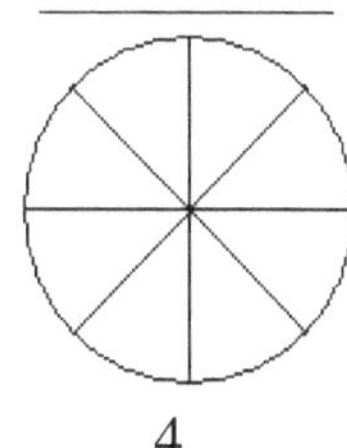 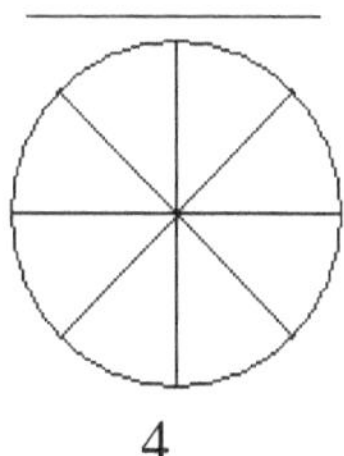

$\frac{2}{4} = \frac{4}{8}$ ________

4.

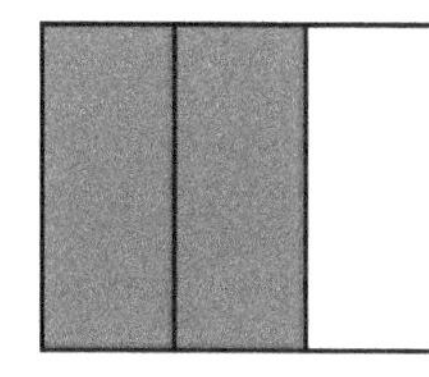 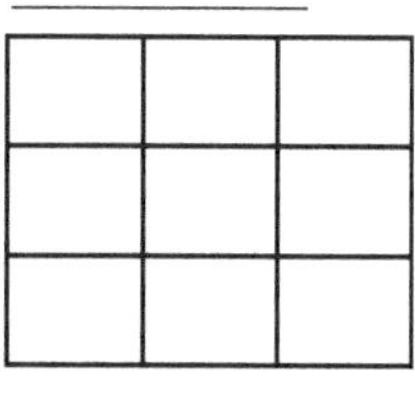

$\frac{2}{3} = \frac{6}{9}$ ________

Student's name: ____________________ Assignment date: ________________

3. Complete the chart then write an equivalent fraction for each fraction.

1 whole									
$\frac{1}{2}$	$\frac{1}{2}$								
$\frac{1}{3}$	$\frac{1}{3}$	$\frac{1}{3}$							
$\frac{1}{4}$	$\frac{1}{4}$	$\frac{1}{4}$	$\frac{1}{4}$						
$\frac{1}{5}$	$\frac{1}{5}$	$\frac{1}{5}$	$\frac{1}{5}$	$\frac{1}{5}$					
$\frac{1}{6}$	$\frac{1}{6}$	$\frac{1}{6}$	$\frac{1}{6}$	$\frac{1}{6}$	$\frac{1}{6}$				
$\frac{1}{7}$	$\frac{1}{7}$	$\frac{1}{7}$	$\frac{1}{7}$	$\frac{1}{7}$	$\frac{1}{7}$	$\frac{1}{7}$			
$\frac{1}{8}$	$\frac{1}{8}$	$\frac{1}{8}$	$\frac{1}{8}$	$\frac{1}{8}$	$\frac{1}{8}$	$\frac{1}{8}$	$\frac{1}{8}$		
$\frac{1}{9}$	$\frac{1}{9}$	$\frac{1}{9}$	$\frac{1}{9}$	$\frac{1}{9}$	$\frac{1}{9}$	$\frac{1}{9}$	$\frac{1}{9}$	$\frac{1}{9}$	
$\frac{1}{10}$	$\frac{1}{10}$	$\frac{1}{10}$	$\frac{1}{10}$	$\frac{1}{10}$	$\frac{1}{10}$	$\frac{1}{10}$	$\frac{1}{10}$	$\frac{1}{10}$	$\frac{1}{10}$

1. $\frac{3}{4} = \frac{6}{8}$
2. $\frac{2}{5} = \frac{4}{10}$
3. $\frac{2}{3} = \frac{4}{6}$
4. $\frac{6}{10} = \frac{3}{5}$
5. $\frac{4}{6} = \frac{2}{3}$
6. $\frac{6}{9} = \frac{2}{3}$
7. $\frac{2}{8} = \frac{1}{4}$
8. $\frac{3}{5} = \frac{6}{10}$
9. $\frac{3}{9} = \frac{1}{3}$
10. $\frac{8}{10} = \frac{4}{5}$
11. $\frac{3}{6} = \frac{1}{2}$
12. $\frac{1}{4} = \frac{2}{8}$
13. $\frac{1}{5} = \frac{2}{10}$
14. $\frac{2}{6} = \frac{1}{3}$
15. $\frac{4}{10} = \frac{2}{5}$
16. $\frac{4}{8} = \frac{1}{2}$

Ho Math Chess Primary Grades Math

Test Review assesssment 何数棋谜低年级数学测试複習考核

Student's name: ____________________ Assignment date: ________________

Comparing fractions using models

1. 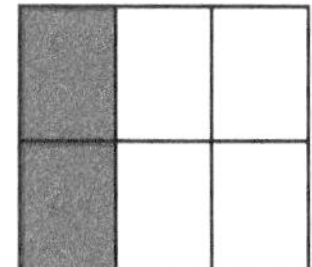 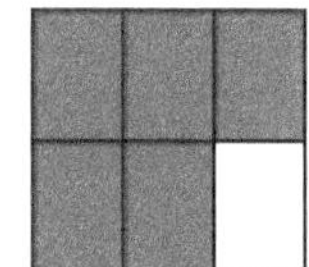

$\frac{2}{6} < \frac{5}{6}$

2. 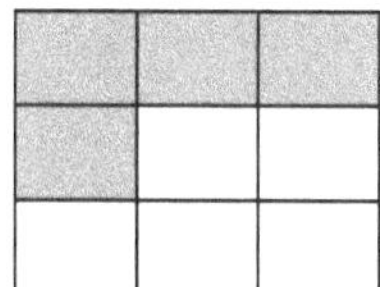 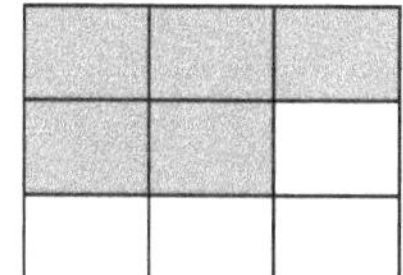

$\frac{4}{9} < \frac{5}{9}$

3. 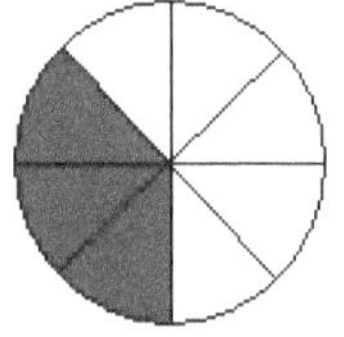 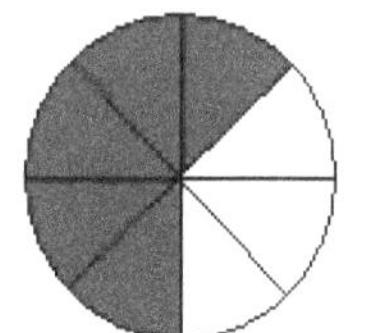

$\frac{3}{8} < \frac{5}{8}$

4. 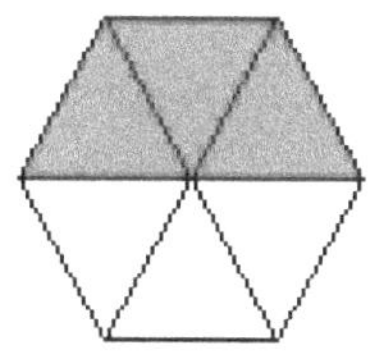 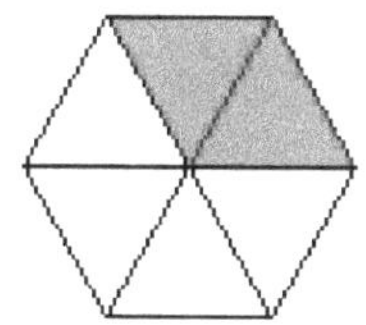

$\frac{3}{6} > \frac{2}{6}$

5. 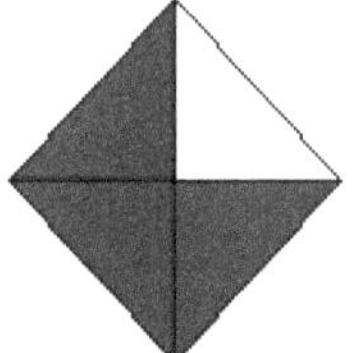 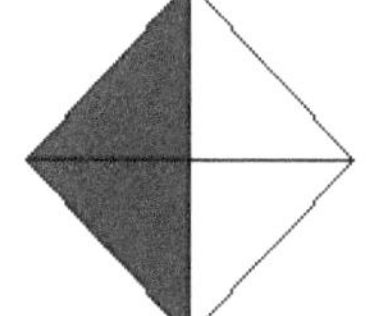

$\frac{3}{4} > \frac{2}{4}$

6.  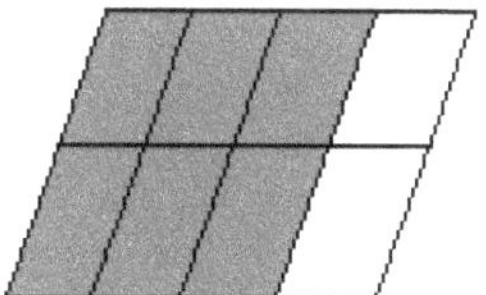 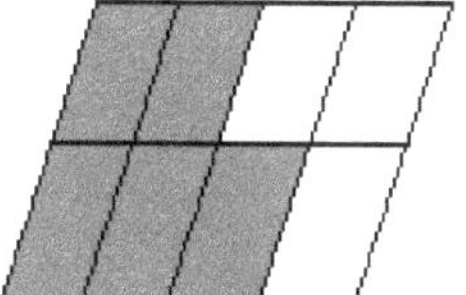

$\frac{6}{8} > \frac{5}{8}$

7. 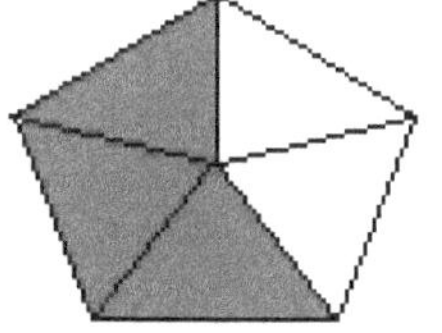 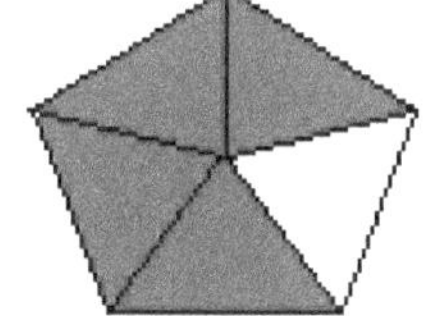

$\frac{3}{5} < \frac{4}{5}$

8. 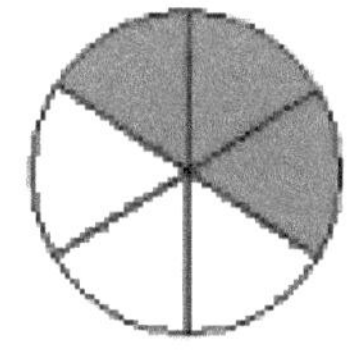 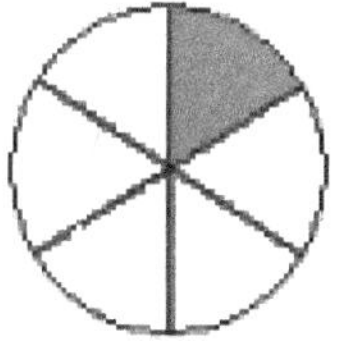

$\frac{3}{6} > \frac{1}{6}$

9. 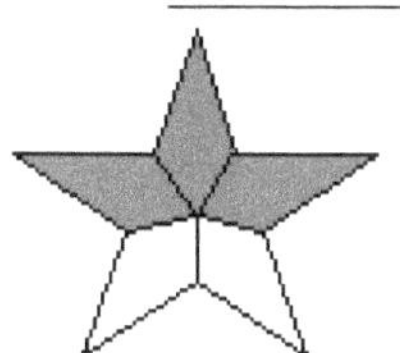

$\frac{3}{5} < \frac{5}{5}$

10.  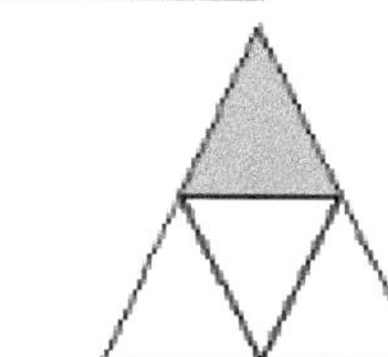

$\frac{2}{4} > \frac{1}{4}$

Student's name: ____________________ Assignment date: ________________

Compare fractions.

1. $\frac{4}{8} \boxed{>} \frac{3}{8}$ >

2. $\frac{3}{5} \square \frac{4}{5}$ <

3. $\frac{1}{4} \square \frac{3}{4}$ <

4. $\frac{3}{3} \square \frac{2}{3}$ >

5. $1\frac{1}{5} \square \frac{3}{5}$ >

6. $2\frac{3}{4} \square 3\frac{2}{4}$ <

7. $\frac{5}{8} \square 4\frac{2}{8}$ <

8. $6\frac{1}{2} \square 3\frac{1}{2}$ >

9. $2\frac{4}{7} \square 2\frac{2}{7}$ >

10. $5\frac{4}{9} \square 5\frac{5}{9}$ <

11. $7\frac{1}{8} \square 1\frac{7}{8}$ >

12. $4\frac{3}{5} \square 3\frac{4}{5}$ >

13. $\frac{15}{7} \square \frac{14}{7}$ >

14. $2\frac{2}{9} \square 1\frac{7}{9}$ >

15. $8\frac{5}{6} \square 4\frac{1}{6}$ >

16. $\frac{11}{3} \square \frac{13}{3}$ <

17. $7\frac{3}{4} \square 4\frac{1}{4}$ >

18. $9\frac{1}{5} \square 7\frac{4}{5}$ >

19. $1\frac{1}{7} \square 2\frac{3}{7}$ <

20. $4\frac{3}{8} \square 3\frac{4}{8}$ >

21. $2\frac{1}{5} \square 3\frac{4}{5}$ <

22. $7\frac{5}{8} \square 7\frac{7}{8}$ <

23. $3\frac{1}{9} \square 2\frac{5}{9}$ >

24. $3\frac{6}{8} \square 4\frac{7}{8}$ <

25. $\frac{7}{4} \square \frac{8}{4}$ <

26. $\frac{6}{5} \square \frac{2}{5}$ >

Student's name: ____________________ Assignment date: ________________

Circling fraction models to match fraction on the left

$\frac{6}{9}$	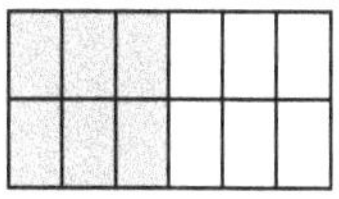 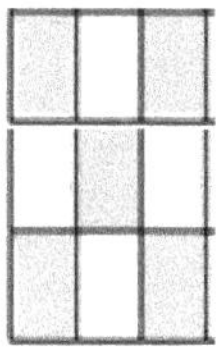  circling the third one.
$\frac{2}{3}$	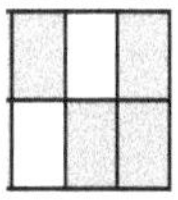 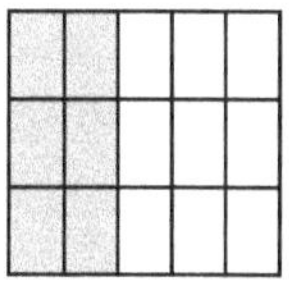 (Think the figure as $\frac{2\ coluns}{5\ columns}$ not $\frac{6}{15}$) 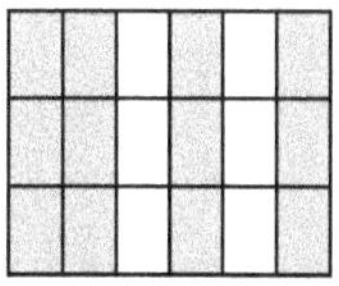 circling the first and the third one. 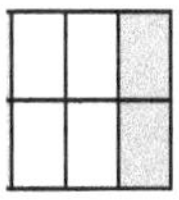
$\frac{3}{9}$	 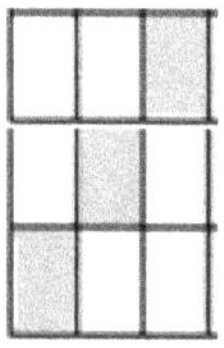 circling both.

Student's name: ____________________ Assignment date: ________________

Circling fraction models to match fraction on the left

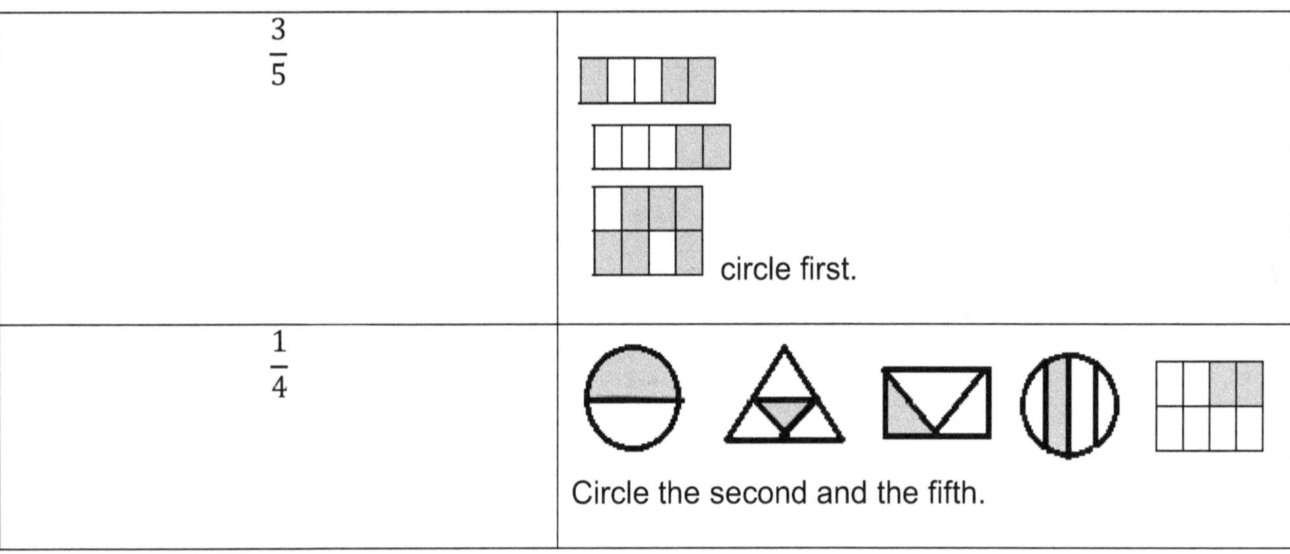

$\frac{3}{5}$	circle first.
$\frac{1}{4}$	Circle the second and the fifth.

Use equivalent fraction to do prediction

Lucy finished $\frac{1}{15}$ of a black and white quilt as shown below. How many white rectangles will be in the finished quilt?

There are 7 white rectangles in the above, which represents $\frac{1}{15}$ of the entire quilt. So the total white rectangles will be $7 \times 15 = 105$.

Lucy finished $\frac{1}{21}$ of a black and white quilt as shown below. How many white rectangles will be in the finished quilt?

There are 10 white rectangles in the above, which represents $\frac{1}{21}$ of the entire quilt. So the total white rectangles will be $19 \times 211 = 210$.

Student's name: ____________________ Assignment date: ________________

Order the following fractions from least to greatest.

1. $\frac{6}{8}, \frac{3}{8}, \frac{5}{8}$

   $\frac{3}{8}, \frac{5}{8}, \frac{6}{8}$

   ____

2. $\frac{2}{7}, \frac{6}{7}, \frac{5}{7}$

   $\frac{2}{7}, \frac{5}{7}, \frac{6}{7}$

   ____

3. $\frac{6}{9}, \frac{3}{9}, \frac{7}{9}$

   $\frac{3}{9}, \frac{6}{9}, \frac{7}{9}$

   ____

4. $\frac{8}{5}, \frac{3}{5}, \frac{1}{5}$

   $\frac{1}{5}, \frac{3}{5}, \frac{8}{5}$

   ____

5. $2\frac{1}{3}, 3\frac{2}{3}, 1\frac{1}{3}$

   $1\frac{1}{3}, 2\frac{1}{3}, 3\frac{2}{3}$

   ____

6. $2\frac{6}{7}, 1\frac{3}{7}, 3\frac{2}{7}$

   $1\frac{3}{7}, 2\frac{6}{7}, 3\frac{2}{7}$

   ____

Order the following fractions from greatest to least.

1. $\frac{2}{6}, \frac{3}{6}, \frac{5}{6}$

   $\frac{5}{6}, \frac{3}{6}, \frac{2}{6}$

   ____

2. $\frac{7}{9}, \frac{3}{9}, \frac{6}{9}$

   $\frac{7}{9}, \frac{6}{9}, \frac{3}{9}$

   ____

3. $\frac{6}{5}, \frac{9}{5}, \frac{4}{5}$

   $\frac{9}{5}, \frac{6}{5}, \frac{4}{5}$

   ____

4. $\frac{15}{8}, \frac{13}{8}, \frac{7}{8}$

   $\frac{15}{8}, \frac{13}{8}, \frac{7}{8}$

   ____

5. $1\frac{3}{7}, 3\frac{2}{7}, 2\frac{5}{7}$

   $3\frac{2}{7}, 2\frac{5}{7}, 1\frac{3}{7}$

   ____

6. $5\frac{1}{8}, 1\frac{7}{8}, 3\frac{5}{8}$

   $5\frac{1}{8}, 3\frac{5}{8}, 5\frac{1}{8}$

   ____

Student's name: ____________________ Assignment date: ________________

Order the following fractions from least to greatest.

1. 13 $\frac{6}{8}, \frac{3}{8}, \frac{5}{8}$

$\frac{3}{8}, \frac{5}{8}, \frac{6}{8}$

____

2. $\frac{2}{7}, \frac{6}{7}, \frac{5}{7}$

$\frac{2}{7}, \frac{5}{7}, \frac{6}{7}$

____

3. $\frac{6}{9}, \frac{3}{9}, \frac{7}{9}$

$\frac{3}{9}, \frac{6}{9}, \frac{7}{9}$

____

4. $\frac{8}{5}, \frac{3}{5}, \frac{1}{5}$

$\frac{1}{5}, \frac{3}{5}, \frac{8}{5}$

____

5. $2\frac{1}{3}, 3\frac{2}{3}, 1\frac{1}{3}$

$1\frac{1}{3}, 2\frac{1}{3}, 3\frac{2}{3}$

____

6. $2\frac{6}{7}, 1\frac{3}{7}, 3\frac{2}{7}$

$1\frac{3}{7}, 2\frac{6}{7}, 3\frac{2}{7}$

____

Student's name: ____________________ Assignment date: ________________

Order fractions with different denominators

$\frac{7}{13}, \frac{6}{10}, \frac{3}{7}$
$\frac{4}{8}, \frac{5}{9}, \frac{3}{6}$
$\frac{4}{5}, \frac{7}{10}, \frac{7}{9}$
$\frac{10}{12}, \frac{8}{10}, \frac{3}{7}$
$\frac{10}{11}, \frac{8}{9}, \frac{3}{8}$
$\frac{8}{12}, \frac{8}{9}, \frac{5}{7}$

Student's name: ____________________ Assignment date: ______________

Model 2 – Choosing one or more equal parts of a set.

The fraction of a set

Example: Find $\frac{2}{4}$ of 12

1. Divide 12 into 4 equal groups.
2. Count the number in each group, which is "3".
3. Times the number with a numerator.
 $3 \times 2 = 6$

○	○	○	○
○	○	○	○
○	○	○	○
$\frac{1}{4}$	$\frac{1}{4}$	$\frac{1}{4}$	$\frac{1}{4}$

$\frac{1}{4}$ $\frac{2}{4}$

Shade or divide the following squares such that the shaded area matches the fraction shown.

$\frac{1}{2}$	$\frac{5}{6}$	$\frac{9}{16}$
$\frac{1}{2}$	$\frac{3}{10}$	$\frac{1}{3}$

Student's name: ____________________ Assignment date: ________________

Shade or divide the following squares such that the shaded area matches the fraction shown.

1. □□□□□ □□□□□ $\frac{3}{10}$ ______

2. □□□□□□□ □□□□□□□ $\frac{3}{14}$ ______

3. □□□□□□ $\frac{5}{6}$ ______

4. □□□□□ $\frac{2}{5}$ ______

5. □□□□□□□ $\frac{4}{7}$ ______

6. □□□□□□ $\frac{4}{6}$ ______

7. □□□□ $\frac{2}{4}$ ______

8. □□□□□ $\frac{3}{5}$ ______

9. □□□□□ □□□□□ $\frac{6}{10}$ ______

10. □□□□ □□□□□ $\frac{4}{9}$ ______

11. □□□ □□□□□ $\frac{3}{8}$ ______

12. □□□□ □□□□□□ $\frac{5}{10}$ ______

13. □□□ □□□□□ $\frac{2}{8}$ ______

14. □□□ □□□□ $\frac{5}{7}$ ______

15. □□□□ $\frac{4}{4}$ ______

16. □□□□□ $\frac{0}{5}$ ______

17. □□□ □□ $\frac{4}{5}$ ______

18. □□ □□□□ $\frac{2}{6}$ ______

Student's name: ____________________ Assignment date: ________________

Converting fraction addition or subtraction to $\frac{a}{b}$

Fraction addition	Fraction subtraction
$1+\frac{1}{3}=\frac{1\times3+1}{3}=\frac{4}{3}$	$1-\frac{1}{3}=\frac{1\times3-1}{3}=\frac{2}{3}$
$1+\frac{1}{4}=$	$1-\frac{1}{4}=$
$1+\frac{1}{6}=$	$1-\frac{1}{6}=$
$1+\frac{1}{6}=$	$1-\frac{1}{6}=$
$1+\frac{1}{7}=$	$1-\frac{1}{7}=$
$1+\frac{1}{10}=$	$1-\frac{1}{10}=$
$2+\frac{1}{6}=$	$2-\frac{1}{6}=$
$3+\frac{1}{6}=$	$3-\frac{1}{6}=$
$2+\frac{1}{7}=$	$2-\frac{1}{7}=$
$2+\frac{1}{8}=$	$2-\frac{1}{8}=$

Ho Math Chess Primary Grades Math

Test Review assesssment 何数棋謎低年级数学测试複習考核

Student's name: ____________________ Assignment date: ________________

Find the fractional part of the number.

Lower-grade students should master $\frac{1}{a}$ × amount first.

1. $\frac{1}{8}$ *of* 16 = 2
2. $\frac{1}{3}$ *of* 15 = 5
3. $\frac{2}{5}$ *of* 20 = 8
4. $\frac{3}{4}$ *of* 16 = 12
5. $\frac{2}{3}$ *of* 18 = 12
6. $\frac{2}{6}$ *of* 30 = 10
7. $\frac{3}{4}$ *of* 12 = 9
8. $\frac{1}{5}$ *of* 45 = 9
9. $\frac{3}{6}$ *of* 24 = 12
10. $\frac{7}{9}$ *of* 54 = 42
11. $\frac{3}{10}$ *of* 30 = 9
12. $\frac{6}{10}$ *of* 50 = 30
13. $\frac{2}{7}$ *of* 28 = 8
14. $\frac{7}{8}$ *of* 32 = 28
15. $\frac{3}{5}$ *of* 50 = 30
16. $\frac{7}{10}$ *of* 80 = 56
17. $\frac{5}{9}$ *of* 36 = 20
18. $\frac{2}{11}$ *of* 33 = 6
19. $\frac{5}{8}$ *of* 80 = 50
20. $\frac{5}{30}$ *of* 180 = 30
21. $\frac{1}{4}$ *of* 40 = 10
22. $\frac{3}{4}$ *of* 12 = 9
23. $\frac{3}{7}$ *of* 70 = 30
24. $\frac{7}{11}$ *of* 55 = 35

Student's name: ____________________ Assignment date: ________________

Fraction and division

$\frac{1}{10}=0.1$	$1\frac{1}{10}=1.1$	$1\frac{1}{100}=1.01$	$1\frac{1}{1000}=1.001$
$\frac{2}{10}=0.2$	$1\frac{12}{10}=1.2$	$1\frac{2}{100}=1.02$	$1\frac{2}{1000}=1.002$
$\frac{3}{10}=0.3$	$1\frac{3}{10}=1.3$	$1\frac{3}{100}=1.03$	$1\frac{3}{1000}=1.003$
$\frac{4}{10}=0.4$	$1\frac{4}{10}=1.4$	$1\frac{4}{100}=1.04$	$1\frac{4}{1000}=1.004$
$\frac{5}{10}=0.5$	$1\frac{5}{10}=1.5$	$1\frac{5}{100}=1.05$	$1\frac{5}{1000}=1.005$
$\frac{6}{10}=0.6$	$1\frac{6}{10}=1.6$	$1\frac{6}{100}=1.06$	$1\frac{6}{1000}=1.006$
$\frac{7}{10}=0.7$	$1\frac{7}{10}=1.7$	$1\frac{7}{100}=1.07$	$1\frac{7}{1000}=1.007$

Student's name: ____________________ Assignment date: ______________

Commonly used unit fractions

Lower grades students are not taught how to do fraction divisions, but sometimes the commonly used unit fractions will appear in the word problems. Some problems do not need division but to think a bit more.

Pauline bus 6 pounds of candy and packs them into $\frac{1}{2}$-pound per bag. How many pounds can she pack? $\frac{1}{2} pound + \frac{1}{2} pound\ need\ 2\ bags$ She will pack 2 bags per pound, so, with 6 pounds, she needs to pack 12 bags.
Pauline bus 6 pounds of candy and packs them into $\frac{1}{3}$-pound per bag. How many pounds can she pack? $\frac{1}{3} pound + \frac{1}{3} pound + \frac{1}{3} pound\ need\ 3\ bags$ 1 pound need 3 bags She will pack 3 bags per pound, so with 6 pounds, she needs to pack 18 bags.
10% + 10% = ? (Answer in fraction)
10% + 1% = ? (Answer in fraction)
100% – 10% = ? (Answer in fraction)
10% × 100% = ? (Answer in fraction)
100% ÷ 10% = ? (Answer in fraction)

Student's name: ____________________ Assignment date: ________________

Test of fraction word problems

Rank the following data from least to greatest in the original data format. $$\frac{4}{4}, \frac{3}{4}. 0.6, 0.8, 25\%, 0.09$$
Kitty started to prepare for her final test from 6 p.m. to 8 p.m. She took a break $\frac{1}{4}$ of the way during her study until the middle of the second half of the study. How many minutes did she take her break during the studyÉ 60 minutes
A bathtub is $\frac{3}{4}$ full after 15 gallons of water have been drained. How much water can it hold when it is full? 60 gallons
A bathtub is $\frac{3}{4}$ full. After 15 gallons of water have been drained, it is half full. How much water can it hold when it is full? 15 gallons refers to $\frac{1}{4}$ of a full bathtub, so the total capacity is 60 gallons
$\frac{1}{3}$ of tulips are red. The rest are 40 white tulips. How many red tulips are there? .

Student's name: ____________________ Assignment date: ________________

Finding the original amount using fraction or ratio

A ratio could often be converted to a fraction, then a Line Segment Diagram or a Division Method (work backwards) could be used to solve the original amount problems.

Cher spent $10 to buy a gift for her sister. This was $\frac{2}{2}$ of her money in her purse. How much did she have originally in her purse?
Jessica went shopping and spent $\frac{1}{3}$ of her money at her lunch break. She had 316 left. How much did she spend on her lunch break?

Student's name: ____________________ Assignment date: ________________

Estimation of fractions 0, $\frac{1}{2}$, and 1 (Faction benchmark)

Example:

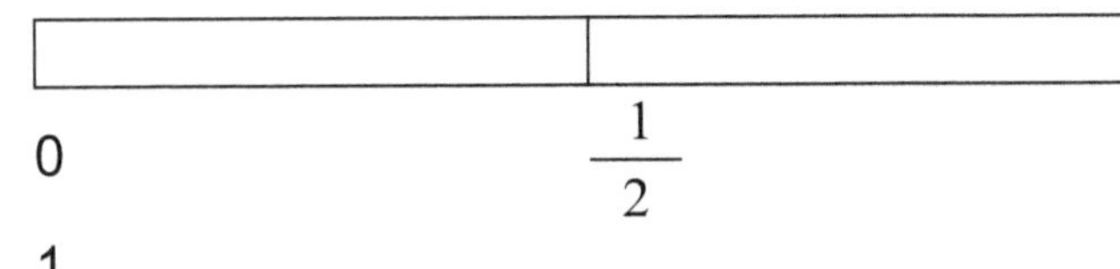

0 $\frac{1}{2}$ 1

Decide whether each fraction is close to 1, $\frac{1}{2}$, or 1

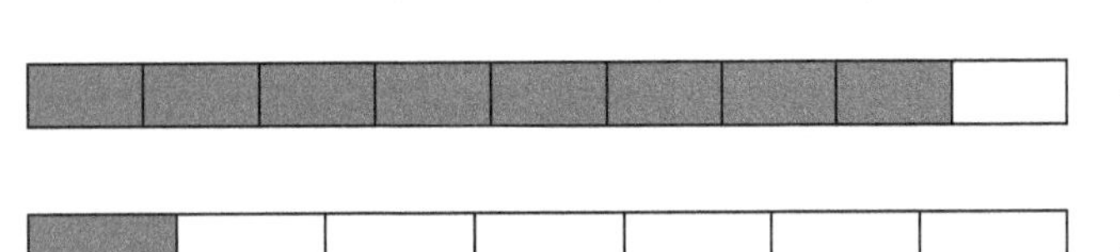

$\frac{3}{5}$ is closer to $\frac{1}{2}$.

$\frac{8}{9}$ is closer to 1.

$\frac{1}{7}$ is closer to 0.

Divide each strip to show a fraction and decide whether it is closer to 0, $\frac{1}{2}$ or 1.

1. $\frac{1}{5}$ is closer to 0 ________

2. $\frac{3}{8}$ is closer to $\frac{1}{2}$ ________

3. $\frac{5}{6}$ is closer to 1 ________

4. $\frac{3}{5}$ is closer to $\frac{1}{2}$ ________

5. $\frac{2}{9}$ is closer to 0 ________

6. $\frac{6}{7}$ is closer to 1 ________

7. $\frac{1}{3}$ is closer to $\frac{1}{2}$ ________

Student's name: ____________________ Assignment date: ________________

Divide each strip to show a fraction and decide whether it is "more than half", "half", or "less than half".

1. $\frac{1}{5}$ [ ] is ________ less than half ______

2. $\frac{3}{8}$ [ ] is ________ less than half ________

3. $\frac{5}{6}$ [ ] is ________ more than half ________

4. $\frac{3}{5}$ [ ] is ________ more than half ________

5. $\frac{2}{9}$ [ ] is ________ less than half ________

6. $\frac{6}{7}$ [ ] is ________ more than half ________

7. $\frac{1}{3}$ [ ] is ________ more than half ________

8 $\frac{5}{10}$ [ ] is ________ half ________

Student's name: ____________________ Assignment date: ______________

Fraction word problem

1. Today is Linda's birthday. She shared her birthday cake with five friends equally. Draw a graph to show how she divided her cake.

2. Sam bought a pizza. He ate 2 eighths of the pizza and gave Linda 3 eighths. What fraction of the pizza did he give to Linda?
$\frac{3}{8}$

3. There are 5 girls and 3 boys in the playground. What fraction of the children are girls?
$\frac{5}{8}$

4. There are 5 apples, 3 pears and 4 oranges in a basket. What fraction of the fruits are pears?
$\frac{3}{12}$

5. There are 7 pieces in a Tangram. Three of them are triangles. The rest are quadrilaterals. What fraction of the Tangram are quadrilaterals?
$\frac{4}{7}$

6. Adam has ten marbles. 2 tenths of them are blue. 3 tenths of them are red. The rest are yellow. Draw a picture to show the marbles. What fraction of the marbles are yellow?
2 blue, 3 red, 5 yellow 1/2

7. 20 minutes is what fraction of an hour?
$\frac{20}{60}$

8. 3 days is what fraction of a week?
$\frac{3}{7}$

Student's name: ____________________ Assignment date: ________________

9. 7 eggs are what fraction of a dozen eggs?

$\frac{7}{12}$

10. How many centimetres are there in 17 millimetres? Write a fraction and a mixed number.

$\frac{17}{10} = 1\frac{7}{10}$

11. How many centimetres are there in 25 millimetres? Write a fraction and a mixed number.

$\frac{25}{10} = 2\frac{5}{10}$

12. How many years are there in 18 months? Write a fraction and a mixed number.

$\frac{18}{12} = 1\frac{6}{12}$

13. Emma had 12 candies. She ate half of them. How many candies did she eat?

6

14. Stanley has 20 books. He gave 2 fifths of them to his sister. How many books did he give to his sister?

8

15. Shirley has a ribbon 50 cm long. She cut 2 fifths of it off. How long is the ribbon now?

30 cm

16. Marko had 15 chocolate bars. He ate 1 fifth of them and gave 3 to Fiona. How many chocolate bars did he leave?

9

Student's name: ____________________ Assignment date: ______________

17. Pauline has walked 7 blocks, and she must walk 10 blocks in total to reach her school. What fraction of distance is left for her to walk?

Answer $\frac{3}{10}$

18. Amanda says $\frac{2}{4}$ of a pie, size is the same as to say $\frac{2}{4}$ of the same pie. Is she right? Explain your reason by drawing a model.

Yes, Amanda is right because 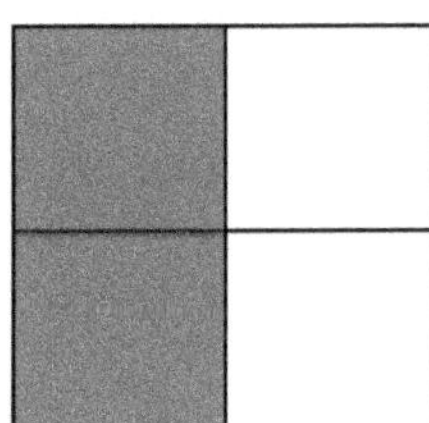 it is equivalent to 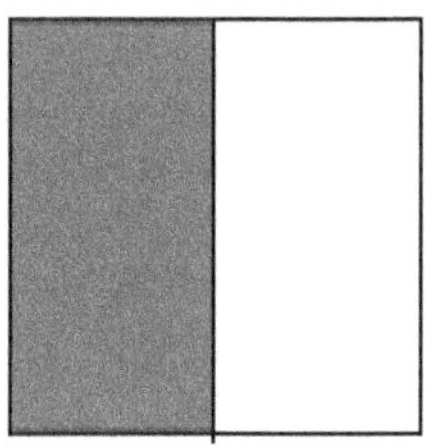

.

19. What fraction of a pit must you order to $\frac{2}{5}$ of a pie, you already ordered to make a whole pie?

$$\frac{3}{5}$$

Student's name: ____________________ Assignment date: ________________

Test of fractions

Result of fraction in English	Arithmetic computation	Graphic representation
One fourth	Not available	
One half	Not available	
Two thirds	Not available	0 1
One third	$\frac{2}{3}-\frac{1}{3}=\frac{1}{3}$	0 1
One half	$\frac{3}{4}-\frac{1}{4}=\frac{2}{4}$	–
One half	$\frac{2}{4}+\frac{2}{4}=1$	+ ? = 1
One half	$2\times\frac{1}{4}=\frac{1}{2}$	2 of $\frac{1}{4}$ =

Student's name: ____________________ Assignment date: ________________

Test of fractions

Fractions	Write the fractions from the least to the greatest
$\frac{9}{2}$ $4\frac{1}{3}$	
$2\frac{2}{3}$ $\frac{7}{3}$	
$\frac{23}{27}$, $\frac{11}{27}$, $\frac{25}{27}$, $\frac{26}{27}$	
$3\frac{3}{7}$, $4\frac{1}{7}$, $3\frac{5}{7}$, $2\frac{6}{7}$	
$\frac{3}{7}$, $\frac{3}{5}$, $\frac{3}{4}$, $\frac{3}{6}$	
$\frac{6}{7}$, $\frac{6}{5}$, $\frac{6}{4}$, $\frac{6}{6}$	
$\frac{8}{9}$, $\frac{8}{11}$, $\frac{8}{13}$, $\frac{8}{10}$	

Write a fraction or a mixed number to make each statement true (more than one answers).

$\frac{8}{8} >$ ______ $\frac{1}{10}$
$1\frac{1}{1} <$ ______ $\frac{5}{2}$
______ $> \frac{4}{7}$ $\frac{5}{7}$
______ $< 1\frac{2}{3}$ $\frac{4}{3}$

Student's name: ____________________ Assignment date: ________________

Test of fractions

<table>
<tr><td>The following figure represents $\frac{3}{7}$ of one whole. It has some part missing, so complete the figure and shaded it, so it shows the shaded part is $\frac{3}{7}$.
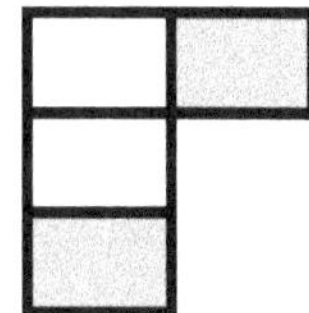</td></tr>
<tr><td>A. Write a fraction between 0 and 1 that is neither closer to 0 nor closer to 1. ________
B. Write a fraction between 0 and $\frac{1}{2}$ that is neither closer to 0 nor closer to $\frac{1}{2}$. ________
C. Write a fraction between 1 and $\frac{1}{2}$ that is neither closer to 1 nor closer to $\frac{1}{2}$. ________</td></tr>
</table>

Fraction equation	Fraction multiplication model
$\frac{1}{2} \times 6 = 3$	$\frac{1}{2}$ of 6
$\frac{3}{5} \times 20 =?$	?
? $\frac{1}{3} \times 12 = 4$	
? $\frac{1}{3} \times 9 = 3$	

Student's name: ____________________ Assignment date: ________________

Test of fractions and fraction pictures

Mixed number	Improper fraction	Fraction picture
$3\frac{1}{2}$answer	$\frac{7}{2}$answer	
$2\frac{3}{4}$answer	$\frac{11}{4}$answer	
$4\frac{2}{3}$answer	$\frac{14}{3}$answer	
$4\frac{2}{3}$answer	$\frac{14}{3}$answer	

One-half plus one and three-quarter is equal to ____________.

Shade $\frac{3}{5}$ of

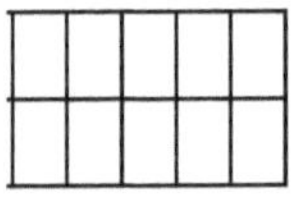

Shade $\frac{4}{10}$ of

Shade $\frac{4}{10}$ of

Shade $2\frac{4}{6}$ of

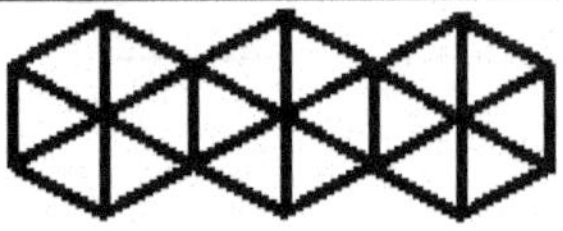

Student's name: ____________________ Assignment date: ________________

Test of fractions using the number line

Fill in the missing fractions on the following number lines.

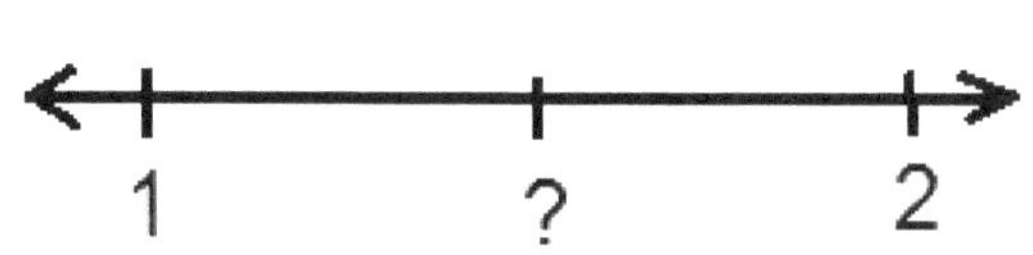

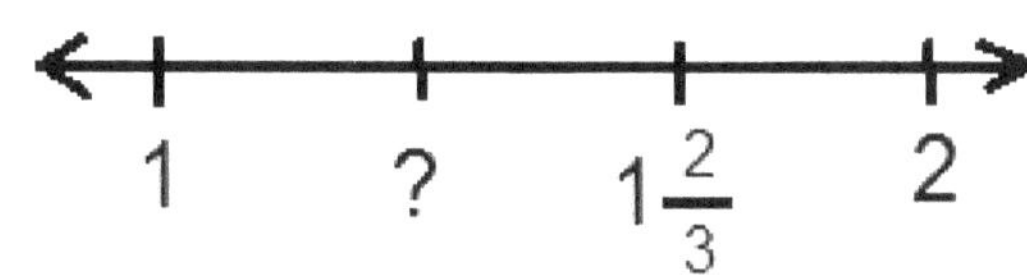

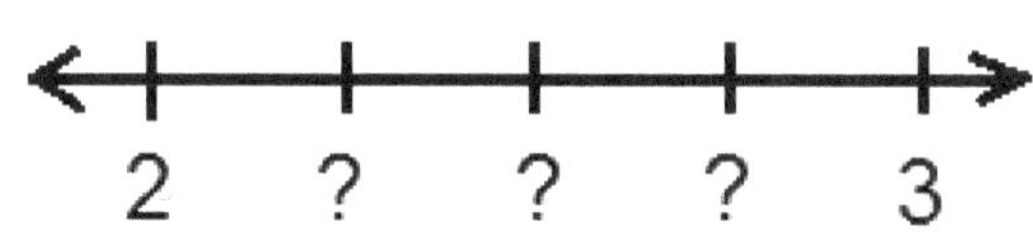

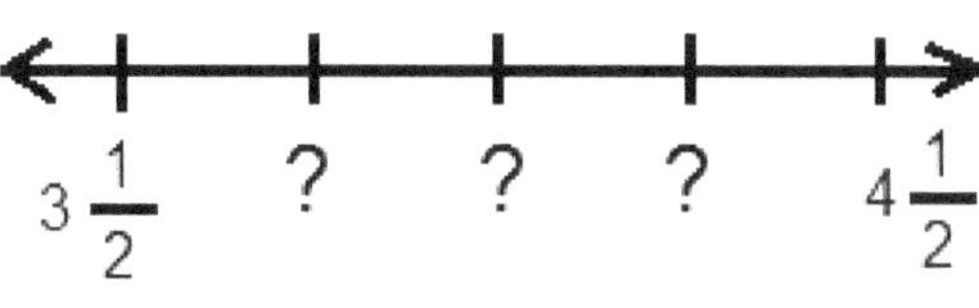

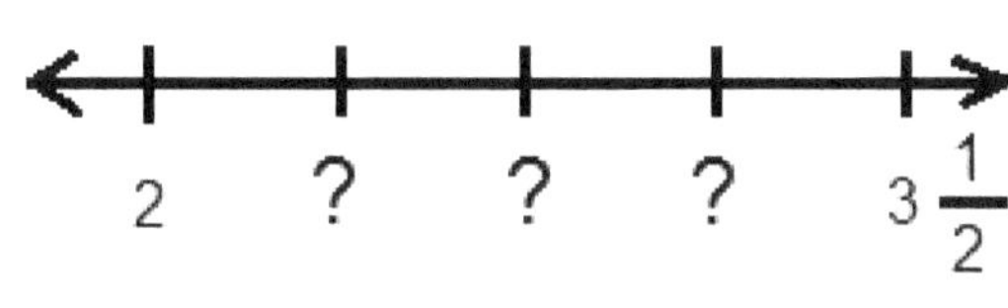

$1\frac{1}{2}$, $1\frac{1}{3}$, $2\frac{1}{4}$, $2\frac{2}{4}$, $2\frac{3}{4}$, $3\frac{3}{4}$, 4, $4\frac{1}{4}$,
$2\frac{3}{8}$, $2\frac{6}{8}$, $3\frac{1}{8}$,
Get the line difference by using the endpoint – start point
$3\frac{1}{2} - 2 = 1\frac{1}{2}$, $1\frac{1}{2} \times \frac{1}{4} = \frac{3}{8}$ which is the gap (quarter) between each point.

Student's name: ____________________ Assignment date: ________________

***** Part 17 Percent *****

Percent means "per hundred" or "out of 100". When a fraction $\frac{a}{100}$ is expressed as a out of 100, then it is called a %. For example, $\frac{2}{100}$ = 2%. The notation is used for easy communication, so the % is often converted to decimal for computation purposes. Since $\frac{2}{100} = 0.02$, We now established the conversion relationship between fraction, percent, and decimal.

When $\frac{a}{b}$ (a over b) is not explained, it could mean the following different meanings:

- a out of b
- a to b (a : b)
- a divided by b
- a times $\frac{1}{b}$
- a favourable outcome out of b possible outcome

For computation purposes, a percent normally is converted to decimal.

fraction	%	decimal	Division
$\frac{1}{10}$			$10\overline{)1}$
$\frac{1}{20}$			$\overline{)}$
$\frac{1}{8}$			$\overline{)}$
$\frac{1}{2}$			$\overline{)}$
$\frac{3}{4}$			$\overline{)}$
$\frac{2}{3}$			$\overline{)}$

Student's name: ____________________ Assignment date: ________________

fraction	%	decimal	Division
		0.4	
		0.12	
		0.01	
		1.5	
		1.05	
6 out of 10			
$2\frac{1}{5}$			
	$33\frac{1}{3}\%$		
X		$0.\overline{3}$	
	455		

Student's name: ____________________ Assignment date: ________________

Computation of percent

Often we translate percent to either divided by 100 or multiplied by $\frac{1}{100}$ in the computation of %.

Original amount × percent = partial amount

In lower grades, most problems are to find the partial amount when a percent is given. A direct method using multiplication could be used to solve it.

Example 1

A dress is selling for $20. If Sophie buys it at a 20% discount, how much will she save and how much will she have to pay?

20 × 0.2 = 4 …… The Amount Sophie will save.
20- 4 = 16 …….. The amount Sophie will have to pay.

Use one statement

Students should also understand that without getting the amount of discount, use the concept of a whole in fraction. How much does Sophie have to pay could also be solved by using only one statement?

20 × 0.8 = 16 … Sophie only pays 80%.

Student's name: ____________________ Assignment date: ________________

Example 2

Twelve students of Alvin's borrowed books for the library, which is 75% of the entire class. How many students in Alvin's class did not borrow any books?

Method 1

Convert the percent to fraction and then convert fraction to groups.

75% = $\frac{3}{4}$ which could mean Alvin's class is divided into 4 groups, and 3 groups of them borrowed books, and the number of students in that 3 groups is 12. To find how many students in each group, we just use $\frac{12}{3}$=4. We know there is only one group of students who did not borrow any books, so the answer is 4.

Method 2

Use the Line Segment Method by drawing line segments.

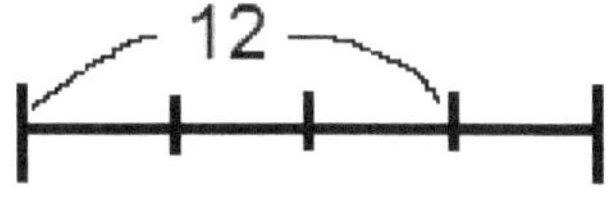

Method 3

A quantity divided by its corresponding value (to work backwards to get the original amount.)

This method is difficult for lower grades students to understand, so we suggest this method for higher grades students.

$12 \div 0.75 = 12 \times \frac{4}{3} = 16$ …. The number of students for the entire class

$16 - 12 = 4$

Student's name: ____________________ Assignment date: ________________

Test of Percent

Information		Problem	Answer
		Find the % of the shaded area. Find % of the not shaded area.	
Annie		Find the letter of n`s percentage in the name as spelled on the left.	
25% 50%		Which one is a larger percentage?	
		Find the percent of shaded squares.	
Annie`s class has 10 boys and 15 girls.		Find the percent of boys in Annie`s class.	

Student's name: ____________________ Assignment date: ________________

Finding equal to, more than, less than of the originals

Emily has 20% of Mable's money. Mable has \$15. How much money does Emily have? $15 \times 0.2 = 3$
Emily has 20% more money than Mable. Mable has \$15. How much money does Emily have? $15 \times 1.2 = 18$
Emily has 20% less money than Mable. Mable has \$15. How much money does Emily have? $15 \times 0.8 = 12$
Emily has as much as $\frac{2}{5}$ of Mable's money. Mable has \$15. How much money does Emily have? $15 \times \frac{2}{5} = 6$
Emily has $\frac{2}{5}$ more money than Mable. Mable has \$15. How much money does Emily have? 15×1.4 $(1\frac{2}{5} = \frac{7}{5})$ $= 21$
Emily has $\frac{2}{5}$ less than Mable. Mable has \$15. How much money does Emily have? $15 \times 0.6 = 9$

Student's name: ____________________ Assignment date: ________________

Percent and line number

Find the answer to each question.

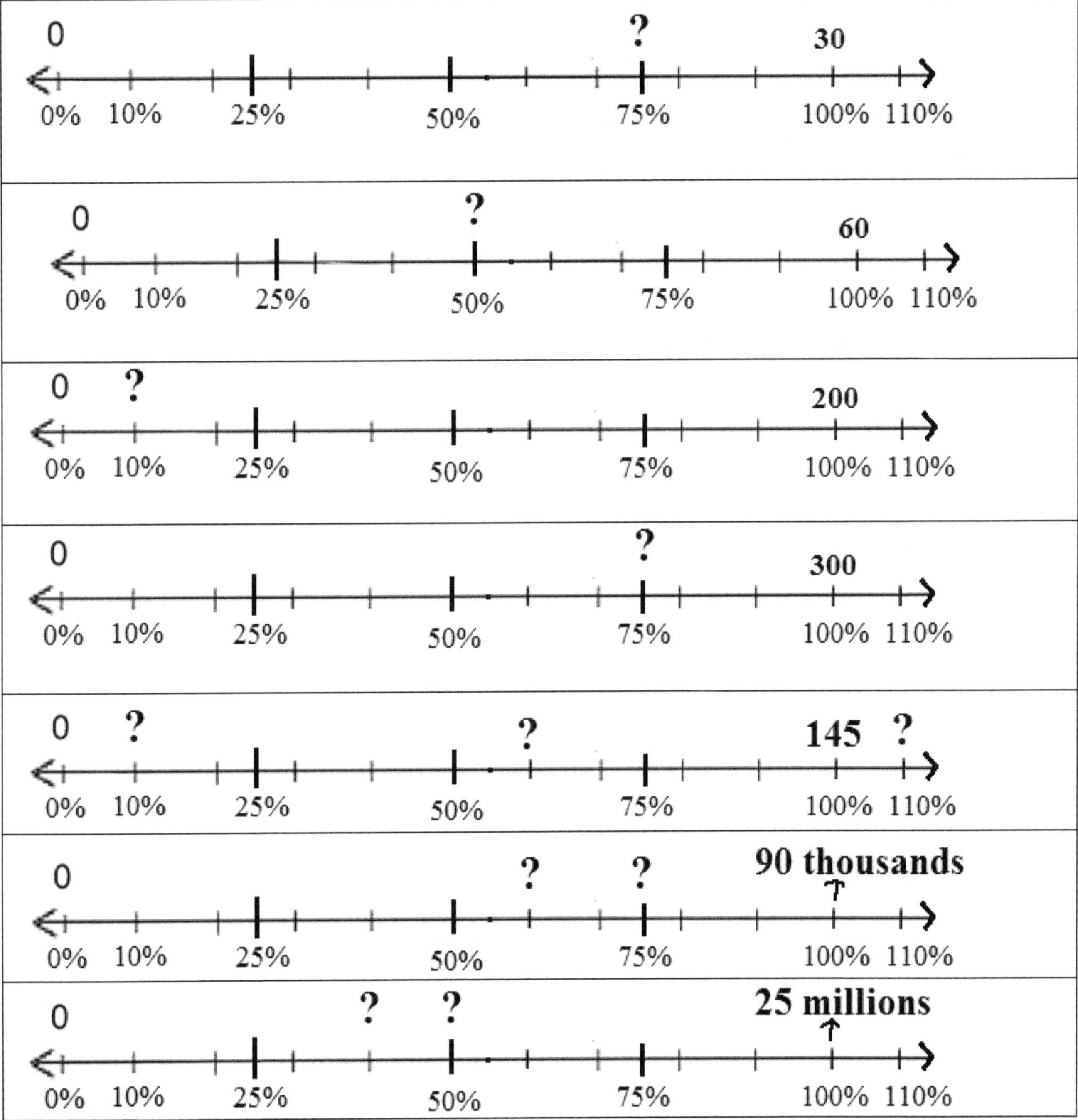

Student's name: ____________________ Assignment date: ________________

Test of percent word problems

Ten percent off is the same as \$15 off what price? $x \times 0.1 = 15$ $x = 15 \div 0.1 = 150$
Adam earns 10% interest in his savings every year. How much interest does he earn for every dollar after one year? 100 ¢ × 0.1 = 10 cents

Student's name: ____________________ Assignment date: ________________

Conversion between fraction, percent, ratio

Original problems	fraction	percent	Alternate problems
3 out of 5 students wear white caps in Heather's class.	The fraction of students wearing white caps = ______. .	The percent of students wearing no-white caps = _____.	Suppose 9 students are wearing white caps in Heather's class. How many total students in Heather's class?

Student's name: ____________________ Assignment date: ________________

Ratio, proportion, rate

The ratio is a general term used to describe the relation of any two or more quantities (or variables). The way to compare two quantities is by a number of different techniques, and this is where the confusion starts. By definition, the ratio is used when 2 or more quantities are compared. Still, in practice, there are many different ways of writing the result of the comparison. For example, the ratio could be described in words, 2 out of 5 children are girls could be written as 2 out of 5 or 2 to 5 or ratio can also be expressed as a symbol such as 2:5. It can also be written as a fractional number $\frac{2}{5}$. Further, the ratio is not limited to just comparing 2 quantities. For example, the number of balls in red: black: white = 2: 3: 4 is a ratio to compare 3 quantities.

In order to make the comparison meaningful, the numbers compared normally have the same measuring unit but not necessarily so all the time. For example, the scale is one type of ratio but is normally expressed in different measuring units and only converted to the same unit when doing calculations. Rate is also one type of ratio but also expressed in different measuring units, but in a special case, that is when b is one.
Whenever any 2 (or more) quantities are compared either in words or in the form of $\frac{a}{b}$ where a and b are whole numbers and $b \neq 0$, the result could be called ratio. Ratio includes fraction, probability, scale, interest rate, rate, speed, or sides/angles ratio of similar triangle etc.

The ratio does not have to be a rational number. For example, the ratio of the circumference to its diameter is π, which is a non-terminating and non-repeating number (irrational number).

The ratio becomes more interesting when it is assumed to be a constant and thus can be used to predict either future a or b - this concept is called proportion.

The ratio is to compare two numbers in a simplified form without any unit. The ratio can be expressed in many ways but often the from $\frac{a}{b}$ is used for calculation. Without any further explanation of the meaning $\frac{a}{b}, \frac{a}{b}$ can be a ratio, fraction, division. Often a ratio is changed to or converted to $\frac{a}{b}$ and calculated as a fraction because we learn all 4 basic operations (+ , −, ×,÷) of fractions.

Because a ratio is reduced form so a ratio problem often could be solved by using the common factor idea.

There is a ratio $a : b$. The difference between the two ratios converted to original numbers could be expressed as follows:

$$ax - bx = x(a - b)$$

Student's name: ____________________ Assignment date: ________________

$\frac{ax-bx}{a-b} = x$ which is the common factor

Example

Two out of 5 students watched TV on the new year`s eve in Linda`s class. How many students did not watch TV if Lina`s class has 25 students?

Convert the wording Two out of 5`` into a fraction $\frac{2}{5}$.
Get the answer by using the concept of fraction. $25 \times \frac{3}{5}$ = 15

Test of ratio word problems

Three times as many pens as erasers	P: E = 3:1	E: P = 1:3
	P = ___ E	E = _____ P

There are 3 boys for every 2 girls in Sarah's class. There are 24 children in her class. How many girls and boys in her class?

There are 19 more boys than girls in Sarah's martial arts class. There are 41 children in her class. How many girls and boys in her class?

There are many ways to solve this problem such as Sum and Difference, multiple methods (turning difference into multiples by subtracting 19, and ratio concept to make boy : girl = 1 : 1)

Student's name: ____________________ Assignment date: ________________

When writing ratio, remember the following points:

The numbers in a ratio should always be given in the same order as the statement stated.
The numbers in a ratio should always give in whole numbers.
The numbers in a ratio should always in simplest form.
The numbers in a ratio added together representing the LCM of a whole set (after reducing).

Proportion

Two equal ratios are called proportion.

Test of ratio, rate, and proportion

Emily collects coins. For every 5 coins, she collects 2 dimes. How many dimes does she have if she has 28 coins?
Kiko, the cat, brings home 3 leaves in 30 minutes. How many leaves will she bring in one and a half hours if she collects leaves at twice the speed of the given rate? 18 leaves

Student's name: ____________________ Assignment date: ________________

***** Part 18 Geometry *****

Lines

Straight-line	Curve	Parallel lines

1. Matching.

Straight lines

Parallel lines

Curve

2. Write the name of the following lines.

curve	parallel lines	straight lines
____________	____________	____________

Student's name: ____________________ Assignment date: ________________

3. What kind of lines does each picture have?

	Straight line	Curve	Parallel lines
		√	
	√		√
	√		
		√	

4. Draw line(s) through the following dots.

Straight line	Parallel lines	Curve
. B . A	. C . D	. E . F

Student's name: ____________________ Assignment date: ________________

Name of lines

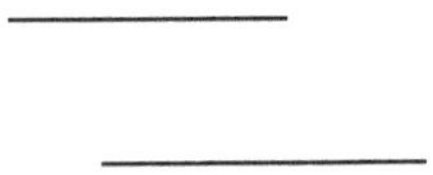 horizontal lines	 vertical lines	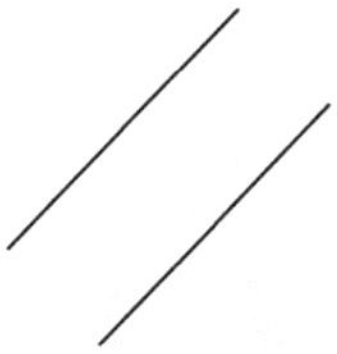 parallel lines
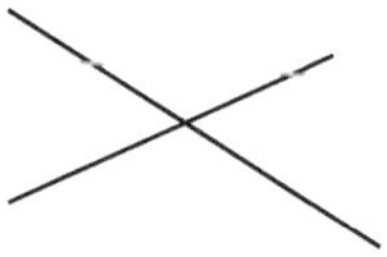 intersecting lines	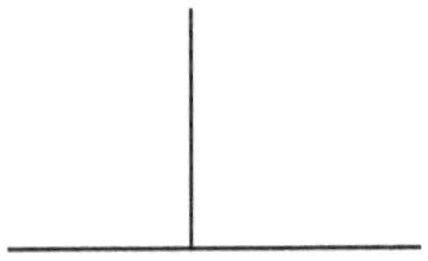 perpendicular lines	

What types of lines can you find in each figure?

	horizontal lines	vertical lines	parallel lines	intersecting lines	perpendicular lines
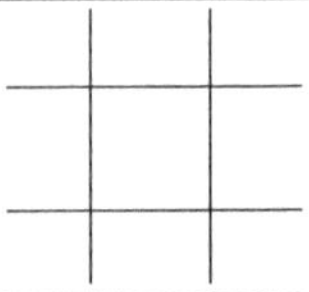	√	√	√	√	√
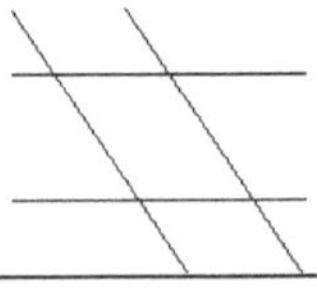	√		√	√	
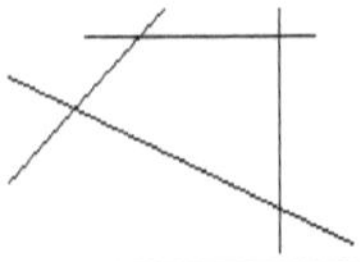	√	√		√	√
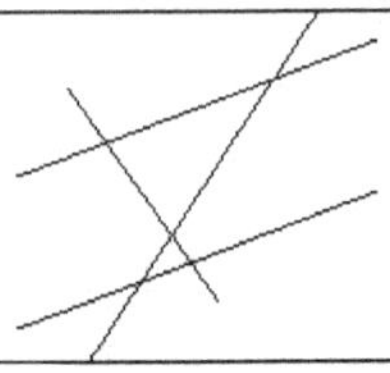			√	√	

Student's name: ____________________ Assignment date: ________________

Angles

An angle is formed by two rays intersected with a common endpoint.

An acute angle is an angle that is less than 90°.

A right angle is an angle that is 90°.

An obtuse angle is an angle that is greater than 90° but less than 180°.

A straight angle is an angle that is 180° exactly.

A reflex angle is an angle that is greater than 180° but less than 360°.

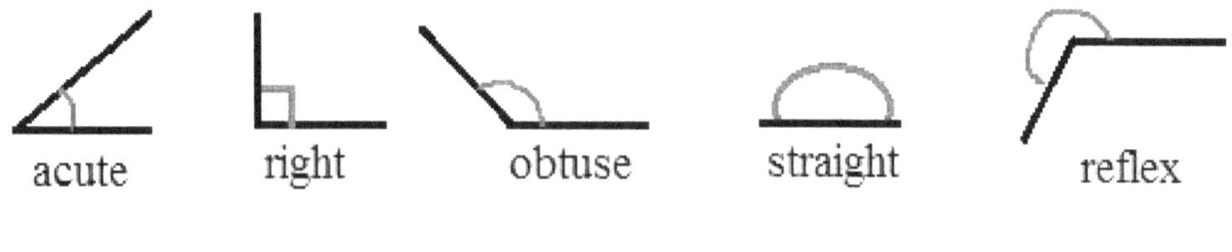

An angle such as B—C (with A, angle 1) can be expressed as ∠B, ∠1, ∠ABC, ∠CBA.

Student's name: ____________________ Assignment date: ________________

1. Arrange the angles in order of size from the largest to the smallest. Put in 1, 2, 3 to show.

a.

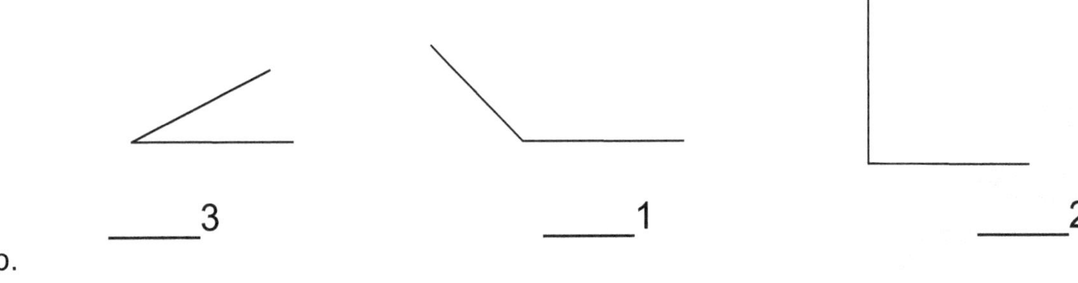

_____3 _____1 _____2

b.

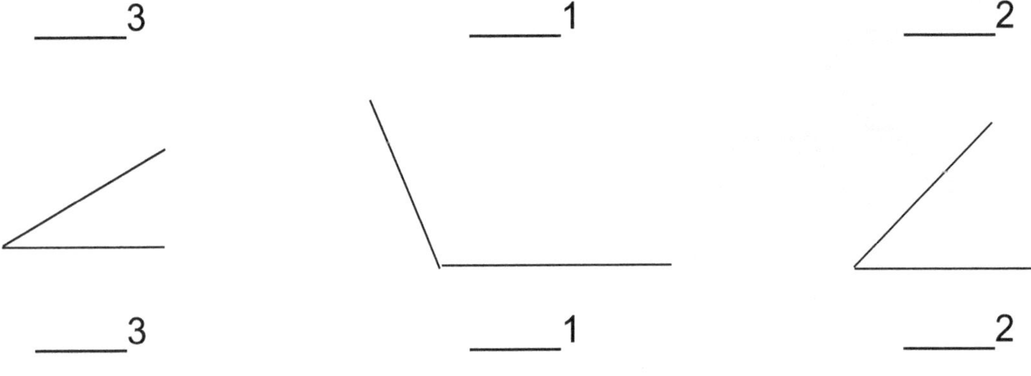

_____3 _____1 _____2

2. Find the number of right angles of the following figures.

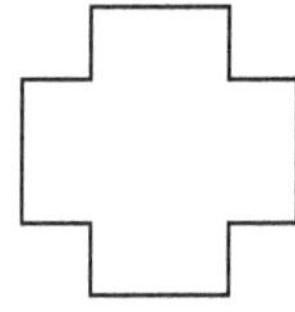

_____4 _____16 _____8

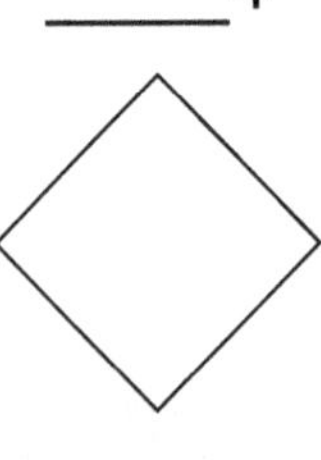

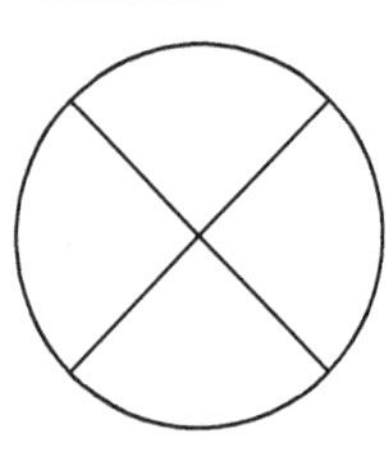

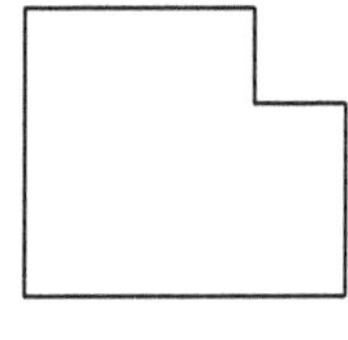

_____4 _____4 _____5

Student's name: ____________________ Assignment date: ________________

Measure the following angles.

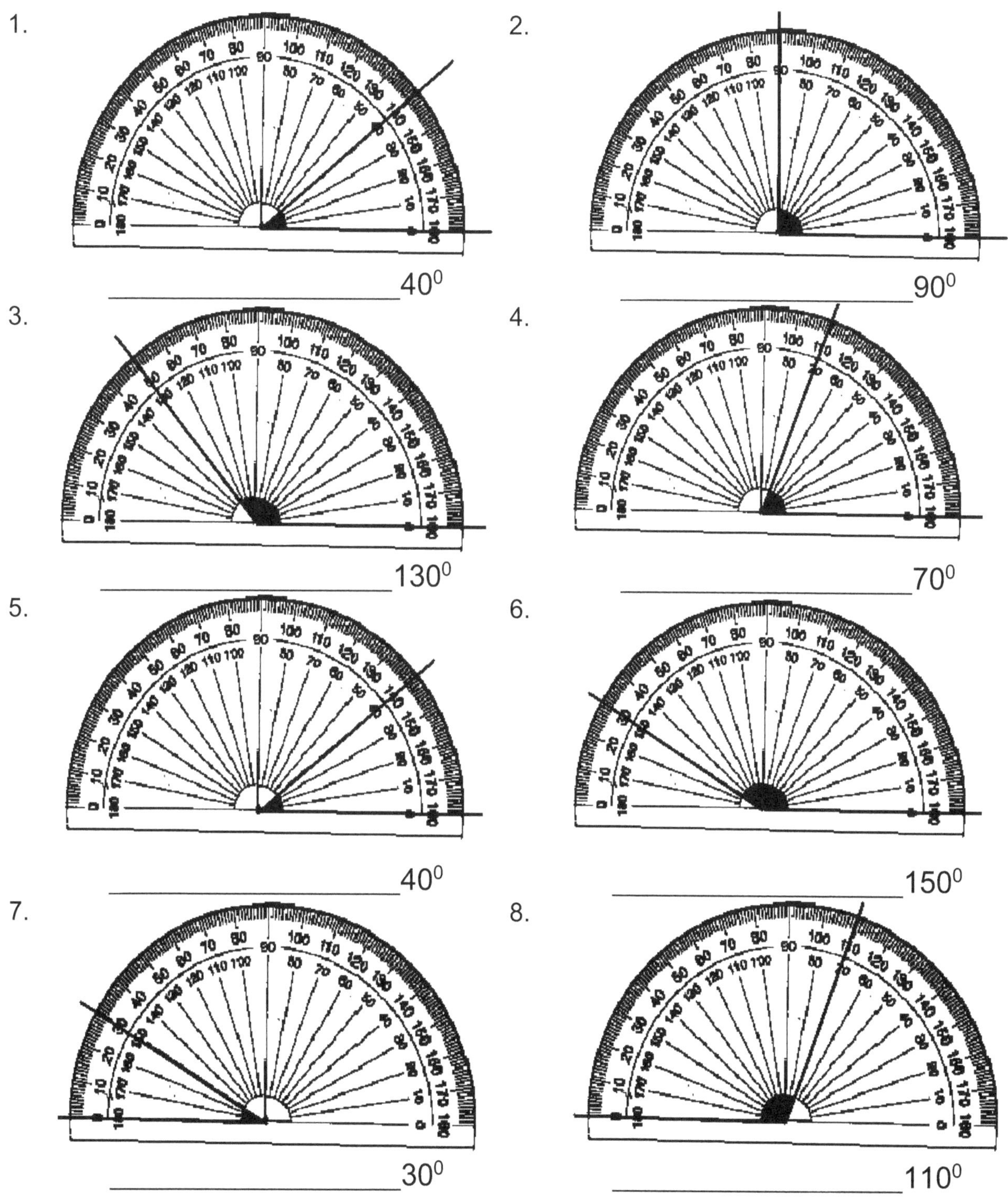

Student's name: ____________________ Assignment date: ________________

Measure the following angles.

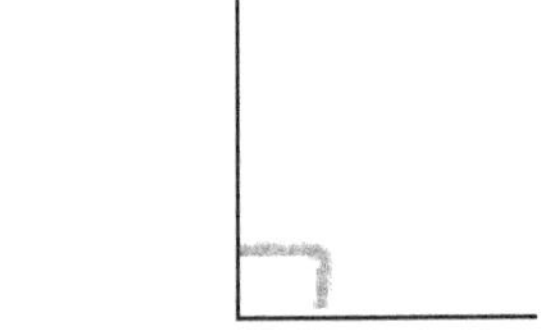

1 ____________ 2 ____________

3 ____________ 4 ____________

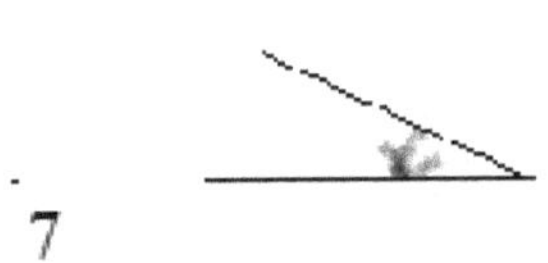

5 ____________ 6 ____________

7 ____________ 8 ____________

40, 180
140, 360
90, 45
25, 145

Student's name: ____________________ Assignment date: ________________

9.

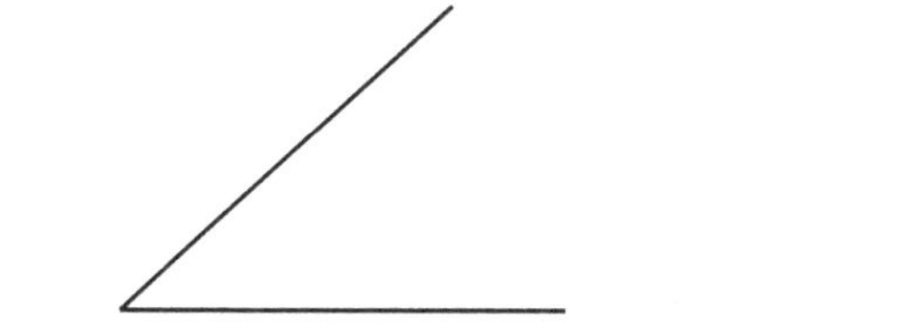

__________________ 40^0

10.

__________________ 27^0

11.

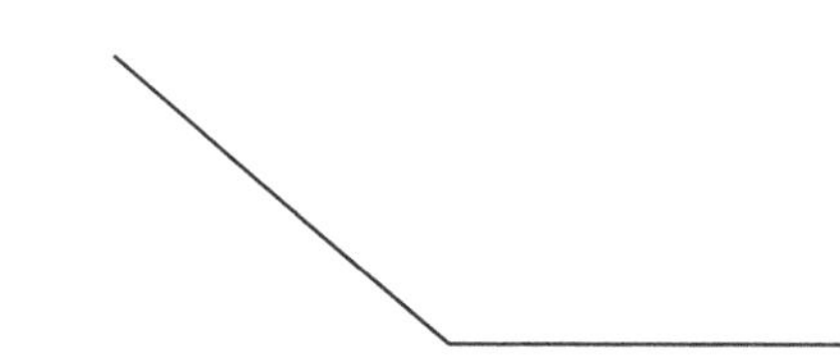

__________________ 140^0

12.

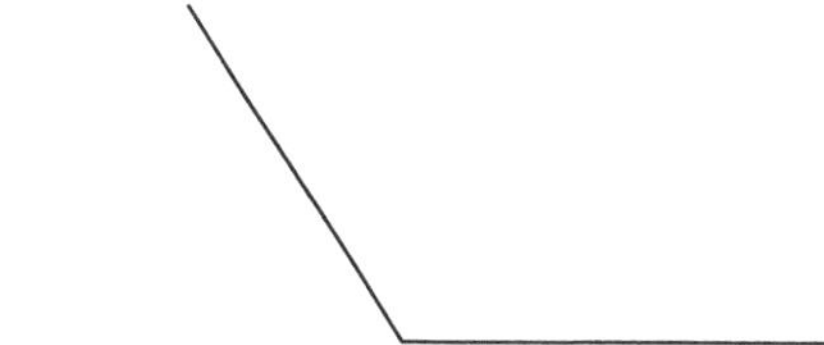

__________________ 125^0

13.

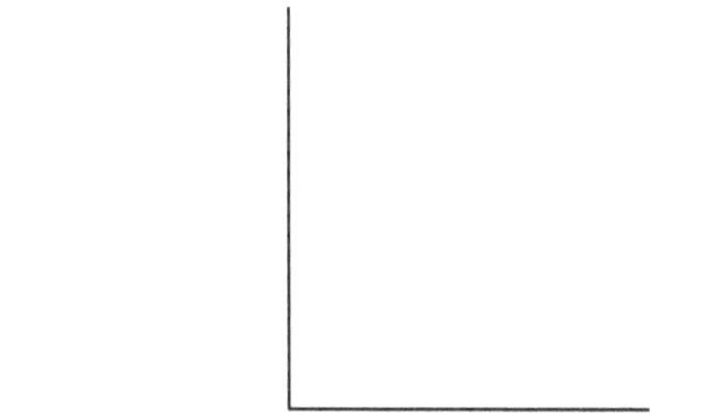

__________________ 90^0

14.

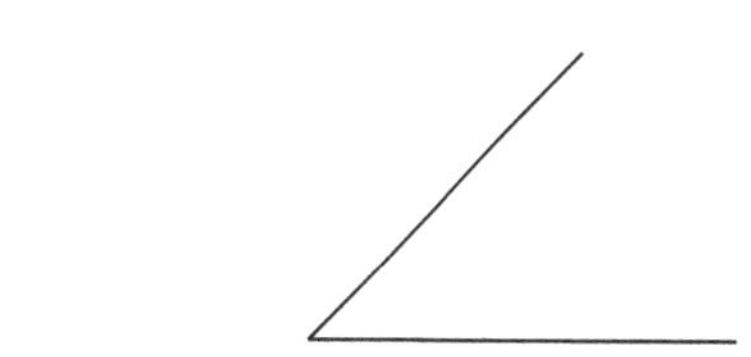

__________________ 45^0

15.

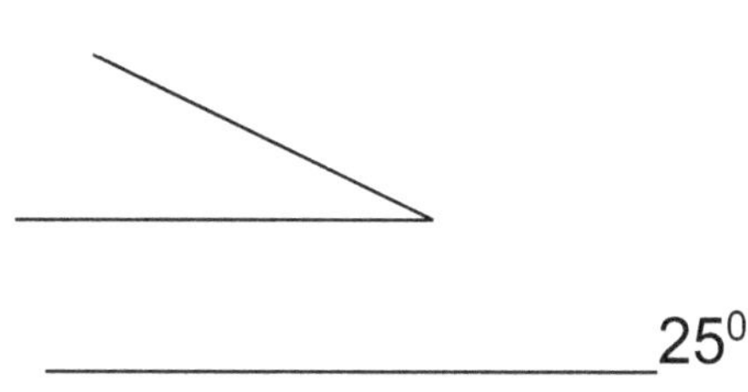

__________________ 25^0

16.

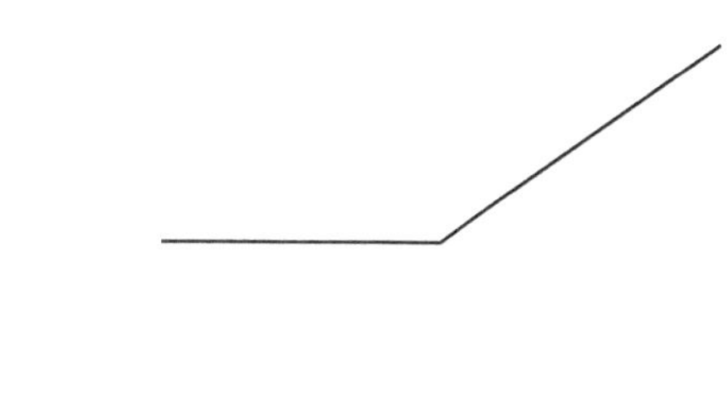

__________________ 145^0

Student's name: ____________________ Assignment date: ________________

Shapes

Circle The number of circle sides does not have a definite answer. It is not a polygon, so that the answer could be 0. If you think of the circle as a disk, then it has an up-side and a down-side. If you think of it as a curve, then it has an inside and an outside. If you think of it as the limit of an n-sided regular polygon, one can justify the answer that the circle has infinitely many infinitesimal sides.	**Triangle** (Three sides)	**Rectangle** (Four sides)
Pentagon (Five sides)	**Hexagon** (Six sides)	**Octagon** (Eight sides)

What types of shapes can you find in each figure?

	Circle	Triangle	Rectangle	Pentagon	Hexagon	Octagon
	√	√	√			
			√			√
	√		√			
	√			√		

Ho Math Chess Primary Grades Math

Test Review assesssment 何数棋謎低年级数学测试複習考核

Student's name: ____________________ Assignment date: ________________

Triangle

Angles sum of a triangle is 180^0. This geometry is often not given in the problems, but students must know in advance.

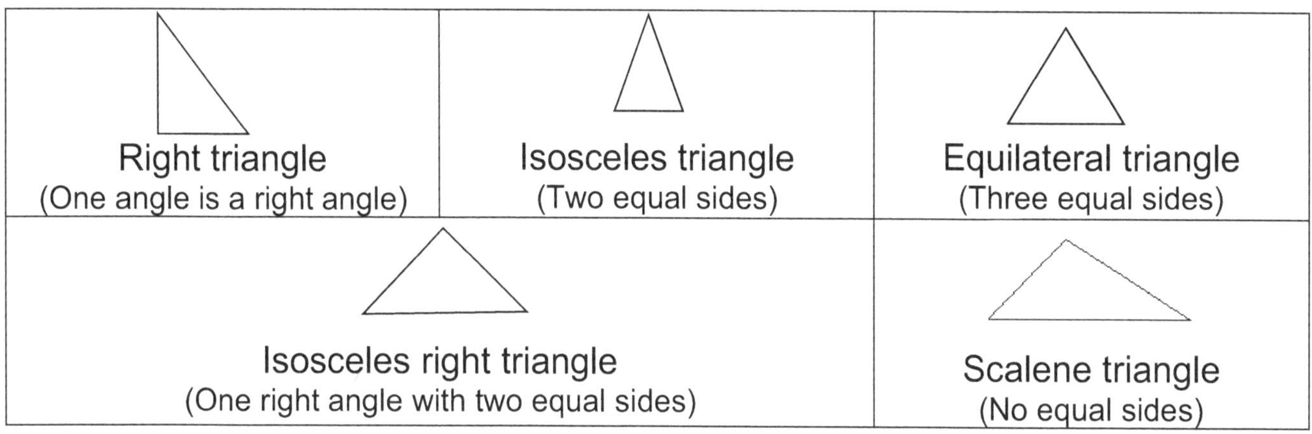

Right triangle (One angle is a right angle)	Isosceles triangle (Two equal sides)	Equilateral triangle (Three equal sides)
Isosceles right triangle (One right angle with two equal sides)		Scalene triangle (No equal sides)

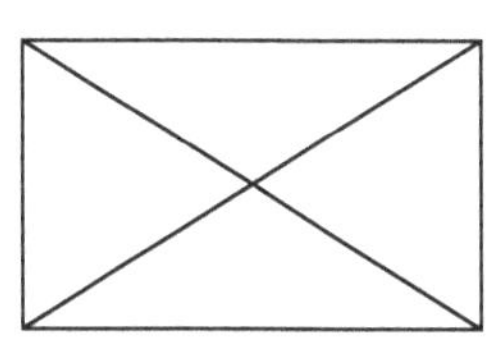

1. There are __4__ right triangles in a rectangle.
2. There are __4__ isosceles triangles in a rectangle.

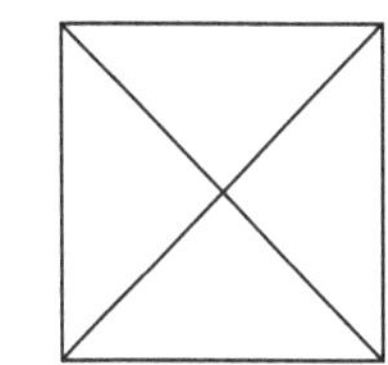

1. There are __8__ isosceles right triangles in a square.

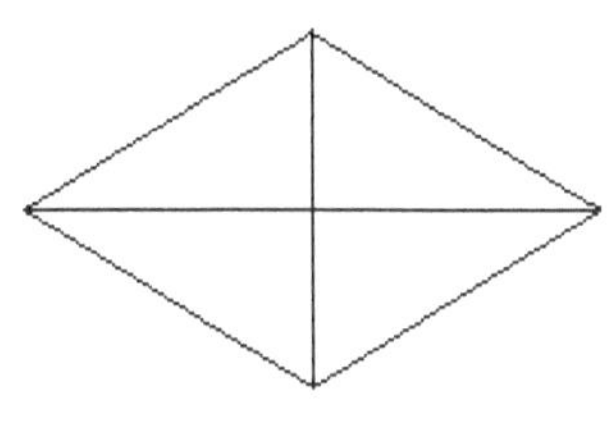

1. There are __4__ right triangles in a rhombus.
2. There are __4__ isosceles triangles in a rhombus.

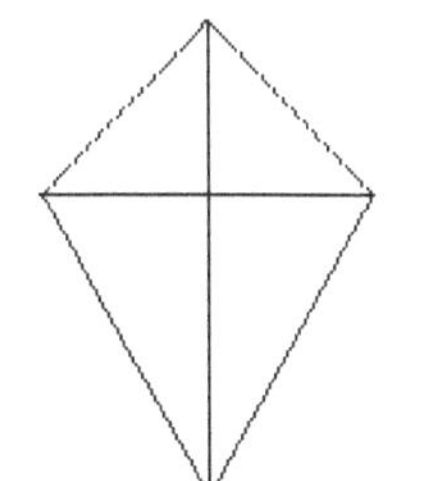

1. There are __4__ right triangles in a kite.
2. There are __2__ isosceles triangles in a kite.

Student's name: ____________________ Assignment date: ________________

Quadrilateral

The quadrilateral progressing diagram

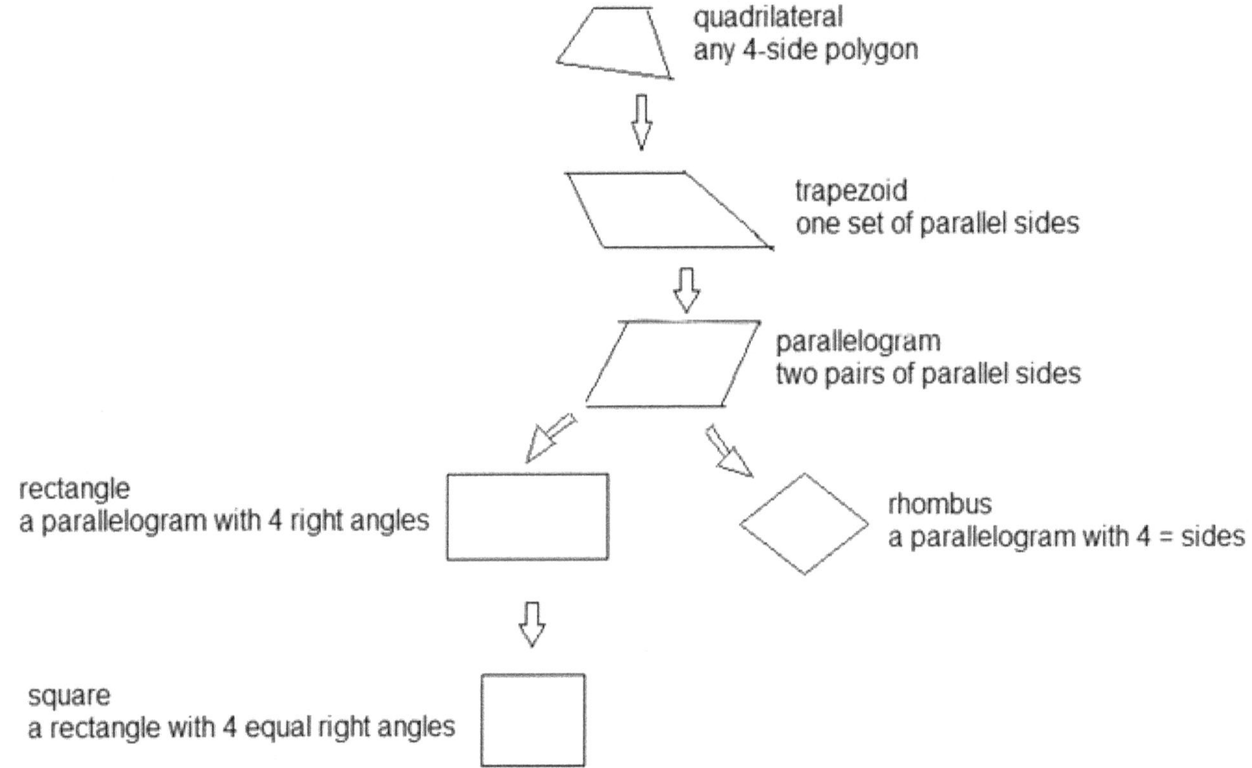

Student's name: ____________________ Assignment date: ________________

Quadrilaterals

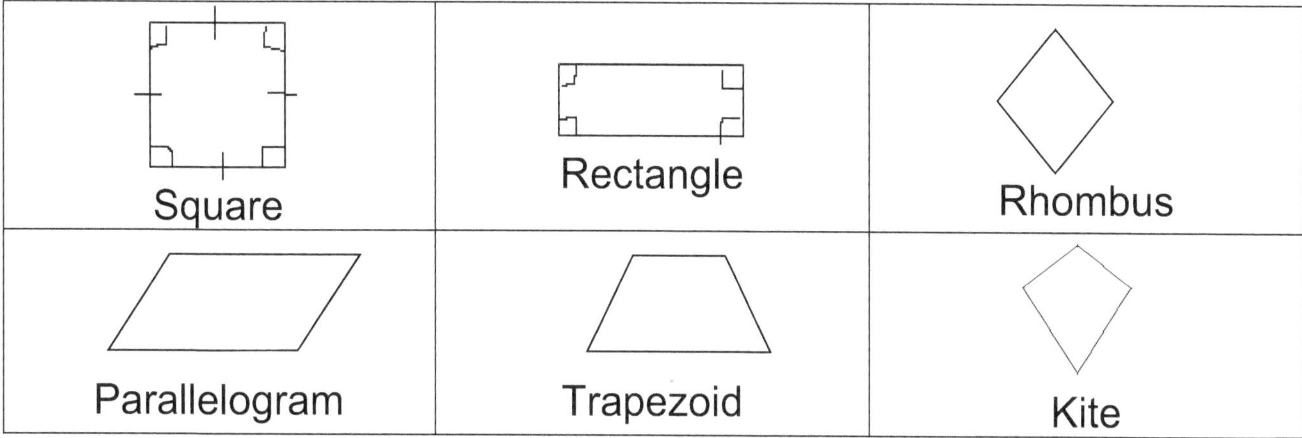

1. How many rectangles can you find?

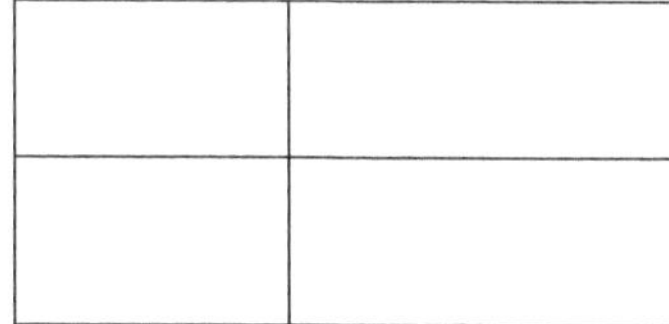

9

2. How many triangles can you find?

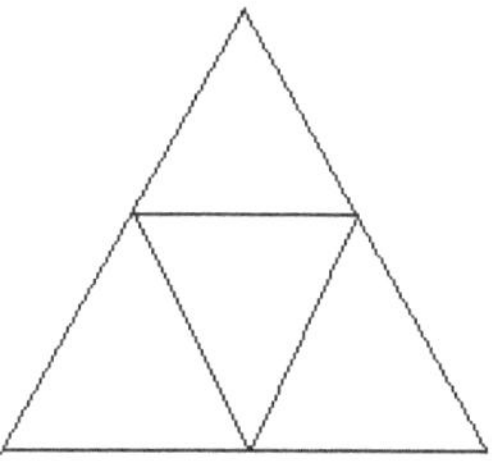

5

3. How many squares can you find?

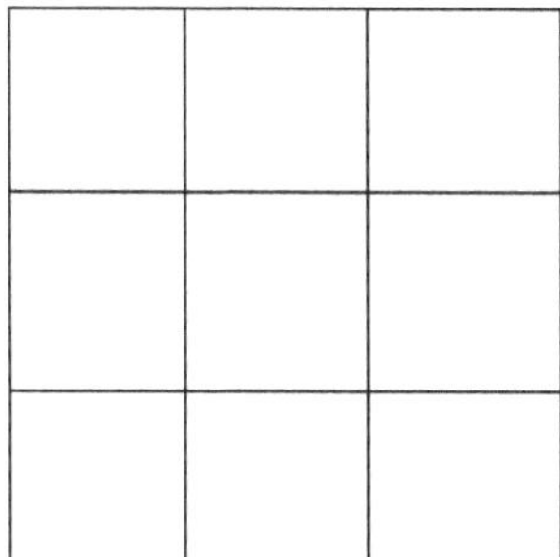

14

Student's name: ____________________ Assignment date: ________________

4. Matching.

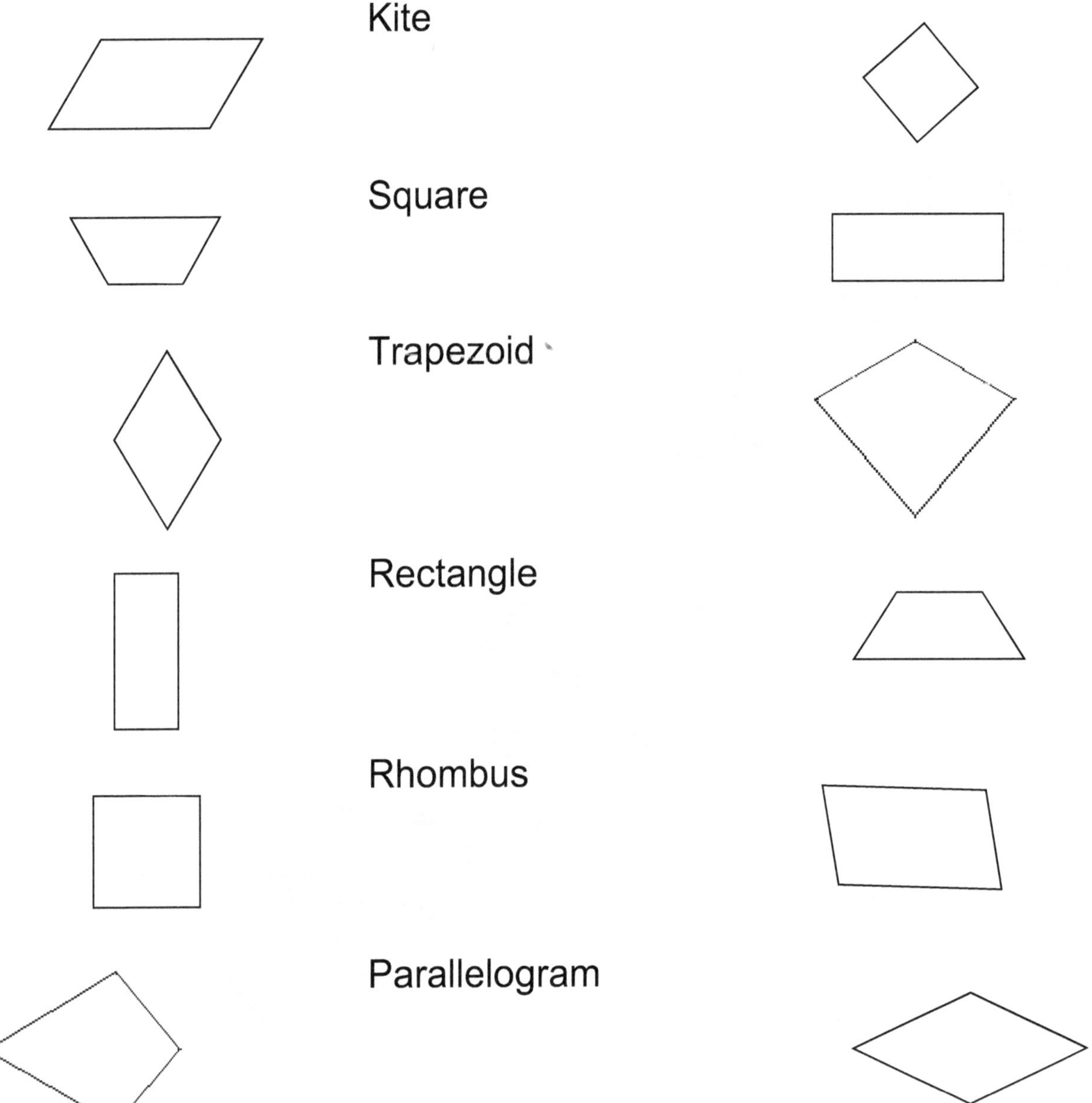

Student's name: ____________________ Assignment date: ________________

Shapes

The figure below is the Chinese Tangram. It is made up of seven pieces. Observe and fill in the blanks below.

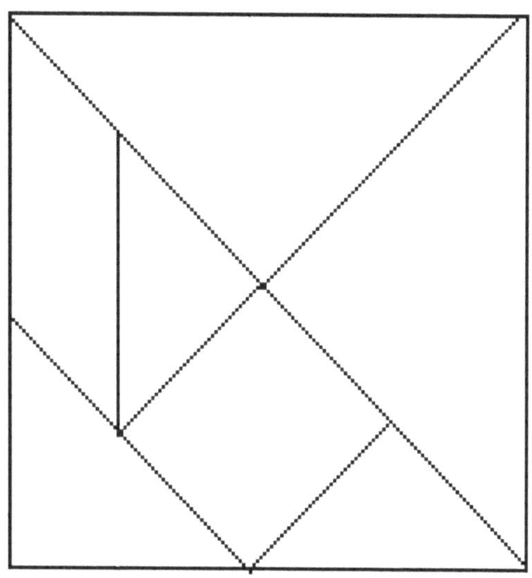

1. There are __7__ triangles in the graph.
2. There are __2__ squares in the graph.
3. There are __1__ parallelograms in the graph.
4. There are __5__ trapezoids in the graph.

Student's name: ____________________ Assignment date: ________________

Complete the following chart to show the property of each quadrilateral.

	Name	# of pairs of parallel sides	# of pairs of equal sides	# of equal angles
	trapezoid	1 pair	None	None
	Rhombus	2 pairs	4 equal sides	2 pairs of opposite angles
	Kite	None	2 pairs	1 pair
	Parallelogram	2 pairs	2 pairs	2 pairs of opposite angles
	rectangle	2 pairs	2 pairs	4 equal angles
	square	2 pairs	4 equal sides	4 equal angles

Student's name: ____________________ Assignment date: ________________

Draw the quadrilateral according to each description.

2 pairs of parallel sides and 2 pairs of equal sides	2 pairs of parallel sides and 4 equal sides
4 right angles and 2 pairs of equal sides	4 right angles and 4 equal sides
2 pairs of opposite equal sides and 2 pairs of opposite equal angles	2 pairs of adjacent equal sides and 1 pairs of opposite equal angles
1 pair of parallel sides and no equal sides	2 pairs of opposite equal angles and 4 equal sides

Student's name: ____________________ Assignment date: ________________

Complementary and supplementary angles

Complementary angles add up to 90^0 $\angle a + \angle b = 90^0$ and each is a complementary angle.	Supplementary angles add up to 180^0 $\angle a + \angle b = 180^0$, and each is a supplementary angle.
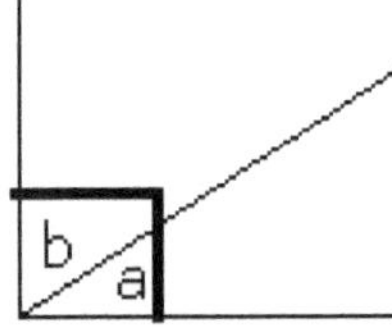	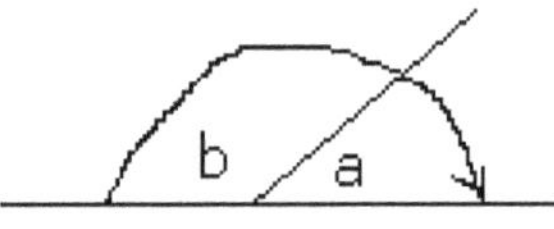

Find the missing angles and state the reason on how to find its size.

1.

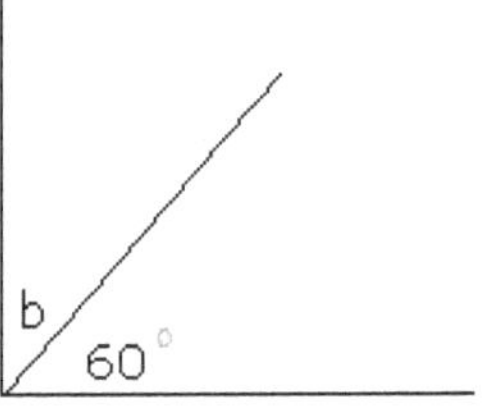

$\angle$ b = __________ 30

Reason: ____________________

2.

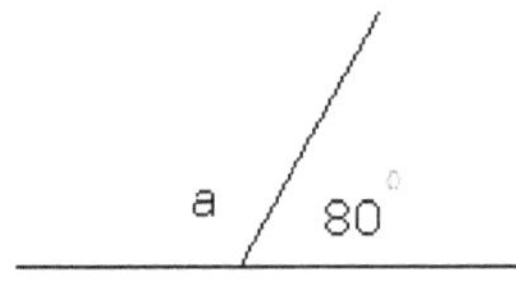

$\angle$ a = __________ 100

Reason: ____________________

3.

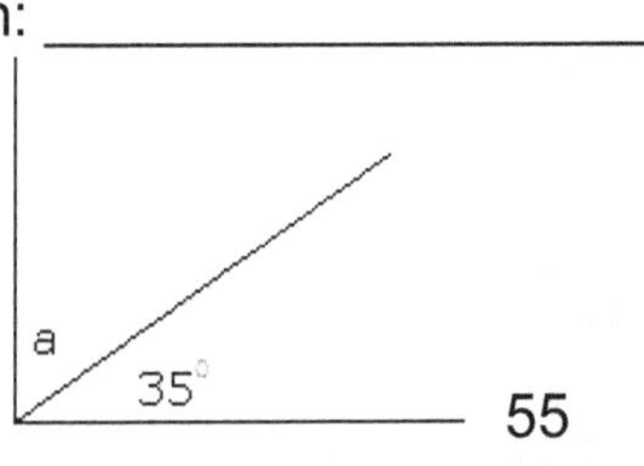

55

$\angle$ a = __________

Reason: ____________________

4.

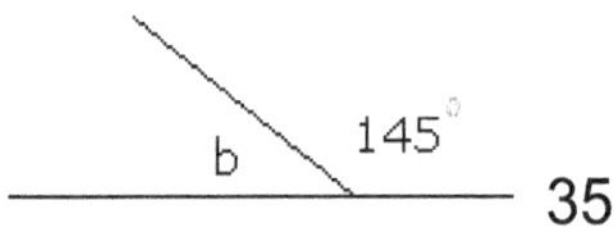

35

$\angle$ b = __________

Reason: ____________________

5.

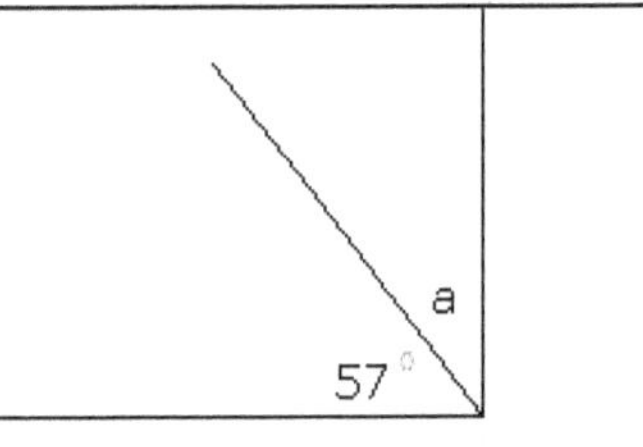

$\angle$ a = __________ 33

Reason: ____________________

6.

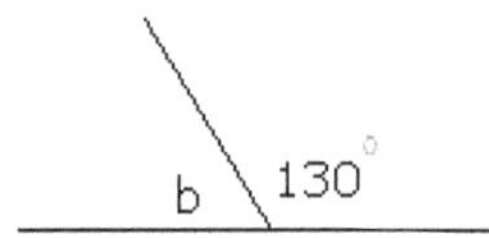

$\angle$ b = __________ 50

Reason: ____________________

Student's name: ____________________ Assignment date: ________________

Adjacent Angles and Angles at a Point

Adjacent angles on a line add up to 180^0 $\angle a + \angle b + \angle c = 180^0$ This is different from the supplementary angles in that this adjacent angles deal with 2 or more angles. All angles must be on the same line. 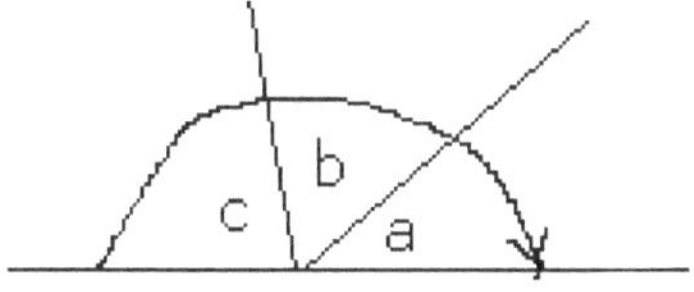	Angles at a point add up to 360^0 $\angle a + \angle b + \angle c + \angle d = 360^0$ 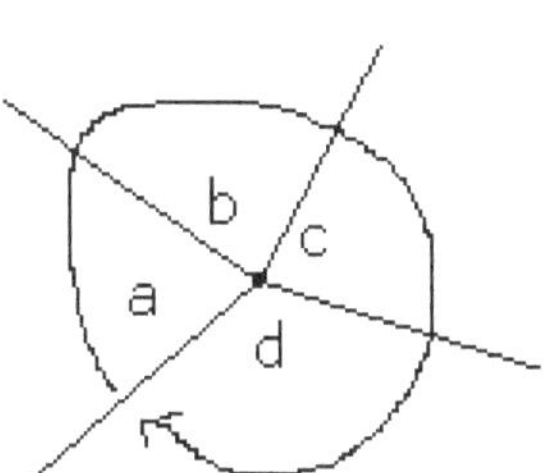

Find the missing angles and state the reason on how to find its size.

7.

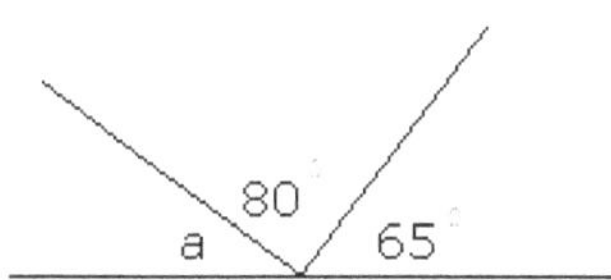

$\angle$ a = __________ 35

Reason: ____________________

8.

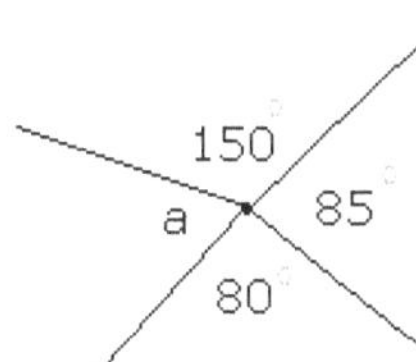

$\angle$ a = __________ 45

Reason: ____________________

9.

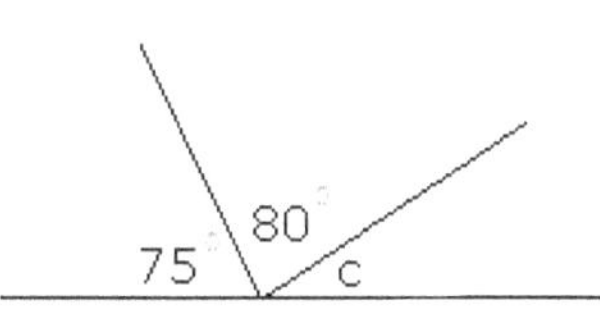

$\angle$ c = __________ 45

Reason: ____________________

10.

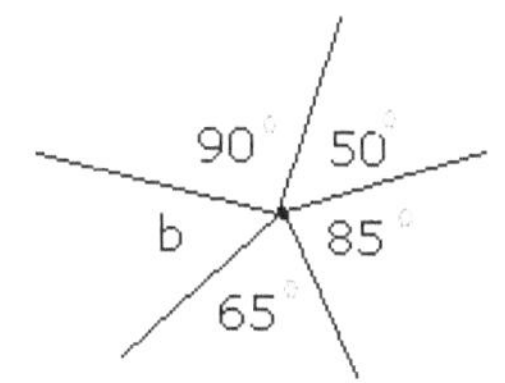

$\angle$ b = __________ 70

Reason: ____________________

11.

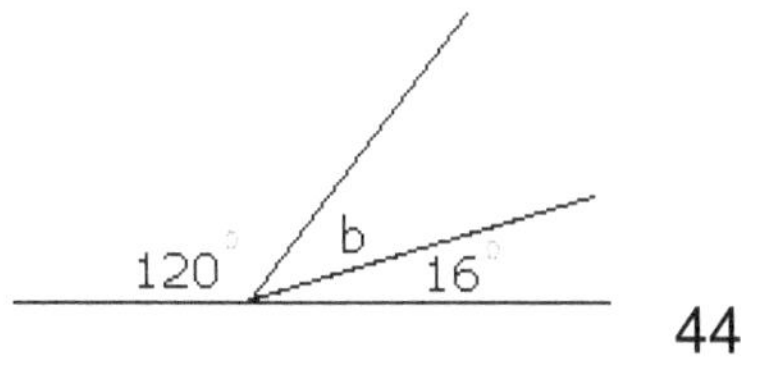

44

$\angle$ b = __________

Reason: ____________________

12.

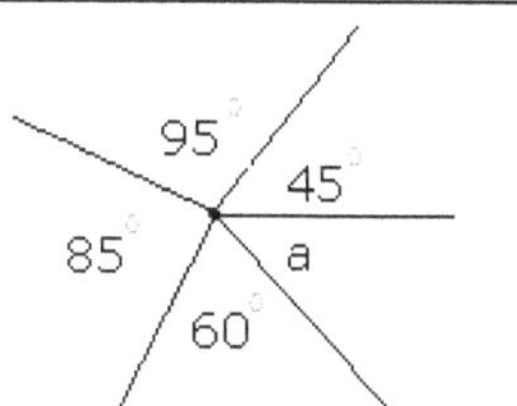

$\angle$ a = __________ 75

Reason: ____________________

Student's name: ____________________ Assignment date: ________________

Opposite Angles

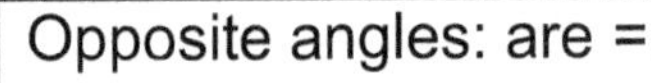
Opposite angles: are =.

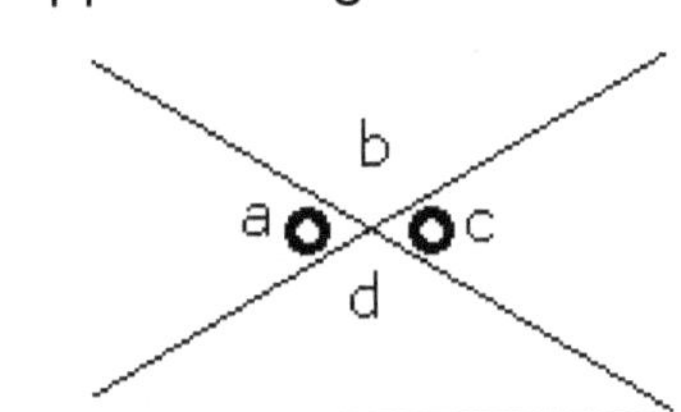

∠ a and ∠ c are opposite angles.

∠ b and ∠ d are opposite angles.

We have: ∠ a = ∠ c, ∠ b = ∠ d

Find the missing angles and state the reason on how to find its size.

13.

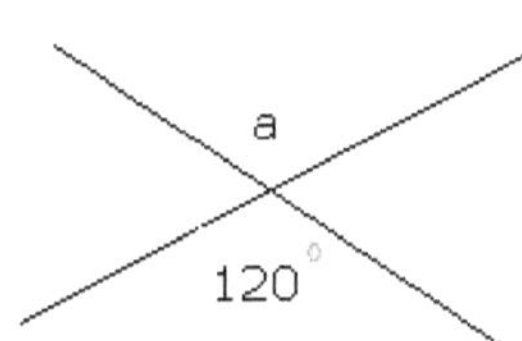

∠ a = __________

Reason: ____________________

14.

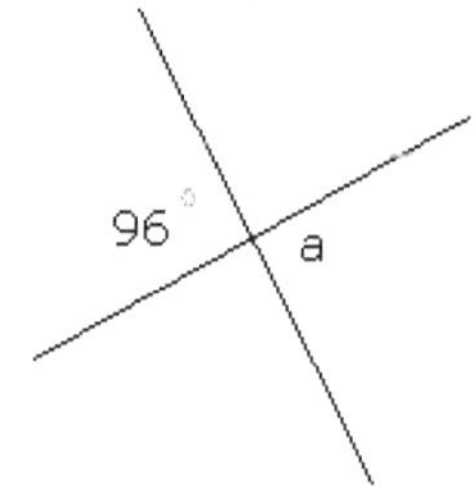

∠ a = __________

Reason: ____________________

15.

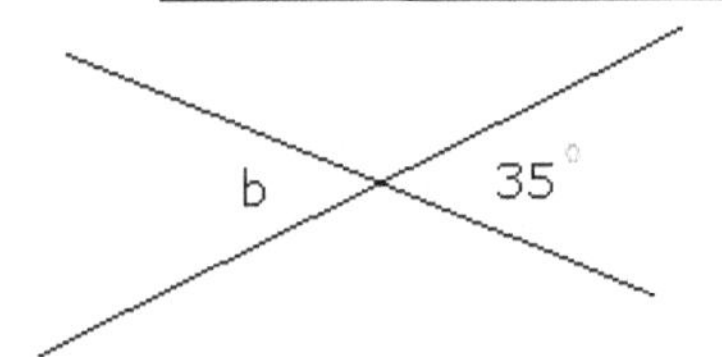

∠ b = __________

Reason: ____________________

16.

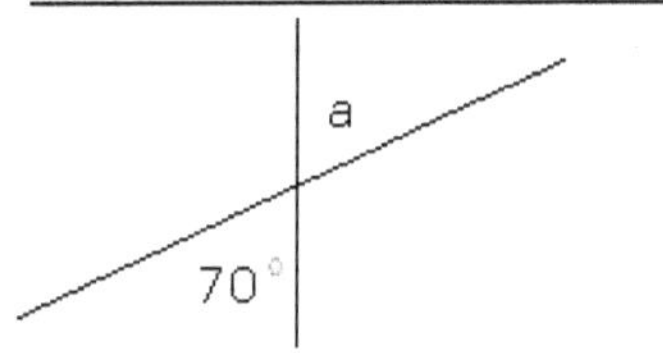

∠ a = __________

Reason: ____________________

17.

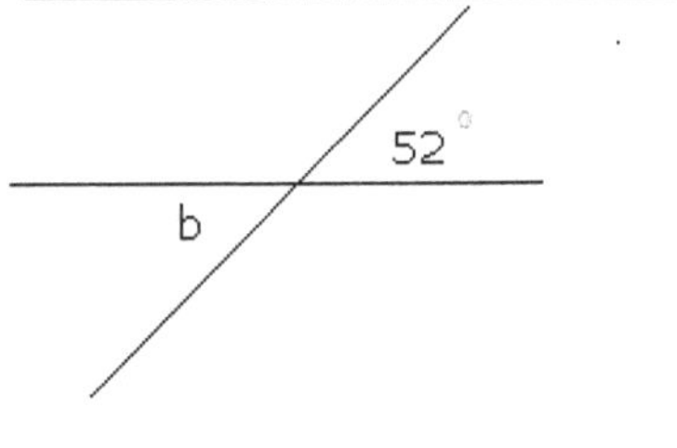

∠ b = __________

Reason: ____________________

18.

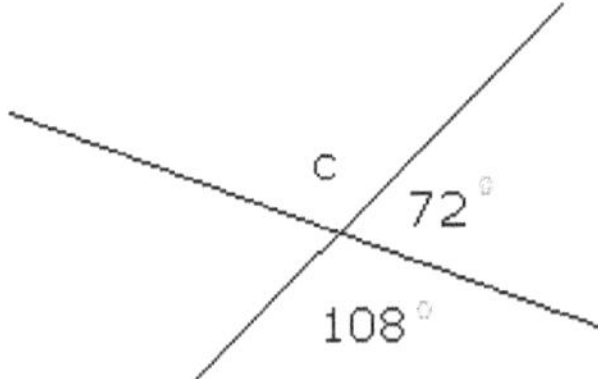

∠ c = __________

Reason: ____________________

Student's name: ____________________ Assignment date: ________________

Corresponding angles

Corresponding angles are =. 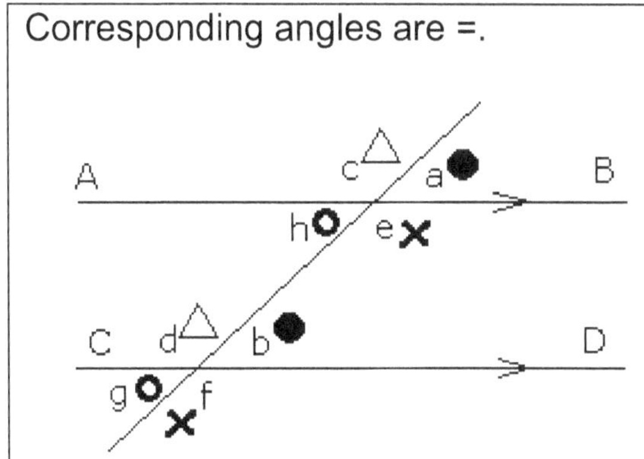 	When AB // CD, then there are 4 pairs of corresponding angles. ∠ a and ∠ b are corresponding angles. ∠ c and ∠ d are corresponding angles. ∠ e and ∠ f are corresponding angles. ∠ g and ∠ h are corresponding angles. We have: ∠ a = ∠ b, ∠ c = ∠ d ∠ e = ∠ f, ∠ g = ∠ h

Find the missing angles and state the reason on how to find its size.

19.

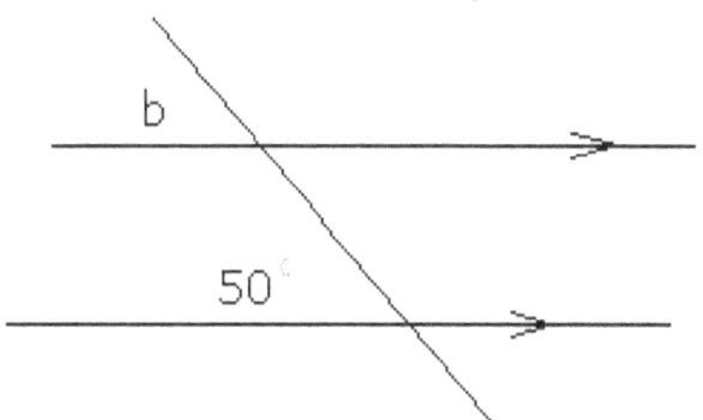

∠ b = __________ 50

Reason: ____________________

20.

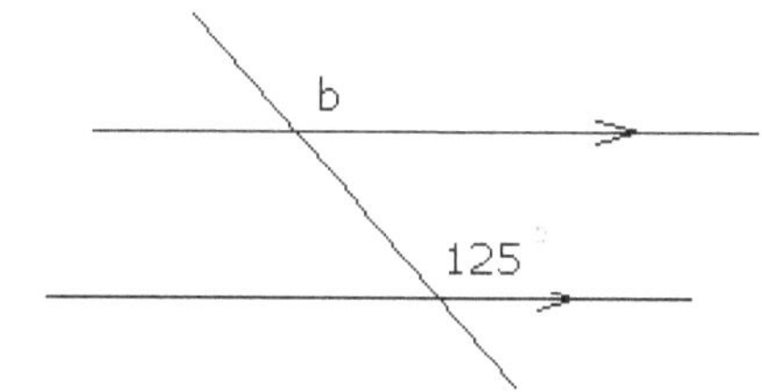

∠ b = __________ 125

Reason: ____________________

21.

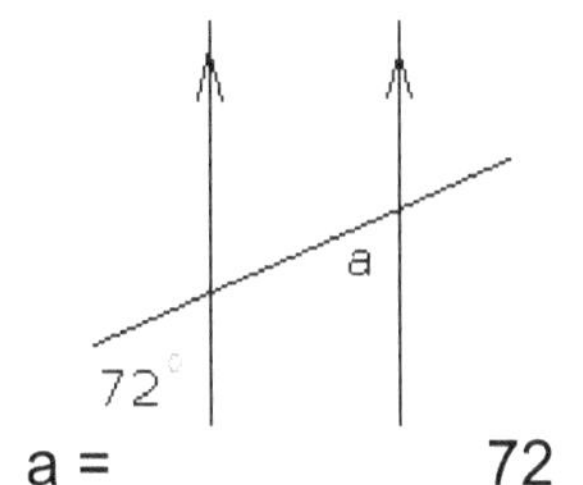

∠ a = __________ 72

Reason: ____________________

22.

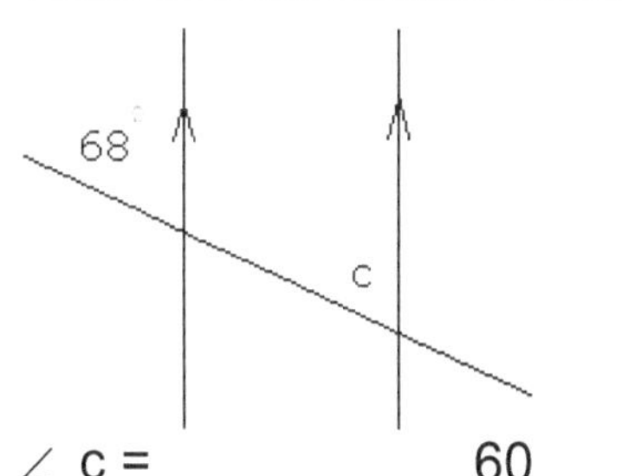

∠ c = __________ 60

Reason: ____________________

23.

87°

d

∠ d = __________ 87

Reason: ____________________

24.

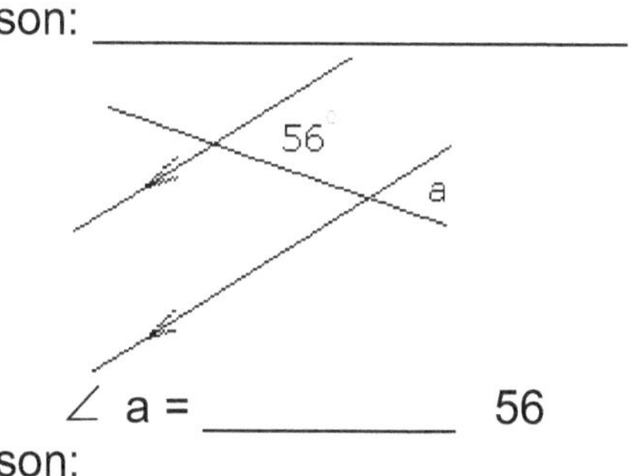

∠ a = __________ 56

Reason: ____________________

Student's name: ____________________ Assignment date: ________________

Alternate Interior Angles

Alternate interior angles are =. 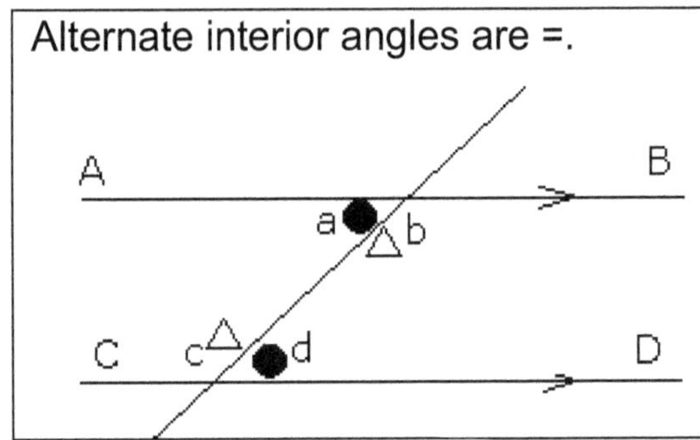	When AB // CD, then ∠ a and ∠ d are alternate interior angles. ∠ b and ∠ c are alternate interior angles. We have: ∠ a = ∠ d, ∠ b = ∠ c

Find the missing angles and state the reason on how to find its size.

25.

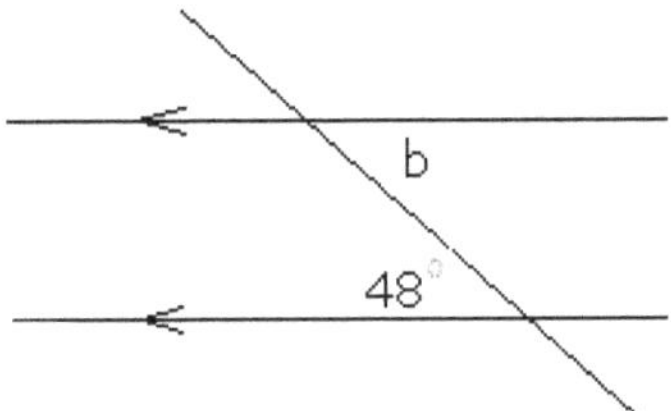

∠ b = __________ 48

Reason: ____________________

26.

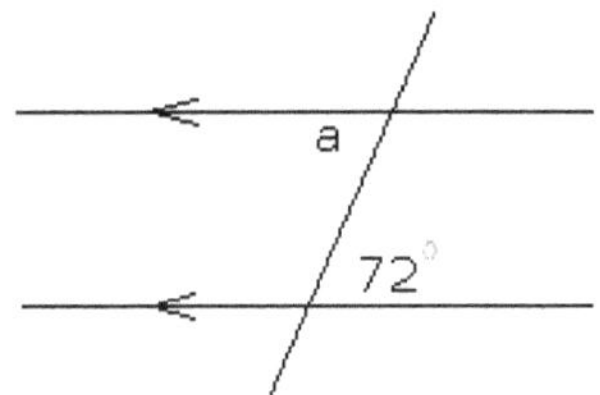

∠ a = __________ 72

Reason: ____________________

27.

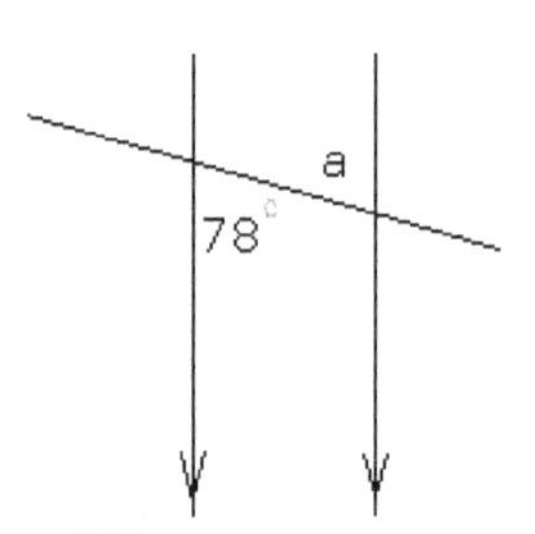

∠ a = __________ 78

Reason: ____________________

28.

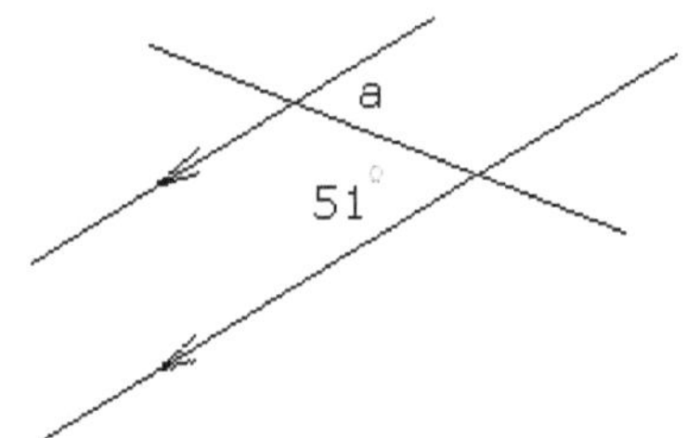

∠ a = __________ 51

Reason: ____________________

29.

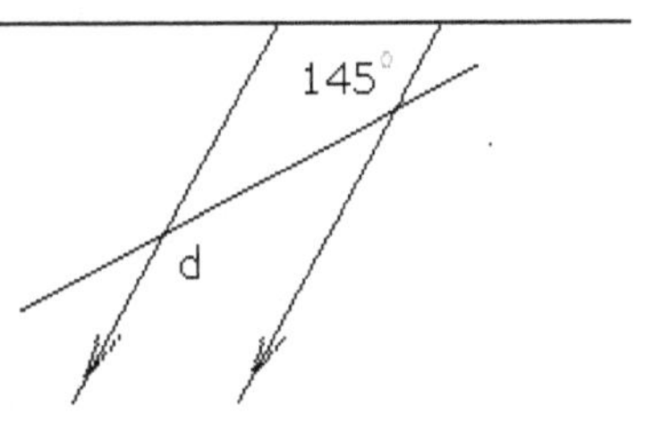

∠ d = __________ 145

Reason: ____________________

30.

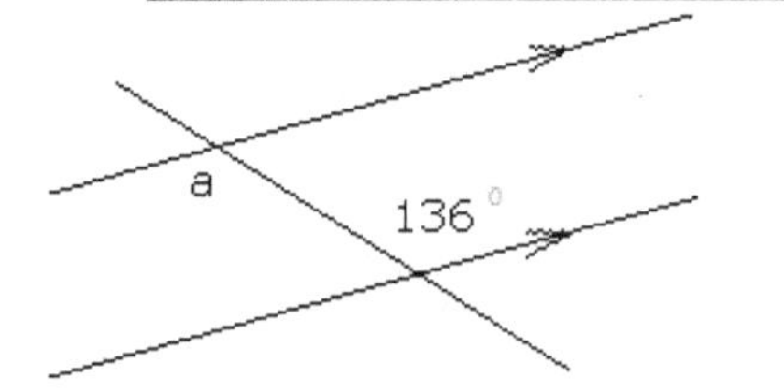

∠ a = __________ 136

Reason: ____________________

Ho Math Chess Primary Grades Math

Test Review assesssment 何数棋谜低年级数学测试複習考核

Student's name: ____________________ Assignment date: ________________

Co-interior Angles

Co-interior angles add up to 180^0.	When AB // CD, then ∠ a and ∠ c are co-interior angles. ∠ b and ∠ d are co-interior angles. We have: ∠ a + ∠ c = 180^0 ∠ b + ∠ d = 180^0

Find the missing angles and state the reason on how to find its size.

31.

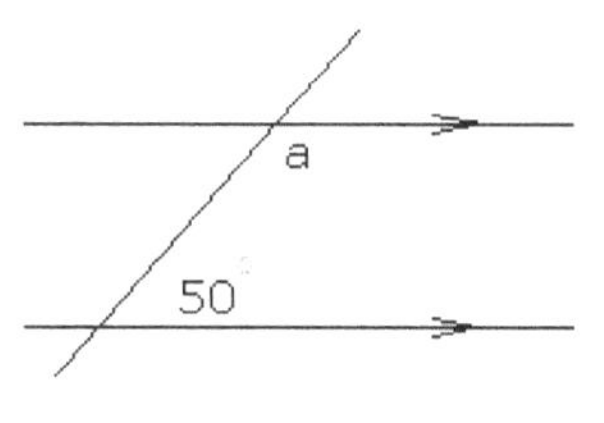

∠ a = __________ 130

Reason: ____________________

32.

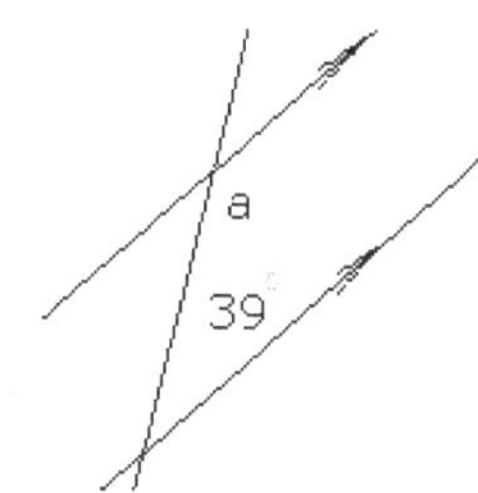

∠ a = __________ 141

Reason: ____________________

33.

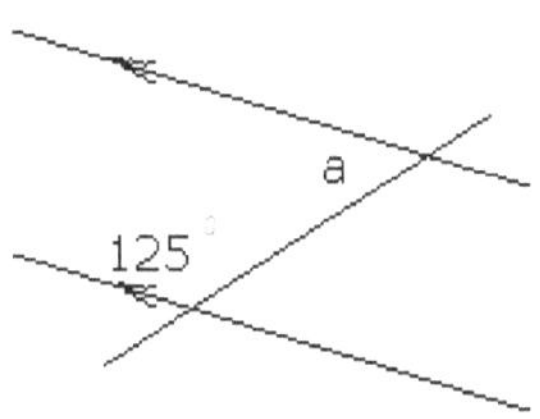

∠ a = __________ 55

Reason: ____________________

34.

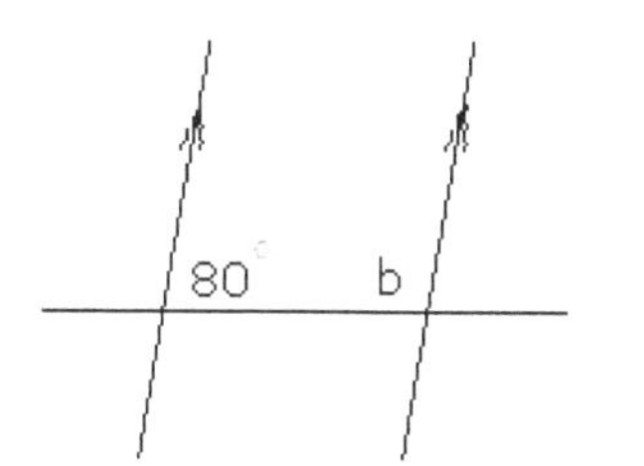

∠ b = __________ 100

Reason: ____________________

35.

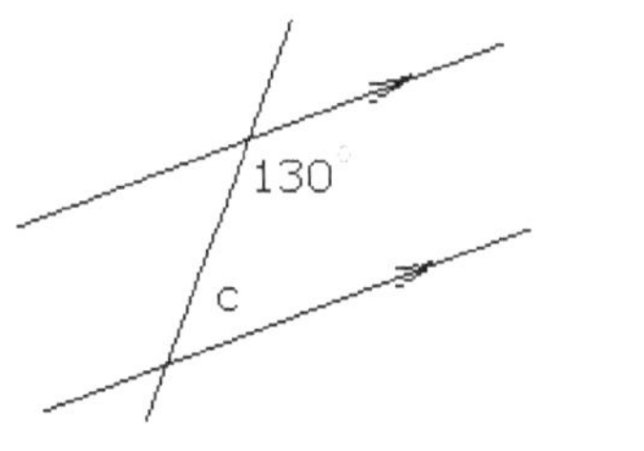

∠ c = __________ 50

Reason: ____________________

36.

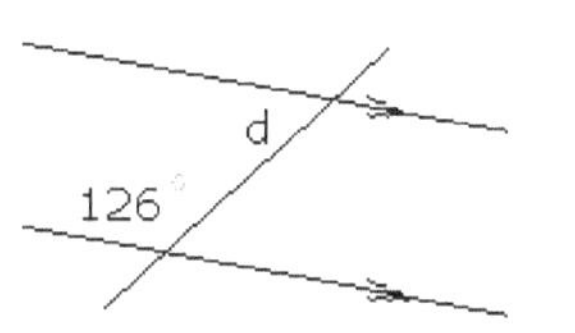

∠ d = __________ 54

Reason: ____________________

Student's name: ____________________ Assignment date: ________________

Test of geometry

What is the perimeter of the following square? The diameter of the circle is 7 cm.  28 cm
The perimeter of a rectangle is 48 cm, and its length is 14 cm. What is the length of its width? 24 – 14 = 10 cm
Two sides of an equilateral triangle are $x-1$ and $13-x$, what is the value of x?
A rectangular shape has an area of 24 cm^2 with an odd number of width value. What could be its dimensions? 24 by 1, 8 by 3
The two sides of an equilateral triangle have lengths of $x+3$ and $19-x$. What is the value of x? 8
Find the perimeter of the following figure. All measures are approximate and are in cm. 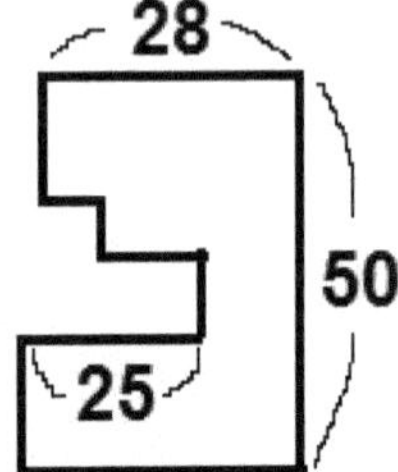 (50+25+28) x2=206 cm

Student's name: ____________________ Assignment date: ________________

Calculate the perimeter of the following figures.

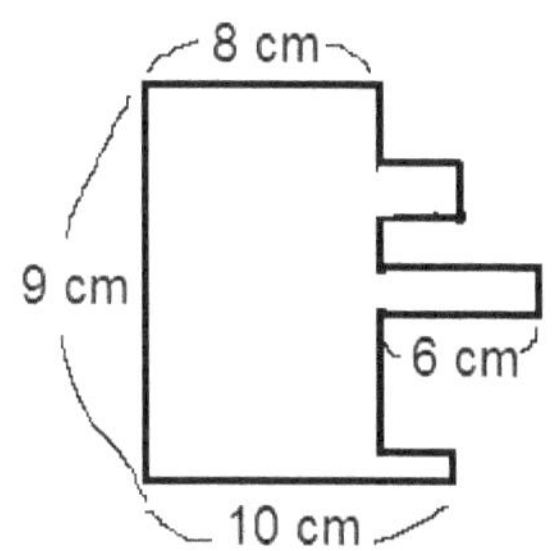

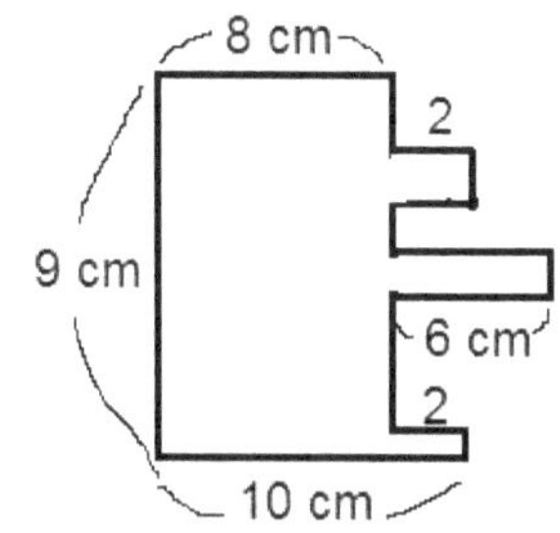

9 + 9 + 10 + 10 + 2 + 6 + 6 + 2 + 2 = 56 cm

How many different rectangles can be made using exactly 24 square tiles placed side by side?

24 = 1 x 24
24 = 2 x 12
24 = 3 x 8
24 = 4 x 6

Four different rectangles.

Student's name: ____________________ Assignment date: ________________

Transformation

Slide (translate)

Horizontal slide

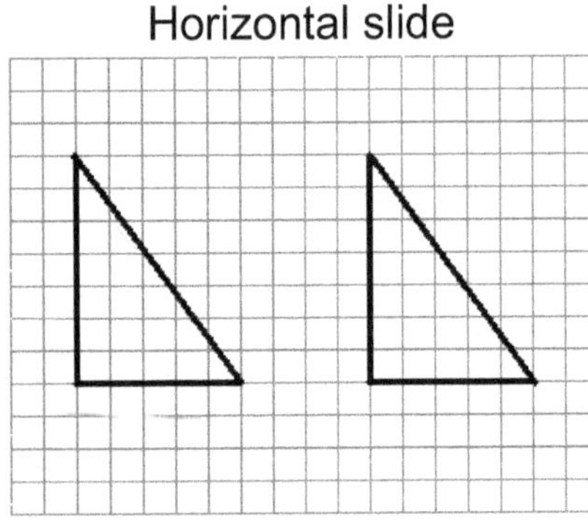

Vertical slide

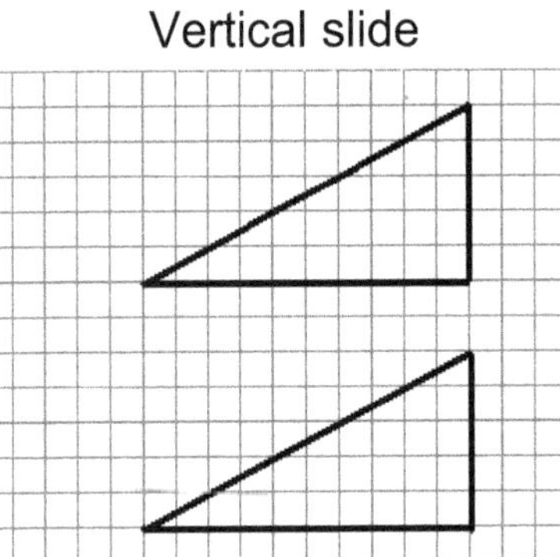

Diagonal slide

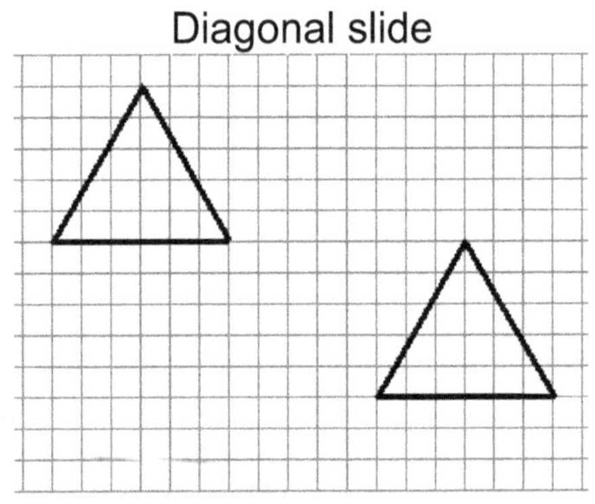

Indicate whether each slide a horizontal, a vertical, or a diagonal slide.

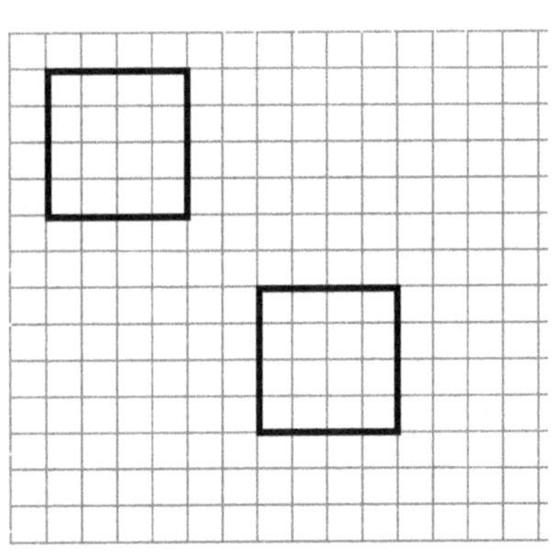

diagonal
____

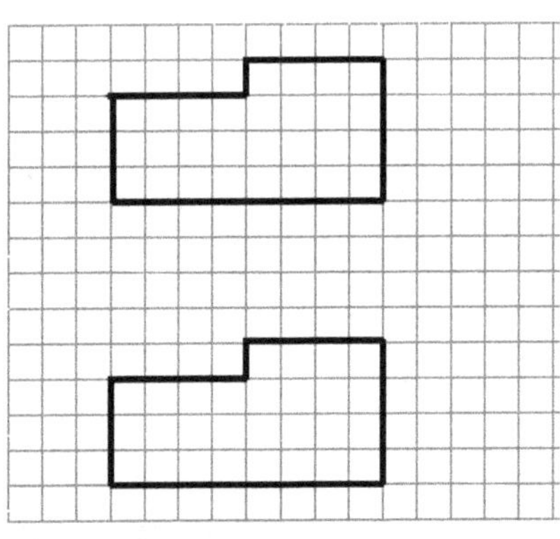

vertical
____

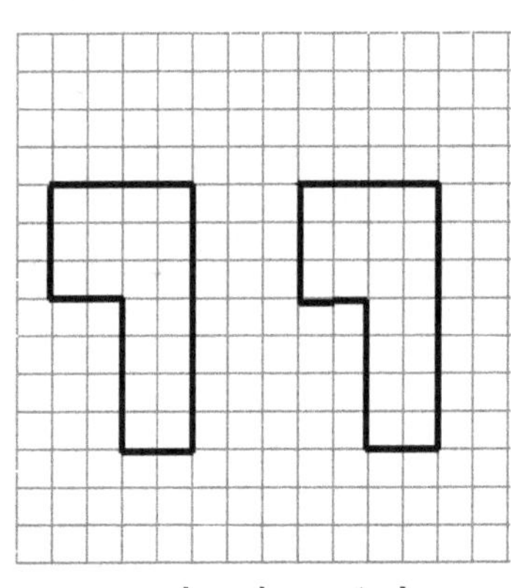

horizontal
____

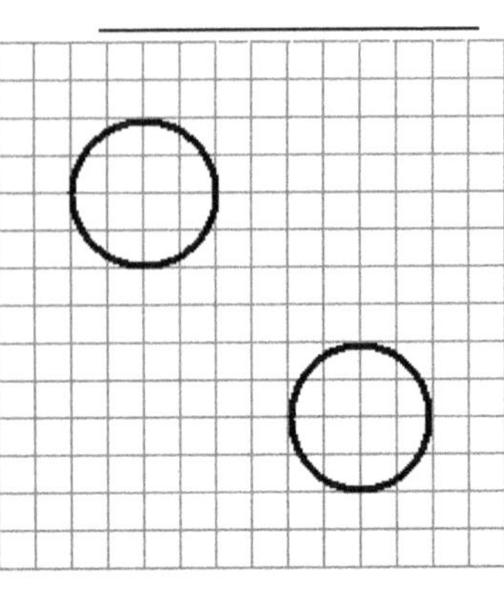

Diagonal
____

horizontal
____

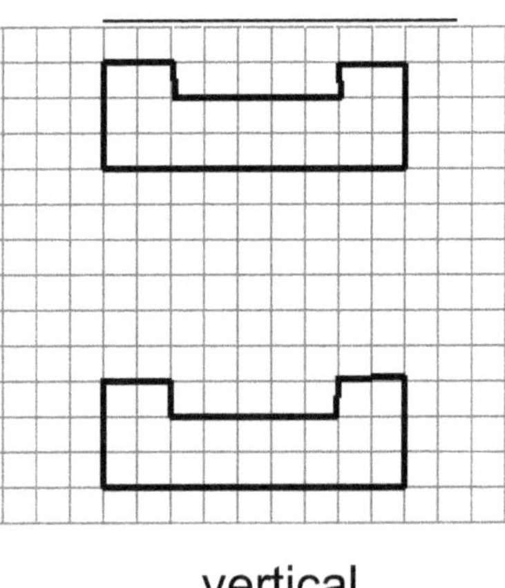

vertical
____

Ho Math Chess Primary Grades Math

Test Review assesssment 何数棋謎低年级数学测试複習考核

Student's name: ____________________ Assignment date: ________________

Turn (rotate)

Point C is the turn centre, figure A is turned from A to B,

A quarter-turn clockwise or a three-quarter turn counter clockwise

Half turn

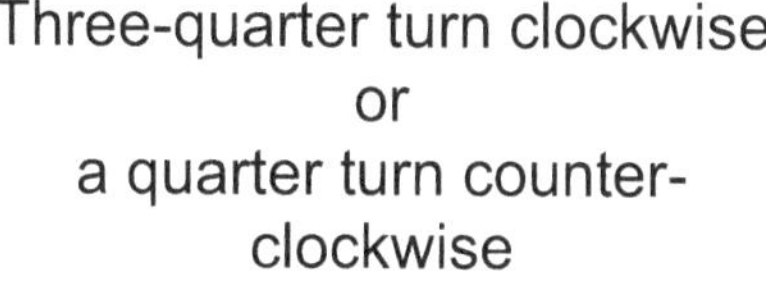
Three-quarter turn clockwise or a quarter turn counter-clockwise

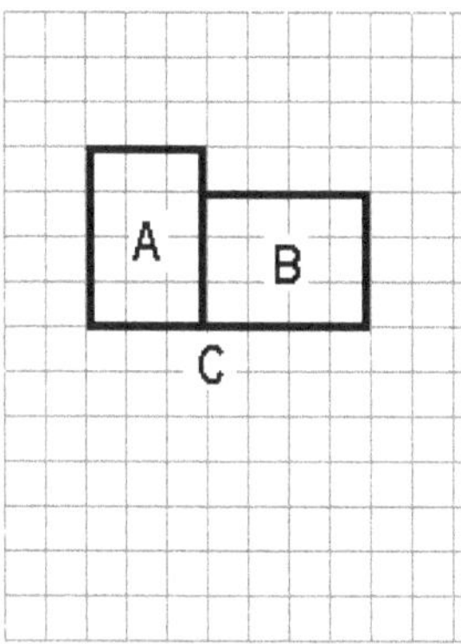

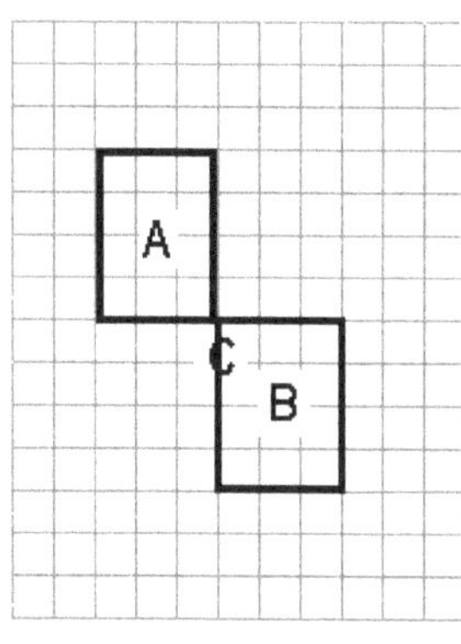

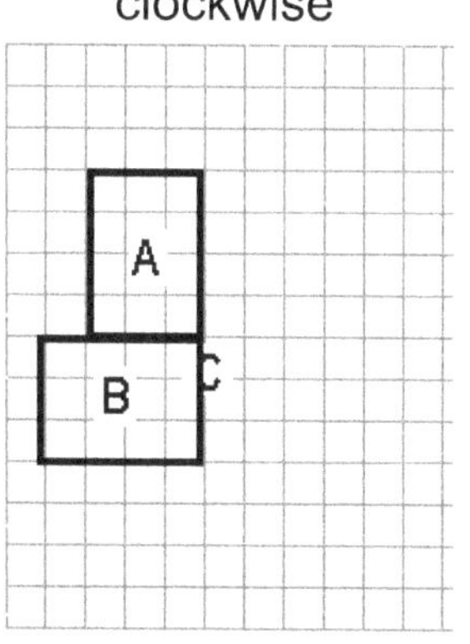

Each figure turned from A to B indicates whether each turn is a quarter-turn clockwise, half turn or a three quarter turn clockwise about point O.

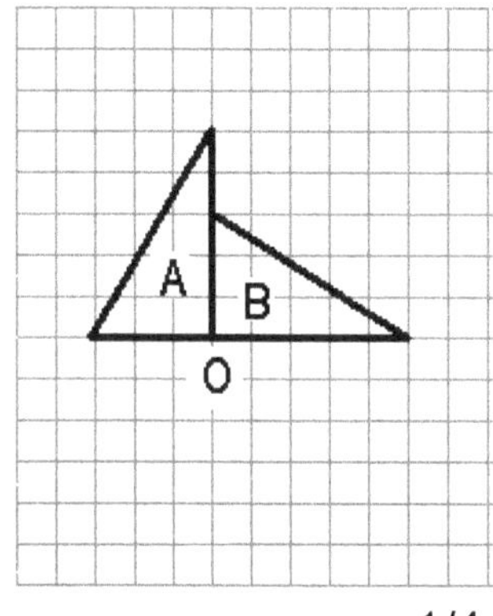

_______________1/4

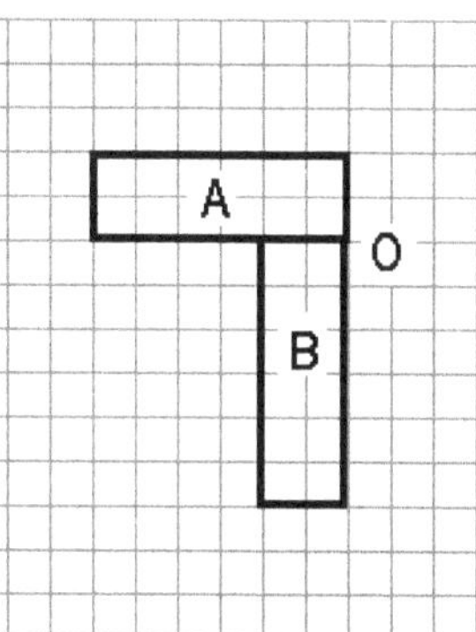

_______________3/4

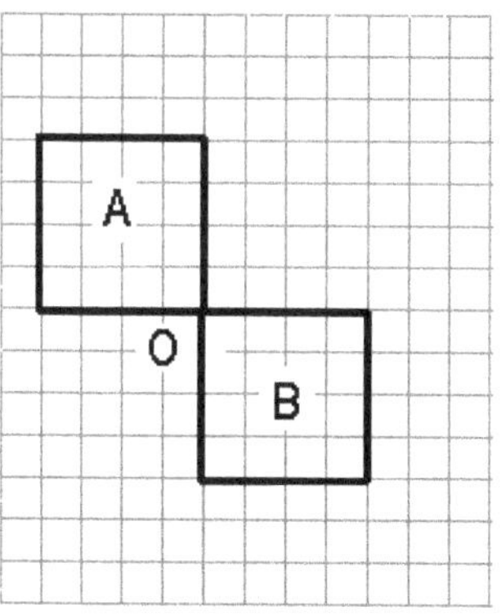

_______________1/2

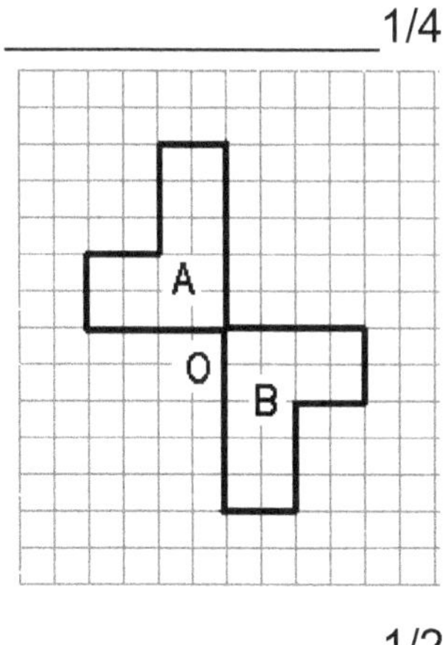

_______________1/2

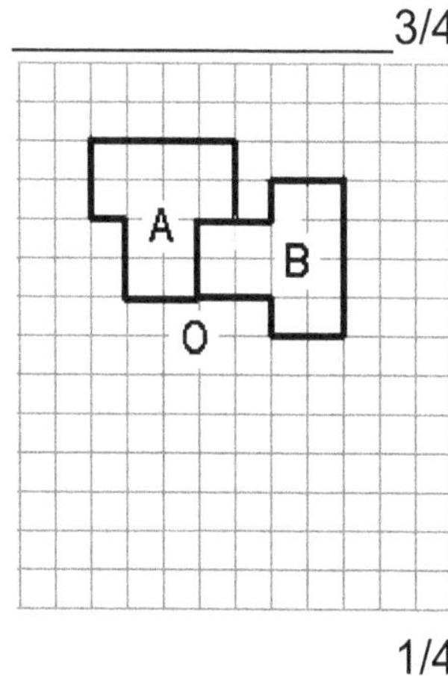

_______________1/4

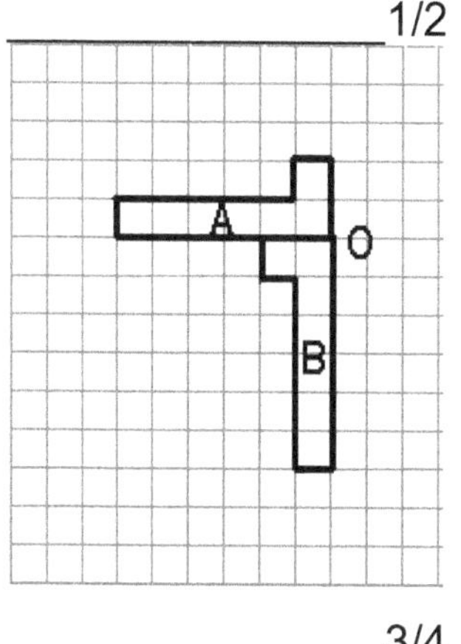

_______________3/4

Student's name: ____________________ Assignment date: ________________

Flip (reflect)

Finish the symmetric shapes below using the straight-line (mirror line) as lines of symmetry. Each vertex (corner) of the original figure flips to the opposite side with the same distance from the line to form an image.

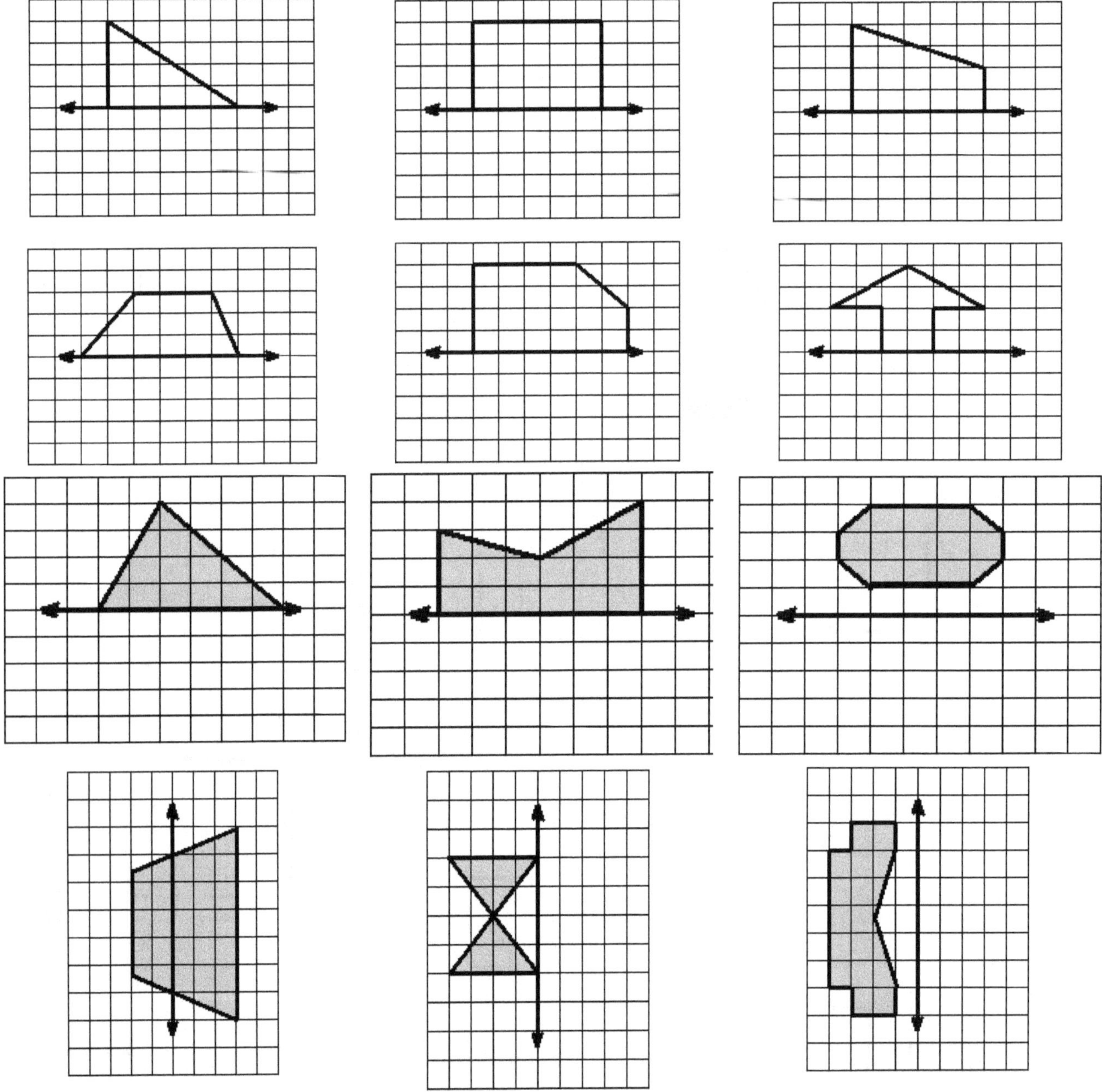

Student's name: ____________________ Assignment date: ________________

Symmetry line

Find the lines of symmetry for these drawings

A	B	C	D

Student's name: ____________________ Assignment date: ________________

Decide whether each figure is a slide, a turn, or a reflection of figure A.

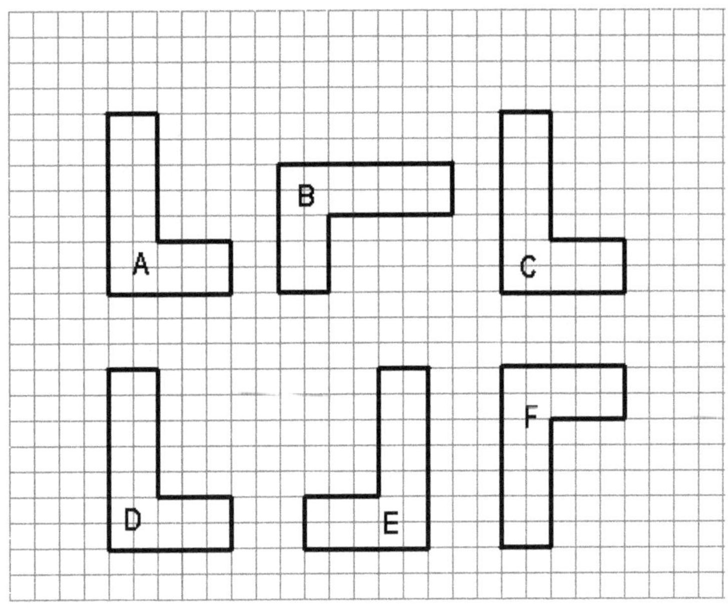

1. Figure B is a ___turn___ of figure A.
2. Figure C is a ___slide___ of figure A.
3. Figure D is a ___slide___ of figure A.
4. Figure E is a ___reflection___ of figure A.
5. Figure F is a ___turn___ of figure A.

Student's name: ____________________ Assignment date: ________________

Congruent Figures (figures with the same size and shape)

If figures have the same size and same shape, then these figures are congruent.
Example:

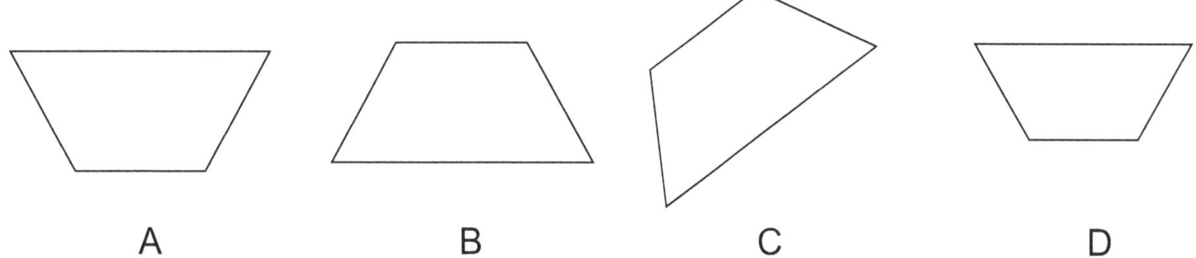

Figures A, B, and C are congruent because they have the same size and same shape.
Figure D is not congruent to A, B, or C, because they have different sizes.

Connect all the pairs of congruent figures.

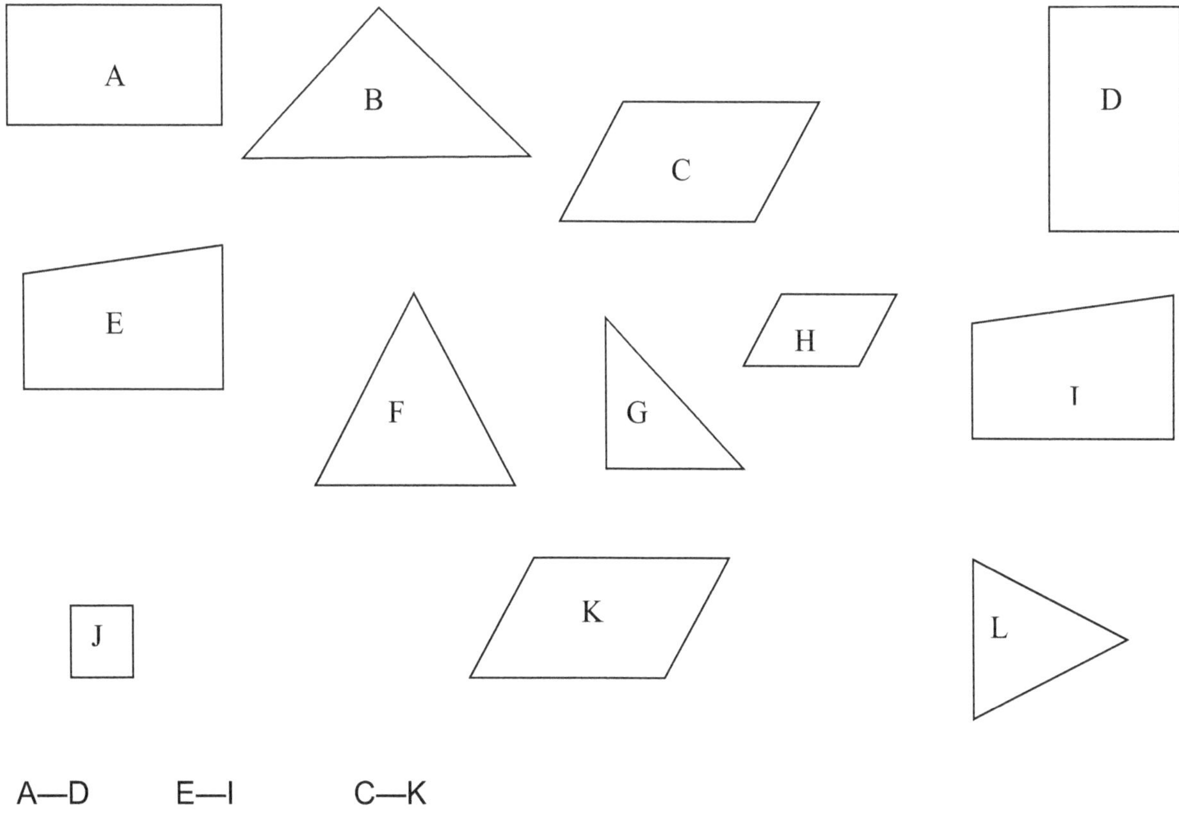

A—D E—I C—K

Student's name: ____________________ Assignment date: ________________

Divide the following figures into 2 congruent parts.

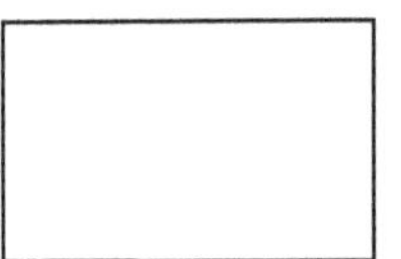 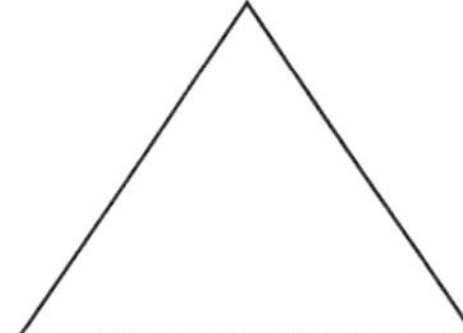 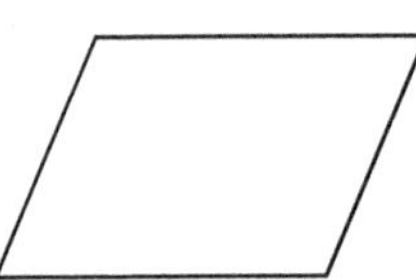 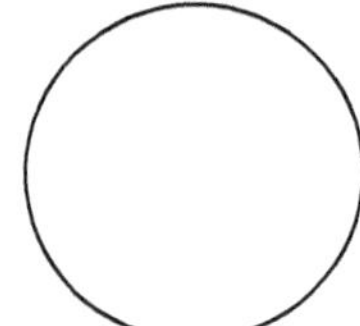

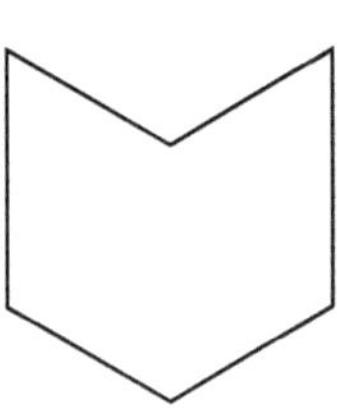 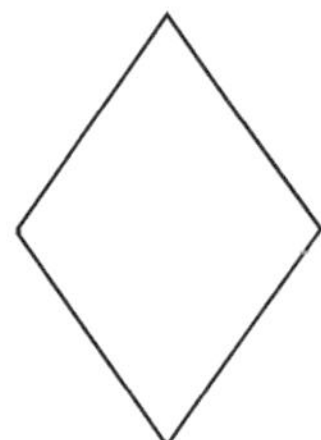 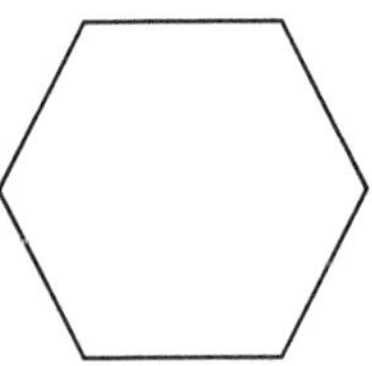 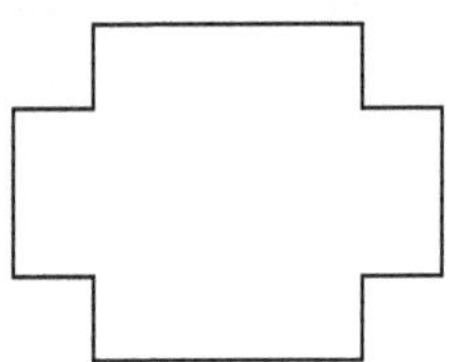

Divide the following figures into 4 congruent parts.

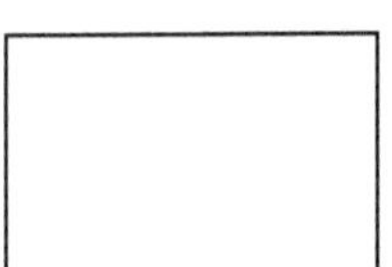 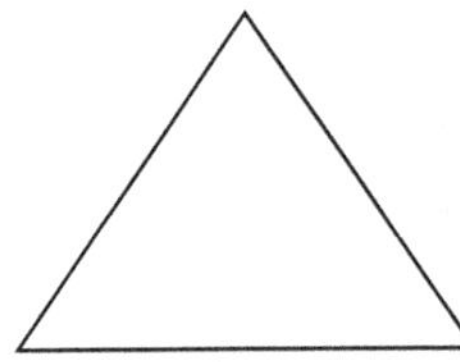 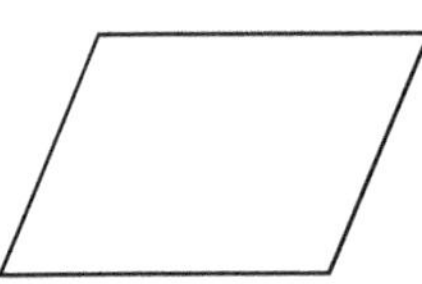 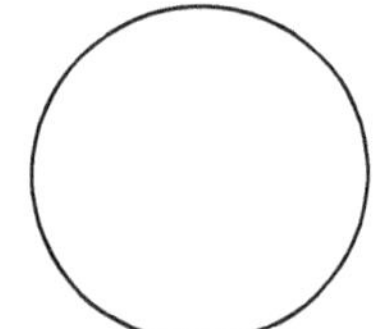

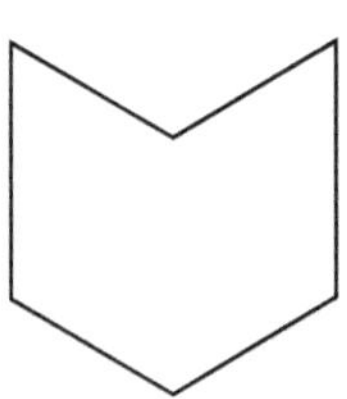 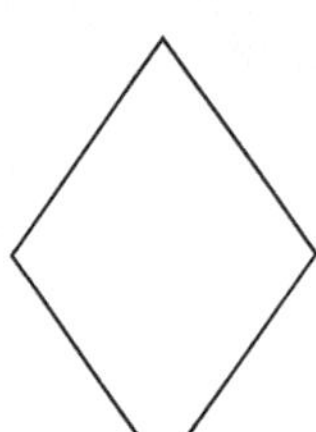 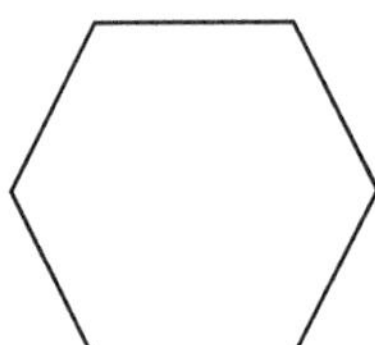 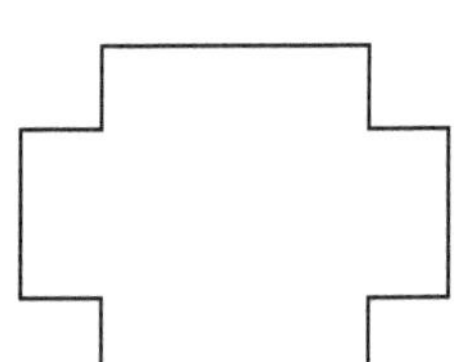

Student's name: ____________________ Assignment date: ________________

Find the figure that is congruent to the left.

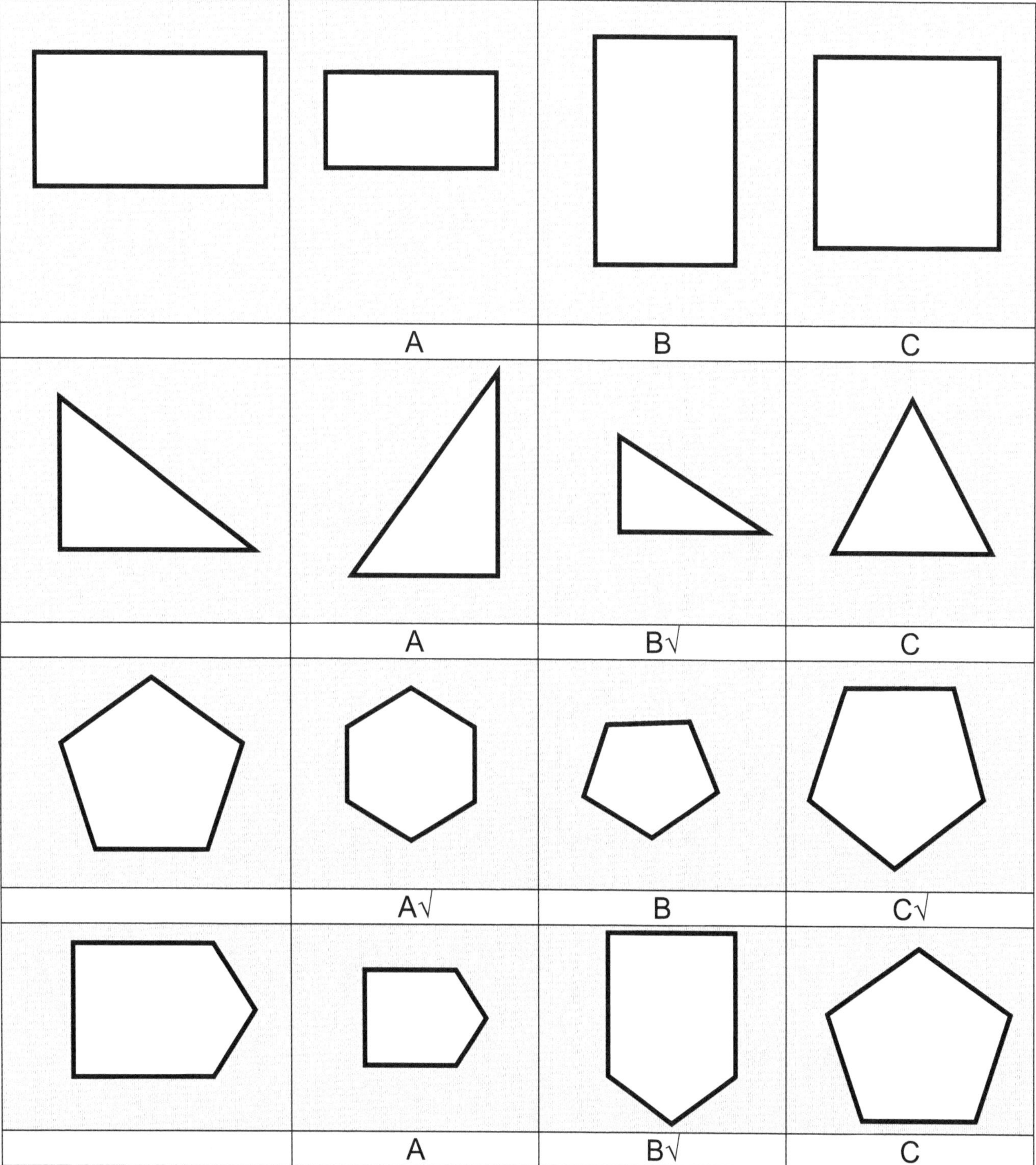

Ho Math Chess Primary Grades Math

Test Review assesssment 何数棋谜低年级数学测试複習考核

Frank Ho, Amanda Ho www.homathchess.com

Student's name: ____________________ Assignment date: ________________

Similar Figures
If all the figures have the same shape but different sizes, then these figures are similar.
Find the figure that is similar to the leftmost.

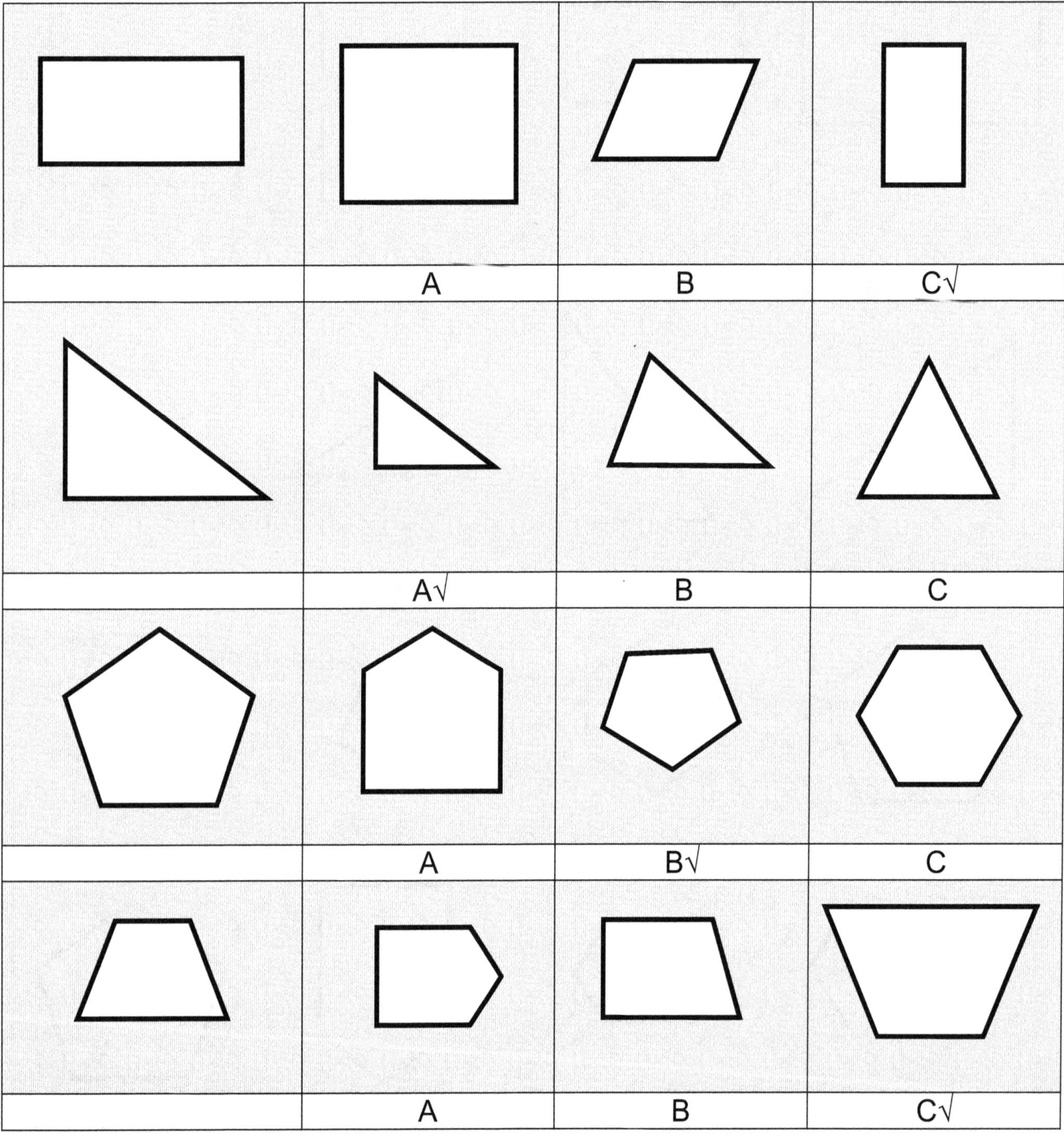

Student's name: ____________________ Assignment date: ________________

Identifying tessellations

A unit shape is a shape that can be repeated over and over to form a pattern. A unit shape can be a composite unit shape, which may consist of two or more basic shapes such as a triangle and a square.

When a unit shape is drawn repeatedly without any gaps between them or any overlaps between them, then the pattern is called tessellation.

Circle the unit shape of the following figures and then complete 3 more patterned unit shapes on the grid.

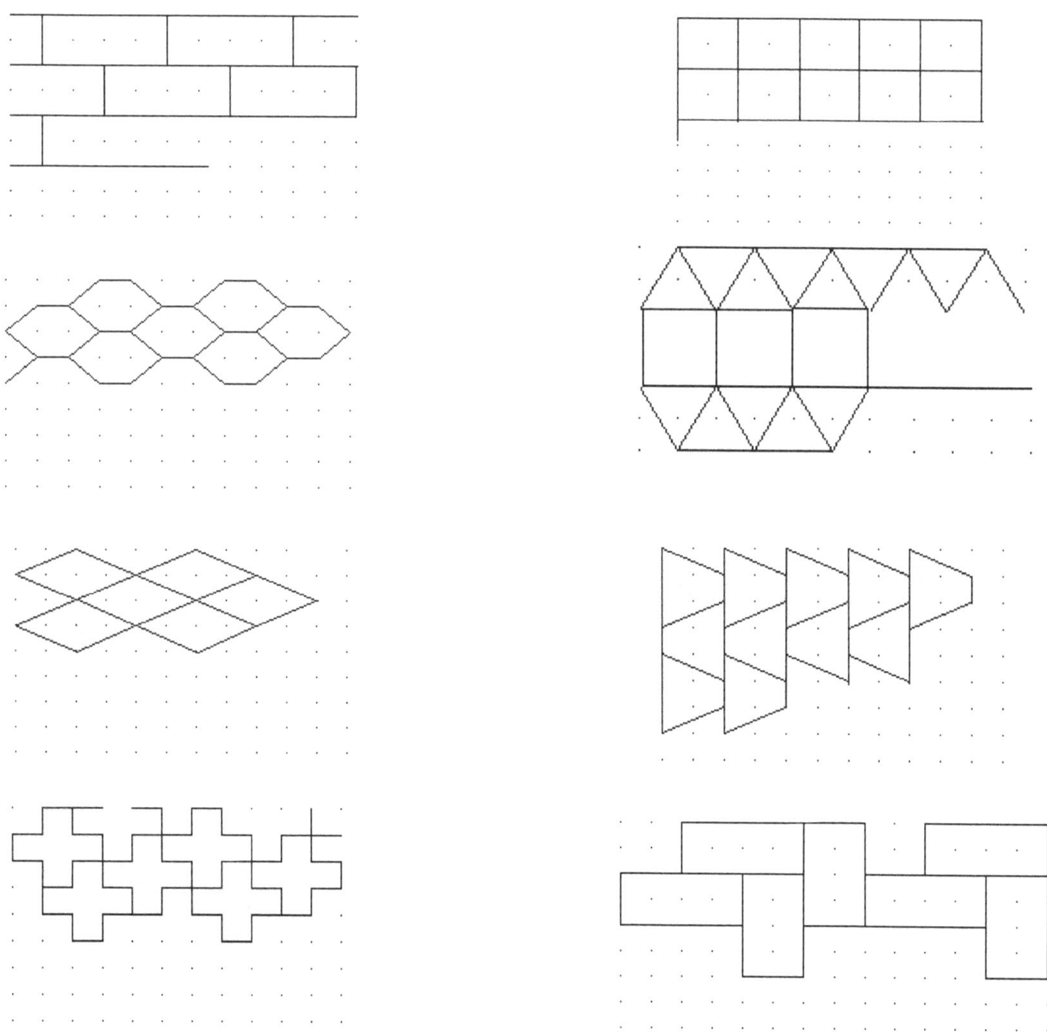

Student's name: ____________________ Assignment date: ________________

Solids

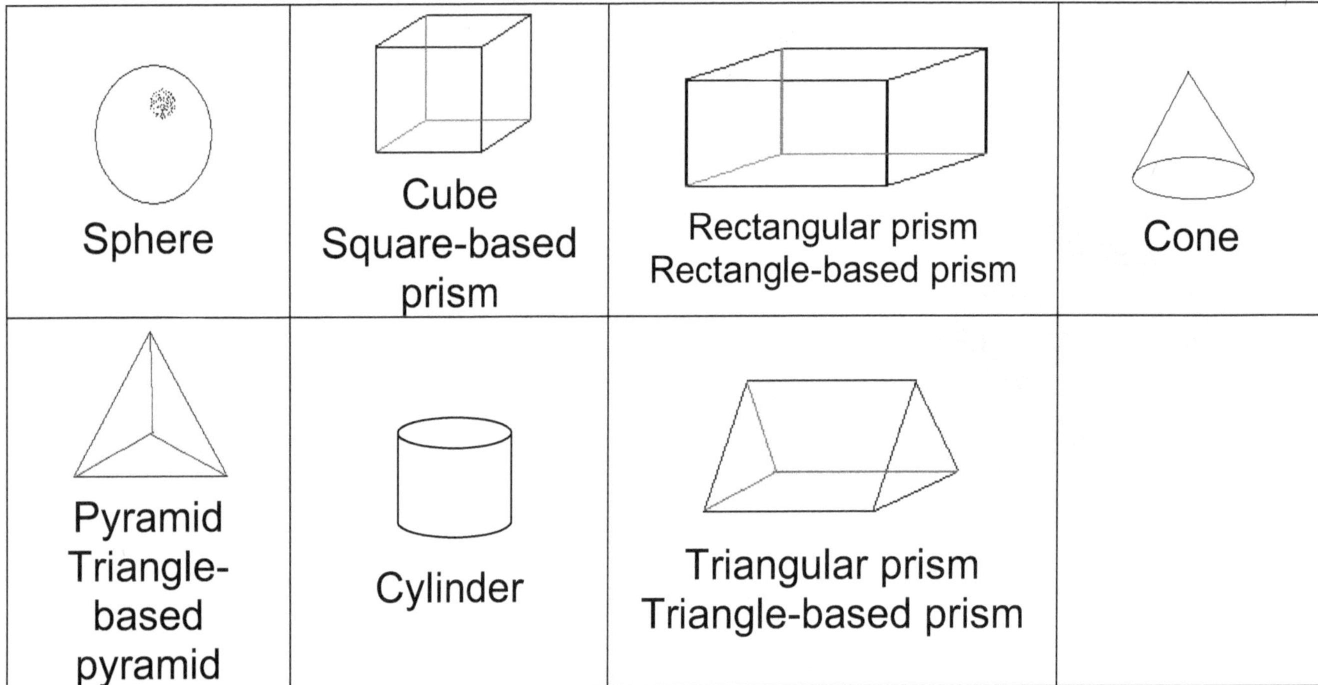

Write the name of the following solids.

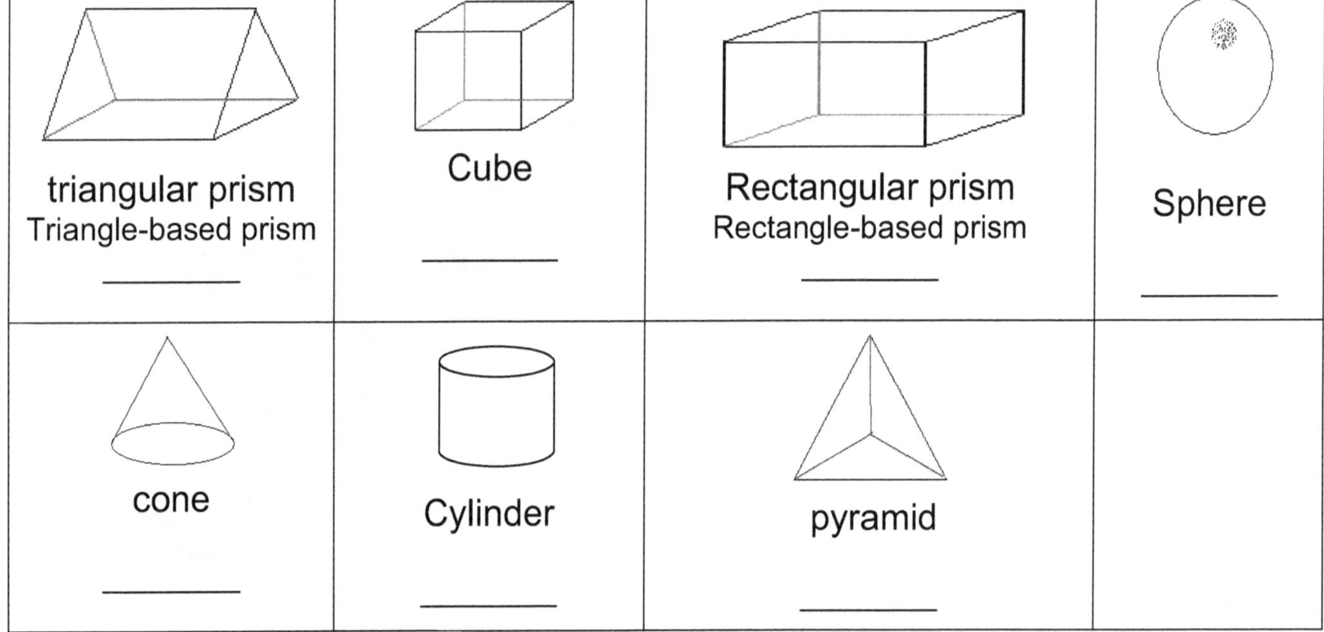

Student's name: ____________________ Assignment date: ________________

Pyramids or Prisms

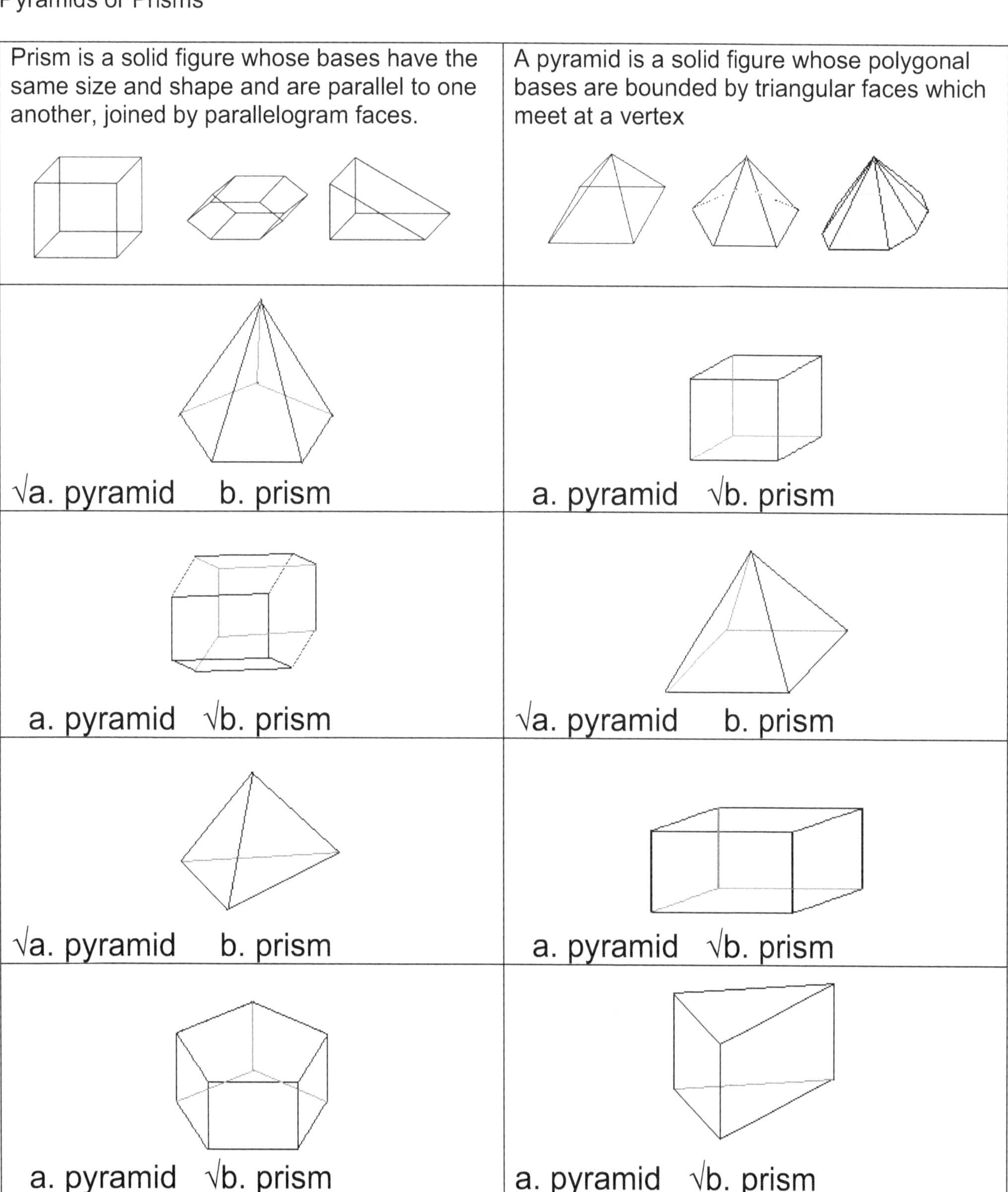

Student's name: ____________________ Assignment date: ________________

Matching left to the right

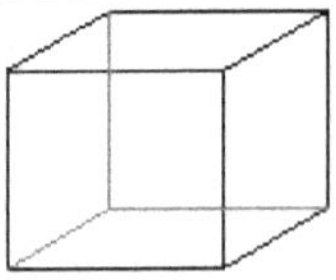	Triangular Prism
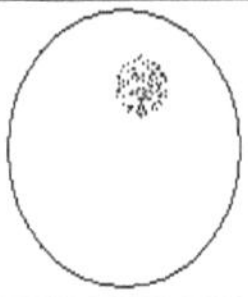	Pyramid
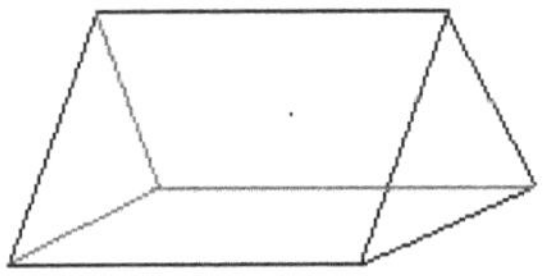	Cube
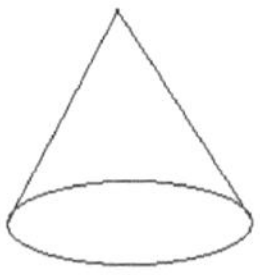	Rectangular prism
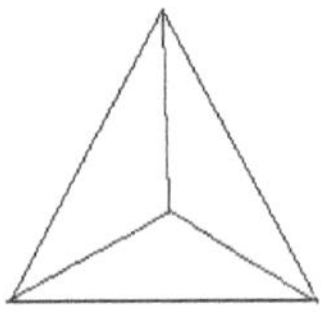	Cone
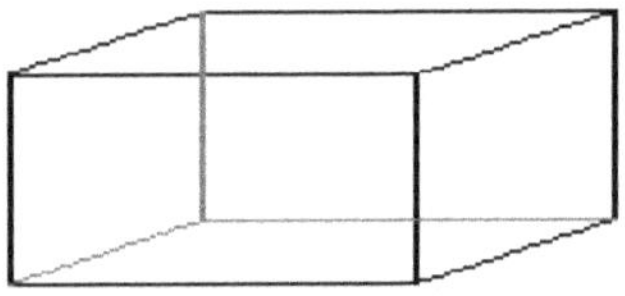	Sphere
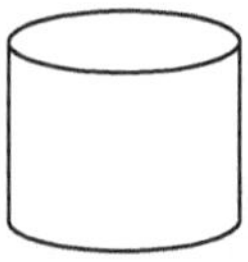	Cylinder

Student's name: ____________________ Assignment date: ________________

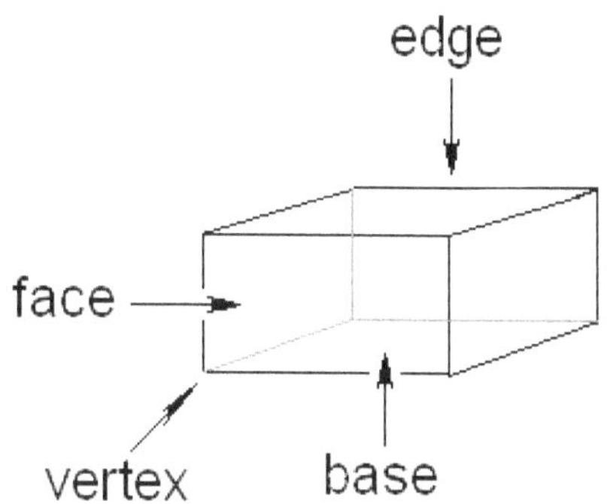

Complete the following chart.

Shape	Name	Number of faces	Number of edges	Number of vertices
	cube	6	12	6
	Triangular prism	5	9	6
	Pyramid	4	6	4
	Rectangula r prism	6	12	8
	Pentagonal prism	7	15	10

Student's name: ____________________ Assignment date: ________________

Matching solids with their tracing faces.

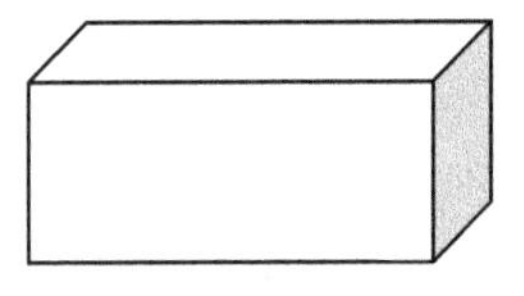
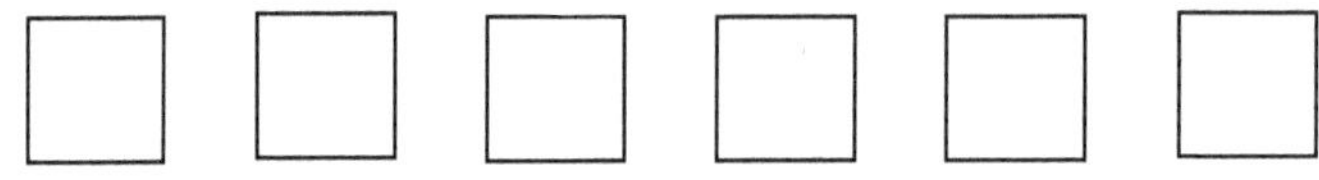
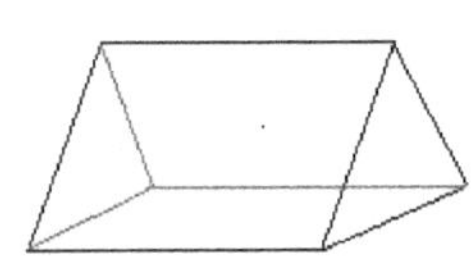

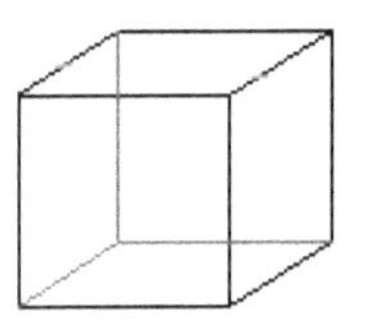
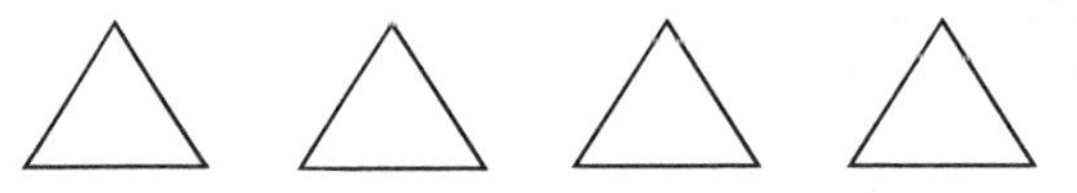
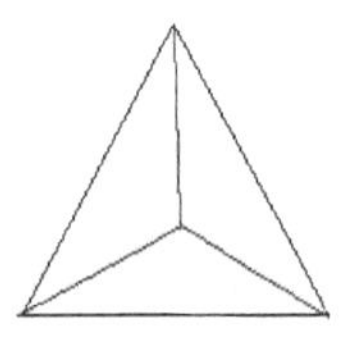
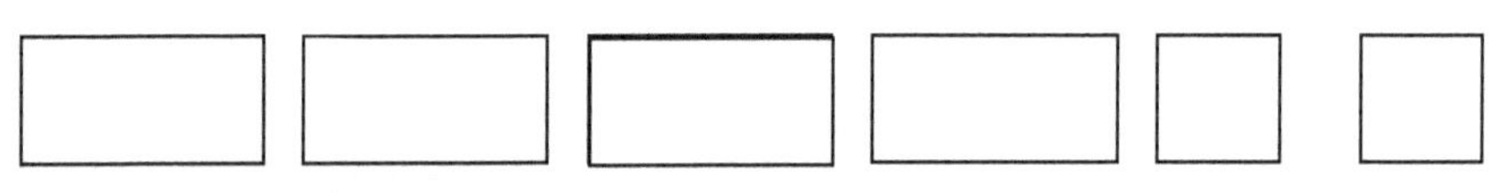
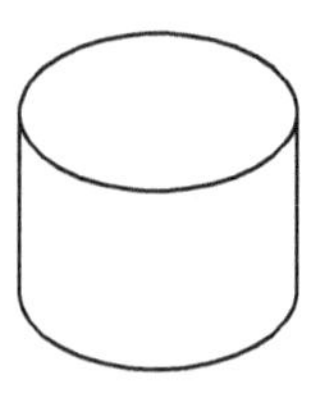
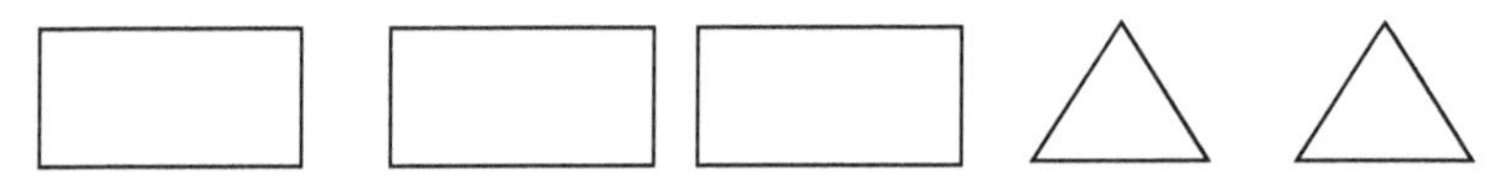
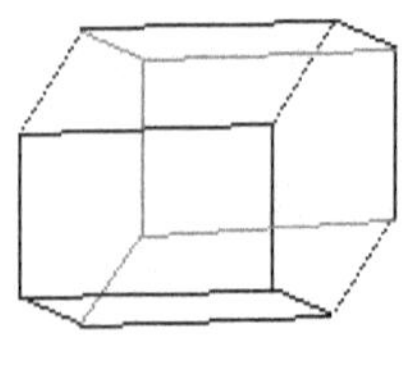
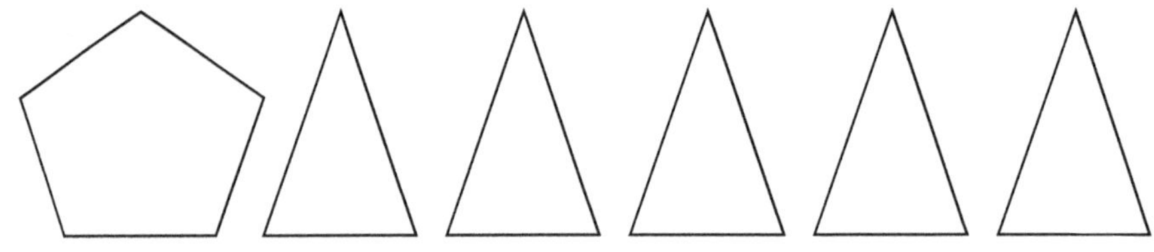
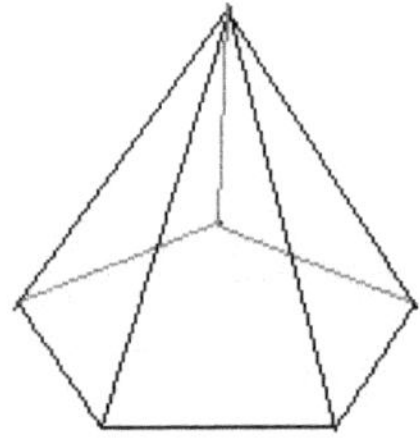
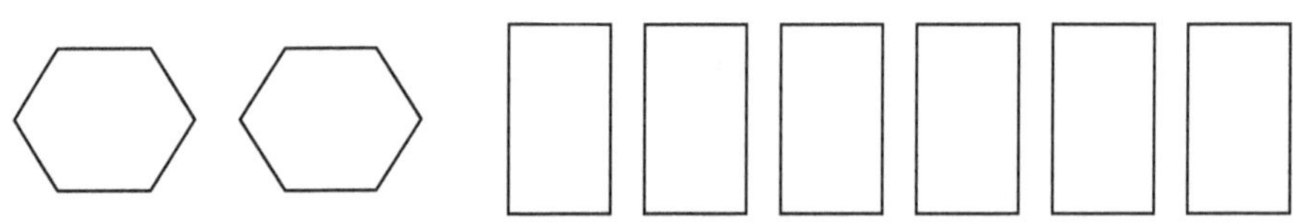

Student's name: ____________________ Assignment date: ________________

Faces of Solids

1.

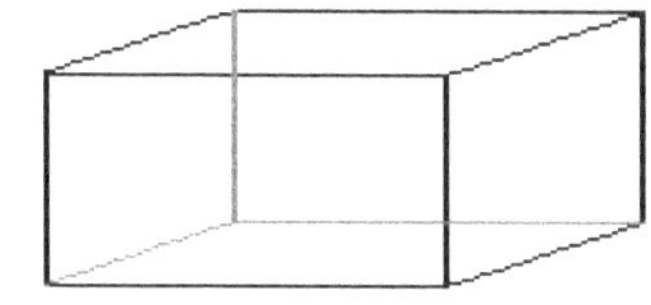

6 rectangular faces

2.

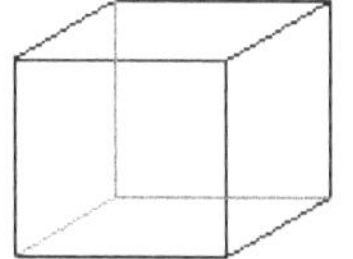

6 square faces

3.

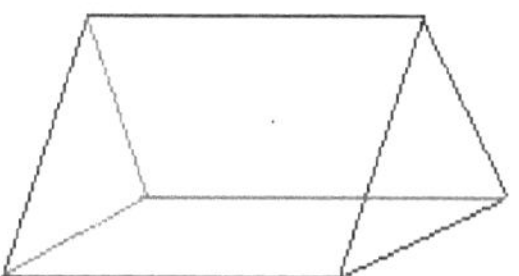

5 triangular faces and 3 rectangular faces

4.

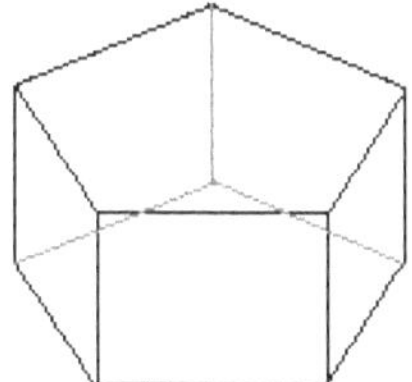

2 pentagonal faces and 5 rectangular faces

5.

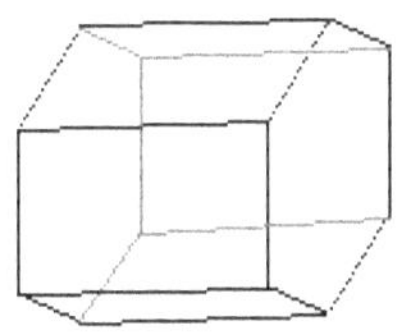

2 hexagonal faces and 6 rectangular faces

6.

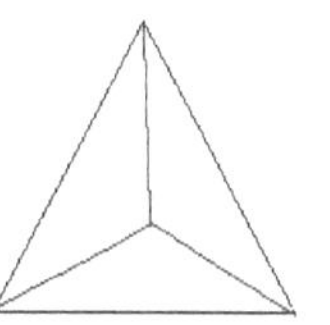

4 triangular faces

7.

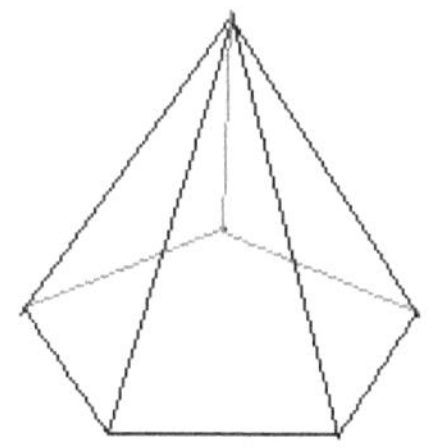

5 triangular faces and 1 pentagonal face

8.

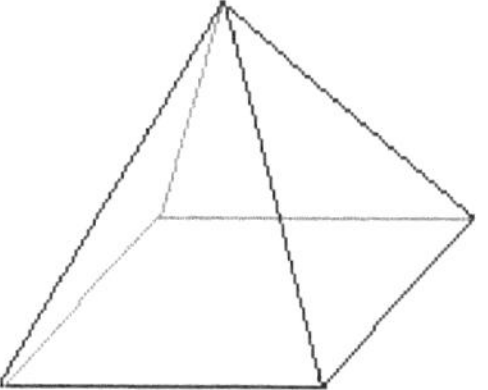

4 triangular faces and 1 square face

Student's name: ____________________ Assignment date: ________________

Nets of Boxes a pattern for a solid

1. Circle the net, which can be folded to each solid?

1.

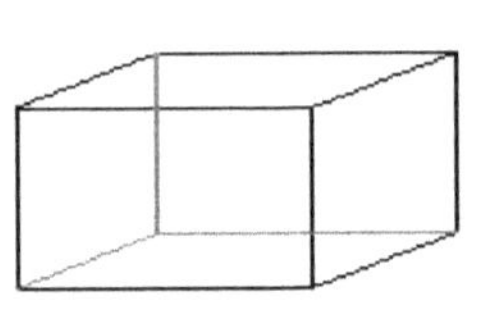
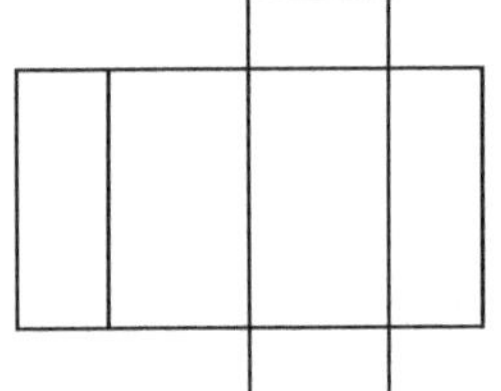
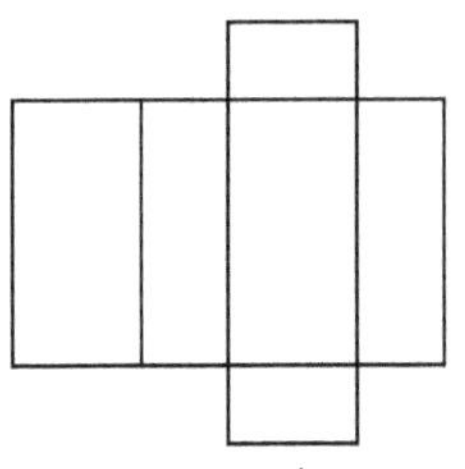
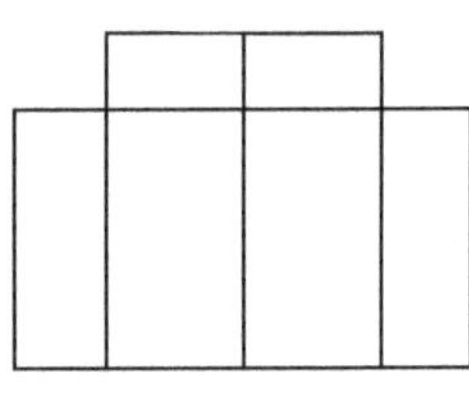

A B√ C

2.

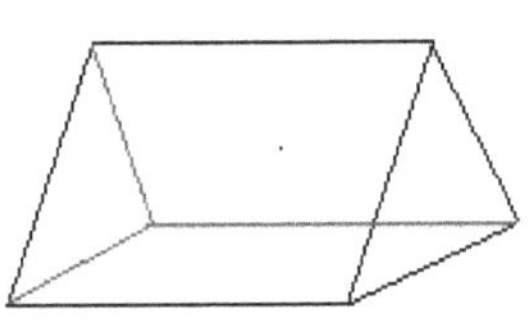
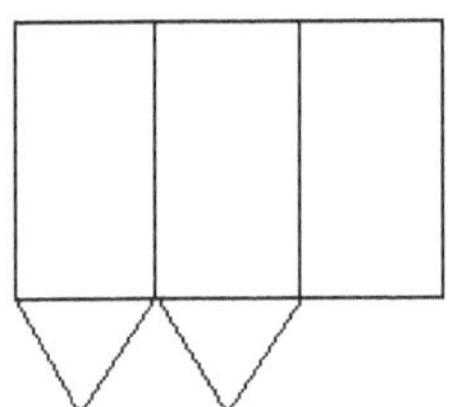
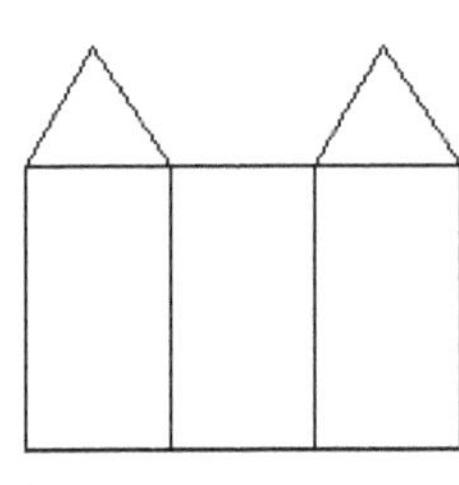
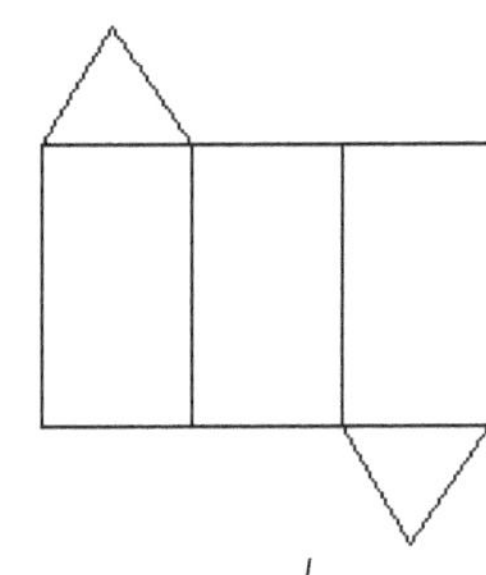

A B C√

3.

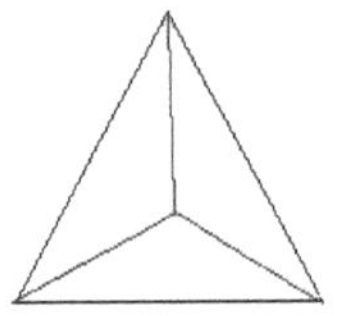
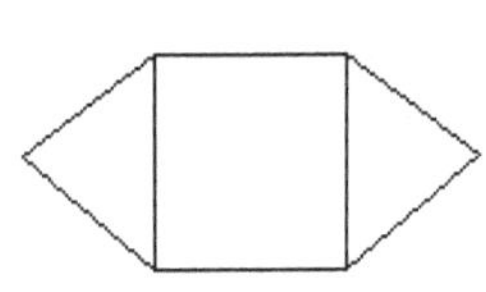
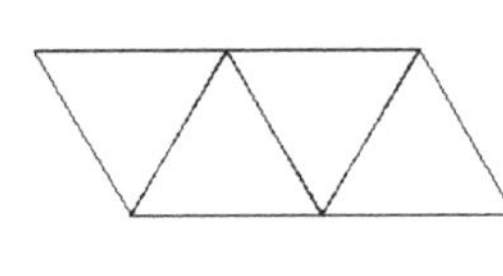
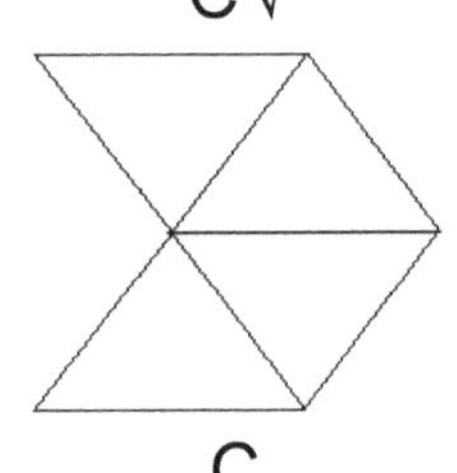

A B√ C

4.

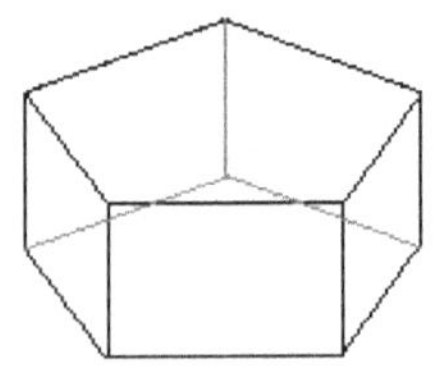
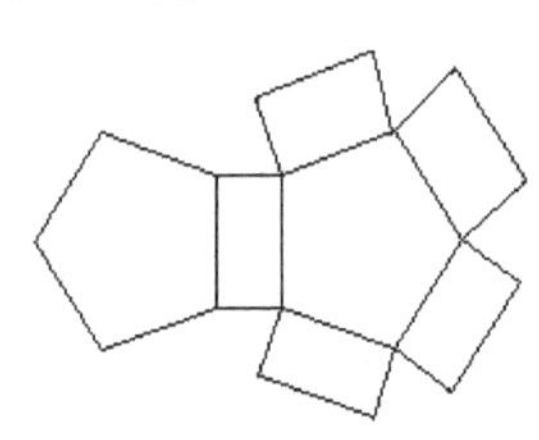
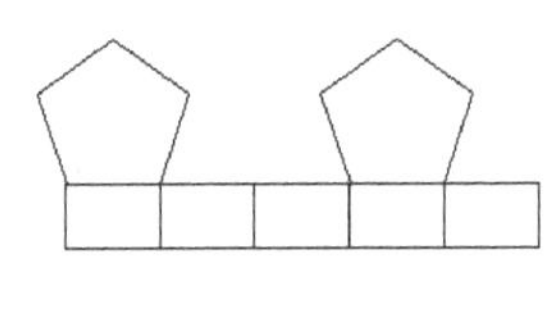
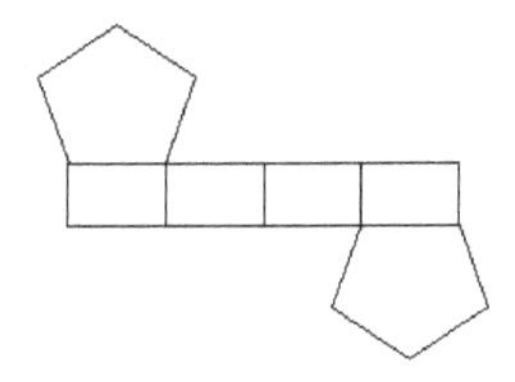

A B C

5.

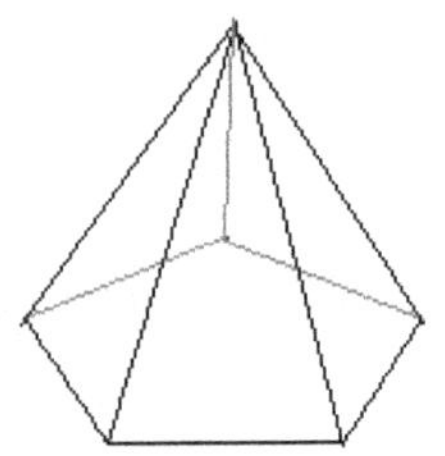
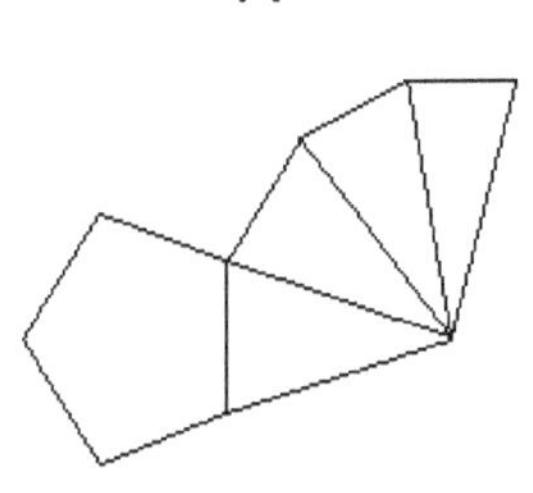
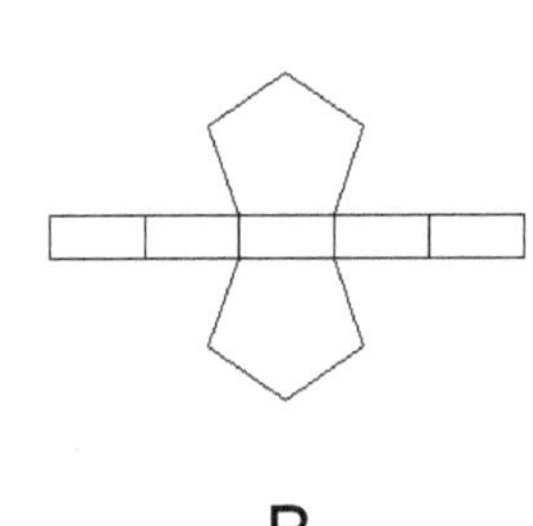
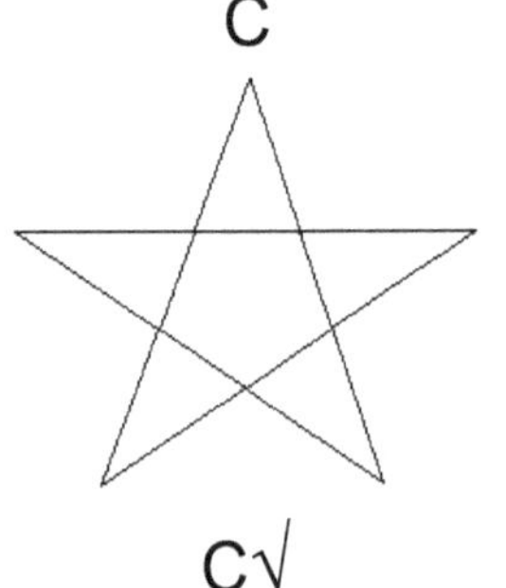

A B C√

Student's name: ____________________ Assignment date: ________________

1. Circle the nets that can be folded into boxes.

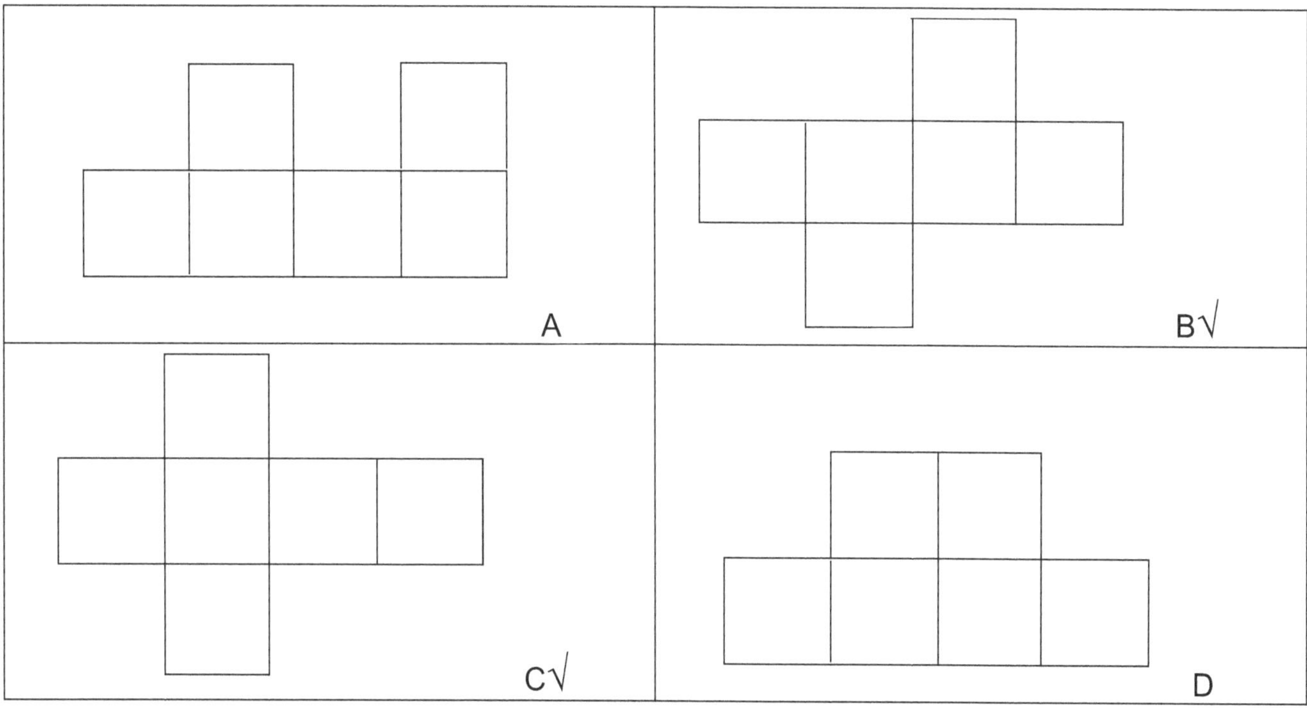

1. The following net makes up the cube.

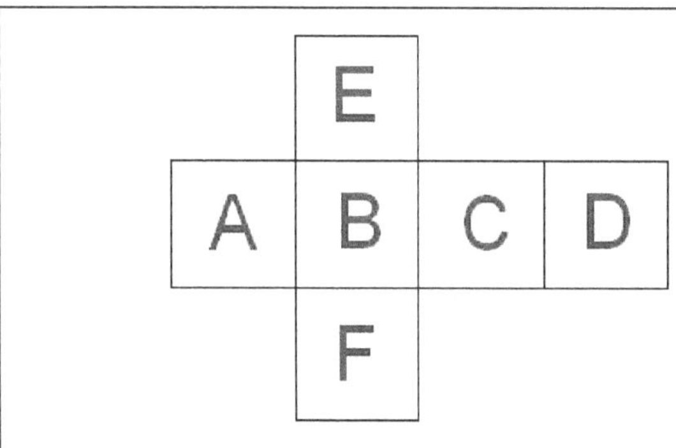

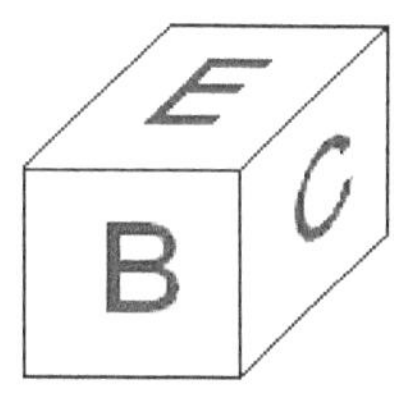

1. Which letter is on the base? F

2. Which letter is opposite the letter "B"? D

3. Which letter is opposite the letter "C"? A

Student's name: ____________________ Assignment date: ________________

Skeletons
A model showing only edges and vertices

Skeleton	Name	Number of vertices	number of edges for each base	Number of edges for side
	Triangular pyramid	4	3 equal edges	3 equal edges
	Rectangular prism	4	2 pairs of equal edges	4 equal edges
	Triangular prism	6	3 equal edges	3 equal edges
	Pentagonal prism	10	5 equal edges	5 equal edges
	Hexagonal prism	12	6 equal edges	6 equal edges
	Hexagonal pyramid	7	6 equal edges	6 equal edges
	Square-based pyramid	5	4 equal edges	4 equal edges

Student's name: ____________________ Assignment date: ________________

***** Part **19** Graph and charts *****

Tally table

Complete the following chart and answer the questions.

1.

Favourite Snack

Snack	Number	Tally
Cookie	7	卌 II
Chip	3	III
Fries	5	卌
Ice cream	9	
Popcorn	4	

1. How many people chose cookies as their favourite snack?
   7 ____________
2. How many people chose either chips or fries?
   8 ____________
3. How many people chose either fries or ice cream?
   14 ____________
4. How many people answered the survey?
   28 ____________

2.

Favourite Colour

Colour	Number	Tally
Red		IIII
Blue		卌 III
Green		III
Yellow		卌 IIII
Purple		II

1. How many people chose blue as their favourite colour?
   8 ____________
2. How many people chose either green or red?
   7 ____________
3. How many more people chose yellow than chose purple?
   7 ____________
4. List the colour in the order of their popularity?
   Yellow, blue, red, green, purple ____________

Student's name: ____________________ Assignment date: ________________

3\. Favourite Food

Food	Number	Tally
Pizzas	15	
Hamburgers	8	
Sandwiches	13	
Pasta	7	
Sushi	6	

1. How many people chose pasta as their favourite food?
   7
   ____
2. How many people chose either pizzas or Sandwiches?
   28
   ____
3. How many fewer people choose sandwiches than chose sushi?
   7
   ____
4. How many people were surveyed?
   49
   ____
5. How many people didn't choose hamburgers as their favourite food?
   41
   ____

4\. Favourite Drinks

Drinks	Number	Tally
Juice		卌 卌 IIII
Lemonade		卌 II
Punch		卌 卌
Tea		III
Coke		卌 II

1. How many people chose coke as their favourite drink? 7
   ____
2. How many people chose either punch or juice? 24
   ____
3. How many people answered the survey?
   41
   ____
4. List the drink in order from least votes to most votes.
   Tea, Lemonade/ Coke, Punch, Juice,
   ____

Student's name: ____________________ Assignment date: ________________

5. Clubs

Clubs	Number	Tally
Drawing	9	
Chess	15	
Dancing	8	
Skiing	6	
Swimming	11	

1. What club is the most popular?
Chess
____
2. If three more people chose the dancing club, how many people would have chosen the dancing club?
____
3. How many more people chose the swimming club than chose the skiing club? 5
____
4. How many people didn't choose the swimming club as their favourite club?
38
____

6. Sales

Sales	Number	Tally
Shirts	5	
Sweaters	2	
Jackets	7	
Coats	3	
Blouses	8	

1. How many shirts were sold? 5
____
2. How many were more blouses sold than sweaters? 6
____
3. If 3 more jackets were sold, how many jackets would have been sold? 10
____
4. How many items were sold totally? 25
____
5. List the sales from the most sold to the least sold.
Blouses, jackets, shirts, coats, sweaters
____

Student's name: ____________________ Assignment date: ______________

Line plots

1.	Books read 5: X X X 6: X X X X X 7: X X X X 8: X X X X X X 9: X X X X X 10: X X	1. How many students read exactly six books? 5 ________ 2. How many students read not less than nine books? 7 ________ 3. How many students read less than seven books? 8 ________ 4. How many students were surveyed? 25 ________
2.	Points scored 3: X X X X X X X 4: X X X X 5: X X X 6: X X 7: X X 8: X	1. What points are most of the teams scored? 3 ________ 2. What points is the champion team scored? 8 ________ 3. What are the total points of all the teams scored? 86 ________

Student's name: ____________________ Assignment date: ________________

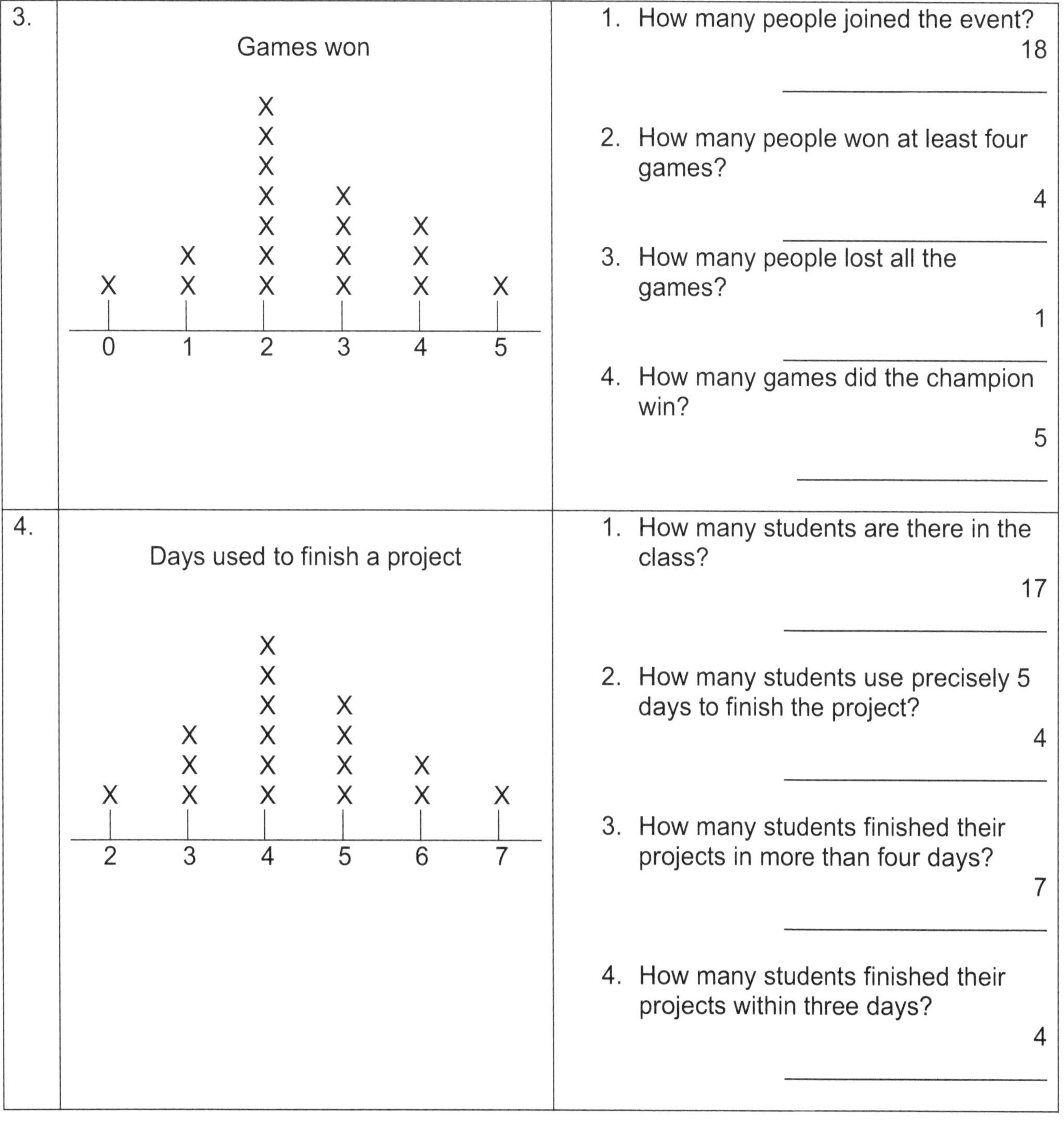

3.

Games won

0	1	2	3	4	5
X	XX	XXXXXXX	XXXXX	XXX	X

1. How many people joined the event? 18
2. How many people won at least four games? 4
3. How many people lost all the games? 1
4. How many games did the champion win? 5

4.

Days used to finish a project

2	3	4	5	6	7
X	XXX	XXXXXX	XXXX	XX	X

1. How many students are there in the class? 17
2. How many students use precisely 5 days to finish the project? 4
3. How many students finished their projects in more than four days? 7
4. How many students finished their projects within three days? 4

Student's name: ____________________ Assignment date: ________________

5. This is a survey about the number of pets a student keeps. Draw a line plot according to the following information.

Family	Number of pets
Tom	2
James	4
John	3
Michael	6
Jimmy	3
Jenny	5
Laura	7
Cindy	3
Andy	5
Victor	4
David	3
Serena	6
Grace	3
Alex	5
Ann	3
Kelly	6
Christine	4
Jason	2

2	3	4	5	6	7
XX	XXXXXX	XXX	XXX	XXX	X

6. A dart competition was held. Draw a line plot according to the following information.
Three students scored five points.
Four students scored six points.
Eight students scored seven points.
Six students scored eight points.
Seven students scored nine points.
Two students scored ten points.

XXX	XXXX	XXXXXXXX	XXXXXX	XXXXXXX	XX

Student's name: ____________________ Assignment date: ________________

Stem-and-leaf plots

1. The following stem-and-leaf graph shows the heights of students in a class. (unit is in cm)

Stem	Leaves
11	8
12	2 4 5 5 9
13	0 8 4 6 6 0 9
14	5 7 3 6 4 6 2 8
15	1 3

1. How many students are 130 cm? 2 ________
2. How many students are between 130 and 139 cm (inclusive)? 7 ________
3. How many students are taller than 150 cm? 2 ________
4. How many students are there in the class? 23 ________

2. The following stem-and-leaf graph shows the score of the students got in a math test. (unit is in cm)

Stem	Leaves
5	1
6	2 8 3 6 9 4
7	0 4 7 2 9 5 3 8
8	1 6 3 0 7 9 5 3
9	2 7 4 1 8
10	0 0

1. How many students failed the test (below 60)? 1 ________
2. How many students got an "A"(at least 86)? 10 ________
3. How many students get full marks? 2 ________
4. How many students are there in the class? 30 ________
5. More students got the sixties or nineties? the sixties ________

Student's name: ____________________ Assignment date: ________________

3. This is a record of the long-jump of a class. Make a stem-and-leaf graph according to the data. Unit is in cm.

104	125	117	121	136
138	107	116	129	109
115	117	125	136	124
109	112	114	126	132
117	127	119	137	125

Stem	Leaves
10	4 7 9 9
11	7 6 5 7 2 4 7 9
12	5 1 9 5 4 6 7 5
13	6 8 6 2 7

4. This is a record of sales in a different department of a store. Make a stem-and-leaf graph according to the data. Unit is in the dollar.

63	62	80	54	43
57	66	61	69	71
70	68	42	49	52
36	68	85	64	39
73	74	36	57	48

Stem	Leaves
3	6 9 6
4	3 2 9 8
5	4 7 2 7
6	2 6 1 9 8 8 4
7	1 0 3 4
8	0 5

5. This is a record of the weight of each apple in a basket. Make a stem-and-leaf graph according to the data. Unit is in gram.

75	81	68	90	108
82	95	79	112	79
98	83	86	105	103
116	86	78	67	102
79	92	95	86	103
98	107	113	104	107

Stem	Leaves
6	8 7
7	5 9 9 8 9
8	1 2 3 6 6 6
9	0 5 8 2 5 8
10	8 5 3 2 3 7 4 7
11	2 6 3

Student's name: ______________________ Assignment date: ________________

Mean and Range

Mean, or average, is the sum of all numbers divided by how many numbers there are.
The range is the difference between the greatest number and the least number.

Find mean and range for each set of numbers.

Example: Find mean and range of 4, 7, 2, 8, and 9.
Sum = 4 + 7 + 2 + 8 + 9 = 30
How many numbers? 5

Mean = $\frac{sum}{\#of\ numbers} = \frac{30}{5}$ = 6

Greatest number = 9
Least number = 2
Range = Greatest number – least number = 9 – 2 = 7

	Numbers	mean	range
1.	5, 16, 7, 10, 12	10	11
2.	6, 13, 9, 8	9	7
3.	3, 15, 8. 12, 9, 13	10	12
4.	5. 12, 3, 8	7	9
5.	10, 15, 16, 9, 5	11	11
6.	8, 11, 15, 12, 7, 13	11	8
7.	24, 18, 19, 16, 13	18	11
8.	18, 22, 25, 23	22	7
9.	11, 16, 9, 22, 12	14	13
10.	13, 16, 15, 18, 13	15	5

Ho Math Chess Primary Grades Math

Test Review assesssment 何数棋謎低年级数学测试複習考核

Student's name: ____________________ Assignment date: ________________

Find mean and range from line plot.

Example: Find mean and range from the line plot below.

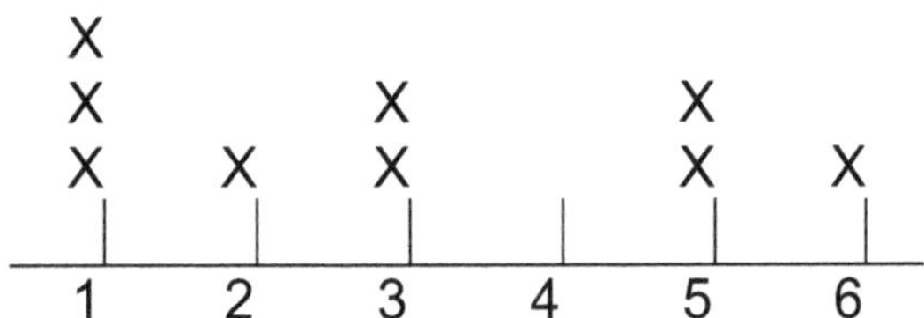

There are 3 of 1, 1 of 2, 2 of 3, 2 of 5 and 1 of 6. So,
Total = $3 \times 1 + 1 \times 2 + 2 \times 3 + 2 \times 5 + 1 \times 6 = 27$
\# of numbers = 3 + 1 + 2 + 1 + 2 = 9

Mean = $\frac{sum}{\#of\ numbers} = \frac{27}{9} = 3$

Greatest number = 6
Least number = 1
Range = Greatest number – least number = 6 – 1 = 5

1.

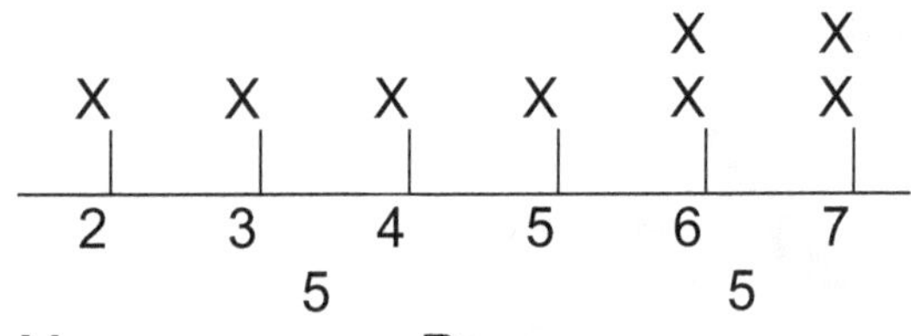

Mean = 5 Range = 5

2.

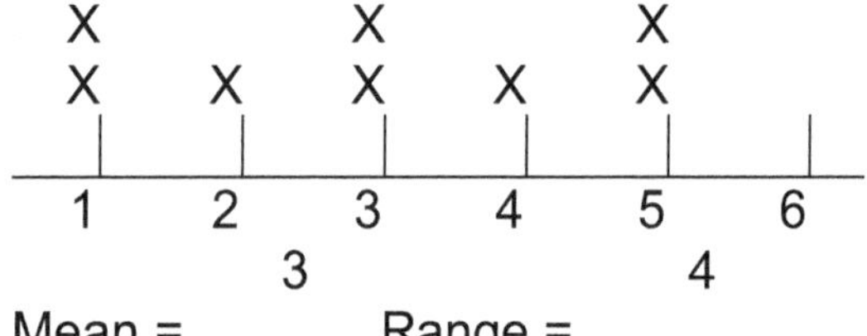

Mean = 3 Range = 4

3.

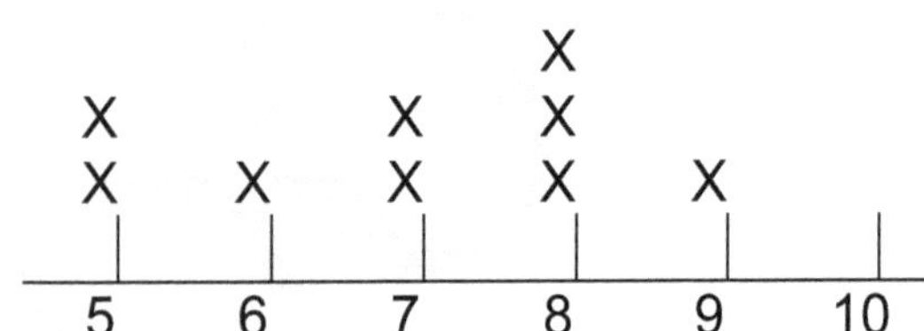

Mean = 7 Range = 4

4.

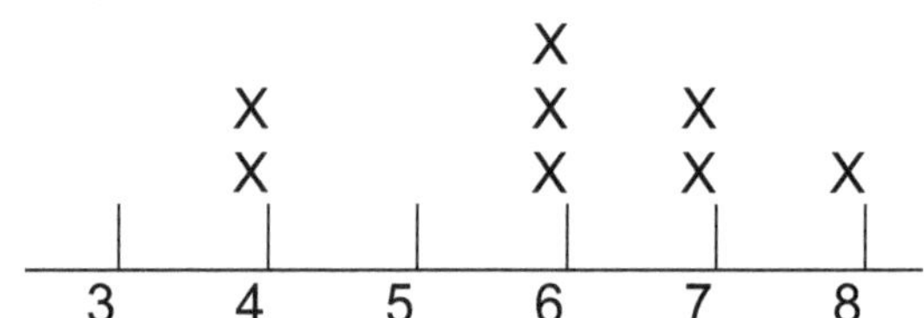

Mean = 6 Range = 4

Student's name: ____________________ Assignment date: ________________

Find mean and range from stem-and-leaf plot.

Example: Find mean and range from the stem-and-leaf plot below.

Stem	Leaves
1	1 4 7
2	0 2 5
3	1

There are 7 numbers in the plot above: 11, 14, 17, 20, 22, 25, and 31.
Total = 11 + 14 + 17 + 20 + 22 + 25 = 140
# of numbers = 7

Mean = $\frac{sum}{\#of\ numbers} = \frac{140}{7} = 20$

Greatest number = 31
Least number = 11
Range = Greatest number – least number = 31 – 11 = 20

1.

Stem	Leaves
2	0
3	3 3 8
4	5 1

35 25
Mean = ______ Range = ________

2.

Stem	Leaves
3	1 0 8
4	2 5
5	4

40 24
Mean = ______ Range = ________

3.

Stem	Leaves
1	4 2 6 2
2	0
3	3 5 4

22 23
Mean = ______ Range = ________

4.

Stem	Leaves
11	2 6
12	3 7 5
13	2 0 7 2 6

127 25
Mean = ______ Range = ________

Student's name: ____________________ Assignment date: ______________

Pictographs

A pictograph uses a pictorial symbol to represent a physical object.

1.

Favourite Colours

Red	▣ ▣
Blue	▣ ▣ ▣ ▣ ▣
Green	▣ ▣ ▣
Yellow	▣ ▣
black	▣

▣ = 10 votes

1. What colour is the most popular?
blue
____
2. How many students take green as their favourite colour?
30
____
3. How many students answered the survey?
125
____
4. List the popularity from greatest to least.
Blue, green, red, yellow, black
____
5. What is the range?
40
____

2.

Favourite Games

Soccer	☼ ☼ ☼ ☼
Basketball	☼ ☼
Hockey	☼ ☼ ☼ ☼ ☼
Tennis	☼ ☼
Swimming	☼ ☼ ☼
Skiing	☼

☼ = 8 students

1. What game is the most popular?
Hockey
____
2. How many more students take hockey as their favourite game than basketball?
24
____
3. How many students answered the survey?
136
____
4. List the popularity from least to greatest.
Skiing, basketball/tennis, swimming, soccer, hockey
____
5. What is the range?
32
____

Student's name: ____________________ Assignment date: ________________

Making pictographs

1.

Favourite Food	# of students
Pizzas	15
Sandwiches	20
Pasta	5
Hamburger	10
Sushi	25

Favourite Food

Pizzas

Sandwiches

Pasta

Hamburger

Sushi

Use  to present 5 students

2.

Name of poultry	# of poultry
Chicken	32
Ducks	8
Goose	20
Turkey	12

Name of poultry

Chicken

Ducks

Goose

Turkey

Use to present 4 poultry

3.

Favourite drink	# of students
Coke	9
Juice	12
Tea	3
Water	6
Punch	15

Favourite drink

Coke

Juice

Tea

Water

Punch

Use to present 3 students.

Student's name: ____________________ Assignment date: ________________

Pictograph problem

1. The fish caught, in average of four years, from 2013 to 2016 is ____________.
2. The fish caught in 2013 is what fraction of the year 2016? ________

Fish caught from 2013 to 2016

Year	Fish
2016	🐟 🐟 🐟 🐟 🐟 🐟 🐟 🐟
2015	🐟 🐟 🐟 🐟
2014	🐟 🐟 🐟 🐟 🐟 🐟
2013	🐟 🐟

🐟 = 2 fish

1. $\frac{20 \times 2}{4} = 10$
2. $\frac{1}{4}$

answer

Student's name: ____________________ Assignment date: ________________

Bar Graphs (Bar Charts)

There is a type of data that has no real numerical meaning of measurement; that is, you cannot use it to do any computation to have a meaningful result. For example, if assigning a numerical value to male = 1 and female = 3, then the average of these two items = 2, which is not meaningful. This type of data is categorical data.

A bar graph, also known as a bar chart, is a graphical display of categorical data using different heights of bars to correspond to the frequency (the number of occurrences) of the amount of data. The higher the bar, the higher the frequency of the data. The lower the bar, the lower the frequency of the data.

The purpose of using a bar chart is to use it to represent data so that it is easier for readers to understand. For example, after collecting the information of Vancouver rainfall by months in a year, we can show the monthly amount of rainfall by the different heights of bars that occurred in different months.

Bar graphs are most commonly drawn vertically, though they can also be depicted horizontally.

Double Bar graph

If there are two different types of categorical data, then a double bar graph can be drawn.

Histogram

If the data are not categorical (such as the scores of a test), then a type of graph called Histogram can be used.

Student's name: ____________________ Assignment date: ________________

How to draw a bar chart?

1. The title of the bar chart and two headings for the vertical axis and horizontal axis must be provided.
2. Decide the scale (number of points) of the vertical axis. Normally, the vertical axis shows the quantity, and the horizontal line shows the category. The origin should normally start with 0.

The size of intervals (the distance between any points) = $\frac{the\ maximum\ value}{the\ number\ of\ interals\ (points\ or\ scales)}$

Normally the lowest scale is below the lowest value in the data, and the largest scale is higher than the maximum value in the data.

3. The horizontal axis shows the number of categorical data, which in turn determines the number of bars.

Example,

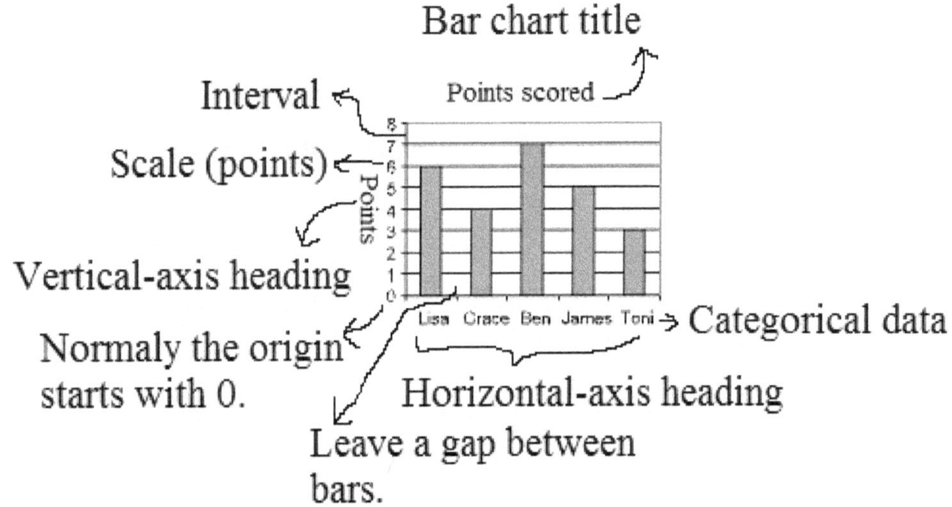

Student's name: ____________________ Assignment date: ________________

1. Vertical bar graph.

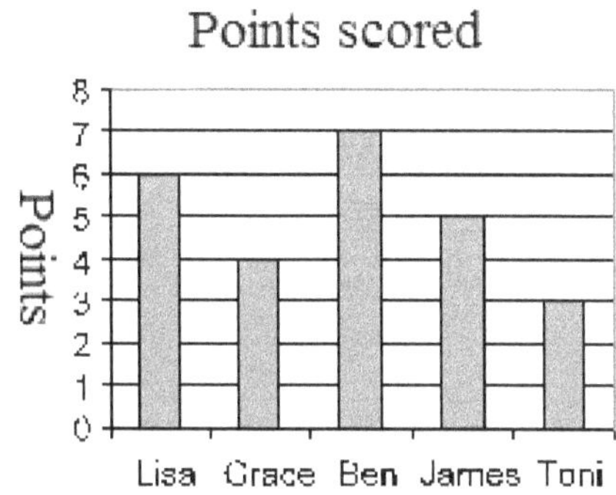

1. Who scored the most points?

Ben ________________

2. What are the total points scored?

25 ________________

3. What are the mean points scored?

5 ________________

4. List the name of students according to their points from least to greatest.

Toni, Grace, James, Lisa, Ben ________________

5. What is the range?

4 ________________

2. Horizontal bar graph.

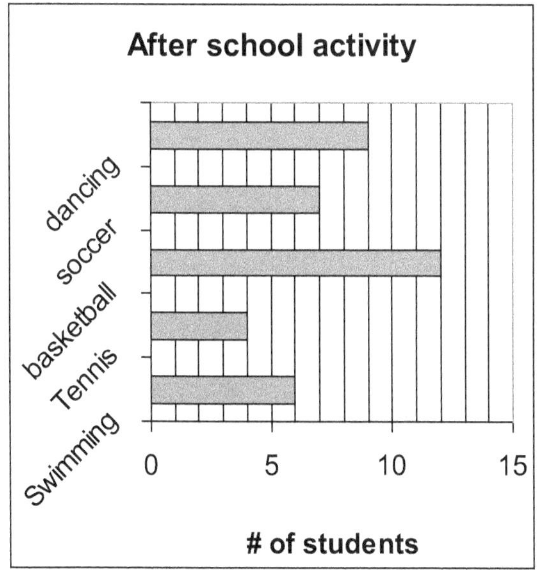

1. What is the most popular activity?

basketball ________________

2. How many more students joined in soccer than tennis?

3 ________________

3. Which activities have at least 7 students joined in?

Basketball, soccer, dancing ________________

4. List the activities according to their popularity from greatest to least.

Basketball, dancing, soccer, swimming, tennis ________________

5. If the scale is 10 at the first grid, instead of 5, the graph would have to be shorter or longer to show the same data?

It would be shorter.

6. What is the range?

________8__

Student's name: ____________________ Assignment date: ________________

Make a bar graph from each below.

1.

Name	# of chin-ups
John	6
Tom	9
Sam	3
Justin	5
Ben	8

Title: ________________

# of chin-ups

12 11 10 9 8 7 6 5 4 3 2 1 0

2.

Fruits in a basket	# of fruits
Orange	5
Apple	8
Pear	2
Peach	9
Plum	6

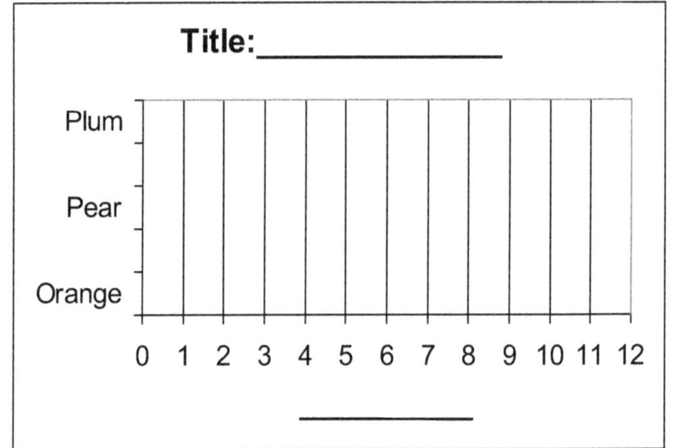

3.

Team	# of games won
Tiger	5
Hunter	8
Eagle	13
Giant	10
Hurricane	9

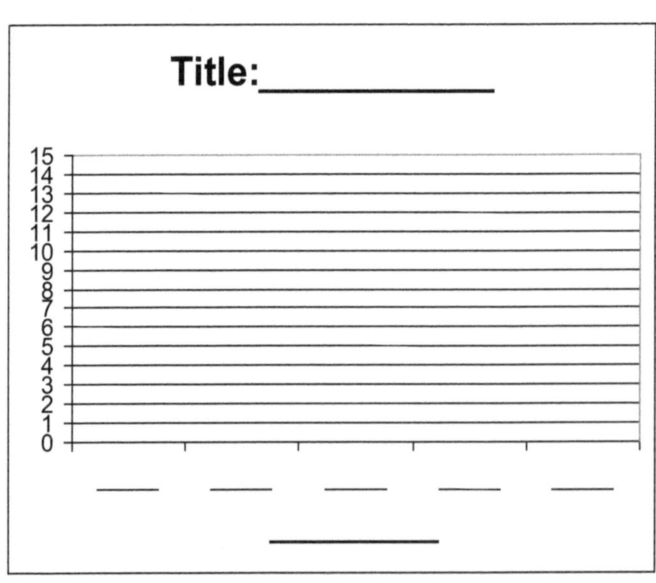

Student's name: ____________________ Assignment date: ________________

Line Graph

The following graph shows the sales of a store from 1998 to 2005.

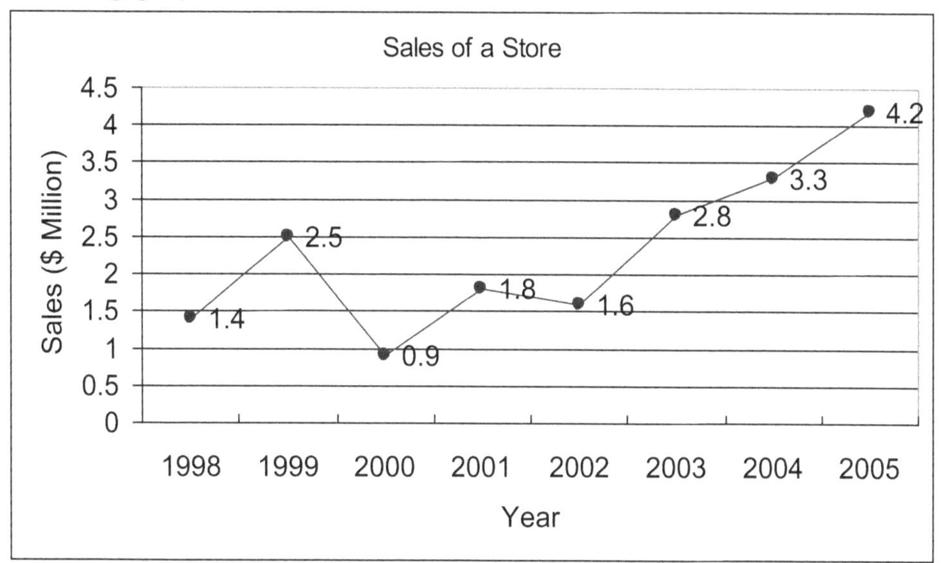

1. In which year did the store make the least amount of sale? 2000

   What was the sale? $0.9 million

2. In which year did the store make the greatest amount of sale? 2005

   What was the sale? $4.2 million

3. Between which two years did the sale of the store rise the most? 2002 & 2003

   How much did it rise? $1.2 million

4. Between which two years did the sale of the store drop the most? 1999 & 2000

   How much did it drop? $1.6 million

5. What can you predict for 2006, rise or drop? rise

Student's name: ____________________ Assignment date: ________________

The following graph shows the average price of a stock from 1995 to 2005. Draw a line graph to describe the change.

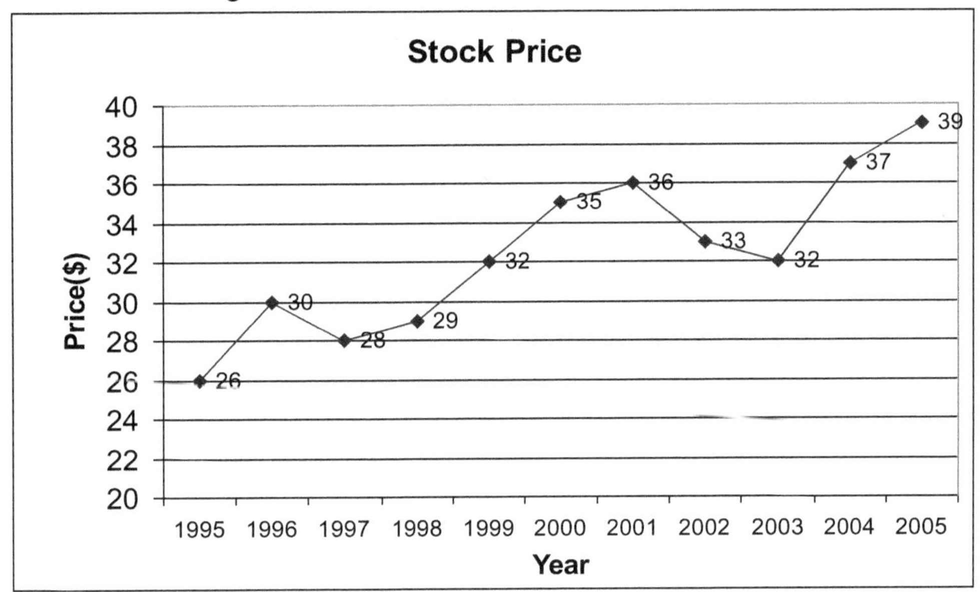

1. What is the highest price of the stock? $39

   In which year? 2005

2. What is the lowest price of the stock? $26

   In which year? 1995

3. Between which two years did the price of the stock rise the most? 2003 & 2004

   How much did it rise? $5

4. Between which, two years did the price of the stock drop the most? 2001 & 2002

   How much did it drop? $3

5. What is the mean (average price)? $32.45

6. What can you predict for 2006, rise or drop? rise

Student's name: ____________________ Assignment date: ________________

Circle Graphs

1. This circle graph shows the pets in a house.

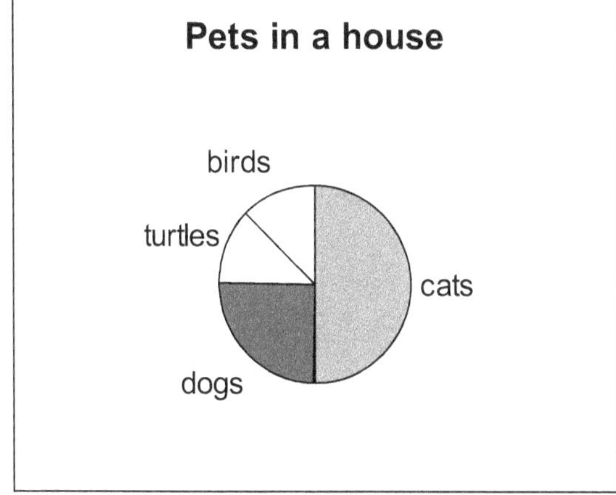

1. What fraction of the pets are cats?

$\frac{1}{2}$

2. What fraction of the pets are dogs?

$\frac{1}{4}$

3. Which two kinds of pets represent $\frac{1}{4}$ the pets?

Birds and turtles

4. What is the greatest number of pets?

cats

2. This circle graph shows the votes of the students in a class on their favourite drinks.

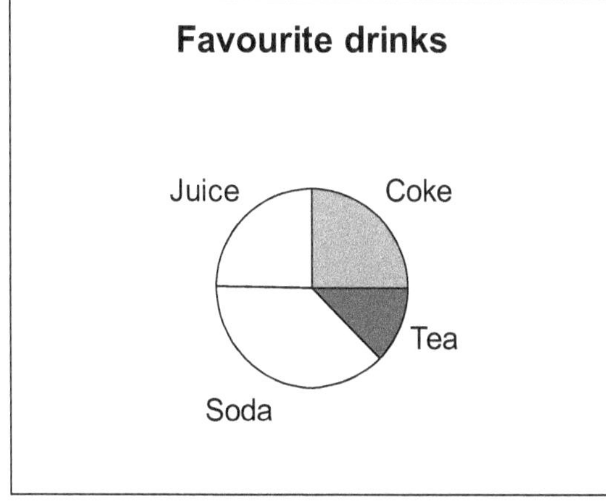

1. What fraction of the class chose juice as their favourite drink?

$\frac{1}{4}$

2. What fraction of the class chose soda as their favourite drink?

$\frac{3}{8}$

3. Do more students like coke or tea?

coke

4. What is the most popular drink?

soda

5. If there are 24 students in the class, how many students chose coke as their favourite drink?

9 students

Student's name: ____________________ Assignment date: ______________

Comparing pictograph, bar chart, line graph, pie chart (circle graph)

1. It is easy to draw a pictograph because each pictorial symbol in the graph represents a value, but to get the actual value, the reader needs to calculate.
2. The bar chart provides a good visual so the reader can see the value of each category immediately, but we can not see the trend as clearly as the line chart, especially since the bar chart is awkward to compare multiple categories. Sometimes the double bar chart is drawn to show the subcategory, but if more categories are needed, then the line chart is better by using different line styles.
3. The pie chart shows something out of the total, and it provides the idea of fraction or % out of the whole.
4. The stem-and-leaf shows the branch data out of the main value. Suppose the details of each main category are needed, then the stem-and-leaf plot is good.

Student's name: ____________________ Assignment date: ________________

Venn diagram

A Venn diagram is a method to sort data using a circle.
For two sets: $n(A \cup B) = n(A) + n(B) - n(A \cap B)$

Part	Square	Black
A	Yes	No
B	Yes	Yes
C	No	Yes
D	No	No

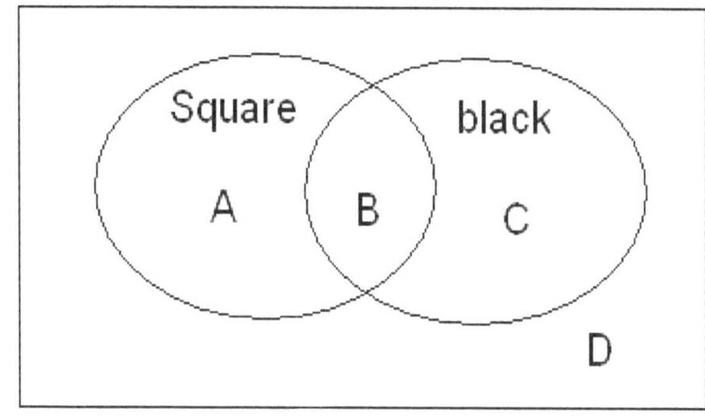

a. Below each object, write the part of the Venn diagram to which it belongs.

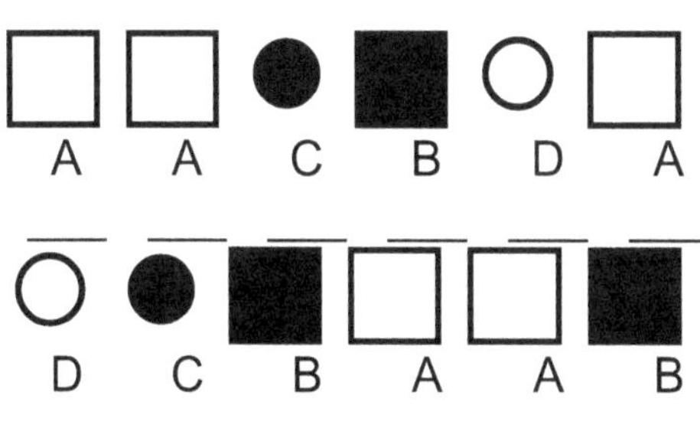

A A C B D A

D C B A A B

B D B B D C

b. Write the number in each part.

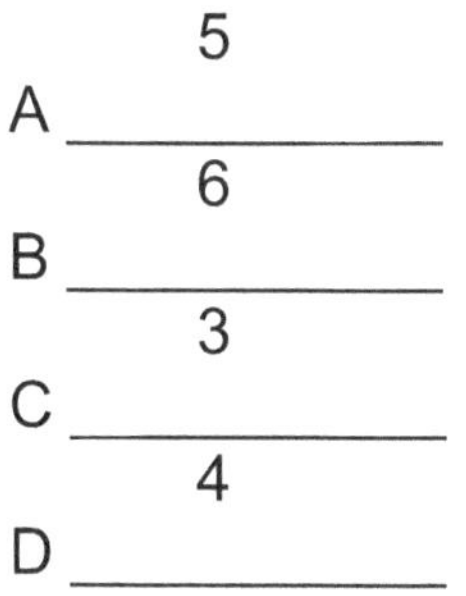

A 5

B 6

C 3

D 4

Tina	James	Melissa	Isabel
English French	English	French	English French
B	A	C	B

Kevin	Justin	Linda	Steven
English French	English	French	English
B	A	C	A

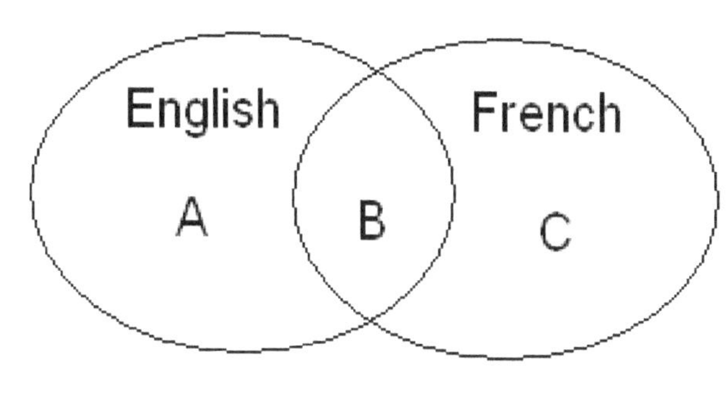

A 3 B 3 C 2

Student's name: ____________________ Assignment date: ________________

3.

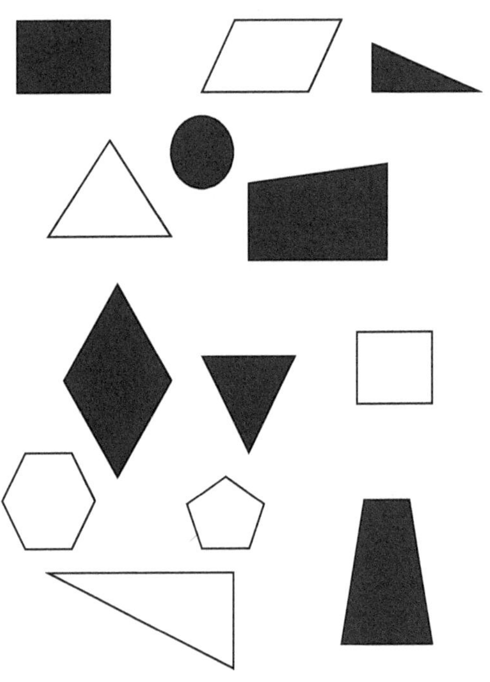

Four sides A B C Black D

Write the number in each part.

A 2

B 4

C 3

D 4

4.

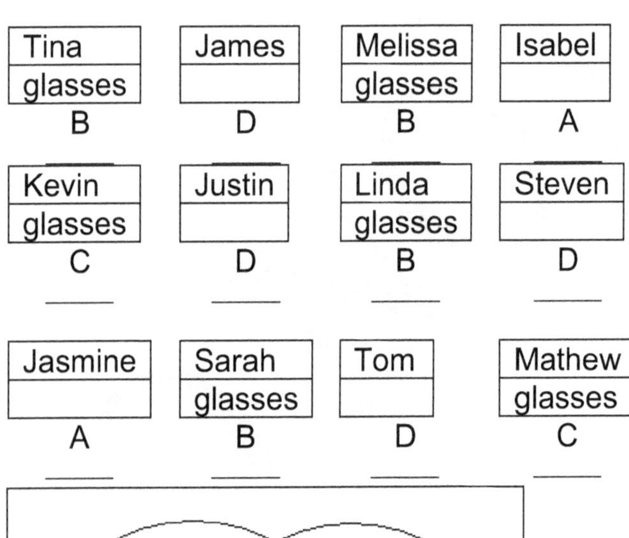

Girls A B C Glasses D

Answer the following questions.

1. How many girls wear glasses? 4

2. How many students wear glasses? 6

3. How many students are there? 12

4. How many boys do not wear glasses? 4

Student's name: ____________________ Assignment date: ________________

5.

There are 47 students in the Ho Math Chess Learning Centre summer program. 18 students took a math class. 12 students took chess class. 21 students did not take math or chess classes. How many students took both math and chess classes?

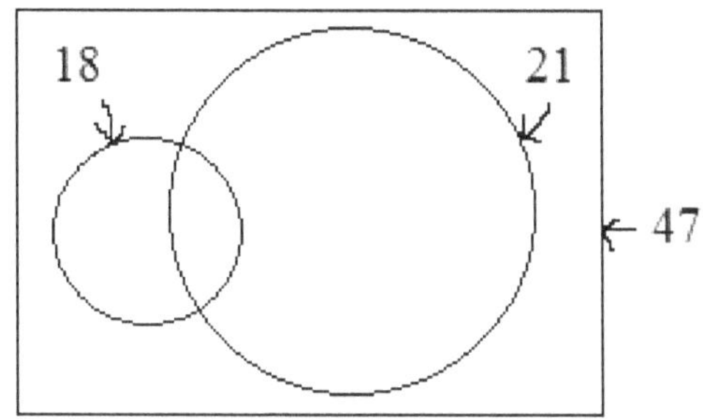

18 +12 + 21 – 47 = 4

Carroll diagram

Sort and classify the following numbers using a Caroll diagram.

3, 50, 293, 98, 390, 879, 175, 46

	Odd	Even
Less than or equal to 100	3,	50, 98, 46
Greater than 100	293, 879, 175	390

Student's name: ____________________ Assignment date: ______________

Temperature

Write the temperatures.

1. 50 ____ ^{0}C

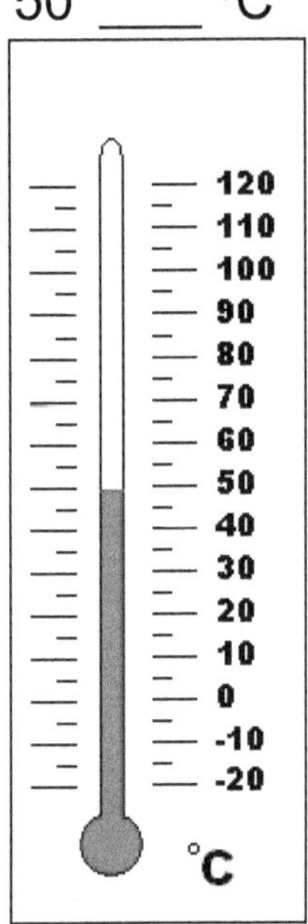

2. 80 ____ ^{0}C

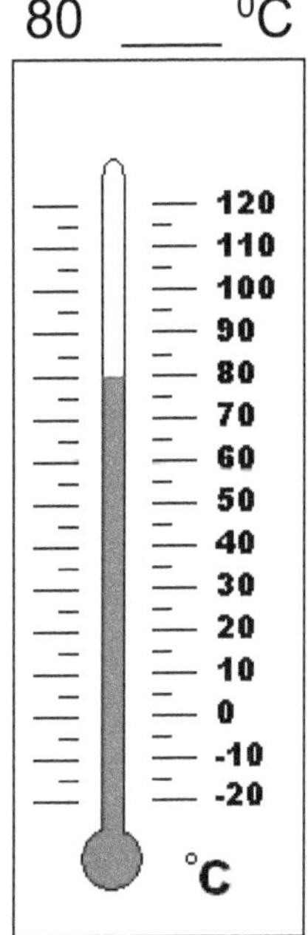

3. 40 ____ ^{0}C

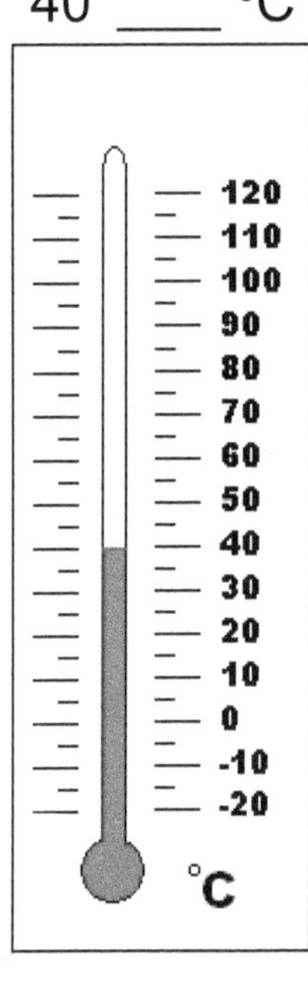

4. 95 ____ ^{0}C

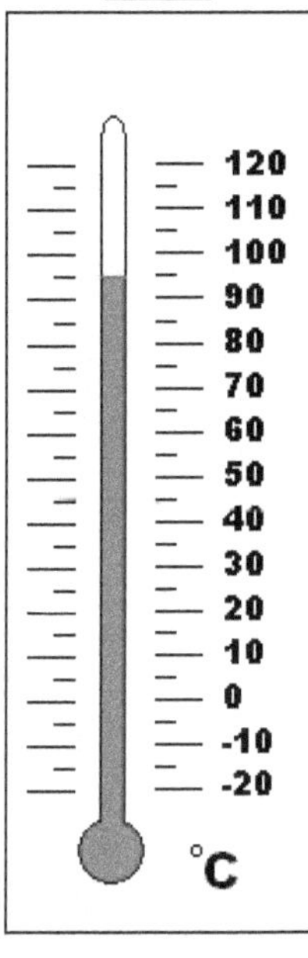

5. 75 ____ ^{0}C

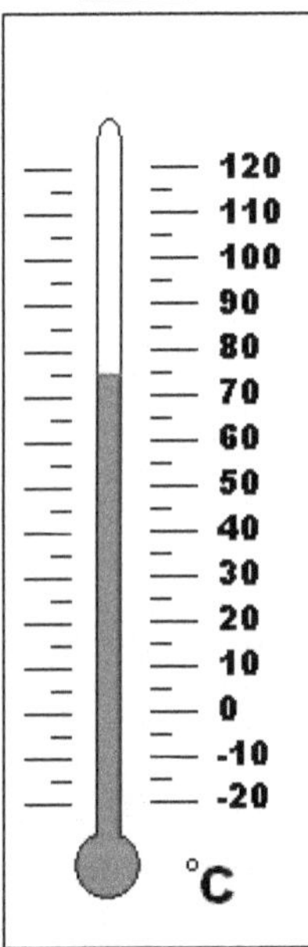

6. 5 ____ ^{0}C

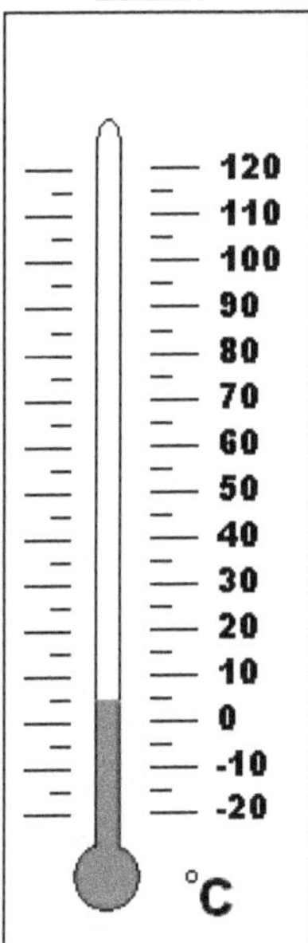

7. 70 ____ ^{0}C

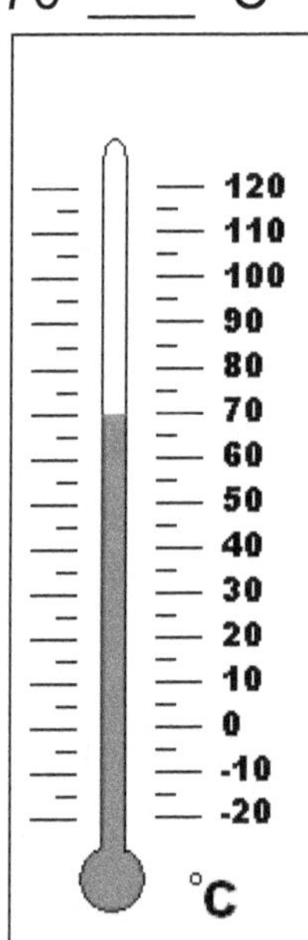

8. 115 ____ ^{0}C

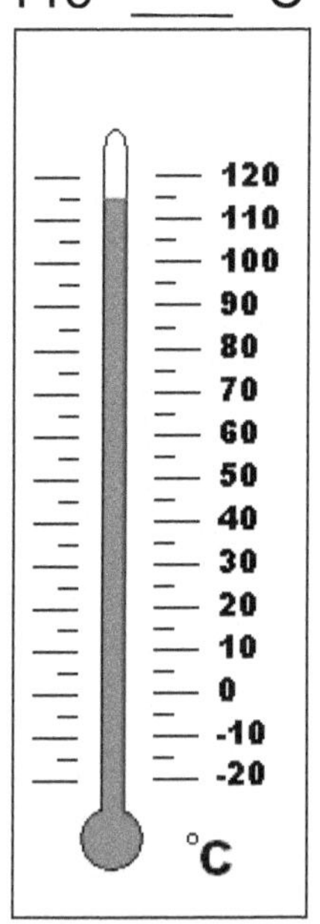

Student's name: ____________________ Assignment date: ________________

Colour the thermometer to show the temperature.

1. 40 ^{0}C

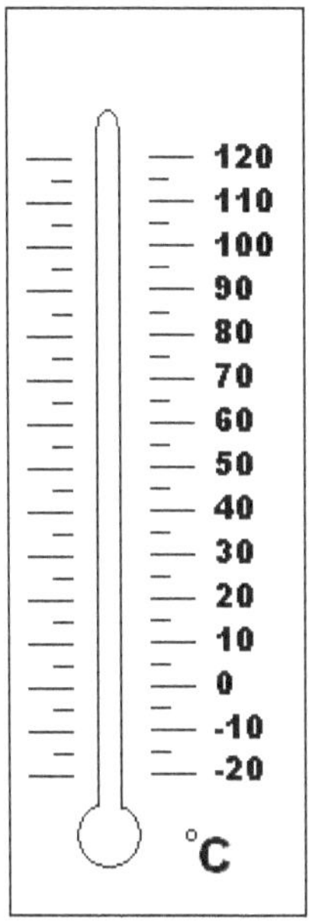

120, 110, 100, 90, 80, 70, 60, 50, 40, 30, 20, 10, 0, -10, -20 °C

2. 80 ^{0}C

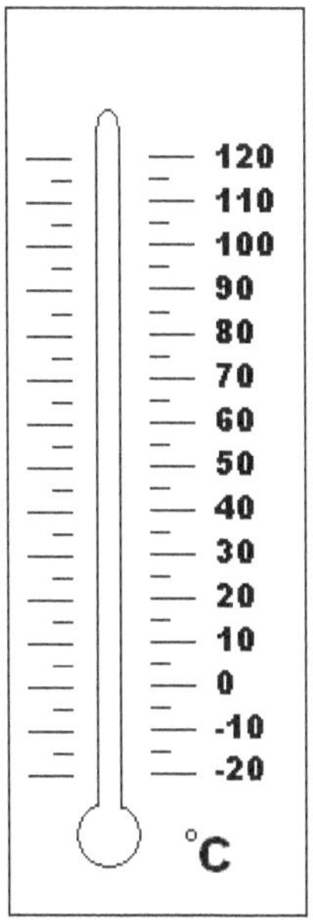

120, 110, 100, 90, 80, 70, 60, 50, 40, 30, 20, 10, 0, -10, -20 °C

3. 55 ^{0}C

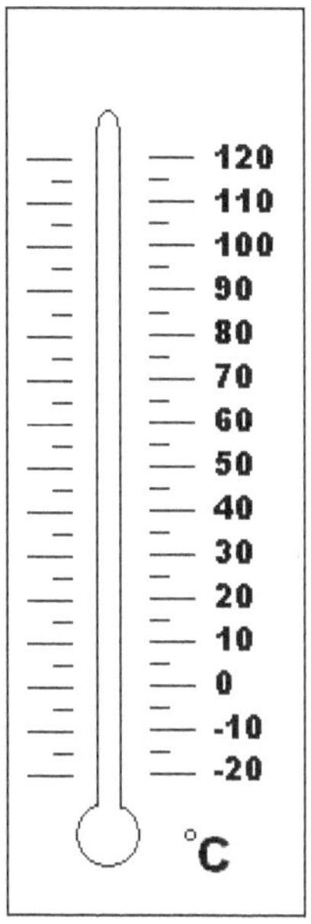

120, 110, 100, 90, 80, 70, 60, 50, 40, 30, 20, 10, 0, -10, -20 °C

4. 75 ^{0}C

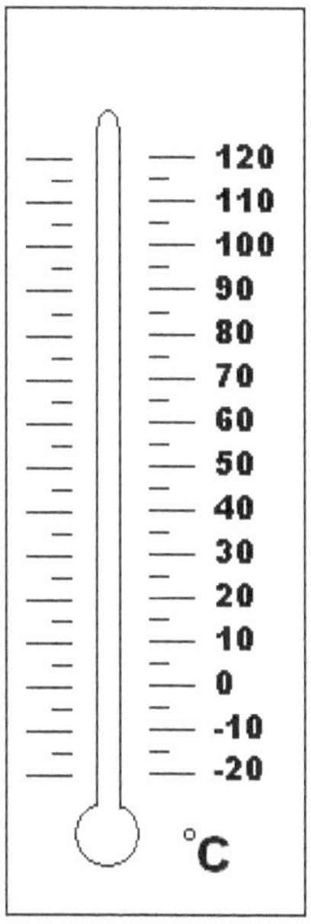

120, 110, 100, 90, 80, 70, 60, 50, 40, 30, 20, 10, 0, -10, -20 °C

5. 5 ^{0}C

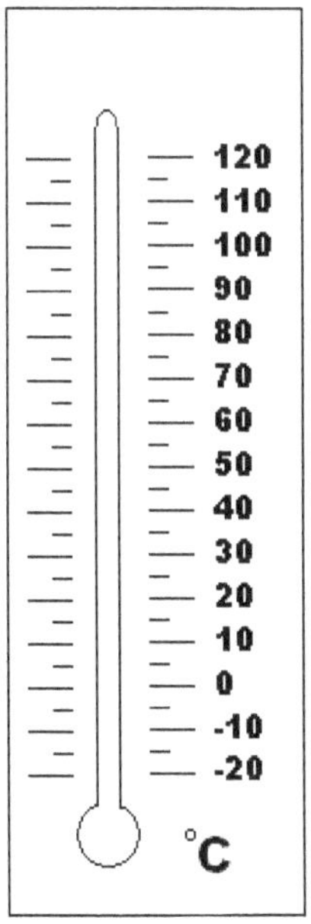

120, 110, 100, 90, 80, 70, 60, 50, 40, 30, 20, 10, 0, -10, -20 °C

6. 60 ^{0}C

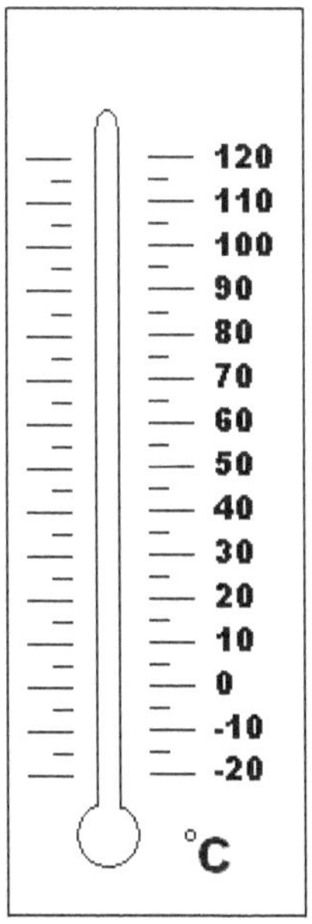

120, 110, 100, 90, 80, 70, 60, 50, 40, 30, 20, 10, 0, -10, -20 °C

7. 95 ^{0}C

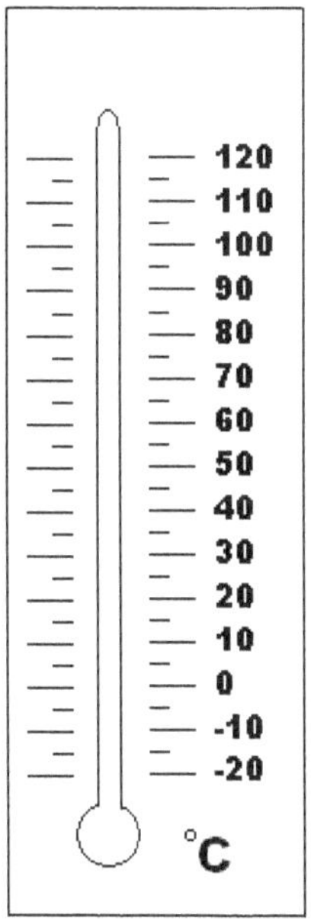

120, 110, 100, 90, 80, 70, 60, 50, 40, 30, 20, 10, 0, -10, -20 °C

8. 100 ^{0}C

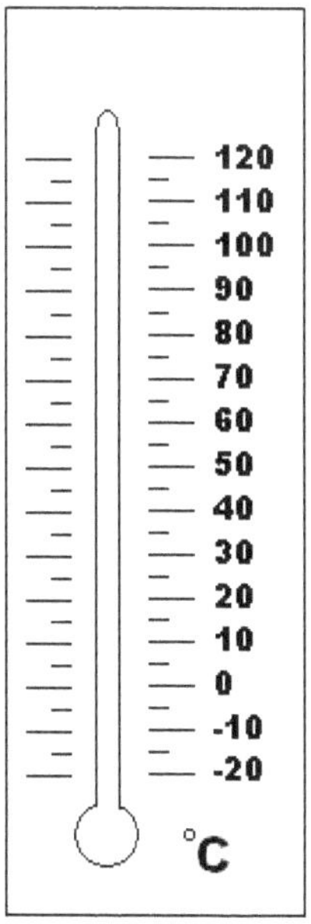

120, 110, 100, 90, 80, 70, 60, 50, 40, 30, 20, 10, 0, -10, -20 °C

Ho Math Chess Primary Grades Math

Test Review assesssment 何数棋謎低年级数学测试複習考核

Student's name: ____________________ Assignment date: ________________

The following thermometers show midnight temperatures in four different cities: Vancouver, Winnipeg, Chicago, and San Carlos.

15 ___ °C 5 ___ °C

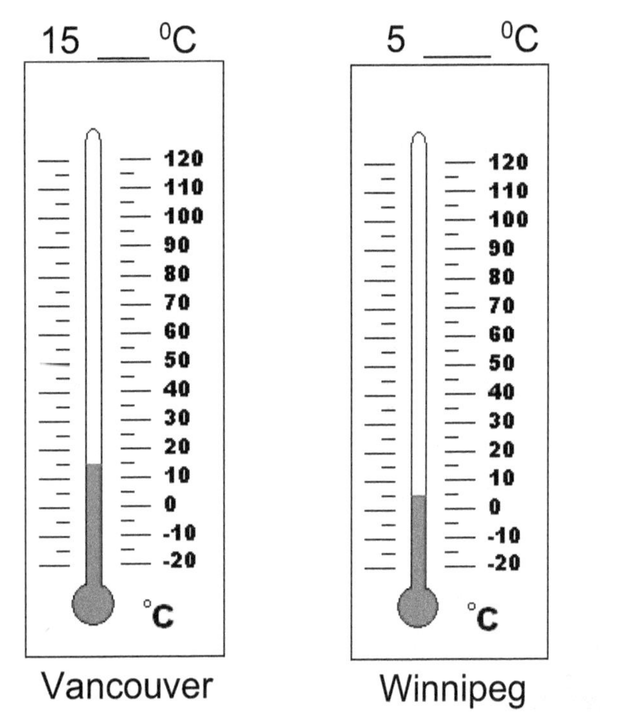

Vancouver Winnipeg

25 ___ °C

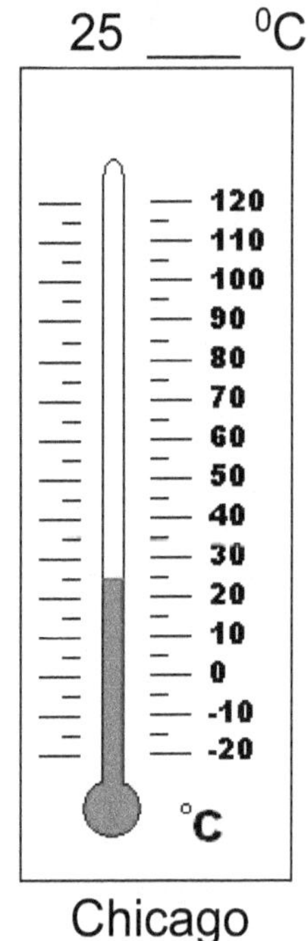

Chicago

30 ___ °C

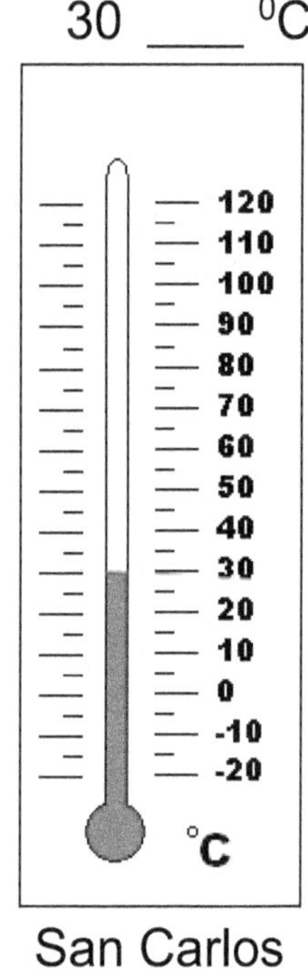

San Carlos

1. What is the temperature of Vancouver? 15^0 C
2. What is the temperature of Chicago? 25^0 C
3. What is the highest temperature? Which city? 30^0 C San Carlos
4. What is the lowest temperature? Which city? 5^0 C Winnipeg
5. How many ^{0}C higher is the temperature of San Carlos than Winnipeg? 25^0 C
6. How many ^{0}C lower is the temperature of Vancouver than Chicago? 10^0 C

Student's name: ____________________ Assignment date: ________________

Cold or hot? Then estimate the temperature.

a. hot√ b. cold

Temperature: ____________ 100^0 C

a. hot b. cold√

Temperature: ____________ 0^0 C

a. hot b. cold√

Temperature: ____________ below 0^0 C

a. hot√ b. cold

Temperature: ____________ 30^0 C

a. hot√ b. cold

Temperature: ____________ 39^0 C

a. hot b. cold√

Temperature: ____________ 0^0 C

Student's name: ____________________ Assignment date: ________________

Directions

The little kitty got lost. Tell her where she should go.

1. If the kitty wants to find the shoe, she should go _________. east
2. If she feels hungry, she should go ________ to buy a burger. West
3. She can go ______ to the shopping mall to buy a cap for herself. South
4. If she wants to go home, she should go _________. North
5. The church is on the ________ of the shopping mall. East
6. The shopping mall is on the ________ of the church. West
7. The bus is on the ________ of the house. East
8. The farm is on the ________ of the house. West
9. The house is on the ________ of the farm. East
10. The dog is on the ________ of the burger store. South
11. If the bus drives to the church, it should go ________. South
12. If the bus heads to the farm, it should go ________. west
13. The dog misses his friends on the farm. He should go ________. north
14. The dog goes east two blocks, then turn north one block, he can find a ________. shoe

Student's name: ____________________ Assignment date: ________________

***** Part 20 Coordinates *****

An ordered pair (x, y) shows the position of a point on a grid. The value of x shows the horizontal distance from the origin. The value of y shows the vertical distance from the origin.

Example: Show the point P (4, 2) on a grid.

Start from the origin, move 4 units to the right and 2 units up.

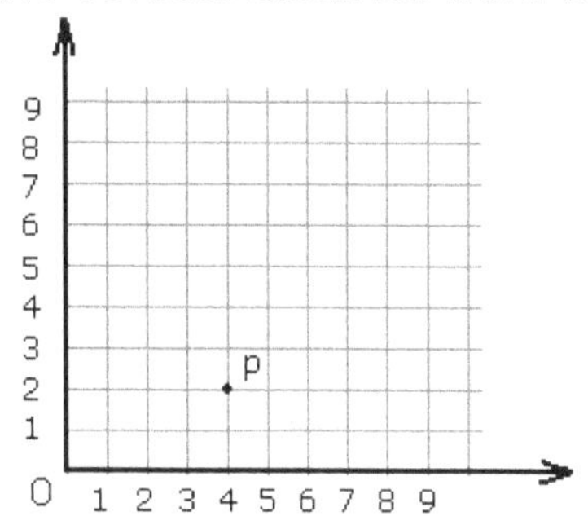

Write the ordered pair of each point on the grid.

1.

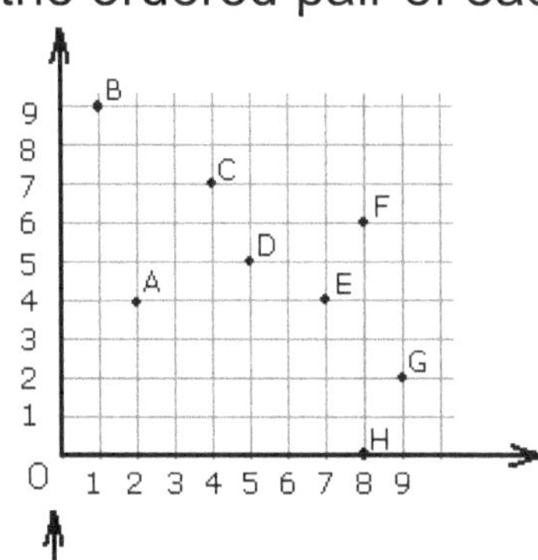

A __________ B __________

C __________ D __________

E __________ F __________

G __________ H __________

2.

M __________ N __________

O __________ P __________

Q __________ R __________

S __________ T __________

Plot each point on the grid and join these points in order.

3. A (2, 5) B (8, 5) C (3, 1)

D (5, 8) E (7, 1) F (2, 5)

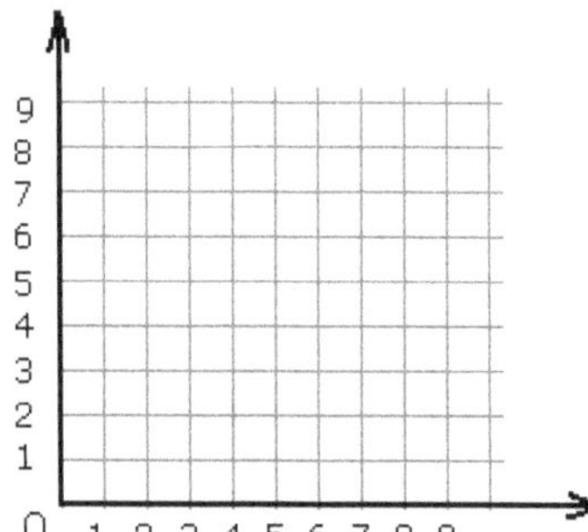

Student's name: ____________________ Assignment date: ________________

4. A (1, 1) B (1, 6) C (4, 3)

D (7, 6) E (7, 1)

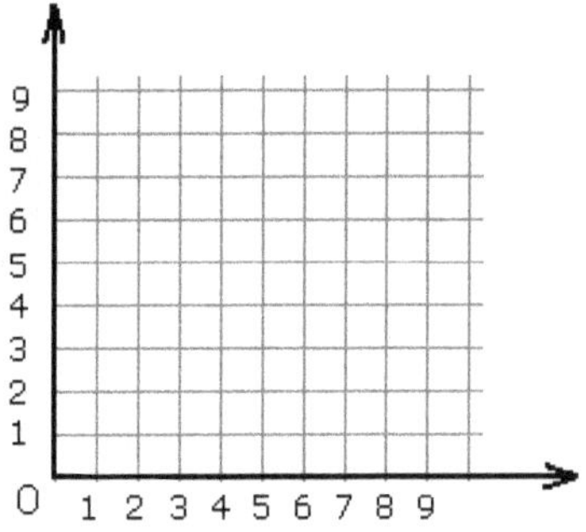

5. A (7, 5) B (2, 5) C (2, 8)

D (7, 8) E (7, 2) F (2, 2)

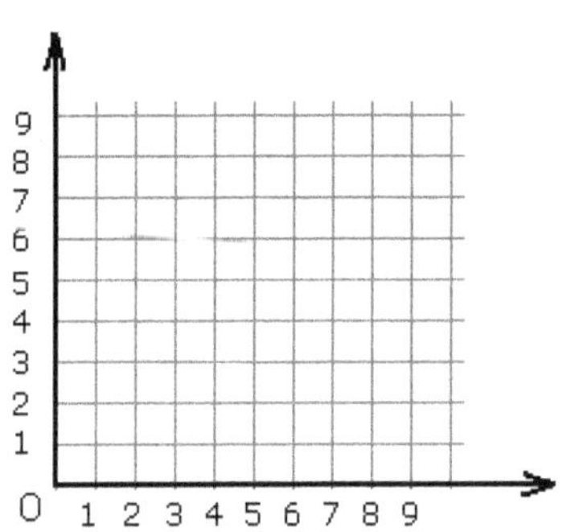

6. A (5, 2) B (3, 5) C (7, 5)

D (5, 2) E (9, 2) F (5, 8)

G (1, 2) H (5, 2)

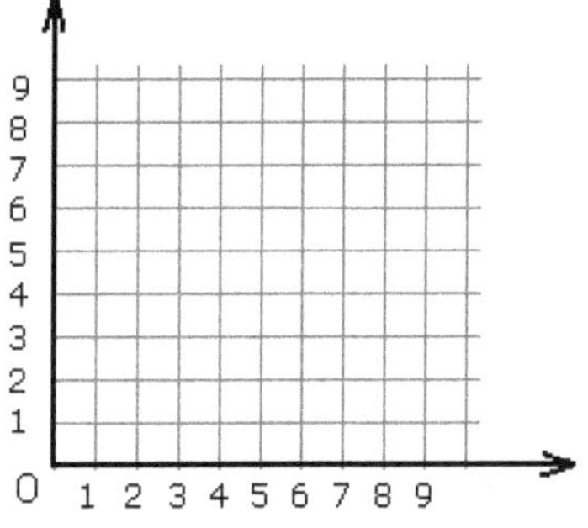

7. A (2, 8) B (3, 8) C (3, 7) D (4, 7)

E (4, 8) F (5, 8) G (5, 7) H (6, 7)

I (6, 8) J (7, 8) K (7, 6) L (6, 6)

M (6, 2) N (7, 2) O (7, 1) P (2, 1)

Q (2, 2) R (3, 2) S (3, 6) T (2, 6)

U (2, 8)

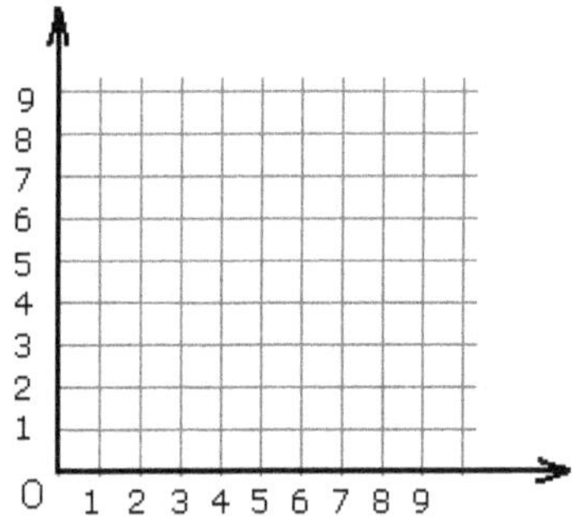

Student's name: ____________________ Assignment date: ________________

***** Part 21 Linear graph relationships *****

Example:

Input	Output	Ordered pairs
2	1	(2 , 1)
3	2	(3 , 2)
4	3	(4 , 3)
5	4	(5 , 4)
6	5	(6 , 5)
7	6	(7 , 6)
8	7	(8 , 7)

Graph ordered pairs.

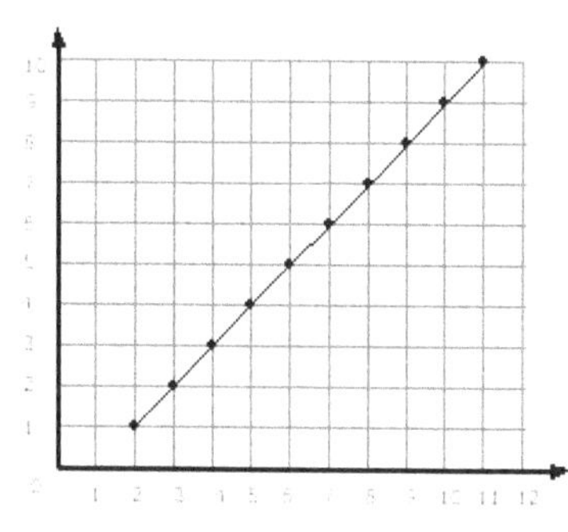

Find the pattern and complete the table. Then graph the relationship.

8.

Input	Output	Ordered pairs
2	1	(2 , 1)
4	2	(4 , 2)
6		
8		
10		
12		
14	7	(14 , 7)
16		

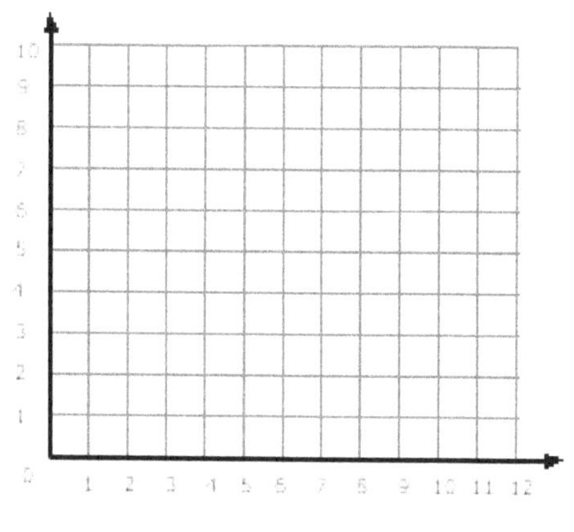

9.

Input	Output	Ordered pairs
1	1	(1 , 1)
2	3	(2 , 3)
3	5	(3 , 5)
4		
5		
6		
7		
8		

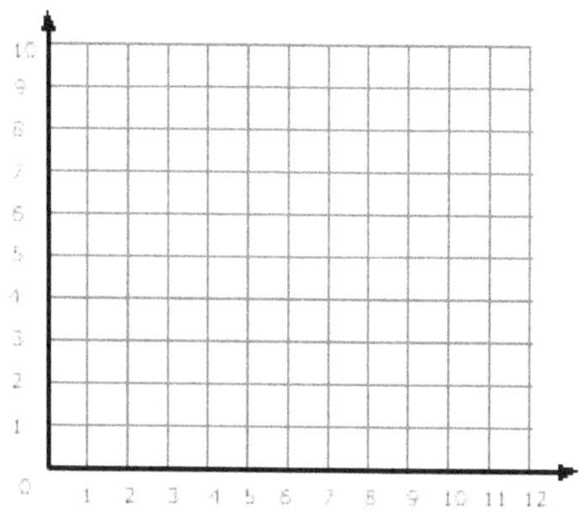

Student's name: ____________________ Assignment date: ________________

10.

Input	Output	Ordered pairs
1	10	(1 , 10)
2	20	(2 , 20)
3	30	
4		
5		
6		
7		
8		

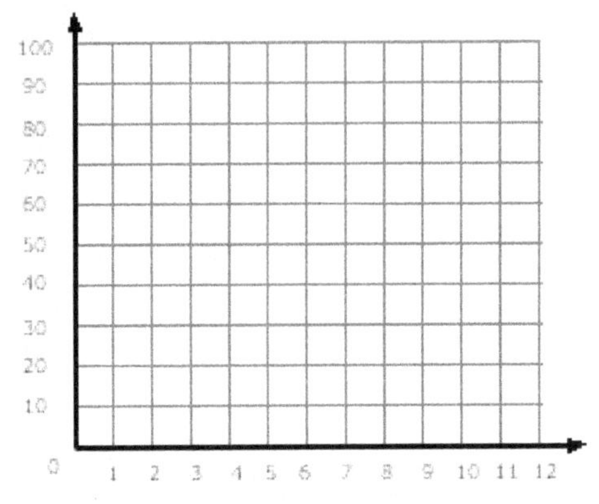

11.

Input	Output	Ordered pairs
1	5	(1 , 5)
2	10	(2 , 10)
3	15	
4		
5		
6		
10		
12		

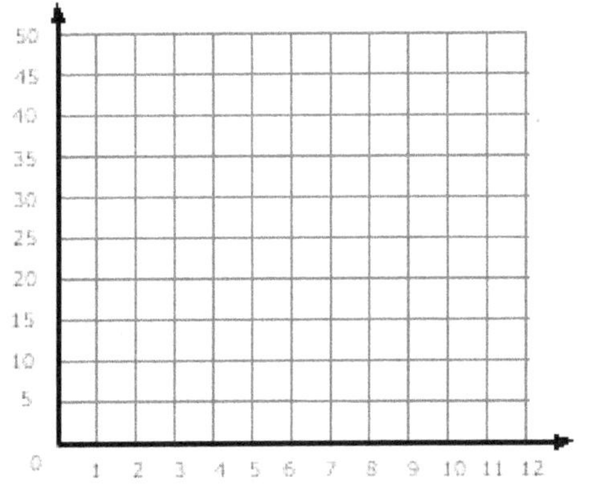

12.

Input	Output	Ordered pairs
1	1	(1 , 1)
2	4	(2 , 4)
3	9	
4		
5		
10		
20		
50		

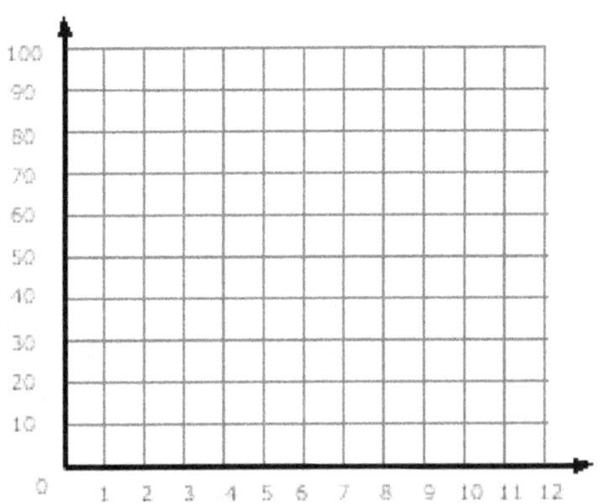

Student's name: ____________________ Assignment date: ________________

13.

Input	Output	Ordered pairs
1	4	(1 , 4)
2	7	(2 , 7)
3	10	
4		
5		
6		
10		
100		

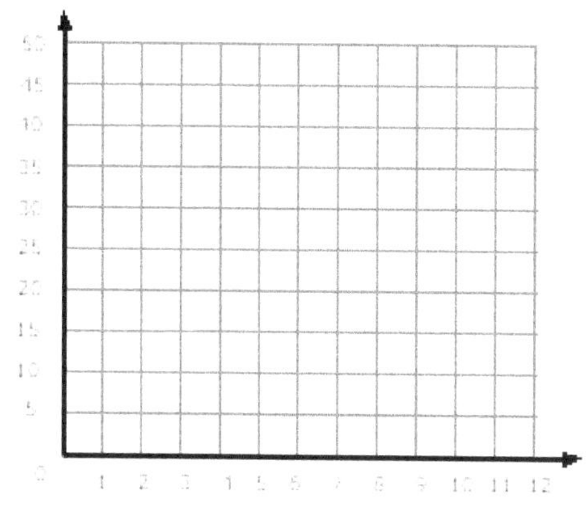

14.

Input	Output	Ordered pairs
1	3	
2	7	
3	11	
4		
5		
6		
10		
20		

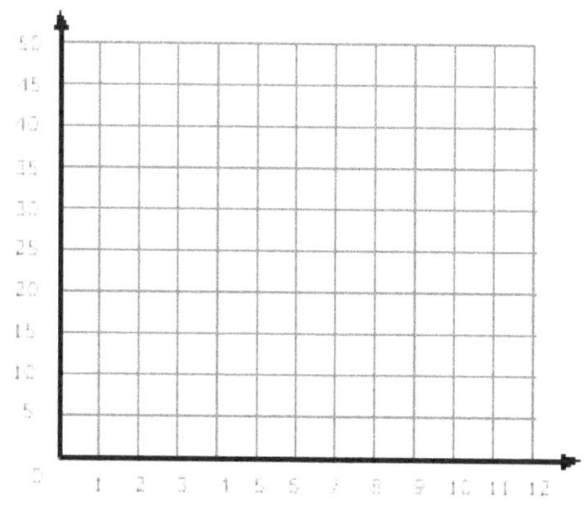

15.

Input	Output	Ordered pairs
5	1	
10	2	
15	3	
20		
25		
30		
50		
100		

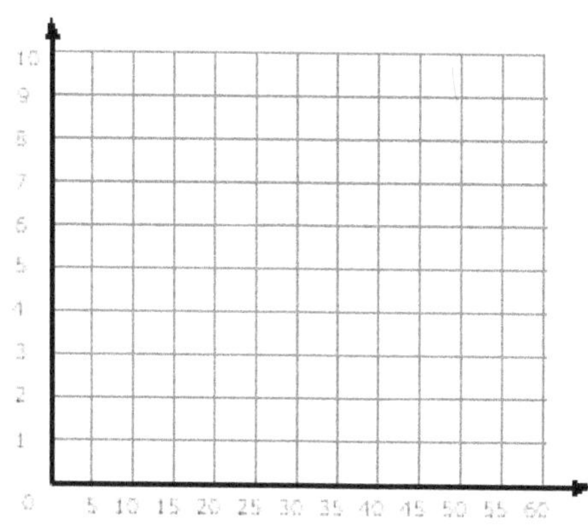

Student's name: ____________________ Assignment date: ________________

***** Part 22 Likelihood or possibility *****

The chance of an event that could happen is "unlikely" if the event is expected to happen less than half of the time.
The chance of an event that could happen is "likely" if the event is expected to happen more than half of the time.
The chance of an event that could happen is "even" if the event is expected to happen exactly half of the time.

Make predictions whether each event is impossible, unlikely, likely, even (exactly half of the time) or certain.

1. Throw a dice, the probability of getting an even number is likely
2. Draw a card from a deck. The probability of getting heart is unlikely
3. There are eight red marbles and one white marble. The probability of picking a white marble is unlikely
4. Throw a coin, the probability of getting a 'head' is even
5. There are three dimes and five quarters. The probability of picking a dime or a quarter is certain
6. Spin a spinner, the probability of getting a '2' is unlikely
7. There are five red marbles and five white marbles. The probability of picking a black marble is impossible
8. Draw a card from a deck. The probability of getting a King is unlikely

Student's name: ____________________ Assignment date: ________________

9. Denny played chess against Benny. Benny won six times and lost two times. The probability for Denny winning the next game is Unlikely ________

10. 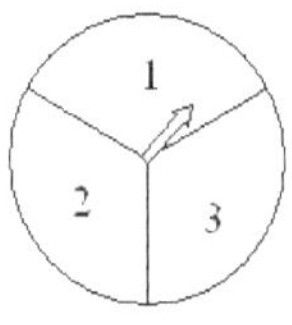

Spin a spinner, the probability of getting a '4' is impossible ________

11. Throw a dice, the probability of getting an odd number is likely ________

12. Throw a dice, the probability of getting a number not less than 5 is unlikely ________

Student's name: ____________________ Assignment date: ________________

Make predictions whether each event is impossible, unlikely, likely, or certain.

1.	A train is faster than a car.	likely
2.	A dog is heavier than a cat.	likely
3.	A cow eats mice.	impossible
4.	Steve can eat twenty eggs for each meal.	impossible
5.	A tree turns green during spring.	certain
6.	The earth rotates around the sun.	certain
7.	Winter is warmer than in summer.	impossible
8.	A cat will take a mouse.	certain
9.	A bird cannot fly.	unlikely
10.	A rabbit runs faster than a turtle.	certain
11.	You will go hiking during summer vacation.	likely
12.	You can write twenty words in a minute.	likely
13.	If Sam doesn't eat for a whole day, he will feel hungry.	certain
14.	If you run, your heart will beat slower.	impossible
15.	A horse is heavier than an elephant.	impossible
16.	A goldfish can live without water.	impossible
17.	A snake has four legs.	impossible
18.	A bicycle has two wheels.	certain
19.	A crow is white.	impossible
20.	Stone is harder than mud.	likely

Student's name: ____________________ Assignment date: ________________

Equal, likely, and unlikely by calculating their chances

1. There are four red marbles and four green marbles in a box. Pick up a marble randomly without looking. The probability of choosing green marble and the red marble is:

   a. equally likely   b. unequally likely

2. There are three nickels, four dimes, and four quarters in a bag. Pick up a coin randomly without looking. The probability of choosing a dime and a quarter is:

   a. equally likely   b. unequally likely

3. Throw a coin. The probability of getting a tail and getting a head is"

   a. equally likely   b. unequally likely

4. 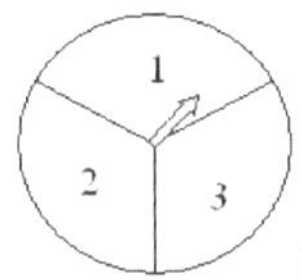

Spin a spinner. The probability of getting a '2' and getting a '3' is:

   √a. equally likely   b. unequally likely

5. 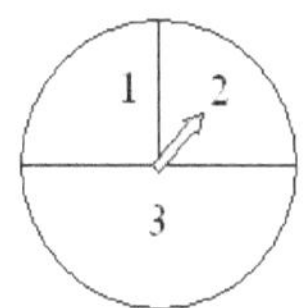

Spin a spinner. The probability of getting a '2' and getting a '3' is:

   a. equally likely   √b. unequally likely

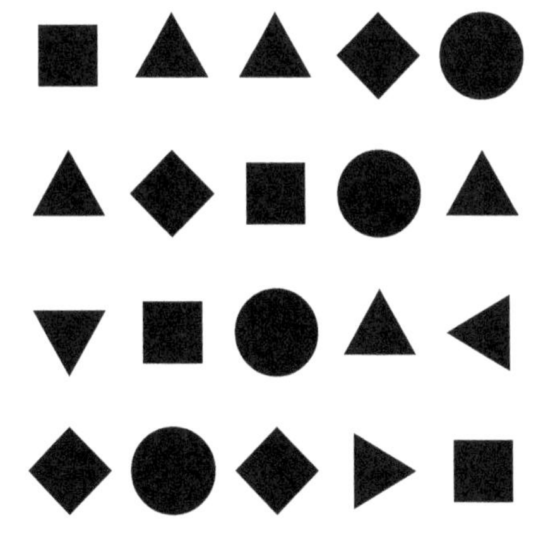

6. From the box to the left, choosing a triangle and a square is:

   √a. equally likely   b. unequally likely

7. From the box to the left, choosing a circle and a square is:

   a. equally likely   √b. unequally likely

8. From the box to the left, choosing a triangle and a circle is:

Student's name: ____________________ Assignment date: ________________

a. equally likely √b. unequally likely

7. Name an event that is (1) impossible, (2) likely, (3) unlikely, (4) certain.

____

Student's name: ____________________ Assignment date: ________________

Likelihood and comparisons on spinners

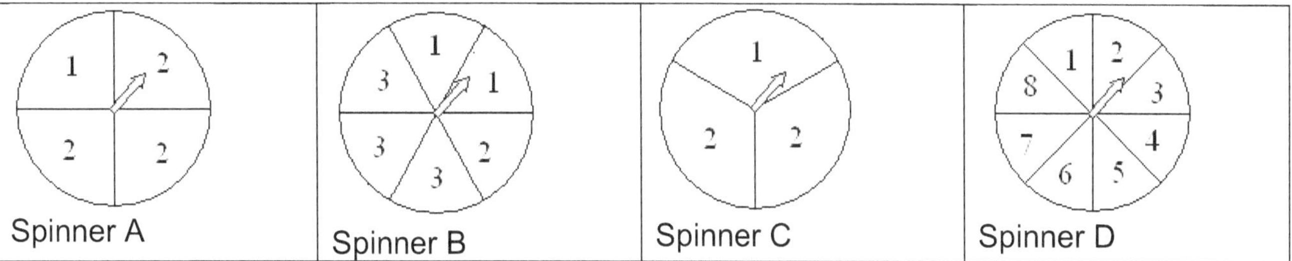

What could be the likely results of 24 spins for the Spinner A if the arrow lands on odd numbers?

What could be the likely results of 24 spins for the Spinner B if the arrow lands on odd numbers?

What could be the likely results of 24 spins for the Spinner C if the arrow lands on odd numbers?

What could be the likely results of 24 spins for the Spinner D if the arrow lands on odd numbers?

What could be the likely results of 24 spins for the Spinner A if the arrow lands on the number 6?

What could be the likely results of 24 spins for the Spinner B if the arrow lands on the number 6?

What could be the likely results of 24 spins for the Spinner C if the arrow lands on the number 6?

What could be the likely results of 24 spins for the Spinner D if the arrow lands on the number 6?

Which spinner would you choose if spinning an even number wins a prize?

What could be the likely results of 16 spins for the Spinner D if the arrow lands on even numbers?

Student's name: ____________________ Assignment date: ______________

***** Part 23 Probability *****

Write the probability of spinning each outcome.

1.	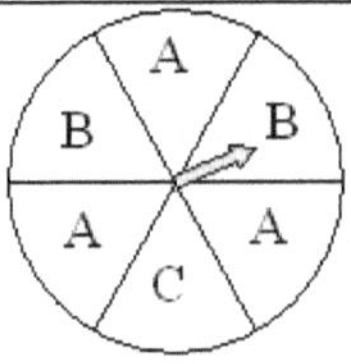 A, B, B, A, C, A	2.	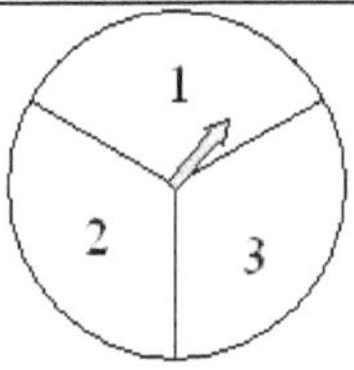 1, 2, 3	3.	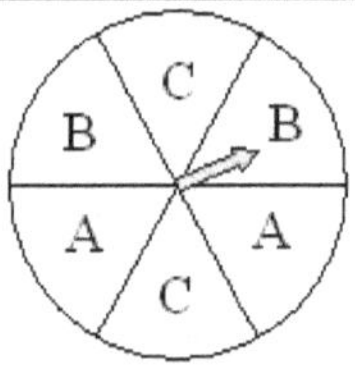 C, B, B, A, C, A	4.	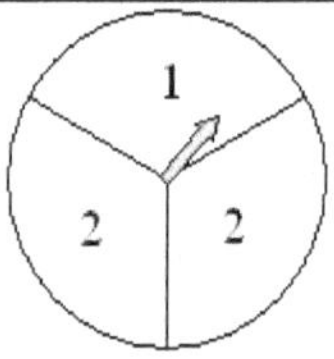 1, 2, 2
	The letter B.		The number 1.		The letter B.		The number 2.
	2 out of 6.		1 out of 3.		2 out of 6.		2 out of 3.
5.	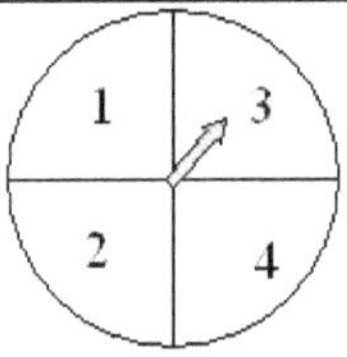 1, 3, 2, 4	6.	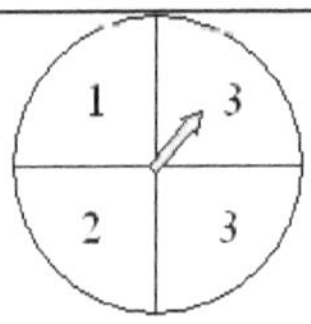 1, 3, 2, 3	7.	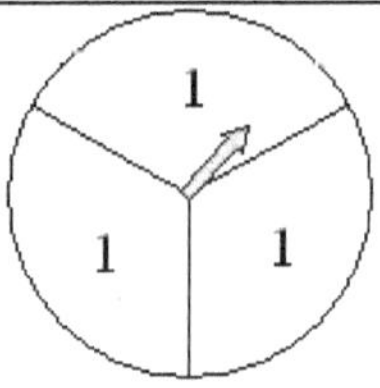 1, 1, 1	8.	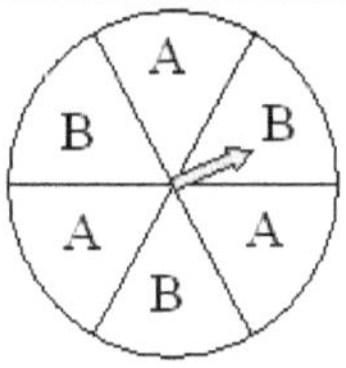 A, B, B, A, B, A
	The number 3.		The number 3		The number 2		The letter B.
	1 out of 4.		2 out of 4.		0 out of 3.		3 out of 6.
9.	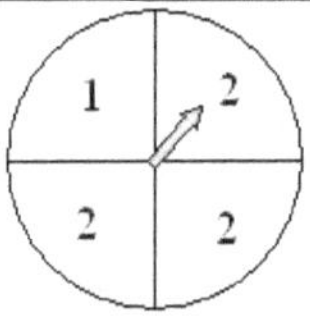 1, 2, 2, 2	10.	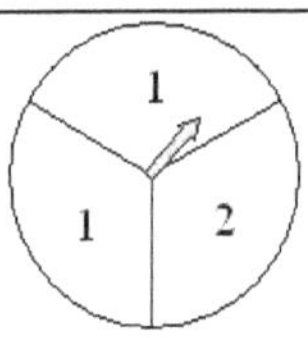 1, 1, 2	11.	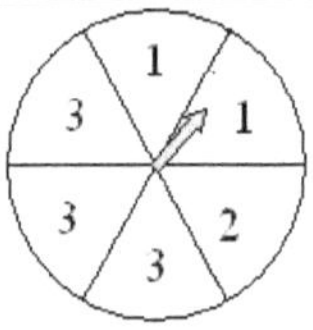 1, 1, 3, 3, 3, 2	12.	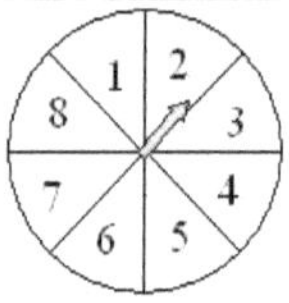 1, 2, 8, 3, 7, 4, 6, 5
	The number 2.		The number 2.		The number 1.		The number 3.
	3 out of 4.		1 out of 3.		2 out of 6.		1 out of 8.
13.	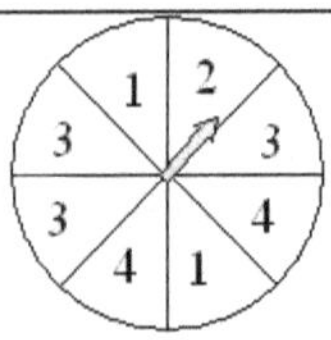 1, 2, 3, 3, 3, 4, 4, 1	14.	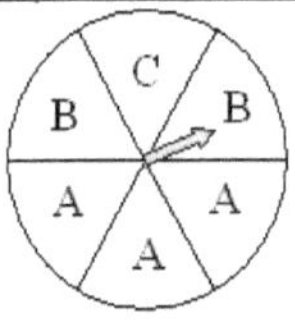 C, B, B, A, A, A	15.	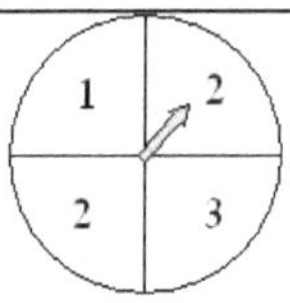 1, 2, 2, 3	16.	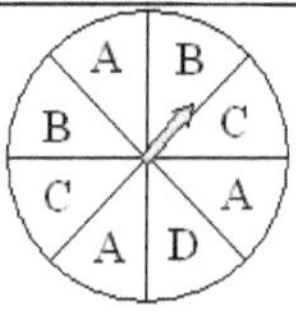 A, B, B, C, C, A, A, D
	The number 4.		The letter A.		The number 2.		The letter B.
	2 out of 8.		3 out of 6.		2 out of 4.		2 out of 8.

Student's name: ____________________ Assignment date: ________________

Write the probability of each outcome.

	Example: Toss a coin. What is the probability of getting a head?
	Total outcomes: head, tail
	The probability of getting a head is: 1 out of 2
1.	Throw a dice. What is the probability of getting '3'?
	1 out of 6
2.	One letter is randomly chosen from the word 'chess'. What is the probability of choosing the letter 's'?
	2 out of 5
3.	There are 12 boys and fifteen girls in the classroom. If one student is randomly chosen, what is the probability of choosing a boy?
	12 out of 27
4.	There are 5 red marbles, 3 white marbles, 4 green marbles, and 2 yellow marbles in a bag. Randomly choose a marble from the bag. What is the probability of choosing a white marble?
	3 out of 14
5.	Throw a dice. What is the probability of getting an even number?
	3 out of 6
6.	One letter is randomly chosen from the word 'butter' what is the probability of choosing the letter 't'?
	2 out of 6
7.	Throw a dice. What is the probability of getting a number not less than 5?
	2 out of 6

Student's name: ____________________ Assignment date: ________________

8.	There are 6 red marbles, 2 white marbles, 7 green marbles, and 5 yellow marbles in a bag. Randomly choose a marble from the bag. What is the probability of choosing a red marble?
	6 out of 20
9.	One letter is randomly chosen from the word 'singing'. What is the probability of choosing the letter 'i?
	2 out of 7
10.	A cube has 6 sides. The sides have the letters 'A', 'B', 'A', 'C', 'A', and 'B'. Throw the dice. What is the probability of getting the letter 'B'?
	2 out of 6
11.	There are 3 pennies, 5 nickels, 9 dimes, and 8 quarters. Pick a coin randomly. What is the probability of picking a quarter?
	8 out of 25
12.	There are 3 pennies, 6 nickels, 4 dimes, and 9 quarters. Pick a coin randomly. What is the probability of picking a penny or a dime?
	7 out of 22
13.	There are 4 red marbles, 5 white marbles, 8 green marbles, and 3 blue marbles in a bag. Choose a marble from the bag randomly. What is the probability of choosing a red or a green marble?
	12 out of 20
14.	One letter is randomly chosen from the word 'noon'. What is the probability of choosing the letter 'n' or 'o'?
	4 out of 4

Student's name: ____________________ Assignment date: ________________

Make predictions.

Example: There are 20 red marbles and blue marbles in a bag. Sam took out a marble, recorded the colour and put it back.

Red	Blue
𝍸	𝍸
	𝍸
	𝍸

The result shows that there are three times as many blue marbles as red marbles. So, Sam predicts 5 red marbles and 15 blue marbles.

1. There are 50 dimes and quarters in a bag. Linda took a coin, made a record, and put it back. The record is shown below. Predict the number of dimes and quarters.

Dimes	Quarters
𝍸	𝍸
𝍸	𝍸
𝍸	

Dimes: 30

Quarters: 20

2. There are 18 red and green tokens in a box. Linda took a token, made a record, and put it back. The record is shown below. Predict the number of red and green tokens.

Red	Green
𝍸	𝍸
𝍸	

Red: 12

Green: 6

Student's name: ____________________ Assignment date: ________________

3.		Spin the spinner 30 times. Prediction how many times the spinner will land on each number. 1: 10 2: 10 3: 10
4.		Spin the spinner 20 times. Prediction how many times the spinner will land on each number. 1: 5 2: 10 3: 5
5.		Spin the spinner 30 times. Prediction how many times the spinner will land on each letter. A: 15 B: 10 C: 5
6.		There are ten shapes in a box. Randomly pick a shape, make a record, and put it back. Repeat 50 times. Prediction how many times each shape will come up. Circle: 10 Square: 20 Triangle: 20
7.		There are 6 cards in a box. Choose a card randomly. Repeat 30 times. Prediction how many times each kind of card will show up. : 15 : 10 : 5

Student's name: ____________________ Assignment date: ________________

According to the experiment result, draw a spinner that matches.

1.

Red	卌 卌
Blue	卌 卌
Yellow	卌 卌

R, Y, B

2.

Red	卌
Blue	卌
Yellow	卌 卌
Black	卌 卌

B, B, B, Y, Y, R

3.

A	10
B	20
C	30

A, B, C, C, C, B

4.

1	卌 卌
2	卌 卌 卌 卌

1, 2, 2, 2, 2, 1

Student's name: ____________________ Assignment date: ______________

5.

A	~~IIII~~ ~~IIII~~
B	~~IIII~~ ~~IIII~~
C	~~IIII~~ ~~IIII~~ ~~IIII~~ ~~IIII~~

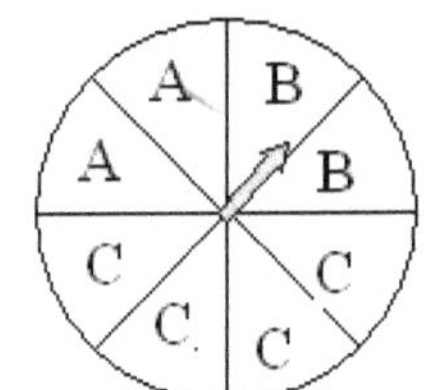

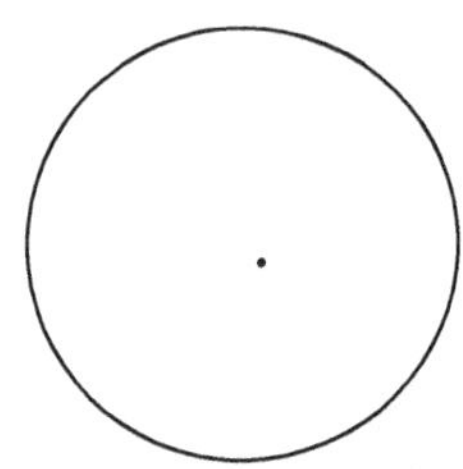

Student's name: ____________________ Assignment date: ________________

Analogue clock Time

Telling time

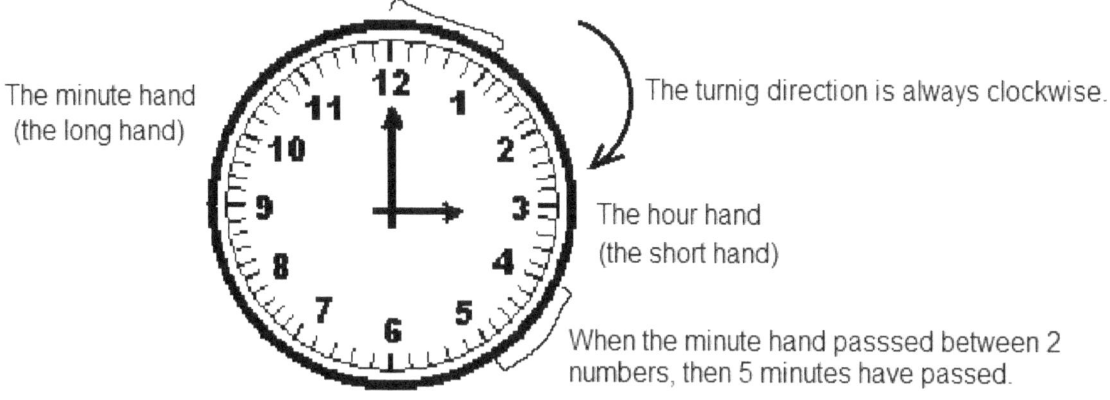

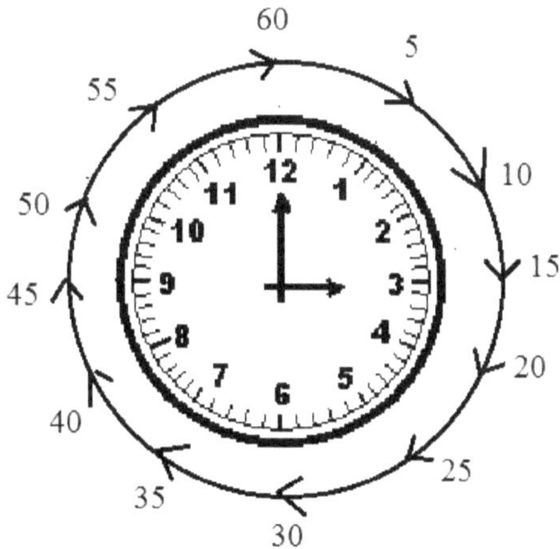

1. If the minute hand is pointing at 12, then the minute is 0 rather than 60 minutes. 12 is only on the clock for displaying to show 60 minutes = 1 hour.

2. By the time the minute hand travels back to the number 2 again, a total of 60 minutes have passed. In this case, the hour hand will increase by 1 hour, and the minute goes back to 0.

Student's name: ____________________ Assignment date: ________________

3. a.m. and p.m. is a 12-hour clock system. The 24 hours of a day are divided into two periods: a.m. (from the Latin ante meridiem, meaning "before midday") and p.m. (post meridiem, "after midday").

4. a.m. (before midday)
   The time from midnight to noon (not including noon) is called a.m.
   For the 12-hour expression, midnight is written as 12 a.m. For 24-hour expression, 12 o'clock midnight is written as 0:0. Often to avoid confusion, 12 o'clock midnight is often written as 12:00 midnight.

5. p.m.
   The time period from 12 o'clock noon to 12 o'clock midnight (not including midnight) is called p.m.
   For the 12-hour expression, 12 o'clock noon is written as 12 p.m. For 24-hour expression, 12 o'clock noon is written as 12:00. Often to avoid confusion, 12 o'clock noon is written as 12:00 noon

6. Students should be encouraged to memorize the times table of 5 instead of using the technique of counting by 5s to calculate the minutes.

Student's name: ____________________ Assignment date: ________________

5's multiples for telling time

5, ☐, 15, ☐, 25, ☐, 35, ☐, ☐, ☐, ☐, ☐, ☐	
☐, ☐, 15, 20, ☐, 30, ☐, ☐, ☐, ☐, ☐, ☐	
☐, ☐, ☐, 20, 25, 30, ☐, ☐, ☐, ☐, ☐, ☐	
☐, ☐, ☐, ☐, ☐, ☐, ☐, ☐, ☐, 50, 55, 60	
☐, ☐, ☐, ☐, ☐, ☐, 35, 40, 45, ☐, ☐, ☐, ☐	
$5 \times 1 =$	$5 \times 3 =$
$5 \times 2 =$	$5 \times 4 =$
$5 \times 3 =$	$5 \times 5 =$
$5 \times 4 =$	$5 \times 6 =$
$5 \times 5 =$	$5 \times 7 =$
$5 \times 6 =$	$5 \times 8 =$
$5 \times 7 =$	$5 \times 9 =$
$5 \times 8 =$	$5 \times 1 =$
$5 \times 9 =$	$5 \times 2 =$
$5 \times 7 =$	$5 \times 6 =$
$5 \times 8 =$	$5 \times 8 =$
$5 \times 9 =$	$5 \times 9 =$
$5 \times 2 =$	$5 \times 3 =$
$5 \times 3 =$	$5 \times 4 =$
$5 \times 4 =$	$5 \times 6 =$
$5 \times 6 =$	$5 \times 5 =$
$5 \times 7 =$	$5 \times 9 =$
$5 \times 8 =$	$5 \times 3 =$
$5 \times 9 =$	$5 \times 4 =$
$5 \times 4 =$	$5 \times 8 =$
$5 \times 5 =$	$5 \times 5 =$
$5 \times 6 =$	$5 \times 2 =$
$5 \times 5 =$	$5 \times 3 =$
$5 \times 6 =$	$5 \times 4 =$
$5 \times 7 =$	$5 \times 7 =$
$5 \times 8 =$	$5 \times 8 =$
$5 \times 4 =$	$5 \times 9 =$

Ho Math Chess Primary Grades Math

Test Review assesssment 何数棋謎低年级数学测试複習考核

Student's name: ____________________ Assignment date: ________________

1.

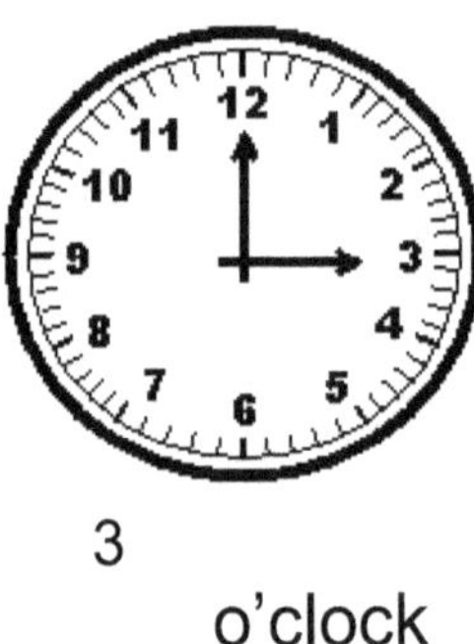

3 ____o'clock

3 : 00

2.

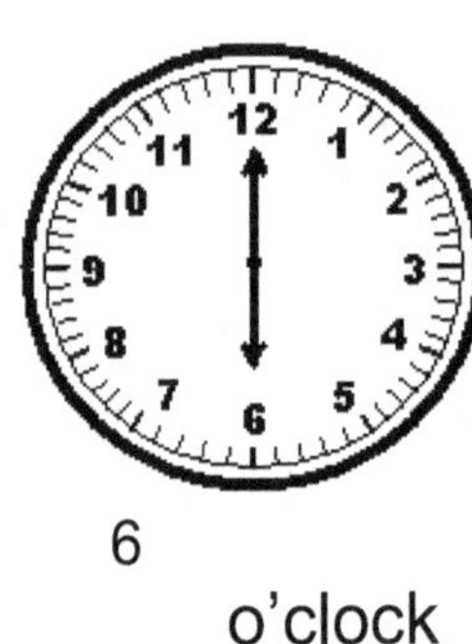

6 ____o'clock

6 : 00

3.

9 ____o'clock

9 : 00

4.

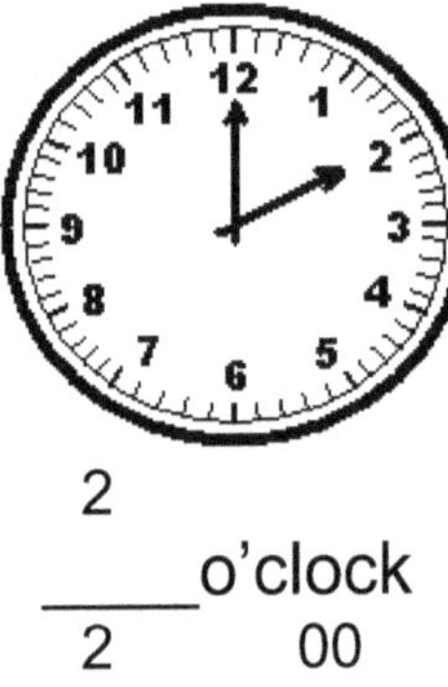

2 ____o'clock

2 : 00

5.

8 ____o'clock

8 : 00

6.

5 ____o'clock

5 : 00

7.

10 ____o'clock

10 : 00

8.

4 ____o'clock

4 : 00

9.

7 ____o'clock

7 : 00

Ho Math Chess Primary Grades Math

Test Review assesssment 何数棋谜低年级数学测试複習考核

Student's name: ____________________ Assignment date: ________________

Telling time

1.

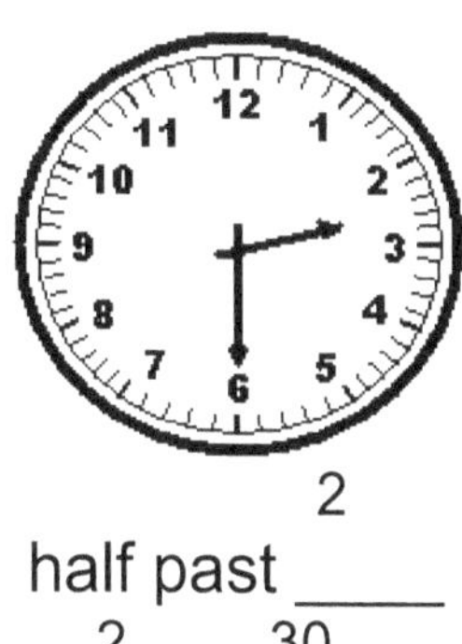

half past ~~2~~ ____

2 : 30

_____ : _____

2.

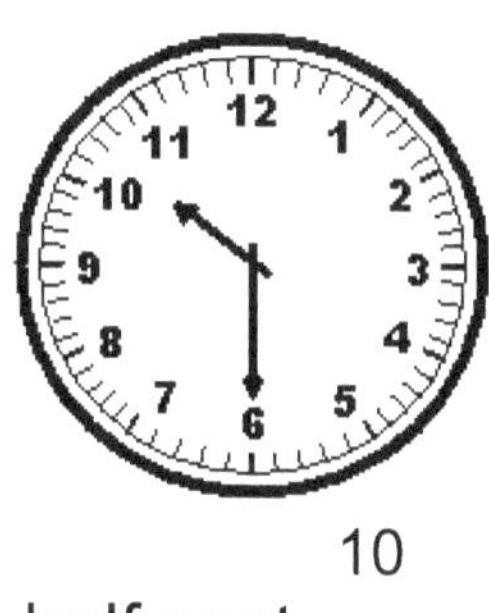

half past 10 ____

10 : 30

_____ : _____

3.

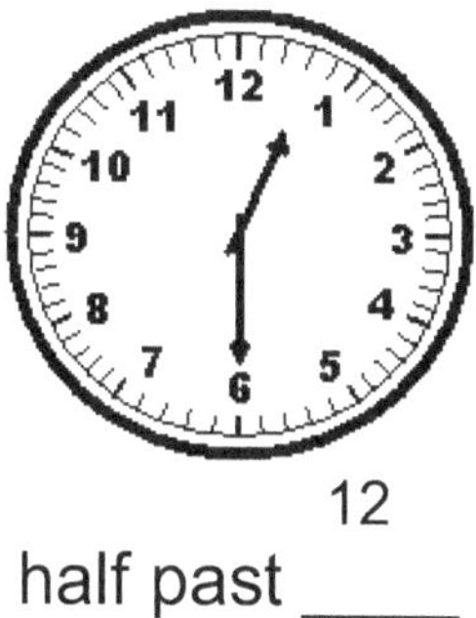

half past 12 ____

12 : 30

_____ : _____

4.

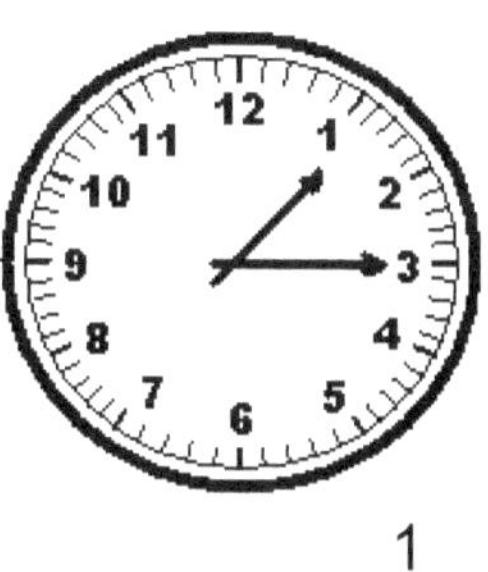

Quarter past 1 ____

1 : 15

_____ : _____

5.

Quarter past 4 ____

4 : 15

_____ : _____

6.

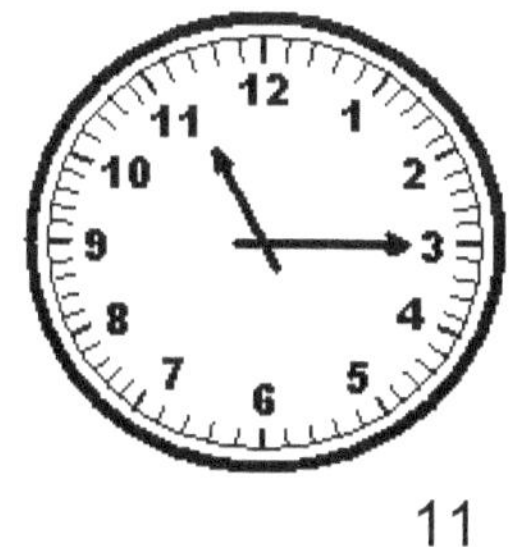

Quarter past 11 ____

11 : 15

_____ : _____

7.

Quarter to 2 ____

1 : 45

_____ : _____

8.

Quarter to 2 ____

1 : 45

_____ : _____

9.

Quarter to 2 ____

1 : 45

_____ : _____

Student's name: ____________________ Assignment date: ________________

What time is it to the nearest 5 minutes?

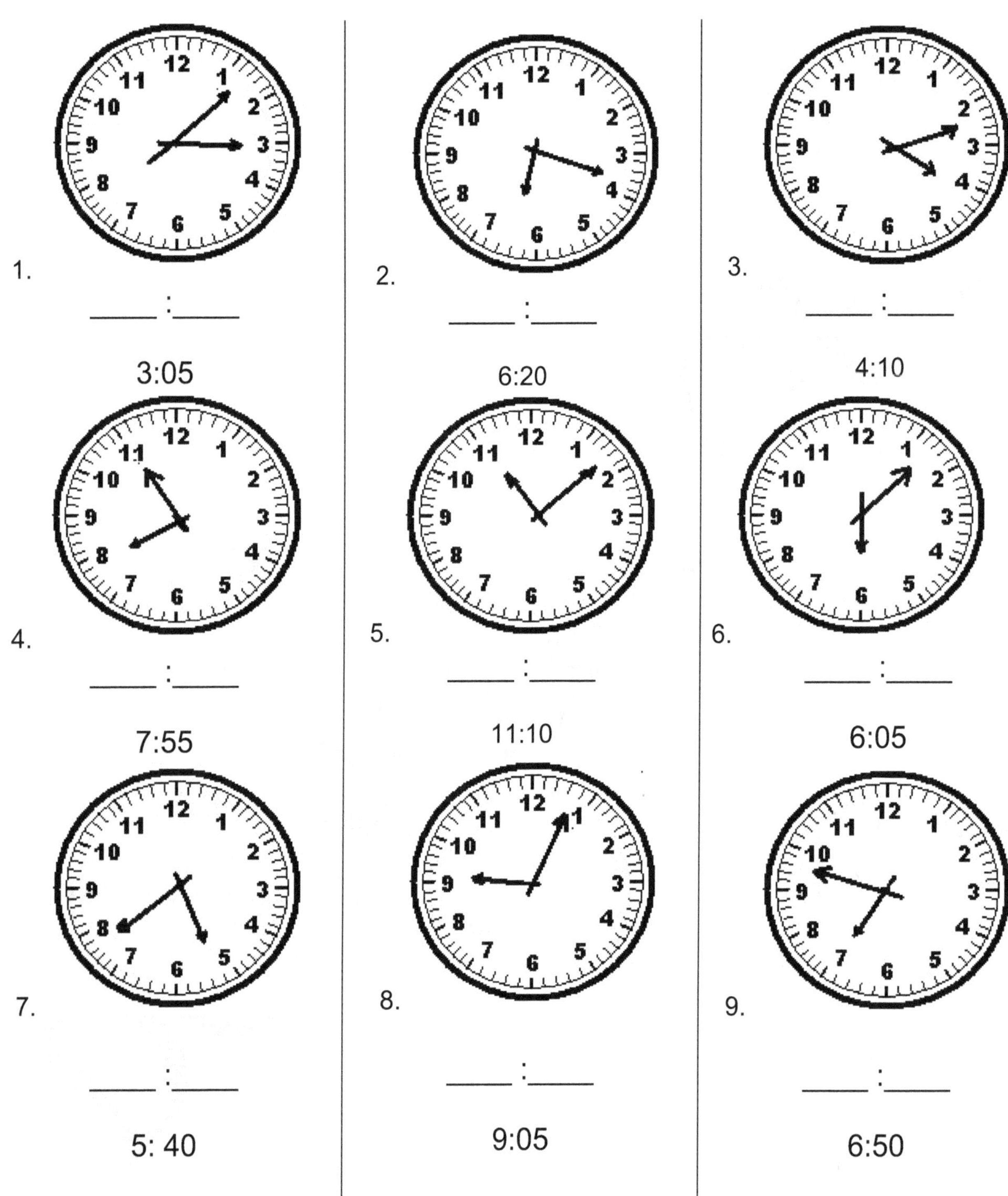

Student's name: ____________________ Assignment date: ________________

Draw the hands on the clock to show the time.

1.

2:02

2.

4:04

3.

5:07

4.

8:24

5.

12:03

6.

3:12

7.

6:36

8.

9:59

9.

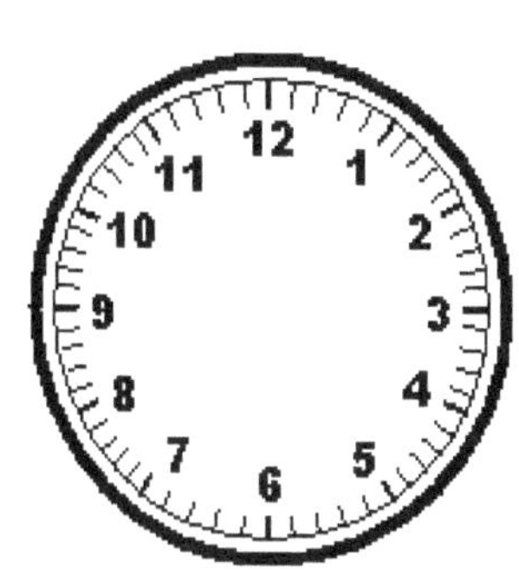

10:37

Student's name: ____________________ Assignment date: ________________

Draw the hands on the clock to show the time.

1.

2:31

2.

half past 5

3.

9:34

4.

quarter past 5

5.

3:11

6.

10:17

7.

1:47

8.

quarter to 4

9.

quarter to 12

Student's name: ____________________ Assignment date: ________________

Draw the hands on the clock to show the time.

1.

2: 07

2.

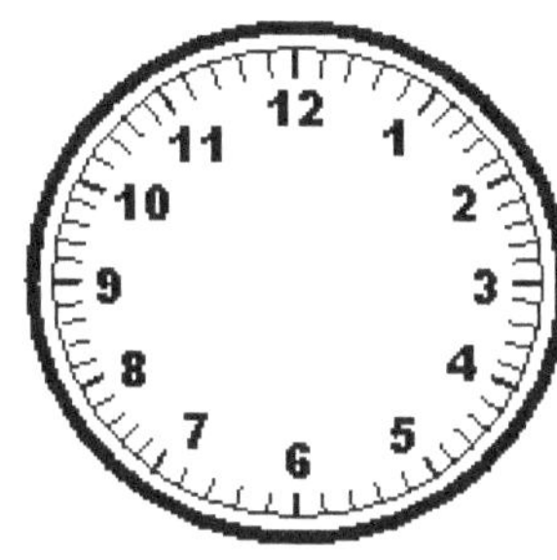

7:13

3.

12:11

4.

9:36

5.

1:44

6.

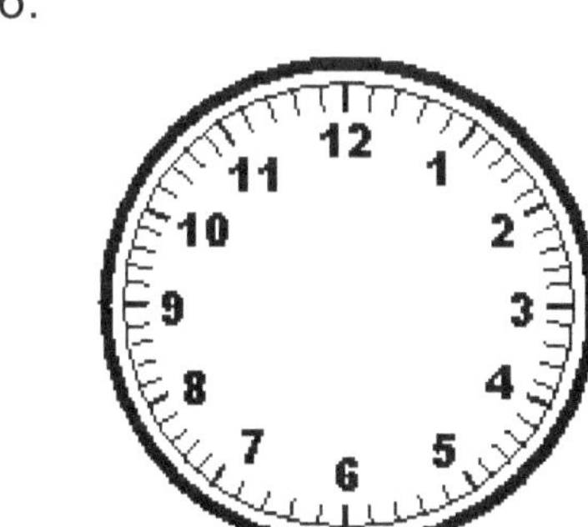

6:26

7.

15 minutes past 7

8.

20 minutes to 8

9.

13 minutes after 5

Student's name: ____________________ Assignment date: ________________

Digital clock Time

01 : 25 am

25 past 1
___ minutes past/to ___
in the morning/afternoon

09 : 55 am

5 to 10
___ minutes past/to ___
in the morning/afternoon

03 : 40 pm

20 to 4
___ minutes past/to ___
in the morning/afternoon

10 : 50 pm

10 to 11
___ minutes past/to ___
in the morning/afternoon

11 : 45 am

15 to 12
___ minutes past/to ___
in the morning/afternoon

04 : 25 pm

25 past 4
___ minutes past/to ___
in the morning/afternoon

07 : 55 pm

5 to 8
___ minutes past/to ___
in the morning/afternoon

06 : 10 am

10 past 6
___ minutes past/to ___
in the morning/afternoon

08 : 40 am

20 to 9
___ minutes past/to ___
in the morning/afternoon

Ho Math Chess Primary Grades Math
Test Review assesssment 何数棋謎低年级数学测试複習考核

Student's name: ____________________ Assignment date: ________________

Time interval (Duration)

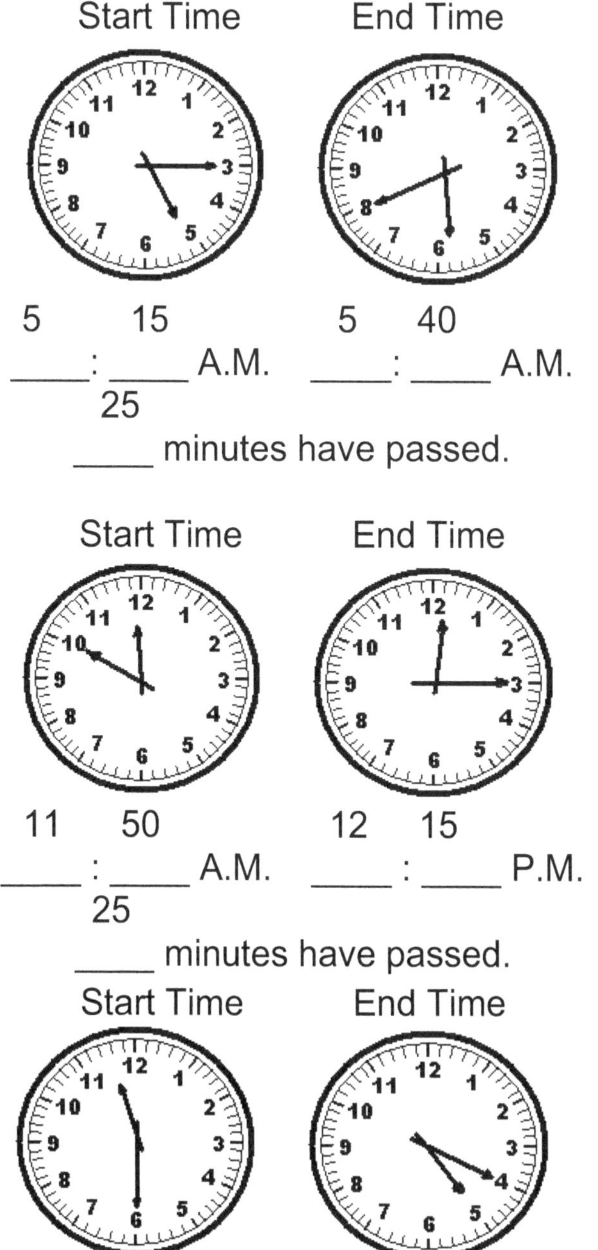

Start Time End Time

5 15 5 40
_____ : _____ A.M. _____ : _____ A.M.
25
_____ minutes have passed.

Start Time End Time

11 50 12 15
_____ : _____ A.M. _____ : _____ P.M.
25
_____ minutes have passed.

Start Time End Time

11 30 5 20
_____ : _____ A.M. _____ : _____ P.M.
350
_____ minutes have passed.

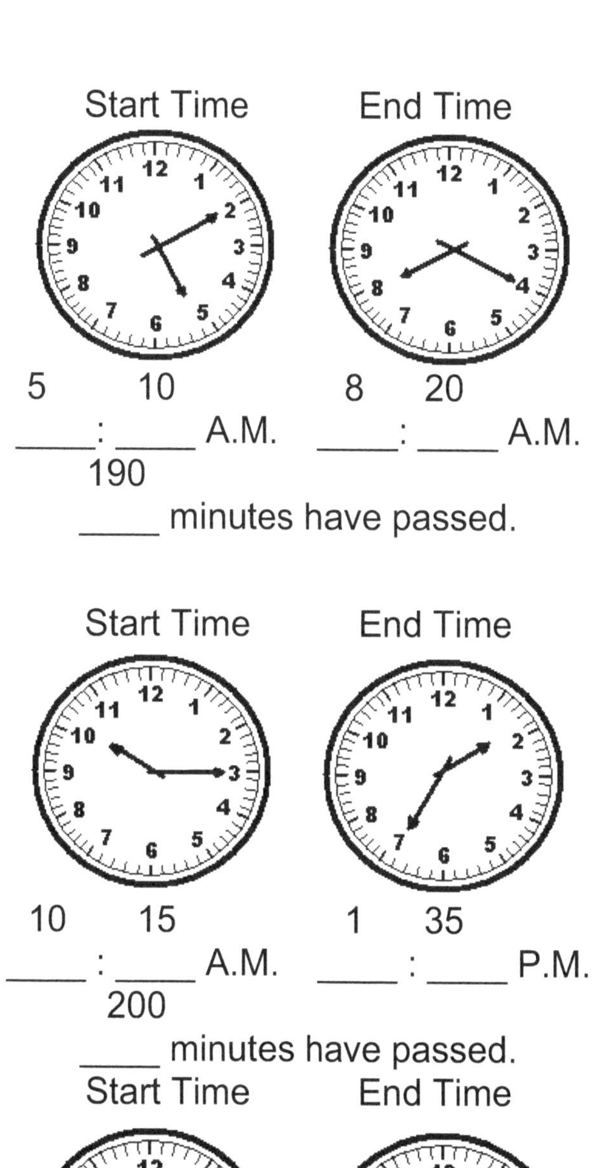

Start Time End Time

5 10 8 20
_____ : _____ A.M. _____ : _____ A.M.
190
_____ minutes have passed.

Start Time End Time

10 15 1 35
_____ : _____ A.M. _____ : _____ P.M.
200
_____ minutes have passed.

Start Time End Time

10 40 4 05
_____ : _____ A.M. _____ : _____ P.M.
325
_____ minutes have passed.

Student's name: ____________________ Assignment date: ________________

Time interval (Duration)

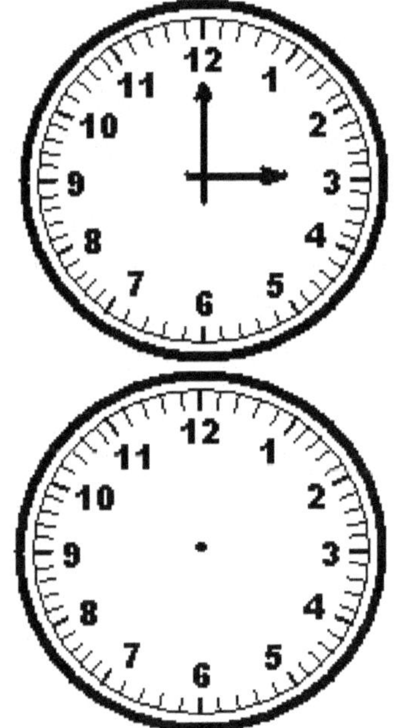

4:15

It will be ________ in 1 hour 15 minutes.

What time was it one and a half hours ago?

_____ 1:30

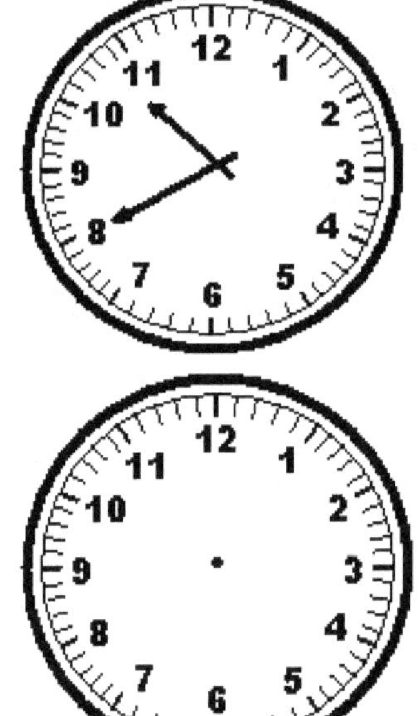

1:00

It will be ________ in 2 hour 20 minutes.

What time was it two and a half hours ago?

_____ 8:10

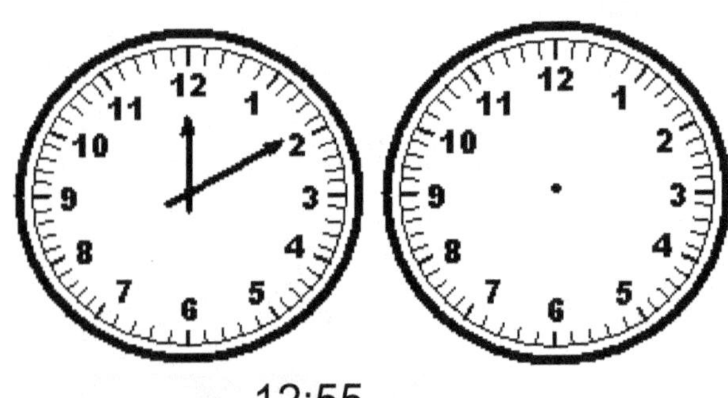

12:55

It will be ________ in 45 minutes.

What time was it two and 55 minutes ago?

_____ 9:15

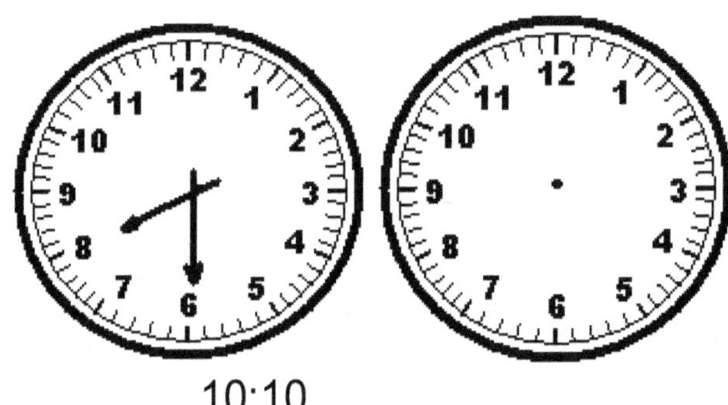

10:10

It will be ________ in 1 hour 40 minutes.

What time was three hours and 20 minutes ago? _____ 4:10

Student's name: ____________________ Assignment date: ________________

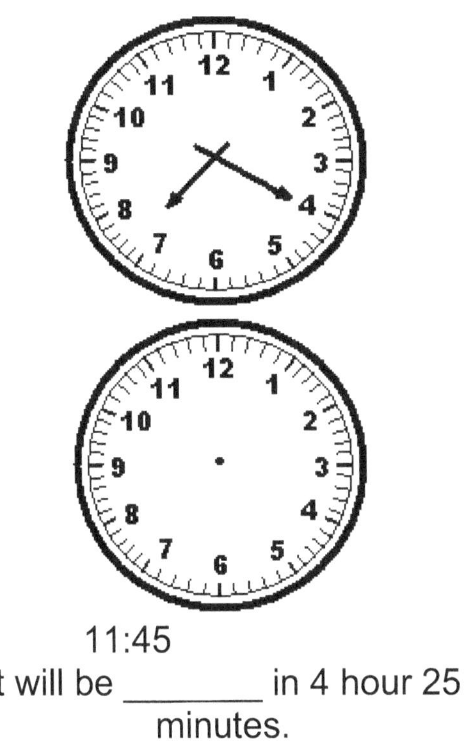

11:45
It will be _______ in 4 hour 25 minutes.

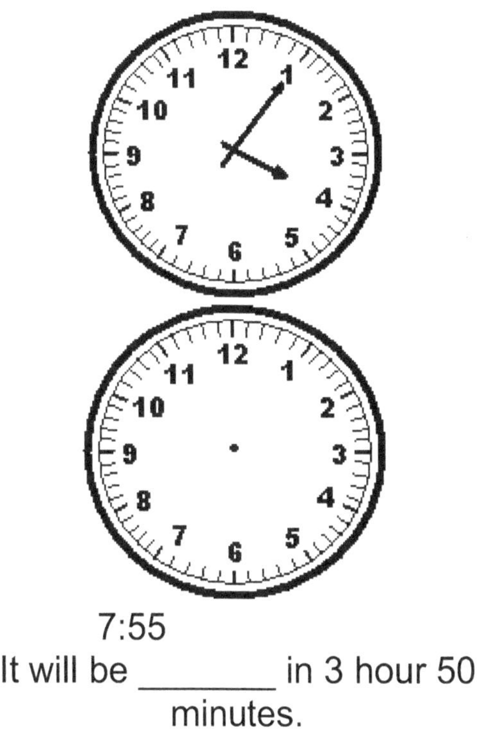

7:55
It will be _______ in 3 hour 50 minutes.

Ho Math Chess Primary Grades Math

Test Review assesssment 何数棋謎低年级数学测试複習考核

Frank Ho, Amanda Ho www.homathchess.com

Student's name: ____________________ Assignment date: ________________

Pattern

Write the time and draw the clock hands on the clock.

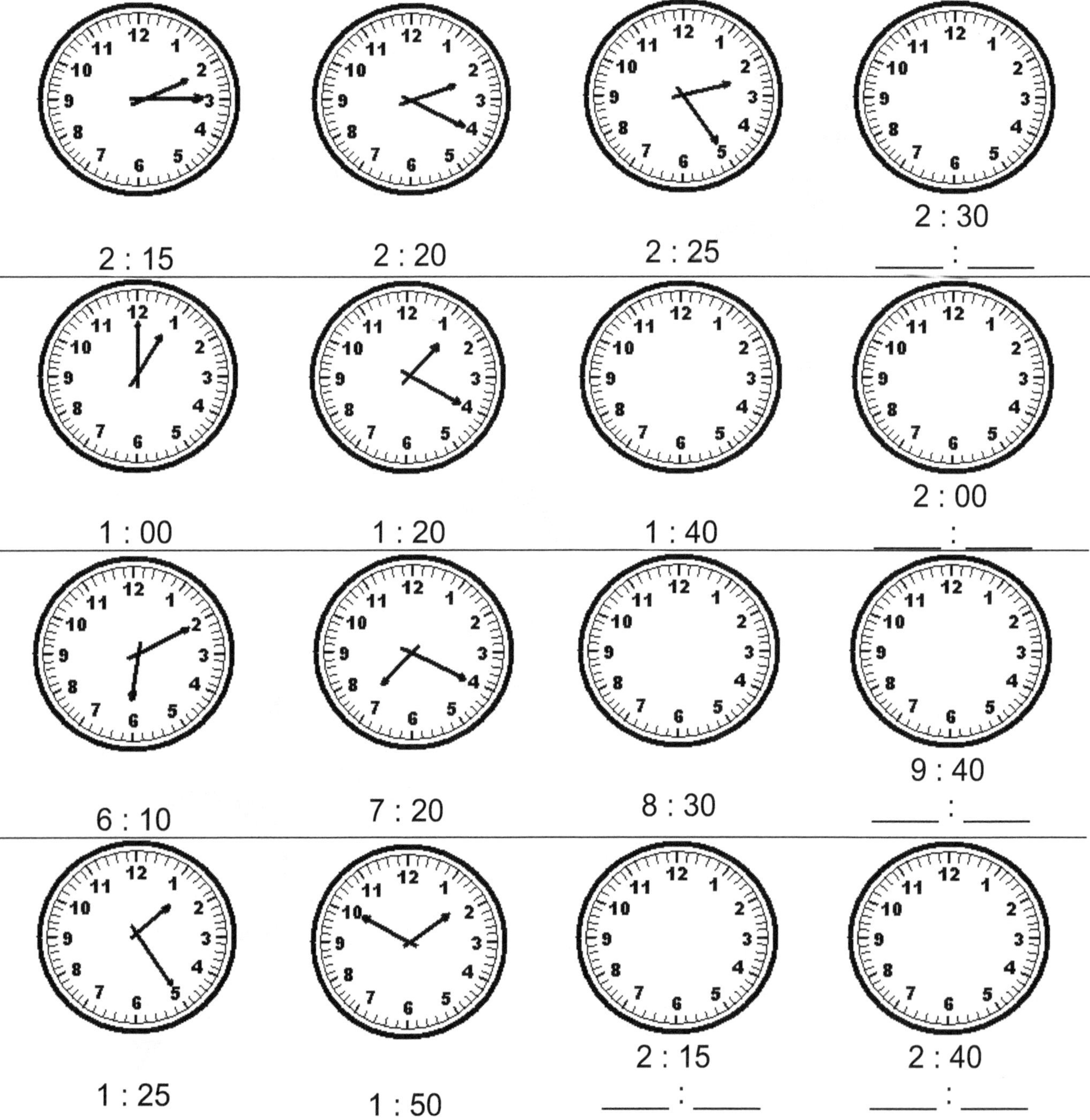

Ho Math Chess Primary Grades Math

Test Review assesssment 何数棋谜低年级数学测试複習考核

Frank Ho, Amanda Ho www.homathchess.com

Student's name: ____________________ Assignment date: ________________

Pattern

Write the time and draw the clock hands on the clock.

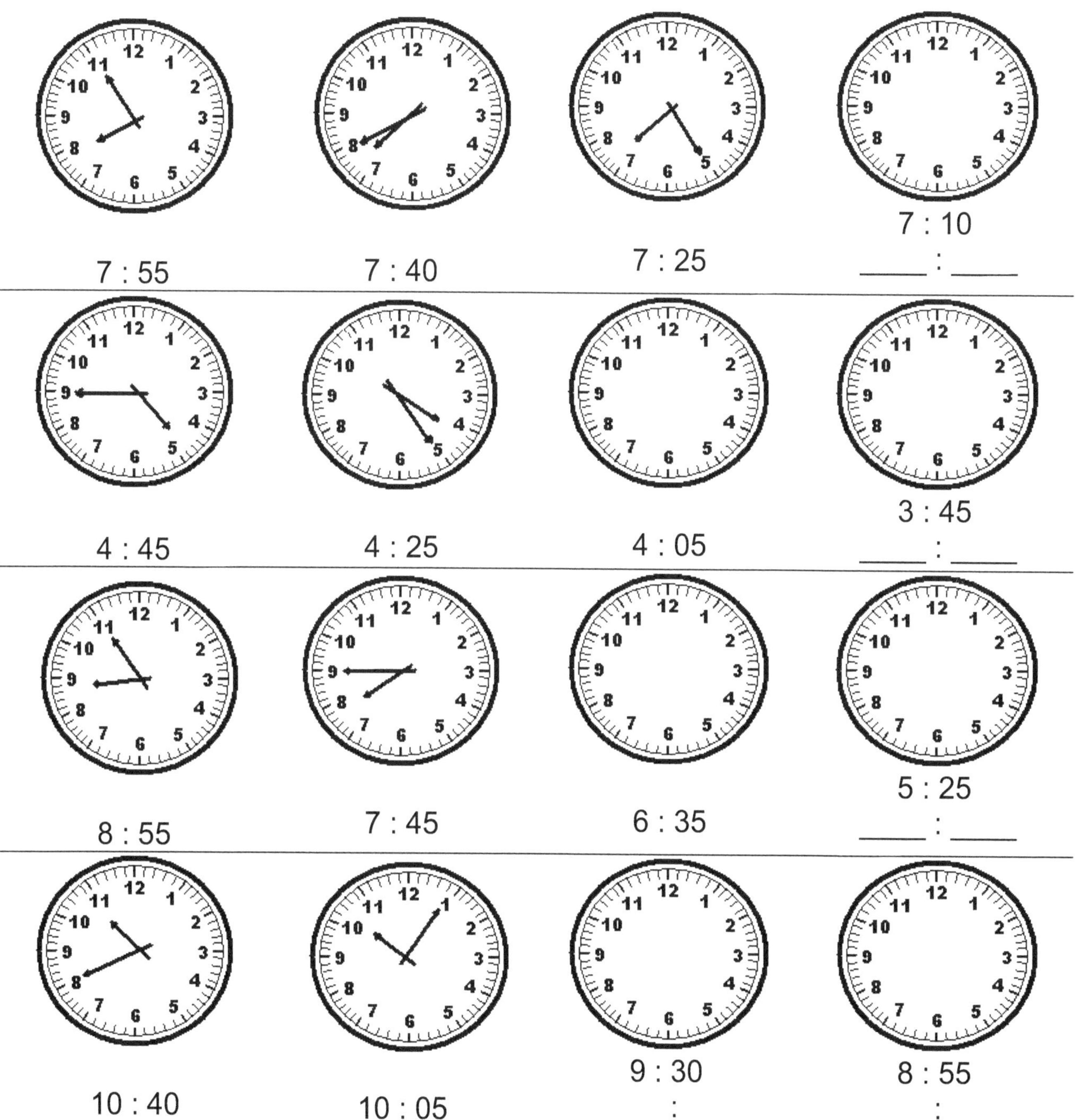

Student's name: ____________________ Assignment date: ________________

Time word problems

1. Adrian started playing piano at 4:00 p.m. He played until 5:30 p.m. How long did he play?

1 h 30 minutes

2. James and John started playing chess at 4:30 p.m. They played until 6:00 p.m. How long did they play?

1 h 30 minutes

3. Jennifer started drawing at 8:50 a.m. She finished at 9:10 p.m. How long did it take her to make?

12 hours 20 minutes

4. The Joe's went to a concert in downtown. The concert started at 4:10 p.m. and finished at 6:30 p.m. How long did the concert last?

2 h 20 minutes

5. Victor started badminton training at 5:45 p.m. He got trained until 7:15 p.m. How much time passed?

1 h 30 minutes

Student's name: ____________________ Assignment date: ________________

Time word problems

1. Robbie plans to travel from Toronto to Seattle. The airplane will take off at 9:45 a.m. The trip will take him four hours and twenty minutes. When will he land on Seattle in Toronto time?

9:45 +4:20 = 14:05 = 2 : 05 p.m.

2. Shirley and Wendy went to a movie. The film started at 3:40 p.m. and would last two and a half hours. When would they get out of the cinema?

6 : 10 p.m.

3. Betty went to school at 8:00 a.m. and went home at 2:30 p.m. How long did she stay at school?

6 h 30 minutes

4. Jonathan plans to go on a vacation in Hawaii from Vancouver. The airplane will take off at 10:00 a.m. He should arrive at the Vancouver international airport one and half an hour earlier before the departure time. It will take the bus for one hour to get to the airport. When should he arrive at the bus stop at the latest?

7 : 30 a.m.

5. A Christmas party will start at 8:00 p.m. It will take the chef two and a half hours to prepare food. When should he start to work?

5: 30 p.m.

6. 1 hour 20 minutes multiplied by 4 = _______ hours _______ minutes

5 hours 20 minutes

Student's name: ____________________ Assignment date: ________________

Calendar

Fill in the following blank.

12
1. There are ____ months in a year.

28 365
2. In a regular year, February has ____ days. A regular year has ____ days.

29 366
3. In a leap year, February has ____ days. A leap year has ____ days.

52
4. There are about ____ weeks in a year.

31
5. January, March, May, July, August, October, and December have ____ days each.

30
6. April, June, September, and November have ____ days each.

7 Tuesday Wednesday
7. There are ____ days in a week. They are Monday, ________, ________,
Thursday Friday Saturday Sunday
________, ________, ________ and ________. I like _______ the best.

Jan 7th
8. Today is January 6th . Tomorrow will be ________. The day after tomorrow
Jan 8th
will be ________.

March 9th
9. Today is March 10th. Yesterday was ________. The day before yesterday
Mar 8th
was ________.

Tuesday
10. Today is Monday. Tomorrow will be ________. The day after tomorrow
Wednesday
will be ________.

Tuesday
11. Today is Wednesday. Yesterday was ________. The day before
Monday
yesterday was ________.

Aug 4th
12. Today is July 25th. It will be ________ in 10 days.

Student's name: ____________________ Assignment date: ________________

13. Today is July 5th. 10 days earlier it was June 25th.

14. Today is Tuesday. It will be Friday in 10 days.

15. Today is Saturday. 10 days earlier it was Wednesday.

16. Today is September 1st. It will be December 10th in one hundred days.

Student's name: ____________________ Assignment date: ________________

Use the calendar of February 2006 to answer the questions.

Sun	Mon	Tue	Wed	Thu	Fri	Sat
			1	2	3	4
5	6	7	8	9	10	11
12	13	14	15	16	17	18
19	20	21	22	23	24	25
26	27	28				

1. There are _____ Sundays in February 2006. 4
2. The date of the first Monday is ________. Feb 6th
3. The date of the second Wednesday is ________. Feb 8th
4. The date one week after February 4 is ________. Feb 11th
5. The date one week before February 4 is ________. Jan 28th
6. The date two weeks after February 23 is ________. Mar 9th
7. The date two weeks before February 23 is ________. Feb 9th
8. The date four weeks after February 23 is ________. Mar 23rd
9. The date four weeks before February 23 is ________. Jan 26th
10. The day 5 days after February 10 is ________. Feb 15th
11. The day 5 days before February 10 is ________. Feb 5th
12. The day 10 days after February 10 is ________. Jan 31st
13. The day 10 days before February 10 is ________. Feb 20th
14. The day 20 days after February 10 is ________. Mar 2nd
15. The day 20 days before February 10 is ________. Jan 21st
16. The day 30 days before February 10 is ________. Jan 11th
17. The day 30 days after February 10 is ________. Mar 12th
18. The day 100 days after February 6 is ________. May 17th

Student's name: ____________________ Assignment date: ________________

Multiple choices

1. There are ____ months with 31 days in one year.

a. 4 b. 5 c. 6 d. 7√

2. There are ____ months with less than 31 days in one year.

a. 4 b. 5√ c. 6 d. 7

3. There are ____ days in February 1978.

a. 28√ b. 29 c. 30 d. 31

4. There are ____ days in February 1984.

a. 28 b. 29√ c. 30 d. 31

5. There are ____ days in August 1991.

a. 28 b. 29 c. 30 d. 31√

6. There are ____ days in September 1992.

a. 28 b. 29 c. 30√ d. 31

7. ____ is a leap year.

a. 1836√ b. 1537 c. 2562 d. 2006

8. ____ is a regular year.

a. 1636 b. 1996 c. 1984 d. 2005√

9. ____ is a leap year.

a. 1998 b. 1999 c. 2000√ d. 2001

10. ____ is a regular year.

a. 2004 b. 2008 c. 2010√ d. 2012

11. There are ____ days from January 1, 2006, to March 31, 2006.

a. 89√ b. 90 c. 91 d. 92

12. There are ____ days from January 1, 2004, to March 31, 2004.

a. 89 b. 90√ c. 91 d. 92

Student's name: ____________________ Assignment date: ________________

Time word problems

1. The Lees will leave for California in 25 days. Today is April 2, 2015. What day will they leave?

   May 7th, 2015

2. Mark will go to a chess tournament held in Germany on June 24, 2016. He plans to get there 3 days ahead of time. The Journey will take him 2 days. What is the date he will go?

   June 19th, 2016

3. Grade 3 students plan to run 1 000 000 metres for Children Federation from June 22. They can run 20 000 metres every day. What date will the event end?

   August 11th

4. Emily planted a crop in her garden on March 25. If the crop grows 3 cm every day, and its full height is 63 cm. What date would the crop reach its full height?

   Apr 15th

5. A baby male kitten was born on October 18th and weighed 200 g. If he gains 4 g each day. In how many days will he reach 3 kg?

   $\frac{3000-200}{4}$ = 700 days

6. Grade 4 students will make 6000 paper airplanes for an airplane flying contest. They can make 150 airplanes every day after school. If they work on it from Monday to Friday every week and expect to complete the entire project by December 5th, should they start working on it at the latest?

   $\frac{6000}{150} = 40\ days$
   Dec has 4 days, Nov has 30 Days, Oct 31, 30, 29, 28, 27, 26
   Oct 26th starts to work on it.

Student's name: ____________________ Assignment date: ________________

Decades, Centuries and Millenniums

1 decade = 10 years
1 century = 100 years
1 millennium = 1000 years

1. It is 2007 this year. It was 1997 one decade ago.
2. It is 2007 this year. It will be 2017 in one decade.
3. It is 2007 this year. It was 1907 one century ago.
4. It is 2007 this year. It will be 2107 in one century.
5. It is 2007 this year. It was 1007 one millennium ago.
6. It is 2007 this year. It will be 3007 in one millennium.
7. 1 millennium = 10 centuries = 100 decades = 1000 years
8. 5 decades is 50 years.
9. 6 centuries are 600 years, 60 decades.
10. There are 2 millenniums in 2000 years.
11. There are 8 centuries in 80 decades.
12. The apple tree was planted 2 decades ago when it was 5 years old.
    It is 25 years old now.
13. That building celebrated its centennial year in 2005. It was established in 1905.
14. The fossil was formed 3 millenniums ago. It is 3000 years old.
15. The antique vase was made in the year 1500. It will have been 52 decades till 2020.
16. This clock was made 4 decades ago. If it is 2008 this year, then it was made in 1968.

Student's name: ____________________ Assignment date: ________________

Test of time
Assume 1 month has 30 days.

5 weeks 3 days – 2 weeks 5 days =? 4 weeks 5 days
21 months 24 days ÷ 6 =? 4 months 4.8 days (4 months 4 days19.2 hours)
20 hours 42 minutes ÷ 5 =? 4 hours 8.4 minutes (4 hours 8 minutes 24 seconds)
21 hours 47 minutes ÷ 7 =? 3 hours 6.7 minutes (3 hours 6 minutes 42 seconds)
18 days 13 hours – 8 days 14 hours =? 9 days 23 hours

clock A

clock B

How many minutes have passed from clock A to clock B? ________________ 30

Student's name: ____________________ Assignment date: ________________

Periodical data

Data appears to repeat the pattern core; then, it is called periodical data such as the calendar data.

Today is Wednesday. What day will it be 10 days after today? 10 divided by 7, the remainder is 3. The day is Saturday.
Today is Wednesday. What day will it be 20 days before today? One more day will be 3 of 7-day cycles, so the day is Thursday.

Student's name: ____________________ Assignment date: ______________

Arrangement

Example

Kitty, Meghan, and Jordan are to sit in a row. How many different ways can they sit together? List all the ways.

Use the Box Method, then multiply all numbers.

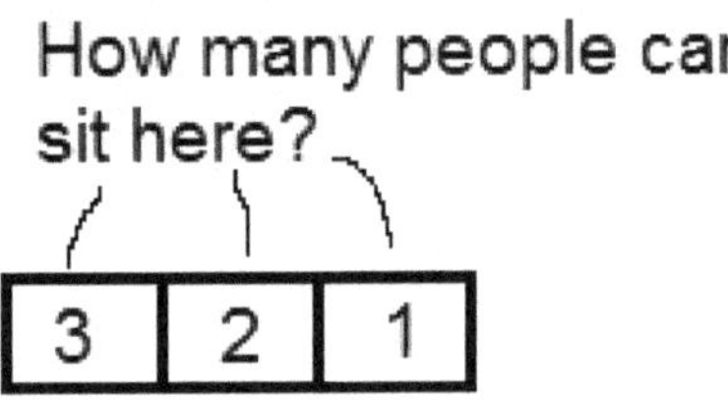

Heather has 2 shirts: red and blue. She also has a pair of pants and a skirt. How many different outfits that can she wear? Use the Multiplication method to get the answer. 2 x 1 x 1 = 2
Oscar has 3 digits: 3, 4 and 6. How many different numbers that he can create without using the same digit twice? 9 3x2+3=9
Oscar has 3 digits: 3, 4 and 6. How many different 3-digit numbers Oscar can create greater than 300 without using the same digit twice? 9 6+(444, 666, 333) = 9
Oscar has 3 digits: 3, 4 and 6. How many different 3-digit numbers Oscar can create less than 400 without using the same digit twice? 3 346, 364, 333
Oscar has 3 digits: 3, 4 and 6. How many different even numbers that he can create without using the same digit twice? 6

Student's name: ____________________ Assignment date: ________________

Combinations using the T-table method

Example

A pencil costs 15 cents and an eraser costs 12 cents. Cindy has 50 cants. Show all the combinations of pencils and erasers that Cindy could buy. Cindy could buy only one item of both.

Use T-table to find four combinations.

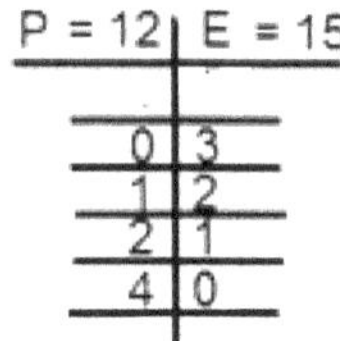

answer

How many different scores of using 2 darts? 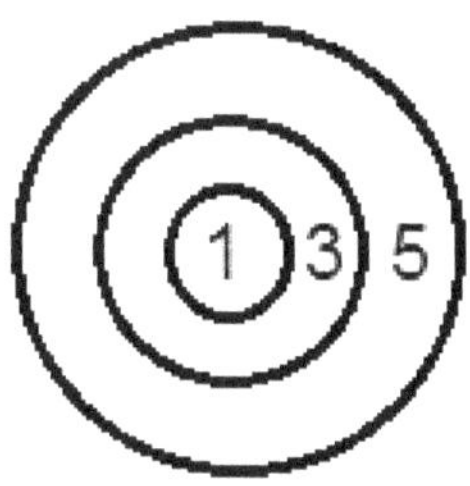 55, 33, 11,53, 51,31
Jessica likes to choose 2 marbles out of a bag with three marbles, red, blue, and white. How many ways can she choose from? 6
Frank has two cats Kiko and Snow, and they like two kinds of cat food shredded or pate salmon. How many different ways can Frank feed his cats? 4
Kevin can choose one course in the morning out of two choices math or choose. He can also choose one activity out of three activities basketball, dance, or drama. How many choices that she can have? List all choices. 6

Student's name: ____________________ Assignment date: ________________

Brent has $0.37 consisting of 4 coins. How many nickels can he have?

none

Sarah got 9 points for throwing darts. There were 2-point and 3-point circles on the dart. How many 2-point darts did she get?

Alvin has $1.05 consists of quarters and dimes. Replace each ? with a number.

Dimes	Quarters	Total values	Total number of coins
?	?	$1.05	6
1	4	$1.05	5
3	3	$1.05	6

A chair can be purchased with the following choices:

Colours: red, blue, black
Sizes: small, medium, large
Material: metal, wood

How many different combinations are possible to choose from?

Student's name: ____________________ Assignment date: ________________

Model problems and strategies
Sum and difference

Some problems are classified as Model word problems in China, frequently appearing in lower grades. This kind of problem can be solved easily by using the algebraic method. Without using algebra, students could be taught with a story on how to solve it.

Example

A cell phone sells $15 more than a graphics calculator. Minnie buys a cell phone and a graphics calculator for a total of $395. How much does each item cost?

We can convert this kind of problem to a ``money dividing problem` that assumes two persons like to share a $395 pot of money and person C likes to have $15 more than person G.

$\frac{395-15}{2} = 190$ ……….. Cost of the graphics calculator
190 + 15 = 205 ……. Cost of the cell phone.

Students should check back the answer because if the cost of the graphics is calculated incorrectly, then the answer of cell phone depending on the cost of the calculator will also be wrong. There is an answer dependency problem here.

Student's name: ____________________ Assignment date: ________________

Floor and lineup problems

City Tower is 150 feet tall above ground and 75 feet below ground. How many feet is the tallest point higher than the lowest point? 150 + 75 = 225
Jocelyn is on the 6th steps of her school stairs. She walks down 3 steps, then up 2 steps. Finally, she walks up the remaining 3 steps to walk into her classroom. How many steps do the stairs have? 6 – 3 + 2 + 3 = 8
Kitty is on the ground floor of a condo. She walks up 7 floors, then down 5 floors, then up 3 floors, then down 2 floors. What floor does Kitty end up on? 7 - 5 + 3 – 2 = 3 4h floor

Student's name: ____________________ Assignment date: ________________

Statistics

Austin scored 2 of 85% and 3 of 95% of his math tests. What was his average (mean) percent score for all five tests?

$$\frac{2 \times 0.85 + 3 \ \times 0.95}{5} = \frac{1.7 + 2{,}85}{5} = \frac{4.55}{5} = 0.91 = 91\%$$

Three numbers are in a ratio of 1 to 2 to 3. The largest of these three numbers is 24. What is the average (mean) of these three numbers?

$\frac{24}{3} = 8$

$\frac{8 \ \times 6}{6} = 8$

The average is 8.

Fernando biked 62 miles to a park in 2 hours. What was his average speed?

62 ÷ 2 = 31 miles / per hour

Kathy bought 6 pencils at $0.75 each and 4 erasers. The average price of these 11 items was $0.66, what was the cost of one eraser?

$0.69

Student's name: ____________________ Assignment date: ________________

Equation word problems

Five years ago, the sum of the ages of Jessica and her twin brother Kevin was 9. How old is Kevin now? $\frac{9-5}{2}+5=7$ 7
Brent is 10 years old. Two years less than two times his age is _______ years old. 18

Student's name: ____________________ Assignment date: ________________

Inequality

The way to sole inequality is the same as the equality equation other than the sign such as $-x > 3$.

$-x > 3$
$x < -3$ (The inequality sign changes.)

Solve $\frac{x}{8} > \frac{1}{2}$ $x>4$
Four times of a whole number is less than 41 but greater than 32. What is the number? 10
If $\frac{3}{4} < x < 0.77$ then x could be ____ (Answer in 2 decimal places.). 0.76
Suppose N is a whole number and is divisible by 2 and is also a multiple of 5. What is N if it is between 10 and 30? 20

-

Student's name: ____________________ Assignment date: _______________

Work backwards

Arithmetic equation usually is working from left to right, so from the operation direction point of view, working backwards is to work from right to left and reverse its operators.

After Yi-yi spent \$9 on food and \$8 on a movie, she had \$29 left. How much money did she have at first? \$46
If 150 × ☐ = 0.135, what is the value of ☐? 0.0009
What is the smallest number that can be added to 50 to produce a number divisible by 8? 6

Student's name: ____________________ Assignment date: ________________

Scale - Making both sides balanced

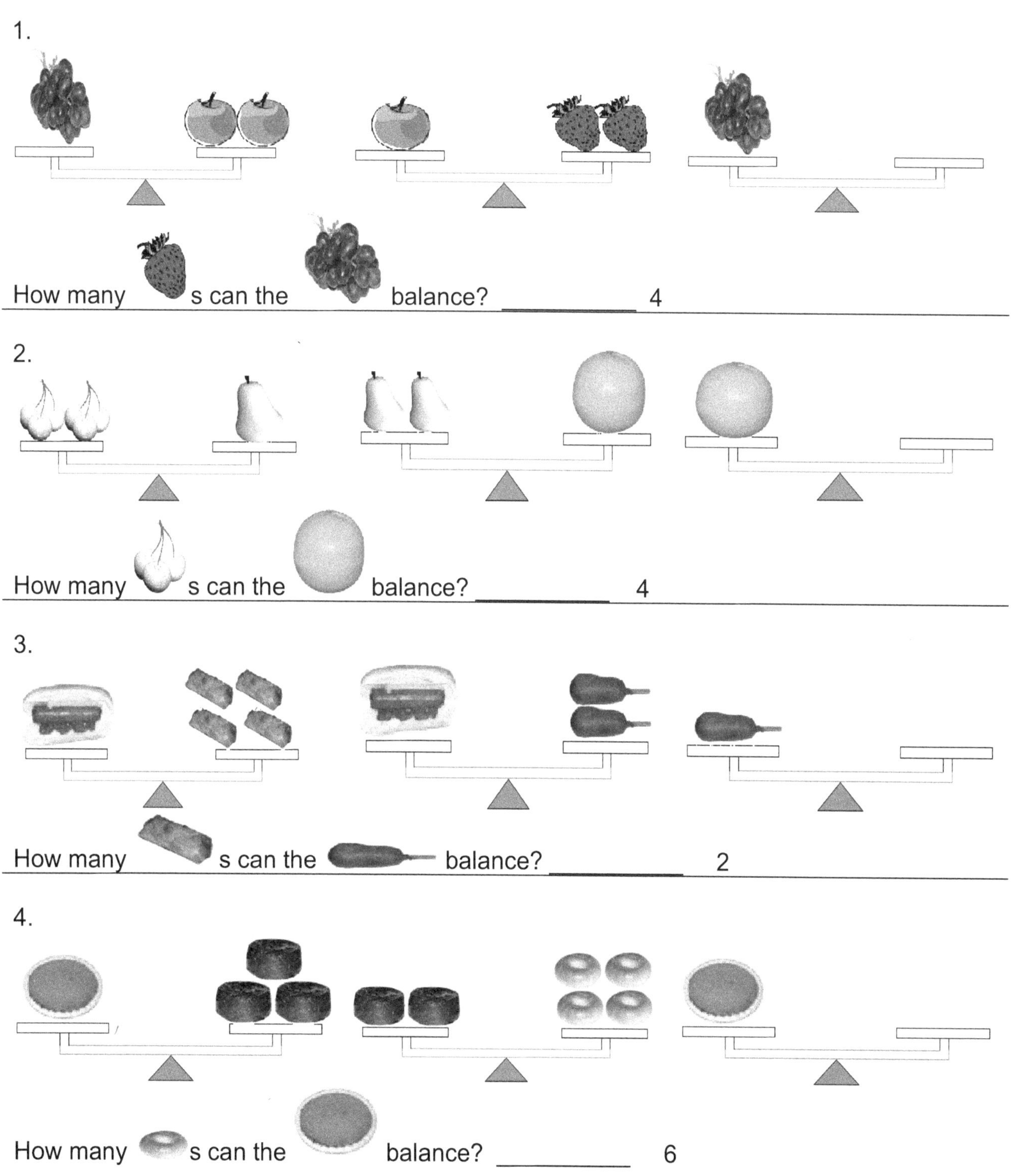

Ho Math Chess Primary Grades Math

Test Review assesssment 何数棋謎低年级数学测试複習考核

Student's name: ____________________ Assignment date: ________________

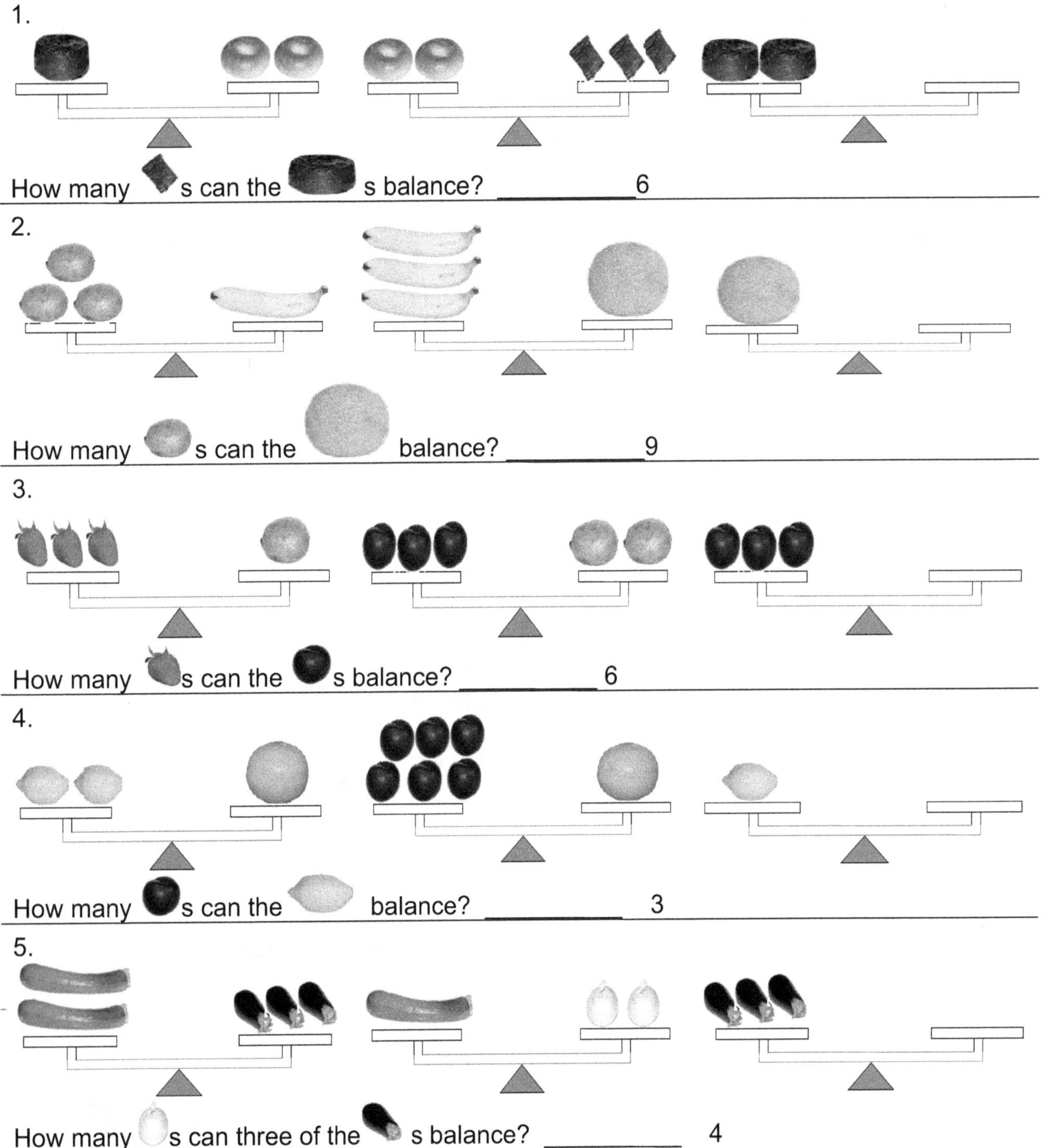

Student's name: ____________________ Assignment date: ________________

Number line

<table>
<tr><td>Number line
A number is drawn as follows to show 1 + 1 = 2.
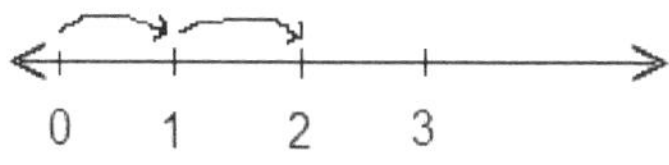</td></tr>
<tr><td>Look at the following diagram and come up with your equation.
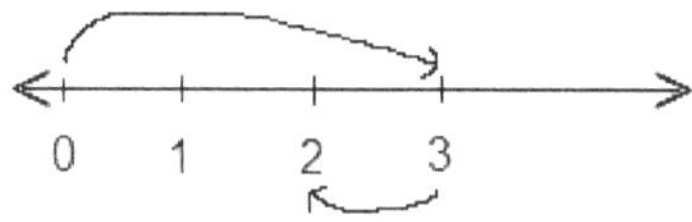
3 - 1 = 2</td></tr>
<tr><td>Write an equation for the following number line.
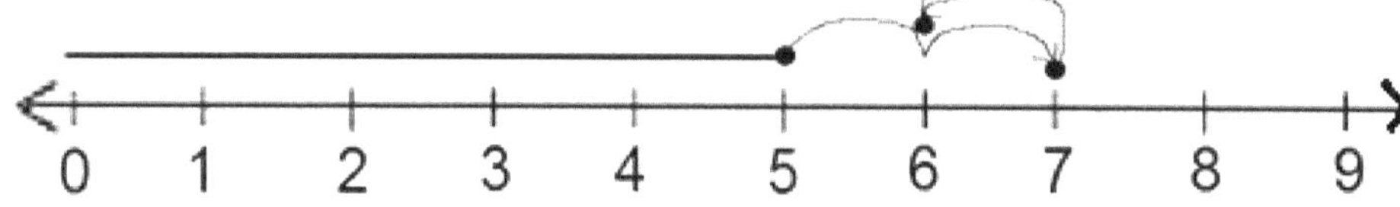
5+2-1=6</td></tr>
<tr><td>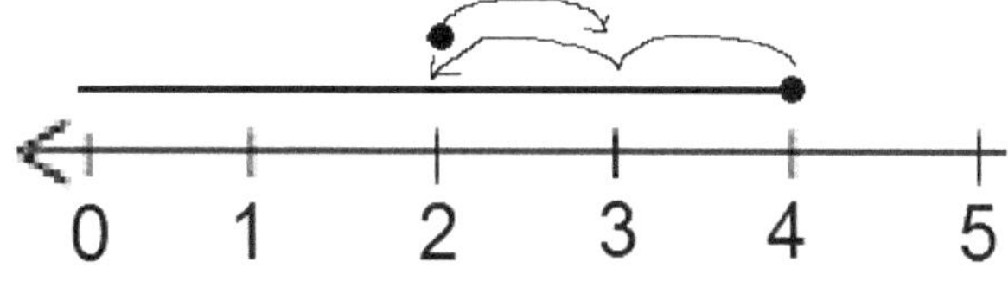
Write the equation for the above number line.
4-2+1=3</td></tr>
</table>

Student's name: ____________________ Assignment date: ________________

Do not always use 1 as an unknown quantity

Adding for less and subtracting for more

We often use "1" as a unit to solve the unknown quantity problem, for example, the work problem, but it is not convenient sometimes. The following example demonstrates the idea of not use "1" as the basic unit.

Example

In the following line segment diagram, the length of AB is 30 cm, the length of AC is equal to the length of DB, the length of the CD is $\frac{1}{2}$ of AC, what is the length of the CD?

Assume AC = DB – 2
CD = 1
Ab is divided into 5 equal parts. Each pat is 6 cm.
CD = 6 × 2 $= 12\ cm.$

Pauline has half as many cat food cans as Elise. Jocelyn has half as many cat food cans as Pauline. Together they have 56 cans. How many cans does each one have? Let Elise = 4 units Pauline = 2 units Jocelyn = I unit $\frac{56}{7} = 8$ Jocelyn Pauline = 8 × 2 = 16 Elise = 16 × 2 = 32
Pauline has 2 less than twice as many cat food cans as Elise. Elise has 6 less than twice as many cat food cans as Jocelyn. Together they have 41 cans. How many cans does each one have? Draw the Line Segment Diagram to solve. 41+ 2 + 6 = 49 $\frac{49}{7} = 7$ Jocelyn $2 \times 7 - 2 = 12$ Elise $2 \times 12 - 6 = 18$ Pauline

Student's name: ____________________ Assignment date: ________________

Word problems

1. Harry Hiker saw 24 caterpillars when he was walking in the forest. When he stopped for lunch, he saw 5 more. How many caterpillars did he see altogether?

   29

2. Wally Walker spotted and picked up 45 leaves on the grass. He then found 23 more in the park. What is the total number of leaves that Wally found?

   68

3. Wendy Watcher saw 12 birds in her backyard today. Yesterday she saw 38 birds at the park. How many birds has she seen in all?

   50

4. Tiffany owns 23 books. She received 2 more today for her birthday. What is the total number of books that Tiffany owns?

   25

Student's name: ____________________ Assignment date: ________________

5. Tyler has 32 baseball cards. His friends give him 20 more. How many baseball cards does he have in all?

   52

6. Christina counted 24 tulips in her garden. Her sister counted 15 roses. What is the sum number of flowers that they counted?

   39

7. Anthony was on a Scouts trip and found 23 small twigs, 34 medium-sized twigs, and 25 large twigs for a campfire. How many twigs did he find altogether?

   82

8. Tom, who was also on the camping trip, saw 10 squirrels climbing trees. He also saw 7 chipmunks scurrying to their homes. How many animals did Tom see in all?

   17

   Which two numbers have a sum of 22 and a difference of 12?

   5, 17, This is a Sum and Difference model problem.

Student's name: ____________________ Assignment date: ________________

9. Jennifer went fishing with her dad, and she caught 3 fish. Her dad caught one. How many fish did Jennifer and her dad catch?

   4

10. Larry, Curly, and Moe were playing a game of darts. Larry scored 10 points, Curly scored 12 points, and Moe scored 8 points. What is the total number of points that they scored?

   30

11. Yumiko helped her mother make four rolls of sushi. Her younger sister helped make two. How many rolls of sushi did Yumiko and her sister help make?

   6

12. Dave found 17 chocolates in the community Easter egg hunt. He also helped his little sister find seven. How many chocolates did he find altogether?

   24

Student's name: ____________________ Assignment date: ________________

***** Part 24 Tests, reviews, and assessments *****

Kindergarten, grade 1 and above

If ◯ = 3, then ◯ + 1 = ______. 4
If ◯ = 4, then ◯ + 1 = ______. 5
If ● = 1, then ◯ = ●●● then ◯ + ● = ______. 4
If ◯ = ●●●, then ◯ + ●● = ______ 5
If ◯ = ●●● and ● = 1, then ◯ – ● = _____ 2
Match left to right by drawing lines. 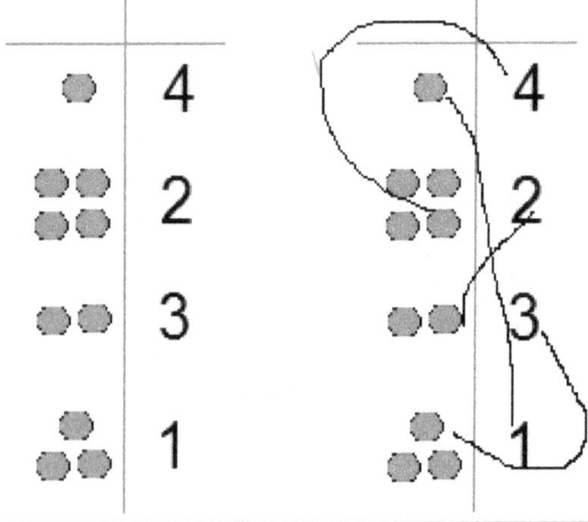 answer
Out of 1, 2, and 3, what numbers added together will give answers of 3? 1, 2

Student's name: ____________________ Assignment date: ________________

Number line
A number is drawn as follows to show 1 + 1 = 2.

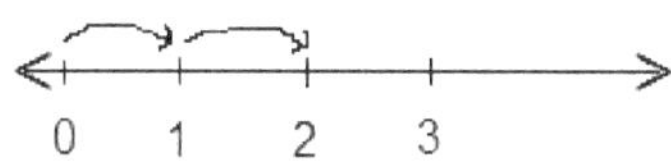

Look at the following diagram and come up with your equation.

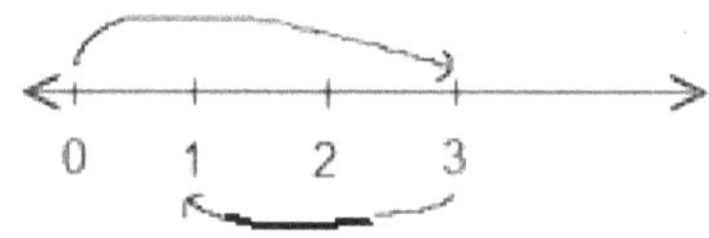

3 - 2 = 1

If the following diagram shows 3 - 1 = 2,

Then what is the value of the following diagram?

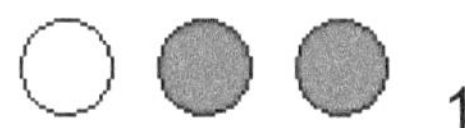

1

What is the value of the following diagram?

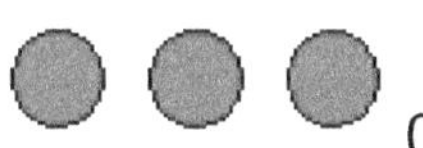

0

Write an equation for the following number line.

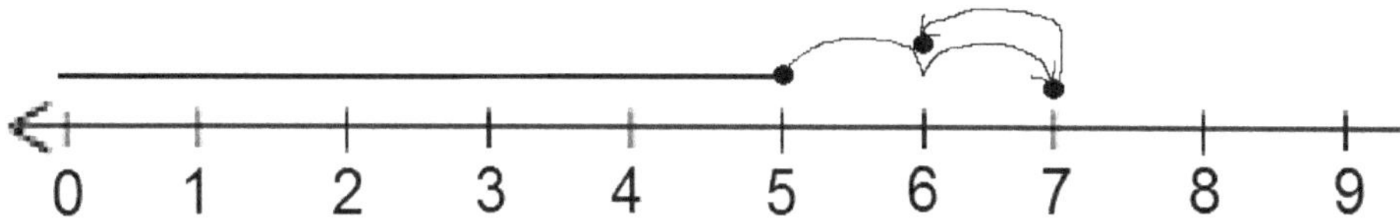

5+2-1=6

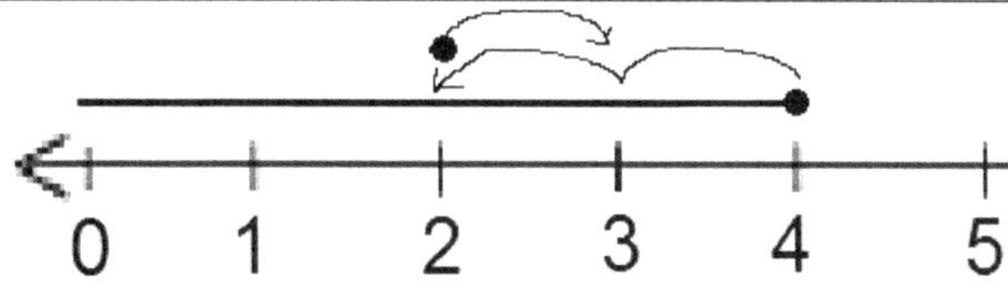

Write the equation for the above number line.

4-2+1=3

Student's name: ____________________ Assignment date: ________________

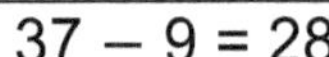

37 – 9 = 28
73 – 4 = 69
45 – 8 = 37
89 +7 = 96
36 – 17 = 29
What is the largest one-digit number? 9
What is the largest two-digit number? 99
What is the smallest two-digit number? 10
Circle the following even numbers. 177, 46, 8, 91, 32, 21 46, 8, 32

Insert >, <, or = in □.

(67 – 19) □ 47 >	(31 – 18) □ 12 >
(77 – 28) □ (37 + 12) =	(34 – 26) □ (17 – 8) <

If ● + ● + ● + ● + 6 = 8 + ● + ● + ●, what is the value of ●?

2

Student's name: ____________________ Assignment date: ________________

Grade 1 and above

▲ – 7 = 16, ▲ + ● = 36 ▲ =? 23 ● = ? 13
▲ + ▲ = 16, ▲ – ● = 8 ▲ =? 28 ● = ? 0
▲ + ▲ = 24, ▲ – ● = 6 ▲ =? 12 ● = ? 6
6+ ▲ = 13, ▲ + ● = 11 ▲ =? 7 ● = ? 4
● – ▲ = 13, 15 – ▲ = 7 ▲ =? 8 ● = ? 21
If ● + ■ + ▲ = 21, ● + ■ = 13, ■ + ▲ =12 What values are ●, ■, and ▲ each? 9, 4, 8
If ▲ + ▲ = 16, ▲ =? 8 ▲ + ● =17, ● =? 9 ● + ■ = 19, ■ =? 10

Student's name: ____________________ Assignment date: ________________

Grade 1 and above

■ + ▲ =12, ■ + ▲ + ▲ + ▲ + ▲ =24 ▲ =? 8 ■ = ? 4
● – ▲ = 4 ● + ● – ▲ = 10 ● =? 6 ▲ =? 2
▲ + ▲ + ▲ =44 ● + ● + ● =23 ▲ – ● =? 7
▲ – ● =10 ▲ + ● =12 ▲ = ? 11 ● = ? 1
What are the odd numbers which are less than 15? 1,3,5,7,9,11,13

Student's name: ____________________ Assignment date: ________________

Grade 1 and above

How many squares are in the following figure? 5
What are the odd numbers which are less than 20? 1, 3, 5, 7, 9, 11, 13, 15, 17, 19
Ethan is in a lineup for a concert. There are 3 people in front of Ethan and 5 people behind Ethan. How many people are in the lineup? 9
Adam is 2 years older than Bob now. How old will Adam be more than Bob next year? 2
Meghan had 17 apples, and she gave two of her friends every 4 apples then. How many apples does she have now? 9
Andrew has $13, and he wishes to buy applications software, which costs $29. How much more he has to save to buy the software he wants to? 29-13 = 16

Student's name: ____________________ Assignment date: ________________

Grade 2

Complete the pattern. 5, 51, 511, 5111, _____ 51111
Compute 17 + 15 + 13 + 11 + 9 + 7 - 16 - 14 - 12 - 10 - 8 - 6 = 6
Complete the pattern. 10, 101, 1011, 10111, ______ 101111
Circle the number which does not belong to the group. 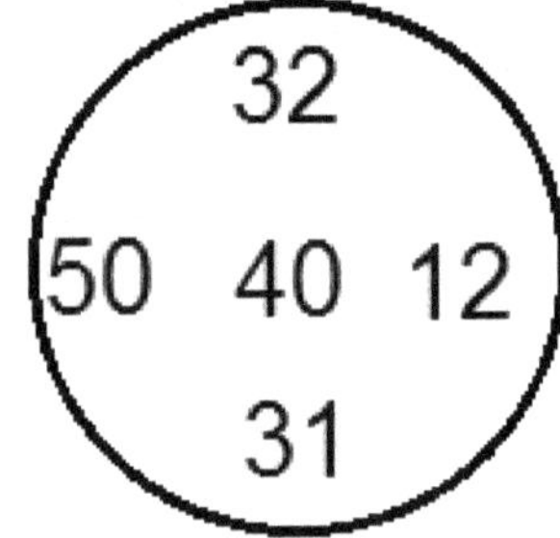 The odd number 31.
Find the next item.   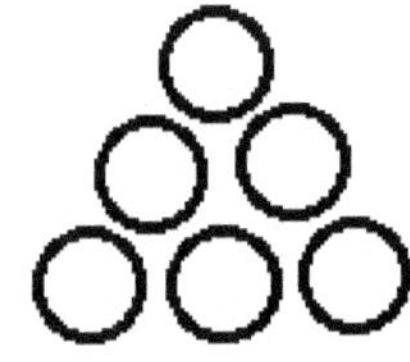 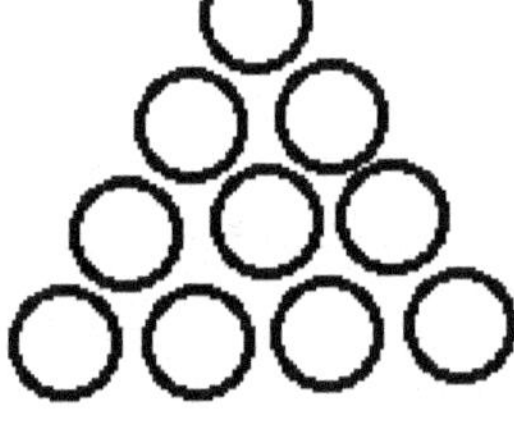 answer
Complete the next number. 88, 96, 11, ______ 69 or 00 A number can be seen the same when sitting across the table.

Student's name: ____________________ Assignment date: ________________

Grade 2 and above

Questions	Solutions
Tammy has 15 books. Tina has 36 books. How many books do they have in all?	51
Mike has 37 stickers. Aaron has 19 stickers. How many fewer stickers does Aaron have than Mike?	18
Sandy Liang has 29 e-mail messages. Jeffrey Lai has 13 e-mail messages less than Sandy. How many messages do they have in all?	45
Jun has 27 cookies, and Veronica has 16 cookies more than Jun. How many cookies they have in all?	70
Shirley has finished reading 119 pages of a book, and there are 293 pages left. What is the total number of pages of the book in all?	412
14 books were sold, and 29 books are left. How many books were there before selling?	43

51, 18, 45, 70, 412, 43

Student's name: ____________________ Assignment date: ________________

Grade 2 and above

10 people got on the bus, 8 people got off the bus, 5 people got off, and the bus was empty. How many people were on the bus initially (excluding the driver)?	
Jerry would have received as many e-mail messages as Julie if he had 16 more messages. Julie had 37 messages. How many messages did Jerry receive?	

3, 21

Student's name: ____________________ Assignment date: ________________

Grade 2 and above

One chick has 2 legs. Three chicks, how many legs? 6
Circle the odd one.
Which figure should be in place of the "?"? = ? answer
What number should replace ⓘ to balance the weights on the scales? 8 + 3 4 + ⓘ 7
I had 2 pairs of gloves. I lost one glove. How many gloves do I have now? 3
I am 8 years old, and my brother is 5 years older than me. How old will my brother be next year? 14
How many rectangles can you see in the following figure? 9

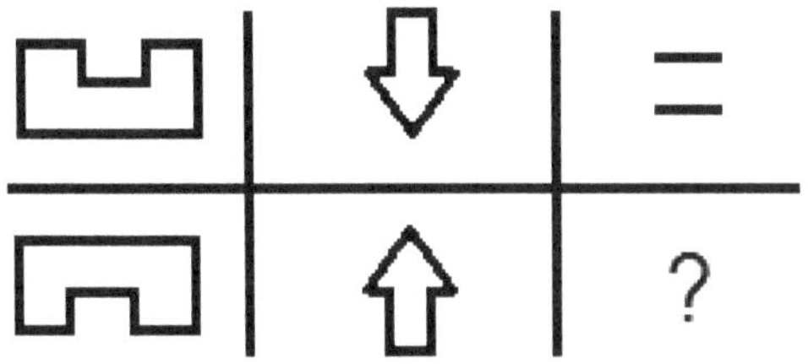

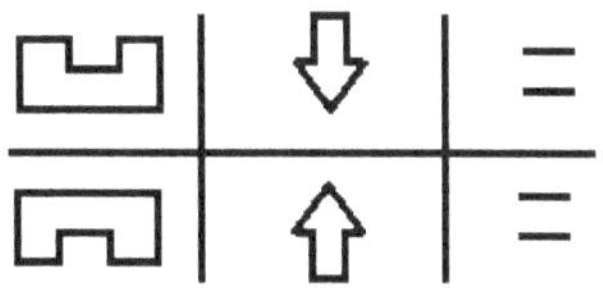

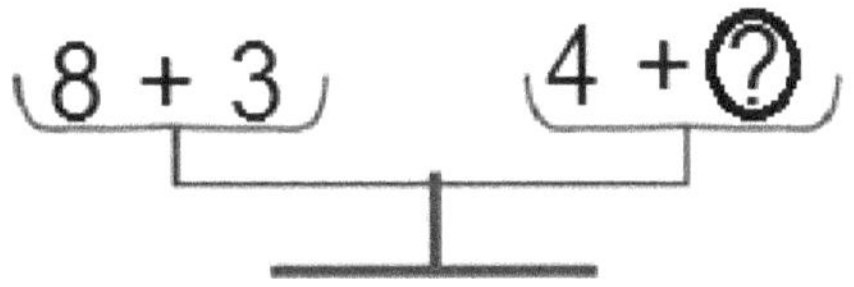

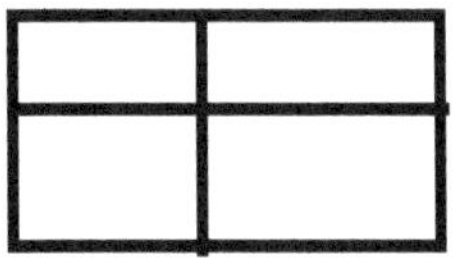

Student's name: ____________________ Assignment date: ________________

Grade 2 and above

After taking six plums from a basket, six were left in the basket. How many plums were in the basket at the beginning? 12
Bob has 14 oranges more than Adam, and Adam has six oranges. How many oranges do they have altogether? 20
Amy has nine more apples than Bryan. Bryan has 3 fewer apples than Cathy. Cathy has 13 apples. How many apples does each one of them have? A=19, B = 10, C = 13
Bill has four more apples than Bob, and Bob has 8 more apples than Coco. Together, all three have 41 apples. How many apples does each one of them have? Coco = 7, Bob = 15, Bill = 19
Some birds were on the tree. Seventeen more birds flew back, and eight flew away. Now there are 24 birds on the tree. How many birds were on the tree originally? 15
Fill in each the same box with the same number. 6 + □ = 13 □ + △ = 12 7, 7, 5

Student's name: ____________________ Assignment date: ________________

Grade 2 and above

If □ = 6 and ○ =3, then □ + ○ =? 9
5 = 7 – □ 2
□ + 3 – 1 = □ + ? 2
6 + 4 + □ = 13 3
7 + 7 + □ = 15 1
8 + 2 + 5 + 5 + □ = 21 1
A half dozen is 6. How many is one dozen? 12
Mom gave me one-half of $4. How much was it? $2
□ □ □ – □ □ □ □ + □ □ □ = ? □ 4
If □ = 2 and ○ =3, then □ + ○ =? 5
4 + □ = 6 2
One dog has 4 legs. If there are 12 legs, then how many dogs are there? 6
One boy has 2 legs. Two boys have ____ legs. 4
One wagon has 4 wheels, ____ wagons have 8 wheels. 2
If □ = 7 and ○ = 5, then □ – ? = ○. 2

Student's name: ____________________ Assignment date: ________________

Grade 2 and above

If 13 + 7 + 6 + ⓞ = 31, then what is ⓞ ? 5
One boy has 2 legs, and one dog has 4 legs. How many legs are there for 2 boys and 2 dogs? 12
The following large square is made of 16 small squares, but some of them are missing. How many small squares are missing? 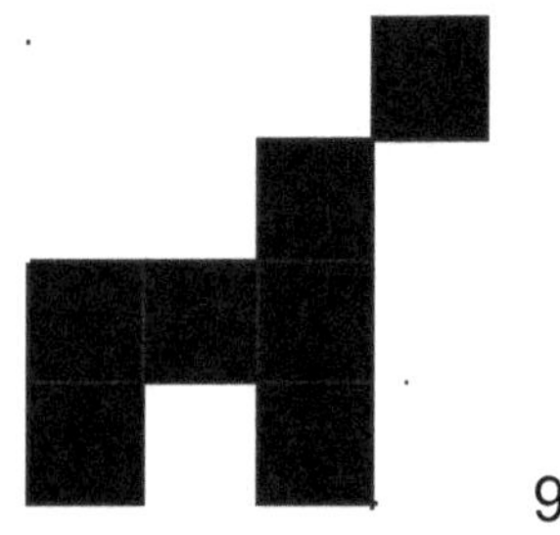 9
Each dot is two points. Find the value of one ⁙ + ⁘ = ○ 18 ○ + □ =31 18+ 13 = 31
What number should replace ⓞ to balance the weights on the scale 3. 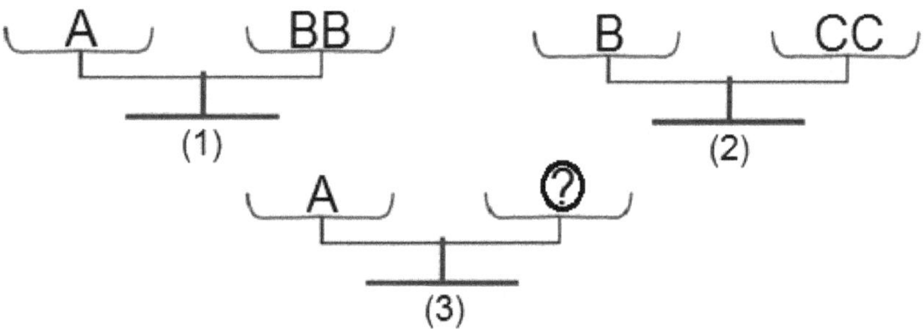 The first two scales are balanced. How many C's are needed to balance the scale 3? 4

Student's name: ____________________ Assignment date: ________________

Grade 2 and above

Which of the following figure has the longest line in the following figures?

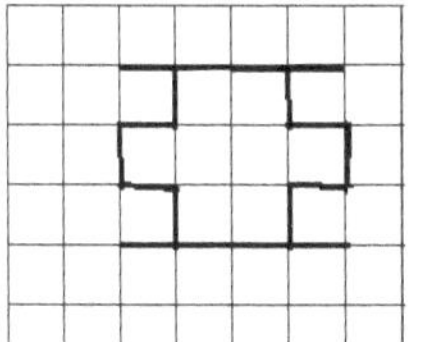 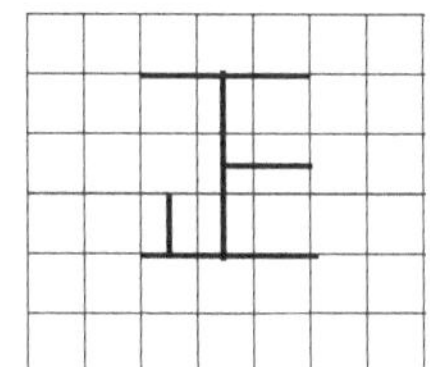 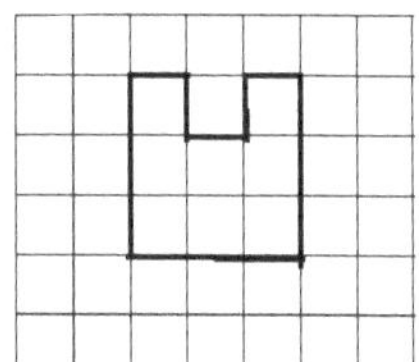 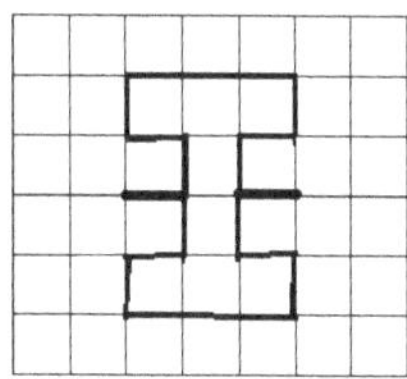

18, 11.5, 14, 20, The last one (The rightmost one.).

Last month, the cats Kiko and Snow together ate 12 cans of fish. This month they ate 5 more cans of fish than the last month. How many cans of fish did they eat in two months?

29

The cat Kiko likes to play with pom-pom balls, but often she lost them, and so far, she has lost 21 pom-pom balls in two months. This month she lost twice as many as the last month. How many pom-pom balls she lost last month?

7

The cat Snow likes to watch leaves falling from trees in the fall by turning his head up and down whenever he sees a leaf falling. This morning he saw 20 leaves falling, and in the afternoon, he saw one less than half of what he saw in the morning. How many leaves fell did Snow see in the morning and the afternoon?

29

The cat Snow likes to jump up to catch his toy. He jumped high 15 times in the morning, which was one more than twice as many times as he jumped in the afternoon. How many times did he jump in the morning and also in the afternoon altogether?
22

Student's name: ____________________ Assignment date: ________________

Find the values of the following figures.

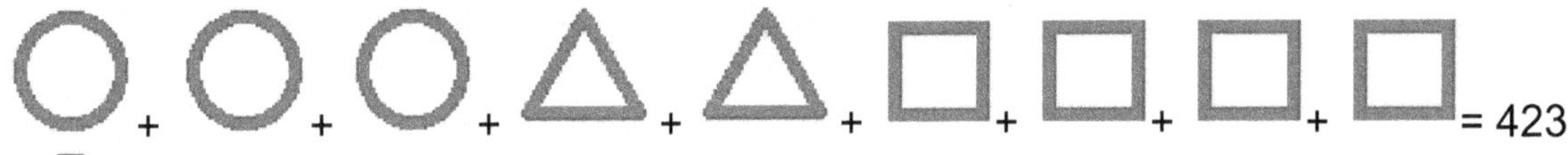

○ = _______ 1

△ = _______ 10

□ = _______ 100

Fill in each square by a number from 1 to 6 such that the sum of each line is 9.

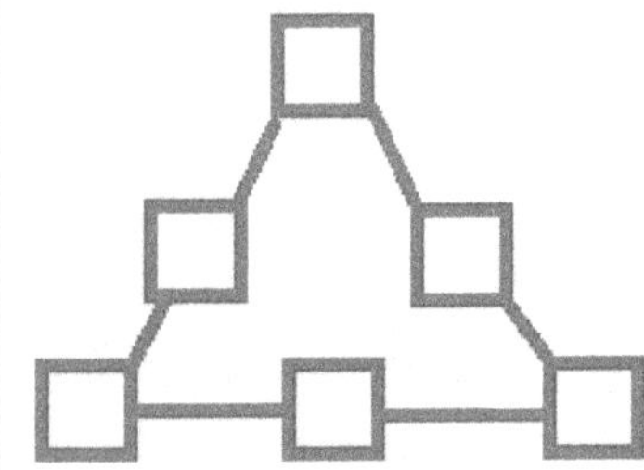

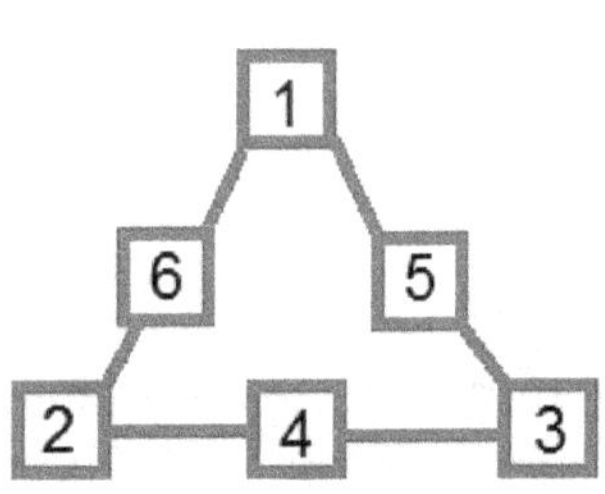

answer

Place the numbers 1, 2, 3, 4, 5 and 6 in the circle so that each line's sum is the same.

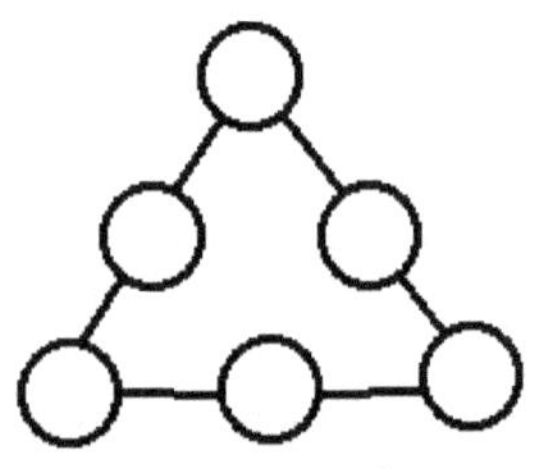

The sum of 1 + 2 + 3 + 4 + 5 + 6 = 21

21 + 3 corner repeated circles must be divisible by 3. The following bold numbers are corner numbers.

21 + 6 = 27 (1, 2, 3)

21 + 9 = 30 (2, 3, 4) (1, 3, 5)

21 + 12 = 33 (2, 4, 6) (3, 4, 5)

21 + 15 = 36 (4, 5, 6)

There are six different answers. The corner numbers are 1, 64, 325.

Student's name: ____________________ Assignment date: ________________

Grade 3 and above

Complete the pattern. 5, 51, 511, 5111, ______ 51111
Compute 17 + 15 + 13 + 11 + 9 + 7 - 16 - 14 - 12 - 10 - 8 - 6 = 6
Complete the pattern. 10, 101, 1001, 10001, ______ 100001
Circle the number which does not belong to the group. 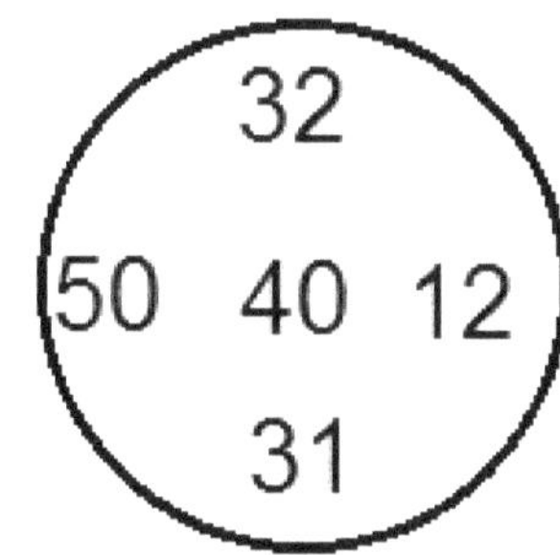 The odd number 31.
Find the next item.   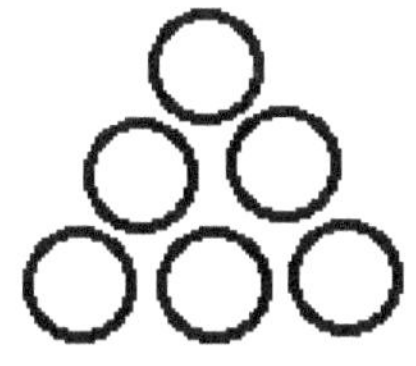 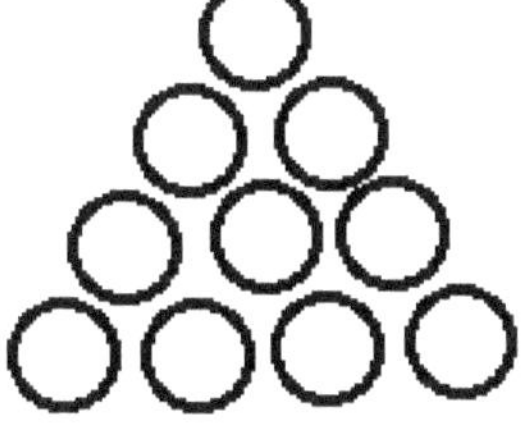 answer
Complete the next number. 88, 96, 11, ______ 69

Student's name: ____________________ Assignment date: ________________

Grade 3 and above

Questions	Solutions
Tammy has 15 books. Tina has 36 books. How many books do they have in all?	51
Mike has 37 stickers. Aaron has 19 stickers. How many fewer stickers does Aaron have than Mike?	18
Sandy Liang has 29 e-mail messages. Jeffrey Lai has 13 e-mail messages less than Sandy. How many messages do they have in all?	45
Jun has 27 cookies, and Veronica has 16 cookies more than Jun. How many cookies they have in all?	70
Shirley has finished reading 119 pages of a book, and there are 293 pages left. What is the total number of pages of the book in all?	412
14 books were sold, and 29 books are left. How many books were there before selling?	43

51, 18, 45, 70, 412, 43

Student's name: ____________________ Assignment date: ________________

Grade 3 and above

10 people got on the bus, 8 people got off the bus, 5 people got off, and the bus was empty. How many people were on the bus originally (excluding the driver)?	
Jerry would have received as many e-mail messages as Julie if he had 16 more messages. Julie had 37 messages. How many messages did Jerry receive?	

3, 21

Student's name: ____________________ Assignment date: ________________

Grade 3 and above

One chick has 2 legs. Three chicks, how many legs? 6
Circle the odd one. 
Which figure should be in place of the "?"? = 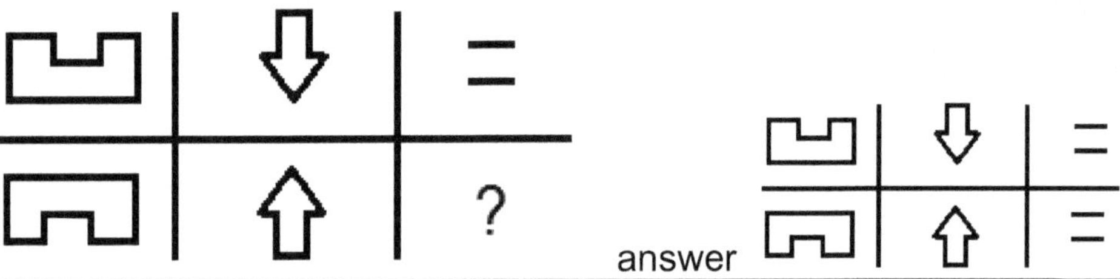
What number should replace ? to balance the weights on the scales? 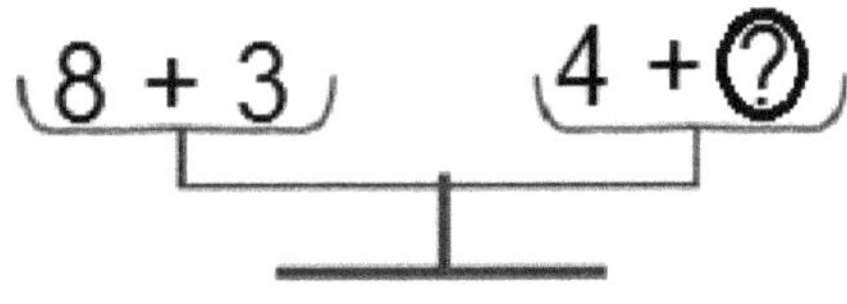 7
I had 2 pairs of gloves. I lost one glove. How many gloves do I have now? 3
I am 8 years old, and my brother is 5 years older than me. How old will my brother be next year? 14
How many rectangles can you see in the following figure? 9 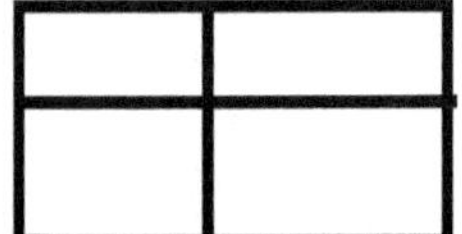

Student's name: ____________________ Assignment date: ________________

Grade 3 or 4

If □ = 6 and ○=3, then □ + ○=? 9
5 = 7 – □ 2
□ + 3 – 1 = □ + ? 2
6 + 4 + □= 13 3
7 + 7 + □= 15 1
8 + 2 + 5 + 5 + □= 21 1
A half dozen is 6. How many is one dozen? 12
Mom gave me one-half of $4. How much was it? $2
□+□+□ –□–□–□–□ + □+□+□ = □ any number
If □ = 2 and ○=3, then □ + ○=? 5
4 + □= 6 2
One dog has 4 legs. If there are 12 legs, then how many dogs are there? 3
One boy has 2 legs. Two boys have ____ legs. 4
One wagon has 4 wheels, ____ wagons have 8 wheels. 2
If □ = 7 and ○= 5, then □– ? = ○. 7-2=5

Student's name: ____________________ Assignment date: ________________

Grade 3 or 4

Tommy sent emails to a dozen of his friends. Half dozen of his friends received one page each, and the other half received two pages each. How many pages did his friends receive from Tommy altogether? 6 x 1 + 6 x 2 = 18 pages
Alvin used matches to build square figures as follows. How many matches will he use for the 21st figure if the pattern continues?  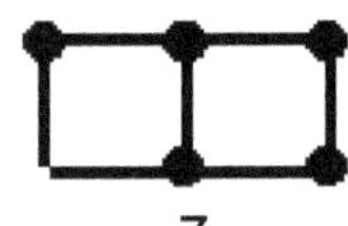 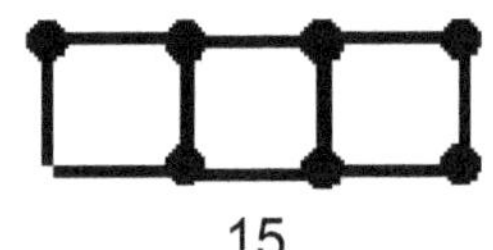 4 7 15 The pattern rule is 4 + 3(n-1) 21st figure= $4 + 3 \times 20 = 64$
Alvin drew squares as follows. How many squares will he draw for the 21st figure if the pattern continues? 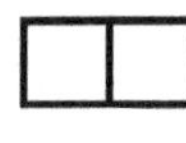 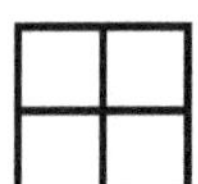 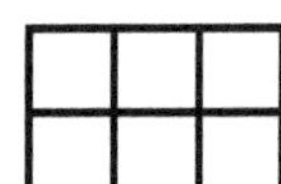 2 squares 4 squares 6 squares 21 rows x 2 columns = 42
Circle the following odd fraction. $\frac{1}{2}$ $\frac{2}{8}$ $\frac{2}{4}$ $\frac{3}{6}$ $\frac{1}{2}$ ($\frac{2}{8}$) $\frac{2}{4}$ $\frac{3}{6}$ answer
Jason left Bapton by bike. He rode for one hour and reached the following sign. How long will take Jason to reach Apaton if he continues to ride at the same speed Bapton ⇦ 30 km 20 km ⇨ Apaton $\frac{20}{30} \times 60$= 40 minutes

Student's name: ____________________ Assignment date: ________________

Grade 3 or 4

Cathy ate $\frac{2}{3}$ of a pizza and later she ate $\frac{1}{6}$ of the same pizza. How much of the pizza did she eat altogether? $\frac{2}{3}+\frac{1}{6}=\frac{5}{6}$
What are the factors of 16? 1, 16, 2, 8, 4
Paint sells in a 5-litre can. Taylor needs 39 litres. How many cans must he buy? $\frac{39}{5}=7.8$ 8 cans must be purchased.
What is the value of the following underlined digit? 7<u>7</u>77 7 hundred
Find the pattern rule of the following pattern and then use the pattern rule to find the next number. 3, 8, 18, 38, ______ The pattern rule is ____________________ Start at 3 and then times 2, add 2 to get the next number. 78
The following shows that one apple is worth 2 pears and three pears are worth 4 oranges.  A. Meghan has 6 apples. Use the above information, how many pears could Meghan get? 12 B. How many oranges could Meghan get? 16

Student's name: ____________________ Assignment date: ________________

Grade 3 or 4

Which of the following fractions is greater than $\frac{1}{2}$?

$\frac{3}{5}$ $\frac{3}{6}$ $\frac{4}{10}$ $\frac{3}{7}$

$\frac{3}{5}$ answer

The scale on a map indicates that 1 cm represents 3 km on the land. If the distance between two towns is 9 cm, how many km are thee between two towns?

27 km. Use the pattern to understand.

An egg pie recipe in the following is for 4 people.

Ingredients	
Eggs	4
Flour	10 cups
Milk	1 cup

Cathy uses the above recipe for 2 people. Find the amount for the ingredients.

Ingredients	
Eggs	?
Flour	?
Milk	?

2, 5, $\frac{1}{2}$

Five thousand raffle tickets numbered 1 to 5000 were sold. The last three digits of 343 received prizes. What numbers had won the prizes? List all winning numbers.

343
1343
2343
3343
4343

Student's name: ____________________ Assignment date: ________________

Ho Math Chess Assessment Grade 1

1. Join dots by numbers starting from 1.

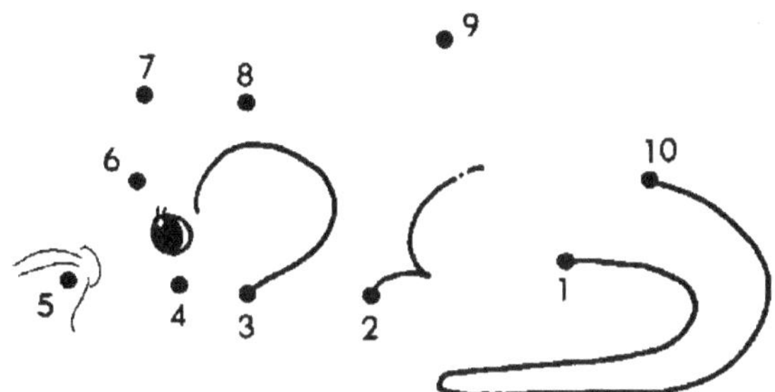

2. Complete each number sequence.
   0, 1, 2, 3, _____, _____, 6, _____
   8, 7, 6, _____, 4, _____, 2
   1, 3, 5, _____, 9

3. Add numbers.

4	7	15	48	64	312	674
+ 3	+ 9	+ 34	+ 39	+ 78	+ 254	+ 739

4. Subtract numbers.

8	79	46	75	638	546
− 3	− 47	− 18	− 49	− 224	− 228

5. Draw the correct sign (<, > or =) to make true sentences
   7 3   6 6   4 9   5 11

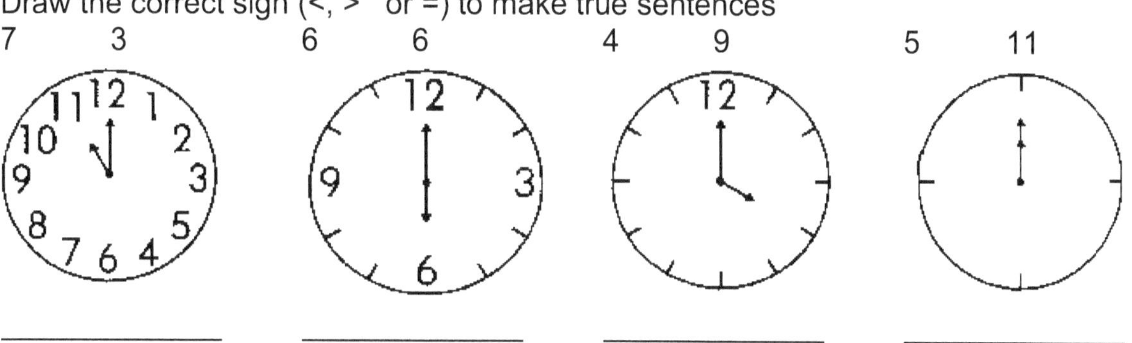

7. Copy a drawing along the symmetry line.

Student's name: ___________________ Assignment date: _______________

Ho Math Chess Assessment Grade 2

1. Fill in the blanks with the missing numbers.
   44 46 ______ 50 52
   996 997 998 999 _______
2. Add numbers.

47	38	36	699	1875
+ 32	+ 84	+ 28	+ 248	+ 5726

3. Subtract numbers.

57	71	84	468	906
– 24	– 26	– 59	– 219	– 578

4. Write numbers in standard form.
   For example, Eight hundred thirty-five 835
   Four hundred twenty-one ________ Nine hundred nine ____________
5. Connect the shapes with their names.

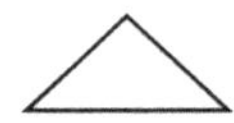  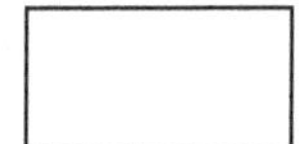 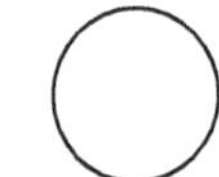 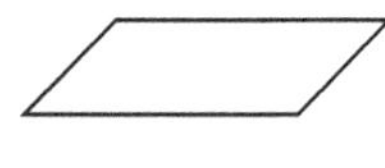

rectangle circle triangle parallelogram square

6. What time is it?

__________ __________ __________ __________

. Multiply numbers.

$5 \times 4 =$ ______	$8 \times 6 =$ ______	$9 \times 7 =$ ______	$7 \times 6 =$ ______
$9 \times 5 =$ ______	$3 \times 7 =$ ______	$6 \times 4 =$ ______	$2 \times 9 =$ ______
$27 \times 6 =$ ______	$35 \times 4 =$ ______	$52 \times 7 =$ ______	$95 \times 6 =$ ______

8. Arrange the angles in order of size. Begin with the smallest one.

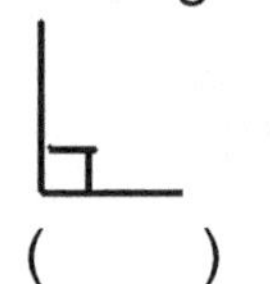 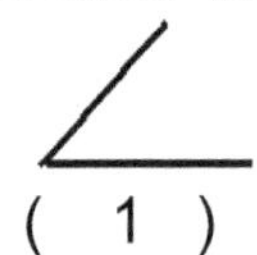 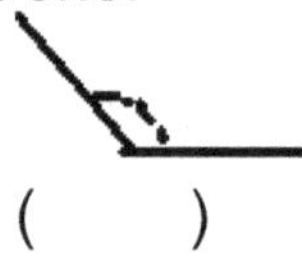

( ) (1) ( )

9. Find the number

$7 + 3 - K - 2 = 1$	$9 - M - 1 = 8$	$A - 2 = 8 - A$
K = ________	M = _______	A = ______

Student's name: ____________________ Assignment date: ________________

Ho Math Chess Assessment Grade 3

1. Write the next three numbers in each sequence.

14, 21, 28, ______, ______, ______

0, 1, 3, 6, 10, 15, ______, ______, ______

2. Add and Subtract

$$\begin{array}{r} 74 \\ -\ 58 \\ \hline \end{array} \qquad \begin{array}{r} \\ -\ 15 \\ \hline 37 \end{array} \qquad \begin{array}{r} 75 \\ +\ \\ \hline 123 \end{array} \qquad \begin{array}{r} 536 \\ +\ \\ \hline 721 \end{array} \qquad \begin{array}{r} 840 \\ -\ \\ \hline 578 \end{array}$$

3 Multiplication

$8 \times 9 =$ _____ $5 \times 7 =$ _____ $9 \times 8 =$ _____ $3 \times 6 =$ _____ $7 \times 6 =$ _____

$35 \times 7 =$ ______ $46 \times 8 =$ ______ $58 \times 26 =$ ______ $356 \times 58 =$ ________

4. Division

$42 \div 6 =$ ______ $448 \div 7 =$ ______ $276 \div 12 =$ ______ $1344 \div 24 =$ ______

5. Write the numbers

Five thousand, four hundred seven ________________

One hundred twenty-two thousand, three hundred forty ________________

6. What fraction of the whole figure is shaded?

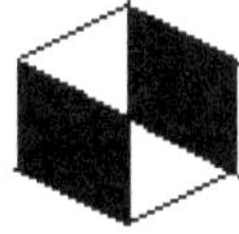 ________

 ________

 ________

 ________

7. Shade the figures as the fractions show

$\frac{4}{9}$

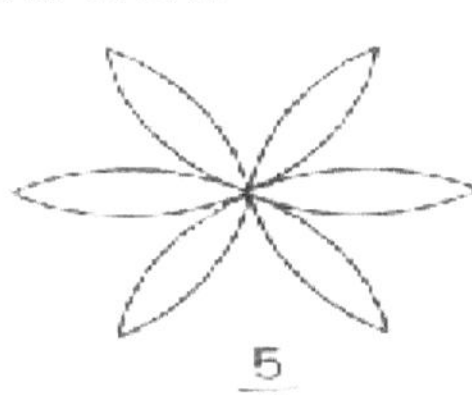

$\frac{5}{6}$

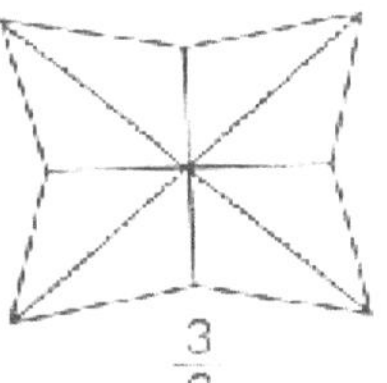

$\frac{3}{8}$

8. Area and Perimeter

Area = ________ square units

Perimeter = ________ units

9. According to the calendar on the right, answer the following questions

The year 1902 began on what day of the week? ____________

What is the date of the second Tuesday in December 1901? __________

What is the date of last Wednesday in November 1901? __________

DECEMBER 1901

S	M	T	W	T	F	S
1	2	3	4	5	6	7
8	9	10	11	12	13	14
15	16	17	18	19	20	21
22	23	24	25	26	27	28
29	30	**31**				

Ho Math Chess Primary Grades Math

Test Review assesssment 何数棋謎低年级数学测试複習考核

Frank Ho, Amanda Ho www.homathchess.com

Student's name: ____________________ Assignment date: ______________

Ho Math Chess Assessment Grade 4

1. Multiplication

$14 \times 53 =$ ________ $37 \times 68 =$ ________

$432 \times 26 =$ ________ $123 \times 456 =$ ________

2. Division

$186 \div 3 =$ ______ $4207 \div 7 =$ ________

$840 \div 24 =$ ______ $735 \div 42 =$ ______

3. Naming the <u>face value</u> of the digit 5

Example, 25.34 <u>five ones</u>

452.36 ________________

34.257 ________________

432.65 ________________

4. Write a name under each shape.

(rectangle, triangle, parallelogram, square)

________ ________ ________ ________

5. Comparing decimal numbers

(Using >, <, or =)

(A) 5.0 5.00 (B) 0.4 0.04

(C) 0.2 0.20000 (D) 0.5 0.500

6. Adding and subtracting Fractions

$\frac{4}{6}+\frac{1}{6}=$ ______ $\frac{7}{10}-\frac{4}{10}=$ ______

$\frac{5}{6}-(\frac{5}{6}-\frac{1}{6})=$ ______

$1\frac{1}{2}+\frac{1}{2}=$ ______

$\frac{2}{5}+\frac{3}{7}=$ ______ $\frac{6}{7}-\frac{4}{5}=$ ______

7. Adding and subtracting decimals

$$\begin{array}{r} 3.4 \\ +\ 6.5 \\ \hline \end{array} \qquad \begin{array}{r} 4.63 \\ +\ 2.59 \\ \hline \end{array} \qquad \begin{array}{r} 0.7 \\ -\ 0.136 \\ \hline \end{array}$$

8. Multiplication and division of decimals

$$\begin{array}{r} 6.48 \\ \times\ 9 \\ \hline \end{array} \qquad \begin{array}{r} 3.2 \\ \times\ 2.8 \\ \hline \end{array} \qquad 2\overline{)4.32}$$

9. Comparing fractions by using pictures

(Using >, < or =)

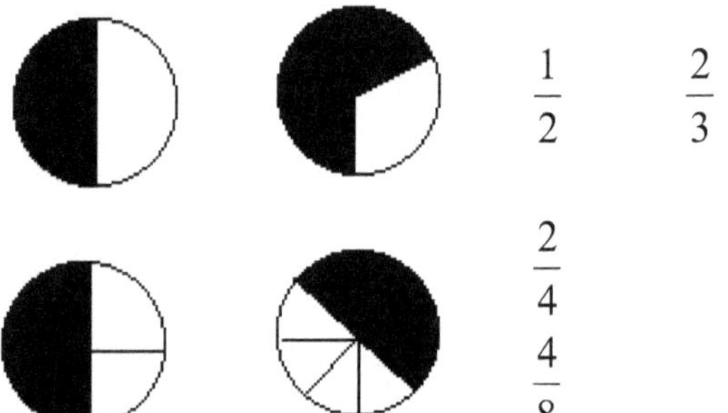

Word problems

1. I wrote 5 consecutive numbers on 5 cards. The sum of the numbers is 15. What numbers did I write on the cards?

2. Bob had 2 tickets for rides at the carnival. Each ride required 1 ticket. There were four rides available for him to take: merry-go-round, ferries wheel, airplane, and roller coaster. How many different ways could Bob use his 2 tickets if each ride needs one ticket?

3. May was arranging coins in the following manner: 1 penny, followed by 2 nickels, followed by 3 dimes, followed by 4 pennies, and then followed by 1 penny, 2 nickels and so on. If she continues in this manner, what coin will be in the thirteenth position?

4. I timed some children walking in the hallway. They walked 5 m in 8 seconds. How far will they walk in 72 seconds?

Student's name: ____________________ Assignment date: ________________

This sheet is for Teachers ONLY

Level 4 and Under Ho Math Chess Assessment
Preparation for Math Assessment

The purpose of Ho Math Chess assessment is not just to find out the potential student's math ability. The equally important purpose is to let the potential student work on a few sample Ho Math Chess problems to taste how Ho Math Chess worksheets are different from other traditional worksheets.

The most common problems that grade 4 and under students often encounter are:

If the student can do 11 – 2, 11 – 3, 36 borrowing subtractions and multiplication facts.

If the student already knows how to play chess, you can show the Ho Math Chess Teaching Set and play half-blind chess or even one-side half-blind chess.

If the student does not know how to play chess or is not interested in playing chess, there is no point in asking them to play chess other than show the Ho Math Chess Teaching Set.

The Assessment is designed to assess cumulative knowledge so you will find out the potential student's weakness and strength.

Students must discover the "fun' after working on Ho Math Chess worksheets, and the teacher should also point out to parents or students how Ho Math Chess worksheets are different from others.

This level 4 Assessment assesses the 4 basic operations of addition, subtraction, multiplication, and division. Not only 4 basic operations are evaluated; the math and chess integrated material is also included to let students understand how Ho Math Chess worksheets are different from others.`

Although level 4 can mean grade 4 in some countries, it is not absolute. Be careful not to dampen the student's enthusiasm if they are already a grade 5 student but are doing a level 4 assessment.

Student's name: ____________________ Assignment date: ________________

This sheet is for Teachers ONLY

Level 4 and Under
Ho Math Chess Assessment

Preparation for Chess Assessment

The teacher can play a short chess game against the potential student and gain a feeling, but to assess the knowledge of check, checkmate, stalemate, castling, or some basic tactics such as fork, pin, discovered check, skewer etc., some test sheets are required to give to the student, In this case, 2-hour assessment is not enough.

Use Ho Math Chess Teaching Set to play the game and introduce half-blind chess or blind chess.
If the student wants to learn chess only, then assign him or her to the chess class taught by the chess teacher.

Student's name: ____________________ Assignment date: ________________

For Students

Level 4 and Under

Ho Math Chess Assessment

www.homathchess.com

Frank Ho, Amanda Ho

Ho Math Chess Learning Centre

fho1928@gmail.com

Please skip any questions you cannot do. This assessment is not intended to evaluate your overall math ability but is specially designed to find out your working on basic math.

Student's name: ____________________ Assignment date: ______________

Assessment of math basics - addition

(♔ = 0, ♙ = 1, ♗ = 3, ♘ = 3, ♖ = 5, ♕ = 9)

(Explain the chess point system to students if they do not know.)

0123456789

(The above is the dotted Arabic numeration for children who like to use fingers. Count dots to replace counting fingers, and then finally, the student should be able to calculate intuitively without using fingers.)

170	123	103	613	23
– 6	– 15	– 18	– 19	– 16
164	108	85	594	7
167	100	15	24	33
– 19	– 8	– 7	– 6	– 14
148	92	8	18	19
45	223	□□□	43	175
– 19	– 114	– 12	– □□	– 17
26	109	221 233	29 14	□□ 158

Student's name: ____________________ Assignment date: ________________

- These sheets evaluate the addition of 1 digit + 1 digit and multi-digit addition and its reverse calculation with or without carrying over. Check carefully and see if the student can do carrying over or not.
- You can see how many digits of addition the student can do and if they can work backwards.
- This sheet also assesses whether the student can convert an abstract symbol to numbers (i.e., chess symbol to its corresponding point). Observe to see if the student knows how to add from the bigger number to the smaller number

Student's name: ____________________ Assignment date: ________________

Assessment of mental math from 1 to 10

Fill in each ____ by a number.

2 numbers	+	−	×	Larger number ÷ smaller number. (use fraction if not divisible.)
__, __ 4, 2	6	2	______ 8	______ 2
______, ______ 6, 3	9	______ 3	18	______ 2
______, ______ 2,1	3	______ 1	______ 2	2
______, ______ 9, 5	14	______	______	$\frac{9}{5}$
______, ______ 8, 7	15	1	______56	______ $\frac{8}{7}$
______, ______ 8, 3	______ 11	5	24	______ $\frac{8}{3}$
______, ______ 9, 3	12	6	______ 27	______ 3
______, ______ 6, 2	______ 8	4	12	______ 3
______, ______ 6, 8	14	2	______ 48	___ $\frac{8}{6} = \frac{4}{3}$

- Observe if the student can do math mentally. It will be helpful to the student to do word problems if the student can do math mentally
- If the student uses fingers to do the computation, these kinds of questions may present some difficulty for students.

Student's name: ____________________ Assignment date: ________________

Assessment of mental math from 11 to 18

Fill in each ____ by a number.

2 numbers	+	−	×	Larger number ÷ smaller number. (use fraction if not divisible.)
__14_, __5___	19	9	______ 70	______ $\frac{14}{5}$
______, ______ 16,8	24	______	128	______ 2
______, ______ 12,4	______ 16	______ 8	48	3
______, ______ 17,9	26	8	______ 153	______ 17/9
______, ______ 18, 9	______ 27	9	______ 162	2
______, ______ 11,7	18	4	______ 77	______ 11/7
______, ______ 13, 5	18	8	______ 65	______ 13/5
______, ______ 14,7	______ 21	______ 7	98	2
______, ______ 18,9	______ 27	9	______ 162	2

- Observe if the student can do math mentally. It will be helpful to the student to do word problems if the student can do math mentally
- If the student uses fingers to do the computation, then these kinds of questions may present some difficulty for students.

Student's name: ____________________ Assignment date: ______________

Assessment of word problems – addition and subtraction

Ho gives 3 sheets of lined paper to Wendy, then each of them has an equal number of sheets. Altogether they have 28 sheets. How many sheets does each have originally? The difference is 6. 28 – 6 = 22 to remove the extra sheets 22/2=11 Andrew = 11 + 6 = 17, Wendy = 11
If I add 4 and subtract 5, then add 7, I will get 22. What number am I? 16
If I subtract 5 and add 17, then subtract 6, I will get 39. What number am I? 33
If Coco gives Meghan 5 cookies and then Meghan gives 3 cookies to Coco, they have the same cookies. Together they have 24 cookies. How many cookies does each of them have in the beginning? The difference is really 4 between 2 persons, but Coco has more. So 24 – 4= 20, 20/2 = 10 this is the amount each person has the equal number of cookies, and it is also Meghan's cookies (Sum and Difference model problem), so it is 10. Cock's cookies = 10 + 4 = 14.
In 5 years, Andrew will be 12 years old, and 5 years ago, Meghan was 5 years old. What is the total age of both Meghan and Andrew now? Andrew's age now is 12- 5 = 7 Meghan's age now 5 + 5 = 10, 10 + 7 = 17

Ho Math Chess Primary Grades Math

Test Review assesssment 何数棋谜低年级数学测试複習考核

Student's name: ____________________ Assignment date: ________________

Spatial relation and logic

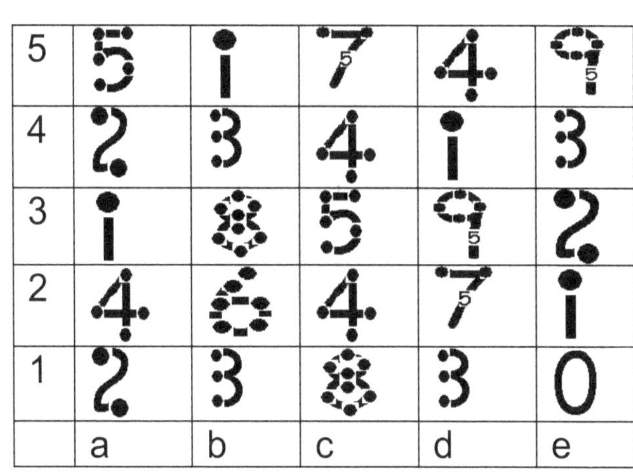

5 is the total of the following 2 numbers.

0	5
5	0
1	4
4	1
2	3
3	2

If you are at a3 and the symbol ✥ 3 indicates to move to the right 3 squares (to reach the square numbered 9), what number will ✥ 2 reach _______ . 3

If you are at a3 and the symbol ⤧ 2 indicates to move diagonally 2 squares (to reach the square numbered 7, what number will ⤧ 2 reach _______ . 2

This sheet is to let the student get a taste of what Ho Math and Chess integrated material is all about.

Student's name: ____________________ Assignment date: _______________

Assessment of multiplication

Fill in each ? by a number such that a1 ╳ a2 = a3 and b1 ╳ b2 = b3.
╳ = a1 ╳ b2, ╳ = b1 ╳ a2.

Example	
<table><tr><td>3</td><td>6</td><td>1</td></tr><tr><td>2</td><td>? 2</td><td>? 1</td></tr><tr><td>1</td><td>? 3</td><td>? 1</td></tr><tr><td></td><td>a</td><td>b</td></tr></table>	╳ + ╳ = __3__ + __2__ = 5 ╳ – ╳ = __3__ – __2__ = 1
<table><tr><td>3</td><td>6</td><td>2</td></tr><tr><td>2</td><td>?</td><td>?</td></tr><tr><td>1</td><td>?</td><td>?</td></tr><tr><td></td><td>a</td><td>b</td></tr></table> 1 2 6 1	╳ + ╳ = ____ + ____ = 13 ╳ – ╳ = ____ – ____ = 11
<table><tr><td>3</td><td>6</td><td>2</td></tr><tr><td>2</td><td>?</td><td>?</td></tr><tr><td>1</td><td>?</td><td>?</td></tr><tr><td></td><td>a</td><td>b</td></tr></table> 3 1 2 2	╳ + ╳ = ____ + ____ = 8 ╳ – ╳ = ____ – ____ = 4

This is to see if the student can do the basics of multiplication and introduce math and chess-integrated problems.
This is the general multiplication. If the student has problems, then use the workbook of Multiplication or use the Test of Future Math Star workbook or High-Performance workbook.
Watch the speed when the student is working on this sheet.

Student's name: ____________________ Assignment date: ________________

Assessment of multiplication

Fill in each ? by a number such that a1 ✕ a2 = a3 and b1 ✕ b2 = b3.

✕ = a1 ✕ b2, ✕ = b1 ✕ a2.

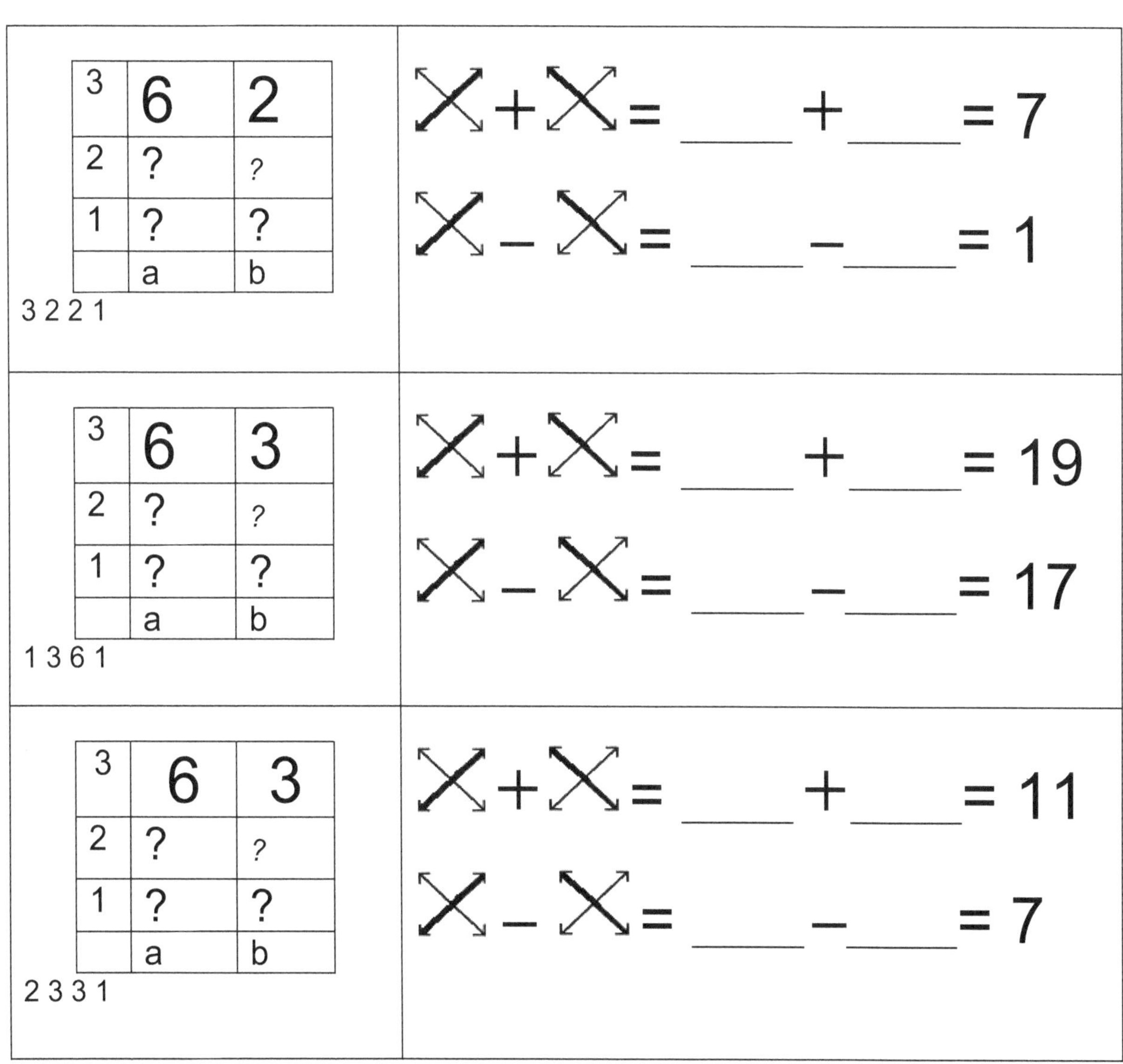

This is to see if the student can do the basics of multiplication and also to introduce the concept of math and chess integrated problems.

Watch the speed when the student is working on this sheet.

Student's name: ____________________ Assignment date: ________________

Assessment of multiplication (order of operations)

3	i	8	5
2	7	6	4
1	2	3	9
	a	b	c

You are at b2 = □.

□ + ✥ × (□ – 1) = ____ + ____ × ____ = ____
□ + ✥ × (□ – 1) = ____ + ____ × ____ = ____
□ + ✥ × (□ – 1) = ____ + ____ × ____ = ____
□ + ✥ × (□ – 1) = ____ + ____ × ____ = ____
□ + ⤧ × (□ – 1) = ____ + ____ × ____ = ____
□ + ⤧ × (□ – 1) = ____ + ____ × ____ = ____
□ + ⤧ × (□ – 1) = ____ + ____ × ____ = ____
□ + ⤧ × (□ – 1) = ____ + ____ × ____ = ____

6+4x5=26, 21. 41, 46, 31, 51, 16, 11

This is to see if the student can do the basics of multiplication and also to introduce the concept of math and chess integrated problems.
Watch the speed when the student is working on this sheet.

Student's name: ____________________ Assignment date: ________________

Whole number multiplying or dividing by a whole number

Horizontal division form	Fraction form	Work Area	Answer in decimal to tenth.	Answer in %
24 ÷ 2	$\frac{24}{2} = \frac{12}{1}$		12.0	1200%
2420 ÷ 11	220/1		220.0	22000%
14670 × 1000	$\frac{14670000}{1}$		14670000.0	1467000000%
170017 ÷ 17	10001/1		10001.0	1000100%
90040523 ÷ 100	$900405\frac{23}{100}$		900405.2	90040523%

This is the general division. If the student has a problem, use Division or use Test of Future Math Star workbooks or High-Performance Math.

Watch and see if the student can handle there are 0's in the middle of the dividend.

What happens when the divisor is 10's power. Does the student know the shortcut way of dividing by 10's power?

Does the student know the shortcut way of multiplying by 10's power?

Student's name: ____________________ Assignment date: ________________

Word problem for multiplication and division

What is the smallest 1-digit number if it divided by 2 the remainder is 1 and divided by 3 the remainder is 2? What is the smallest 2-digit number when it is divided by 2 the remainder is 1 and divided by 3, the remainder is 2? 5, 11 (1, 3, 5, 7, 9, 11) (3, 5, 7, 9, 11)
,
How many different pairs of outfits can Melody have if she has 3 different kinds of skirts and 5 kinds of T-shirts? 15
The cost of each ticket for a child is $5 and for each adult is $7. What is the average cost per ticket if a family of 2 children and 2 adults bought tickets for every member of the family? $6

This is to evaluate the student's multiplication or division ability.

Student's name: ____________________ Assignment date: ________________

Ho Math Chess grades assessment answers 各年级考核答案

Ho Math and Chess

Joining

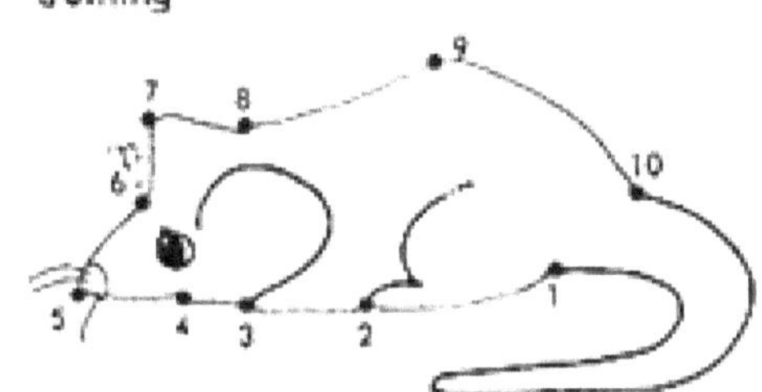

Complete each sequence

0, 1, 2, 3, 4, 5, 6, 7

8, 7, 6, 5, 4, 3, 2

1, 3, 5, 7, 9

Add

4 + 3 = 7

7 + 9 = 16

15 + 34 = 49

48 + 39 = 87

64 + 78 = 142

312 + 254 = 566

674 + 739 = 1413

Subtract

8 − 3 = 5

79 − 47 = 32

46 − 18 = 28

75 − 49 = 26

638 − 224 = 414

546 − 228 = 318

Draw the correct sign (<, > or =) to make true sentences

4 < 9

Write the time

11:00

6:00

4:00

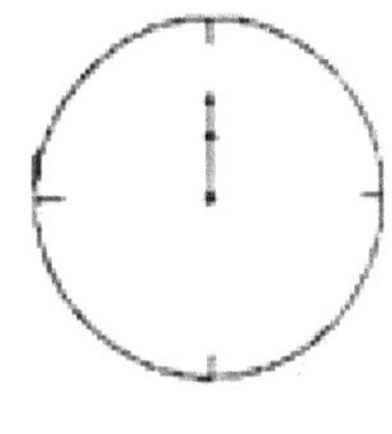

12:00

Ho Math Chess Primary Grades Math Test Review assesssment 何数棋謎低年级数学测试複習考核

Student's name: ____________________ Assignment date: ______________

Ho Math and Chess

1. Fill in the blanks with the missing numbers.

   44 46 <u>48</u> 50 52

   996 997 998 999 <u>1000</u>

2. Add

47	38	36	699	1875
+ 32	+ 84	+ 28	+ 248	+ 5726
79	122	64	947	7601

3. Subtract

57	71	84	468	906
− 24	− 26	− 59	− 219	− 578
33	45	25	249	328

4. Write the numbers

   For example: Eight hundred thirty five <u>835</u>

   Four hundred twenty one <u>421</u> Nine hundred nine <u>909</u>

5. Identify the shapes

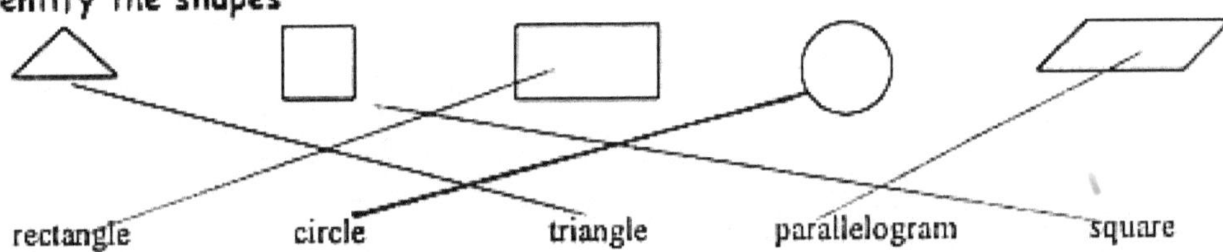

6. What time is it?

 <u>7:30</u>

 <u>11:00</u>

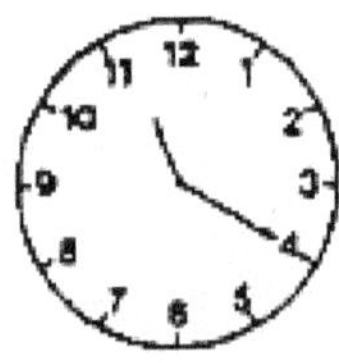 <u>11:20</u>

 <u>12:50</u>

7. Multiply

5 × 4 = <u>20</u>	8 × 6 = <u>48</u>	9 × 7 = <u>63</u>	7 × 6 = <u>42</u>
9 × 5 = <u>45</u>	3 × 7 = <u>21</u>	6 × 4 = <u>24</u>	2 × 9 = <u>18</u>
27 × 6 = <u>162</u>	35 × 4 = <u>140</u>	52 × 7 = <u>364</u>	95 × 6 = <u>570</u>

8. Arrange the angles in order of size. Begin with the smallest one.

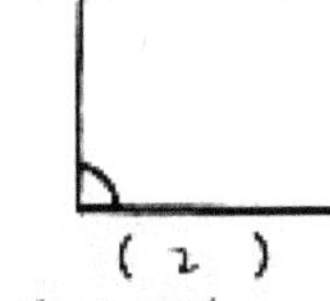 (2)

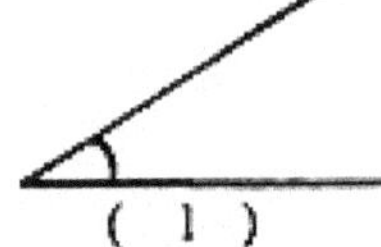 (1)

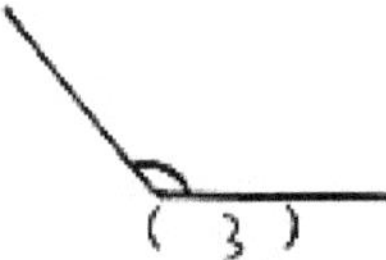 (3)

9. Find the number

7 + 3 − K − 2 = 1	9 − m − 1 = 8	A − 2 = 8 − A
K = 7	m = 0	A = 5

Student's name: ____________________ Assignment date: ________________

5

Ho Math and Chess

1. Write the next three numbers in each sequence.

14, 21, 28, __35__, __42__, __49__

0, 1, 3, 6, 10, 15, __21__, __28__, __36__

2. Add and Subtract

$$\begin{array}{r} 74 \\ -58 \\ \hline 16 \end{array} \qquad \begin{array}{r} 52 \\ -15 \\ \hline 37 \end{array} \qquad \begin{array}{r} 75 \\ +48 \\ \hline 123 \end{array} \qquad \begin{array}{r} 536 \\ +185 \\ \hline 721 \end{array} \qquad \begin{array}{r} 840 \\ -262 \\ \hline 578 \end{array}$$

3. Multiplication

$8 \times 9 =$ __72__ $5 \times 7 =$ __35__ $9 \times 8 =$ __72__ $3 \times 6 =$ __18__ $7 \times 6 =$ __42__

$35 \times 7 =$ __245__ $46 \times 8 =$ __368__ $58 \times 26 =$ __1508__ $356 \times 58 =$ __20648__

4. Division

$42 \div 6 =$ __7__ $448 \div 7 =$ __64__ $276 \div 12 =$ __23__ $1344 \div 24 =$ __56__

5. Write the numbers

Five thousand, four hundred seven __5407__

One hundred twenty two thousand, three hundred forty __122,340__

6. What fraction of the whole figure is shaded?

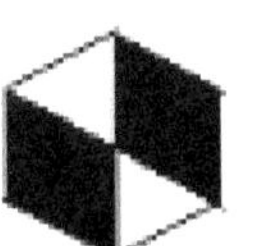 $\frac{4}{6}$   $\frac{1}{5}$  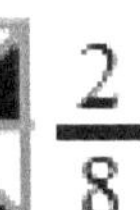 $\frac{2}{8}$  $\frac{2}{6}$

7. Shade the figures as the fractions show

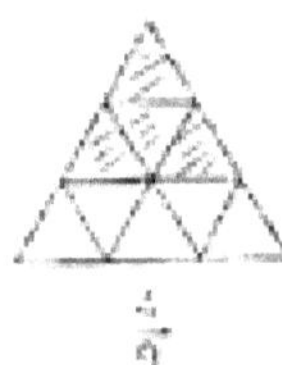

$\frac{4}{9}$

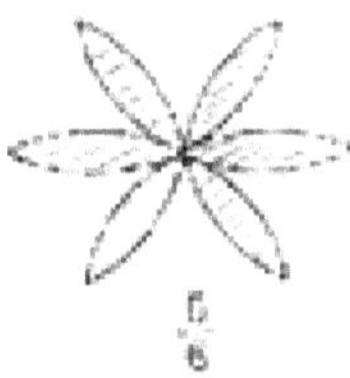

$\frac{5}{6}$

$\frac{3}{8}$

8. Area and Perimeter

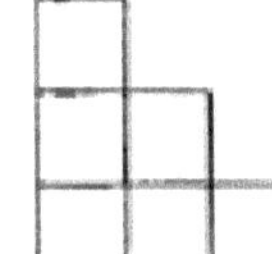

Area = __6__ square units

Perimeter = __12__ units

9. According to this calendar, answer the following questions

The year 1902 began on what day of the week? __Wednesday__

What is the date of the second Tuesday in Dec, 1901? __10th__

What is the date of last Wednesday in Nov, 1901? __27th__

Student's name: ____________________ Assignment date: ________________

Ho Math and Chess 4

1. **Multiplicaion**

$14 \times 53 =$ 742 $37 \times 68 =$ 2516

$432 \times 26 =$ 11232 $123 \times 456 =$ 56088

2. **Division**

$186 \div 3 =$ 62 $4207 \div 7 =$ 601

$840 \div 24 =$ 35 $735 \div 42 =$ 17R21

3. Name the face value of 5.

25.34 5 ones

452.36 5 tens

34.257 5 hundredths

432.65 5 hundredths

4. **Identifying shapes**

(rectangle, triangle, parallelogram , square)

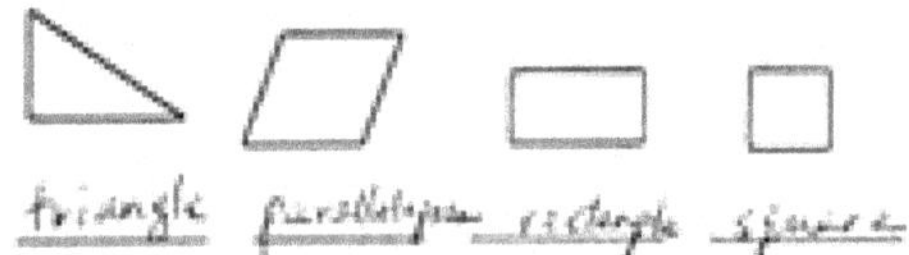

triangle parallelogram rectangle square

5. **Compare decimal numbers**

(Using >, <, or =)

50 (<) 500 0.4 (>) 0.04

0.2 (=) 0.20000 0.5 (=) 0.500

6. **Adding and subtracting Fractions**

$\frac{4}{6} + \frac{1}{6} =$ 5/6 $\frac{7}{10} - \frac{4}{10} =$ 3/10

$\frac{5}{6} - (\frac{5}{6} - \frac{1}{6}) =$ 1/6 $1\frac{1}{2} + \frac{1}{2} =$ 2

$\frac{2}{5} + \frac{3}{7} =$ 29/35 $\frac{6}{7} - \frac{4}{5} =$ 2/35

Adding and subtracting decimals

3.4	4.63	0.7
+ 6.5	+ 2.59	− 0.136
9.9	7.22	0.564

8. **Multiplication and division of decimals**

6.48	3.2	2.16
× 9	× 2.8	2) 4.32
58.32	8.96	

9. **Compare fraction by drawing pictures**

(Using >, < or =)

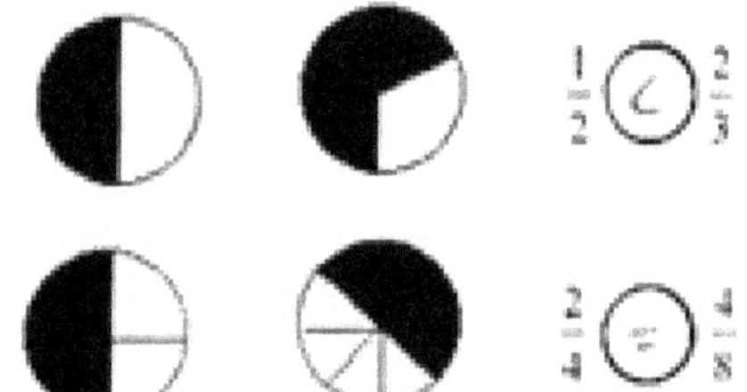

$\frac{1}{2}$ (<) $\frac{2}{3}$

$\frac{2}{4}$ (=) $\frac{4}{8}$

Problem-Solving

1. I wrote 5 different numbers on 5 cards. The sum of the numbers is 15. What numbers did I put on the cards?

1, 2, 3, 4, 5

2. Bob had 2 tickets for rides at the carnival. There were 4 rides he could take: merry-go-round, ferries wheel, airplanes, and roller coaster. How many different ways could Bob use his 2 tickets?

6

3. May was arranging coins in the following manner: 1 penny, followed by 2 nickels, followed by 3 dimes, followed by 4 pennies and so on. If she continues in this manner, what coin will be in the thirteenth position?

nickel

4. I timed some children walking in the hallway. They walked 5 m in 8 s. How far will they walk in 72 s?

Student's name: ____________________ Assignment date: ________________

Introducing Ho Math Chess™

Ho Math Chess™ = math + puzzles + chess

Frank Ho, a Canadian math teacher, intrigued by math and chess relationships after teaching his son chess, started Ho Math Chess™ in 1995. His long-term devotion to research has led his son to become a FIDE chess master and Frank's publications of over 20 math workbooks. Today Ho Math Chess™ is the world's largest and the only franchised scholastic math, chess and puzzles specialty learning center with worldwide locations. Ho Math Chess™ is a leading research organization in math, chess, and puzzles integrated teaching methodology.

There are hundreds of articles already published showing chess benefits children and that math puzzles are an excellent way of improving brainpower. So, by integrating chess and mathematical chess puzzles, the learning effect is more significant.

Parents send their children to Ho Math Chess™ because they like Ho Math Chess™ teaching philosophy – offering children problem-solving questions in a variety of formats. The questions could be pure chess, chess puzzles or mathematical chess puzzles in the nature of logic, pattern, tree structure, Venn diagram, probability and many more math concepts.

Ho Math Chess™ has developed a series of unique and high-quality math, chess, and puzzles integrated workbooks. Ho Math Chess™ produced the world's first workbook Learning Chess to Improve Math. This workbook is not only for learning chess but also for enriching math ability. This sets Ho Math Chess apart from other math learning centers, chess club, or chess classes.

The teaching method at Ho Math Chess™ is to use math, chess, and puzzles integrated workbooks to teach children fun math. The purposes of Ho Math Chess™ teaching method and workbooks are to:

- Improve math marks.
- Develop problem-solving and critical thinking skills.
- Improve logic thinking ability.
- Boost brainpower.

Testimonials, sample worksheets, reports, and franchise information can be found at www.homathchess.com.

More information about Ho Math Chess™ can also be found from the following publications:

1. Why Buy a Ho Math Chess™ Learning Centre Franchise: A Unique Learning Centre?
2. Ho Math Chess™ Sudoku Puzzles Sample Worksheets
3. Introduction to Ho Math Chess™ and its Founder Frank Ho

The above publications can be purchased from www.amazon.com.

www.ingramcontent.com/pod-product-compliance
Lightning Source LLC
LaVergne TN
LVHW081400110826
845149LV00010B/1623

* 9 7 8 1 9 8 8 3 0 0 3 5 1 *